BRASSEY'S
GUIDE TO
WAR
FILMS

ALUN EVANS

Brassey's
Washington, D.C.

ISBN 1-57488-263-5   (alk.paper)

Printed in Hong Kong on acid-free paper that meets the American National
Standards Institute Z39-48 Standard.

Brassey's
22841 Quicksilver Drive
Dulles, Virginia 20166

First Edition

10 9 8 7 6 5 4 3 2 1

A cursory look will show you why this cross between a dictionary and a guide to war films is a little bit different. War in the movies has been the subject of many fine books, but this one has been compiled like nothing else. It brings together the interests of the film-goer and the military historian without marginalising either; I hope, too, it will be of interest to anyone who loves a good browse.

I have attempted to cover over 3,000 titles from all around the world. No other catalogue of war pictures is so comprehensive yet so catholic in its scope. While some books of war films deal with national films only, and others define 'war' pictures as only those depicting World Wars I and II, I have taken a wider view. There is no right or wrong with such arbitrary delineations, of course. Suffice to say I could not omit **The 300 Spartans**, **Chimes of Midnight** or **Zulu** from any reckoning I have of what is, or is not, a war movie. It has got me into hot water over the months: there have been times, when reviewing a picture or article, I have noticed a compelling argument for including a film which previously was not within my parameters — parameters which I was then tempted to re-draw. I have remained pretty faithful to my original premise, however. Basically I have included movies which portray battles, the effects of war, the psychology of waging war and the psychology of war on people — hence the dangerous crossover with the genres of espionage, romance, melodrama, historical

adventure, westerns, fantasy, comedy and musical. If you think about it, very few movies classed as 'war' pictures contain none of the above.

The book is split into two main sections; the A–Z is an alphabetical listing of the most appropriate 2,000 films (as per the above philosophy and the following constrictions); thereafter there are indexes listing the films by period and then by director.

I have had to make some hard and fast rules, if only to comply with the spirit of the book's title. Every picture listed uses drama to tell its tale (including many documentaries which are identified in the A–Z by italicisation of their titles). Because of this, some elastication of the facts is obvious, and in many more cases fictional scenarios are based on real events — there wouldn't be a Hollywood otherwise. I have excluded pictures, however, which have no basis whatsoever in truth, or those, such as wartime comedies and musicals, for which war is purely a vehicle for the plots and players. (Some borderline cases may have a mention in in the indexes if there is some degree of authenticity or fact — **The Sound of Music** springs to mind.)

The decision also had to be taken to omit many fine foreign-language pictures, simply because of lack of space; many are, however, listed in the indexes for further reference. Westerns are only included where the U.S. Army comes into conflict with Native Americans: spy films where they specifically relate to authentic wars (the Cold War being an exception here

as that would entail a whole sub-genre on its own!).

As many more pictures have been made of conflicts which are topical, or of recent history, it's hardly surprising there is not a glut of celluloid on the Punic Wars or the Wars of the Roses. For that reason, some semi-mythical romances from the historical archive have been included to provide a semblance of events from those times to create a rolling historical narrative of wars and warfare in the cinema.

Entries in the A–Z listing (see guide below) carry a star rating. Having commented on the films, I decided it would also be helpful to readers to highlight the 'better' pictures and the real turkeys. The industry norm is to use stars, and I have opted for a range of nil to five: from the ridiculous to the sublime, respectively.

Some readers may disagree with the logic of all this — and I would love to hear from anyone via the publisher.

Thanks go to to Martin Windrow, whose idea this project first was, for his correcting of the proofs and technical tit-bits; and thanks again to my family for their forebear-(with a sore head)-ance, especially Caryl, my wife.

We are grateful to all the companies and individuals who have given us permission to reproduce their photographs, particularly KOBAL. Every effort has been made to trace the copyright and obtain permission to publish these stills, but where this has not been possible, may we offer our thanks here. Credits are given with individual stills.

GUIDE TO ENTRY LAYOUT

ADDRESS UNKNOWN ◄——————————————► **TITLE** If it is in italics it is a ***DOCUMENTARY***

★ *William Cameron Menzies — U.S., 1944* [70min] ◄—— ◄ *Director — country of origin, date of release* [approximate

★ Kressman Taylor's popular novel adapted into a neat running times (except for some B-movies, foreign films
thriller by Menzies. The story is fairly familiar for the and documentaries]
times — Nazi anti-semitism in the late '30s; American ◄—— ◄ Editorial
naiveté until it's too late, predictable stuff.

With *Paul Lukas, Carl Esmond, Peter Van Eyck, Mady* ◄—— ◄ *List of stars*
Christians, Morris Carnovsky

DE AANSLAG See **The Assault**

DIE ABENTEUER DES WERNER HOLT
See **The Adventures of Werner Holt**

ABOVE and BEYOND
Melvin Frank/Norman Panama — U.S., 1952 [120min]
Biopic of *Enola Gay* pilot, Col Paul Tibbetts, and how the
Hiroshima bombing affected him. Pretty boring fare, but the
right kind of Hollywood fodder for the days of McCarthy and
Stalin.
With *Robert Taylor, Eleanor Parker, James Whitmore*

ABOVE SUSPICION
Richard Thorpe — U.S., 1943 [90min]
MacMurray and Crawford on honeymoon on the Continent
get involved with Nazis. He's an Oxford don just before the
outbreak of war who is not all he seems and helps the British
Secret Service to track down one of their missing spies. Played
for laughs as much as suspense.
With *Fred MacMurray, Joan Crawford, Basil Rathbone, Conrad
Veidt*

ABOVE US THE WAVES
The little action of the 'Phoney War' was still too much for some. Rank

ABOVE US THE WAVES
Ralph Thomas — GB, 1955 [100min]
Royal Navy mini-submariners cripple the German pocket-
battleship *Tirpitz* in a Norwegian fjord in September 1943.
This effectively bottled up the warship for the rest of the war,
and it was finally sunk (after several attempts) by Lancaster
bombers in November 1944.
   It's a pity Thomas doesn't do the action justice, but it does
have a cast of the best of British stiff upper lips.
With *John Mills, John Gregson, Donald Sinden, James Robertson
Justice*

ABRAHAM LINCOLN
D.W. Griffith — U.S., 1930 [95min]
Lincoln's election to the U.S. Presidency on an anti-slavery
ticket in 1860 was the catalyst for the American Civil War and
the secession of the Southern states. Precious little action and
much talk from the master of silent spectacles.
With *Walter Huston, Una Merkel, Edgar Dearing*

ABYSSINIA
Roman Karmen — USSR, 1939
The other side of the coin. Whereas **The Great Challenge**
and **The Path of the Heroes**, made by Italians, justified and
glorified Mussolini's annexation of Abyssinia, this Soviet
documentary ridiculed the fascists' attempt at petty imperialism
and magnified the plight of the conquered Africans.

ACCEPTABLE LEVELS
John Davies — GB, 1983 [100min]
A British documentary film crew arrive in contemporary
Belfast to film on an aspect not specifically related to the
troubles — but witness a child killed by the security forces.
Well-made, 'worthy', if somewhat predictable.
With *Andrew Rashleigh, Kay Adshead, Sally McCafferty*

ACCIDENTAL LEGEND (aka 'Fei Tian')
Wang Shaudi — China, 1996 [120min]
Highly visual comic adventure set in early 1900s northern China.
The peasants are revolting and the Manchu dynasty crumbling.
With *René Liu, Niu Chenze, Chang Shih*

L'ACCOMPAGNATRICE See **The Accompanist**

THE ACCOMPANIST (aka 'L'Accompagnatrice')
Claude Miller — France, 1992 [110min]
A tale of self-sacrifice, clandestine love and ultimately
collaboration in German-occupied Paris in WW2. The atmos-
phere created is OK, but it's the human drama here that
matters most.
With *Richard Bohringer, Elena Safonova, Romane Bohringer,
Bernard Verley*

ACCORDING TO THE CODE
Charles Michelson — U.S., 1916
Love between North and South in the War of Secession.
Familiar plot involves husband dying and widow marrying the
guy who was injured. Not too demanding, and has several
good action scenes.
With *Lewis Stone, Marguerite Clayton*

ACE ELI AND RODGER OF THE SKIES
See **The Great Waldo Pepper**

ACE OF ACES
J. Walter Ruben — U.S., 1933 [75min]

Blood-lust overtakes a meek sculptor when he has the Hun in his sights in this WW1 aviation drama.

If you weren't Wild Bill Wellman in those days, chances are you purloined your aerial sequences. Walter Ruben found Hughes' **Hell's Angels** ripe for the picking.

With *Richard Dix, Elizabeth Allan, Theodore Newton, Ralph Bellamy*

ACES HIGH
Jack Gold — GB, 1976 [115min]

A rather late but worthy British entry into the almost fashionable sub-genre of WW1 flying films (**The Blue Max, Von Richthofen and Brown**), but not as good as either: and itself a virtual remake of **Journey's End** taken out of the trenches. TV director Gold employed Peter Allwork as action photographer — just as Corman did in **VR and B**.

Reasonable action sequences, with some good and some very approximate replica aircraft.

With *Malcolm McDowell, Christopher Plummer, Simon Ward, John Gielgud, Trevor Howard, Ray Milland*

ACROSS THE PACIFIC
Roy del Ruth — U.S., 1926

The Philippines at the turn of the century. The Pacific arm of the Spanish-American War is over, but the natives are still hostile — especially to the Americans. Blue plays a U.S. spy seeking out the rebel leader.

With *Monte Blue, Myrna Loy, Walter McGrail*

ACROSS THE PACIFIC
John Huston — U.S., 1942 [100min]

Warners using the studio-system economies of scale? Not only did Huston reunite Bogart, Astor and Greenstreet from *The Maltese Falcon* a few months earlier, WB gave him the old film title from 1926 and Blue (in a bit part) as well. At least the story is different, with pre-Pearl Harbor Japanese spies on the Panama Canal this time (a theme close to U.S. hearts — **Betrayal from the East** ★ from William Berke in 1945 also covered it).

Incidentally, Warners remade the *Falcon* from their 1931 original, directed by — yes — del Ruth.

With *Humphrey Bogart, Mary Astor, Sydney Greenstreet, Sen Yung, Monte Blue*

ACTION IN THE NORTH ATLANTIC
Lloyd Bacon — U.S., 1943 [130min]

High on propaganda, this is the story of the U.S. Merchant Marine's 'liberty ships' and the Murmansk run during the U-boat blockade in WW2. Massey's ship (Bogart is his first mate) is sunk as the Nazis toy with the convoy. the action is plentiful and the realism is attained through its documentary style and attitude.

With *Humphrey Bogart, Raymond Massey, Alan Hale*

ACES HIGH
Dogfights over France during World War 1. The action is reasonably good and some of the aircraft quite convincing. EMI

ADDRESS UNKNOWN
William Cameron Menzies — U.S., 1944 [70min]

Kressman Taylor's popular novel adapted into a neat thriller by Menzies. The story is fairly familiar for the times — Nazi anti-semitism in the late '30s; American naiveté until it's too late, predictable stuff.

With *Paul Lukas, Carl Esmond, Peter Van Eyck, Mady Christians, Morris Carnovsky*

ADIEU BONAPARTE (aka 'Al-wedaa ya Bonaparte')
Youssef Chahine — Egypt/France, 1984 [120min]

Sprawling account of Napoleon's 1798 campaign in Egypt, seen through today's Egypt — gay love scenes and all. Patrice Chéreu makes his mark as Napoleon.

With *Michel Piccoli, Mohsen Mohiedine, Mohensa Tewfik, Patrice Chéreu*

ADOLF HITLER — MY PART IN HIS DOWNFALL
Norman Cohen — GB, 1972 [100min]

Impossible to be funnier than Spike Milligan's own war autobiographies, but as a British comedy film it just gets by. Where it does score, however, is in evoking the mood of those tentative early weeks and months of WW2 — the Phoney War, call-up, training to be soldiers. Jim Dale plays Spike, and Spike plays his Dad.

With *Jim Dale, Spike Milligan, Arthur Lowe, Bill Maynard, Windsor Davies*

ADVANCE TO THE REAR (aka 'Company of Cowards?')
George Marshall — U.S., 1964 [95min]

Civil War western about incompetent Union officers sent west on a mission designed to take them out of the fray — only for them to trap a Confederate spy.

In all a pleasing comedy from the veteran Marshall, which borders on satire.

With *Glenn Ford, Stella Stevens, Melvyn Douglas, Jim Backus, Alan Hale, Joan Blondell*

ADVENTURE FOR TWO See **The Demi-Paradise**

ADVENTURE IN IRAQ See **The Green Goddess**

ADVENTURES OF BUFFALO BILL
Theodore Wharton — U.S., 1914
Interesting in its coverage of the U.S. Cavalry's massacre of the Sioux at Wounded Knee in December 1890 (see also **Soldier Blue**). With Cody as consultant as well as star, the outcome was a somewhat sanitized version of events.
With *William Cody, Chief Running Hawk*

ADVENTURES OF CASANOVA
Roberto Gavaldon — U.S., 1948 [85min]
Excuse for a naughty, swashbuckling spectacular from a second division studio which is unsatisfactory at all levels. Casanova, a Venetian, was both a soldier and spy, among the many and varied entries on his CV, and this poor fare attempts to locate him in the Kingdom of Sicily, where he is somehow involved in a side-show of the War of Austrian Succession (see **A Celebrated Case** for more direct coverage of that particular war).
With *Arturo de Cordova, Lucille Bremer, Turhan Bey*

THE ADVENTURES OF GERARD
Jerzy Skolimowski — GB/Italy/Switzerland, 1970 [90min]
Conan Doyle's hussar in an international co-production romp through the Peninsular War. An unusual vehicle for a normally serious director, who at the time was exiled from Poland — perhaps that's why. Some surprisingly good costumes, based on contemporary Dighton paintings.
With *Peter McEnery, Claudia Cardinale, Eli Wallach, Jack Hawkins, John Neville*

THE ADVENTURES OF GERARD
Gerard (Peter McEnery) demonstrating how hussars get into big girls' blouses! UA

ADVENTURES OF MICHAEL STROGOFF
See **The Soldier and the Lady**

THE ADVENTURES OF ROBIN HOOD
Michael Curtiz/William Keighley — U.S., 1938 [100min]
Five-star entertainment (nominated for Best Picture Oscar and Korngold's score won an Academy Award), but gets a big zero for history. Probably the most famous swashbuckler of them all, featuring the best swashbuckler of them all.

The legend of Robin Hood is loosely set in England of the 1190s at a time of Saxon unrest with their Plantagenet overlords. Prince John is looking after things while King Richard is having the dickens of a job finding his way back from the Crusades. While the Cœur de Lion is ensnared in Austria, John declares himself ruler, supported by Norman nobles like Guy of Gisbourne and the Sheriff of Nottingham. Robin of Loxley, although a nobleman, has no truck with this, gathers a group of like-minded individuals around him, and begins to put together (unofficially!) Richard's ransom.
With *Errol Flynn, Olivia de Havilland, Basil Rathbone, Claude Rains, Alan Hale, Ian Hunter*

The saga of Robin Hood has been told and re-told many times on film — some are set in more historically-correct scenarios than others, while some are just ludicrous. Curtiz's version was partly based on Sir Walter Scott's **Ivanhoe ★★** filmed under that title by Richard Thorpe in 1952 (105min), with Robert Taylor, Joan Fontaine, Elizabeth Taylor and George Sanders. (A short-lived UK TV series based on Scott's character made the name of Roger Moore in 1958; whilst a superior TV movie, again bearing the same title, and starring a particularly glossy cast [James Mason, Anthony Andrews, Sam Neill, Michael Hordern, Lysette Anthony, Olivia Hussey], was released in 1982, directed by Douglas Camfield.) Other Robin Hood-related titles include:

Robin Hood ★★★ (Allan Dwan — U.S., 1922 [125min]) With *Douglas Fairbanks, Wallace Beery*
The Bandit of Sherwood Forest ★ (George Sherman/Henry Levin — U.S., 1946[85min]) With *Cornel Wilde, Anita Louise*
Prince of Thieves ★★ (Howard Bretherton — U.S., 1948 [70min]) With *Jon Hall, Patricia Morison*
Rogues of Sherwood Forest (Gordon Douglas — U.S., 1950 [80min]) With *John Derek, Alan Hale*
Robin Hood's son (!), King John and Magna Carta.
The Story of Robin Hood and his Merrie Men ★★ (Ken Annakin — GB, 1952 [85min]) With *Richard Todd, Peter Finch*
Men of Sherwood Forest ★ (Val Guest — GB, 1956 [75min]) With *Don Taylor, Reginald Beckwith*
Son of Robin Hood (George Sherman — GB, 1958 [75min]) With *David Hedison*
Even less historically factual (impossible!) than the putative offspring's outing above!
The Sword of Sherwood Forest ★★ (Terence Fisher — GB, 1960 [80min]) With *Richard Greene* (on the back of 143 TV episodes), *Peter Cushing*
Robin and Marian ★★★ (Richard Lester — U.S., 1976 [105min]) With *Sean Connery, Audrey Hepburn*
Robin Hood ★★ (John Irvin — U.S., 1991 [105min]) With *Patrick Bergin, Uma Thurman*
Robin Hood: Prince of Thieves ★★★ (Kevin Reynolds — U.S., 1991[145min]) With *Kevin Costner, Morgan Freeman*
Popular vehicle for a star that, at the time, could do no wrong.

Ineptly spoofed by Mel Brooks in *Robin Hood: Men in Tights* (1993), with Cary Elwes.
TV versions include the above-mentioned Richard Greene in *The Adventures of Robin Hood* (1955-59) and *Robin of Sherwood* with Michael Praed (who was replaced by Jason Connery) between 1984 and 1986.

THE ADVENTURES OF TARTU (aka 'Tartu')
Harold S. Bucquet — GB, 1943 [105min]
Donat saves the day in more ways than one in this very thin spy caper based in WW2 Czechoslovakia. He's the only good thing about it.
With *Robert Donat, Valerie Hobson*

THE ADVENTURES OF WERNER HOLT
(aka 'Die Abenteuer des Werner Holt')
Joachim Kunert — FRG, 1963 [165min]
Serious, over-long adaptation of Dieter Noll's autobiography about a young German finally understanding the horrors of Nazism while serving on the Russian Front in 1943.
With *Klaus-Peter Thiele, Manfred Karge*

THE ADVENTURESS See I See a Dark Stranger

AERIAL GUNNER
William H. Pine — U.S., 1943 [80min]
Routine Pacific actioner from WW2. A U.S. bomber is forced by Japanese fighters to land behind enemy lines. Morris gives his life to save Arlen — a life-long rival.
With *Chester Morris, Richard Arlen, Lila Ward*

AEROGRAD (aka 'Frontier')
Alexander Dovzhenko — USSR, 1935 [80min]
An early anti-facist tract from the Soviet master, wrapped in a suspenseful and visually-striking 'Japanese spies try to sabotage Siberian airport' scenario.
   With the Japanese already occupying neighbouring Manchuria, the Soviet film-makers were turning away at last from the Revolution and Civil War and starting to consider potential threats from outside their borders.
With *Semyon Shagaida, Stepan Shkurat, Sergei Stolyarof*

THE AFFAIR
Paul Seed — GB, 1995 [105min]
A disappointing attempt to address an interesting and much overlooked subject — racism towards black GIs stationed 'over here' in WW2.
With *Kerry Fox, Courtney B. Vance*

L'AFFAIRE DU COURRIER DE LYON
Claude Autant-Lara/Maurice Lehmann — France, 1937 [100min]
Five robbers attack the treasury courier on his way to support Napoleon in Italy in 1796. They are arrested — but one is actually a doppelganger. Guess who gets executed?
With *Pierre Blanchar, Dita Parlo, Sylvia Bataille*

L'AFFICHE ROUGE See The Red Poster

THE AFRICAN QUEEN
John Huston — GB, 1951 [105min]
The film with all the credentials: a script from that quintes-sential movie critic, James Agee, based on a Forester yarn; Jack Cardiff's amazing jungle camerawork; and Huston eliciting career-best performances from Bogart and Hepburn. Based in equatorial Africa during WW1, Bogart, an old sweat eking out a living along the waterways, wreaks revenge for the killing of Hepburn's brother (Morley) by German troops. The climactic scrap between the 'Queen' and the German gunboat tops a marvellous filmic experience. It won Bogart his only Oscar, and provided nominations for Hepburn, Huston and Agee.
With *Humphrey Bogart, Katharine Hepburn, Robert Morley*

THE AFRICAN QUEEN
Bogart and Hepburn, uncharacteristically quiet for once as they drag the 'Queen' through the swamps around Lake Victoria. United Artists (cour-tesy KOBAL)

AFRODITE DEA DELL'AMORE
See **Aphrodite, Goddess of Love**

AGAINST ALL FLAGS
George Sherman — U.S., 1952 [85min]
One of Flynn's last run-outs as a top-knotch swashbuckler, almost replaying his **Captain Blood** role: a pirate captain attacking Spanish shipping on behalf of the British Crown in the 17th century.
With *Errol Flynn, Maureen O'Hara, Anthony Quinn*

Updated in 1967 as **The King's Pirate**, with Doug McLure, by Don Weis [100min], but set during the Napoleonic Wars.

AGAINST THE WIND
Charles Crichton — GB, 1947 [95min]
Rather unusual topic for Ealing Studios and its director *(The Lavender Hill Mob, A Fish Called Wanda)*. It's a sharp WW2 spy thriller based in London which has as its plot a traitor in a school for saboteurs.
With *Simone Signoret, Robert Beatty, Jack Warner, James Robertson Justice, Gordon Jackson*

AGONIA See Agony

AGONY
(aka 'Agonia', 'Rasputin') See **Rasputin and the Empress**

AGUIRRE, DER ZORN GOTTES
See **Aguirre, Wrath of God**

AGUIRRE, WRATH of GOD
(aka 'Aguirre, Der Zorn Gottes')
Werner Herzog — West Germany, 1972 [95min]
A massive cinematic achievement. Senses are numbed by the presence of Kinski's megalomanic Conquistador fighting the overwhelming barriers — natural and man-made — placed before him in his quest for El Dorado. (It is 1560 and Pizarro's brother is leading an expedition in search of the legendary site in Peru). Herzog harnesses these huge forces with the help of Thomas Mauch's imaginative camera and a haunting score from Popol Vuh.
With *Klaus Kinski, Ruy Guerra, Del Negro, Helena Rojo*

AI TO SHI NO KIROKU See **Heart of Hiroshima**

AIR AMERICA
Roger Spottiswoode — U.S., 1990 [120min]
Tawdry, unfunny war comedy involving CIA pilots smuggling supplies into Laos during the Vietnam War.
With *Mel Gibson, Robert Downey Jr, Nancy Travis*

AIR FORCE
Howard Hawks — U.S., 1943 [125min]
Teamwork is the propaganda message in this flag-waver. We follow the sorties of a Flying Fortress across the length and breadth of the Pacific theatre, hearing much ensemble Jap bad-mouthing along the way, while, as skilfully as ever, Hawks stitches in the newsreel action scenes.
With *John Ridgley, Gig Young, Arthur Kennedy, John Garfield, Charles Drake*

EL ALAMEIN
Fred F Sears — U.S., 1953 [65min]
Unlikely story of an American tank parts engineer and a sole tank crew holding off Rommel's crack Afrika Korps until relieved. El Alamein? Well, they had to call this second feature something, although it really is against the Trades Descriptions Act.
With *Scott Brady, Edward Ashley, Rita Moreno*

THE ALAMO
John Wayne — U.S., 1960 [195min]
The end of Travis, Bowie and Crockett at the little mission. It is 1836 and General Santa Anna's hordes have headed north to put those dratted Texicans down for good. Col Travis' task — hold them up until Sam Houston can rustle up a proper army. Texas' independence is not far off.

The Duke's directorial debut (he only did direct once more — see **The Green Berets**) owes a lot to mentor John Ford, who was on hand for some of the time, and isn't half as bad as some made out. It is too long, with one or two interminable intermissions, but it has an epic sweep to it and a fine sense of colour (the Mexican uniforms are a definite highlight). The action is also first rate.
With *John Wayne, Richard Widmark, Laurence Harvey, Richard Boone, Frankie Avalon, Linda Cristal*

THE ALAMO
Part of Santa Anna's 7,000-troop assault on the old mission. United Artists (courtesy KOBAL)

Other pictures involving the Battle of the Alamo and Texas' independence include:
The Martyrs of the Alamo ★ (Christy Cabanne — U.S., 1915) With *Walter Long*
The Heroes of the Alamo (Harry Fraser – U.S., 1938) With *Lane Chandler* (as Crockett)
Man of Conquest ★★ (George Nicholls — U.S., 1939 [100min]) With *Richard Dix, Joan Fontaine*
Concerns the life and times of Texas' first leader, Sam Houston.
Lone Star ★★ (Vincent Sherman — U.S., 1952 [90min]) With *Clark Gable, Ava Gardner*
More about Sam Houston.
The Man from the Alamo ★★★ (Budd Boetticher — U.S., 1953 [80min]) With *Glenn Ford, Julie Adams*
Davy Crockett (1955) See separate entry
The Last Command ★★ (Frank Lloyd — U.S., 1955 [110min]) With *Ernest Borgnine*
Deals with the role of Jim Bowie.
The First Texan ★★ (Byron Haskin — U.S., 1956 [80min]) With *Joel McCrea, Jeff Morrow*
About Houston again.

ALBERT RN (aka 'Break to Freedom')
Lewis Gilbert — GB, 1953 [90min]
The latest in the line of British POW stories after **The Captive Heart** and **The Wooden Horse** (see also **The Colditz Story**). They are almost a genre apart from their U.S. counterparts, though. The British 'grin and bear it', 'don't let them grind you down' attitude is balanced by a public school sense of humour. This one is based on the true story of an escape from a naval prison camp by means of a lifelike dummy taken on parade to hide the escaper's absence. In comparison, in **Stalag 17** from the same year, the POWs seem to be spray-coated with an arrogant sheen — indeed cynical individualism — as they ridicule their captors, and themselves. The two caricatures are beautifully obvious in the apotheosis of POW films, John Sturges' **The Great Escape**.
With *Jack Warner, Anthony Steel, Robert Beatty, William Sylvester, Anton Differing, Eddie Byrne*

ALEXANDER NEVSKY

Sergei Eisenstein — USSR, 1938 [110min]

Eisenstein at his most cinematic — a magnificent swathe of landscape, climate and people. A timely reminder to Nazi Germany, Nevsky is the Russian prince called upon to lead his people against the invading Teutonic Knights in 1242. With the Red Army at his disposal, Eisenstein's recreation of the battle on frozen Lake Peipus is a masterpiece on a huge scale — yet pays the precisest attention to detail.

With *Nikolai Cherkassov, Nikolai Okhlopkov, Andrei Abrikosov, Dmitri Orlov*

ALEXANDER THE GREAT

Robert Rossen — U.S., 1956 [135min]

A literate sword-and-sandal movie? This comes quite close to it, but in its attempt it bogs down the action and adds an unwanted 20 minutes to its length. Burton goes slightly over the top as the Boy Wonder conquering most of the known world back in the 4th century BC, but the battle scenes are fine and historically it's fairly accurate — perhaps that's where its major cinematic fault lies.

With *Richard Burton, Frederic March, Danielle Darrieux, Claire Bloom, Harry Andrews, Stanley Baker*

ALFRED THE GREAT

Clive Donner — GB, 1969 [120min]

One of a very few pictures made world-wide, which deal with factual history in the Dark Ages. Even the glut of 1980s sword-and-sorcery tales were mostly later-medieval in basis. Unfortunately Donner has not made the most of his rare opportunity, with '60s icon Hemmings badly miscast as the king uniting England in 871.

His feel for the action sequences suggests that the sparse numbers and spartan, rather 'impressionist' costumes (with unusually sombre-looking Vikings) were the result of budgetary pressure, not a striving for realism. Notable only for Ian McKellen's film debut.

With *David Hemmings, Michael York, Colin Blakely, Prunella Ransome, Julian Glover, Ian McKellen*

AN ALIEN ENEMY

William A. Seiter — U.S., 1918
Standard WW1 espionage drama with a German POW camp scene.

With *Louise Glaum* (playing two roles), *Thurston Hall*

ALL-OUT ATTACK ON SINGAPORE

Koji Shima — Japan, 1943
Using actual locations, Shima was influenced by contemporary documentaries like *Occupation Sumatra*. The aim — to glorify the Japanese conquest of South East Asia in 1942.

ALL QUIET ON THE WESTERN FRONT

Lewis Milestone — U.S., 1930 [130min]

The archetypal anti-war movie.

Erich Maria Remarque's tale of German youth callously sacrificed for their country's honour is the basis for this film, which is the most famous of several WW1 pictures (see **West Front 1918, Journey's End, Tell England**) to be made at this time of reflection and foreboding of war to come — a hiatus before events in Manchuria, Abyssinia, Spain and the Rhineland were to bring back the horrors of 1914-18.

Telling the now-famous tale of a group of young German soldiers on the Western Front from 1916 to the end of the war, and its systematic decimation, it is full of symbolism pointing out war's contradictions and ultimate inanity.

The film is a landmark for technical innovation and still powerful set pieces, Milestone's imaginative direction won an Oscar for himself and the picture — awarded to a war film for the first time.

Naturally the film was banned in Germany with the advent of the Nazis to power in 1933. It was also Universal's biggest production for 30 years to come, until **Spartacus**, due to the crippling box office disaster of *King of Jazz*: and the studio's only Best Picture Oscar until *The Sting* in 1973. Probably in everyone's 'Most Moving Picture' Top Ten.

With *Lew Ayres, Louis Wolheim, John Wray, Slim Summerville, Russell Gleason, Raymond Griffith*

A totally irrelevant TV version, starring Richard Thomas, was released in 1979.

ALL THE YOUNG MEN

Hall Bartlett — U.S., 1960 [85min]

Cheap Korean War actioner used to air the issue of racial prejudice in battle. Look out for Ingemar Johansson, World Heavyweight Boxing Champion until Floyd Paterson won it back that same year, in a fairly kooky cast list.

With *Alan Ladd, Sidney Poitier, James Darren, Glenn Corbett, Mort Stahl, Ingemar Johansson*

ALL THE YOUNG MEN
Death in the Korean snow. Columbia

ALL THROUGH THE NIGHT
★ *Vincent Sherman — U.S., 1942* [105min]
★ Odd blend of comedy-spy-gangster movie set in and around New York just before the Americans enter WW2. Bogey foils the Hollywood Nazis in their attempt to blow up a battleship.
With *Humphrey Bogart, Conrad Veidt, Peter Lorre*

ALLEGHENY UPRISING (aka 'The First Rebel')
★ *William A. Seiter — U.S., 1939* [100min]
★ Interesting only for its subject matter and the timing of its release. As a film it's pretty average, with Trevor joining Wayne (on the back of *Stagecoach*) in the Pennsylvania backwoods fighting everybody in sight, viz the oppressive British and the marauding Indians, in a prologue to the French and Indian Wars. Several scenes were edited due to British protestations (for bad Britain read Nazi Germany).
With *John Wayne, Claire Trevor, Brian Donlevy, George Sanders*

AL-RISALAH See Mohammad, Messenger of God

ALVAREZ KELLY
★ *Edward Dmytryk — U.S., 1966* [115min]
★ Based on a true story from the American Civil War, Holden is in charge of a cattle drive taking beef to the Union, which gets stolen by the Confederates.
With *William Holden, Richard Widmark, Janice Rule, Patrick O'Neal*

AL-WEDAA YA BONAPARTE See Adieu Bonaparte

AMBUSH
★ *Sam Wood — U.S., 1949* [90min]
★ Last picture for Sam Wood (*A Night at the Opera, King's Row,* **For Whom the Bell Tolls**, and a piece of **Gone with the Wind** when Victor Fleming fell ill).

THE AMERICANIZATION OF EMILY
US forces come ashore on Omaha Beach in this 1964 black comedy.
MGM

Solid Western set in the Apache troubles of the last decades of the 19th century (the whites having the higher moral ground, of course) with a couple of good action sequences involving the Cavalry.
With *Robert Taylor, John Hodiak, Arlene Dahl*

AMBUSH BAY
Ron Winston — U.S., 1966 [110min] ★
High on action, low on sense: U.S. Marines on a special mission in Japanese-occupied Philippines.
With *Mickey Rooney, Hugh O'Brian, James Mitchum*

AMERICA (aka 'Love and Sacrifice')
D. W. Griffith — U.S., 1924 [120min] ★
Having dealt with the internecine rivalries in **Birth of a** ★
Nation, Griffith addresses the pure embryo of American ★
nationhood a century earlier. The American Revolution was all about democracy, so Griffith keeps on telling us, which is why *America* was banned in Britain. The imperialists are painted in a pretty dark shade of black, while heroes of the Revolution take centre screen. In style, the film is very similar to his 1915 landmark, but lack of imagination made this his last silent epic.
With *Neil Hamilton, Carol Dempster, Lionel Barrymore*

AN AMERICAN GUERRILLA IN THE PHILIPPINES
(aka 'I Shall Return') ★
Fritz Lang — U.S., 1950 [105min] ★
Lang's only venture into the Pacific theatre of WW2. Indeed ★
his only other pure action Hollywood War film was **Hangmen also Die** about the Heydrich affair. The British title gives the plot away — Power leading a group of U.S. Marines who are supporting Filipino guerrillas against the Japanese, awaiting the return of General MacArthur following the fall of Bataan.
With *Tyrone Power, Tom Ewell, Micheline Presle, Robert Barrat,*

THE AMERICANIZATION OF EMILY
Arthur Hiller — U.S., 1964 [115min] ★
A Paddy Chayevsky *(The Hospital, Network)* script fails to save ★
this hit-and-miss black comedy of events surrounding the D-Day landings. Andrews confirms she's only Oscar material when there's an o/d of saccharine. Garner, as usual, is good.
With *James Garner, Julie Andrews, James Coburn, Melvyn Douglas, Joyce Grenfell*

THE AMERICANO
John Emerson — U.S., 1916 [60min] ★
Produced by D. W. Griffith with **Gone with the Wind**'s director, ★
Victor Fleming, behind the camera, this loose historical ★
vehicle for Fairbanks is concerned with the revolution in Patagonia, leading up to its partitioning between Chile and Argentina in 1902. Many action films of Hollywood's silent era dealt with rumblings in Latin America — mostly in unnamed countries.
Revolutions were commonplace in the early decades of the 20th century in Nicaragua, Guatemala, Haiti, Cuba and of course Mexico, and being within the U.S. sphere of influence made films on these topics interesting to the American public.
With *Douglas Fairbanks Sr, Alma Rubens*

AMNESIA
Gonzalo Justiniano — Chile, 1994 [90min] ★
A dramatic attempt, using flashback techniques, to rationalize atrocities in post-Allende Chile through the revenge taken by

a former soldier on his one-time brute of a sergeant.
With *Julio Jung, Nelson Villagra, Pedro Vicuna*

THE ANDERSON PLATOON
See ***The Anderson Section***

THE ANDERSON SECTION
(aka 'The Anderson Platoon') See ***317e Section***

ANGEL (aka 'Danny Boy')
Neil Jordan — Ireland, 1982 [90min]
Jordan's (*Mona Lisa*, **The Crying Game**, *Interview with a Vampire*) directorial debut sees Rea in troubled Ulster avenging murders that he has witnessed. John Boorman, director of **Hell in the Pacific**, *Deliverance*, **Excalibur** and **Hope and Glory** produced: cinematographer Chris Menges (**The Killing Fields**, **The Mission**) directed photography. It all promised so much more.
With *Stephen Rea, Alan Devlin, Veronica Quilligan, Peter Caffrey, Ray McAnally*

THE ANGEL WORE RED
Nunnally Johnson — U.S., 1960 [105min]
Spanish Civil War romantic hodgepodge. Johnson, who scripted such films as *The Grapes of Wrath, Tobacco Road*, **The Desert Fox** and even **The Dirty Dozen**, directed few films — and it shows.
Brief, quite interesting action footage of this rarely filmed war, e.g. Nationalist fighter aircraft.
With *Ava Gardner, Dirk Bogarde, Joseph Cotten, Vittorio de Sica*

ANGELS ONE FIVE
George More O'Ferrall — GB, 1952 [100min]
Box-offices in Britain were stormed for this low-key, very British RAF drama set at the time of 'the Few'. It made a change from the Hollywood WW2 and Korean War air pictures inundating the local Roxy, I suppose. You could have probably named the principals in ten guesses.
Bad model work of German aircraft in flying sequences, but made with genuine Hurricanes (ex-Portuguese air force).
With *Jack Hawkins, John Gregson, Michael Denison*

THE ANGRY HILLS
Robert Aldrich — GB/U.S., 1959 [105min]
Set during the German invasion of Greece in late 1940; Mitchum is a U.S. war correspondent caught up in espionage. Baker (uncharacteristically) plays a softy Gestapo officer.
After **Apache**, *Kiss me Deadly* and **Attack!**, this was very disappointing fare from Aldrich, who was hardly to regain such form again, although he at least became gratuitously violent in **The Dirty Dozen**.
With *Robert Mitchum, Stanley Baker, Gia Scala, Elisabeth Mueller*

AN ANNAPOLIS STORY (aka 'The Blue and the Gold')
Don Siegel — U.S., 1955 [80min]
Unimaginative Korean War story about recently-trained navy flyers.
With *John Derek, Kevin McCarthy, Diana Lynn*

AN-NASR SALAH AD-DIN See **Saladin**

ANNI DIFFICILI See **The Difficult Years**

ANOTHER TIME, ANOTHER PLACE (1958)
See **Another Time, Another Place** (1983)

ANOTHER TIME, ANOTHER PLACE
Michael Radford — GB, 1983
Poignant love story between a Scottish famer's wife and an Italian POW, towards the end of WW2. Emphasis here on the 'imprisonment' metaphor, and how it affects them both. Stunning depiction of the harsh landscape.
With *Phyllis Logan, Giovanni Mauriello*

A WW2-background romance with the same title, set in rural Cornwall, was made in 1958 by Lewis Allen, with Lana Turner and Barry Sullivan. Only notable for an early outing by a young Sean Connery as a killed war correspondent.

ANTONY AND CLEOPATRA See **Cleopatra** (1963)

ANZIO (aka 'The Battle for Anzio')
Edward Dmytryk — Italy, 1968 [115min]
Based very loosely on war correspondent Wynford Vaughan Thomas' memoirs and with a starry cast — what went wrong? Journeyman Dmytryk and an appalling script completely undo Thomas' sentiments so that his words sound pompous and pretentious. We are left with another run-of-the-mill U.S. invasion (sub-**The Longest Day** standard) picture. The only good thing to say for it is that some attempt was made at accurate costume.
With *Robert Mitchum, Robert Ryan, Peter Falk, Arthur Kennedy*

APACHE
Robert Aldrich — U.S., 1954 [90min]
After **Broken Arrow**, Hollywood started to take the Indian's point of view for a change and a more balanced approach comes through in this sombre Western. Lancaster plays a renegade Apache who after playing havoc with his Army pursuers, is surprisingly allowed to live.
With *Burt Lancaster, Jean Peters, John McIntyre, Charles Buchinsky (Bronson)*

APACHE DRUMS
Hugo Fregonese — U.S., 1951 [75min]
Typical Western with no real interest except that it fictionalizes an incident in the life of Victorio, a real-life Apache chief almost as powerful as Geronimo or Cochise.
With *Stephen McNally, Willard Parker, Coleen Gray*

APACHE RIFLES
William H. Witney — U.S., 1964 [90min]
Cavalry v Indians vehicle for Murphy, who is suitably sensitive to the Red Men's predicament.
With *Audie Murphy, Michael Dante, L. Q. Jones, Linda Lawson*

APHRODITE, GODDESS OF LOVE
(aka 'Afrodite Dea Dell'Amore', 'Slave Women of Corinth')
Mario Bonnard — Italy, 1958 [90min]
Don't be put off by the yucky title — this story of how the Governor of Corinth in Nero's day coped with a local uprising is surprisingly jolly. Sergio Leone had a hand in the script.
With *Isabelle Corey, Antonio de Teffe, Irene Tunc, Ivo Garrani*

The Battle of Corinth — Mario Costa, 1962 with Jacques Sernes, covered similar ground, but very badly.

APOCALYPSE NOW

Francis Ford Coppola — U.S., 1979 [155min]

Echoing the hellish river journey in Conrad's *Heart of Darkness*, Coppola's flawed epic took films about the Vietnam War to a pretentious full stop. It would not be until the mid-1980s and the advent of cut-no-ice movies like **Full Metal Jacket, Hamburger Hill** and **Platoon** that the Vietnam War would receive serious, straightforward attention from film-makers again.

An operatic, hallucinogenic, at times mesmeric piece of filmmaking, it is, nevertheless, more concerned with its own style in portraying the madness of war, than with the madness itself. Brando's maverick colonel is one of the most bizarre and incomprehensible (in more ways than one) characters ever created for the screen. Still, the helicopter attack by Duvall's Air Cavalry unit is an unforgettable set-piece. Vittorio Storaro picked up an Academy Award for Cinematography, and Coppola (for Direction, and with John Milius for Script), Duvall and the picture itself, all were nominated.

With *Martin Sheen, Robert Duvall, Marlon Brando, Frederic Forrest, Dennis Hopper, Sam Bottoms*

APPOINTMENT IN BERLIN

Alfred E. Green — U.S., 1943 [75min]

Double propaganda and double agent. Sanders is WW2 RAF officer seemingly diametrically opposed to the 'Careless talk' ethos. In fact he talks so much the Nazis offer him a job as a Lord Haw Haw-type, but little do they know . . .

With *George Sanders, Gale Sondergaard, Marguerite Chapman, Onslow Stevens*

APPOINTMENT IN LONDON

Philip Leacock — GB, 1952 [95min]

Not a sequel to the previous entry, this fairly run-of-the-mill tract deals with a British bomber squadron in 1943.

With *Dirk Bogarde, Ian Hunter, Dinah Sheridan, Bryan Forbes*

APPOINTMENT WITH VENUS (aka 'Island Rescue')

Ralph Thomas — GB, 1951 [90min]

Could have come from Ealing Studios, but this is a Thomas/Betty Box production and just as amusing. The plot? Niven has to abduct a Jersey cow from under the noses of the Nazis occupying the Channel Islands. Oddly tense, too.

With *David Niven, Glynis Johns, Kenneth More*

L'ARBRE DE GUERNICA

Fernando Arrabal — France/Spain, 1975 [105min]

Love among the German bombs on Guernica in Franco's 1937 purge of the Basque country. Arrabal was pretty smart to bring this out so soon after the dictator's death. See Resnais' documentary, ***Guernica***.

With *Mariangela Melato, Ron Faber*

ARCH OF TRIUMPH

Lewis Milestone — U.S., 1948 [120min]

Milestone tried to recreate magic with another Erich Maria Remarque story (see **All Quiet on the Western Front**) but this time it fell flat. Now it's love in Paris in June 1940, refugees, camps, flashbacks — but it's all so droopy and dull.

With *Ingrid Bergman, Charles Boyer, Charles Laughton*

ARCHANGEL

Guy Maddin — Canada, 1990 [90min]

APOCALYPSE NOW
Lt Willard's (Martin Sheen) riverboat on its journey through hell.
Omni Zoetrope

Maddin veers towards the absurd in this tale of a WW1 Canadian soldier allied to the Whites of Arkhangelsk against the Bolsheviks in 1918. Enjoy the amazing battle sequences in the snow, though, to get you through the confusing bits.

With *Kyle McCulloch, Kathy Marykuca, Sarah Neville, Ari Cohen*

ARE WE ALL MURDERERS?

(aka 'Nous Sommes Tous des Assassins')

André Cayette — France, 1948 [115min]

Disturbing tale of a natural born killer plying his trade for the Resistance in 1944 Occupied France. Cayette draws a parallel to four years of Gestapo tactics, but pulls back from adopting the interrogative case in the French title.

With *Mouloudji, Raymond Pellegrin, Claude Laydu*

ARGIE

Jorge Blanco — GB, 1985 [75min]

Drunken one-man Argentinian would-be hit squad in Britain at the time of the Falklands War of 1982. Totally exploitative and pointless. One of a very few films to emerge from the conflict — none of which deal with events directly (see **For Queen and Country**).

With *Jorge Blanco, Christine von Schreitter*

ARISE MY LOVE

Mitchell Leisen — U.S., 1940 [115min]

Highly-watchable romantic comedy set at the end of the Spanish Civil War and the beginning of WW2. Reporter Colbert rescues idealistic Milland from the grips of the fascists, and after meandering around Europe listening to the rumblings of the Nazi steam-roller getting under way, they sail back to the States. Their ship, the *Athena*, is torpedoed by a U-boat: Milland promptly joins the RAF whilst Colbert reports the dastardly act to the world. At the time, as effective a piece of U.S. anti-isolationist propaganda as any newsreel.

The script by Charles Brackett and Billy Wilder was based on the Oscar-winning original story by Benjamin Glazer and John S. Toldy: Oscar nominations were received by Charles Lang (Cinematography), Victor Young (Score) and for art direction.
With *Claudette Colbert, Ray Milland, Dennis O'Keefe, Walter Abel*

ARIZONA BUSHWACKERS
Lesley Selander — U.S., 1968 [85min]
A late Selander — but no better than the rest. Interesting concept, though — the story involves the preposterous (but probably true) notion that Abe Lincoln in the Civil War, with his jails filled to overflowing with Rebs, selected some for law-enforcement work in other parts of the Union unaffected by conflict, subject to the signing of an oath of allegiance.
With *Howard Keel, Brian Donlevy, Yvonne de Carlo, John Ireland, Scott Brady*

ARIZONA RAIDERS See **Quantrill's Raiders**

ARMAGEDDON See *The Battle of Jutland*

L'ARMEE DES OMBRES
See **The Army in the Shadows**

ARMORED ATTACK See **The North Star**

ARMORED COMMAND
Byron Haskin — U.S., 1961 [105min]
The Ardennes, December 1944. Before the German counter-attack in the **Battle of the Bulge**, a **Mata Hari**-type siren infiltrates a U.S. post. More cloak and dagger than action. Burt Reynolds' second feature.
With *Howard Keel, Tina Louise, Burt Reynolds, Earl Holliman*

ARMS AND THE WOMAN See **Mr Winkle goes to War**

ARMY (aka 'Rikugun')
Keisuke Kinoshita — Japan, 1944
One of a series of anti-Allies films produced by Japan during WW2. This considers U.S. attempts to restrict the size of the Imperial army in the run-up to the conflict, as it tells the tale of a Japanese family over three generations sending its sons off to war.
With *Kinuyo Tanaka, Chisu Ryu, Ken Mitsuda, Kazumasa Hoshino*

ARMY-NAVY SCREEN MAGAZINE
Leonard Spiegelgass (prod) — U.S., 1943+
An increasingly-important 'two-way' series of WW2 newsreels produced exclusively for U.S. forces by Hollywood writer Spiegelgass but inspired by Frank Capra (see also **Why We Fight**).

THE ARMY IN THE SHADOWS
(aka 'L'Armeé des Ombres)
Jean-Pierre Melville — France, 1969 [145min]
Film-noirish homage to the French Resistance in Lyon during WW2 — a long time in gestation for the director.
Although quite gruesome in parts, and certainly harrowing, the film has a gripping narrative and is a worthy testimony to its subject.
With *Lino Ventura, Simone Signoret, Jean-Pierre Cassel*

ARROWHEAD
Charles Marquis Warren — U.S., 1953 [105min]
An early run-out for Heston as a Cavalry Scout in the 1880s who was brought up by Apaches. Palance is the treacherous chief and Keith the soldier intent on persuading him to move to a Florida reservation. Pretty ordinary stuff.
With *Charlton Heston, Jack Palance, Katy Jurado, Brian Keith*

ARSENAL
Alexander Dovzhenko — USSR, 1929 [100min]
Much acclaimed by Eisenstein, this epic poem broke the creative bounds of Soviet cinema. The film looks passionately at life in a Ukraine munitions factory — tracing the story from WW1 to the 1917 revolution, and a tragic, yet heroic workers' rebellion in 1918 against the Whites.
With *S. Svachenko, A. Buchma, M. Nademsky*

ASCENDANCY
Edward Bennett — GB, 1982 [85min]
Slight essay concerning the standpoint of the English upper classes in 1920s Ireland. Tries to be arty in the style of Peter Greenaway, but falls between this and any substantive views on the troubles.
With *Julie Covington, Ian Charleson*

ARMORED COMMAND
Americans surprised by a German Panzer counter-attack in the Ardennes.
Allied Artists

THE ASCENT (aka 'Voskhozhdenie')
Larissa Shepitko — USSR, 1976 [105min]
A powerful account of the partisans and the occupying Germans in Belorussia, as it was then, in 1943. 'White' Russia is symbolised by the snowscape and sharply-focused through the monochrome camera work. The heroism of the partisan captured by the Nazis borders on the religious.
With *Boris Plotnikov, Sergei Yakovlev, Vladimir Gostjuchin*

THE ASCENT
Donald Shebib — U.S., 1994 [95min]

That truth is stranger than fiction there is no doubt. Who would have dreamed up this scenario? Italian prisoners in a British East African POW camp in WW2 challenge the Brits to a race to scale Mount Kenya.
With *Vincent Spano, Ben Cross, Tony Lo Bianco, Rachel Ward*

ASHES AND DIAMONDS (aka 'Popiol i Diament')
Andrzej Wajda — Poland, 1958 [105min]
This, the third part of Wajda's wartime trilogy (**A Generation, Kanal**) sees an opening out of style. Not really a 'war' film, it deals with the 'what happens next' question on the first day of peace in Poland in 1945. The hero knows how to kill his enemies, by who are his enemies now? Expert film-making.
With *Zbigniew Cybulski, Ewa Krzyzanowska, Adam Pawlikowski*

ASSASSIN OF THE TSAR (aka 'Tsareubiitsa')
Karen Shakhnazarov — GB/USSR, 1991 [105min]
Unusual and unsuccessful attempt to recreate the demise of the Romanovs in 1918 in the mind of a mental patient.
With *Malcolm McDowell, Oleg Yankovsky, Armen Dzhigarkhanyan*

ASSASSINATION (1964)
(aka 'Atentat') See **Hangmen also Die**

ASSASSINATION (1975) See **Assassination at Sarajevo**

ASSASSINATION AT SARAJEVO (1975) (aka 'Atentat u Sarajevu', 'The Day that Shook the World', 'Assassination')
Veljko Bulajic — Yugoslavia/Czechslovakia, 1975
Uninspired attempt to portray those days in late June 1914 — and one day in particular — which saw the end of Archduke Franz Ferdinand, and the beginnings of WW1.
With *Christopher Plummer, Florinda Bolkan, Maximilian Schell*

ASSIGNMENT IN BRITTANY
The Bosch about to be assailed by survivors of Agincourt! MGM

THE ASSAULT (aka 'De Aanslag')
Fons Rademakers — Holland, 1986 [150min]
Intelligent, thought-provoking film which stole the Best Foreign Film Oscar. De Lint is haunted throughout his life by Nazi killings which occurred in front of his eyes in occupied Holland during WW2. Works equally well as a taut thriller.
With *Derek de Lint, Marc van Uchelen, Monique Van de Ven, John Kraaykamp*

ASSIGNMENT IN BRITTANY
Jack Conway — U.S., 1943 [95min]
Ludicrous premise of a Free French officer remaining in France to fight the Germans — based on a Helen McInnes yarn.
With *Jean-Paul Aumont, Susan Peters, Signe Hasso, Reginald Owen*

THE ASSISI UNDERGROUND
Alexander Ramati — Italy/U.S., 1985 [180min]
The Golan-Globus caravan of mediocrity continues with this awful yarn. This time they've really indulged writer-director Romati in attempting to make this work as a feature film; a TV movie; even a TV mini-series. In any format the story, concerning Assisi clerics smuggling out Jews from under the noses of the Nazis, is utterly vacuous. The cast have all seen, and have all been, better.
With *Ben Cross, James Mason, Irene Papas, Maximilian Schell, Simon Ward*

AT DAWN WE DIE See **Tomorrow We Live**

ATENTAT See **Assassination** (1964)

ATENTAT U SARAJEVU See **Assassination at Sarajevo**

ATLANTIC CONVOY
Lew Landers — U.S., 1942
Typical low-budget Landers about a spy under suspicion in an Icelandic weather station in WW2. No surprises in either the plot or the acting.
With *John Beal, Bruce Bennett, Larry Parks, Lloyd Bridges*

ATTACK!
Robert Aldrich — U.S., 1956 [105min]
Primeval Aldrich — this is a ruthless, somewhat Fuller-esque, bloody war film of a type not seen too often in the mid-50s. The Battle of the Bulge is again the focus of film-makers (see **Battleground, Battle of the Bulge, A Midnight Clear**) and the theme is cowardice.
  Albert as the yellow captain, and Palance as his stinging lieutenant, give riveting performances and the action sequences are certainly vivid.
With *Jack Palance, Eddie Albert, Lee Marvin, Buddy Ebsen, Richard Jaeckel*

ATTACK AND RETREAT See **Italiano Brava Gente**

ATTACK: INVASION OF NEW BRITAIN
Frank Capra (prod) — U.S., 1944
An almost hour-long WW2 documentary made by the U.S. Office of War Information and supervised by Frank Capra. This type of 'front-line' documentary scored with audiences because it was basically honest, and pulled very few punches. (See also **The Battle of San Pietro, The Memphis Belle, The Fighting Lady**).

ATTACK FORCE Z
Tim Burstall — Australia/Taiwan, 1981 [110min]
An unimportant foray by Australian cinema to put its slant on the Pacific War. A small commando group are behind Japanese lines trying to find a plane that's crashed. Interesting to see one or two up-and-coming Antipodeans in the cast.
With *John Phillip Law, Mel Gibson, Sam Neill*

THE ATTACK LASTED FIVE DAYS
Ting Shan-Si — China/Japan, 1977
Surprising co-production by the protagonists re-enacting a Japanese attack on a small Chinese force on the outskirts of Shanghai in 1937 during the Sino-Japanese War.
With *Kuo Chuan, Hsiung, Lin Chin Hsia*

ATTACK ON THE IRON COAST
Paul Wendkos — GB/U.S., 1967 [90min]
Ordinary WW2 actioner sees Bridges as a Canadian leading a commando raid on a French port during WW2. A sort of Ste Nazaire meets Dieppe.
With *Lloyd Bridges, Andrew Keir, Sue Lloyd, Mark Eden, Maurice Denham*

ATTILA '74
Michael Cacoyannis — Greece, 1975
Greek Cypriot documentary — naturally not very complimentary to the Turks — who invaded the island's north shore in 1974. Cacoyannis is not too coherent in some passages, and he lets sentiment overshadow political point-making.

ATTILA THE HUN (aka 'Attilio Flegello di Dio')
Pietro Francisci — France/Italy, 1954 [80min]
The 'Scourge of God' is the subject of a picture that becomes a bridge between the de Mille-type Hollywood spectacle and the more prosaic Italian cinema sword-and-sandal vehicles for Steve Reeves and Gordon Scott, over the following decade. Attila invades Italy in 452AD, and puts some pressure on Emperor Valentinian III.
With *Anthony Quinn, Sophia Loren, Irene Papas*

Meanwhile, back in Hollywood, Douglas Sirk released **The Sign of the Pagan** ★ [90min], also concerning Attila, at roughly the same time, with toughies Chandler and Palance. Difficult to say which is worse.

ATTILIO FLAGELLO DI DIO See Attila the Hun

AU REVOIR, LES ENFANTS
Louis Malle — France, 1987 [105min]
Malle's beautiful film about Catholic and Jewish schoolfriends during the German occupation of France in WW2 earned an Oscar nomination for Best Foreign Film and one for his own script.
   A deeply-felt excursion through some very personal, but never sentimental reminiscences.
With *Gaspard Manesse, Raphael Fejtö, Francine Racette*

AU REVOIR, MON AMOUR (aka 'He Rijun Zai Lai')
Tony Au — Hong Kong, 1991 [125min]
Tale of love between a night-club singer and a Chinese patriot complicated by the introduction of a Japanese officer. Some action between-times, though.
With *Anita Mui, Tony Leung, Hidekazu Akai*

AUCTION OF SOULS (aka 'Ravished Armenia')
Oscar Apfel — U.S., 1919
An extraordinarily bold film for Hollywood at any time, but especially during the silent period. Here we have just about the only record of the ethnic cleansing and genocide of Armenians in the crumbling Ottoman Empire.
   This dramatized account centres on the 1915 atrocities when some 600,000 Armenian Christians were massacred by the Turks under cover of WW1.
With *Irving Cummings, Aurora Mardiganian, Anna Q. Nelson, Howard Davies*

AUFUHR IN DAMASKUS See Tumult in Damascus

AUS EINEM DEUTSCHEN LEBEN
See **Death is my Trade**

AUSTERLITZ (aka 'The Battle of Austerlitz')
Abel Gance — France/Italy/Leichtenstein/Yugoslavia, 1959 [165min]
Gance (**J'Accuse**, **Napoleon**) was 70 when he attempted the epic swirl of romantic history once more. The result showed that his greatest days were behind him — his own script causing all kinds of confusion. Napoleon's great victory over the Russians and Austrians in 1805 is reduced to a Who's Who? of world cinema stars. Alexander (**Superman**) Salkind co-produced.
With *Pierre Mondy, Jack Palance, Orson Welles, Leslie Caron, Claudia Cardinale, Rossano Brazzi, Vittorio de Sica*

AVANTI-POPOLO
Rafi Bukaee — Israel, 1986 [90min]
The Six Days' War, 1967. Two Egyptian soldiers can't see much sense in war as they retreat to the Suez Canal. Painfully slow.
With *Salim Daw, Suhel Hadad*

THE AVENGERS See The Day will Dawn

AVENTURE MALAGACHE See Lifeboat

LES AVENTURES DE TILL L'ESPIEGLE
Gerard Philipe — France, 1956 [95min]
A Flemish folk hero getting into a few scrapes during the Netherlands War of Independence from Spain, 1567–1648. Charles de Coster's tale was also the subject of a Richard Strauss tone poem *Till Eulenspiegel* (1894–95).
With *Gerard Philipe, Jean Vilar*

AVRIANOS POLEMISTIS See Tomorrow's Warrior

AWAY ALL BOATS! [115min]
Joseph Pevney — U.S., 1956
The story of a U.S. attack transport ship with the Pacific fleet in WW2. The action sequences are good, particularly the kamikaze scene, but 11 years after the War, does the patter really have to be quite so jingoistic?
With *Jeff Chandler, George Nader, Julie Adams, Lex Barker*

AY! CARMELA
Carlos Saura — Spain, 1990 [105min]
A rather shallow political comedy from Saura, which sees a vaudeville troop entertain both sides in the Spanish Civil War. It fails to get its message across, but remains quite watchable.
With *Carmen Maura, Andres Pajares, Gabino Diego*

A BRIDGE TOO FAR
Michael Caine stars in a film that's definitely for war buffs only (see p. 32).

BA WANG BIE JI See **Farewell My Concubine**

BABETTE GOES TO WAR
See **The Crossing of the Rhine**

BABY BLUE MARINE
John Hancock — U.S., 1976 [90min]
Marine comes home from WW2 and claims to be a hero. Hancock has also tried to weave in a Vietnam anti-guilt thread, but give me **Hail the Conquering Hero** every time.
With *Jan-Michael Vincent, Glynnis O'Connor, Katherine Helmond, Richard Gere*

BACK DOOR TO HELL
Monte Hellman — U.S., 1964 [70min]
WW2 Philippines — routine U.S. patrol. Nothing really more interesting to say, except that both Nicholson and Hellman (who went on many years later to produce Tarantino's well-received *Reservoir Dogs*) were from the Roger Corman school of hard knocks.
With *Jimmie Rodgers, Jack Nicholson, John Hackett*

BACK TO BATAAN
Edward Dmytryck — U.S., 1945 [95min]
The Duke organizes native resistance to the Japanese during the period from the fall of the Philippines (May 1942) to the landings on Leyte (October 1944). Enough said.
With *John Wayne, Anthony Quinn, Beaulah Bondi*

BACKGROUND TO DANGER
Raoul Walsh — U.S., 1943 [80min]
Eric Ambler's novel *Uncommon Danger* was the source: Nazi spies in Turkey — Greenstreet and Lorre on hand. More was expected. Walsh directs with his usual zest, but thoughts naturally turn to what Hitchcock might have done with this.
With *George Raft, Brenda Marshall, Sydney Greenstreet, Peter Lorre*

BAD COMPANY
Robert Benton — U.S., 1972 [90min]
Draft-dodging, 1860s-style. Benton's and David Newman's *(Bonnie and Clyde)* script is influenced by the themes of the day; they write their escapees from the Civil War in the east into *B&C*-style adventures in the Old West. Not a 'war' picture as such, but an entertaining debut for Benton as director.
With *Jeff Bridges, Barry Brown, Jim Davis, David Huddleston, John Savage*

A BAG OF MARBLES (aka 'Un Sac de Billes')
Jacques Doillon — France, 1975 [100min]
Charming comedy-adventure of two young Jewish boys fleeing Paris during the German occupation for the relative freedom of the Midi.
With *Paul-Eric Schulman, Richard Constantini, Joseph Goldenberg, Reine Bartève*

BALLAD OF A SOLDIER (aka 'Ballada o Soldate')
Grigori Chukrai — USSR, 1959 [90min]
A humanist stance grafted on to the typical Soviet realist style gives a gentle charm and even a mild comedic undertone to this wonderfully crafted picture. A Russian soldier, after performing heroics against German tanks on the Eastern Front in WW2, is allowed leave. An episodic journey home results in his eventual stay being all too brief, and probably his last. The director's and Valentin Yoshov's script was nominated for an Oscar: almost unheard of, especially at the time.
With *Vladimir Ivashov, Zhanna Prokhorento, Antonina Maximova*

THE BALLAD OF BERLIN (aka 'Berliner Ballade')
Robert Stemmle — Germany (American Zone), 1948 [75min]
Arguably the best picture to sum up the lot of the German people so demoralised at the end of WW2 — and certainly the most stylish. It provides an early role for Frobe (*Goldfinger*). Heavily satirical and set to '30s Berlin cabaret-style music, it articulates the problems far better than most straightforward

accounts from German cinema at this time. See also **Somewhere in Berlin** (Soviet Zone) and **In Those Days** (British Zone) for examples of cinema sponsored by the differing occupying powers.
With *Gert Frobe, Tatiana Sais*

BALLADA O SOLDATE See **Ballad of a Soldier**

BALTIC DEPUTY (aka 'Deputat Baltiki')
Josef Heifitz/Alexander Zharki — USSR, 1937 [100min]
Parable of the Russian Revolution, concerning the egalitarian ethos, simply but effectively told, with Cherkassov (title roles of **Alexander Nevsky**, **Ivan the Terrible**) as the professor eating humble pie and joining his comrades — but eventually representing them in the Soviet.
With *Nikolai Cherkassov, M. Damasheva, A. Melnikov, Boris Liavanov*

THE BAMBOO PRISON
Lewis Seiler — U.S., 1954 [80min]
An interesting, if unsubtle, attempt to address an important issue: one of the first Korean War POW pictures to raise the subject of brainwashing and collaboration (see **The Manchurian Candidate**). Set at the Panmunjon peace talks.
With *Robert Francis, Brian Keith, E.G. Marshall*

BANDIDO
Richard Fleischer — U.S., 1956 [90min]
1916 — Mitchum and Scott are rival mercenaries running guns to rebels in the Mexican Revolution. The rest is hokey action. Still better than **Il Mercenario** [105min] and **Compañeros** [120min], a pair of spaghetti Westerns on the same lines, directed by Sergio Corbucci (1968 and 1970) with Franco Nero and the ubiquitous Jack Palance, and with Ennio Morricone scores for good measure.
With *Robert Mitchum, Gilbert Roland, Zachary Scott*

THE BANDIT OF ZHOBE
John Gilling — GB, 1959 [80min]
Epitomizes hopeless attempts by the British cinema to revive the '30s genre of 'empire' films around this time on the back of the much better **Zarak**. With *Victor Mature, Anthony Newley, Anne Aubrey*

Terence Fisher's **The Stranglers of Bombay** ★ [80min], starring Guy Rolfe and Allan Cuthbertson, was released the same year: Gilling's other embarrassment, **The Brigand of Kandahar** [80min], with Oliver Reed and Ronald Lewis, came out in 1965). Still all 19th century curry.

THE BANDIT OF SHERWOOD FOREST
See **The Adventures of Robin Hood**

BAPTISM OF FIRE (aka 'Feuertaufe')
Hans Bertram — Germany, 1940
Powerful, hate-filled epic of a documentary praising the Luftwaffe's destruction of Warsaw and with a narrative that provocatively taunts and threatens Britain.
Typical of German self-congratulation at the time (see also **Victory in the West**).

THE BARBARIAN AND THE LADY
See **The Rebel Son**

THE BARBARY PIRATE
Lew Landers — U.S., 1949
The Mediterranean c1790. Barbary Coast pirates are causing a nuisance to shipping and a youthful US of A is having none of it. By 1800 the U.S. was at war with the state of Tripoli, and a national hero was made of Stephen Decatur, following his bold move in 1804 to enter Algiers harbour and set alight the captured U.S. frigate *Philadelphia*, before going on to more heroics in the War of 1812.
With *Donald Woods, Trudi Marshall, Stefan Schnabel*

Other pictures which featured the U.S.–Tripoli (Tripolitan) War, or skirmishes related to it, include*:*
The Man Without a Country ★★ (Ernest C. Warde — U.S., 1917) With *H. H. Herbert*
Updating of Edward Hale's novel, putting his hero Philip Hale in a WW1 context.
(Rowland V. Lee — U.S., 1925) With *Edward Hearne*
(*The Man Without a Country* — TVM — Delbert Mann, U.S., 1973 With *Cliff Robertson*)
Old Ironsides ★ (James Cruze — U.S., 1926) [110min] With *Charles Farrell, Wallace Beery*
Tripoli ★★ (Will Price — U.S., 1950) [95min] With *John Payne, Maureen O'Hara*
Yankee Pasha ★★ (Joseph Pevney — U.S., 1954) [85min] With *Jeff Chandler, Rhonda Fleming*

BARBED WIRE
Rowland V. Lee/Erich Pommer — U.S., 1927 [85min]
A film released at a time which was, in retrospect, reflective rather than accusing of WW1 adversaries. Germany would not achieve its high international profile again for another six years, and this POW saga asks French captors to accept a German prisoner into their village at the end of the War. Originally a 1923 novel by pacifist Hall Caine; the POW camp was located on the Isle of Man.
With *Pola Negri, Clive Brook*

BAREFOOT BATTALION
Greg Tallas — Greece, 1954 [90min]
True story of a band of urchins causing problems for Nazis in occupied Greece. Could have been done better.
With *Maria Costi, Nico Fermas, Stavros Krozos*

BARRICADE
Gregory Ratoff — U.S., 1939 [70min]
Nonsense with Americans caught up in civil strife in 1920s China.
With *Alice Faye, Warner Baxter, Charles Winninger, Arthur Treacher*

BARRY LYNDON
Stanley Kubrick — GB, 1975 [185min]
Interesting in that the eponymous hero fought for both the Prussians and the Franco-Austrian side in the European Seven Years' War (aka The Third Silesian War), 1756–63, just about the only English-speaking feature film to pay lip-service to this theatre of the war.

Lyndon is Thackeray's Irish rake who scams his way across war-torn Europe, but Kubrick, being Kubrick, comes up with an atypical picture book of a movie — much closer to bizarre Greenaway than the lighthearted Lester approach to period extravaganzas.

BARRY LYNDON
Lyndon's Prussian regiment defending against the French during the Seven Years' War.
WB/Hawk/Peregrine

The result is a visual treat, but the director's own script is let down by O'Neal's wooden delivery. It received a Best Picture nomination as did Kubrick (for both adapted script and direction), and walked away with all the arty statuettes — cinematography, score, art direction and costume design.
With *Ryan O'Neal, Marisa Berenson, Patrick Magee, Hardy Kruger, Steven Berkoff, Leonard Rossiter*

BASTOGNE See **Battleground**

THE BAT SQUADRON (aka 'Geschwader Fledermaus')
Erich Engel — East Germany, 1958
Unusual GDR propaganda feature. Hero, on the colonists' side in the French-Indochina War, changes heart when U.S. support planes for the French start carrying arms as well. He deserts and joins the communist North Vietnamese liberationists.

BAT 21
Peter Markle — U.S., 1988 [105min]
Intelligent attempt, based on a true story, to put war into the perspective of a service non-combatant. Hackman is a missiles expert lost behind enemy lines during the Vietnam War, witnessing from both sides the horrors that take place.
With *Gene Hackman, Danny Glover*

BATAAN
Tay Garnett — U.S., 1943 [115min]
In essence this is **The Lost Patrol** updated and moved to the Philippines theatre of WW2 (although actually only the MGM backlot!).

Lots of heroic jumping around and flagwaving. See also **Back to Bataan, Cry Havoc**.
With *Robert Taylor, George Murphy, Thomas Mitchell, Lloyd Nolan, Robert Walker*

LA BATAILLE
Nicolas Farkas — France, 1933 [90min]
Claude Farrère's love story is based on board a Japanese warship in the Russo-Japanese War of 1904-5. One of only a few feature films made concerning the conflict (see **Jack London**) — all the more surprising then that there were three versions of it.
Farkas's was the improved French sound version of Edouard-Emile Violet's 1923 silent original (starring Sessue Hayakawa, Felix Ford); Robert Stevenson made the English language edition, **The Battle ★★** [85min], in 1934 with Merle Oberon.
With *Charles Boyer, Annabella, Valery Ikijinoff, Betty Stokefield, John Loder*

LA BATAILLE DE L'EAU LOURDE
See **The Battle for Heavy Water**

LA BATAILLE DU FEU
Maurice de Canogne — France, 1948
Lives of French fire officers during the German occupation in WW2.
With *Pierre Larquey, Nicole Maurey, Noelle Norman, Roland Armontel, Jean Gaven, Gabrielle Fontan*

LA BATAILLE DU RAIL
René Clément — France, 1945 [85min]

Clément's minor masterpiece of reconstruction is probably the finest tribute to the French Resistance immediately after WW2.

Taking actual events and faithfully replaying them with amateur actors, Clément makes railway workers his core subject, but his tribute goes further to become a valuable contemporary recounting of events.
With *Salina, Daurand, Lozatch, Tony Laurent*

LA BATALLA DE CHILE See **The Battle of Chile**

LA BATTAGLIA DI ALGERI
See **The Battle of Algiers**

LA BATTAGLIA DI MARATONA
See **The Giant of Marathon**

THE BATTLE
(aka 'Hara Kiri', 'Thunder in the East') See **La Bataille**

THE BATTLE AND FALL OF PRZEMSYL
American Correspondent Film Co — U.S., 1915
Quite a rarity — an American-produced (but European-compiled) documentary on activities on the Eastern Front in the Great War. It deals with the taking of Przemsyl in Galicia by Russian forces in March 1915 after they had laid siege for six months, and the subsequent retaking of the city by Austrian and German troops.

Albert K. Dawson, through the same production company, took the story on to the fall of Lemberg, then Warsaw in *The Battles of a Nation ★★★* later that year. Documentaries like these woke up America — and particularly American film-makers — to the great events taking place in Europe; and over the following 12 months, before the U.S. entered the War, more pictures were made on WW1 than the Mexican Revolution (which wasn't the case before that).

BATTLE AT APACHE PASS
George Sherman — U.S., 1952 [85min]
Civil War and revolting Apaches (again). The U.S. Cavalry had its work cut out in the 1860s. After behaving badly (although Sherman does adopt the fashionable 'let's be fair to the Indian' approach), **Geronimo** (leader of the Mogollon branch of the Chiricahua Apaches) is banished by the more moderate Cochise. Chandler reprises his role from **Broken Arrow** with noble profile.
With *Jeff Chandler, John Lund, Beverly Tyler, Bruce Cowling, Richard Egan, Susan Cabot*

BATTLE AT BLOODY BEACH
Herbert Coleman — U.S., 1961 [80min]
Very ordinary Murphy vehicle set in the Japanese-occupied Philippines during WW2.
With *Audie Murphy, Gary Crosby, Dolores Michaels*

BATTLE CIRCUS
Richard Brooks — U.S., 1953 [90min]
M★A★S★H without the martinis, Hawaiian shirts and gags. A mobile field hospital in Korea is as gory and as grim as it should be, with Bogart only tearing himself out of his surgeon's smock to flirt with June Allyson. Good helicopter rescue sequences.
With *Humphrey Bogart, June Allyson, Keenan Wynn*

BATTLE CRY
Raoul Walsh — U.S., 1955 [150min]
Blood and lust would-be epic in Saipan with U.S. Marines in 1944. Leon Uris (**Exodus**) 'developed' the lame script from his own, much better, first novel.
With *Van Heflin, Aldo Ray, Mona Freeman, Nancy Olsen*

THE BATTLE CRY OF PEACE
Wilfred North — U.S., 1915 [120min]
Produced and scripted by war pictures pioneer, now rabid Hun-hater, Stuart Blackton, this most unsubtle of the many WW1 'preparedness' pictures being made in the then neutral U.S.A. caused a tremendous reaction at the box office — and in public debate throughout the land. Henry Ford, for one, spoke out against its belligerence. The film depicts a 'Prussian-looking' invasion by sea off New York City, with all kinds of atrocities against civilians ensuing.

There is apparently no connection between the original novel (*Defenseless America*) by Hudson Maxim, of the Maxim machine-gun family, and the message of the film to mobilize the nation. The film is now apparently lost.
With *Charles Richman, Norma Talmadge, L. Rogers Lytton, Charles Kent, James Morrison*

BATTLE FLAME
RG Springsteen — U.S., 1959 [80min]
Routine low-budget action drama set behind the lines in Korea, with the U.S. Marines rescuing some comely nurses.
With *Scott Brady, Robert Blake, Elaine Edwards*

THE BATTLE FOR ANZIO See **Anzio**

THE BATTLE FOR BERLIN See **Liberation**

THE BATTLE FOR HEAVY WATER
(aka 'La Bataille de L'Eau Lourde', 'Operation Swallow')
Titus Wibe Muller — France/Norway, 1947 [95min]
The true story of the **Heroes of Telemark**. Virtually a documentary in its faithful reconstruction of events and its use of the actual Norwegian partisans who took part in the 1943 raid on a German heavy water (an atomic bomb requirement) plant in the Telemark Mountains as 'actors'.

Amazing mountaineering feats are required to reach the plant after the partisans parachute on to treacherous snow-fields. The visual effect is stunning. Supervised by Jean Dréville, who would later liaise with Soviet film-makers on **Normandie-Niemen**.

BATTLE FOR OUR SOVIET UKRAINE
See *Battle for the Ukraine.*

THE BATTLE FOR POWDER RIVER See **Tomahawk**

THE BATTLE FOR THE MARIANAS
U.S. Marine Co — U.S., 1944
Exciting front-line documentary covering the bloody battles for Saipan, Tinian and Guam. Six Marine photographers were killed for their art.

BATTLE FOR THE UKRAINE
(aka 'Bitva Nashu Sovietskayu Ukrainu', 'Battle for our Soviet Ukraine', 'Ukraine in Flames')
Yulia Solntseva — USSR, 1943

By 1943 Soviet cineastes were profoundly influenced by the technical skill of Capra's **Why We Fight** series of U.S. war documentaries. Supervised by Solntseva's husband, maestro Alexander Dovzhenko (**Arsenal, Aerograd**), who employed 24 cameramen to cover this theatre of war, it tells the story of how Soviet forces gradually began to free the Ukraine from the grip of the Germans. Dovzhenko's own *Victory in the Ukraine* ★★★ (1945) provides a suitable companion piece.

BATTLE FORCE See **The Great Battle**

BATTLE HELL See **Yangtse Incident**

BATTLE HYMN
★ *Douglas Sirk — U.S., 1957* [110min]
★ Hudson is the WW2 flyer who turned to the cloth, salving conscience for his accidental bombing of a German orphanage by setting one up in Korea during the war there. Based on the true story of Dean Hess.
With *Rock Hudson, Martha Hyer, Dan Duryea*

BATTLE INFERNO
★ (aka 'Stalingrad', 'Hunde, Wollt ihr Ewig Leben')
★ *Frank Wisbar — West Germany, 1959*
★ Following the Soviet view of things in **The Battle of Stalingrad**, here is a German perspective on the 1943 engagement, reconstructed in a documentary style by Wisbar.

BATTLE OF ALGIERS
Street fighters going to work by bus during the Algerian bid for independence from France in 1957. The film is shot entirely in black and white and manages to be remarkably even-handed in its analysis of the bitter conflict. Casbah/Igor (courtesy KOBAL)

One of several WW2 movies made by Germans in the late '50s (see **The Bridge**) with a definite anti-war message. Even so it lacks the power of Vilsmaier's 1992 epic, just called **Stalingrad**.
With *Joachim Hansen, Peter Carsten, Horst Frank*

THE BATTLE OF ALGIERS
(aka 'La Battaglia di Algeri', 'Maarakat Alger') ★
Gilles Pontecorvo — Algeria/Italy, 1965 [135min] ★
A remarkable achievement in film. Pontecorvo's honest, extra- ★
ordinarily even-handed, but politically provocative portrayal of ★
events in French-colonial Algeria in 1957 pre-empts, and out- ★
does, Costa-Gavras (*Z*, **Missing**).

Stylistically based in Rossellini-type Italian neo-realism, the film is shot in black and white to create a sense of newsreel immediacy in the action shots; while editing reminiscent of Eisenstein allows for character development not usually associated with this kind of picture.

It lost out at the Oscars that year for Best Foreign Film to *A Man and a Woman*, and was also nominated for Franco Solinas' script and Pontecorvo's bravura direction. Consolation came in the Golden Lion award at Venice. Former Algiers city ALN leader Yacef Saadi was co-producer, and played himself; yet the film still makes the French paratroop colonel a balanced character, and allows him a speech justifying the torture of terrorist suspects — an event which is unflinchingly shown.
With *Yacef Saadi, Brahim Haggiag, Jean Martin, Tommaso Neri*

THE BATTLE OF ANCRE See **The Battle of Arras**

THE BATTLE OF ARRAS
J.B. McDowell/Geoffrey Malins — GB, 1917 ★
The first stirrings of the British documentary. Malins and ★
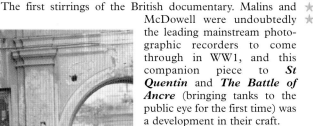
McDowell were undoubtedly the leading mainstream photo- ★
graphic recorders to come through in WW1, and this companion piece to *St Quentin* and *The Battle of Ancre* (bringing tanks to the public eye for the first time) was a development in their craft.

In the previous year cinema audiences had gasped at the sheer power — albeit very raw in cinematic terms — of their ground-breaking *The Battle of the Somme*.

THE BATTLE OF AUSTERLITZ See **Austerlitz**

BATTLE OF BLOOD ISLAND
Joel Rapp — U.S., 1960
Dreadfully scripted, directed and acted. These are the plus points of this risible tale of lost GIs on some Pacific island full of Japs, sometime in WW2.
With *Richard Devon, Ron Kennedy*

BATTLE OF BLOOD ISLAND
Both U.S. and Japanese try to bury their heads in the sand after the rushes! Filmgroup

BATTLE OF BRITAIN (1943) See *Why We Fight*

THE BATTLE OF BRITAIN
Guy Hamilton — GB, 1969 [130min]
Very expensive to make, and although the fine production values manifest themselves best in Freddie Young's stirring aerial sequences, this attempt to cover the dark days of 1940 is nevertheless plodding in tempo and perhaps should have been sub-titled 'The Longest Finest Hour'. Self-congratulatory it has to be, but more might have been made of the Polish and Czech contributions in supplementing 'the Few'.

The plethora of star performances pale after a while, but Robert Shaw is the pick of the bunch, and Olivier is fine as Dowding. The film gathered the largest number of flying WW2 aircraft up to this date — both original Spitfires, Hurricanes and a Junkers Ju52, and re-engined Spanish Messerschmitt Bf109s and Heinkel He111s. For its day the model work was good.
With *Laurence Olivier, Michael Caine, Robert Shaw, Kenneth More, Susannah York, Christopher Plummer, Ralph Richardson, Michael Redgrave*

THE BATTLE OF CHILE (aka 'La Batalla de Chile')
Patricio Guzman — Chile, 1978
A hugely accessible and surprisingly unbiased documented history of the Allende overthrow in 1973. Divided into three separate feature length documentaries (**The Insurrection of the Bourgeoisie**, **The Coup d'Etat**, **The Power of the People**) it tells of the events that took power away from the socialists and ushered in 16 years of Augusto Pinochet's brutal military dictatorship.

THE BATTLE OF CHINA See *Why We Fight*

BATTLE OF CORINTH
(aka 'Il Conquistadore di Corinto')
See **Aphrodite, Goddess of Love**

THE BATTLE OF EL ALAMEIN
Giorgio Ferroni — France/Italy, 1968 [105min]
Cheeky whitewashing attempt by the Italian cinema to distance their nation from the WW2 Axis. In this picture about the turning point in the Desert War, it's the British and the Germans who are made to look like the logical allies, rather than the Germans and Italians.
With *Michael Rennie, Robert Hossein, Frederick Stafford, George Hilton*

THE BATTLE OF GALLIPOLI See **Tell England**

THE BATTLE OF GETTYSBURG
Thomas Ince — U.S., 1914
This was the only feature made about one of the pivotal battles in the War of Secession (a short was made in 1936) until Ronald Maxwell's four-hour *tour de force*, **Gettysburg**, in 1993. At its time, Ince's raw, often horrific and often fictional representation of accounts was the longest feature yet on the Civil War. Ince had come to prominence in 1912 with a short, *Custer's Last Raid*, and went on to direct one of the silent era's greatest pictures, **Civilization**, in 1916.
With *Willard Mack, Charles French, Enid Bennett, Herschal Mayall*

THE BATTLE OF JUTLAND
H. Bruce Woolfe — GB, 1921
If Malins and McDowell brought the immediate reality of WW1 to British cinema audiences, then, with the help of hindsight and no lack of imagination, Woolfe's work in the '20s added another dimension to the war documentary. The great sea battle was his first canvas, upon which he mixed newsreels and graphics — often animated for effect. He followed this with **Armageddon** (1923 — about Allenby in Palestine) and **Zeebrugge** (1924), introducing re-enactions and scale models; and collaborated with Walter Summers on films such as **The Battles of the Coronel and Falkland Islands**. ★★★★

THE BATTLE OF MIDWAY
John Ford — U.S., 1942
One of WW2's most famous documentaries, it left Ford wounded in hospital but won him the first of consecutive Oscars for Best Documentary (see also **December 7th**). Mighty popular, not least for the first portrayal of a major American victory — indeed the turning point in the Pacific — but also because of Ford's use of his 'stock' cast like Henry Fonda and Donald Crisp in narration.

THE BATTLE OF MIDWAY (1976) See **Midway**

THE BATTLE OF NERETVA
Veljko Bulajic — Italy/U.S./W.Germany/Yugoslavia, 1969 [105min]
Nominated for Best Foreign Film by the Academy, this account of the Yugoslav partisans blocking Nazi progress in the Balkans in WW2 was savagely cut from its epic three hours 'for commercial reasons', making it too often unintelligible. Action scenes are well above average.
With *Yul Brynner, Curt Jurgens, Orson Welles, Hardy Kruger, Sylva Koscina, Franco Nero*

THE BATTLE OF OKINAWA
(aka 'Gekido no Showashi — Okinanwa Kessen')
Kihachi Okamoto — Japan, 1971

Rather straightforward approach to the downfall of the last of the islands before Japan proper in the biggest land battle of the Pacific War. Told from a controlled Japanese viewpoint, with the inhabitants of the island brought into the plot; Japanese troops are depicted as heroic but without the maniacal stereotyping of Western pictures.

With *Keiju Kobayashi, Tatsuya Nakadai, Tetsuro Tamba, Yuzo Kayama*

BATTLE OF RUSSIA See *Why We Fight*

THE BATTLE OF SAN PIETRO
John Huston — U.S., 1944

Huston's courageously clear-eyed work created waves within the U.S. military hierarchy, but remains one of the most telling documentaries of WW2. Reporting the taking of a strategic Italian village by the Americans in 1944, Huston highlights the U.S. dead and the demoralizing effect on the inhabitants. It is still a most powerful indictment on the futility of war.

THE BATTLE OF STALINGRAD
Vladimir Petrov — USSR, 1950

Overlong semi-documentary made to the greater glorification of Stalin. The large-scale battle scenes are brutal, however, and project the necessary horror one would expect when witnessing so savage a conflict. Not as effective as **The Great Turning Point**.

With *Alexei Diki*

THE BATTLE OF THE BULGE
Ken Annakin — U.S., 1965 [165min]

Highly-fictionalised sprawling drama concerning the Allies' unwillingness to accept that the Germans would consider a major counter-attack in the Ardennes forest in December 1944. Fonda plays the intelligence officer trying to convince the doubting Thomases, while Shaw has to knock his rookie Tiger tank commanders into shape — with the aid of a stirring score incorporating the WW2 'Panzer Song' march.

King Tigers are played by M47 Pattons, and the M4 Shermans, for some unknown reason, by M24 Chaffees. On other levels Annakin's film took too many liberties with the truth for some, and may have sped the release of the *Battle of the Bulge — The Brave Rifles* **** a no-holds barred documentary from Lawrence Mascott the following year. Whatever, it is certainly no **Battleground**.

With *Henry Fonda, Robert Shaw, Robert Ryan, Dana Andrews, Telly Savalas, Charles Bronson, Ty Hardin*

THE BATTLE OF THE BULGE — THE BRAVE RIFLES
See *The Battle of the Bulge*

BATTLE OF THE CORAL SEA
Paul Wendkos — U.S., 1959 [85min]

Sub-standard sub story. Captain Robertson badly needs to get information on the Japanese Fleet in 1942, but gets captured in the process. He valiantly escapes, like all Allied heroes do, to get his message back.

With *Cliff Robertson, Gia Scala, Teru Shimada*

THE BATTLE OF THE COMMANDOS
(aka 'The Legion of the Damned')
Umberto Lenzi — Italy, 1969 [95min]

One of Palance's 'wandering in the wilderness' films. Even while out of favour for the best part of 30 years, he always found work — of a sort. Usually this sort. He leads a commando group out to disable a big gun in Normandy before D-Day. No credit was given to **The Guns of Navarone**.

With *Jack Palance, Curt Jurgens, Tomas Hunter*

THE BATTLE OF THE RIVER PLATE
(aka 'The Pursuit of the Graf Spee')
Michael Powell/Emeric Pressburger — GB, 1956 [120min]

An unsatisfactory last P-P collaboration (see **One of Our Aircraft is Missing**, **The Life and Death of Colonel Blimp** for superior offerings). Studio-bound, with a strange line in artificially-induced Prussian chivalry, both dialogue and action are muddled.

It's a shame, as very few good war-at-sea pictures have been produced, and as this was the main action of the Phoney War of 1939, it is doubly so.

With *John Gregson, Anthony Quayle, Ian Hunter, Peter Finch, Bernard Lee*

THE BATTLE OF THE SOMME
J.B. McDowell/Geoffrey Malins — GB, 1916

Acclaimed by Lloyd George among others, this was the first British feature length documentary of WW1. It was no more than an elongated newsreel, and although it portrayed death and deprivation in the trenches it pulled up short of the real horror stories revealed by other nations' works.

Malins and McDowell reached their peak with *The Battle of Arras* in the following year.

BATTLE OF THE 38TH PARALLEL
Lin Kwon Taek — South Korea/U.S., 1976 [90min]

The horrors of the Korean War as seen through the eyes of a young Korean girl. Unusual insight from within.

With *Kin Chang Sook*

THE BATTLE OF THE V1
(aka 'Missiles from Hell', 'Unseen Heroes')
Vernon Sewell — GB, 1958 [110min]

Low-budget actioner depicting the Polish underground's assault on the German rocket base of Peenemunde in WW2. Much more polished, with better production values — although having a greater licence in characterization — the tale was subsequently made into better cinema a few years later in **Operation Crossbow**.

With *Michael Rennie, Patricia Medina, Esmond Knight, Christopher Lee*

BATTLE SQUADRON LUTZOW
(aka 'Bomber Squadron (Wing) Lutzow') See **DIII 88**

BATTLE STATIONS
Lewis Seiler — U.S., 1956 [80min]

Another Seiler cheapie. It depicts life on a U.S. Pacific aircraft carrier in WW2 and relies heavily on newsreel footage for action sequences.

With *John Lund, William Bendix, Richard Boone*

BATTLE STRIPE See **The Men**

BATTLE TAXI
Herbert L. Strock — U.S., 1954 [80min]

The Korean War movie was now a popular Hollywood genre,

and technology had moved on, allowing film-makers new angles like jet planes and, in this instance, helicopters.

B-movies like this should be short and diverting. This fails on both counts.

With *Sterling Hayden, Arthur Franz, Marshall Thompson*

BATTLE ZONE
Lesley Selander — U.S., 1952 [80min]
As routine as anything churned out by Selander. Boring story of a couple of war cameramen in Korea and their girl.
With *John Hodiak, Stephen McNally, Linda Christian*

BATTLEGROUND (aka 'Bastogne')
William Wellman — U.S., 1949 [120min]
As good a picture on **The Battle of the Bulge** as any until **A Midnight Clear**, and one of the best-ever devoted to WW2's European theatre. Wellman takes a bunch of non-stars and paints a harrowing picture of men in battle when the odds are against them. Robert Pirosh's script is telling — he fought at **Bastogne** — and it won him an Oscar, as did Paul C. Vogel for his vivid camera work. Nominees were: Best Picture, Wellman, Whitmore (Supporting Actor) and John Dunning (Editing).
With *Van Johnson, John Hodiak, Ricardo Montalban, George Murphy, James Whitmore*

THE BATTLES OF A NATION
See **The Battle and Fall of Przemysl**

THE BATTLES OF CHIEF PONTIAC
Felix Feist — U.S., 1952 [75min]
An attempt to make a confection out of some unpalatable history that fails miserably. The chief of the Ottawa Indians was a real character, allied to the French in the French and Indian Wars (Seven Years' War), who fought a lone battle against the victorious British after France capitulated in 1763. In this nonsense, however, a Hessian mercenary, supposedly on the side of the British, tries to undermine their peace talks with Pontiac.
With *Lex Barker, Lon Chaney Jnr, Helen Westcott*

THE BATTLES OF THE CORONEL AND FALKLAND ISLANDS
Walter Summers — GB, 1927
A landmark for British war films, this documentary/reconstruction of the two 1914 sea battles took the bare realism of the newsreel-type feature into the land of semi-documentary. Actors, and hence semi-fictitious sub-plots, were introduced almost apologetically to infill those periods for which actual footage was unavailable. Supervised by the daring H. Bruce Woolfe (**The Battle of Jutland**), this 1927 effort followed the mixed reviews of their previous collaborations, **Ypres ★★** (1925) and **Mons ★★** (1926).

THE BATTLESHIP POTEMKIN
Sergei Eisenstein — USSR, 1925 [75min]
The picture that appears in all the Top Tens. Its power and vigour are still there to witness today, but it will always be remembered for Eisenstein's revolutionary cross-cutting scene on the Odessa Steps — a technique still used by modern film-makers, as witnessed in the station shoot-out scene in *The Untouchables* (Brian de Palma, 1987). The Navy's mutiny at Kronstadt was a catalyst for change in Tsarist Russia, and a

BATTLE STATIONS
Crew doing just that, with varying degrees of enthusiasm. Columbia

centre-point of the first, the 1905, Revolution. It arose due to the general disgust at the outcome of the Russo-Japanese War, and shook the seemingly solid foundations of the monarchy which would eventually crumble just over a decade later.
With *Alexandr Antonov, Grigori Alexandrov, Vladimir Barski, Midhail Gomorov*

BAVU
Stuart Paton — U.S., 1923
Ill-considered Hollywoodization about rough Russian peasants, mobs, revolutionaries, aristos, etc, circa 1917.
With *Wallace Beery, Estelle Taylor, Forest Stanley*

BEACH OF THE WAR GODS
Wang Yu — Hong Kong, 1972 [100min]
The 'One-armed Swordsman' set in reasonably accurate historical context. The kung-fu comic cuts are pasted on to a late-16th century canvas when China was ravaged by a series of piratical Japanese raids which so severely weakened the Ming dynasty that it was not to survive.
With *Wang Yu, Lung Fei, Tien Yeh*

BEACH RED
Cornel Wilde — U.S., 1967 [105min]
A surprising directorial offering from ex-matinee idol Wilde. A pacifist tract set in the WW2 Pacific, which doubles as a potent allegory for the way the Vietnam War was shaping up. Influenced by the Fuller-Aldrich school of brutality.
With *Cornel Wilde, Rip Torn, Jean Wallace*

BEACHHEAD
Stuart Heisler — U.S., 1953 [90min]
Better-than-average WW2 yarn set in the Japanese-occupied Solomon Islands.
With *Tony Curtis, Frank Lovejoy, Mary Murphy*

THE BEAST (aka 'The Beast of War')
Kevin Reynolds — U.S., 1988 [110min]
Unusual offering which considers the Soviet invasion of Afghanistan. It centres on a tank and its crew becoming gradually ensnared, then taunted, by Afghan rebels intent on revenge for atrocities inflicted on a local village. Their fear is tangible. A welcome addition to the genre, made with Israeli Army co-operation.
With *Stephen Baldwin, George Dzundza, Jason Patric*

THE BEAST OF BUDAPEST
Harmon C. Jones — U.S., 1958 [70min]
Stridently anti-communist attempt to portray events in Hungary in 1956. Important in that it is the only Western feature film directly based on the uprising.
With *Gerald Milton, John Hoyt*

THE BEAST OF WAR See **The Beast**

BEASTS OF BERLIN
(aka 'Goose Step', 'Hitler — Beast of Berlin')
Sherman Scott — U.S., 1939
An early attempt to focus U.S. popular opinion against Nazi aggression in the early days of WW2 in Europe. It met with violent opposition from pro-German factions in America, hence the diluted title under which it was finally released.
With *Roland Drew, Alan Ladd, Steffi Duna*

BEAU GESTE (1926) See **Beau Geste** (1939)

BEAU GESTE
William Wellman — U.S., 1939 [120min]
P.C. Wren's hero remade from Brenon's original and the best-known of several versions (the 1966 version is desperately

bad). The Geste brothers leave England for the French Foreign Legion and a veritable Hollywood genre is created — especially during the inter-war period.
Wellman's effort was definitive enough (remember the chilling opening scene with the ramparts manned by corpses?) to staunch the output of Legion pictures until the 1950s (Robert Florey's work excepting — see the following list). Oscar nominations for Donlevy (Best Supporting Actor) and for art direction.
With *Gary Cooper, Ray Milland, Brian Donlevy, Robert Preston, J. Carroll Naish*

Other versions:
Beau Geste ** (Herbert Brenon — U.S., 1926 [120min], with *Ronald Colman, Ralph Forbes*)
Beau Geste * (Douglas Heyes — U.S., 1966 [105min], with *Telly Savalas, Guy Stockwell*)
Wren's companion novels **Beau Sabreur** ** (John Waters, 1928 [85min], with *Cooper* and *Noah Beery*) and **Beau Ideal** ** (Brenon, again, 1931 [75min], with *Forbes* and *Loretta Young*) were also filmed, but with less success.
Other films featuring the French Foreign Legion, (most ostensibly set on the southern Algerian/Moroccan frontier in c1890-1914 or in the Moroccan Riff War of 1925-6, but usually with only the faintest of nods towards historical accuracy — exceptions are commented on, or referred to separate entries), include:
Under Two Flags — Three versions: i) ** J. Gordon Edwards (U.S., 1916) With *Theda Bara, Herbert Hayes*; ii) ** Tod Browning (U.S., 1922) With *Priscilla Dean, James Kirkwood*; iii) *** Frank Lloyd (U.S., 1936) [110min] With *Claudette Colbert, Ronald Colman*
The Winding Star (John Griffith Wray — U.S., 1926) With *Alma Rubens, Edmund Lowe*
Hell's Island * (Edward Sloman — U.S., 1930) With *Jack Holt, Ralph Graves*
Morocco *** (Josef von Sternberg — U.S., 1930) [95min] With *Marlene Dietrich, Gary Cooper*
With credits like this, it's just a bit more than a Foreign Legion picture — Dietrich was launched in the U.S. with this, even though *The Blue Angel* was completed first, and Michael Curtiz went on to develop the backdrop for **Casablanca** some years later.
Renegades ** (Victor Fleming — U.S., 1930) [85min] With *Warner Baxter, Myrna Loy*
Le Sergent X ** (Vladimir Strijewski — France, 1931) [90min] [120min] With *Suzy Vernon, Jean Angelo*
Le Grand Jeu *** — two versions: i) Jacques Feyder (France, 1933) With *Pierre-Richard Wilm, Marie Bell*; ii) ** Robert Siodmark (Italy/France, 1953) With *Jean-Claude Pascal, Gina Lollobrigida* (aka 'Card of Fate')
Trouble in Morocco (Ernest Schoedsack — U.S., 1937) With *Jack Holt, Nae Clarke*
Drums of the Desert (George Waggner — U.S., 1940) With *Ralph Byrd, Lorna Gray*
Rogues' Regiment ** (Robert Florey — U.S., 1947) [85min] With *Dick Powell, Vincent Price*
Concerns Nazi-hunting after WW2, with the Legion based in Saigon.
Outpost in Morocco * (Robert Florey — U.S., 1949) [90min] With *George Raft, Marie Windsor*
Ten Tall Men ** (Willis Goldbeck — U.S., 1951) [95min] With *Burt Lancaster, Gilbert Roland*

BEAU GESTE
Dean Stockwell takes over the machine gun against the RIF. Universal

Desert Legion * (Joseph Pevney — U.S., 1953) [85min] With *Alan Ladd, Richard Conte*
Fort Algiers (Lesley Selander — U.S., 1953) [85min] With *Yvonne de Carlo, Raymond Burr*
One of half a dozen pictures Selander prefixed with the word 'Fort'!
Desert Sands (Lesley Selander — U.S., 1955) With *Ralph Meeker, J. Carroll Naish*
China Gate See separate entry
Desert Hell * (Charles Marquis Warren — U.S., 1958) [80min] With *Brian Keith, Barbara Rush*
Legion of the Doomed (Thor Brooks — U.S., 1958) [75min] With *Bill Williams*
The Legion's Last Patrol See separate entry
March or Die ** (Dick Richards — GB, 1977) [105min] With *Gene Hackman, Catherine Deneuve*

Also, the comedy entrants: Laurel and Hardy's *Beau Hunks* (1931) and *The Flying Deuces* (1939); items from Abbot and Costello (. . . *In the Foreign Legion*, 1950) and the *Carry On* Team (— *Follow that Camel*, 1966); Marty Feldman's *The Last Remake of Beau Geste* (1977); and the operetta — three versions of the *Desert Song* (Roy del Ruth, 1929; Robert Florey, 1943; and Bruce Humberstone, 1953)!

BEAU GESTE (1966) See **Beau Geste** (1939)

BEAU IDEAL See **Beau Geste** (1939)

BEAU SABREUR See **Beau Geste** (1939)

BEAUTIFUL PEOPLE
Jasmin Dizdar — GB, 1999
Gentle, rather than biting, political allegory about the Balkans in the 1990s; its complex cross-narrative being both its strength and its weakness. Set mainly in the UK, it involves, for instance, two fighting Bosnians, one a Serb, the other a Croat, ending up in hospital with a Welsh nationalist; and a Bosnian refugee who wants an abortion, having been a victim of wartime rape; a BBC newsman filming in Bosnia a drug-crazed English footballer supporter who got on the wrong plane after a World Cup Qualifier in Holland; and a succession of leg amputations.
   With me so far? Quite! having said all that, some of the messages do hit home.
With *Rosalind Ayres, Linda Bassett, Charlotte Coleman, Edin Dzandzanovic, Walentine Giorgiewa, Nicholas Farrell, Dado Jehan, Gilbert Martin, Nicholas McGaughey, Danny Nussbaum*

THE BED SITTING ROOM See **Dr Strangelove**

THE BEDFORD INCIDENT
James B. Harris — GB, 1965
Sub-Strangelove nuclear madness about a U.S. destroyer firing a missile at a Soviet submarine. Suffers from comparison with Kubrick's masterpiece and with **Fail Safe**; but the neuroses of the time make it more tense than the late cold-war movies, **The Hunt for Red October** *** (John McTiernan, U.S., 1990 [135min], with Sean Connery and Alec Baldwin) and **Crimson Tide** ** (Tony Scott — U.S., 1995 [115min], starring Gene Hackman and Denzel Washington).
With *Richard Widmark, Sidney Poitiers, James MacArthur, Eric Portman*

BEFORE THE RAIN (aka 'Pred Dozdot')
Milcho Manchevski — France/GB/Macedonia, 1994 [115min]
Through three separate but ultimately intertwined stories, Manchevski depicts the effects of the Yugoslavian civil war on a Macedonian village. Very moving, if constantly morose.
With *Katrin Cartlidge, Rade Serbedzija, Gregoire Colin*

BEFORE WINTER COMES
J. Lee(-)Thompson — GB, 1968 [105min]
Lack-lustre WW2 drama which deals with displaced persons in Austria in 1945 — the scenario which later became better known with the controversy over the British return of Cossacks and others to the Communist powers.
With *David Niven, Topol*

THE BEGGAR OF CAWNPORE
Charles Swickard — U.S., 1916
Romance and drug-abuse at the time of the Indian Mutiny (1857-8). The Battle of Cawnpore and other skirmishes get rare cinema coverage.
With *H.B. Warner, Lola May*

THE BEGINNING OR THE END
Norman Taurog — U.S., 1947 [110min]
Atom bomb experiments go wrong in WW2 America. Tragedy in more ways than one.
With *Brian Donlevy, Robert Walker, Godfrey Tearle*

THE BEGUILED
Don Siegel — U.S., 1971 [110min]
American Civil War used as a backdrop for erotic melodrama. Eastwood, a Northerner wounded, vulnerable, is nursed back to health by ladies of a Southern seminary. He abuses their hospitality and revenge is wreaked upon him. By no means the usual Siegel-Eastwood mix *(Coogan's Bluff, Dirty Harry)* that cinema-goers had come to expect.
With *Clint Eastwood, Geraldine Page, Elizabeth Hartman*

A similar tale, updated to WW2 France, appears in Peter Duffel's 1985 picture, **Letters to an Unknown Lover** (with Cheri Lunghi, Yves Benyton) when an escapee from a German POW camp inveigles his way into the house and minds of two beautiful sisters.

BEHIND ENEMY LINES See **POW: The Escape**

BEHIND THE LINES See **Viva Villa!**

BEHIND THE RISING SUN
Edward Dmytryk — U.S., 1943 [90min]
Blatant propagandist fare from Dmytryk (see also **Hitler's Children**) as he follows a Japanese-American family through the Sino-Japanese War and beyond Pearl Harbor.
With *J. Carroll Naish, Tom Neal, Robert Ryan*

BEHOLD A PALE HORSE
Fred Zinnemann — U.S., 1964 [120min]
The Spanish Civil War has not ended. 20 years later, Peck is still carrying grudges from his exiled base in France. Newsreel action and poor plot dilute the intended morality play.
With *Gregory Peck, Omar Sharif, Anthony Quinn*

BEIQING CHENGSHI See **A City of Sadness**

A BELL FOR ADANO

★ *Henry King — U.S., 1945* [105min]

★ Minor atmospherics in a small Italian town in 1944, with U.S. occupiers trying to prove they are nicer than previous fascist and Nazi tenants. Popular at the time.
With *John Hodiak, William Bendix, Gene Tierney, Richard Conte*

THE BELLS GO DOWN

★ *Basil Dearden — GB, 1943* [90min]

★ Morale-booster with fire-fighting heroics during London's
★ Blitz. Not without humour, as you would expect with Trinder in the lead.
With *Tommy Trinder, James Mason, Mervyn Johns*

THE BELLS HAVE GONE TO ROME

★ (aka 'A Harangok Romaba Mentek')

★ *Miklos Jancso — Hungary, 1958*

★ Jancso's first film as director sees a group of teenage partisans in WW2 Hungary ease the path of Soviet 'liberators' by defying the Germans.
With *Miklos Gabor, Ferenc G. Deak*

BELOVED ENEMY

★ *H.C. Potter — U.S., 1936* [90min]

★ The Irish troubles came more into Hollywood's focus after Ford's remake of the **Informer**. This heavily-romanticised tale of love and betrayal, loosely based on the **Michael Collins** story, was pretty average, though.
With *Merle Oberon, Brian Aherne, David Niven, Donald Crisp*

The general theme of cross-loyalty love was revisited later that year by Brian Desmond Hurst's British picture, **Ourselves Alone** [85min], starring Niall MacGinnis and Antoinette Cellier.

THE BELOVED VAGABOND See If I Were King

BENGAL BRIGADE
Different Indian chief — but same ploy. Universal-International

BEN-HUR (1926) See **Ben-Hur** (1959)

BEN-HUR

William Wyler — U.S., 1959 [215min] ★
Wyler remade Fred Niblo's 1926 silent version [115min] ★
(with *Ramon Novarro* and *Francis X. Bushman*) reasonably ★
faithfully, but in a more grandiose, if pedestrian, manner. ★
These pictures about the epic tale of a noble Jew, and the ambitious Roman who grew up with him, have some of the most famous action sequences ever filmed. They will be best remembered for the climactic chariot race (2nd Unit help from Andrew Marton and Sergio Leone), but should not be overlooked for the compulsive sea battle between the Romans and Greek pirates. The tension as the galley builds up to 'ram speed' is magical cinema.

Niblo's version was released a year or so too early to be considered for the first Academy Awards; but the '59 vintage won a record 11 Oscars — matched only by James Cameron's *Titanic* in 1997 — including Best Picture, Actor (Heston), Director, Supporting Actor (Griffith), Robert Surtees' Cinematography and Miklos Rosza's Score.
With *Charlton Heston, Stephen Boyd, Jack Hawkins, Hugh Griffith, Haya Harareet, Martha Scott, Sam Jaffe*

BENGAL BRIGADE (aka 'Bengal Rifles')

Laslo Benedek — U.S., 1954 [85min] ★
More sub-standard Hollywood heroics around the time of the Indian Mutiny. Anotherdull Eastern-Western.
With *Rock Hudson, Torin Thatcher, Arlene Dahl*

BENGAL RIFLES See **Bengal Brigade**

BEQUEST TO THE NATION

(aka 'The Nelson Affair') See **That Hamilton Woma**

BERLIN

Yuli Raizman — USSR, 1945 ★
The newsreel cameras of 40 front-liners capturing the last ★
days of Berlin in 1945, featuring ★
the cremation of the Göbbels ★
family and the raising of the Red Flag over the Reichstag.

BERLIN CORRESPONDENT

Eugene Forde — U.S., 1942 ★
[70min]
One of a glut of ernest but nevertheless unintentionally funny American-in-pre-WW2-Germany spy films and a suitable cast for such an effort.
With *Dana Andrews, Virginia Gilmore, Sig Rumann*

BERLIN VIA AMERICA

Francis Ford — U.S., 1918 ★
John's brother, Francis, also ★
starred in this WW1 flag-waver as a primordial cross between James Bond and Indiana Jones.

Having cleverly infiltrated himself into von Richthofen's

Flying Circus as an ace pilot, he spies for the Allies then returns to the States where he continues to battle with his Prussian counterpart.
With *Francis Ford, Jack Newton, Edna Emerson*

BERLINER BALLADE See **The Ballad of Berlin**

BESATZUNG DORA See **Garrison Dora**

THE BEST OF ENEMIES
Guy Hamilton — Italy/U.S., 1961 [105min]
Low-key anti-war drama, with a British and Italian officer crossing more verbal swords than literal ones, set unusually in 1941 Abyssinia.
With *David Niven, Alberto Sordi, Michael Wilding, Harry Andrews*

THE BEST YEARS OF OUR LIVES
William Wyler — U.S., 1946 [180min]
One of Hollywood's best-loved films of the '40s, and just about the best made on the plight of the war veteran, despite the plethora of more 'in your face' examples of the genre made after Korea and, especially, Vietnam.
    With sentimentality restrained, the varying stories of three home-comers produced a second of three Oscars for Wyler (see also **Mrs Miniver, Ben-Hur**) and awards for Best Picture, Robert Sherwood's Script, the Score, Best Actor for March and Best Supporting Actor for amateur Russell — who, left with no hands after a flying accident, was given the award as a gesture to maimed servicemen everywhere.
With *Frederic March, Myrna Loy, Dana Andrews, Teresa Wright, Virginia Mayo, Harold Russell, Hoagy Carmichael*

BETRAYAL FROM THE EAST
See **Across the Pacific** (1942)

BETRAYED
Gottfried Reinhardt — U.S., 1954 [110min]
WW2 tale of resistance and spies, of the type produced a decade earlier.
With *Clark Gable, Victor Mature, Lana Turner*

BETROGEN BIS ZUM JUNGSTEN TAG
See **Duped Till Doomsday**

BETWEEN HEAVEN AND HELL
Richard Fleischer — U.S., 1956 [95min]
Wagner is the privileged Southerner put firmly in his place in the classless U.S. Army in the Pacific in WW2. War and comradeship make him a better man.
With *Robert Wagner, Broderick Crawford, Buddy Ebsen, Brad Dexter*

BEYOND RANGOON
John Boorman — U.S., 1995 [95min]
Boorman is to be applauded for his attempt to mix the message and entertainment so seamlessly. In the end, partly because of Arquette's failure to convince, and partly because the reality of repression is still there in modern-day Myanmar, it doesn't quite make the Burmese problem of the late 1980s urgent or relevant enough.
With *Patricia Arquette, Frances McDormand, U Aung Ko, Spalding Gray*

THE BIG PARADE
John Garfield takes a German trench position. This anti-war picture is notable for its gruesome (for its time) battle scenes. MGM (courtesy KOBAL)

THE BIG BLOCKADE
Charles Frend — GB, 1941 [75min]
An Ealing Studio contribution to the war effort. Presented in a series of sketches in a documentary fashion, it instructs its audience in the importance of keeping Nazi naval activities in check.
With *Leslie Banks, Michael Redgrave, John Mills, Will Hay*

THE BIG PARADE
King Vidor — U.S., 1925 [115min]
Considering it was contrived as an anti-war picture, it may be surprising that Vidor gave Hollywood a new direction with the WW1 Western Front action picture; which as a genre was gradually becoming less and less marketable as 1918 receded and audiences wanted to forget the nightmare. More realistic battle scenes, aimed at invoking the horrors of war, proved to be enormously attractive at the box office.
    The biggest-earning silent picture of all time: **What Price Glory?** was hot on its heels.
With *John Gilbert, Renée Adoré, Hobart Bosworth*

THE BIG RED ONE
Samuel Fuller — U.S., 1980 [110min]
The picture that brought Fuller's WW2 œuvre full circle. In this sprawling account of his own First Infantry Division (the Big Red One is emblazoned on the soldiers' sleeves) fighting from North Africa, through Italy, and on into Germany after D-Day, Fuller's realistic, anti-heroic style is fully consummated. Elements of the **Steel Helmet**, **Fixed Bayonets** and **Merrill's Marauders** are all here, in this, one of the most telling movies ever made about the War in Europe. We are allowed to get into the psyche of the GI — his loves, his hates, his prejudices, his smalltalk — but mostly his fear.

Marvin, himself a wounded Marine infantry veteran of the Pacific campaign, gives one of his best roles as the gritty sergeant — a role originally earmarked for John Wayne before Fuller's 1945 plans to make the film were scuppered.
With *Lee Marvin, Mark Hamill, Robert Carradine, Stephane Audran*

BILLY BUDD
Peter Ustinov — GB, 1962 [125min]
Ustinov's ambitious attempt to adapt Herman Melville's novel for the big screen really doesn't work. The story about the killing of a tyrannical master-at-arms on a British warship during the French Revolutionary Wars is, frankly, much more enjoyable as opera. Everyone, including Benjamin Britten agreed. Debutant Stamp received early recognition with an Oscar nomination.
With *Robert Ryan, Peter Ustinov, Terence Stamp, Melvyn Douglas*

BIRDY
Alan Parker — U.S., 1984 [120min]
William Wharton's post-WW2 trauma novel has been sensitively updated by Parker to become one of the most intelligent and compelling Vietnam veteran pictures yet made.
Modine and Cage give powerful performances as the (respective) mental and physical embodiment of the horrors of war, and though not mainstream enough for Hollywood the film was awarded the Special Grand Jury Prize at Cannes.
With *Matthew Modine, Nicholas Cage*

THE BIRTH OF A NATION (aka 'The Clansman')
D. W. Griffith — U.S., 1915 [185min]
Soon to be eclipsed by Eisenstein (who was to learn much from his techniques, especially from **Intolerance** made the following year), and commercially raped by de Mille, the power, eloquence and sheer cinematic, technical innovation of Griffith's masterwork is, however, still there for all to see.
Thomas Dixon's 'The Clansman' gave Griffith the outline and original title for this epic saga of bigoted late-19th century America. Abused blacks, the emergence and acceptance of the Ku Klux Klan — these are unsavoury sub-themes to the stirring heart of the movie, the War of Secession, 1861-5. Griffith took the War of Independence as a theme in **America**, a loose 'prequel' made several years later.
With *Lillian Gish, Henry Walthall, Mae Marsh, Miriam Cooper, Donald Crisp, Raoul Walsh, Robert Harron, Wallace Reid*

THE BIRTH OF A RACE
John W. Noble — U.S., 1919
Over-ambitious, and in part raising a stifled giggle today, this portmanteau history of mankind somehow leaves the cradle of civilization at around about the death of Christ, crosses the Atlantic and picks up again as a pacifist vehicle depicting events from the American Civil War and WW1!
With *John Reinhardt, Jane Grey*

BIRUMA NO TATEGOTO See **The Burmese Harp**

THE BISHOP'S CANDLESTICKS See **Les Misérables**

BISMARK
Wolfgang Liebeneiner — Germany, 1940
The first of two films about the Iron Chancellor (the other being **The Dismissal** ★★★ aka 'Die Entlassung', 1942, with

Emil Jannings) directed by Liebeneiner, was aimed to pump up nationalist fervour in the early part of the war. The 1940 picture covers the historical rise of Bismark, the coercing and allying of once-mighty Austria, and the Franco-Prussian War.
With *Paul Hartmann, Friedrich Kayssler, Maria Koppenhofer*

A 1975 Anglo-American documentary, **Bismark: Germany from Blood and Iron** ★★ directed by John Irvin, studies the Iron Chancellor's early domestic achievements.

BISMARK: GERMANY FROM BLOOD AND IRON
See **Bismark**

THE BITTER TEA OF GENERAL YEN
See **Shanghai Express**

BITTER VICTORY
Nicholas Ray — France/U.S., 1957 [100min]
Tawdry tale set behind enemy lines in WW2 Libya.
With *Richard Burton, Curt Jurgens, Ruth Roman*

BITVA ZA NASHU SOVIETSHAYU UKRAINU
See **Battle for the Ukraine**

BIZALOM See **Confidence**

BLACK AND WHITE IN COLOUR
(aka 'La Victoire en Chantant')
Jean-Jacques Annaud — France/Ivory Coast/Switz., 1976 [100min]
Interesting for its location (French West Africa v Togoland), but nothing more than an antiquated French farce, as sleepy colonials wake up to the events of 1915. It was given the Best Foreign Film Oscar, nevertheless.
With *Jean Carmet, Jacques Dufilho, Catherine Rouvel*

THE BLACK ARROW (aka 'The Black Arrow Strikes')
Gordon Douglas — U.S., 1948 [75min]
Cheapie adaptation of a Robert Louis Stevenson romance set in merrie England during the Wars of the Roses. Apart from Shakespearean sources (see **Richard III**), cinema has avoided the Yorkist and Lancastrian civil wars, but this is a rarity of historical — certainly not cinematic — importance only.
With *Louis Hayward, Janet Blair*

THE BLACK ARROW STRIKES See **The Black Arrow**

THE BLACK BOOK (aka 'The Reign of Terror')
Anthony Mann — U.S., 1949 [90min]
Mann's first collaboration with writer Philip Yordan (see also **El Cid**, **The Fall of the Roman Empire**) is not as broad an epic as the future enterprises, but at least the camera-work in this piece about the goings-on of Robespierre in the National Assembly following the 1789 revolution in France, is first-rate. Historically hokey, however.
With *Robert Cummings, Arlene Dahl, Richard Basehart*

THE BLACK FOX
Louis Clyde Stoumen — U.S., 1961
Winner of a Best Documentary Oscar; Marlene Dietrich narrates this newsreel compilation on the ascent of Hitler to power, which parallels Göthe's fable about cunning Reynard the Fox. One of many documentaries on Hitler (see also **Nuit**

et Brouillard, *Mein Kampf*, *The Double-Headed Eagle*, *Swastika*, etc) between 1955 and 1975 (see **The Hitler Gang** for a fuller list).

BLACK RAIN (aka 'Kuroi Ame')
Shohei Imamura — Japan, 1988 [125min]
Striking in parts, melodramatic for most, this is the tale of a Hiroshima family witnessing the dropping of the first A Bomb, and how its after-effects contaminate, then destroy them.

The best sequences are the haunting mushroom cloud scenes at the beginning — it frankly loses its way afterwards.
With *Yoshiko Tanaka, Kizuo Kitamura, Etsuko Ichihara*

BLACK ROSES (aka — 'Roses Noires', 'Did I Betray?')
Jean Boyer/Paul Martin — France, 1935 [100min]
A romance involving a Russian dancer and a Finnish patriot during the Finns' passive resistance against Russification in 1903. Made simultaneously by Martin in a German version (**Schwartze Rosen**) with Harvey and Willie Fritsch; and in English with Esmond Knight playing opposite Harvey.
With *Lillian Harvey, Jean Galland, Jean Worms*

THE BLACK SHIELD OF FALWORTH
See **The Dark Avenger**

THE BLACK WATCH
John Ford — U.S., 1929
Very early Ford talkie which sends McLaglen and a small force of Scottish soldiers during WW1 to quell another rebel uprising in India, while the rest of the Blackwatch regiment is shipped off to the trenches in Flanders. Lots of Fordisms, but lots of rough edges too.
With *Victor McLaglen, Myrna Loy, David Rollins*

BLACKOUT See **Contraband**

DIE BLECHTROMMEL See **The Tin Drum**

BLOCKADE
William Dieterlie — U.S., 1938 [85min]
It was, I suppose, bold of Hollywood to make a picture about the on-going Spanish Civil War (there was one previous fatuous attempt in 1937 with **The Last Train from Madrid**), but any thoughts of it being provocative in any way were strangled by the Hays Office.

In case it offended either side, neither the fascists nor communists were allowed to be mentioned! Spies, a U-Boat blockade and the lovely Carroll are the high spots — and not necessarily in that order.
With *Henry Fonda, Madeleine Carroll, Leo Carrillo*

BLOOD AND STEEL See **The Fighting Seabees**

BLOOD OATH
Stephen Wallace — Australia, 1990 [110min]
Fairly routine (except for the Australian viewpoint) account of an atrocities trial — a Japanese POW camp commandant is accused of mass murder.

Brown gives his usual high-compression performance; and the script does at least address the way wartime certainties collided with the realities of immediate post-war politics and pragmatism enters the fray.
With *Bryan Brown, George Takei, Terry O'Quinn, Jason Donovan*

BLOOD ON THE SUN
Frank Lloyd — U.S., 1945 [95min]
Fiction highlighting fact, but a strange release date. One would have thought that the unearthing of the Tanaka Plan (aired in true historical context in **The Battle of China** episode of Capra's **Why We Fight** series) might have received dramatic attention by Hollywood before Pearl Harbor, rather than at the end of the war.

The Tanaka Plan, the blueprint for Japanese world domination — which actually specified the taking out of Pearl Harbor — was uncovered in 1927, but this dramatisation has Cagney as a U.S. newspaper man in '20s Japan printing the story. As an action-suspense movie it has its moments.
With *James Cagney, Sylvia Sidney, Wallace Ford*

BLOODY SNOW (aka 'Soiouz Veliksgo Dela')
Grigori Kozintsev — USSR, 1929
A real rarity. Kozintsev (**The New Babylon**) deals with the military conspiracy against Tsar Nicholas I in 1827 with all the realism and striking cinematography of the Russian cinema of the time.
With *K. Khoklov, S. Magarill, Pyotr Sobolevsky*

THE BLUE AND THE GOLD See **An Annapolis Story**

THE BLUE MAX
John Guillermin — U.S., 1966 [155min]
Classic aerial sequences of dog-fights over WW1 France rescue this fairly dreadful account of ambition, lust and class values in the German officer ranks.

An impressive stable of flying replica aircraft include Pfalz DIIIs, Fokker DVIIs, Fokker Triplanes and SE5s. Peppard is suitably arrogant in the role of the upstart hero, possibly too much so, as the audience doesn't deeply care when he gets his come-uppance from the urbanely Prussian Mason, who turns in his reliable smooth baddie performance.
With *George Peppard, Ursula Andress, James Mason, Jeremy Kemp*

THE BOAT See **Das Boot**

BOB HAMPTON OF PLACER
See **They Died with Their Boots On**

LA BOCA DEL LOBO See **The Lion's Den**

BODY AND SOUL
Alfred Santell — U.S., 1931 [80min]
Another post-**Wings** rip-off, with Bogart in only his third film role. This time it's the Royal Flying Corps in combat over France in WW1.
With *Charles Farrell, Elissa Landi, Humphrey Bogart, Myrna Loy*

THE BOER WAR
George Melford — U.S., 1914
Not surprisingly, more films came out of Hollywood about the roughly contemporaneous and not too far away Spanish-American War than the Boer War an ocean away over in Southern Africa.

This exception to the rule, however, could have used any conflict as the background to a morals and bravery soaper of less than the highest quality — even for its time.
With *William Brunton, Edward Clisbee*

THE BOLD AND THE BRAVE
Lewis R. Foster — U.S., 1956 [85min]
Low on action, high on crap-game drama, this story of GIs in the Italian campaign of WW2 gained an Oscar nomination for Rooney and Robert Lewin's script.
With *Wendell Corey, Mickey Rooney, Don Taylor, Nicole Maurey*

BOMB AT 10.10
Charles Damic — Yugoslavia, 1966 [85min]
Yugoslavian partisans fight the Nazis, helped by an American escapee from a POW camp. Rubbish.
With *George Montgomery*

BOMBARDIER
Richard Wallace — U.S., 1943 [100min]
Somehow this recruiting officer's prop showing young bomber crews over Japan in 1943 was big business in U.S. box-offices. Clichéd script and wooden acting were subordinate to stuffing the Japs.
With *Pat O'Brien, Randolph Scott, Anne Shirley, Robert Ryan*

BOMBER SQUADRON (WING) LUTZOW
See **Battle Squadron Lutzow**

BOMBER'S MOON
Charles Fuhr — U.S., 1943 [70min]
An American flyer is shot down over Germany and falls in love with a fellow prisoner who happens to be Russian. She escapes to Holland, he to England, in this attempt to cover as many nations and nationalities as possible in 70 minutes. Count 'em.
With *George Montgomery, Annabella, Kent Taylor*

BOMBS OVER BURMA
Joseph H. Lewis — U.S., 1942 [65min]
In April 1942 the Japanese took control of the Burma road — the only land connection left between the Allies and beleaguered China. This low-budget concoction about Chinese spies along the road was more bad news for the Allies.
With *Anna May Wong, Noel Madison*

BOMBSIGHT STOLEN See **Cottage to Let**

BON VOYAGE See **Lifeboat**

BONNIE PRINCE CHARLIE
Anthony Kimmins — GB, 1948 [140min]
The picture that became the laughing stock of British cinema, mainly because of Niven's miscasting and the amazing repertory theatre sets. Over 20 minutes was later cut and America thought it quite reasonable fare. Indeed, the scenes depicting Culloden, if not accurate, are at least shot with some flair by Robert Krasker; but it was said that producer Alexander Korda never recovered from the initial criticism and derision.
With *David Niven, Margaret Leighton, Jack Hawkins*

DAS BOOT (aka 'The Boat')
Wolfgang Petersen — West Germany, 1981 [150min]
The work which made Petersen (*Shattered, In the Line of Fire, Outbreak*) hot property in Los Angeles. Marvellous sets and camerawork evoke the claustrophobic chaos of a U-boat at battle stations like no other film on submarine warfare, as we follow a voyage in 1941.

Falls down, though, on weak characterization for a film of such length. Oscar nominations in five categories including direction, adapted screenplay (again Petersen) and cinematography (Jost Vacano).
With *Jürgen Prochnow, Herbert Gronemeyer, Klaus Wennemann*

BORDER RIVER
George Sherman — U.S., 1954 [80min]
Action adventure with Confederates stealing Union gold in the Civil War, then going to Mexico (in rebellion against Maximilian) to buy arms for the conflict. Except some have other ideas for the gold . . .
With *Joel McCrea, Yvonne de Carlo*

BORDER STREET
Aleksander Ford — Poland, 1948
One of several excellent Polish post-war productions (see also **The Last Stage**) before the advent of Wajda, Ford's story about the Warsaw uprising of the Ghetto Jews strikes a blow for both humanity and the cinema. Life in the Ghetto is realistically and hauntingly described. Not exactly **Schindler's List**, but belongs to that rare category.
With *Maria Broniewska, Jurek Zlotnicki, Wladyslaw Godik*

BORN FOR GLORY See **Brown on Resolution**

BORN ON THE FOURTH OF JULY
Oliver Stone — U.S., 1989 [145min]
The second, and most complete film in Stone's loose Vietnam trilogy (see also **Platoon**, **Heaven and Earth**), is based on a true story. One of the few films dealing with the trauma of friendly fire (see **Battle Hymn**, **Courage under Fire**). It develops Stateside into a powerful drama with the disabled vet coming up against, and overcoming, the gamut of put-downs at home to find a focus in his life again as an anti-war campaigner.

BONNY PRINCE CHARLIE
Jacobite war chants. British Lion/Lion

Cruise proves he can act, and was deservedly nominated at the Oscars, as was the picture itself among a total of eight. Only Stone (as director) and editing (David Brenner, Joe Hutshing) attained the ultimate award, though.
With *Tom Cruise, Bryan Larkin, Raymond J. Barry*

THE BOXER
Jim Sheridan — GB/Ireland, 1997 [115min]
After 14 years in a British prison, an IRA man returns to Belfast and seeks to take up boxing again. He finds that the troubles are now so ingrained into local society that he cannot break free from his past. Day-Lewis gives his expected fine performance and Sheridan's atmospheric backcloth is unnervingly accurate.
With *Daniel Day-Lewis, Emily Watson, Brian Cox*

BOXER REBELLION See 55 Days at Peking

BOY SOLDIER
Karl Francis — GB, 1986 [100min]
The Irish troubles as seen by others in the so-called Celtic fringe of Britain. A Welsh soldier imprisoned for murder in Belfast finds himself drawn more to the separatist viewpoint — symbolised by his withdrawal into the Welsh language. An intelligent angle, although the film is flawed through a lack of objectivity as it develops.
With *Richard Lynch, Bernard Latham, Dafydd Hywel*

THE BOYS IN COMPANY C
Sidney J. Furie — U.S., 1978 [175min]
Tough Vietnam action-drama which pre-empts the gritty films of almost a decade later (**Hamburger Hill, Platoon, Full Metal Jacket**), and was certainly not in tune with flavour-of-the-month sermonising vet movies like **The Deer Hunter** and **Coming Home**. Coarse and quite basic, it has no pretensions, but does hit out at nit-picking officers — in fact officers, officiousness and routines in general.
With *Stan Shaw, Andrew Stevens, James Canning, James Whitmore Jnr*

BRADDOCK: MISSING IN ACTION III
See **Missing in Action**

BRADY'S ESCAPE (aka 'The Long Ride')
Pal Gabor — Hungary/U.S., 1984 [95min]
Odd release from 1984, this is a throwback to the '40s and '50s WW2 dramas of Yanks shot down behind enemy lines. This time it is slightly different — the hero is rescued by Magyar cowboys and makes his escape on horseback (!) — but ignore the accents, scenery and costumes and it's still the same old plot underneath.
With *John Savage, Kelly Reno*

THE BRAND OF COWARDICE
See **Viva Villa!**

BRAVE WARRIOR See The Buccaneer

BRAVEHEART
Mel Gibson — U.S., 1995 [175min]
Gibson's grotty-Scotty fantasy in the late 13th century tale of 'Auld Enemy' bickering earned five Oscars — including Best Picture, Gibson (as director) and John Toll's photography.

BRAVEHEART
Wallace's followers celebrate. 20CF

Edward I of England proclaimed himself King of Scotland after the battle of Dunbar in 1296, and only a rag-tag bunch of demi-nobles under Wallace continued to rebel. Wallace won a morale-boosting victory at Stirling Bridge the following year, before being heavily defeated and executed by the English after Falkirk in 1298 — the catalyst for the Scottish barony under Robert the Bruce to enter the fray, which would lead, by 1314, to Bannockburn.

When it concentrates on the wild and woolly action sequences and the brooding Highland scenery the picture achieves some sense of period, though the late 20th century political cant put in a 13th century mouth is simply absurd. Wallace v Longshanks was never like this, but the battle scenes are rousing and riveting and Mel's first effort at direction gets ten-out-of-ten for its pacing. Spoiled by the romantic fantasy between Wallace and his dead wife.
With *Mel Gibson, Patrick McGoohan, Sophie Marceau, Ian Bannen, Alun Armstrong*

BREAK TO FREEDOM See Albert RN

BREAKER MORANT
Bruce Beresford — Australia, 1980 [105min]
A thoughtful, somewhat old-fashioned court-martial drama set in the Boer War and featuring a handful of Australian volunteers in the cause of the Empire.

Excellently played and directed, the story however disappointingly treats the alleged atrocities (the killing of Boer prisoners) with kid gloves. The screenplay, adapted from the Kenneth Ross play, received an Oscar nomination for Beresford, along with Jonathan Hardy and David Stevens.
With *Edward Woodward, Jack Thompson, John Waters, Bryan Brown, Charles Tingwell, Terence Donovan*

BREAKOUT See Danger Within

BREAKTHROUGH
Lewis Seiler — U.S., 1950 [90min]
A post-D Day tale of U.S. infantry definitely surplus to requirements.
With *David Brian, John Agar*

THE BREAKTHROUGH (1969) See Liberation

31

BREAKTHROUGH (1979) See **Sergeant Steiner**

THE BREATH OF THE GODS See **Jack London**

THE BRIDGE

Bernhard Wicki — West Germany, 1959 [105min]
After acting in one of the most moving of 1950s West German anti-war films, **The Last Bridge**, Wicki took the helm in another powerful piece on the insanity of Germany's war with the world.

The futility of the defence of the homeland in 1945 is heavily underscored here, with several conscripted and pathetically-armed youths dying to defend a bridge from American tanks. Nominated for Best Foreign Film Oscar.
With *Vokler Bohnet, Fritz Wepper, Michael Hinz*

THE BRIDGE AT REMAGEN

John Guillermin — U.S., 1968 [115min]
Just like the last entry — another bridge in Germany in 1945. But the pictures have absolutely nothing else in common: Guillermin's is a '60s stylized WW2 action picture with plenty of cynicism and very, very loud action sequences based on the true story of the battle for the last bridge over the Rhine.

Vaughn, as the German officer in charge of the bridge, represents the humanist thread in the picture as he defies orders to blow it so as to provide an escape route for thousands of retreating soldiers. In the end he delays too long and the Americans take the bridge intact.
With *George Segal, Bradford Dillman, Ben Gazzara, Robert Vaughn*

THE BRIDGE ON THE RIVER KWAI

Col Nicholcon (Alec Guinness) leading his men in this study of obsession: but is it collaboration? Columbia (courtesy KOBAL)

THE BRIDGE ON THE RIVER KWAI

David Lean — GB, 1957 [160min]
A war movie masterpiece — the first of several 20th century war-related epics from Lean (**Lawrence of Arabia**, **Dr Zhivago** and **Ryan's Daughter**). Very British, yet Hollywood-appealing in the only character that doesn't work — Holden's knowing Yank — it combines a cinematic and technically brilliant action picture with the psychological tortures of war.

Guinness' performance is peerless as the stiff-upper-lipped CO of British prisoners at a Japanese POW camp in 1943 Burma — taking his men on a roller-coaster of emotions from **The Colditz Story**-style non-co-operation stance to the Britisher's 'pride in a job well done' as they build 'their' bridge. The irony goes one stage further in the spectacular and tense climax — but by this time Guinness' Col Nicholson is so far obsessed that his action becomes almost predictable.

Oscars all round (seven in all), for Guinness, Lean, the picture, the adapted screenplay by Pierre Boulle from his novel, Carl Foreman (**The Guns of Navarone**, **The Victors**) and Michael Wilson; also for Jack Hildyard's camera-work, editing, and the famous score by Malcolm Arnold. Sessue Hayakawa was also nominated for his performance as the camp commandant — a long way from his Hollywood silent days.
With *Alec Guinness, William Holden, Jack Hawkins, Sessue Hayakawa, James Donald, Geoffrey Horne, Andre Morrell*

BRIDGE TO THE SUN

Etienne Pèrier — U.S., 1961 [110min]
A picture that takes as its subject an American woman living in Japan during WW2 — and indirectly, but not too subtly, lambasts U.S. chauvinism.
With *Carroll Baker, James Shigeta*

A BRIDGE TOO FAR

Richard Attenborough — GB/U.S., 1977 [175min]
Or, as some wag put it, 'A film too long'. Attenborough's sprawling and episodic account of Operation 'Market Garden' — the taking of the Rhine bridge at Arnhem in September 1944 and ancillary targets — is militarily accurate and provides some outstanding combat scenes (particularly the house-by-house fighting in Arnhem town). It falls down as effective cinema, though, in trying to involve, over three hours, a non-specialist audience in the sheer detail of a multi-faceted operation and a multitude of (mostly) bemused star names.

Acting parts are at a premium — ask Caan and Redford — with the best bits saved for Brits Fox and Hopkins and Dutchman(!) Olivier. Ultimately a disappointing attempt to reproduce **The Longest Day**-type adaptation of a Cornelius Ryan story — it's a film for war movie buffs only. With *Dirk Bogarde, Sean Connery, Gene Hackman, Edward Fox, Ryan O'Neal, Laurence Olivier, Anthony Hopkins, Michael Caine, Hardy Kruger, Robert Redford, Elliott Gould, Liv Ullman, Maximilian Schell, James Caan*

A documentary reconstruction, using many of the actual Arnhem vets, called **Theirs is the Glory ★★★**, came out in 1946, directed by Brian Desmond Hurst.

THE BRIDGES AT TOKO-RI

Mark Robson — U.S., 1954 [105min]
Based on a James Michener novel, this is at least one film on the Korean conflict to be recommended — it manages to entertain while driving the message home. Won an Oscar for

its use of special effects, and the battle sequences, especially the aerial ones, are particularly good.
With *William Holden, Gene Kelly, Frederic March, Mickey Rooney, Earl Holliman*

THE BRIGAND OF KANDAHAR
See **The Bandit of Zhobe**

BRITAIN CAN TAKE IT See **London Can Take It**

BRITISH AGENT
Michael Curtiz — U.S., 1934 [75min]
Early attempt at the espionage genre from Curtiz (**Casablanca**, **Passage to Marseilles**) which previews his flare quite neatly. Howard is the Brit embroiled in pre-Revolutionary Russia in a picture let down by its blatant anti-communist stance.
With *Leslie Howard, Kay Francis, Irving Pichel, J. Carroll Naish*

BRITISH INTELLIGENCE
(aka 'Enemy Agent') See **Three Faces East**

BRITTON OF THE SEVENTH
See **They Died with Their Boots On**

BROKEN ARROW
Delmer Daves — U.S., 1950 [90min]
Earnest Cavalry v Indians Western credited with being the first Hollywood picture to take the side of the Red Man since the Dark Ages. Pretty drab because of it, but its seriousness elicited a script nomination for Michael Blankfort. The cinematography of Ernest Palmer was also recognized by the Academy, as was Chandler's first stab at playing Cochise (see also **Battle at Apache Pass, Taza Son of Cochise**).
   There was a1953 'B' picture called **Conquest of Cochise** [70min] by cheesy director William Castle in which John Hodiak broke Chandler's monopoly. (Not to be confused with John Woo's *Broken Arrow* of 1996, starring John Travolta and Christian Slater.)
With *James Stewart, Jeff Chandler, Debra Paget, Will Geer*

BROKEN LULLABY See **The Man I Killed**

BROWN ON RESOLUTION
(aka 'Born for Glory', 'Forever England')
Walter Forde — GB, 1935 [80min]
C.S. Forester's famous yarn of a solo Jack Tar holding a German warship under siege in the Mediterranean in WW1. Remade and updated to WW2 as **Single-Handed** (aka **Sailor of the King**) [85min] by Roy Boulting in 1953, with Jeffrey Hunter as a not-so British hero.
With *John Mills, Betty Balfour, Jimmy Hanley*

THE BRYLCREEM BOYS
Terence Ryan — GB, 1995 [105min]
It could only happen in Ireland. During WW2, British and Germans are interned in the same prison camp.
   Could have been a good idea for a film — could have been a good film — fails on both counts..
With *Gabriel Byrne, Bill Campbell, William McNamara*

THE BUCCANEER
Cecil B. de Mille — U.S., 1938 [125min]

A rousing action adventure set in the U.S.-British War of 1812 shows the best side of de Mille. For once his spectacle is directed with pace, and the lavishness of the sets and expansive action scenes are in harmony with the overall scale. The quality of Victor Milber's photography received an Oscar nomination, typified in the Battle of New Orleans sequence. Remade without the verve 20 years later by Anthony Quinn (a supporting actor in the '38 version and this time produced by de Mille) [120min], with Yul Brynner in the March role as Jean Laffite.
With *Frederic March, Franciska Gaal, Akim Tamiroff, Walter Brennan, Anthony Quinn*

Other films concerning the War of 1812 include:
Captain Caution ** (Richard Wallace — U.S., 1940) [85min] With *Victor Mature*
Magnificent Doll ** (Frank Borzage — U.S., 1946) [95min] With *Ginger Rogers*
The Fighting Kentuckian *** (George Waggner — U.S., 1949) [100min] With *John Wayne*
The Last of the Buccaneers * (Lew Landers — U.S., 1950) [80min] With *Paul Henreid*
Brave Warrior (Spencer G. Bennet — U.S., 1952) [75min] With *Jon Hall*
Mutiny ** (Edward Dmytryk — U.S., 1952) [75min] With *Mark Stevens*

THE BUCCANEER (1958) See **The Buccaneer** (1938)

THE BUGLER of ALGIERS See **Love and Glory**

BUGLES IN THE AFTERNOON
See **They Died with Their Boots On**

A BULLET FOR THE GENERAL
(aka 'El Chucho', '¿Quién Sabe?')
Damiano Damiani — Italy, 1966 [135min]
Relatively thoughtful spaghetti Western developing Leone's favourite themes of corruption and death in revolutionary Mexico, with Damiani using every contour of the formidable Volonté (*A Fistful of Dollars*) and Kinski (**Aguirre — Wrath of God**) façades for effect.
   There is also a grossly-cut version which loses the impact of the original.
With *Gian-Maria Volonté, Klaus Kinski, Martine Beswick*

IL BUONO, IL BRUTTO, IL CATTIVO
See **The Good, The Bad and The Ugly**

THE BURGOMASTER OF STILEMONDE
George J. Banfield — GB, 1928
One of several mediocre WW1 dramas (this time based in German-occupied Belgium) made by British cineastes in the renaissance of the action, but not necessarily anti-German, cinema between **The Big Parade** and **All Quiet on The Western Front**.
   The best of a pretty poor bunch set on the Western Front at this time, apart from this, were Sinclair Hill's **The Guns of Loos** ** (1927) [90min] and Victor Saville's **The W Plan** ** (1930) [105min], both starring (coincidentally, honest!) the author's favourite, Madeleine Carroll (the former was her debut role), with Brian Aherne also in the latter.
With *Sir John Martin Harvey, A.B. Imeson*

BURMA CONVOY

Noel Smith — U.S., 1941 [70min]
Pre-Pearl Harbor flagwaver as American volunteers supply the Chinese via the Burma Road in the Sino-Japanese War.
With *Charles Bickford, Cecil Kellaway*

BURMA VICTORY

Roy Boulting — GB, 1945
One of the most satisfying of WW2 documentaries; Boulting chronologically unfolds the drama of the Burma theatre over the previous three years, chillingly capturing the singular trauma of jungle warfare. A worthy companion piece to his **Desert Victory**.

THE BURMESE HARP (aka 'Biruma no Tategoto')

Kon Ichikawa — Japan, 1956 [115min]
Ichikawa's brilliant, horrifying anti-war masterpiece was deservedly nominated for Best Foreign Film by the Academy. It tells of a Japanese soldier staying on in Burma after the war, retiring into Buddhism and burying the war dead. Its strength lies in Ichikawa's ability to convey its pacifist message without undue sentiment.
With *Shoji Yasui, Rentaro Mikuni, Tatsuya Mihashi*

THE BURNING SKY (aka 'Moeru Ozora', 'Flaming Sky')

Yutaka Abe — Japan, 1940
Abe made several heavily-nationalistic movies portraying Japan's air prowess over the Pacific early in WW2. Other titles included **Nippon's Young Eagles ★★** (1941) and **South Seas Bouquet ★★**(1942) — but here the action takes place against the Chinese in the Sino-Japanese War.

BURNING SANDS

George Melford — U.S., 1922
A rarity from Hollywood, or from anywhere — a drama based on the Sanusi Moslem uprising in 1917 Egypt. Cinematically acceptable for its day, it remains the only film directly covering this offshoot action of the WW1 Middle East theatre.
With *Milton Stills, Louise Dresser*

BYE BYE BLUES

Anne Wheeler — Canada, 1989 [115min]
Well-liked in Canada at the time, Ms Wheeler's film about the little wife running the home while her husband is away defending King and Empire in WW2, and not knowing his fate, is no more than a throwback to many similar plots devised during WW1, let alone the '40s — where this really belongs.
With *Michael Ontkean, Rebecca Jenkins*

CABARET

Bob Fosse — U.S., 1972 [125min]
Apart from it having the most interesting of Dietrich-esque performances from Minnelli, this is one of the most atmospheric pictures made outside of Germany about the rabble-rousing beginnings of Nazism in the late Weimar Republic, and is chronologically and atmospherically an unknowing sequel to Dietrich's own groundbreaking *The Blue Angel* (Josef von Sternberg, 1930).

As well as Oscars for editing, sound, score and art direction, the *tour de force* performances by Minnelli and Grey were also rewarded, as was Fosse's Direction and Geoffrey Unsworth's Cinematography, making eight statuettes in all.
With *Liza Minelli, Joel Grey, Michael York, Helmut Greim*

CABEZA DE VACA

Nicolas Echevarria — Mexico/Spain, 1990 [110min]
A long but always interesting picture about the contretemps between Spanish Conquistadores and Florida natives in the 1520s. Unconventional, but riveting for most of its length. Based on a handed-down tale.
With *Juan Diego, Daniel Jimenez Cacho, Roberto Sosa*

LA CADUTA DEGLI DEI See **The Damned** (1969)

CAESAR AND CLEOPATRA See **Cleopatra** (1963)

THE CAINE MUTINY

Edward Dmytryk — U.S., 1954 [125min]
Like **Billy Budd**, this 'mutiny' picture has war as a backdrop (WW2 this time) and similarly depicts the tensions aboard ship during impending conflict. The film is then taken over by a pedestrian courtroom drama made famous by the respective real-life and dramatic deterioration of Bogart and his character Captain Queeg. Age and the onset of cancer had made Bogie vulnerable for the first time in a lead role, but his creaking performance still earned him an Oscar nomination.
With *Humphrey Bogart, José Ferrer, Fred MacMurray, Van Johnson, Tom Tully, E.G. Marshall, Claude Akins, Lee Marvin*

CAIRO

W.S. Van Dyke — U.S., 1941 [100min]
Come the desert war, come Hollywood's interest in a part of the world where previously only the Foreign Legion lived. This is a spoofy spy comedy set behind the British lines in 1941.
With *Jeanette MacDonald, Robert Young, Lionel Atwill*

CAL

Pat O'Connor — GB, 1984 [100min]
Rather more than the love story between the widow of an assassinated Protestant and a young Catholic youth who was an accessory to the deed, this is a well-written and well-acted tale of guilt and morality during the darkest days of the troubles in Ulster. Quite classy.
With *Helen Mirren, John Lynch, Donal McCann, Ray McAnally*

CALIFORNIA See **Kit Carson**

CALIFORNIA CONQUEST See **Kit Carson**

A CALIFORNIA ROMANCE See **Kit Carson**

THE CALL TO ARMS
Cecil Hepworth — GB, 1902
Shortly after J. Stuart Blackton (see **Tearing Down the Spanish Flag**) pioneered the medium of film for propaganda purposes during the Spanish-American War, Hepworth knocked out this inflammatory anti-Boer piece in Britain. This followed his own **Wiping Something off the Slate ★★** (1900), and along with James Williamson's **The Soldier's Return ★★** (1902) marked British film-makers' start in dramatising events from South Africa. All these films were of a reconstruction or semi-documentary type, and the actors used were amateurs or actual soldiers. Documentaries such as Joseph Rosenthal's **A Skirmish with the Boers near Kimberley by a Troop of Cavalry Scouts attached to General French's Column ★★** had started to feed back since 1898, often with titles longer than their running times!

LES CAMISARDS
Réné Allio — France, 1972 [100min]
Detached, somewhat stylized piece of French cinema on a fairly obscure (to non-French cinema-goers) piece of French history. 'Les camisards' — Huguenots who fled to the Cevenne after 1685 when Louis XIV revoked the Edict of Nantes (1598) — take their toll of the Royalist forces in a long campaign of guerrilla warfare. The film depicts this action quite well and the period feel is fine — but the sometimes obtuse handling can be annoying. The camisards' revolt began in earnest in 1702, but fizzled out eight years later.
With *Philippe Clevennot, Jacques Debary, Gérard Desarthe*

IL CAMMINO DEGLI EROI See **The Path of the Heroes**

CAMP DE THIAROYE
Ousmane Sembène/Thierno Faty Sow — Algeria/Sengal/Tunisia, 1988 [150min]
The empire strikes back. Sembène — long the guiding light in West African cinema — and Sow highlight colonial racism in the French forces in WW2, when having been called up in 1939, African soldiers returning to Camp Thiaroye at the end of the war are discriminated against. The resultant explosion of hate culminates in appalling tragedy. Sembène exposed the recruiting of black French West Africans in his 1972 film, **Emitaï ★★★** [105min].
With *Ibrahima Sane, Sigiri Bakara, Hamed Camara*

THE CAMP ON BLOOD ISLAND
Val Guest — GB, 1958 [80min]
Exploitative Japanese POW camp drama with stereotyped national caricatures. Fairly odious Hammer production, of a type which, thankfully, they were on the point of eschewing for another, more acceptable kind of gore.
With *Andre Morrell, Carl Mohner, Barbara Shelley*

CAMPAIGN IN POLAND See **Victory in the West**

CAMPANADAS A MEDIANOCHE
See **Chimes at Midnight**

CAMPANEROS
(aka '¡Vamos a Matar, Campañeros!') See **Bandido**

THE CAMPBELLS ARE COMING
Francis Ford — U.S., 1915
The Indian Mutiny of 1857-58, interesting in the ferocity of its action sequences, courtesy of its director and star — the brother of John.
With *Francis Ford, Grace Cunard*

THE CANADIANS See **They Died with Their Boots On**

CANARIS (aka 'Canaris Master Spy')
Alfred Wiedenmann — West Germany, 1954 [90min]
Rambling biopic of the *Abwehr* boss when the only WW2 pictures to come out of Germany took an anti-Nazi stance.
With *O.E. Hass, Martin Held, Barbara Rutting*

CANARIS MASTER SPY See **Canaris**

CANDLELIGHT IN ALGERIA
George King — GB, 1943 [85min]
British venture into the WW2 desert war spy film sub-genre. At least Mason ought to have known better.
With *Carla Lehmann, James Mason*

LE CAPORAL EPINGLE See **The Elusive Corporal**

CAPTAIN BLOOD (1924) See **Captain Blood** (1935)

CAPTAIN BLOOD
Michael Curtiz — U.S., 1935 [120min]
First starring roles for 26-year-old Flynn and 19-year-old de Havilland which made their careers. Flynn plays Peter Blood in this boisterous remake of David Smith's 1924 silent version — a man wrongly transported to the Caribbean in the reign of James II. He turns to piracy and is then at odds with the British establishment until the Glorious Revolution of 1688, when he is pardoned by William and Mary. Nominated for Best Picture.
With *Errol Flynn, Olivia de Havilland, Basil Rathbone*

Sloppily remade as **Fortunes of Captain Blood** by Gordon Douglas in 1952 [90min], with Louis Hayward and Patricia Medina. **Son of Captain Blood** [Tulio Demicheli, 1962 — 95min] is set two decades later with its background in the War of the Spanish Succession; it stars Flynn's son Sean and Ann Todd, and is also pretty awful.

CAPTAIN CAUTION See **The Buccaneer**

CAPTAIN EDDIE
Lloyd Bacon — U.S., 1945 [105min]
Quite boring picture about the true-life exploits of WW1 leading American air ace, Eddie Rickenbacker.
With *Fred MacMurray, Lynn Bari, Charles Bickford, Thomas Mitchell*

CAPTAIN FROM CASTILE
Henry King — U.S., 1947 [140min]
Epic but empty tale of the Inquisition and Cortés' Conquistadores. Alfred Newman's score was nominated.
With *Tyrone Power, Jean Peters, Lee J. Cobb, Cesar Romero*

CAPTAIN FURY
Hal Roach — U.S., 1939 [90min]

Interesting, if inopportune stab at Britain's colonial tyranny during the 19th century. This Aussie Western looks at the plight of Irish rebel prisoners transported to a penal colony Down Under.

Its rip-roaring action made it popular at the box-office, but not in Britain's War Cabinet Office.

With *Brian Aherne, Victor MacLaglen, Paul Lukas, June Lang, John Carradine*

CAPTAIN HORATIO HORNBLOWER, RN
Raoul Walsh — GB, 1951 [115min]

Walsh brought Hollywood to Blighty to make this yarn about our naval hero during the Napoleonic Wars. Crash-bang stuff without the 'British' heroism for which C.S. Forester's novels were renowned.

With *Gregory Peck, Virginia Mayo, Robert Beatty, James Robertson Justice*

A lack-lustre British TV series, *Hornblower* with Ioan Gruffydd and Robert Lindsay, was screened in 1999.

CAPTAIN LIGHTFOOT
Douglas Sirk — U.S., 1955 [90min]

One of those lavish costume dramas that silky Sirk was famous for, except that it's a rather daft film that casts Hudson as a son of Tara, and the plot — about the serious subject of Irish rebellion in the 19th century — is even dafter.

With *Rock Hudson, Barbara Rush, Jeff Morrow, Kathleen Ryan*

CAPTAIN NEWMAN, MD
David Miller — U.S., 1963 [125min]

Pre-**M★A★S★H** army hospital drama with an almost sanctimonious Dr Peck fighting bureaucracy. Based Stateside in WW2, it doesn't have the same impact as the Altman classic, but did produce some good performances, with Darin nominated for the Best Supporting Actor Oscar.

With *Gregory Peck, Tony Curtis, Angie Dickinson, Bobby Darin, Eddie Albert, Robert Duvall*

CAPTAIN SWAGGER
See **Lafayette Escadrille**

A CAPTAIN'S HONOUR
See **L'Honneur d'un Capitaine**

CAPTAINS OF THE CLOUDS
Michael Curtiz — U.S., 1942 [115min]

Corny WW2 Cagney caper sees the irrepressible star flying bombers over the Atlantic after being busted by the Royal Canadian Air Force. We even get Churchill's 'We will fight them on the beaches . . .' speech in the soundtrack.

Sol Polito and Wilfrid C. Kline were nominated for the excellent photography, though, and Curtiz directs the aerial sequences with characteristic gusto.

With *James Cagney, Dennis Morgan, Brenda Marshall, Alan Hale*

THE CAPTIVE
Cecil B. de Mille — U.S., 1915

A rare feature to be made in the west on the Balkan War of 1912-13 (**An Unforgettable Summer** is placed another

THE CAPTIVE HEART
The pioneer of WW2 Camp pictures. Ealing

decade on), albeit using the conflict as background only. The Balkan League of Greece, Bulgaria, Montenegro and, most belligerently, Serbia, threw out the weakened Ottoman Empire before squaring up to each other in a prelude to Sarajevo and all that.

With *Blanche Sweet, House Peters*

THE CAPTIVE HEART
Basil Dearden — GB, 1946 [110min]

The daddy of the British POW movie, predating **The Wooden Horse** by four years. In many ways this remains the purest of its type, with a balance between the semi-documentary style and the seemingly unruffled British sense of humour which its future derivatives could not match.

Let down by a romantic (through correspondence) sub-plot involving Czech impostor Redgrave and the widow of the Brit whose papers he acquired.

With *Michael Redgrave, Basil Radford, Jack Warner, Mervyn Johns, Gordon Jackson, Jimmy Hanley*

CAPTIVE HEARTS
Paul Almond — U.S., 1987 [95min]

Romance involving an American airman shot down over Japan in WW2 and reprieved from execution. Strange film for the time, and not that interesting anyway.

With *Pat Morika, Chris Makepeace, Michael Sarrazin*

CAPTURED
Roy del Ruth — U.S., 1933 [70min]

Unsatisfactory WW1 POW melodrama where British chums fall out over a woman and the camp commandant chats to the hero about their Oxford days.

With *Leslie Howard, Douglas Fairbanks Jnr, Paul Lukas*

Maurice Elvey also directed a WW1 POW drama in his 1938 **Who Goes Next?** ★★ with Jack Hawkins — much the same.

LES CARABINIERS (aka 'The Riflemen', 'The Soldiers')
Jean-Luc Godard — France/Italy, 1963 [75min]
Surreal anti-war statement in a style we've come to expect from Godard. In a mythical war of the future we see a couple of unsavoury soldiers exploit the situation, with archive action footage providing a background.
With *Marino Masé, Albert Juross*

CARD OF FATE See **Le Grand Jeu** (1953)

CARDIGAN
John W. Noble — U.S., 1922
Events leading up to the start of the American War of Independence and seemingly taking into account everything and everybody involved at the time. The battles at Lexington and Concord are featured, as is Paul Revere's ride. The Indians are also in there somewhere.
With *William Collier Jr, Betty Carpenter*

CARGO OF INNOCENTS See **Stand by for Action**

CARL PETERS See **The Riders of German East Africa**

CARLA'S SONG
Ken Loach — GB/Germany/Spain, 1996 [125min]
After a quarter of a century of creating very English working-class dramas (from *Poor Cow* and *Kes* in the '60s to *Riff Raff* and *Raining Stones* in the '90s), this was Loach's third picture in seven years looking at strife away from England. In 1990 he came out with **Hidden Agenda** about the Irish troubles; in 1995 **Land and Freedom** considered the Spanish Civil War. Here Loach looks at Nicaragua through the eyes of a Scot who has fallen in love with Sandinista refugee Carla and follows her back to Latin America.

The film works least-well of the three, mainly because we are not allowed to get involved as much, but also because of the schizoid approach — scenes of Loch Lomond and love in the Lowlands make up half the picture: incongruously, troubled 1987 Managua the rest. *The Full Monty*-Carlyle is beginning to compile an impressive portfolio of parts.
With *Robert Carlyle, Oyanka Cabezas, Scott Glenn*

CARNIVAL IN FLANDERS See **La Kermesse Héroïque**

CARREFOUR DES PASSIONS
See **Crossroads of Passion**

CARTHAGE IN FLAMES See **Hannibal**

CARVE HER NAME WITH PRIDE
Lewis Gilbert — GB, 1958 [120min]
McKenna plays real-life SOE heroine Violette Szabo, the English wife of a French soldier, who was eventually shot after capture by the Gestapo. One of several British heroine biopics of the 1950s (see also **Odette**, **The Inn of the Sixth Happiness**).
With *Virginia McKenna, Paul Scofield, Jack Warner*

CASABIANCA
Georges Péclet — France, 1950 [85min]
The story of the Free French submarine *Casabianca*'s escape from Toulon harbour in 1942 and its part in the reoccupation of Corsica in September 1943 — de Gaulle's first foothold on his way back to the motherland.
With *Paulette Andrieux, Pierre Dudan, Gérard Landry*

CASABLANCA
Michael Curtiz — U.S., 1942 [100min]
The film for all occasions. Along with **Gone with the Wind** and *Citizen Kane*, more words have been written about this set of happy coincidences — serendipity really — than anything else on celluloid. The pinnacle of Curtiz's career, the pace of its simple love story is less frenetic than in pictures by his alter ego (**Captain Blood**, **The Charge of the Light Brigade**, **The Adventures of Robin Hood**, etc). But rarely — if ever — has a simple love story contained such elements of drama, suspense and intrigue. Bogart and Bergman gel perfectly, and the range of fascinating characters involved throughout the entire film accentuate its multi-layered composition.

The film is the story of a U.S. ex-pat running a bar in Vichy-governed Morocco during pre-Pearl Harbor WW2, meeting the love of his life all over again (against a background of Gestapo fiends; Free- and collaborating-French; various refugees; and German underground escapees — all from the turmoil in Europe), works equally well as an allegory.

Cynical Rick is the symbol of U.S. isolationism between 1939 to 1941: 'I stick my neck out for nobody'. He does, however, smooth the waters for those in conflict by providing a means out of Casablanca to neutral Lisbon, echoing Uncle Sam's materiel support for besieged Britain and other acts of an anti-Nazi nature. Oscars for picture, Curtiz, and Julius J. Epstein, Philip G. Epstein and Howard Koch for their adaptation of Murray Bennett's play *Everybody Comes to Rick's*; Bogart and Rains were nominated as actors. As time goes by, it is a picture that remains timeless.
With *Humphrey Bogart, Ingrid Bergman, Claude Rains, Paul Henreid, Sydney Greenstreet, Peter Lorre, Conrad Veidt, Dooley Wilson, S.Z. Sakall*

THE CASE OF SERGEANT GRISCHA
Herbert Brenon — U.S., 1930 [80min]
Anti-war story using a Russian soldier to symbolise the mass mistreatment of POWs by the Germans in WW1. Brenon (see **Beau Geste**) was not really jumping on to Milestone's band-wagon in this year of **All Quiet . . .** he was previously responsible for the famous pacifist tract **War Brides** in 1916.
With *Chester Morris, Betty Compson, Jean Hersholt*

CAST A GIANT SHADOW
Melville Shavelson — U.S., 1966 [140min]
Palestine, 1947. Jews and Arabs contest the 'homelands' with the mandated British as piggy-in-the-middle. Douglas plays an American Jewish WW2 vet called upon to train the proto-Israeli soldiers, battling with his conscience in the shape of former superior Wayne (told in flashback), before finally committing himself fully to the struggle. Starry cast — including the British military stock company. Plenty of exciting action sequences.
With *Kirk Douglas, Angie Dickinson, Senta Berger, Frank Sinatra, John Wayne, (Chaim) Topol, James Donald, Gordon Jackson, Michael Hordern, Jeremy Kemp*

CASTLE KEEP
Sydney Pollack — U.S., 1969 [105min]
WW2 curio, much-loved in France, but it bombed elsewhere. An allegorical tale of U.S. troops (New World culture) defending

CASABLANCA
Bogart, Rains, Henreid and Bergman in one of the greatest films of all time. Warner Brothers (courtesy KOBAL)

a 10th-century Belgian chateau and all its priceless treasures (Old World culture) against the on-coming German forces (barbarians). Pollack's attempt to adapt William Eastlake's fantasy novel doesn't quite come off, but the picture is different enough for cult status to set in. It could yet have a longer shelf-life than more high-profile mainstream WW2 productions. (See also **The Keep**.)
With *Burt Lancaster, Peter Falk, Patrick O'Neal, Jean Pierre Aumont, Bruce Dern, Astrid Heeren*

CASUALTIES OF WAR
Brian de Palma — U.S., 1989 [115min]
Not in the same league as **Platoon**, **Hamburger Hill** or **Full Metal Jacket**, the other Vietnam war pictures from the same period. This attempt to discuss morality in a war zone, when not just extremely dull, is typical de Palma of that time — nauseating. Penn steals the show as the sadistic rapist sergeant: Fox is overwhelmed as the goody-goody side-kick. The terrible thing is, both characters are so pukey in their polarized stances, no-one cares who's good or bad.
With *Michael J. Fox, Sean Penn, Thuy Thu Le*

CATCH-22
Mike Nichols — U.S., 1970 [120min]
Nichols was Hollywood's boy wonder in the late '60s, receiving an Oscar nomination, then the statuette itself, for his first two ground-breaking movies, *Who's Afraid of Virginia Woolf* and *The Graduate*, respectively. Despite using Buck Henry (*The Graduate*) again to adapt, in this case, Joseph Heller's blacker-than-black comedy, Nichols fails to recreate the sweep of probably *the* novel depicting WW2 hell, and instead shoots it episodically in a series of cameos and vignettes.

The main theme revolves around bomber crewman Yosserian (Arkin) trying to get to the end of his tour of duty in Italy, by hook or by crook. Catch-22? To quote Heller: ' . . . [a man] would be crazy to fly more missions and sane if he didn't, but if he was sane he'd have to fly them. If he flew them he was crazy and didn't have to; but if he didn't, he was sane and had to'!

Good performances from Arkin, and Voight as the spiv selling parachutes for stocking material, and some super verbal interplays and stunning sight gags make a long and frustrating film periodically watchable. Aviation buffs will enjoy a sky full of B-25 Mitchells.
With *Alan Arkin, Martin Balsam, Richard Benjamin, Art(hur) Garfunkel, Jon Voight, Jack Gilford, Buck Henry, Paula Prentiss, Orson Welles, Anthony Perkins, Bob Newhart, Martin Sheen*

CATHERINE THE GREAT (aka 'The Rise of Catherine the Great') See **The Scarlet Empress**

CAVALCADE
Frank Lloyd — U.S., 1932 [110min]
Oscar-winning Noel Coward *Upstairs Downstairs*-type saga of an upper-class London family with references (documentary-style), to the Boer War and WW1. More stagey melodrama than action, it went down well in Hollywood (Louella Parsons preferred it to **Birth of a Nation**), and as well as the picture itself the Academy recognized Lloyd and William Darling's art direction. Wynyard received a nomination.
With *Clive Brook, Diana Wynyard, Ursula Jeans*

CAVALRY ATTACK See **The Last Outpost** (1951)

THE CAVERN
Edgar G. Ulmer — Italy/U.S., 1966 [95min]
Poor end of WW2 drama in the Italian Alps. Cast of those who have been there, will never get there, and will one day make it big on TV, says it all.
With *John Agar, Rosanna Schiaffino, Brian Aherne, Larry Hagman*

CEASE FIRE
Owen Crump — U.S., 1953
3-D documentary view of action in the run-up to the Korean War peace talks at Panmunjom. (Not to be confused with the dramatic Vietnam 'vet-coming-home' feature by David Nutter in 1985, starring Don Johnson.)

A CELEBRATED CASE
George Melford — U.S., 1914
Rare cinematic treatment of the Battle of Fontenoy (1745) during the War of Austrian Succession, when the Duke of Cumberland's force of English, Dutch, Hanoverians and Austrians succumbed to the French army of Marshal Saxe. Told, as usual, through a tale of personal romance, this is the only Hollywood treatment of this important 18th century conflict among the Hapsburg family and friends, although **The Adventures of Casanova** and **General Crack** allude to fringe arguments.
With *Alice Joyce, James B. Ross*

LA CHAGRIN ET LA PITIE See *Grief and Pity*

LA CHANSON DE ROLAND
Frank Cassenti — France, 1978 [110min]
The legend of Roland, nephew of Charlemagne, has its base in historical fact. The Frankish scholar Einhard refers to his death at the hands of Basques in the Pyrenees, and this tale describes (apart from his role at court) Roland's accompaniment of Charlemagne to Spain in 778 to fight the Moors, only to be ambushed and killed on his return to what is now France. (Previously aired in Pietri Francisci's **Roland and the Paladins of France ★** [100min] in 1956 with Rick Battaglia and Rosanna Schiaffino.)
With *Klaus Kinski, Dominique Sanda, Alain Cluny*

CHAPAYEV
Georgi and Segei Vasiliev — USSR, 1934 [95min]
A rare drama about the Revolution and Civil War in Russia, unfettered by Eisenstein-type documentary realism. It tells of Chapayev, a Red Army officer up against the Whites in 1919, and conveys a strain of humanism and individuality of a style not seen too often since Tsarist days.
With *Boris Babochkin*

THE CHARGE AT FEATHER RIVER
Gordon Douglas — U.S., 1953 [95min]
When the 3-D craze was at its zenith, this was probably the best spectacle made for the system, with audiences ducking from U.S. cavalry charges, flying Cheyenne tomahawks and arrows — even baccy sputum. Historically unidentifiable, though.
With *Guy Madison, Frank Lovejoy, Helen Westcott, Vera Miles*

THE CHARGE OF THE LANCERS
William Castle — U.S., 1953 [75min]
Derivative, sometimes unconsciously funny action adventure based on the Crimean War with a none-too-original title. At least it throws in a French angle, with Aumont as the French captain who gets the gypsy girl (girl? Goddard was 42 at the time), then rescues a British officer who has secrets of a new Russian cannon which could affect the imminent British assault on Sebastopol.
With *Paulette Goddard, Jean Pierre Aumomt, Richard Stapley*

THE CHARGE OF THE LIGHT BRIGADE
Michael Curtiz — U.S., 1936 [115min]
Flynn and de Havilland's second starring outing with the master action director after **Captain Blood** and before the climactic **The Adventures of Robin Hood**. Hollywood hokum at its very best — to hell with the history.
  Set initially in pre-Mutiny India, the scene changes to the Crimea quite late into the picture, but it will then always be remembered for its epic set piece — Tennyson's version of the Six Hundred riding hell for leather into the Valley of Death (for which Curtiz was indebted to his Second Unit Director, B. Reeves Easton). The film picks up where **Lives of a Bengal Lancer** left off in paving the way for the very best of the so-called 'empire' films of the late '30s — **The Four Feathers** remake and **Gunga Din**. The only recognition from the Academy was a nomination for Max Steiner's music.
With *Errol Flynn, Olivia de Havilland, Patric Knowles, Donald Crisp, C. Aubrey Smith, Henry Stephenson, David Niven, Nigel Bruce, C. Henry Gordon*

Not really a remake, Tony Richardson's 1968 film of the same title [140min], with Trevor Howard, Vanessa Redgrave, John Gielgud, David Hemmings, and Harry Andrews, sticks a lot closer to the history-book account of this action in the Battle of Balaclava. But in de-Hollywoodising it he should have been more careful with its plot and overall demeanour. In style, it could be the director's '*Tom Jones* II' (with scenes linked by animated interludes), whilst the storyline is so jumbled, it's little wonder the British commanders were so confused. The 'charge' itself is its biggest saving grace (although Howard as the brave but wooden-headed Cardigan and Gielgud as the senile Raglan are excellent), and has been avidly scrutinised by war movie buffs. It is typically '60s anti-heroic in manner, though, and Hemmings, as the principal anti-hero, and his comrades, go through slaughter-by-numbers.

THE CHARGE OF THE LIGHT BRIGADE (1968)
See **The Charge of the Light Brigade** (1936)

CHARGE OF THE LIGHT BRIGADE
Nolan — David Hemmings — is passed by the survivors of the charge.

CHARLEY ONE-EYE
Don Chaffey — GB/U.S., 1972 [105min]
Violent U.S. Civil War piece involving desertion, racism and bounty hunters. Different.
With *Richard Roundtree, Roy Thinnes, Nigel Davenport*

THE CHARTERHOUSE OF PARMA
See **La Chartreuse de Parme**

LA CHARTREUSE DE PARME
(aka 'The Charterhouse of Parma')
Christian-Jaque — France, 1948 [170min]
Unhappy portrayal of Stendahl's novel about Fabrice del Dongo, or Fabrizio, which puts the Battle of Waterloo association on a par with Richard Lester filming Dumas.
With Gérard Philippe, Louis Salou

CHASING THE DEER
Graham Holloway — GB, 1994 [95min]
Attempt to film Bonnie Prince Charlie's revolt and the Battle of Culloden very cheaply. Result: Bonnie Prince Charlie's revolt and the Battle of Culloden look as if they've been made on the cheap. For a few dollars more, or less (?), the TV production *Culloden*, directed by Peter Watkins, is much better. Shame for the solid leads.
With *Brian Blessed, Iain Cuthbertson*

CHE!
Richard Fleischer — U.S., 1969 [95min]
The turgid biopic of the revolutionary icon of the '60s, Che Guevara (remember the psychedelic LSD-driven poster design?), and his romanticised involvement with Castro's Cuban Revolution in 1958-59.

Palance makes a bizarre Castro. It was quite apparent that the Hollywood establishment was uncomfortable making pictures about the Reds so close by — but it was hip to cover this subject, however ambivalently, in this year of the *Stones in the Park* and *Woodstock* concerts.
With *Omar Sharif, Jack Palance, Robert Loggia, Woody Strode*

THE CHESS PLAYERS
(aka 'Shatranj Ke Khilari')
Satyajit Ray — India, 1977 [130min]
Indian master film-maker Ray handled subjects relating to the British Raj very rarely — it's an area he was obviously uneasy with as this film shows. In attempting to symbolise British expansion in the Oudh of 1856 through the figures on a chessboard, the effect is quite puerile. On another level, however, as a mild comedy of obsessed Lucknow nabobs playing constant chess, ignorant of the British plans to deprive them of their estates, and that within months the sepoys' mutiny would begin, it works quite well. Good to look at, too.
With *Sanjiv Kumar, Saeed Jaffrey, Richard Attenborough, Amjad Khan, Shaban Azmi*

CHETNIKS (aka 'Chetniks — the Fighting Guerrillas')
Louis King — U.S., 1942 [75min]
Routine action with Hollywood paying lip-service to the smaller European nations embroiled in the struggle against the Nazis. This was before they realised that the Chetniks were in fact Serbian separatists, after which they only supported Tito, a Croatian, and his united Yugoslavian partisans. But hang on, wasn't he communist . . . ?
With *Philip Dorn, Anna Sten*

CHETNIKS — THE FIGHTING GUERRILLAS
See **Chetniks**

CHEYENNE AUTUMN
John Ford — U.S., 1964 [170min]
Ford's personal apology to the Native American? In his last Western, beautifully shot by Oscar-nominated William Clothier, we see *his* Monument Valley for the last time, we see Widmark and Stewart in somewhat remorseful roles, and we see the noble savage portrayed as a hunted victim, badly let down by Washington. Overlong and episodic, it is not up amongst the Ford classics (**She Wore A Yellow Ribbon**, **The Searchers**, for example) but a Ford Western it is, and in parts it's as elegaic as his best work. The story is based on the true case of the Cheyenne who surrendered to the cavalry in 1877

and were taken from their Yellowstone, Montana, hunting grounds to a bald plateau in Oklahoma. After a decade of broken promises to improve their lot, they decide to up sticks and go home. The army is sent out to intercept them.
With *Richard Widmark, Carroll Baker, James Stewart, Karl Malden, Dolores del Rio, Edward G. Robinson, Sal Mineo*

CHICAGO JOE AND THE SHOWGIRL
Bernard Rose — GB, 1989 [105min]
An unusual and unpalatable WW2 exploitation piece. Yank 'over here' teams up with a young trollop to commit a series of crimes culminating in murder. Supposedly based on fact, it evokes nothing more than film-noirish clichés of unreality. Poor all round.
With *Keifer Sutherland, Emily Lloyd, Patsy Kensit*

CHIEF CRAZY HORSE
See **They Died with Their Boots On**

CHILDREN OF HIROSHIMA (aka 'Genbaku No Ko', 'Children of the Atom Bomb') See **Hiroshima**

CHILDREN OF THE ATOM BOMB
See **Children of Hiroshima**

CHIMES AT MIDNIGHT
(aka 'Campanadas a Medianoche', 'Falstaff')
Orson Welles — Spain/Switzerland, 1966 [120min]
Welles concertinas the Bard's five plays involving Sir John Falstaff (plus supplements from Holinshed's *Chronicles*) into a shambolically-edited two hours or so. That should be enough said, but Welles was nothing if not a maverick and this film has always something interesting to revisit. The bloody, muddy Battle of Shrewsbury (1403) which ends *Henry IV, Part 1*, and which sees Prince Hal beat Hotspur in single combat, is one of the goriest and most brutally-intensive encounters ever filmed: after which, recuperating (supposedly) in the Cotswolds, Sir John meets an old friend with whom he had heard 'the chimes of midnight' (from *Henry IV, Part 2*). See also **Henry V**.
With *Orson Welles, Keith Baxter, John Gielgud, Jeanne Moreau, Margaret Rutherford*

CHINA
John Farrow — U.S., 1943 [80min]
Interest in the Japanese run-up to Pearl Harbor became good box-office after the dirty deed was done. This was one of several anti-Japanese pictures made on the Sino-Japanese War.
Others of the time included **China Girl ★★** (Henry Hathaway, 1942 [90min], with George Montgomery) and **China Sky ★** (Ray Enright, 1945 [80min], starring Randolph Scott). Farrow's excursion to the conflict features loads of heroics involving Ladd, who was then big box-office.
With *Alan Ladd, Loretta Young, William Bendix*

CHINA CARAVAN See **A Yank on the Burma Road**

CHINA GATE
Samuel Fuller — U.S., 1957
One of a few U.S. dabbles into the proto-Vietnam situation, viz the French-Indochina Wars (see also **Jump into Hell**, **Lost Command**). Fuller is, as usual, one of the first ashore (his **Steel Helmet** was one of the first movies to look at the Korean War), and tells the tale of a Foreign Legion patrol blowing up a commie arms dump in straightforward fashion. Not one of his best, however. For a list of more traditional Foreign Legion movies, see **Beau Geste** (1939).
With *Gene Barry, Angie Dickinson, Nat 'King' Cole, Lee Van Cleef*

CHINA GIRL See **China**

CHINA SKY See **China**

CHINA VENTURE
Don Siegel — U.S., 1953 [85min]
Early directorial run out for Siegel (*Riot in Cell Block 11, Invasion of the Body Snatchers, Dirty Harry*) wasn't overly sprightly. Ordinary WW2 fodder of U.S. Marines snatching a Japanese admiral shot down over China.
With *Edmond O'Brien, Barry Sullivan*

CHEYENNE AUTUMN
The lengthening shadows say it all for Sal Mineo (left) and Ricardo Montalban. WB

EL CID
The 'Cid' joins forces with the Moors before the Battle of
Valencia. Allied Artists (courtesy KOBAL)

CHINA'S LITTLE DEVILS
Monta Bell — U.S., 1945 [75min]
Tokyo Joe v Our Gang. Child guerrillas emerge from missionary
Carey's charge in WW2 China to wreak revenge on their
heinous Japanese occupiers.
With *Harry Carey Sr, Paul Kelly, Ducky Louie (!)*

CHISTOHE NEBO See The Clear Skies

CHOCOLATE AND SOLDIERS
Také Sado — Japan, 1941
The Sino-Japanese War from the Japanese perspective.
Sentimental story, aimed at patriotic families, of a father at the
Front who sends his son chocolate wrappers — when the
chocolate company find out they sponsor the boy's education.
The father, is, of course, killed.

THE CHORALE OF LEUTHEN See Fridericus

CHRONIQUE DES ANNEES DE BRAISE
Mohamed Lakhdar Hamina — Algeria, 1975 [170min]
Seen through the eyes of a shepherd boy, the turmoil in
French Algeria from the outbreak of WW2 to the day the
colonial war broke out in 1954.
Epic political history but rather self-indulgent at nearly
three hours.
With *Jorgo Voyagis, Larbi Zekkal*

EL CHUCHO
See A Bullet for the General

EL CID
*Anthony Mann — Italy/U.S.,
1961* [185min]
The first of two overlong but
historically-interesting projects
Mann undertook with producer
Samuel Bronston (see also **The
Fall of the Roman Empire**).
Rodrigo Díaz de B(V)ivar
(c1043-99) received the nick-
name the 'Cid' (from the Arabic
Sidi — Lord) after fighting for
the Moorish king of Zaragoza:
the film (eventually) deals with
the expulsion of the Moors after
Valencia in 1094, and the siege
and later battle sequences are
particularly well done.
The Cid rides into his last
battle — posthumously —
ahead of his men. A truely epic
film.
With *Charlton Heston, Sophia
Loren, Raf Vallone, Genevieve
Page*

LA CIOCIARA
See **Two Women**

CIRCLE OF DECEIT (aka 'Die Fälschung')
Volker Schlondorff — France/West Germany, 1981 [110min]
Provocative and physically brave dramatisation of events in the
Lebanese civil war (it was filmed on the streets of Beirut
before the cease fire), with actual footage from the horrors to
support it. Makes Costa-Gavras seem like weak beer. Polish
director, Skolimowski (**The Adventures of Gerard**) appears
as a press cameraman. (**War Zone ★★**, directed by Nathaniel
Gutman in Germany in 1986 [100min], and starring a
bemused Christopher Walken, covers a similar theme, but
cannot compete with its tautness or veracity.)
With *Bruno Ganz, Hanna Schygulla, Jerzy Skolimowski*

CIRCLE OF DECEPTION
Jack Lee — GB, 1960 [100min]
Workaday behind-German-lines WW2 espionage drama with
a cast that would learn to do better for itself.
With *Bradford Dillman, Harry Andrews, Robert Stephens, Suzy
Parker, Paul Rogers*

A CITY OF SADNESS (aka 'Beiqing Chengshi')
Hou Xiaoxian — Taiwan, 1989 [160min]
Somewhat cryptic in its approach (it certainly benefits from a
second viewing) Hou's account of the political comings and
goings between the Japanese withdrawal from Formosa in
1945 and Chiang Kai-Shek's presence four years later is told
through the daily life of a family — its members representative
of different island milieu of the time. The Venice Film Festival
awarded the picture the Golden Lion.
With *Tony Leung, Xin Shufen, Li T'ien-lu*

CIVILIZATION
Thomas Ince — U.S., 1916 [70min]
Ince's *pièce de résistance* needed directorial help from others

42

such as Reginald Barker (**The Coward**). Made at the height of WW1 in Europe, it was anti-German, as many Hollywood pictures were becoming, but was also blatantly pacifist with effective religious imagery. President Wilson appeared in it, thus seemingly endorsing its sentiment (a factor in his re-election that November?), only to send the Doughboys in the following year anyway.
With *Herschell Mayall, Enid Markey, Lola May, Howard Hickman, J. Barney Sherry*

THE CLANSMAN See **Birth of a Nation**

THE CLAY PIGEON
Richard Fleischer — U.S., 1949 [65min]
Benefiting from a Carl Foreman script (**The Men**, *High Noon*, **Bridge on the River Kwai**, **The Guns of Navarone**, **The Victors**) and a young Fleischer (**Bandido**, **Tora! Tora! Tora!**) this 'B' movie turns out to be one of the more interesting and intelligent WW2 vet pictures, with Williams as the amnaesic sailor court-martialled for treason.
With *Bill Williams, Barbara Hale*

THE CLEAR SKIES (aka 'Chistohe Nebo')
Grigori Chukhrai — USSR, 1961
Anti-Stalinist tract about a downed WW2 pilot, feared dead, but imprisoned by the Germans. On returning home he is branded a traitor and banished from the Party, to be reinstated into the Soviet air force only after Stalin's death.
With *Yevgeni Urbanski*

CLEOPATRA (1934)
See **Cleopatra** (1963) *Cecil B. de Mille — U.S., 1934*

CLEOPATRA
Joseph L. Mankiewicz — U.S., 1963 [245min]
What more can be said of the *Heaven's Gate* of its day — apart from that it didn't (quite) put the studio (Paramount) out of business? (It did in fact just about break even at the box-office.) The waste is legendary, the length interminable, the stars abominable — is there anything good about it? Well, it did win the Oscar for Cinematography for Leon Shamroy, as well as for its lavish art direction: and it is better than the vulgarly ostentatious 1934 fare from the master of kitsch (100min) from de Mille with Claudette Colbert and Henry Wilcoxson.
In that earlier (almost totally) fabricated account of the Queen of the Nile and Rome's straying triumvir, Antony, millions of extras are seemingly employed to titillate the audience's senses — something the Hays Office was about to stamp out. One thing it does have in its favour — it is mercifully short. Nominated for Best Picture, its only Oscar went to Victor Milner for his photography.
Mankiewicz's monolith is, to be fair, quite accurate histori-cally; the Battle of Actium (31BC) is reasonably re-enacted, and it is the only picture to cover fully the history of Julius Caesar's last years and both his and Antony's involvement with the Egyptian queen.
With *Elizabeth Taylor, Richard Burton, Rex Harrison, Pamela Brown, George Cole, Hume Cronyn, Kenneth Haig, Martin Landau, Roddy McDowell*

The director's own **Julius Caesar** *** (1953 — 120min), which won nominations for Best Picture and its star Marlon Brando (it also starred John Gielgud and James Mason), and

a thin remake by Stuart Burge in 1969 [115min], ** with Richard Johnson, Jason Robards, Charlton Heston and Gielgud again, were more-or-less faithful Shakespearean reproductions up to the Battle of Philippi (42BC).
The bard's work was again covered by Heston (as director and lead) in the 1972 international production of **Antony and Cleopatra** **** [170min] — with Hildegarde Neil as Cleopatra — which places events several years later. (William Castle's hopeless **Serpent of the Nile** from 1953 [80min], with Rhonda Fleming and William Lundigan as C & A, is pure hokum: **The Legions of Cleopatra** [Vittorio Cottafavi — Italy, 1959, with Linda Cristal — 100min], is just an excuse for a bunch of Cinecittà extras to put on togas.)

CLIVE OF INDIA
Richard Boleslawski — U.S., 1934 [90min]
Dated attempt to portray the life and times of the founder of British India. With more emphasis on the love angle than on action, it at least considers the siege of Trichonopoly (1741) before romance takes over.
With *Ronald Colman, Loretta Young, Colin Clive*

CLOAK AND DAGGER
Fritz Lang — U.S., 1946 [105min]
Disappointing Lang espionage drama with Cooper dropped behind German lines in WW2 to find a scientist.
With *Gary Cooper, Lili Palmer, Robert Alda*

THE CLOCK (aka 'Under the Clock')
Vincente Minelli — U.S., 1945 [90min]
Famous — and in fairness, just about the least mawkish or sentimental — WW2 Stateside leave-romance picture. The clock is the one at Grand Central Station, New York City, which acts as a time-ticking backdrop to Walker's 48-hour leave, in which he meets and marries Garland.
With *Judy Garland, Robert Walker*

CLOSELY OBSERVED TRAINS
(aka 'Ostra Sledovane Vlaky')
Jiri Menzel — Czechoslovakia, 1966 [90min]
The deserved winner of the 1967 Oscar for Best Foreign Film is set in a rural railway station in occupied Czechoslovakia, and is a charming, gentle comedy more concerned with pubescence and rites of passage than the war, which seems to pass it by — until the tragic *dénouement*.
With *Vaclav Neckar, Jitka Bendova, Vladimir Valenta, Josef Somr*

COCKLESHELL HEROES
José Ferrer — GB, 1955 [95min]
Successful foray into direction by Puerto Rican Ferrer, even though pointing a bunch of Brit Marines in the right direction (in this case to Bordeaux harbour to limpet-mine blockading Nazi warships) was not obvious material. Popular with school kids of the author's vintage, and a fairly accurate account of the real raid.
With *José Ferrer, Trevor Howard, Victor Maddern, Anthony Newley, Peter Arne, Dora Bryan*

CODE NAME: EMERALD
Jonathan Sanger — U.S., 1985 [95min]
WW2 espionage drama filmed about 25 years too late. It has nothing further to add to the sub-genre.
With *Ed Harris, Horst Buccholz, Max von Sydow, Helmut Berger*

CLOSELY OBSERVED TRAINS
What is this fascination with trains? Ceskoslovensky Film

COLD DAYS (aka 'Hideg Napok')

Andras Kovacs — Hungary, 1966
Gripping re-enaction of atrocities perpetrated by Horthy's pro-German Hungarian troops in WW2 Yugoslavia — a powerful study of guilt and responsibilities in war.
With *Zoltan Latinovits, Ivan Darvas, Adam Szirtes*

THE COLDITZ STORY

Guy Hamilton — GB, 1954 [95min]
Arguably the best of the British POW dramas of the '50s, this adaptation of Maj Pat Reid's memoirs, whilst told in docudrama fashion, has no shortage of humour either — although somewhat clichéd for modern audiences.

It became the inspiration for a popular BBC TV series in the 1970s, *Colditz*, with Robert Wagner and David McCallum. (See **The Captive Heart**, **The Wooden Horse**, **Albert RN**.)
With *John Mills, Eric Portman, Christopher Rhodes, Lionel Jeffries, Ian Carmichael, Bryan Forbes, Anton Diffring*

COLONEL REDL (aka 'Redl Ezredes', 'Oberst Redl')

Istvan Szabo — Austria/Hungary/West Germany, 1984 [150min]
Szabo's impressive next picture on the back of **Mephisto** again stars Brandauer in a huge performance. This time he plays the eponymous 'hero' who rises through the military ranks of the Hapsburg Empire after the Franco-Prussian War, becoming head of Military Intelligence before WW1. Nominated for Best Foreign Film Oscar, it also took the Jury Prize at Cannes.
With *Klaus-Maria Brandauer, Armin Mueller-Stahl, Gudrun Landgrebe*

The combination of Szabo and Brandauer shone brightly one more time in 1988 in the Oscar-nominated [Foreign Film] **Hanussen** [115min], where Brandauer moves from a WW1 hospital into the society of Nazi ascendancy through his remarkable powers of clairvoyance.

IL COLOSSO DI RHODI
See **The Colossus of Rhodes**

THE COLOSSUS OF RHODES

(aka 'Il Colosso de Rhodi')
Sergio Leone — Italy, 1960 [130min]
Well above-average classical saga out of the Rome studios with Rhodian Greeks defending their island from invading Phoenicians in the 4th century BC. Leone was well-versed in this Italian speciality dish as he had worked on the **Ben-Hur** chariot race the previous year, before moving on to creating his own sub-genre — the spaghetti Western (*A Fistful of Dollars*, **The Good, the Bad and the Ugly**, *Once Upon a Time in the West*).
With *Rory Calhoun, Lea Masari, Georges Marschal*

COLUMN SOUTH

Frederick de Cordova — U.S., 1953 [85min]
The Navajo tribe gets a rare outing in this routine Murphy vehicle of Army versus Indians. The outbreak of the Civil War adds a deviating undercurrent to events.
With *Audie Murphy, Robert Sterling, Joan Evans, Ray Collins, Dennis Weaver*

COMANCHE

George Sherman — U.S., 1956 [85min]
Sherman made two films directly about the plight of the Comanche Indians in the late 19th century. His earlier **Comanche Territory** ★ (1950 [75min] with Maureen O'Hara) told the tall tale of Jim Bowie (Macdonald Carey) and a bunch of white renegades; the 1956 picture, while still quite hokey, at least deals with events of 1875 and Chief Quanah Parker. Both feature battles with the U.S. Army.

André de Toth's **The Last of the Comanches** ★ (1952- aka 'The Sabre and the Arrow' — 85min) with Broderick Crawford, is of no historical relevance whatsoever.
With *Dana Andrews, Kent Smith, Henry Brandon, Nestor Paiva, John Litel*

COMANCHE TERRITORY See **Comanche**

COMBAT SQUAD

Cy Roth — U.S., 1953 [70min]
Been-here-before Korean War picture with absolutely nothing to commend it.
With *John Ireland, Lon MacCallister*

COME AND SEE (aka 'Idi i Smotri')
Elem Klimov — USSR, 1985 [140min]
Another extremely powerful picture from Klimov, some ten years after **Agony**. This time the agony is set on the Polish-Byelorussian border in 1943, unsurprisingly depicting appalling German atrocities in Soviet villages.
With *Alexei Kravchenko, Olga Miranova*

COME SEE THE PARADISE
Alan Parker — U.S., 1990 [135min]
Not afraid to deal with difficult subjects (*Midnight Express, Mississippi Burning*) Parker turns his attention to Japanese-American internment in the U.S. during WW2. The project fails this time — not enough historical punctuation in what develops into pure melodrama.
With *Dennis Quaid, Tamlin Tamita, Sab Shimono*

COMING HOME
Hal Ashby — U.S., 1978 [130min]
Good performances (both Voight and Fonda picked up Oscars) can't save this archetypal Vietnam War vet picture from its cloying sentimentality.
  Fonda falls for paraplegic vet Voight while vet husband (Dern) goes mad and drowns himself. Dog-fighting with **The Deer Hunter** in the same year in an Academy probably riddled with guilty patriotism, it lost out for the picture, director and supporting actor awards, although — somewhat bafflingly — collecting the statuette for the multi-fingered script.
With *Jane Fonda, Jon Voight, Bruce Dern*

A COMING OUT PARTY See **Very Important Person**

COMMAND DECISION
Sam Wood — U.S., 1949 [110min]
Starchy Ops Room drama with Gable very concerned at the casualty rate suffered by daylight bombing raids over Germany in WW2.
With *Clark Gable, Walter Pidgeon, Van Johnson, Brian Donlevy*

COMMANDO See **The Legion's Last Patrol**

COMMANDO SUICIDA See **Suicide Commando**

COMMANDOS See **The Legion's Last Patrol**

THE COMMANDOS STRIKE AT DAWN
John Farrow — U.S., 1942 [100min]
Early recognition of the use of commando raids into Nazi-occupied Europe benefiting from a script by Irwin Shaw (**The Young Lions**). Muni organizes Norwegian partisans to support a British commando mission launched by the Royal Navy. Not bad.
With *Paul Muni, Anna Lee, Lillian Gish, Cedric Hardwicke, Robert Coote*

COMPANEROS See **Bandido**

COMPANY OF COWARDS?
See **Advance to the Rear**

COMRADESHIP See **Kameradschaft**

UN CONDAMNE A MORT S'EST ECHAPPE
See **A Man Escaped**

CONFESSIONS OF A NAZI SPY
Anatole Litvak — U.S., 1939 [110min]
Very serious attack by Warner Brothers on the Third Reich. Certainly the most damning picture to come out of Hollywood up to this time, it tells (unlike some other tongue-in-cheek 'message' movies of the '30s) of a network of Nazi spies in America, and how Hoover's G-Men track them down. Sol Polito's monochrome photography evokes an early *film noir* style, and refugee Litvak directs his best Hollywood work to date — before getting involved with Capra's **Why We Fight** documentaries.
With *Edward G. Robinson, Francis Lederer, Paul Lukas, George Sanders*

CONFIDENCE (aka 'Bizalom')
Istvan Szabo — Hungary, 1979 [115min]
Taut political thriller based in WW2 occupied Hungary with the hero and heroine avoiding both Nazis and the underground. Good forerunner to **Mephisto** from Szabo.
With *Ildiko Bansagi, Peter Andorai*

CONFIDENTIAL AGENT
Herman Shumlin — U.S., 1945 [120min]
A Spanish Civil War story with a difference — and also a decent adaptation of a Graham Greene story. Boyer is the Loyalist spy attempting to spike fascist attempts to buy munitions from Britain in 1937. It hardly seems credible now.
With *Charles Boyer, Lauren Bacall, Peter Lorre, Katina Paxinou*

CONFIRM OR DENY
Archie Mayo — U.S., 1941 [80min]
OK, but a bit of a daft story of London in the Blitz, a U.S. war correspondent and Nazi plans for Operation 'Sea Lion'. Samuel Fuller, inauspiciously, had a hand in the script. He would come to write a little better with time.
With *Don Ameche, Joan Bennett, Roddy McDowall*

THE CONFORMIST (aka 'Il Conformista')
Bernardo Bertolucci — France/Italy/W. Germany, 1969 [110min]
Visually striking parable of the perniciousness of fascism in Italy seen through the eyes of an intelligent man — from initiation into the party, through informing and assassination, to eventual decline in 1943. A startling film from Bertolucci (Oscar-nominated for his adapted script), who developed the Italian fascist scene in the more-obliquely political **The Spider's Stratagem *** (aka 'Strategia del Ragno' [95min]) with Giulio Brogi and Alida Valli the following year, before taking on a whole new bundle of taboos in his next picture, *Last Tango in Paris*.
With *Jean-Louis Trintignant, Stefania Sandrelli, Gastone Moschin*

IL CONFORMISTA See **The Conformist**

THE CONQUEROR
Dick Powell — U.S., 1956 [110min]
It has been mooted that Powell, Wayne and Hayward all died of cancer brought on by shooting this picture on a former atomic bomb testing site. It may be that producer Howard Hughes' and Powell's choice of location was an error only secondary to releasing the film at all.

THE CONFORMIST
The Assassination of Professor Quadri (Enzo Tarascio) by Fascists.
Mars/Marianne/Maran

With Wayne determined to play Genghis Khan as some kind of dislocated late 12th-century Doc Holliday, and a script discarded by an infants' play-group, history has not been served well. The extraordinary 'plot' had something to do with Mongols v Tartars, with the Mongols going on to win by an own goal. Utter tosh.
With *John Wayne, Susan Hayward, Pedro Armendariz, Agnes Moorhead*

THE CONQUEROR WORM See **Witchfinder General**

CONQUEST (aka 'Marie Walewska')
Clarence Brown — U.S., 1937 [115min]
Historical romance done with typical MGM flounce (Cedric Gibbons received yet another Oscar nomination for his sets). Napoleon's love-life gets more footage than the battle scenes. Boyer also gained a nomination.
With *Greta Garbo, Charles Boyer*

THE CONQUEST OF ALBANIA
(aka 'La Conquista de Albania')
Alfonso Ungria — Spain, 1982 [120min]
Overlong Spanish epic depicting Charles II of Navarre's campaign in the Balkans in the 14th century and his attempt to place his son on the throne.
With *Xavier Elloriaga, Klara Badiola*

CONQUEST OF COCHISE
See **Broken Arrow**

LA CONQUISTA DE ALBANIA
See **The Conquest of Albania**

IL CONQUISTADORE DI CORINTO
See **The Battle of Corinth**

CONSPIRACY OF HEARTS
Ralph Thomas — GB, 1960 [115min]
Completely derivative WW2 adventure with nuns smuggling Jews out of fascist Italy.
With *Lilli Palmer, Sylvia Sims*

THE CONSPIRATORS
Jean Negulesco — U.S., 1944 [100min]
Casablanca in Lisbon. Henreid, Greenstreet and Lorre as well — but that's about all in this WW2 spy drama involving the Dutch underground. Lisbon, in neutral Portugal, acted as a crossroads for much of the shady cloak-and-dagger goings on in early WW2 Europe, and became much-romanticised in the movies. This, believe it or not, is one of the better films.
With *Hedy Lamarr, Paul Henreid, Sydney Greenstreet, Peter Lorre*

Other WW2 espionage thrillers focusing on Lisbon include:
One Night in Lisbon ** (Edward H. Griffith — U.S., 1941 [95min]) With *Madeleine Carroll, Fred MacMurray*
The Lady has Plans ** (Sidney Lanfield — U.S., 1942 [75min]) With *Paulette Goddard, Ray Milland*
Storm Over Lisbon * (George Sherman — U.S., 1944 [85min]) With *Richard Arlen, Erich von Stroheim*
The Lisbon Story (Paul Stein — GB, 1946 [105min]) With *Patricia Burke, David Farrar*
Crossroads of Passions ** (aka 'Carrefour des Passions' [110min]) (Ettore Giannini — France, 1947) With *Viviane Romance, Clément Duhour*
The Secret Door (Gilbert Kay — GB, 1964 [70min]) With *Robert Hutton, Sandra Dorne*

CONTRABAND (aka 'Blackout')
Michael Powell — GB, 1940 [90min]
Atmospheric spy comedy set in the early days of WW2 in London, with Veidt playing a Dane who exposes a Nazi espionage ring. Good star performances from the leads of Powell's previous **The Spy in Black**.
With *Conrad Veidt, Valerie Hobson, Esmond Knight*

CONVOY
Pen Tennyson — GB, 1940 [90min]
Not to be confused with Peckinpah's 1978 blip — this was one of only two feature films (*The Proud Valley* with Paul Robeson being the other) from Tennyson, who was killed shortly afterwards. It deals with the biggest news of the early war in Britain — the threat of the German 'pocket battleships' to the merchant convoys. Quite tense in parts.
With *Clive Brook, John Clements, Edward Chapman*

CORIOLANUS — HERO WITHOUT A COUNTRY
(aka 'Thunder of Battle')
Georgio Ferroni — France/Italy, 1965 [100min]
Rather late entry into the sword-and-sandal genre of Italian cinema, this is, nevertheless, one of the better type — and there is every chance that there was, historically, a character in 5th century Rome who can be correlated with the Coriolanus legend. A theme also developed by Shakespeare, it tells of our hero banished from Rome, leading, in revenge, the Volsci tribe to the city gates, only to pull up short of invading.
With *Gordon Scott, Alberto Lupo*

CORREGIDOR

William Nigh — U.S., 1943 [75min]
Nigh was the first to cash in on the fall of this Philippines island to the Japanese in May 1942, but turned it into a turgid romance. Marginally more informative was **The Eve of St Mark** ★★ (John M. Stahl, 1944 — 95min — with William Eythe and Anne Baxter), but obviously the last battle of the Philippines didn't grab the filmmakers like **Bataan**. (See also **They Were Expendable**.)
With *Elissa Landi, Otto Kruger, Donald Woods*

CORVETTE K-225 (aka 'The Nelson Touch')

Richard Rosson — U.S., 1943 [95min]
Fairly realistic and quite exciting naval drama in WW2 Atlantic. Scott is the skipper of the British corvette escorting convoys from Canada. Tony Gaudio's photography received an Oscar nomination.
With *Randolph Scott, James Brown, Ella Raines, Andy Devine*

THE COSSACKS (1928) See **The Cossacks** (1959)

THE COSSACKS

Giorgio Rivalta — Italy, 1959 [115min]
Italian period romp around the fringes of the Crimean War, with newly-crowned Tsar Alexander II the historical nub. Pretty awful, but no worse than a silent film of the same name (*George Hill*, 1928, starring John Gilbert) which covers quarrels between Cossacks and Turks from an indeterminable age.
With *Edmund Purdom, John Drew Barrymore*

COTTAGE TO LET (aka 'Bombsight Stolen')

Anthony Asquith — GB, 1941 [90min]
Popular WW2 comedy-thriller with a juvenile Cole creating the prototype of the Flash Harry/Arthur Daley Cockney incarnations which were to serve him so well throughout his acting life. He was learning well from his mentor Sim, who was having huge fun in what was his first lead role. The title gives a clue to the (Scottish) rural location and the U.S. alternative alludes to the plot, as Glasgow Nazis do their worst. Great cast enjoy themselves.
With *Alastair Sim, John Mills, Leslie Banks, George Cole, Michael Wilding*

COUNT FIVE AND DIE

Victor Vicas — GB, 1959 [90min]
Military intelligence yarn, quite suspenseful in parts, concerning leaked information about D-Day.
With *Nigel Patrick, Jeffrey Hunter*

COUNTER-ATTACK (aka 'One Against Seven')

Zoltan Korda — U.S., 1945 [90min]
Much was expected of Korda in Hollywood after his British successes with *Sanders of the River* and **The Four Feathers**, but this WW2 sabotage drama (Allied team v Germans) was no more than routine.
With *Paul Muni, Marguerite Chapman, Larry Parks*

COUNTERFEIT COMMANDOS
See **Inglorious Bastards**

THE COUNTERFEIT TRAITOR

George Seaton — U.S., 1962 [140min]
Good to look at with some useful performances, but this tale of a Swedish double agent in WW2 is too long and generally unexciting.
With *William Holden, Lilli Palmer, Hugh Griffith*

COUNTERPOINT

Ralph Nelson — U.S., 1967 [105min]
Perhaps the tallest of the tall tales told about the **Battle of the Bulge**. Heston is the Bernstein-type conductor of a U.S. symphony orchestra captured by Germans while touring Belgium in late 1944 — can you believe it?
With *Charlton Heston, Maximilian Schell, Kathryn Hays, Anton Diffring, Leslie Neilson*

THE COUP D'ETAT See **The Battle of Chile**

LE COUP DE SIROCCO

Alexandre Arcady — France, 1979 [100min]
Drama depicting the lives of *les pieds-noirs* in 1954 on the outbreak of the France-Algerian War.
With *Roger Hanin, Marthe Villalonga*

COURAGE UNDER FIRE

Edward Zwick — U.S., 1996 [115min]
Friendly fire is the main sub-plot in this, one of Hollywood's rare forays into Operation 'Desert Storm'. Washington teams up again with Zwick (**Glory**) in a morality tale, told in action-filled flashbacks, about a posthumous recommendation made for the Medal of Honor to be given to a female helicopter pilot — while he, himself, is pursued by a journalist who wants to know the truth about a tank incident in which Washington was implicated. An intelligent film, spoiled by a saccharine-soaked finale.
With *Denzel Washington, Meg Ryan, Lou Diamond Phillips, Scott Glenn*

THE COURIER TO THE TSAR
See **The Soldier and the Lady**

THE COURT-MARTIAL OF BILLY MITCHELL

(aka 'One Man Mutiny')
Otto Preminger — U.S., 1955 [100min]
Serious, stagey but effective reconstruction of a true event. General Mitchell was court-martialled in 1925 for accusing the U.S. military of incompetence and lack of foresight in not developing its air force against a potential Japanese strike. With Cooper in the lead, you always get integrity. Oscar nominations for Emmet Lavery's and Milton Sperling's script.
With *Gary Cooper, Rod Steiger, Charles Bickford, Ralph Bellamy, Elizabeth Montgomery*

THE COWARD

Reginald Barker — U.S., 1915
Thomas Ince (**The Battle of Gettysburg, Civilization, The Zeppelin's Last Raid**) had a hand in scripting this salutary tale of cowardice and heroism in the War of Secession (1861-65). Allegorically, a 'preparatory' tract for the moral courage Americans would, need in the imminent future.
With *Charles Ray, Frank Keenan*

THE CRANES ARE FLYING (aka 'Letyat Zhuravli')

Mikhail Kalatozov — USSR, 1957 [95min]
Barrier-breaking Soviet film which picked up the Best Picture award at Cannes. Could have been made in Hollywood, so

high are the production values, so unobtrusive is the State. Russian realism has, thankfully, been retained in the grim if derivative love story of boy going off to the Front, girl told he's dead so she marries one of his unsavoury relatives. It is the filmmaker's concern for the individual as an individual that is the real breakthrough here.
With *Tatiana Samoilova, Alexei Batalov, Vasili Merkuriev*

CRASH DIVE
Archie Mayo — U.S., 1943 [105min]
Colour comes to submarine warfare in this exciting and entertaining early example of the ilk, with Andrews commanding a U.S. sub up against German mines and depth charges during WW2.
With *Dana Andrews, Tyrone Power, Anne Baxter*

THE CRIMES OF DR MABUSE
See **The Testament of Dr Mabuse**

THE CRIMSON BLADE See **The Scarlet Blade**

CRIMSON ROMANCE
David Howard — U.S., 1934 [70min]
WW1 aerial warfare curio in that before the U.S. enters the war, Americans Lyon and Bush join the German air force. Lyon then swaps colours when the Yanks join the fray, while Bush is predictably killed.
With *Ben Lyon, James Bush, Eric von Stroheim*

CRIMSON TIDE See **The Bedford Incident**

THE CRISIS
Colin Campbell — U.S., 1915
Early screening of Winston Churchill's American Civil War novel which was swamped by Griffith's **Birth of a Nation**.
With *George W. Fawcett, Bessie Eyton*

LES CROIX DE BOIS
(aka 'Wooden Crosses') See **The Road to Glory**

CROMWELL
Ken Hughes — GB, 1970 [140min]
So few films have been made about the English Civil War that you know you'll be disappointed when an over two-hour epic biopic on its central figure is made. Cromwell as a character has no charisma, so any actor would be on a hiding to nothing, as Harris — attempting to play the administrator-politician as a warlord — certainly is. The picture turns out to be a dramatised history lesson. Nino Novarese did scoop the costume design Oscar, however.
With *Richard Harris, Alec Guinness, Robert Morley, Dorothy Tutin*

CROOKS' TOUR See **Night Train to Munich**

CROSS OF IRON
Sam Peckinpah — GB/West Germany, 1977 [135min]
Just as **Major Dundee** and **The Wild Bunch** weren't straightforward Western-War films, no-one should have expected Peckinpah's only WW2 picture to be mainstream either. It is difficult to watch the director's proclivity for blood and gore without wincing now and again, but in amongst its visual horrors the strong anti-war message hits like a howitzer. A superb cast, with Coburn, as the anti-Nazi German on the

Russian Front in 1943, acting out of his skin. It may not be everybody's cup of tea, but there's no denying its individuality and power.
With *James Coburn, Maximilian Schell, James Mason, David Warner*

Andrew McLaglen's 1979 follow up, with Coburn replaying the eponymous **Sergeant Steiner ★★** (115min — featuring heavyweights Burton, Mitchum, Steiger and Jurgens), is a disappointing affair; with the director's knack of derivation failing, yet again, to be masked by the presence of a starry cast.

THE CROSS OF LORRAINE
Tay Garnett — U.S., 1943 [90min]
Kelly thankfully doesn't dance and sing in this piece of anti-German propaganda. Set in a POW camp for French soldiers, he and Aumont escape to chivvy up the resistance thereabouts. Lorre is the sadistic Nazi officer who tortures our hero. It is *not* a comedy.
With *Gene Kelly, Jean-Pierre Aumont, Cedric Hardwicke, Peter Lorre*

CROSSING PARIS (aka 'La Traversée de Paris')
Claude Autant-Lara — France, 1956 [80min]
Colourful depiction of black market life in German-occupied Paris in WW2.
With *Jean Gabin, Bourvil*

THE CROSSING OF THE RHINE
(aka 'Le Passage du Rhin')
André Cayette — France/Italy/West Germany, 1960 [125min]
During the 1950s, French cinema gave us some memorable and poignant images of WW2 in movies such as Clément's **Les Jeux Interdits**, **A Man Escaped** (Robert Bresson) and Resnais' **Hiroshima, Mon Amour**. Then in 1959 came the Brigitte Bardot vehicle **Babette Goes to War** (Christian-Jaque [105min]) which opened the door for all kinds of lesser offerings — of which this vacuous tale of two French soldiers meeting again in 1945 is just one.
With *Charles Aznavour, Nicole Courcel, Georges Rivière*

CROSSROADS OF PASSIONS
(aka 'Carrefour des Passions') See **The Conspirators**

THE CROUCHING BEAST
W. Victor Hanbury — GB, 1935 [80min]
A not very plausible WW1 espionage drama set in Turkey.
With *Fritz Kortner, Wynne Gibson*

THE CRUEL SEA
Charles Frend — GB, 1952 [125min]
Hugely popular recounting of the Battle of the Atlantic — Britain's WW2 efforts to keep supply convoys afloat — is a superbly-directed, well put-together piece of dramatised documentary. With a script out of Nicholas Monserrat by Eric Ambler (Oscar-nominated) and a stoic cast of Britain's best stiff upper lip stable, how could the U-boats ever gain the upper hand?

The unsentimental grimness of Monserrat's semi-autobiographical novel is largely preserved and, considering its time, the viewpoint is relatively classless.
With *Jack Hawkins, Donald Sinden, Stanley Baker, Denholm Elliott, Virginia McKenna, Moira Lister, Alec McCowen*

CROSS OF IRON
Stomach-churning realism from Peckinpah on the Eastern Front. EMI-Rapid Film/Terra Filmkunst

THE CRUSADES
★ *Cecil B. de Mille — U.S., 1935*
★ Working his way around the Med (see **Cleopatra**, 1935), de Mille alights a millennium or so later on the shores of the Levant. Not that his sense of period is strong enough to detect too much of a difference. The film is absolutely typical de Mille — at least he is consistently full of hokum. There is no attempt to tell it as it was if it gets in the way of the sweep and spectacle of a good story.

Wilcoxson graduates from Mark Antony to kingship in the form of Richard the Lionheart to lead the Holy War against **Saladin**'s infidels in the last decade of the 12th century. The rest is colourful pap on a grand scale, albeit beautifully photographed by Oscar nominee Victor Milner — who just failed to win twice running.
With *Henry Wilcoxson, Loretta Young, C. Aubrey Smith, Ian Keith, Alan Hale*

Other pictures considering the Crusades include:
The Golden Horde See separate entry
Richard the Lion-Hearted ★★ (Chet Webey — U.S., 1923) With *Wallace Beery*
King Richard and the Crusaders ★★★ (David Butler — U.S., 1954) [115min] With *Rex Harrison, Virginia Mayo, George Sanders*
The Saracen Blade ★ (William Castle — U.S., 1954) [75min] With *Ricardo Montalban*

Saladin ★★★ (Youssef Chahine — Egypt, 1963) With *Ahmed Mazhar*
As polarized a view as any western (Christian) version — except it's the opposite pole.
Lionheart ★★ (Franklin J. Schaffner — U.S., 1987) [105min] With *Eric Stoltz, Gabriel Byrne*
Use's King Richard's Crusade for an irrelevant subplot.
Also, most movies involving **Robin Hood** and **Ivanhoe** — see **The Adventures of Robin Hood**.

CRY HAVOC
Richard Thorpe — U.S., 1943 [95min]   ★
Unusual in that it has all-female cast as nurses who do what   ★
they can at the fall of **Bataan**, it is too wordy to be exciting.
With *Margaret Sullavan, Ann Sothern, Joan Blondell, Fay Bainter, Marsha Hunt, Ella Raines*

CRY OF BATTLE
Irving Lerner — U.S., 1963 [100min]   ★
Standard war drama set in post-Pearl Harbor Philippines with ★
Heflin as an objectionable old sweat, MacArthur as the wimp, Moreno the obligatory head-turner.
With *Van Heflin, Rita Moreno, James MacArthur*

THE CRYING GAME
Neil Jordan — GB, 1992 [110min]   ★
Political thriller that works on several levels. Jordan's very bold   ★
polemic hits out at both the British authorities and the IRA in   ★
what is basically a story of love and friendship against a back- ★
cloth of hate, race and homophobia. Rea is superb as the
guilty, confused IRA volunteer, disillusioned with the wanton

CUSTER OF THE WEST
Robert Shaw (as Custer) getting some retaliation in first before the Little Bighorn. Cinerama/Security

killing on both sides, who falls for the lover of a kidnapped black British soldier killed while escaping from his custody.

Acting all round is excellent, with Oscar nominations for Rea and Davidson, the picture, Jordan's direction and editor Kant Pan. Jordan himself walked away with the award for the terrific script.

With *Stephen Rea, Jaye Davidson, Forest Whitaker, Miranda Richardson, Adrian Dunbar, Jim Broadbent*

CUBA
Richard Lester — U.S., 1979 [120min]

Lester is usually colourful — if sometimes off-beam, as he is here. This attempt to portray Castro's revolution via a romantic comedy meant the location and event could have been anywhere and anything.

The director's brand of '60s satire (**How I Won the War**) is *passé* in 1979, and Connery (as a British mercenary training Batista's rag-bag forces) had been in something of a shallow career slump since **The Man who Would be King** — and didn't really find his feet again until *The Name of the Rose* in 1986.

With *Sean Connery, Brooke Adams, Jack Weston, Hector Elizondo, Denholm Elliott, Martin Balsam, Chris Sarandon*

CUBA SI!
Chris Marker — France, 1961

Revealing documentary about the Castro revolution, which today is still powerful in content; and in technique it can still educate.

CUSTER OF THE WEST
Robert Shaw (as Custer) getting some retaliation in first before the Little Bighorn. Cinerama/Security

CUBAN REBEL GIRLS
Barry Mahon — U.S., 1959 [70min]

Interesting only that it was filmed while the communist revolution was taking place and received the backing of Castro — and it was Flynn's last film. What a terrible way to go.

With *Errol Flynn, Beverly Aadland*

CUP FINAL (aka 'G'mar Giviya')
Eran Riklis — Israel, 1991 [110min]

Retreating from a sortie into Lebanon in 1982, an Israeli soldier is captured by Palestinians. He finds that hate turns gradually to respect through their mutual love of soccer. Simplistic parable, but makes — through taut direction and fine acting — a moving and thought-provoking film.

With *Moshe Igvi, Muhammad Bacri, Salim Dau*

CUSTER OF THE WEST
See **They Died with Their Boots On**

D

D III 88
Herbert Maisch — Germany, 1939

This German aerial flagwaver about the need for discipline was overshadowed by its sequel **Battle Squadron Lutzow** ★★★ (aka 'Bomber Squadron [or Wing] Lutzow') — Hans Bertram, 1940 — which was punctuated by actual Luftwaffe footage of the Battle of Poland in August 1939. Both pictures shared the same stars.

With *Christian Kayssler, Heinz Welzel, Hermann Braun*

DAD'S ARMY
Norman Cohen — GB, 1971 [95min]

Croft and Perry's famous BBC TV comedy series translates quite well to the big screen, although for the aficionado of the TV version much of the mystery camouflaged by the restrictions imposed by that medium is maddeningly lifted, making subsequent TV viewing not quite the same again, although still enjoyable.

The film is included here for its faithful replication of life in a quiet southern England seaside town during WW2, half-expecting a German invasion any minute (as well as a some-what jaundiced view of the Home Guard), which few films have managed — or bothered — to achieve (c/f **Millions Like Us, Mrs Miniver**).

With *Arthur Lowe, John Le Mesurier, Clive Dunn, John Laurie, James Beck, Arnold Ridley, Ian Lavender, Bill Pertwee*

THE DAM BUSTERS
Bombs away — but aah, that theme tune! Associated British

DALEKA CESTA See **Distant Journey**

THE DAM BUSTERS
Michael Anderson — GB, 1954 [125min]

Tribute to Barnes Wallis' bouncing bombs; and Guy Gibson and the Lancaster crews who dropped them on the Möhne and Eder Dams in May 1943. A big box-office favourite in Britain, with schoolboys everywhere whistling Eric Coates' theme as they winged across school playgrounds, it is now quite dated, sentimental and a little chauvinistic.

Technically very good for its time, however, and the raid itself is unbearably tense. In 1954 the RAF still had a few real Lancasters to lend to filmmakers; the spectacle could never be repeated today.

With *Richard Todd, Michael Redgrave, Derek Farr, Patrick Barr, Raymond Huntley, George Baker*

THE DAMNED (1947) See **Les Maudits**

THE DAMNED
(aka 'La Caduta degli Dei', 'Götterdämmerung')
Luchino Visconti — Italy/West Germany, 1969 [85min]

Visconti develops the decadence of the late *Risorgimento*, hinted at in **The Leopard**, into downright rottenness in 1933 Germany. Weimar's gone, the Nazis are about to infight (the SS will shortly annihilate the SA Brownshirts), and Bogarde and Rampling oversee some serious pseudo-pornographic imagery — which eventually manifested itself even more disgustingly when they come together again in the so-called Nazi-guilt post-war picture, **The Night Porter** ★ (Liliana Cavani, 1973 — 120min). A film which definitely grabs you — however perversely — with lots of colour everywhere. A bit like a psychedelic yawn, really. Nominated for its script (Visconti and two others).

With *Dirk Bogarde, Ingrid Thulin, Helmut Berger, Umberto Orsini, Renauld Verley, Charlotte Rampling*

DANCES WITH WOLVES
Kevin Costner — U.S., 1990 [180min]

Costner discarded the Indian label and introduced the Native American to cinema audiences through this rambling, some-times incoherent, often didactic — but definitely 'landmark' — Western, which trawled seven Oscars (including Best Picture and Director) from 12 nominations. It also made Costner a full Sioux in the process, a testimony to the history-book style of the piece. He plays a Union officer wounded in the Civil War, sent out West where he becomes neighbourly to Sioux braves and an old wolf, and lives as a (19?)90s-style environmentalist and general good sort. It is the Whites, including the U.S. Cavalry, that are demonized here — with the indigenous people accorded a dignity close to deference, and Pawnee raiders carefully segregated from the attractive Sioux to take sole responsibility for any unavoidable Native American savagery. The Western *has* come a long way since **Broken Arrow**.

That this film is different, there is no doubt, but despite the reasonable handling of the action and battle scenes it is far too long (especially the four-hour director's cut) and lacking in the pace and drama required to make it a great Western. Other Academy Awards included Michael Blake's script (?), the cinematography of Dean Semler, John Barry's score, and finally, the editing.

With *Kevin Costner, Mary McDonnell, Graham Greene*

DANGER WITHIN (aka 'Breakout')
Don Chaffey — GB, 1958 [100min]
Partly written by an 'inmate' of the **Wooden Horse** and **The Colditz Story**, Bryan Forbes, this is an above-average WW2 POW drama, with British officers attempting to identify a traitor in the ranks who is forewarning the guards' of escape attempts. At this time Britain could turn out, at the drop of a hat, at least five equally-strong leads whose upper lips could be counted upon not to quiver.
With *Richard Todd, Michael Wilding, Richard Attenborough, Bernard Lee, Dennis Price, Donald Houston*

DANGEROUS BEAUTY See **The Honest Courtesan**

DANGEROUS MOONLIGHT (aka 'Suicide Squadron')
Brian Desmond Hurst — GB, 1941 [100min]
Always to be remembered for Addinsell's *Warsaw Concerto*, this 'Pole flying for the RAF in the Battle of Britain who can play the piano a bit' romance would otherwise not pass muster.
With *Anton Walbrook, Sally Gray*

DANGEROUSLY THEY LIVE
Robert Florey — U.S., 1941 [75min]
Routine WW2 spy drama involving Nazis dastardly fitting up a young British girl.
With *John Garfield, Raymond Massey, Nancy Coleman*

DANIEL BOONE
David Howard — U.S., 1936 [75min]
For such a legend in America's emerging West, Boone has not been very well served by Hollywood. In this, and in another stab in **Daniel Boone, Trail Blazer** ★ (Albert C. Gannaway and Ismael Rodriguez, 1956 [75min], starring Bruce Bennett, Lon Chaney Jnr), he is given the low-budget, 'B' movie treatment. Both pictures centre on his leading settlers through Indian country and the Cumberland Gap into Kentucky in 1775, and the building of a stockade which is defended against the local hostiles throughout the ensuing Revolutionary War. Boone, incidentally, fought with the British against the French at Fort Duquesne in 1755.

There was a 1950 bomb, directed by Reginald Leborg and starring David Bruce, called **Young Daniel Boone** [70min], alluding to earlier involvement in the French and Indian Wars, but Hollywood, it would seem, was generally keener on his real-life descendants, Pat and Richard.
With *George O'Brien, Heather Angel, John Carradine*

DANIEL BOONE, TRAIL BLAZER See **Daniel Boone**

DANIEL TAKES A TRAIN (aka 'Szerencses Daniel')
Pal Sandor — Hungary, 1983 [90min]
Hungarian liberalism was flourishing sufficiently for this morality tale of the 1956 uprising to be told with limited censorship. Two teenagers — one a deserter from a group of rebel soldiers — taking one of the last trains allowed to leave for Vienna, wrestle with their consciences. Should they fight for their country or choose liberty?
With *Peter Rudolf, Sandor Zsoter*

DANNY BOY See **Angel**

DANTON (1930) See **Danton** (1982)

DANTON (1932) See **Danton** (1982)

DANTON
Andrzej Wajda — France/Poland, 1982
Wajda's first non-Polish picture may still perhaps allegorically allude to his country at that time. Instead of the communist government of General Jaruzelski v Solidarity's Lech Walesa, read the National Assembly's Robespierre v the People's Danton. Superficially, however, the tale of Danton's infighting during the early years of France's First Republic (1792-94) is told in a straightforward, rather un-Wajda-like way, and confines itself to the jaw-jaw of the Revolution.

Earlier versions (in German by Hans Berendt in 1930 ★★; in French by André Roubaud [100min] ★★ two years later) at least devote some footage to the street scenes.
With *Gérard Depardieu, Wojciech Pszoniak, Anne Alvaro*

DARBY'S RANGERS
William Wellman — U.S., 1957 [120min]
Col William Darby was in 1942 assigned the job of training an American precursor of a Special Forces unit based on the British commando system. The title 'Rangers' was lifted from the *ad hoc* forces of militia raised in various U.S. conflicts since the time of the French and Indian Wars, such as Rogers' Rangers (see **Northwest Passage**, **Fort Ti**). Darby's men go on to see action in the desert and the Sicilian invasion. Average fare, but based on fact.
With *James Garner, Etchika Choureau, Jack Warden, Edward Byrnes, Stuart Whitman*

THE DARK ANGEL (1925) See **The Dark Angel** (1935)

THE DARK ANGEL
Sidney Franklin — U.S., 1935 [105min]
Remake of the George Fitzmaurice silent smash (1925 [85min] ★★★ with Ronald Colman and Vilma Banky) which is just a well-made WW1 sniffler concerning love and honour in war. Oberon received an Oscar nomination reprising the Banky role, and the award for art direction went to Richard Day.
With *Frederic March, Merle Oberon, Herbert Marshall*

THE DARK AVENGER (aka 'The Warriors')
Henry Levin — GB, 1955 [85min]
British attempt by Middle Ages fan Levin (**Genghis Khan**) to put a crumbling Flynn back into the saddle for the last time. This time the ageing swashbuckler takes on the role of Edward the Black Prince, defending his recently awarded principality of Aquitaine towards the end of his life against the French in the Hundred Years' War.

Whether by design or by the producer's opportunism, Flynn was then 46 — the age Edward died — thereby lending a modicum of authenticity to this reasonably jolly medieval romp.
With *Errol Flynn, Peter Finch, Joanne Dru, Yvonne Furneaux, Michael Hordern*

A year before, Rudolph Maté had Tony Curtis and Janet Leigh (the two big heart-throb stars of the period) starring in **The Black Shield of Falworth** [100min], depicting fairly well life and strife in late medieval England, despite Curtis' much-quoted 'castle of my fadda' speech.

THE DARK COMMAND See **Quantrill's Raiders**

DARK JOURNEY
Victor Saville — GB, 1937 [80min]
Unusual star pairing, unusual location (Stockholm), unusual release date. Romantic melodrama masquerading as a WW1 espionage adventure. Guess which one's the German.
With *Vivien Leigh, Conrad Veidt*

DARK OF THE SUN see The Mercenaries

DARLING LILI
Blake Edwards — U.S., 1969 [135min]
Included for some passable WW1 flying sequences — the rest is a mish-mash of romantic comedy and a musical vehicle for the director's recent wife.
With *Julie Andrews, Rock Hudson, Jeremy Kemp*

THE DAUGHTER OF MATA HARI
See Mata Hari's Daughter

DAUGHTERS OF CHINA (aka 'Zhonghua Nuer')
Ti Chang/Ling Tsu-Feng — China, 1949
The new communist regime wasted no time cinematically lambasting the Japanese with whom they were at war between 1937 and 1945. This story is of the heroism of eight young Chinese girls who gave their lives for their country.
With *Zhang Zheng, Yu Yang*

DAVID
Peter Lilienthal — West Germany, 1979
Harrowing tale of WW2 Berlin, and the survival throughout the war of a young Jewish boy.
With *Maro Fischel*

DAVY CROCKETT
Norman Foster, U.S., 1955 [95min]
Originally made for TV by Foster (the man credited with directing the Welles classic, **Journey into Fear**), Disney chopped up the episodes and set it in front of cinema audiences, who lapped it up. Coonskin hat manufacture went into orbit. Parker plays the hero in mostly fictionalised tales (although not so far from the mark as in some of the **Alamo**-related pictures) set in the early decades of the 19th century. Indian fighter, raconteur, Congressman, freedom fighter — the Tennesseean was everyone's favourite hero for some time. The same studio brought out less-popular sequels — *Davy Crockett, King of the Wild Frontier* and *Davy Crockett and the River Pirates* — again with Parker (who also played **Daniel Boone** on TV in the 60s). The Crockett-hype was preceded, in 1950, by Lew Landers' and serial king Ford Beebe's down-market (**Davy Crockett,**) **Indian Scout** [70min], starring George Montgomery — getting it's slicker title when reissued to cash in on the Disney bonanza.
With *Fess Parker, Buddy Ebsen*

DAVY CROCKETT, INDIAN SCOUT
(aka 'The Indian Scout') See **Davy Crockett**

DAWN (1930) See Nurse Edith Cavell

DAWN (1933) See Morgenrot

THE DAWN PATROL (1930)
See **The Dawn Patrol** (1938)

THE DAWN PATROL
Time for a swift one between sorties in the 1930 version. WB

THE DAWN PATROL
Edmund Goulding — U.S., 1938 [105min]
It's surprising the difference eight years makes. Goulding's remake of Howard Hawks' early talkie semi-classic is also a commendable upgrade — particularly in the reworking of John Monk Saunders' original Oscar-winning storyline, but also in the acting.
The 1930 version [90min] **** starring Richard Barthelmess and Douglas Fairbanks Jr of the RFC over Flanders in WW1 did, however, provide much of the footage of the aerial action for Goulding's exciting picture. Both pictures stand out as fine examples of early aerial war dramas, on a par with **Wings** and **Hell's Angels**.
With *Errol Flynn, Basil Rathbone, David Niven, Donald Crisp, Barry Fitzgerald*

THE DAWNING
Robert Knights — GB, 1988 [95min]
Splendid acting from young and old (this was Howard's last picture) make this drama in Ireland's south during the emergence of the IRA in the 1920s eminently watchable. Knights also gets a nice period feel to the piece.
With *Rebecca Pidgeon, Anthony Hopkins, Jean Simmons, Trevor Howard, Hugh Grant, Adrian Dunbar*

THE DAY ENGLAND FELL
Shigeo Tanaka — Japan, 1942
Wartime Japanese propaganda tract depicting the odious British colonialism in Hong Kong before it was 'liberated' in 1941.

A DAY IN OCTOBER
Kenneth Madsen — Denmark/U.S., 1990 [90min]
Intelligent drama of a Danish Jewess who harbours a wounded resistance fighter during the German occupation in WW2. Well-acted piece, based on a true story.
With *D. B. Sweeney, Kelly Wolf, Daniel Benzali*

D-DAY: 6TH OF JUNE
Don't let this invasion action fool you. 20CF

THE DAY THAT SHOOK THE WORLD
See **Assassination at Sarajevo**

THE DAY WILL DAWN (aka 'The Avengers')
Harold French — GB, 1942 [100min]
British piece of WW2 propaganda about Norwegian partisans taking on a U-boat base with the commandos coming to the rescue in the nick of time.
With *Ralph Richardson, Deborah Kerr, Roland Culver, Bernard Miles*

DAYS OF GLORY
Jacques Tourneur — U.S., 1944 [85min]
A first screen appearance for Peck lights up this OK tribute to our Soviet cousins in their bid to hurl back the Hun in WW2. Better fare than Milestone's ingratiating **The North Star**.
With *Tamara Toumanova, Gregory Peck*

DAYS OF HOPE See (L')Espoir

D-DAY THE SIXTH OF JUNE
Henry Koster — U.S., 1956 [105min]
What a waste of a good title. The mostly newsreel action sequences take a back seat to Taylor's and Todd's romantic recollections of Wynter.
With *Robert Taylor, Richard Todd, Dana Wynter, Edmond O'Brien*

DE L'ENFER A LA VICTOIRE See **From Hell to Victory**

DEAD PRESIDENTS
Allen and Albert Hughes — U.S., 1995 [120min]
Violent and unpleasant vet thriller with the premise of a black soldier returning home and entering a life of crime after his

hell in Vietnam. Nihilistic hard work, saved only by effective, if harrowing, war scenes and a clever heist plot.
With *Larenz Tate, Keith David, Chris Tucker*

DEAR AMERICA: LETTERS HOME FROM VIETNAM
Bill Coutourie — U.S., 1987
Amateur actors blend with newsreel footage, and actors who have 'been there' cinematically (de Niro, Robin Williams, Martin Sheen and others) narrate the correspondence. Very effective.

DEATH IS CALLED ENGELCHIN
(aka 'Smrt Sirika Engelchen')
Jan Kadar/Elmar Klos — Czechoslovakia, 1963
Story of nationalist unrest during the last months of the Nazi occupation of Czechoslovakia and before the reinstatement of the eastward-looking Benes as head of the fragile federation in April 1945.
With *Jan Kacer, Eva Ploakova, Otto Lackovic*

DEATH IS MY TRADE
(aka 'Aus Einem Deutschen Leben')
Theodor Kotulla — West Germany, 1977 [145min]
Unsatisfactory and unsavoury attempt to purge the national guilt by way of an idealist WW1 soldier, Franz Lang, progressing to concentration camp commandant in WW2 by always, and only, obeying orders.
With *Götz George, Kai Taschner, Elisabeth Schwartz*

DEATH OF A SOLDIER
Phillipe Mora — Australia, 1985 [95min]
Courtroom drama based on a true story. U.S. soldiers are billeted in Melbourne in 1942 waiting to be shipped out to Guadalcanal after the Battles of the Coral Sea and Midway had stopped Japanese momentum. U.S.-Aussie rapport is not too good and when a GI kills three local women the ensuing trial is a sensitive affair. Good plot which deserved better execution (duly carried out on Brown).
With *James Coburn, Reb Brown, Bill Hunter, Terence Donvan*

DECEMBER 7TH
John Ford — U.S., 1942
This powerful Ford documentary for the War and Navy Departments was as propagandist as any Axis production of the time. A mixture of newsreel and re-enaction, it tells the tale of Pearl Harbor reasonably comprehensively but is constantly punctuated by claims of Japanese treachery. It won Ford Best Documentary Oscar for the second year running (see **Battle of Midway**).

DECISION BEFORE DAWN
Anatole Litvak — U.S., 1951 [120min]
WW2 espionage tale — one of the first post-war films to

explore the psyche of the anti-Nazi German, eg the dilemma: morality, or patriotism at all cost?

Not particularly gripping as a spy story (of captured flyer, Werner, dropping back into the Fatherland to collect information for the Allies), even if it did collect Best Picture and Editing nominations at the Oscars.
With *Oskar Werner, Richard Baseheart, Gary Merrill, Hildegarde Neff*

DECOY See **Mystery Submarine** (1962)

THE DEEP SIX
Rudolph Maté — U.S., 1958 [110min]
Pretty awful story of USN gunnery officer in the Pacific in WW2 trying to reconcile killing with his Quaker ideals.
With *Alan Ladd, William Bendix, Keenan Wynn*

THE DEER HUNTER
Michael Cimino — U.S., 1978 [180min]
A cornerstone of the Vietnam war movies cenotaph — probably along with **Apocalypse Now**, **Full Metal Jacket** and **Born on the Fourth of July**, this — like the others — is a memorable, yet deeply flawed picture. No Vietnam picture has yet come through on all sides, and this one fails to address the involvement of the U.S. — and stereotypes the Viet Cong as latter-day Japanese prison camp sadists. (Paradoxically, the Russian roulette scene where the guards bet on the outcome is one of the most suspenseful in any movie depicting the horrors of war.)

Winner of the New York Critics Award before collecting the Best Picture Oscar; Walken won a Best Supporting Actor statuette against nominations for de Niro and Streep. The precocious Cimino picked up the Direction Oscar in only his second film at the helm (*Thunderbolt and Lightfoot* the other, four years earlier) before setting out on the disastrous trail to *Heaven's Gate*. His *magnum opus* (to date) therefore remains this often stunningly-shot epic of male bonding in peace and war — from Pennsylvania to Vietnam and back.
With *Robert de Niro, John Cazale, Meryl Streep, Christopher Walken, John Savage*

THE DEMI-PARADISE (aka 'Adventure for Two')
Anthony Asquith — GB, 1943 [115min]
Rather silly propaganda peace in which a Russian engineer is sent to Britain to develop a new propeller. Turns into a light satire of no particular relevance.
With *Laurence Olivier, Penelope Dudley Ward, Marjorie Fielding, Margaret Rutherford, Leslie Henson*

LES DEMONS DE L'AUBE
See **The Demons of the Dawn**

THE DEMONS OF THE DAWN
(aka 'Les Démons de l'Aube')
Yves Allegret — France, 1945 [100min]
Interesting little film which develops the relationship of a French commando officer and a member of the Resistance after D-Day.
With *Simone Signoret, Georges Marschal, André Valmy*

DEPUTAT BALTIKI See **Baltic Deputy**

LE DERNIER METRO See **The Last Metro**

DESERT ATTACK See **Ice Cold in Alex**

THE DESERT FOX (aka 'Rommel, Desert Fox')
Henry Hathaway — U.S., 1951 [90min]
Standard early '50s fare lifted from oblivion by the remarkable Mason, who reprised his role of Rommel in **The Desert Rats**. Opens with a (ground-breaking pre-credits) sequence where commandos attempt to assassinate Rommel, before dealing routinely with North Africa, Normandy, the 20th of July plot and Rommel's eventual forced suicide.
With *James Mason, Jessica Tandy, Cedric Hardwicke, Luther Adler*

DESERT HELL See **Beau Geste** (1939)

DESERT LEGION See **Beau Geste** (1939)

DESERT PATROL See **Sea of Sand**

THE DESERT RATS
Robert Wise — U.S., 1953 [90min]
Focusing on the siege of **Tobruk** in 1942, Wise cashes in on the box-office success of the **Desert Fox**. In many ways this is a better picture, however, with Richard Murphy nominated by the Academy for his script.
With *Richard Burton, James Mason, Robert Newton, Chips Rafferty*

DESERT SANDS See **Beau Geste** (1939)

DESERT VICTORY
Roy Boulting — GB, 1943
Variety hailed Boulting's documentary masterpiece as 'the greatest battle film of the war'. The thrilling chase across the North African desert of WW2, with Montgomery's 8th Army pursuing the Afrika Korps from **El Alamein** to Tripoli, is evocatively shot — especially the night scenes — accompanied by William Alwyn's superb score.

The effect on morale in Britain, celebrating its first real victory after three years of war, cannot be overstated. The Americans were so impressed they hired Boulting to work with none other than Frank Capra for the less-imaginative **Tunisian Victory** ★★★ the following year.

THE DESERTER
Burt Kennedy — U.S., 1971 [100min]
Savage Western, using the U.S. Cavalry v Apache conflicts after the U.S. Civil War as background. The film disappoints and is not very good despite (after the weak lead) a sterling cast of reliable 'Westerners'.
With *Bekim Fehmiu, Richard Crenna, Chuck Connors, John Huston, Ricardo Montalban, Brandon de Wilde, Slim Pickens, Ian Bannen, Woody Strode*

THE DESERTER AND THE NOMADS
(aka 'Zbehovia a Poutnici')
Juro Jakubisco — Czechoslovakia/Italy, 1968 [100min]
Curious anti-war trilogy which is definitely not mainstream, particularly in the second (WW2) and third (WW3) stories.

Easily the best tale of the lot — and the one told most accessibly — is the deserter's tale from WW1, which opens the picture.
With *Stefan Ladizinsky, August Kubán, Gejza Ferenc*

DESIREE

★ *Henry Koster — U.S., 1954* [90min]
Gaining an Oscar nomination for art direction sums up this costume drama, supposedly about the romance between the eponymous heroine and Napoleon. Brando's lack of interest renders his performance risible. Lots of talk about Bonaparte's conquests, on and off the battlefield, but little action anywhere.
With *Marlon Brando, Jean Simmons, Merle Oberon, Michael Rennie*

THE DESPERADOS
See **Quantrill's Raiders**

DESPERATE JOURNEY

★
★ *Raoul Walsh — U.S., 1942* [110min]
★ 'Now for Australia and a crack at those Japs!' Flynn's famous last words as he reincarnates **Captain Blood** and **Robin Hood** in WW2 Germany as a shot-down bomber pilot creating havoc behind the lines. As a flagwaver it's a swashbuckling action-adventure *par excellence.*
With *Errol Flynn, Ronald Reagan, Raymond Massey, Alan Hale, Nancy Coleman, Arthur Kennedy, Sig Rumann*

DESTINATION GOBI

★ *Robert Wise — U.S., 1953* [90min]
★ Why is it that the true stories are often the most far-fetched? If someone invented a plot about Mongols fighting the Japanese in WW2 supported by the U.S. Navy in the middle of the Gobi Desert, who would believe it? Well, the Navy apparently was there in the role of a meteorological team which was overtaken by events. The reliable Widmark helps the yarn along.
With *Richard Widmark, Don Taylor, Casey Adams*

DESTINATION TOKYO

★ *Delmer Daves — U.S., 1943* [135min]
★ Grant plays the role of a submarine commander somewhat differently to the later **Operation Petticoat**, which was made for laughs. Here he keeps the body and soul of his crew together as they penetrate Japanese waters on a spying mission prior to the first bombings of Japan in WW2. Quite tense, especially in the minefield scenes, but at over two hours under water, the audience begins to get the bends.
With *Cary Grant, John Garfield, Alan Hale, Dane Clark*

DESTROYER
William A. Seiter — U.S., 1943 [100min]
Soupy actioner involving Robinson as WW1 salt having to prove himself all over again in WW2.
With *Edward G. Robinson, Glenn Ford, Marguerite Chapman*

DEUTSCHLAND IM HERBST
See **Germany, Pale Mother**

THE DESERT RATS
Savage defence of the British position. 20CF

DEVIL IN THE FLESH See **Le Diable au Corps**

THE DEVIL WITH HITLER
See **Hitler — Dead or Alive**

THE DEVIL'S BRIGADE
Andrew V. McLaglen — U.S., 1968 [130min]   ★
If it wasn't based on historical fact, this could have been just ★ a cheap rip-off of the **Dirty Dozen**, right down to the appearance of Jaeckel. Robertson's crack Canadian commandos have to work with Holden's dog-pack and together they implausibly crack German defences around Monte Cassino in 1943. One cringes to think what both Canadian and U.S. veterans of the real General Fredrick's remarkable 1st Special Service Force must have made of this.
With *William Holden, Cliff Robertson, Vince Edwards, Claude Akins, Richard Jaeckel, Carroll O'Connor*

THE DEVIL'S DISCIPLE
Guy Hamilton — GB, 1959 [80min]   ★
Shaw's sparkling play uninterestingly transferred to the ★ screen. Set in the American War of Independence, the moral is that even the reprobates of society can have a sense of honour (in this case Dick Dudgeon, who lays down his life for a rebel cleric). Olivier plays General Burgoyne.
With *Burt Lancaster, Kirk Douglas, Laurence Olivier, Janette Scott, Harry Andrews*

DEVIL'S DOORWAY
Anthony Mann — U.S., 1950 [85min]   ★
Broken Arrow is regarded as *the* first pro-Indian film of ★ modern cinema, but if this elegy had a bit more puff Mann's effort might well be remembered. Taylor is the hard-

done-by Shoshone despised on all sides — blue, grey and red — after his Civil War heroics.
With *Robert Taylor, Louis Calhern, Paula Raymond*

THE DEVIL'S GENERAL (aka 'Des Teufels General')
Helmut Kautner — West Germany, 1955 [120min]
Anti-Hitler piece with Jurgens as the Luftwaffe hero (based on the life of Ernst Udet) so disillusioned with the Nazi high command that he arranges for the escape of Jews before eventually taking his own life.
With *Curt Jurgens, Victor de Kowa*

THE DEVIL'S OWN
Alan J. Pakula — U.S., 1997 [110min]
Hollywood's understanding of foreign conflicts is often at kindergarten level — and never more so than when dealing with Ireland. Pakula just rescues this as a picture by taking Pitt, as an aggrieved nationalist sympathiser (with an accent from hell,) out of Ulster and allows him to fester in a New York environment, from where he attempts to ship arms to the IRA. Had he stayed in Ireland the picture would have run out of clichés and stereotypes before an hour was up. In any case, it is the work of a filmmaker in decline (*Klute, The Parallax View, All the President's Men*, **Sophie's Choice**, etc) and Ford's performance is really its only beacon of light.
With *Harrison Ford, Brad Pitt, Margaret Colin, Treat Williams*

LE DIABLE AU CORPS (aka 'Devil in the Flesh')
Claude Autant-Lara — France, 1947 [110min]
Famous French WW1 weepie with hidden meanings every-where. Panned by the critics — loved by the punters.
With *Micheline Presle, Gérard Philipe, Jacques Tati*

LE DIABLE DE SIBERIE See **Rasputine** (1938)

THE DEVILS BRIGADE
Roberston and Holden lead their rival 'teams'. UA

LE DIALOGUE DES CARMELITES
Phillipe Agostini/R.L. Bruckberger — France/Italy, 1959 [115min]
Earnest novel by Gertrude von le Fort makes for pretentious cinema. Carmelite nuns head for the guillotine at the Place de la Révolution in 1792. Poulenc had the right idea when he took Bruckberger's and Agostini's scenario and Georges Bernanos' script and created a fine opera, which premiered fully two years before this straight film version was released.
With *Jeanne Moreau, Alida Valli, Pascal Audret, Madeleine Renaud*

DIAMONDS OF THE NIGHT (aka 'Demanty Noce')
Jan Nemec — Czechoslovakia, 1964
Notable film about two escapees from a concentration camp train in WW2 and their struggle for survival in enemy country, before being recaptured by armed German citizenry.
With *Ladislav Jansky, Antonin Kumbera*

THE DIARY OF ANNE FRANK
George Stevens — U.S., 1959 [170min]
Much revered at the time, Stevens' filming of the recovered diary of a young Jewish girl in hiding in WW2 Amsterdam is still moving today. Anne Frank and her family's attempt to hide from the Nazis ends at Auschwitz, and Stevens was nominated for his ability to retain much of the diary's poignancy.

The picture itself was nominated, as was Wynn for Best Supporting Actor, and Alfred Newman's score: and the movie did win four Oscars. Statuettes were awarded to William Mellor's photography (although Jack Cardiff was also involved), for art direction — and to Winters (Best Supporting Actress) for her memorable performance as Mrs van Daan.
With *Millie Perkins, Josef Schildkraut, Shelley Winters, Richard Beymer, Ed Wynn*

DIAS CONTADOS See **Running Out of Time**

DID I BETRAY? See **Black Roses**

DIEN BIEN PHU
Pierre Schoendoerffer — France, 1992
Schoendoerffer was actually wounded and captured at the defining battle against the Viet Minh in 1954, which led to the Geneva Accords and the resultant French exodus from Indochina (Vietnam). His atmosphere and authenticity are what you might expect, therefore, but a lack of budget denies the scope required to emulate the scale of the battle.

Schoendoerffer's earlier **317e Section**, if anything, is a better film, but as one of only a few battle pictures from the French-Indochina War this one should not be overlooked.
With *Patrick Catalifo, Jean-François Balmer, Donald Pleasence, Ludmila Mikel*

THE DIFFICULT YEARS
(aka 'Anni Difficili') See **Living in Peace**

DIMANTY NOCE See **Diamonds of the Night**

DIPLOMATIC IMMUNITY
Sturla Gunnarsson — Canada, 1991 [95min]
Canadian diplomat in civil war-torn El Salvador experiences the hypocrisy as well as the brutality of war. A thinking

THE DIRTY DOZEN
Well, 14 actually, including Marvin and Jaeckel. A favourite with many film enthuasiasts. MGM

person's picture with the politics playing as big a part as the action.
With *Wendel Meldrum, Michael Hogan, Michael Riley, Ofelia Medina*

THE DIRECTION OF THE MAIN BLOW
See **Liberation**

THE DIRTY DOZEN
Robert Aldrich — GB/U.S., 1967 [150min]
Despite plenty of adverse criticism surrounding the glorification of killing, the degradation of women and the abuse of the criminal justice system — for starters! — this was definitely a return to form for Aldrich (**Apache, Attack!**, etc) and defined the style of the Hollywood WW2 war picture for a decade or so to come.

As well as spawning many imitators (**The Devil's Brigade, Dirty Heroes, A Reason to Live, a Reason to Die**, etc) there were three much inferior TV movie spin offs: *The Next Mission, The Deadly Mission* and *The Fatal Mission* — all with the wonderful Borgnine as General Worden. The tale of how a bunch of death-rowers are reprieved for a special mission to decimate the German officer corps prior to D-Day is well-known — but the arguments about the morality of the motives are more powerful.

However morally wrong it might be to consider the *Dozen* in the same way as the *Seven Samurai* or their alter egos, *The Magnificent Seven*, that is how cinema audiences down the years have pigeon-holed it. Regardless of its tawdry under-tones, it is essentially a tale of adventure, humour and heroism against overwhelming odds — a roller-coaster comic strip yarn for grown-ups. It's tie-breaking failing, however, is in the

assumption that it's acceptable to use bad people to do really bad things in the cause of doing good.

Cassavetes was nominated for best supporting actor.
With *Lee Marvin, Ernest Borgnine, Charles Bronson, Robert Ryan, Donald Sutherland, Jim Brown, John Cassavetes, Richard Jaeckel, Telly Savalas, George Kennedy, Clint Walker, Trini Lopez, Ralph Meeker*

DIRTY HEROES
Alberto DeMartino — Italy, 1969 [105min]
Poor copy of the **Dirty Dozen**. This time a group of convicted criminals become commandos in Nazi-held Holland in WW2.
With *Frederick Stafford, Daniella Bianchi, Curt Jurgens, John Ireland, Adolpho Celi*

DISHONORED
Josef von Sternberg — U.S., 1931 [90min]
Dietrich went right to the top with this after softening up Hollywood with *The Blue Angel* and **Morocco** the previous year — playing the WW1 German secret agent X-27. Pretty drab affair otherwise.
With *Marlene Dietrich, Victor MacLaglen, Lew Cody*

THE DISHONORED MEDAL
Christy Cabanne — U.S., 1914
Early silent which is interesting on two counts: director-to-be Walsh (**They Died with Their Boots On**, *High Sierra*, **Objective Burma**, *White Heat*, etc) in an acting role, aged 27; and the scene — the Algerian holy war against the French colonists (presumably at the time of Abd Al-Qadir in the 1840s) — one of only a few pictures on the subject (Chester Franklin and Frances Marion's **Song of Love** ** with Joseph Schildkraut and Norma Talmadge, developed the theme in 1924).
With *George Gebhart, Miriam Cooper, Raoul Walsh*

THE DISMISSAL
(aka 'Die Entlassung') See **Bismark**

DISTANT DRUMS
Raoul Walsh — U.S., 1951 [100min]
This time the opponents for the U.S. cavalry are the Seminole Indians of the Florida Everglades — an unusual setting for otherwise standard fare with the added attraction of Coop. (See also **Seminole**.)
With *Gary Cooper, Mari Aldon, Richard Webb*

DISTANT JOURNEY (aka 'Daleka Cesta')
Alfred Radok — Czechoslovakia, 1949
Harrowing picture about daily life in a Nazi concentration camp during WW2.
With *Blanka Waleska, Otomar Krejca*

A DISTANT TRUMPET
Raoul Walsh — U.S., 1964 [115min]
It's the Chiricahua Apaches who cop it from the U.S. Army on this occasion. Unlike Walsh's **Distant Drums**, though, there was no Gary Cooper to bale out this no-better-than-standard fare.
With *Troy Donahue, Suzanne Pleshette*

DIVE BOMBER
Michael Curtiz — U.S., 1941 [135min]
Not strictly a war picture, but the combination of Curtiz and Flynn testing the medical stresses on bomber crews just before Pearl Harbor speaks volumes for the U.S.' mental state of preparedness for warfare.
With *Errol Flynn, Fred MacMurray, Ralph Bellamy*

DIVIDE AND CONQUER See Why We Fight

THE DIVINE LADY See That Hamilton Woman

DR PETOIT
Christian de Chalonge — France, 1990 [100min]
Really a murder flick with the added spice of German-occupied Paris in WW2 as a backdrop, and under the guise of escaping Jews. Could have been made by Hammer.
With *Michel Serrault, Pierre Romans*

DR STRANGELOVE: or, How I Learned to Stop Worrying and Love the Bomb
Stanley Kubrick — GB, 1963 [95min]
Message movie of the highest order, which hit the spot at the height of Cold War shadow boxing, but remains a major cult movie today. It takes the nuclear holocaust as a searing black comedy (c/f the contemporaneous **Fail Safe**) and is made up of a montage of memorable images (Sellers — in one of the

DOCTOR ZHIVAGO
Demonstrators about to charged by tsarist cavalry. MGM

three roles he plays — as the paraplegic, self-strangulating ex-Nazi scientist; Wynn's manic attack on a Coca Cola machine; Pickens, astride the determining nuke, rodeo-fashion — to name just a few).
Kubrick undoubtedly went completely over the top, but it is hard to imagine a film of its time spelling out the menace and absurdity of global self-destruction more eloquently. (A case may also be put for that classic of the absurd, the Milligan and Antrobus play, **The Bed Sitting Room ★★★★** [90min], a WW3 satire dealing with post-holocaust relationships, directed by the surrealist swami of the swinging '60s, Dick Lester, and featuring hilarious performances from Ralph Richardson and Michael Hordern).
Oscar nominations for picture, Kubrick's script (with Terry Southern and Peter George — from the latter's novel, *Red Alert*), Kubrick's direction, and Sellers: it won the best film BAFTA.
With *Peter Sellers, George C. Scott, Sterling Hayden, Keenan Wynn, Peter Bull, Slim Pickens, James Earl Jones*

DOCTOR ZHIVAGO
David Lean — U.S., 1965 [190min]
Boris Pasternak's epic romantic novel of Russia in WW1 and through the Bolshevik Revolution is appallingly bowdlerised by Robert Bolt, who with true Hollywood logic picked up the script Oscar (he was only nominated for the much more lucid **Lawrence of Arabia** — but the balance was returned in 1966 with his superb *A Man for All Seasons*). After **Lawrence** and **The Bridge on the River Kwai**, this was also a disappointing outing for Lean (who went downhill further with the turgid **Ryan's Daughter**), despite several high quality, trademark, exterior sequences.
At well over three hours — definitely a steppe too far. The acting is also patchy, with Sharif lightweight and Guinness uncharacteristically low-key. Courtenay, a little better, was nominated for Best Supporting Actor: the picture, its editing and sound, and Lean's direction were also nominated. Academy Awards, apart from Bolt, went to Freddie Young's sumptuous cinematography and Maurice Jarre's sickly score, and for art direction and costume design. Pretty to watch, then; pretty awful to listen to.
With *Omar Sharif, Julie Christie, Geraldine Chaplin, Alec Guinness, Rod Steiger, Tom Courtenay, Ralph Richardson, Rita Tushingham*

THE DOGS OF WAR See The Mercenaries

DOLLAR MAMBO
Paul Leduc — Mexico, 1993 [80min]
Cabaret sketches, not for the squeamish, portraying events before and during the U.S. invasion of Panama and the extrication of Manuel Noriega in December 1989-January 1990.
With *Dolores Pedro, Roberto Sosa, Raul Medina*

DON'T CRY, IT'S ONLY THUNDER
Peter Werner — U.S., 1982 [110min]
Over-sentimental melodrama of U.S. medic in Vietnam getting too attached to young orphan girl, with a predictable outcome.
With *Dennis Christopher, Susan Saint James, Lisa Lu*

DON'T LOOK NOW . . . WE'RE BEING SHOT AT
(aka 'La Grande Vadrouille')
Gerard Oury — France, 1966 [130min]

Curious collaboration of French farce and Blake Edwards-style '60s romp, and a suitably inane English title. Funny only in patches; T-T frenetically leads a few RAF johnnies shot down over Paris in WW2 to freedom.
With *Terry-Thomas, Bourvil*

DON'T PANIC, CHAPS!
George Pollock — GB, 1959 [85min]
A fascinating idea of British and German troops finding themselves watching each other in some Adriatic WW2 backwater, and agreeing to sit out the war in peace. Played more for laughs (not many) than message, this concept was more astutely realised in Boorman's **Hell in the Pacific**.
With *Dennis Price, George Cole, Thorley Waters, Harry Fowler*

THE DOOMED BATTALION
Cyril Gardner — Germany/U.S., 1932 [75min]
Unusual location in WW1 — the Austrian-Italian front in the Alps. Hollywood bought Trenker's original German script and got him to reprise his role in English. Remade and relocated to the Russo-Finnish War as **Ski Patrol ★** (Lew Landers, 1940, featuring Philip Dorn), the earlier version contains genuinely exciting action scenes of battles in the snow.
With *Luis Trenker, Tala Birell, Victor Varconti, Albert Conti*

THE DORA CREW See **Garrison Dora**

EL DORADO
Carlos Saura — France/Spain, 1988 [125min]
Not to be confused with Howard Hawks' film (a remake of his earlier *Rio Bravo*), Saura's version of the quest for Latin American gold by Pizarro's men is more a social commentary on contemporary Spain than the visual mauling we get from Hertzog's **Aguirre, Wrath of God**. Antonutti more understated as Aguirre than the demonic Kinski, but very good, all the same.
With *Omero Antonutti, Eusebio Poncela, Lambert Wilson*

DOUBLE CRIME IN THE MAGINOT LINE
(aka 'Double Crime sur la Ligne Maginot', 'Treachery Within')
Felix Gandera — France, 1939 [85min]
Interesting only for its location and date, this spy story (and the fortification) was totally *passé* by the middle of 1940.
With *Victor Francen, Jacques Baumer*

DOUBLE CRIME SUR LA LIGNE MAGINOT
See **Double Crime on the Maginot Line**

THE DOUBLE-HEADED EAGLE
Lutz Becker/Philippe Mora — West Germany, 1973
The first part of an anthropological study by German students, covering the rise of Hitler from 1918 to 1933, is interesting for its unusual footage, including the Hitler 'face in the crowd' scene from a rally in 1919. The second part, with Mora this time supported by Becker, entitled **Swastika ★★★** deals with the period from 1933 and uses much of Eva Braun's 'home-movie' footage. Both are disturbing in their portrayal of the Nazi leadership as schizophrenic monsters/ordinary guys.

DRAGON SEED
Harold Bucquet/Jack Conway — U.S., 1944 [145min]
Anti-Japanese propaganda set in 1937 China, just after the invasion. Reasonably done by a better-than-average cast, but finally outstays its welcome. MacMahon was nominated as Best Supporting Actress, and Sidney Wagner for his camerawork.
With *Katharine Hepburn, Walter Huston, Lain MacMahon, Turhan Bey, Agnes Moorhead, J. Carroll Naish*

DRAGONFLY SQUADRON
Lesley Selander — U.S., 1954 [80min]
Another Selander cheap exploitation piece — this time South Korean pilots receive U.S. training in time to combat the inevitable attack from the north.
With *John Hodiak, Barbara Britton, Bruce Bennett*

DRAKE OF ENGLAND
(aka 'Drake the Pirate', 'Elizabeth of England')
Arthur Woods — GB, 1935 [105min]
An attempt to cash in on the success of Tudor films such as *The Private Life of Henry VIII*, but this was no Korda production, and the tale of Drake's rebuffing of the Spanish Armada comes across as a static history lesson.
With *Matheson Lang, Athene Seyler, Donald Wolfit, Jane Baxter*

DRAKE THE PIRATE See **Drake of England**

THE DRESSMAKER
Jim O'Brien — GB, 1988 [90min]
The thinking person's **Yanks**? Beautifully atmospheric and authentically recreating wartime Liverpool, O'Brien's first film is impressive, if somewhat claustrophobic, in its story of GIs and homely Scouse lasses. The characterisations and terrific ensemble acting stand out.
With *Joan Plowright, Billie Whitelaw, Jane Horrocks, Tim Ransom, Pete Postlethwaite*

THE DRUM (aka 'Drums')
Zoltan Korda — GB, 1938 [95min]
North-West Frontier action during the British Raj. Jolly fun for most of the time with only loose historical references.
With *Roger Livesey, Sabu, Raymond Massey, Valerie Hobson*

DRUM BEAT
Delmer Daves — U.S., 1954 [110min]
Peace between the Cavalry and the Modoc Indians of California and Oregon breaks down in 1869. Chief Bronson leads his braves against the whites.
With *Alan Ladd, Audrey Dalton, Marisa Pavan, Robert Keith, Charles Bronson*

DRUMS See **The Drum**

DRUMS ALONG THE MOHAWK
John Ford — U.S., 1939 [105min]
Typically Fordian in its expansive outdoor feel, this story of settlers in 18th century (in what is now) upstate New York alludes to, but does not get directly involved in, the ongoing War of Independence. Instead it is more akin to stories set 20 years before in the French and Indian (Seven Years) War, with all the action taking place between the white and the Native American factions.

Laced with the humour and humanity that would stamp Ford's pictures thereafter, it threw up an Oscar nomination for character actress Oliver in a supporting role.
With *Henry Fonda, Claudette Colbert, Edna May Oliver, John Carradine, Ward Bond*

Stealing some of Ford's footage, the feud between the white settlers and the Mohawk Iroquois natives is continued in the mediocre **Mohawk ★★** directed in 1956 by Kurt Neumann (80min) featuring Scott Brady and Rita Gam.

DRUMS IN THE DEEP SOUTH
William Cameron Menzies — U.S., 1951 [85min]
Routine actioner from the War of Secession based around a small band of Confederates attempting to impede Sherman's march on Atlanta in 1864. It is hard to believe that Menzies, who also took the credit of production designer here, received a special Oscar for the same role in **Gone With the Wind**.
With *James Craig, Barbara Payton, Guy Madison*

DRUMS OF THE DESERT See **Beau Geste** (1939)

DUCK SOUP
Leo McCarey — U.S., 1933
Marx Brothers in a book on war movies? **A Night in Casablanca ★★★** (Archie Mayo, 1946 — 85min) was primarily a vehicle for Groucho, Chico and Harpo, with defeated Nazis, espionage and black marketeering as background themes; but *Duck Soup* holds its own with any satire on war. It may not be as black as more modern attempts to ridicule war for what it is, but just with the line 'There must be a war — I've paid a month's rent on the battlefield' (Groucho), the arrow has found its mark. The film savagely attacks militarism, fascism (it was banned in Italy and Germany) and political

DRUMS ALONG THE MOHAWK
Redskins complicating the American Revolution. 20CF

posturing in the course of pillorying war itself — but always in a mercilessly funny way. The last, and probably the best film of their early period, which included *Animal Crackers* and *Horse Feathers*, before they signed with MGM.
With *Groucho, Chico, Harpo* and *Zeppo Marx, Margaret Dumont, Louis Calhern, Edgar Kennedy, Raquel Torres*

DUEL AT DIABLO
Ralph Nelson — U.S., 1965 [105min]
In an attempt to add new spices to the Western mix, two European actors (Travers and Andersson) are drafted in; Poitier adds a third colouring to the pot; and army scout Garner's Comanche wife has been killed by the Apaches. Otherwise, much as before (Cavalry is ambushed by Apaches, etc), but of good quality all round.
With *James Garner, Sidney Poitier, Bibi Andersson, Dennis Weaver, Bill Travers*

THE DUELLISTS
Ridley Scott — GB, 1977 [100min]
Enigmatic tale of two officers in Napoleon's army fitfully duelling over a period of a decade and a half. Looks very good, but whereas Keitel treads water, Carradine is sunk by the talent around him. Why do they duel? Ask Scott (*Alien, Blade Runner, Thelma and Louise*), for whom this was not an auspicious debut movie. The accurate subtleties of costume are a treat for Napoleonic buffs, however, for whom this has become a cult movie; and the duels themselves are often excitingly handled.
With *Keith Carradine, Harvey Keitel, Albert Finney, Edward Fox, Robert Stevens, Tom Conti, Cristina Raines*

DUNKIRK
Leslie Norman — GB, 1958 [135min]
One of the last of the '50s-style of stoic, black-and-white British war films (**The Cruel Sea, The Dam Busters, Ice Cold in Alex, Reach for the Sky**, etc), solidly directed by Barry's dad, Leslie. It tells a fairly faithful tale of the evacuation of the French beaches in May/June 1940 from the British point of view, and the documentary-style tormenting of the dune-huddled masses by screeching Stukas is effectively done. The armada of little ships which came to the rescue of the doomed British Expeditionary Force (Operation Dynamo) was also covered in **Mrs Miniver**.
With *John Mills, Richard Attenborough, Bernard Lee, Robert Urquhart*

The uninspired **Weekend in Dunkirk ★★** by Henri Verneuil in 1965 [120min], with Jean-Paul Belmondo and Catherine Spaak, told the tale from the

point of view of a group of French soldiers on the beaches. To British eyes its main delight may be the hilarious contrast between two British officer characters played, in one case, by the French-speaking English gentleman Ronald Howard (son of Leslie), and in the other by a small, dark French actor lurking behind a truly memorable moustache.

DUPED TILL DOOMSDAY
(aka 'Betrogen bis zum Jungsten Tag')
Kurt Jung-Alsen — East Germany, 1957
A rare East German WW2 picture which is rather anti-Nazi and not just pro-communist, telling of duplicity within the ranks.
With *Wolfgang Kieling, Rudolph Ulrich, Hans-Joachim Martens*

DURING ONE NIGHT
Sidney J. Furie — GB, 1961 [80min]
Sorry tale of an American flyer going AWOL in WW2 Britain, from the director who knocked out the sub-Hammer *Doctor Blood's Coffin* and the Cliff Richard showcase *The Young Ones* in the course of the same year. Hard to believe that this is the same man who would go on to direct *The Ipcress File*.
With *Don Borisenko, Susan Hampshire*

DVADTSAT DNEI BEZ VOINI
See **Twenty Days without War**

THE EAGLE AND THE HAWK
Stuart Walker — U.S., 1933 [70min]
Heavy melodrama in the skies over Flanders in WW1. Following in the wake of **Wings** and **The Dawn Patrol**, the twist here is Grant's rigging of March's suicide to make it look like a glorious war death. Lifted by good words well played.
With *Frederic March, Cary Grant, Carole Lombard*

THE EAGLE AND THE HAWK
Lewis R. Foster — U.S., 1949 [85min]
Paramount reused the title for a completely different story. This time it's about gun-running to **Juarez**'s rebels in Maximilian's Mexico of the 1860s — but not such good cinema as its namesake.
With *John Payne, Dennis O'Keefe, Rhonda Fleming*

THE EAGLE HAS LANDED
John Sturges — GB, 1976 [135min]
Sturges' last film was something of a return to form, invoking memories of his considerable heyday as an action director (*Gunfight at the OK Corrall, The Magnificent Seven*, **The Great Escape**). The plot from Jack Higgins' novel is totally ludicrous (the team which miraculously rescued Mussolini get the short straw after some misdemeanours, and are ordered to kill or kidnap Churchill). It, is nevertheless, in the right hands, as at home on the big screen as in any *Boys' Own* comic. Sturges keeps the twists of geographical location (Eastern Front, Berlin, Ireland, Alderney, Norfolk) in cohesive check without making the thing episodic, while the acting is fine (especially Pleasence as a shrewish Himmler, and the excellent Duvall as the *Abwehr* officer).

It is the director's panache in the action sequences that comes shining through, however. For real buffs there is plenty of convincing German, U.S. and British kit, worn and handled as if the actors were accustomed to it. (Industry insiders also cherish the edit which has a famous British stuntman machine-gunning himself as both a German and an American in the same sequence.)
With *Michael Caine, Donald Sutherland, Robert Duvall, Jenny Agutter, Donald Pleasence, Anthony Quayle, Jean Marsh, Larry Hagman*

EAGLE IN A CAGE
Fielder Cook — GB, 1970 [105min]
Wordy insight into Napoleon's incarceration on St Helena after Waterloo. Good for those who like their history lessons preached — and, as you would expect, the cast is fine.
With *John Geilgud, Ralph Richardson, Kenneth Haigh, Billie Whitelaw*

EAGLE SQUADRON
Arthur Lubin — U.S., 1942 [100min]
Hollywood recognized Britain's plight in the dark years of WW2 in several ways. The **Mrs Miniver**-type picture hit home to U.S. audiences what was really happening (albeit with

more than a pinch of schmaltz); others, like this, spoke of direct action by Americans, individually or in groups, in fighting alongside Britain against the Nazi aggressor. This picture acknowledges the part played by U.S. flyers in the RAF before Pearl Harbor. In reality three Eagle Squadrons were formed, and were absorbed into the USAAF in 1942 — Spitfires and all. Not really much of a film, though.
With *Robert Stack, Diana Barrymore, John Loder, Eddie Albert, Nigel Bruce, Leif Erikson*

EAST OF SUDAN
Nathan Juran — GB, 1964 [95min]
Derivative and outmoded adventure story based in Gordon's Sudan of the 1880s (footage was used from the 1939 classic **The Four Feathers**). Puerile pap bordering on plagiarism.
With *Anthony Quayle, Sylvia Sims, Jenny Agutter, Derek Fowlds*

EAST OF THE RISING SUN See **Malaya**

EDGE OF DARKNESS
Lewis Milestone — U.S., 1943 [125min]
In 1943, Milestone was determined to tell American audiences how the rest of the world was doing against Hitler. With classics like **All Quiet on the Western Front**, **The General Died at Dawn** and *Of Mice and Men* behind him, he used his esteemed position to portray Russians in **The North Star**, and Norwegians (creating their own underground) in this picture, as the heroes we all know they were — but also as backward, unsophisticated rustics. This condescension is not cynical, for the projects are conceptually laudable, but the ignorant arrogance of Hollywood (the 'why research the detail when audiences will accept the stereotypes they understand' syndrome) put paid to the credibility of both ventures.
With *Errol Flynn, Ann Sheridan, Walter Huston, Nancy Coleman*

EAGLE HAS LANDED
American Rangers try to evict Michael Caine's German paras from the village church. ITC/Associated General

DIE EHE DER MARIA BRAUN
See **The Marriage of Maria Braun**

EIGHT IRON MEN
Edward Dmytryk — U.S., 1952 [80min]
Routine (Dmytryk's middle name?) war-jaw of fruity GIs pinned down in a bombed-out building somewhere in WW2 Italy.
With *Bonar Colleano, Arthur Franz, Lee Marvin, Richard Kiley*

1812
Vassili Goncharov/Kai Hansen/Alexander Vralsky — Russia, 1912
An early Russian film to mark the anniversary of Napoleon's Pyrrhic victory at Borodino, the razing of Moscow by the withdrawing Russians, and the horrific French retreat through the snow. Cinematically, only of historical interest.

1871
Kenneth MacMillan — GB, 1989 [100min]
History leading up to the formation of the Paris Commune in 1871, told in an ambitiously Brechtian style as a series of theatrical sketches. Beginning with the overthrow of Maximilian by **Juarez** in Mexico, it traces events through the Franco-Prussian War to the defeat of Napoleon III at Sedan, the setting up of the Third Republic and the end of the Communards. Interesting, if pompous. Documentarist Becker (**The Double-Headed Eagle**) has a small role.
With *Roshan Seth, John Lynch, Timothy Spall, Ian McNeice, Med Hondo, Lutz Becker*

1860 (aka 'Mille Ottocento Sessanta')
Alexander Blasetti — Italy, 1934 [80min]
During the prologue to WW2 the future antagonists produced many nationalistic tracts, eulogizing their countries' histories, heroes and battles of the past. One of the very best was from Rossellini's mentor Blasetti about the glorious climax to the *Risorgimento* in 1860. Italian nationhood is in sight at last, having spent the best part of the 19th century uniting her medieval city states (many of whom were vassals of the Hapsburg Empire) and Napoleonic-French kingdoms — following the Treaty of Paris and the various European upheavals of 1848. Told through the lives of a Sicilian peasant and his wife. Garibaldi is portrayed as a model for Mussolini.
With *Aida Bellia, Giuseppe Gullino*

84 CHARLIE MOPIC
Patrick Duncan — U.S., 1988 [95min]
Commendable attempt to show the horrors of the Vietnam War through the eyes of an army cameraman, for once getting under the skin of the small units that patrolled the pernicious jungle. The budget may have been small — but not the idea.
With *Richard Brooks, Christopher Burgard, Jonathan Emerson, Jason Tomlins, Nicholas Cascone*

ELENI
Peter Yates — U.S., 1985 [115min]
Important in being one of only a few films to concentrate on the run-up to the Cold War. Based on semi-fact, the picture brings out early atrocities in the Greek Civil War which began between the communists and others when the British liberated the country in December 1944. As a film, it is rather plodding.
With *Kate Nelligan, John Malkovich, Linda Hunt, Ronald Pickup, Rosalie Crutchley*

ELENYA

Steve Gough — GB, 1992 [80min]

International production of a slow-moving, somewhat dated tale, told in flashback, of a young Welsh girl of Italian 'Bracchi'-shop background, hitting back at the xenophobic jibes of the locals by caring for a German flyer shot down over Wales in WW2. It does possess an inner strength and sensitivity, however.

With *Margaret John, Klaus Berendt, Pascal Defogue Jones, Seirol Tomos*

ELIZABETH OF ENGLAND See Drake of England

THE ELUSIVE CORPORAL

(aka 'Le Caporal Epinglé', 'The Vanishing Corporal')

Jean Renoir — France, 1962 [105min]

Despite its trademark humanity and idiosyncrasies, this is not the Renoir of **La Grande Illusion** or **La Règle du Jeu**. Played as a light comedy, it tells the tale of three French soldiers escaping from a German POW camp in WW2, and finding their way back to Paris.

With *Jean-Pierre Cassel, Claude Brasseur, Claude Rich, O.E. Hasse*

THE ELUSIVE PIMPERNEL
See **The Scarlet Pimpernel**

EMITAI See Camp de Thiaroye

THE EMPEROR'S NAKED ARMY MARCHES ON

(aka '*Yuki Yukite Shingun*')

Kazuo Hara — Japan, 1987

Bizarre documentary with WW2 vet Kenzo Okuzaki verbally assaulting his wartime contemporaries. He is attempting to ascertain the truth behind a government-suppressed rumour of murder and cannibalism among Japanese soldiers in New Guinea in 1945. The undertow washes out the Japanese dilemma of guilt for the way the Empire conducted the war.

EMPIRE OF THE SUN

Steven Spielberg — U.S., 1987 [150min]

This is Spielberg's visible stepping stone from Peter Pan director to the consummate handler of some of the most poignant, yet strident, war pictures ever made (**Schindler's List**, **Saving Private Ryan**). An audaciously rule-breaking film in its casting and lack of plot, J.G. Ballard's autobiographically-influenced story of the poor little rich Brit boy (wonderfully interpreted by Bale) growing up in a world of street-wise Yank POWs in WW2 China is still a Spielberg visual treat. It introduces a cynicism unseen before in his movies, however, as well as a sense of sophistication — definite signs of growing up. Winner of six (mainly technical) Oscars, but including Allen Daviau's cinematography and John Williams' score.

With *Christian Bale, John Malkovich, Miranda Richardson, Nigel Havers*

THE END OF ST PETERSBURG

(aka 'Konyets Sankt-Peterburga')

Vsevolod Pudovkin — USSR, 1927

A masterpiece of Russian cinema made to celebrate the tenth anniversary of the Bolshevik Revolution — and, as such, is *just* a little biased towards the proletariat. Starting in 1914, the build-up to the events of 1917 is seen through the eyes of a peasant youth, who eventually becomes involved. Amateur actors add to the realism and the imagery is visually striking.

With *Ivan Chuvalov, Vera Baranovskaya*

THE ENEMY

Fred Niblo — U.S., 1928

Two years before **All Quiet on the Western Front**, this silent WW1 melodrama pictures the war through the eyes of an Austrian couple — he goes off to war, she ends up in a bordello — following a trend of sympathetic movies begun by Griffith's **Isn't Life Wonderful?**

With *Lillian Gish, Ralph Forbes*

ENEMY AGENT (1940) See British Intelligence

ENEMY AGENT

Lew Landers — U.S., 1940 [65min]

Not to be confused with the British title of **British Intelligence** from the same year, this is quite a perky (making a change for Landers) espionage second feature involving aircraft secrets.

With *Richard Cromwell, Philip Dorn*

THE ENEMY BELOW

Dick Powell — U.S., 1957 [100min]

After the mauling **The Conqueror** received, Powell could be forgiven for not ever returning to the helm again. This is much better, to his credit, although it does turn out eventually as a South Atlantic battle of manners between destroyer captain Mitchum, and Prussian man of honour Jurgens, skippering the U-boat. Quite restrained.

With *Robert Mitchum, Curt Jurgens, Al (David) Hedison, Theodore Bikel*

THE ENEMY GENERAL

George Sherman — U.S., 1960 [75min]

Spies and counterspies in WW2 involving the **OSS** and a senior Nazi officer renowned for atrocities, picked up by the Americans who have run him as a double agent. Chewy plot which could have done with a firmer hand.

With *Van Johnson, Jean-Pierre Aumont, Dany Carrel, J. van Dreelen*

ENGLAND MADE ME

Peter Duffell — GB, 1972 [100min]

Excellent period piece based, not too pedantically, on another of Graham Greene's tales of an Englishman abroad. York is in Isherwood's Germany at the break-up (literally) of the Weimar Republic by Hitler's thugs. A sort of **Cabaret** without the songs, the mood is just right.

With *Peter Finch, Michael York, Hildegard Neil, Michael Hordern, Joss Ackland*

THE ENGLISH PATIENT

Anthony Minghella — U.S., 1996 [160min]

In this 1996 multi-Oscar winner (nine in all) Minghella has interwoven the threads, both in his adapted script (nominated) and through his direction (won), of Michael Ondaatje's Booker Prize-winning novel, with sublime skill. The balance of mystery and suspense, relating to goings on before WW2 and the romance between the disfigured 'British officer' and his nurse during the Allied race north through Italy, is just about right. One always feels it falls into the category of a 'woman's picture', nevertheless; and for those who care, the chronology of WW2 is ludicrously altered to serve the demands of the love

affair. Apart from picture and director, other major Oscars went to Binoche as Best Actress and for the evocative camera skills of John Seale, while statuettes were also awarded for editing, production design, music, sound and costume design. Fiennes and Scott-Thomas were also nominated.
With *Ralph Fiennes, Juliette Binoche, Willem Dafoe, Kristin Scott-Thomas, Naveen Andrews, Colin Firth, Julian Wadham, Jürgen Prochnow*

ENSIGN PULVER See **Mister Roberts**

ENTEBBE: OPERATION THUNDERBOLT
See **Operation Thunderbolt**

DIE ENTLASSUNG See **The Dismissal**

L'EQUIPAGE (1927) *See* **The Woman I Love**

L'EQUIPAGE (1934) *See* **The Woman I Love**

L'EQUIPAGE (1980) *See* **The Woman I Love**

ERA NOTTE A ROMA (aka 'Night in Rome')
Roberto Rossellini — France/Italy, 1960 [120min]
Rossellini's piece may be more sophisticated than the realism which characterised his end of WW2 masterworks, **Open City** and **Paisà**, but fails to deliver the same power. Almost a straightforward thriller; the tribulations of the British, Russian and U.S. POW escapees thrown together display enough trademark humanism to betray the filmmaker.
With *Leo Genn, Giovanna Ralli, Sergei Bondarchuck, Hannes Messemer, Peter Baldwin*

ERIK THE CONQUEROR See **The Vikings**

EROICA (aka 'Heroism')
Andrzej Munk — Poland, 1957 [85min]
Munk was the realist to Wajda's romanticist in the early post-war period of Polish filmmaking. The two stories which make up this picture poke fun at the Polish underground, then satirise Polish POWs in a savage black farce.
With *Barbara Polomska, Edward Dziewonski, Leon Niemczyk*

ES GESCHAH AM 20 JULI See **Jackboot Mutiny**

ESCAPE
Mervyn Le Roy — U.S., 1940 [105min]
Hollywood anti-Nazi tract, with Taylor rescuing his imprisoned mother (the inappropriately-named Nazimova) from Germany before WW2. Standard fare.
With *Robert Taylor, Norma Shearer, Conrad Veidt, Alla Nazimova*

ESCAPE FROM FORT BRAVO
John Sturges — U.S., 1953 [100min]
Early Sturges with lots of bang-bang and a plot which sees the Civil War antagonists set aside their differences temporarily to fight off a bunch of Mescalero Apaches. Goodish Western — with a message for an America on another kind of red alert?
With *William Holden, Eleanor Parker, John Forsythe*

ESCAPE IN THE DESERT
Edward A. Blatt — U.S., 1945 [80min]
Awful update of the *Petrified Forest* with Dorn (in the original Bogart role) as a Dutch flyer, somehow coming across a bunch of Nazi POW escapees in the heart of an American desert. Serendipity?
With *Philip Dorn, Helmut Dantine, Alan Hale, Jean Sullivan*

ESCAPE OF THE AMETHYST See **Yangste Incident**

ESCAPE TO ATHENA
George P. Cosmatos — GB, 1979 [115min]
Peppered with Second Division actors, or those about to be relegated, this Alistair MacLean-type yarn set in a German POW camp in WW2 Greece is 20 years out of date, and not even worthy of the genre.
With *Roger Moore, David Niven, Telly Savalas, Claudia Cardinale, Stefanie Powers, Richard Roundtree, Elliott Gould, Sonny Bono, Anthony Valentine*

ESCAPE TO GLORY (aka 'Submarine Zone')
John Brahm — U.S., 1940 [75min]
The one that didn't get away. A passenger ship high-tailing it out of Europe in September 1939 is in mid-Atlantic when war breaks out. The supposedly neutral Americans then square up to a U-boat.
With *Pat O'Brien, Constance Bennett*

ESCAPE TO VICTORY See **Victory**

ESCUADRILLA (aka 'Squadron')
Antonio Román — Spain, 1941
Rare (Nationalist) Spanish film about the air battles of the Spanish Civil War. The aerial sequences are quite good, but the plot is as puerile and as propagandist as any produced anywhere else at the time. C/f **(L')Espoir**.
With *Alfredo Mayo, Luchy Soto, José Nieto.*

ESPIONAGE AGENT
Lloyd Bacon — U.S., 1939 [85min]
Sub-**Foreign Correspondent** guff, warning of U.S. isolationism. McCrea at least got into the swing of things for Hitch's cracker the following year.
With *Joel McCrea, Brenda Marshall, Jeffrey Lynn, George Bancroft*

(L')ESPOIR (aka 'Days of Hope', 'Man's Hope')
André Malraux — France, 1939 [75min]
Perhaps more documentary than drama (original combatants took on the acting roles), this anti-fascist film of the Spanish Civil War was more amazing for the making than its effect. It took another 18 months to complete after the original filming was halted when Franco's forces attacked Barcelona. The battle scenes are the more powerful for the rudimentary approach.
With *Andres Majuto, José Sempre, Nicholas Rodriguez*

ETAT DE SIEGE See **State of Siege**

UN ETE INOUBLIABLE
See **An Unforgettable Summer**

THE ETERNAL SEA
John H. Auer — U.S., 1955 [95min]
Biopic of Admiral John M. Hoskins, following his career through adversity in WW2 (when he lost a leg) to triumph in Korea (where his USS *Princeton* becomes one the first carrier

bases for the devastating U.S. jets). Pretty humourless.
With *Sterling Hayden, Alexis Smith, Dean Jagger*

EUROPA, EUROPA
Agnieska Holland — France/Germany, 1991 [110min]
Mephisto-style true story of a young German Jew surviving in the Nazi era by taking amazing risks, such as becoming a member of the Hitler Youth. Unusual story, unusually made.
With *Marco Hofschneider, Julie Delpy, Hans Zischler*

THE EVE OF ST MARK See **Corregidor**

EVERY BASTARD A KING
Uri Zohar — Israel, 1970 [95min]
Poor love story, interesting only for its Six Day War (1967) backdrop.
With *Pier Angeli, William Berger*

EVERY TIME WE SAY GOODBYE
Moshe Mizrahi — U.S., 1986 [95min]
Just about as bad as it gets. Hanks (with an RAF officer's accent that might be described as distinctive) falls for a Sephardic (strictly non-mingling) Jewess in 1942 Jerusalem. Grating.
With *Tom Hanks, Cristina Marsillach*

EXCALIBUR See **Knights of the Round Table**

THE EXILE
Max Ophuls — U.S., 1947 [90min]
Writing the role for himself, Fairbanks plays it (surprisingly) for chat rather than action in a fairly loose rendering of Charles II's flight in 1651 after the Battle of Worcester, and his sojourn in Holland.
With *Douglas Fairbanks Jr, Paule Croset (Paula Corday), Maria Montez, Henry Daniell, Nigel Bruce, Robert Coote*

EXODUS
Otto Preminger — U.S., 1960 [220min]
Leon Uris' epic novel is given the Dalton Trumbo treatment, but even this most articulate of scriptwriters (**A Guy Named Joe**, *Roman Holiday*, **Spartacus**) cannot stop Preminger's juggernaut running for almost four hours.

The (one-sided) story of the birth of Israel focuses on the anti-British feelings fanned by the moral blackmail represented by a ship-load of post-Holocaust would-be immigrants, and the heroics of the small bands of Jewish guerrillas organised by the emerging Haganah. Ernest Gold won an Oscar for Best Score, while Mineo was nominated for Best Supporting Actor and Sam Leavitt for Cinematography.
With *Paul Newman, Eva Marie Saint, Ralph Richardson, Lee J. Cobb, Peter Lawford, Sal Mineo, Hugh Griffith*

EYE OF THE NEEDLE
Richard Marquand — GB, 1981 [115min]
Director Marquand went on to promise much before his untimely death in 1987 (*The Return of the Jedi, Jagged Edge*) but this adaptation of Ken Follett's WW2 espionage story was only just on par. Sutherland plays a German spy again (see **The Eagle has Landed**).
With *Donald Sutherland, Kate Nelligan, Ian Bannen, Christopher Cazenove*

EXCALIBUR
The death of Arthur. WB/Orion

A FACE IN THE RAIN
Irvin Kershner — U.S., 1963 [80min]
WW2 espionage in Italy. Calhoun parachutes behind German lines and has to hole up after things go wrong. Average.
With *Rory Calhoun, Marina Berti*

FAIL SAFE
Sidney Lumet — U.S., 1964 [110min]
Dr Strangelove without the humour would probably be too simplistic, but in its way Lumet's film about the difficulty of stopping Armageddon once control is lost is equally powerful. The developing master of sweaty situations on film (*Twelve Angry Men*, **The Hill**, *Serpico*, *Dog Day Afternoon*, etc) maintains the suspense throughout, with Hagman particularly sudorous in the end.
With *Henry Fonda, Dan O'Herlihy, Walter Matthau, Larry Hagman*

THE FALL OF A NATION
Bartley Cushing — U.S., 1916
With a plotline not too dissimilar from **The Battle Cry of Peace** (the invasion of America by Germany again), Thomas (**The Clansman**) Dixon's screenplay is, however, one of anti-pacifism, bordering on paranoia. 'Preparedness', here, is not so much for the inevitable entry of the U.S. into WW1, but for a nervous breakdown.
With *Arthur Shirley, Lorraine Huling, Flora MacDonald*

THE FALL OF BERLIN (aka 'Padeniye Berlina')
Mikhail Chiaureli — USSR, 1949 [160min]
Overlong propaganda piece, glorifying the achievements of Stalin. The battle scenes are terrific, but the whole thing doesn't really flow between dramatic and documentary stitching. The summit reconstructions are interesting, however, with not only Stalin, but Hitler, Churchill and others represented.
With *Boris Andreyev, Mikhail Gelovani, Victor Stanitsin,*

THE FALL OF THE ROMAN EMPIRE
Anthony Mann — U.S./Spain, 1964 [185min]
Erudite (thanks to Philip Yordan's and Ben Barzman's script) rather than exciting, Mann takes on the 2nd century Roman Empire of Marcus Aurelius and his heir Commodus. The few battle scenes — in the forests of the German frontier — are well-staged, and the picture's scholarly look at the decline of the Empire and the glimpse of the on-coming 3rd century chaos places it well above the average 'sword-and sandal' saga.
With *Alec Guinness, Sophia Loren, Christopher Plummer, Stephen Boyd, James Mason, Anthony Quayle, Omar Sharif, Mel Ferrer*

THE FALL OF THE ROMANOFFS
Herbert Brenon — U.S., 1917
Anti-Bolshevik treatment of the Russian Revolution, with Brenon exceedingly quick off the mark. Esther Shub's **The Fall of the Romanov Dynasty** *** (USSR, 1927), more documentary than drama, provides interesting polarity. Loses out to the sophistication of the much later **Nicholas and Alexandra**. See also **Rasputin and the Empress**.
With *Edward Connolly, Alfred Hickman*

THE FALL OF THE ROMANOV DYNASTY
See **The Fall of the Romanoffs**

THE FALLEN SPARROW
Richard Wallace — U.S., 1943 [95min]
Curio which qualifies for early *film noir* status — and a gold star for an original story-line. It's about an American veteran of the Spanish Civil War who walked off with the battle flag of a German unit fighting on the side of Franco. Nazi spies track him down to New York . . .
With *John Garfield, Maureen O'Hara, Walter Slezak*

DIE FALSCHUNG See **Circle of Deceit**

FALSTAFF See **Chimes at Midnight**

FAREWELL AGAIN (aka 'Troopship')
Tim Whelan — GB, 1937 [85min]
Like **Cavalcade** before it, Whelan wanted to tell the world that Britain and its international influence were still intact. The tale of a group of soldiers with six hours shore leave in Blighty from a transport ship, taking them from India to God-knows-where, is less important than the message. Solid cast and support (James Wong Howe's camera — he of the *Thin Man*, *The Prisoner of Zenda*, *King's Row*, etc: Richard '*Warsaw Concerto*' Addinsell's score).
With *Flora Robson, Leslie Banks, Robert Newton, Sebastian Shaw, Martita Hunt, John Laurie*

FAREWELL MY CONCUBINE (aka 'Ba Wang Bie Ji')
Chen Kaige — China/Hong Kong, 1993 [155min]
The story of China from the 1920s to 1977 through the eyes of two close friends and actors from the Peking Opera, with the personal interrelationship mirroring the turbulence of the civil wars and the attentions of the Japanese. More mainstream than some of Kaige's other works, its homosexuality and operatic backcloth still make it quite inaccessible to the out-and-out action war movie fan.

Very long, this is a roller-coaster history, some bits bad, but more good: it won a Best Foreign Film Oscar nomination and one for Gu Changwei's camerawork. It also walked off with the *Palme d'Or* at Cannes.
With *Leslie Cheung, Zhang Fengyi, Gong Li*

A FAREWELL TO ARMS
Frank Borzage — U.S., 1932 [80min]
Although remade with a bigger budget and to nearly double the length [150min], Charles Vidor's 1957 ** version of Hemingway's famous novel, with Rock Hudson and Jennifer Jones, pales in comparison to Borzage's atmospheric and sensuous original adaptation.

The story of the wounded U.S. ambulanceman falling for his English nurse in WW1 Italy, then deserting to find her, is one of the most moving of war romance pictures, with the actors on top form, and Borzage as sentimental as usual, but never better.

Received nominations for Best Picture and, surprisingly, only art direction: Charles Lang's cinematography won the only statuette.
With *Gary Cooper, Helen Hayes, Adolphe Menjou*

Variants on the same theme were Michael Curtiz's **Force of Arms** ** made in 1951 with William Holden and Nancy Olsen [100min]; Attenborough's **In Love and War**; and, of course, **The English Patient**.

A FAREWELL TO ARMS (1957)
See **A Farewell to Arms** (1932)

A FAREWELL TO THE KING
John Milius — U.S., 1988 [115min]
Based on a Pierre Schoendoerffer novel — he of **317e Section**, **The Anderson Section** and **Dien Bien Phu** directorial fame — this is a cross Conrad-Kipling piece of whimsy, borrowing cinematically from **Apocalypse Now** and **The Man Who Would be King**. Nolte has delusions of grandeur after deserting into the Borneo forests when the Japanese invade in 1942: Havers parachutes in to persuade him, now king of the local headhunters, to lead his new people in battle against the bemused Japs. Lovely thought, but Milius, who had a hand in the **Apocalypse** script (as well as writing and directing such dainties as *Conan the Barbarian* and **Red Dawn**), is typically heavy-handed with pen and camera.
With *Nick Nolte, Nigel Havers, Frank McRae, James Fox*

FATHER GOOSE
Ralph Nelson — U.S., 1964 [115min]
Unsatisfactory late comedy for Grant, who just hasn't the material this time, despite an Oscar for its writers! S.H. Barnett, Peter Stone and Frank Tarloff collected their award in a year when all the major nominated pictures relied on adapted scripts *(My Fair Lady, Mary Poppins, The Night of the Iguana, Goldfinger)*. The irrelevant tale of sot Grant as observer on some Pacific island for the Australian navy in WW2, hampered by school teacher Caron and six of her best, does not warrant two hours of tedium. The lighter moments are all too infrequent, as is the action — when it finally arrives.
With *Cary Grant, Leslie Caron, Trevor Howard*

FEAR AND DESIRE
Stanley Kubrick — U.S., 1953 [70min]
Kubrick's rough first film, which nevertheless sets out his stall about the absurdity of war in future projects (**Paths of Glory**, **Dr Strangelove**, **Barry Lyndon**, **Full Metal Jacket**). This low-budget fantasy is about no war in particular — the abstraction makes its point without political or other overtones.
With *Frank Silvera, Kenneth Harp, Paul Mazursky, Virginia Leith, Steve Coit*

FEI TIAN See **Accidental Legend**

FEUERTAUFE See *Baptism of Fire*

UNE FEMME FRANÇAISE (aka 'A French Woman')
Regis Wargnier — France/GB/Germany, 1994 [100min]
'Emmanuelle takes on the Army' could be another sub-title, in this series of sexual vignettes depicting the waywardness of a French soldier's wife over the years. Beginning at the start of WW2 when Auteuil becomes a German POW, and progressing through his postings (the Allied occupation of Berlin, the Middle East, Indochina and finally Algeria), the catalogue of Béart's affairs while her husband serves his country may be looked on as an allegory of French double values under German occupation, and/or symbolic of social strife in the post war period. It is happier, however, at base level.
With *Emmanuelle Béart, Daniel Auteuil*

THE FIFTH DAY OF PEACE
Giulliano Montaldo — Italy, 1972 [100min]
Shambolic attempt to recreate the feelings of defeated German soldiers wandering around Italy after the WW1 armistice.
With *Richard Johnson, Franco Nero*

THE 5TH OF NOVEMBER See **Hennessy**

THE FIFTH OFFENSIVE
Stipe Delic — Yugoslavia, 1973
Unremarkable pay-day for the declining Burton about Tito's partisans in WW2 Yugoslavia.
With *Richard Burton, Irene Papas*

55 DAYS AT PEKING
Nicholas Ray — Spain/U.S., 1963 [155min]
One of only a few films about the 1900 Boxer Rebellion, but easily the most famous (W.S. Van Dyke's **Foreign Devils** ** made in 1928 with Tim McCoy and Claire Windsor, is another example: Chag Che's Hong Kong picture of 1979, **Boxer Rebellion** ***, gives the Chinese viewpoint). The combination of Philip Yordan (script) and Samuel Bronston (producer) did not have the sure handling of Anthony Mann at the helm this time (as in **El Cid** and **The Fall of the Roman Empire**) and Ray's lead is somewhat plodding. The action sequences are good as Heston leads the resistance to the uprising from the U.S. Embassy. Nominated only for Dimitri Tiomkin's music.
With *Charlton Heston, David Niven, Ava Gardner, Flora Robson, John Ireland, Paul Lukas, Harry Andrews, Robert Helpmann*

THE FIGHTER
Herbert Kline — U.S., 1952 [80min]
Jack London's *The Mexican* provided the basis for this story of a prize-fighter getting involved in revolution in the Porfirio Diaz-dictated Mexico of the early years of the 20th century. Not as informative politically, nor as good a film, as the almost contemporaneous Kazan picture, **Viva Zapata!**
With *Richard Conte, Vanessa Brown, Lee J. Cobb, Frank Silvera*

FIGHTER ATTACK
Lesley Selander — U.S., 1953 [80min]
Jolly Selander, for once, as Hayden, shot down over Italy in WW2, joins the partisans in a spot of sabotage. The fighters are based on Corsica. Brisk.
With *Sterling Hayden, J. Carroll Naish, Joy Page*

FIGHTER SQUADRON
Raoul Walsh — U.S., 1948 [95min]
Typical Walsh blood and thunder with cocky USAAF pilots fighting the Germans up to and including D-Day. Look out for Rock Hudson in a small part debut.
With *Edmond O'Brien, Robert Stack, John Rodney, Henry Hull*

THE FIGHTING COASTGUARD
Joseph Kane — U.S., 1951 [85min]
A look at the U.S. Coastguard performing in the Pacific after Pearl Harbor. Quite routine.
With *Brian Donlevy, Forrest Tucker, Ella Raines, Richard Jaeckel*

THE FIGHTING GUARDSMAN
Henry Levin — U.S., 1945 [85min]
Cheap and cheerful swashbuckler with a cast-iron 'B' movie cast. Hokum with historical hooks, as a French aristo joins the great unwashed in some pre-Revolutionary uprising against Louis XVI.
With *Willard Parker, Anita Louise, George Macready*

THE FIGHTING KENTUCKIAN See **The Buccaneer**

THE FIGHTING LADY
Louis de Rochemont — U.S., 1944
Popular documentary, shot in vivid colour by Edward J. Steichen, about U.S. aircraft carrier in combat off Guam in WW2 — including attacks from Japanese planes.

THE FIGHTING O'FLYNN
Arthur Pierson — U.S., 1949 [95min]
Fairbanks vehicle based in Ireland in the 1790s, where he defeats the traitorous Greene and foils an invasion plot by Napoleon. Many a buckler is swashed.
With *Douglas Fairbanks Jr, Helena Carter, Richard Greene, Patricia Medina*

THE FIGHTING PIMPERNEL See **Pimpernel Smith**

THE FIGHTING PRINCE OF DONEGAL
Michael O'Herlihy — GB, 1966 [105min]
Throwback heroics, Disney-style, with McEnery trying to stir up clan hatred against the English in Elizabethan Ireland. Daffy Irish accents. OK for under-14s who have dropped history at school.
With *Peter McEnery, Susan Hampshire, Tom Adams, Gordon Jackson*

THE FIGHTING SEABEES
Edward Ludwig — U.S., 1944 [100min]
When Wayne's Construction Battalion (the CBs or Seabees) keep getting beaten up by the Japanese in the Pacific, he's had enough. He invests in a programme of combat training for his men, who on their return to the front give the Japs what for. With oodles of eulogies and even a Seabees song to sing, you can't fail to leave the Roxy dewy-eyed and with the Stars and Stripes fluttering. Even so, it is better than the appalling **Blood and Steel** (Bernard Kowalski, 1959 [65min], with John Lupton, James Edwards), which covers similar ground.
With *John Wayne, Susan Hayward, Dennis O'Keefe*

THE FIGHTING 69TH
William Keighley — U.S., 1940 [90min]
Archetypal Cagney character — all mouth and bravado until faced with the action — with an heroic twist at the end. With Pat O'Brien again as his spiritual oppo (as in *Angels with Dirty Faces*), the coward of the WW1 trenches sees the light and becomes a dead hero.
With *James Cagney, Pat O'Brien, George Brent, Alan Hale, Jeffrey Lynn*

THE FIGHTING SULLIVANS See **The Sullivans**

FIGURES IN A LANDSCAPE
Joseph Losey — GB, 1970 [110min]
Shaw's own adaptation of Barry England's suspenseful novel about two Brits escaping from an unidentified Far Eastern prison camp relocates them (presumably for budget and logistical reasons) to 'somewhere' in Totalitarianville, east of the Iron Curtain, Europe.
Not a lot makes sense, but the hunters and the hunted are visualised by Losey as effectively as in any 'breakout' scenario previously filmed.
With *Robert Shaw, Malcolm McDowell*

FILM D'AMORE E D'ANARCHIA
See **Love and Anarchy**

LA FIN DES ROMANOFF See **Rasputine** (1938)

THE FINAL COUNTDOWN
Don Taylor — U.S., 1980 [105min]
TV sci-fi style, fairly effective on the big screen because of the size of its subject — USS *Nimitz*. The carrier ploughs through a time portal to end up at Pearl Harbor on 6 December 1941. Unsatisfactory ending spoils a scrumptious idea.
With *Kirk Douglas, Martin Sheen, Katharine Ross, James Farentino, Ron O'Neal, Charles Durning*

THE FINEST HOUR
Shimon Dotan — U.S., 1991 [105min]
The first (exploitative) picture on the Gulf War is a rehash of wartime *ménages à trois* throughout the ages. This time, two U.S. Navy SEALS are the protagonists, predictably thrown together in a dangerous mission.
With *Rob Lowe, Gale Hensen, Tracy Griffith, Eb Lottimer*

FIRE OVER ENGLAND
William K. Howard — GB, 1936 [90min]
Spirited, though somewhat dated account of the Spanish Armada's attempt to invade England in 1588. Cardboard sets have to be allowed for, but there is much else to enjoy.
With *Flora Robson, Laurence Olivier, Leslie Banks, Vivien Leigh, Raymond Massey, James Mason*

FIRES ON THE PLAIN (aka 'Nobi')
Kon Ichikawa — Japan, 1959 [110min]
Even more passionately pacifist than his **Burmese Harp**, Ichikawa's harrowing story of Japanese soldiers involved in murder and cannibalism at Leyte Gulf in 1945 is totally uncompromising in its stance. One of the most visually-powerful anti-war films ever made.
With *Eiji Funakoshi, Osamu Takizawa, Mickey Curtis*

FIRES WERE STARTED (aka '*I Was a Fireman*')
Humphrey Jennings — GB, 1943
Famous documentary extolling the virtues of London's firemen during the Blitz. Inspiring to the population then, it now seems slightly jingoistic (in a 'no surrender' way), but it was the kind of inverted propaganda upon which backs-to-the wall Britain thrived, while being at the same time entirely baffling to the aggressor. See also ***Britain Can Take It***, **A Silent Village**.

FIRST BLOOD See **Rambo: First Blood Part Two**

FIRST COMES COURAGE
Dorothy Arzner — U.S., 1943 [90min]
Norway is the basis for another Hollywood WW2 propaganda

piece, this time with Oberon as the suspected Quisling — but of course she's not really.
With *Merle Oberon, Brian Aherne*

THE FIRST OF THE FEW (aka 'Spitfire')

Leslie Howard — GB, 1942

Howard starred in his last film about the man who designed the Spitfire (R.J. Mitchell), before, ironically, being shot down himself in 1943.

Sturdy biopic, which starts with the Schneider Trophy days of the Supermarine S-6 seaplane — the startpoint for the Spitfire — through the ups and downs of testing and increasing ill-health, to the final gratification of success in the Battle of Britain. Good performances, although the few action sequences once war starts are only average.
With *Leslie Howard, David Niven, Rosamund John, Roland Culver*

FIRST KNIGHT See **Knights of the Round Table**

THE FIRST REBEL See **Allegheny Uprising**

THE FIRST TEXAN See **The Alamo**

FIRST TO FIGHT

Christian Nyby — U.S., 1967 [95min]

Our U.S. war hero returns from bloody battle in Guadalcanal to collect his Medal of Honor. He gets married during furlough, but when he returns to Saipan he finds he hasn't got the stomach for the fight any more. After much ridicule and contempt he finds his true self again.

Psychological dramas like this were done much better when the facts were fresh in the '40s.
With *Chad Everett, Marilyn Devlin, Dean Jagger, Gene Hackman*

FIRST KNIGHT
Lancelot (Richard Gere) defends Camelot. A modern attempt to recreate the legend. Columbia/Tri-Star

THE FIRST WORLD WAR

Laurence Stallings — U.S., 1934

A timely piece of caution by playwright Stallings. Using footage from several countries, and tracing the origins of the conflict back into the 19th century, the visionary title of this documentary says it all.

FIRST YANK INTO TOKYO

Gordon Douglas — U.S., 1945 [80min]

Inadvertently, the first feature film to use the Hiroshima bomb in its plot — the storyline was changed just before the film was released to cash in on the biggest news of the century. Otherwise just a routine espionage movie with Neal 'face-lifted' (to look like an oriental) into Japan to rescue an engineer.
With *Tom Neal, Barbara Hale, Richard Loo, Marc Cramer*

5 BRANDED WOMEN

Martin Ritt — Italy/U.S., 1960 [100min]

Tough and brutal — and that's only the women — in this all-action tale of Yugoslavian partisans in WW2. Gritty plot about fraternisation with the enemy and lots of noisy action.
With *Sylvana Mangano, Vera Miles, Barbara Bel Geddes, Jeanne Moreau, Richard Basehart, Van Heflin, Harry Guardino, Steve Forrest*

FIVE FINGERS

Joseph L Mankiewicz — U.S., 1952 [110min]

Intrigue in WW2 Turkey, involving a British Embassy mole and the *Abwehr*, and based on a true story. Good of its kind, with Mason immaculate as usual. Academy award nominations went to Mankiewicz and to Michael Wilson's script.
With *James Mason, Michael Rennie, Danielle Darrieux*

FIVE GRAVES TO CAIRO

Billy Wilder — U.S., 1943 [95min]

Superior espionage drama in the Libyan desert after the fall of Tobruk. Part written by Wilder (as in every film he directed), the dialogue and plot are a cut above the norm: von Stroheim's characterisation of Rommel is so different from that of James Mason in **The Desert Fox** and **The Desert Rats** as to be memorable, if hardly convincing. Oscar nominations for John Seitz (cinematography), as well as art direction and editing.
With *Franchot Tone, Anne Baxter, Akim Tamaroff, Erich von Stroheim, Peter van Eyck*

FIVE MAN ARMY

Don Taylor — U.S., 1970 [105min]

Following in the wake of the **Wild Bunch**, this totally derivative tale of a train carrying government gold, and its robbery for the benefit of the 1913 Mexican Revolution, has absolutely nothing to commend it.
With *Peter Graves, James Daly, Bud Spencer (Carlo Pederseri)*

FIVE MEN FOR HELL

Frank Kramer — Italy, 1968 [100min]

Cheapie WW2 thriller based in 1944 Italy involving an American unit trapped by Germans. You get what you pay for.
With *Klaus Kinski, Margaret Lee, John Garko, Nick Jordan*

FIXED BAYONETS!

Samuel Fuller — U.S., 1951 [95min]

Made quickly on the heels of the **Steel Helmet**; Fuller was

determined to take the Korean War to U.S. audiences and ram it down their throats. This rough, tough picture of survival on the battlefield overrides the cheap backlot sets to mark Fuller as a unique and disturbing maker of war films.
With *Richard Basehart, Gene Evans, Michael O'Shea*

THE FLAG LIEUTENANT
Maurice Elvey — GB, 1926
The popular Drury and Tover 'empire' play was filmed three times: in 1919 with George Wynn; this — the best, although still silent, version; and a 1933 talkie [85min] with Edwards replaying the branded coward-turned-hero and also directing this time. Elvey's version has the greatest dynamism, however, and the storming of the British outpost in some far-flung part of Asia is genuinely exciting. The three versions once again emphasised the need to remind Britons of their imperial heritage, and that their place in the world after the Great War was still one of some importance.
With *Henry Edwards, Fred Raynham*

THE FLAME AND THE ARROW
Jacques Tourneur — U.S., 1950 [90min]
With the 12th century Wars of the Lombard League and the 13th century conflicts between the Holy Roman Empire and the Papacy as the source material, all Tourneur has done is to find another location for the **Robin Hood/William Tell**-type hero — acrobatically played by Lancaster. Lip service to history is barely paid, as the director blends the swashbuckling with little more than a circus act. Oscar nominations for Ernest Haller's lensing and Max Steiner's score.
With *Burt Lancaster, Virginia Mayo, Robert Douglas, Nick Cravat*

THE FLAME OF CALCUTTA
Seymour Friedman — U.S., 1953 [70min]
Cinematic licence is again taken with history in this poor second feature based in India at the time of the Seven Years War (1756-63).
With *Denise Darcel, Patric Knowles*

FLAME OF THE DESERT
Reginald Barker — U.S., 1919
Romance against the backdrop of espionage and native uprising in WW1 North Africa. Set at the time of the Sanusi Arabs' rebellion (orchestrated by the Turks) against the British administration in Egypt, the soppy plot is secondary to this historical backwater, which, of course, was topical at the time.
With *Geraldine Farrar, Lou Tellegen.*

FLAME OVER INDIA See North-West Frontier

FLAME TOP (aka 'Tulipää')
Pirjo Honkasalo/Pekka Lehto — Finland, 1980 [135min]
Life and times of writer and entrepreneur and hero of the Finns, Maiju Lassiler, recalls his fight against Russification and exploits in his country's civil war of 1918. Worthy rather than inspiring, it is beautifully shot against the Finnish landscape, but is eventually defeated by its unnecessary length.
With *Asko Sarkola*

THE FLAMING BULGE See Liberation

THE FLAMING FRONTIER
See They Died With Their Boots On

FLAMING SKY See The Burning Sky

THE FLAMING YEARS
(aka 'Povest Plammenykh Let', 'Story of the Turbulent Years')
Yulia Solntseva — USSR, 1961
Heroics of Soviet soldiers in WW2 epitomised by the Ukrainian, Ivan Orlyuk. Solntseva was the widow of early Mosfilm pioneer Alexander Dovzhenko (**Arsenal**, **Aerograd**), who wrote the screenplay, but died in 1956. Commentary by Sergei Bondarchuk (**War and Peace**, **Waterloo**).
With *Nikolai Vingrnovsky, Boris Andreyev, Zinaida Kirienko*

FLAMMENDE BERGE See William Tell

FLAT TOP
Lesley Selander — U.S., 1952 [85min]
Typical Selander country of recycled story (**The Flying Leathernecks**?), wonderful 'B' picture dialogue and cheap stunts, as the 'flat top' (the aircraft carrier) and its men of the U.S. Navy take on the Japanese — and inevitably each other — one more time.
   Meanwhile MacArthur is on his way 'back' (to the Philippines).
With *Sterling Hayden, Richard Carlson, Keith Larsen*

THE FLEMISH FARM
Jeffrey Dell — GB, 1943 [80min]
Unusual story of a Belgian pilot fighting from Britain, returning to his German-occupied home to dig up his old squadron's standard, buried when Belgium was blitzkrieged in 1940. Quite a literal flagwaver, this one.
With *Clive Brook, Clifford Evans, Jane Baxter*

FLIGHT
Frank Capra — U.S., 1929 [110min]
Silent Hollywood made several dramas alluding to various civil wars and rebellions in Latin America. At one time, just before the U.S. entry into WW1, movies about the Mexican Revolution and mayhem in other (thinly disguised) fictitious countries were as commonplace as American Civil War tracts — and certainly thicker on the ground than the 'minor' event occurring in Europe at the time.
   There are no prizes for guessing the country in this early Capra talkie about U.S. air involvement against the left-wing 'bandits', though. It's the Nicaragua of the mid-20s, and Señor Sandino is knocking at the door.
With *Jack Holt, Lila Lee, Ralph Graves*

Other pictures which considered, or alluded to, the Sandino rebellion in Nicaragua between 1925 and 1933 (usually with U.S. *in situ* or its intervention), include:
The Marines are Coming ★ (David Howard — U.S., 1935) With *William Haines*
The Marines Fly High ★★ (George Nicholls Jr/Ben Stoloff — U.S., 1940) [70min] With *Richard Dix*

FLIGHT COMMAND
Frank Borzage — U.S., 1940 [115min]
Recruitment poster heroics from brash trainee naval pilot Taylor. One of those 'look how strong our armed forces are' be-prepared movies before Pearl Harbor.
With *Robert Taylor, Ruth Hussey, Walter Pidgeon, Red Skelton*

FLIGHT FOR FREEDOM
Lothar Mendes — U.S., 1943 [100min]
Shallow WW2 espionage plot is eked from shreds of fact — an amalgamation of events from the lives of two famous flying women (Amelia Earhart and Jacqueline Cochran). Our heroine flies behind Japanese lines to gather information.
With *Rosalind Russell, Fred MacMurray, Herbert Marshall*

FLIGHT LIEUTENANT
Sidney Salkow — U.S., 1942 [80min]
Ford becomes a WW2 hero after crashing his plane in this dreadful propagandist nonsense.
With *Glenn Ford, Pat O'Brien, Evelyn Keyes, Larry Parks, Lloyd Bridges*

FLIGHT NURSE
Allan Dwan — U.S., 1953 [90min]
Dwan had more than competently handled many films in his long career, from **Robin Hood** in 1922 to **Sands of Iwo Jima** in 1949. This romantic acknowledgement of the role of front-line nurses in Korea finishes well down the list of his better pictures, however.
With *Joan Leslie, Forrest Tucker*

FLIGHT OF THE INTRUDER
John Milius — U.S., 1991 [115min]
Right-wing director Milius (**Red Dawn**, **A Farewell to the King**) went a mission too far with this unauthorised bombing raid on Hanoi in the Vietnam War. Besides which, it's plain boring. These days any director can put night-over-the-target pyrotechnics on screen, but since the advent of computer effects the law of diminishing returns is merciless.
With *Danny Glover, Willem Dafoe, Brad Johnson, Rosanna Arquette*

FLY BY NIGHT (aka 'Secrets of G32')
Robert Siodmark — U.S., 1942 [75min]
Clever, sub-Hitchcock espionage thriller, with Carlson on the run from a Nazi spy ring. Quite suspenseful, despite its obvious pittance of a budget.
With *Robert Carlson, Nancy Kelly, Albert Basserman*

FLYING FORTRESS
Walter Forde — GB, 1942 [110min]
Excruciating flagwaver about a Canadian hero in Bomber Command in WW2. Sludgily romantic and incompetently risible.
With *Richard Greene, Carla Lehmann, Basil Radford*

FLYING LEATHERNECKS
Nicholas Ray — U.S., 1951 [100min]
Using newsreel footage from the *Korean* War, this is a tale of conflicts within the command of Marine pilots at the Battle of Guadalcanal! Wayne and Ryan fight tooth and nail, but also find time to biff the Japs, in what is really a pretty ordinary, if brutal, war movie.
With *John Wayne, Robert Ryan, Don Taylor, Janis Carter*

THE FLYING MISSILE
Henry Levin — U.S., 1950 [90min]
Daft picture about Ford's experiments to fire rockets from the deck of his submarine in WW2.
With *Glenn Ford, Viveca Lindfors, Henry O'Neill*

FLYING TIGERS
David Miller — U.S., 1942 [100min]
Tribute to Chennault's Air Volunteer Group, American pilots who joined Chiang Kai-Shek's Chinese air force during the Sino-Japanese War. **God is my Co-Pilot** takes on the story after 1942. Good aerial action, shame about the script. Victor Young's score received an Oscar nomination.
With *John Wayne, John Carroll, Anna Lee*

FOOLS OF FORTUNE
Pat O'Connor — GB, 1990 [110min]
Well-made period piece, excellently acted, about the Irish troubles in the 1920s. The Republicanism is well-evoked, while the Black and Tans paint an evil picture. The balance is, however, generally maintained, but it is a feeling for the age that best comes across.
With *Julie Christie, Iain Glen, Mary Elizabeth Mastrantonio, Michael Kitchen, Niamh Cusack*

FOR BETTER, FOR WORSE
Cecil B de Mille — U.S., 1919
Heavily melodramatic, but one of the first pictures to consider WW1's disabled veterans. Variants of this plot have been over-used ever since Tennyson popularised it through his tragic hero *Enoch Arden*: girl marries hero who goes off to war instead of man who decides to stay; hero gets so badly injured he wants his wife to think he's dead; wife takes up with the other man; hero gets better and comes home (complete with wooden arm!) to find his wife betrothed.
With *Elliot Dexter, Gloria Swanson, Tom Forman*

FOR FRANCE
Wesley Ruggles — U.S., 1917
Anti-Hun propaganda piece with doughty Doughboys in WW1 pulling out all the stops to liberate the brave French from the bestial grip of the Prussians.
With *Edward Earle, Betty Howe, Arthur Donaldson*

FOR FREEDOM
Maurice Elvey/Castleton Knight — GB, 1940 [90min]
Semi-documentary flagwaver to celebrate Britain's first major WW2 success — the scuttling of the *Admiral Graf Spee* in December 1939. Dealt with more studiously in **The Battle of the River Plate**.
With *Will Fyffe, Anthony Hulme, E.V.H. Emmett, Guy Middleton*

FOR QUEEN AND COUNTRY
Martin Stellman — GB/U.S., 1988 [105min]
Washington returns to London as a hero from the Falklands War in 1982, only to run into a barrage of clichés supposedly declaiming the state of Thatcher's Britain. Everything's against him; he's black, from Brixton, and being a St Lucian he hasn't officially been a British citizen since 1979. He's harrassed by the police, hasn't got a job, and considers himself at the bottom of the pile.
Very few films have been made about the conflict in the South Atlantic, and this is really a socio-political by-product. It should have worked better for the director, who impressed with his screenplay for *Defence of the Realm*.
With *Denzel Washington, Amanda Redman, George Baker*

FOR THE FREEDOM OF THE EAST
See **For the Freedom of the World**

FOR THE FREEDOM OF THE WORLD
Ira M. Lowry — U.S., 1918
WW1 propaganda piece, concentrating on **The Slacker** element Stateside, and the poor European countries under the heel of the Kaiser.
With *E.K. Lincoln, Romaine Fielding, Jane Adler*

As if reluctant to under-use such a noble title, Lowry directed **For the Freedom of the East ★★** the following year (with Robert Elliott and Lady Tsen Mei), about intrigues in China between America and Germany in WW1.

FOR THOSE IN PERIL
Charles Crichton — GB, 1944 [70min]
Quiet debut for Crichton (**Against the Wind,** *The Lavender Hill Mob, The Titfield Thunderbolt, A Fish Called Wanda*), concerning the exploits of the air-sea rescue services in WW2. Told in typical semi-documentary style, this was one of only a handful of British films made during 1944 and 1945.
With *David Farrar, Ralph Michael, Robert Wyndham, John Slater*

FOR VALOUR
Albert Parker — U.S., 1917
Canadian soldier, the son of a Boer War veteran, brings honour to his troubled family after winning a Victoria Cross in Flanders in WW1. (Not to be confused with the Ben Travers' Boer War/WW1 farce for Tom Walls and Ralph Lynn in 1937 [95min], also directed by Walls.)
With *Richard Barthelmess, Winifred Allen, Henry Weaver*

FOR WHOM THE BELL TOLLS
Sam Wood — U.S., 1943 [170min]
Wood's would-be epic version of Hemingway's Spanish Civil War novel does not sit happily in the medium of film, despite the professional way all and sundry have gone about their business. Much fence-sitting as Cooper (again the Hemingway hero, see **A Farewell to Arms**) joins the Loyalist partisans and falls in love with Bergman. The romance becomes centre-screen thereafter, with the action patchy.

Despite nine nominations, only Paxinou picked up an Oscar as Best Supporting Actress. Among the nominations were: the picture; Cooper and Bergman for actor and actress; Tamaroff — supporting actor; Ray Rennahan — for photography; and Victor Young for the score.
With *Gary Cooper, Ingrid Bergman, Akim Tamaroff, Arturo de Codova, Katina Paxinou*

FORBIDDEN
Anthony Page — GB/West Germany, 1984 [115min]
Somewhat of an irrelevance in the '80s, this is a standard WW2 drama about the German underground in Berlin, which may have been of interest 25 years before.
With *Jacqueline Bisset, Jurgen Prochnow, Irene Worth, Peter Vaughan*

One of four films of the same title since 1932. If they were all mixed together, then distilled for the best bits, you'd still get a rotten movie.

FORBIDDEN GAMES See **(Les) Jeux Interdits**

FORCE OF ARMS See **A Farewell to Arms**

FORCE TEN FROM NAVARONE
See **The Guns of Navarone**

FOREIGN CORRESPONDENT
Alfred Hitchcock — U.S., 1940 [120min]
Hard on the heels of *Rebecca*, his first Hollywood venture, Hitchcock's odyssey through memorable set pieces (trains, windmills, Westminster Cathedral, crashing planes, etc) makes it *the* No.1 WW2 espionage thriller — even though it takes place strictly in the months of appeasement and diplomatic scurrying shortly before the outbreak of hostilities in 1939. Not without propaganda ('The lights are out everywhere . . .' speech at the end — Göbbels loved it, but banned it), it is first and foremost a glorification of all that is Hitchcock's lighter side, with suspense, romance, humour all blended in a perfect confection.

McCrea is one of the master's best heroes, and the support from Basserman and Sanders, particularly, is a joy, as events

FOR WHOM THE BELL TOLLS
Partisans in belligerent pose. Paramount

turn from England to Holland, with McCrea's reporter becoming further and further embroiled in the diplomatic skulduggery.

With *Joel McCrea, Laraine Day, Herbert Marshall, George Sanders, Albert Basserman, Edmund Gwenn*

FOREIGN DEVILS See **55 Days at Peking**

THE FOREMAN WENT TO FRANCE
(aka 'Somewhere in France')
Charles Frend — GB, 1941 [85min]
Probably the first Ealing comedy, based on fact, about a Welsh engineer going to France to bring back war machinery exported there just before the German blitzkrieg. Wonderfully evocative of the innocence and ignorance of what Britain was symbolically up against, while at the same time painting the first pictures of fleeing refugees and the chaos of invasion.
With *Clifford Evans, Constance Cummings, Gordon Jackson, Tommy Trinder, Robert Morley*

FOREVER AFTER
Harmon Weight — U.S., 1926
Silent WW1 romantic drama with plenty of well-crafted action sequences and heroics galore in the trenches.
With *Lloyd Hughes, Mary Astor*

FOREVER AND A DAY
René Clair/Cedric Hardwicke/Edmund Goulding/Frank Lloyd/ Robert Stevenson/Victor Saville/Herbert Wilcox — U.S., 1942 [105min]
Hollywood charity jamboree made (mostly) by starry ex-pat Europeans, with the history of a London family from the Napoleonic Wars to the Blitz told in a series of sketches. One for the collection.
With *Anna Neagle, Ray Milland, Claude Rains, C Aubrey Smith, Ian Hunter, Jesse Matthews, Cedric Hardwicke, Buster Keaton, Ida Lupino, Brian Aherne, Merle Oberon, Nigel Bruce, Roland Young, Gladys Cooper, Robert Cummings, Robert Coote, Elsa Lanchester, Donald Crisp, Sara Allgood*

FOREVER ENGLAND See **Brown on Resolution**

FOREVER IN LOVE See **Pride of the Marines**

FORT ALGIERS See **Beau Geste** (1939)

FORT APACHE
John Ford — U.S., 1948
The first of Ford's elegiac Cavalry trilogy starring Wayne (see also **She Wore a Yellow Ribbon**, **Rio Grande**), when men were men and the Red Men were all bad. Accepting the chauvinism of the day, the Ford western — for there is no mistaking his mark — was tailor-made for the cinema, with its epic sweep of landscape and the lazy drawl and sprawl of dialogue.

Wayne plays veteran major to Fonda's paranoid colonel as the Cavalry try to coax Cochise and his Apaches to the peace-pipe — only to end up in a disastrous massacre, for which Fonda's blame is honourably concealed. Like all Ford's best Cavalry westerns, this owes a good deal — in characters and tone — to the atmospheric original short stories of James Warner Bellah.
With *Henry Fonda, John Wayne, Shirley Temple, Pedro Armendariz, Ward Bond, Victor MacLaglen, John Agar*

Other pictures, which have titles prefixed by '**Fort**' and deal with Cavalry v Indian themes include:
Fort Defiance ★ (John Rawlins — U.S., 1951) [80min] With *Dane Clark, Ben Johnson* (fighting Navajo Indians)
Fort Osage (Lesley Selander — U.S., 1952) [70min] With *Rod Cameron*
Fort Yuma ★ (Lesley Selander — U.S., 1955) [80min] With *Peter Graves* (Apaches)
Fort Dobbs ★★ (Gordon Douglas — U.S., 1957) [90min] With *Clint Walker, Virginia Mayo, Brian Keith* (Comanches)
Fort Bowie ★★ (Howard H Koch — U.S., 1958) With *Ben Johnson* (Apaches)
Fort Massacre ★★★ (Joseph M. Newman — U.S., 1958) [80min] With *Joel McCrea, Forrest Tucker* (Apaches)
Fort Courageous (Lesley Selander — U.S., 1965) With *Fred Beir, Donald Barry*
Fort Utah ★ (Lesley Selander — U.S., 1968) [85min] With *John Ireland, Virginia Mayo*
Fort Vengeance See **They Died with Their Boots On**

FORT BOWIE See **Fort Apache**

FORT COURAGEOUS See **Fort Apache**

FORT DEFIANCE See **Fort Apache**

FORT DOBBS See **Fort Apache**

FORT-DU-FOU
Léo Joannon — France, 1962 [85min]
Psychological drama involving a garrison of French soldiers and Vietnamese Catholic refugees besieged at Fort-du-Fou by the Viet Minh at the end of the French-Indochina War.
With *Jacques Harden, Alain Saury, Nguyen Thi Tuyet, Foun Sen*

FORT MASSACRE See **Fort Apache**

FORT OSAGE See **Fort Apache**

FORT TI
William Castle — U.S., 1953 [75min]
'Ti' is short for Ticonderoga, or Fort Carillon as it was to the French before the British took it from them in 1759 during the French and Indian part of the Seven Years War. This film is accurate enough to include the part played by Rogers' Rangers — a rag-bag outfit of colonial volunteers fighting with the British — but is hampered by a puerile script, insipid acting and its attempt, seemingly at all costs, to cash in on the 3-D craze (the front row of the stalls ducking and diving hither and thither again).

The Rogers character is first seen on screen in the infinitely better **Northwest Passage**.
With *George Montgomery, Joan Vohs*

FORT UTAH See **Fort Apache**

FORT VENGEANCE
See **They Died with Their Boots On**

FORT YUMA See **Fort Apache**

THE FORTUNES OF CAPTAIN BLOOD
See **Captain Blood**

FORTY-EIGHT HOURS
See **Went the Day Well?**

THE FORTY-FIRST (aka 'Sorok Pervyi')
Yakov Protazanov — USSR, 1927 [80min]
Although remade by Grigori Chukrai in 1956 **★★★** it was
Protazanov's powerful parable of loyalty and honour in the
Russian Civil War that first broke on international audiences.

The story of the Red Army girl falling for a White lieutenant
and then killing him — her 41st kill — was just one of a stream
of important pictures to come out of Soviet Russia in the late
'20s, from people like Dovzhenko, Pudovkin and Eisenstein.
With *Ada Voitsik, Ivan Kovan-Samborsky*

THE FORTY-FIRST (1956) See **The Forty-First** (1927)

49TH PARALLEL (aka 'The Invaders')
Michael Powell — GB, 1941 [125min]
British propaganda at its best. Still quite subtle today, this
Academy Award-nominated picture exudes a real fear that the
old order will be forever lost if the Americans don't enter the
war. Taken at another level, Emeric Pressberger's Oscar-
winning story is imaginatively handled, in almost
Hitchcockian fashion, by Powell.

The yarn of a beached U-boat crew trying to escape from
Canada into neutral America is excitingly told through an
intelligent script (Oscar nomination for Rodney Ackland) and
top-notch ensemble acting.
With *Eric Portman, Anton Walbrook, Leslie Howard, Raymond
Massey, Laurence Olivier, Finlay Currie, Niall McGinnis, Glynis
Johns*

FORTY THOUSAND HORSEMEN
Charles Chauvel — Australia, 1940 [100min]
A very early Australian attempt at a mass-market picture, this
tale based on the famous Australian Light Horse's exploits in
WW1 Palestine is full of primitive action sequences — but no
worse for that. (See also **The Lighthorsemen, Gallipoli**.)
With *Chips Rafferty, Betty Bryant, Grant Taylor*

THE FOUNTAIN
John Cromwell — U.S., 1934 [85min]
Dated, very soupy WW1 melodrama involving a British
woman, her badly injured German pilot husband and her
former boyfriend.
With *Ann Harding, Brian Aherne, Paul Lukas*

THE FOUR DAYS OF NAPLES
Nanni Loy — Italy, 1962 [120min]
Semi-documentary reconstruction of the Battle of Naples in
1943, when the populace erupted against its Nazi occupiers.
Has all the gritty realism of a mid-40s Rossellini. Nominated
for Best Foreign Film and Loy's own script.
With *Lea Massari, Frank Wolff*

THE FOUR FEATHERS (1915)
See **The Four Feathers** (1939)

THE FOUR FEATHERS (1921)
See **The Four Feathers** (1939)

THE FOUR FEATHERS (1929)
See **The Four Feathers** (1939)

THE FOUR DAYS OF NAPLES
German tanks fight back against the Italian uprising of 1943. Titanus-
Metro

THE FOUR FEATHERS
Zoltan Korda — GB, 1939 [130min]
The fourth, and by far the best version of A.E.W. Mason's tale
of cowardice and glory set against a backdrop of the Victorian
English class system and the Sudan campaign, which
culminates with the Battle of Omdurman in 1898.

The action is terrific and much footage was used for later,
inferior pictures. Direction, the vivid colour photography
(with a young Jack Cardiff involved), and all-round acting is
first class. Not one Oscar nomination, though (nor for **Gunga
Din** — another top-class adventure along the same lines) in a
year when Academy members were spoilt for choice (**Gone
With the Wind**, *The Wizard of Oz, Wuthering Heights, Mr Smith
Goes to Washington, Stagecoach, Goodbye Mr Chips* — these were
just some of the ten nominees for Best Picture)**.**
With *John Clements, Ralph Richardson, C. Aubrey Smith, June
Duprez, John Laurie*

Other versions of the **Four Feathers** were: two Hollywood
silents made in 1915 **★★** and 1921 **★★★**; the Richard Arlen-Fay
Wray early talkie **★★** (1929), directed by Lothar Mendes,
Merion C. Cooper and Ernest Schoedsack; a poor 1956
remake, entitled **Storm Over the Nile ★** (Terence Young)
[105min] with Anthony Steel, Laurence Harvey, Ronald
Lewis and Ian Carmichael; and even a spirited TV movie
directed by Don Sharp in 1977, featuring a strong (TV) cast
— Beau Bridges, Simon Ward, Robert Powell, Richard
Johnson, Harry Andrews and Jane Seymour.

THE FOUR HORSEMEN OF THE APOCALYPSE
Rex Ingram — U.S., 1921 [150min]
The Four Horsemen of the Book of Revelation — Conquest,
Slaughter, Famine and Disease. Ingram's interpretation of

THE FOUR FEATHERS
British troops attack a native village in the Sudan. London

Vicente Blasco Ibáñez's 1916 novel may not have got around fully to all of them — but did cover the war-related first two in some depth.

The story is of a French family fleeing the Franco-Prussian War in 1870, and settling in Argentina. It then finds itself torn apart when one faction of the family returns to France while another settles in Germany. Come 1914 they are on opposite sides and, inevitably, all perish.

With *Rudolph Valentino, Alice Terry, Alan Hale, Jean Herscholt, Wallace Beery, Nigel de Brulier*

Remade — somewhat pointlessly, as the '21 version will always be remembered for Valentino's imprint — by Vincente Minnelli in 1961 ★★ [155min], starring some golden oldies (Glenn Ford, Charles Boyer, Paul Henreid, Lee J. Cobb, Paul Lukas and Ingrid Thulin), but updated to WW2.

THE FOUR HORSEMEN OF THE APOCALYPSE (1961) See **The Four Horsemen of the Apocalypse (1921)**

FOUR SONS
John Ford — U.S., 1928 [100min]
Hollywood's sympathetic period to WW1 Germany, before the rise of Hitler, had already produced Griffith's **Isn't Life Wonderful?** and would shortly come up with the daddy of them all — **All Quiet on the Western Front**. In between, Ford's anti-war tract is thematically similar to **The Four Horsemen of the Apocalypse** in that members of the same family are on different sides — with those still living in Germany coming off worse.
With *Margaret Mann, James Hall, Francis X Bushman*

Also like **Four Horsemen . . .** , this was remade (in 1940 by Archie Mayo [90min] ★★ with Don Ameche, Alan Curtis and Sig Rumann) in a WW2 setting.

FOUR SONS (1940) See **Four Sons (1928)**

1492: CONQUEST OF PARADISE
Ridley Scott — U.S., 1992 [155min]
The best of the spate of commemorative pictures made to celebrate 500 years of contact with the New World. The use of the word 'conquest' in the title points to incidents between Columbus' pioneers and the indigenous American — a sort of *hors d'œuvres* to the main course of atrocities indulged in by Cortés and his Conquistadores a few decades later.
With *Gérard Depardieu, Armand Assante, Sigourney Weaver, Fernando Rey*

THE FOURTH WAR
John Frankenheimer — U.S., 1990 [90min]
Poor attempt to fantasise about future war, by placing abrasive ex-Vietnam and ex-Afghanistan veterans nose-to-nose across the German-Czech border towards the end of the Cold War.
With *Roy Scheider, Harry Dean Stanton, Jurgen Prochnow*

THE FOX OF GLENARVON
Max Kimmich — Germany, 1940
Out and out propagandist stirring by ministry-propelled Kimmich (he was Göbbels' brother-in-law), about alleged British atrocities in Ireland during the 1920s. His **My Life for Ireland** ★★ (1941) covered a similar theme.

FOXHOLE IN CAIRO
John Moxey — GB, 1960 [80min]
Intelligent but dull rendering of a true spy story in the North African desert of WW2. The British are trying to confuse Rommel (Lieven) with useless information.

Early, pre-**Zulu**, run-out for Caine. (Interestingly, both this and **The English Patient** are loosely based on the supposed exploits of the same actual German agent, the Hungarian Count Laszlo Almaszy.)
With *James Robertson Justice, Albert Lieven, Niall MacGinnis, Adrian Hoven, Peter van Eyck, Michael Caine*

FRAGMENTS OF ISABELLA
Ronan O'Leary — Ireland, 1989 [80min]
An unique experience. Isabella Leitner's autobiographical tale, already adapted for the stage, of escape from the Belsen death march, is a filmed monologue, sensitively delivered by Reidy. Interspersed by newsreel footage, the overall effect is quite moving.
With *Gabrielle Reidy*

FRAULEIN
Henry Koster — U.S., 1958 [100min]
Second rate, cheap WW2 escape movie, with American POW Ferrer assisted by a conscientious German woman.
With *Dana Wynter, Mel Ferrer*

FRAULEIN DOKTOR see **Mademoiselle Docteur**

FREEDOM RADIO
Anthony Asquith — GB, 1941 [95min]
Inverted propaganda picture about secret radio broadcasts

THE FOUR HORSEMEN OF THE APOCALYPSE
Conquest and destruction: the Book of Revelation manifested in WW1 France. One of the landmark films of family strife in times of war where nobody ends up happily. Metro (courtesy KOBAL)

from Vienna to like-minded Germans who opposed the Nazis. Wooden.
With *Diana Wynyard, Clive Brook, Raymond Huntley*

A FRENCH WOMAN See **Une Femme Française**

FRIDERICUS
Johannes Meyer — Germany, 1936
One of several films issued in a state of nationalistic frenzy during the Third Reich. Preceded by **The Chorale of Leuthen ✳✳✳** (Carl Froelich, 1933) and followed by Veit Harlan's **The Great King ✳✳** in 1942, this was the third film about the great Reich-builder, Frederick the Great. All the films tell the story of the Prussians' great victory at Leuthen, against the odds, over the Austrians in 1757, during the continental European aspect of the Seven Years' War; and generally portray the Emperor as the Führer's natural antecedent.
With *Otto Gebühr, Hilde Körber, Lil Dagover*

FRIENDLY ENEMIES (1914)
See **Friendly Enemies** (1942)

FRIENDLY ENEMIES
Allan Dwan — U.S., 1942 [95min]
A more contemplative update of George Melford's 1925 ✳✳ [70min] WW1 comedy drama featuring vaudevillians, Joe Weber and Lew Fields. The picture deals with the relationship between German-American businessmen at the outbreak of war, and the consequences of their actions.
With *Charles Winninger, Charlie Ruggles*

FRIENDLY PERSUASION
William Wyler — U.S., 1956 [140min]
Gooey soap about a Quaker family in the War of Secession and the examination of their consciences. Played for laughs as much as tears, it sits uncomfortably between a serious look at pacifist sects in time of war and *The Waltons*.

The action 'twixt North and South is minimal. It did, however, receive five Academy Award nominations: the picture; Wyler; black-listed Michael Wilson for the script; Perkins for supporting actor; Dimitri Tiomkin/Paul Francis Webster for the song *Thee I Love — QED!*
With *Gary Cooper, Dorothy Maguire, Anthony Perkins, Marjorie Main, Richard Eyer*

FRIENDSHIP'S DEATH
Peter Wollen — GB, 1987 [80min]
Paterson is a journalist covering the Israel-Arab War of Attrition in 1970, when he comes across a young woman taken by a PLO patrol. She is not all she seems — indeed, is she human as we know it?

Quirky and highly original, the picture cleverly allows us to consider the foibles and follies of the human race by stepping outside ourselves.
With *Bill Paterson, Tilda Swinton*

THE FROGMEN
Lloyd Bacon — U.S., 1951 [95min]
The heroics of under-water demolition teams in the U.S. Navy's Pacific fleet in WW2. Story was strong enough to earn an Academy Award nomination for Oscar Millard.
With *Richard Widmark, Dana Andrews, Gary Merrill, Jeffrey Hunter, Robert Wagner*

FROM HELL TO VICTORY (aka 'De L'Enfer à la Victoire')

Umberto Lenzi as Hank Milestone — France/Italy/Spain, 1979 *[100min]*

You would have thought that Peppard would have had enough of post D-Day France after **The Victors**, but here he is doing it all over again in one of those pretty appalling international productions. Heavy-handed support and a daft script don't help.

With *George Peppard, George Hamilton, Horst Buchholz, Jean-Pierre Cassel, Capucine, Sam Wanamaker*

FROM HERE TO ETERNITY

Fred Zinnemann — U.S., 1953 [120min]

Winner of the 1953 Best Picture at the Oscars — and of six others, including Sinatra and Reed (Best Supporting Actor and Actress), Zinnemann, Daniel Tardash's script, Burnett Guffey (camera) and for editing.

Barracks brutality, sexual and rank tensions over-heating before and during the attack on Pearl Harbor; the picture has something for everybody, and with its good production values it's as smooth as anything Hollywood could offer at the time. Packed with memorable scenes — none more so than the stars' hugely suggestive (for the time) roll-about in the Hawaiian surf.

With *Burt Lancaster, Deborah Kerr, Frank Sinatra*

FROM MAYERLING TO SARAJEVO

Max Ophuls — France, 1940 [90min]

Master French director Ophuls' languid costume-drama history, depicting the decline of Austria-Hungary from the death of Crown Prince Rudolf to that famous assassination in the Balkans on 28 June 1914, is secondary to the real-life drama he experienced getting the film made.

Starting in 1939, Ophuls lost key cast members to conscription when war broke out in August. He eventually finished it in early 1940, only after getting the government's permission to leave his sector of the Front, whereafter it was promptly banned by the occupying Germans. The film was eventually premiered in May 1945.

With *Edwige Feuillère*

FROM TEXAS TO TOKYO See **We've Never been Licked**

FRONT-LINE GIRLFRIENDS
See **The Girl from Leningrad**

FRONTIER See **Aerograd**

THE FRONTIERSMAN

Reginald Barker — U.S., 1927

This is an unusual little film in that it looks at Andrew Jackson's campaign against the Creek Indians in 1813, during the United States-British War — not a conflict that has had much cinematic coverage. The War of 1812, very confusingly rambled on, rather low-key, until 1815.

With *Tim McCoy*

FRONTOVYYE PODRUGI
See **The Girl from Leningrad**

THE FUGITIVE (1910)
See **The Fugitive** (1947)

THE FUGITIVE

John Ford — U.S., 1947 [105min]

Not to be confused with D. W. Griffith's 1910 ★★★ Civil War drama with Kate Bruce and Edward Dillon, nor the Harrison Ford-Tommy Lee Jones thriller, directed by Andrew Davis in 1993; Ford's **The Fugitive** is a very loose adaptation of Graham Greene's *The Power and the Glory* — a tale of betrayal in revolutionary Mexico. It's good to look at, at least, and it does have some of Ford's stock actors on board — but what a liberty he's taken with the story.

With *Henry Fonda, Dolores Del Rio, Pedro Amendariz, J. Carroll Naish, Ward Bond*

FUGITIVE ROAD

Frank Strayer — U.S., 1934 [70min]

Excuse for a romantic comedy at an Austria-Italy border post in WW1. Not that funny either.

With *Eric von Stroheim, Wera Engels, Leslie Fenton*

FULL METAL JACKET

Stanley Kubrick — GB/U.S., 1987 [115min]

Shot entirely in Kubrick's adopted England, this is one of the most numbing war pictures ever made — and against some in the Vietnam genre, that is saying something. Not falling into the trap of devoting his two hours or so to the conflict in 'Nam, the first half of the film is devoted to the conditioning recruits require to take such trauma when they arrive. The Parris Island boot camp takes away any character the Marine rookies have, to the point of dehumanising them: the second half shows how their brutalised personalities function under the pressure of street-fighting in Hue during Tet 1968.

Distasteful to many, perhaps, but few can put across war's overt brutality better. Kubrick, along with Michael Herr and Gustav Hasford — who wrote the original novel — were nominated for an adapted screenplay Oscar.

With *Matthew Modine, Adam Baldwin, Vincent D'Onofrio, Lee Ermey*

GABY See **Waterloo Bridge** (1940)

THE GALLANT BLADE
Henry Levin — U.S., 1948 [80min]
As the Thirty Years' War fizzled out, many offshoot conflicts remained. This depicts some nonsense between France and Spain in 1648 — all in the cause of making a pretty lousy swashbuckling movie.
With *Larry Parks, Marguerite Chapman, George Macready, Victor Jory*

THE GALLANT HOURS
Robert Montgomery — U.S., 1959 [115min]
Biopic of Admiral 'Bull' Halsey, and earnest attempt to show his strategy against Yamamoto in 1942. Unfortunately it's all talk and no action.
With *James Cagney, Dennis Weaver, Richard Jaeckel*

GALLIPOLI
Peter Weir — Australia, 1981 [110min]
Weir had come to notice for his evocative *Picnic at Hanging Rock*, and now his buddy movie, from sprint race meetings in Australia to bloody death in the Dardanelles in 1915, enhanced his stock even further. It was also another step to world stardom for Gibson, who was already in the middle of his *Mad Max* trilogy.
   The picture is segmented, so that the thrilling battle sequences are kept until the very end, and it loses its way slightly in the middle where the troops train in the Egyptian desert. It is one of several thoughtful Aussie war pictures from around that same time (see also **Breaker Morant**, **The Odd Angry Shot**, **The Lighthorsemen**), and always good to watch.
With *Mark Lee, Mel Gibson, Bill Hunter, Bill Kerr*

The Battle of Gallipoli was previously the focus, and alternative title, of Asquith's **Tell England**.

GANG WAR
See **Odd Man Out**

THE GARDEN OF THE FINZI-CONTINIS
Vittorio de Sica — Germany/Italy, 1970 [95min]
A sense of torpid doom descends over a landed Jewish family in 1938 Italy. As the prospect of a concentration camp comes ever closer, all the family can do is to closet themselves behind the high wall of their estate and hopelessly wish that Mussolini and Hitler will pass them by.
   With de Sica directing something of real worth after many years of frustrating fare, the picture collected the Best Foreign Film Oscar, and was nominated for the multi-handed screenplay. With *Dominique Sanda, Lino Capolicchio, Helmut Berger, Fabio Teste, Romolo Valli*

GARDENS OF STONE
Francis Coppola — U.S., 1987 [110min]
The end product of the Vietnam War. Coppola's first direct foray into the conflict since **Apocalypse Now** is a much more straightforwardly presented picture — concerned with the army's need to bring their boys back and bury them at home. It also portrays Caan as the training sergeant vet, who doesn't believe in the cause for which his trainees are being prepared. Weak, as it doesn't really know which point to make its main theme.
With *James Caan, Anjelica Huston, James Earl Jones, Dean Stockwell, Mary Stuart Masterson*

GARRISON DORA
(aka 'Besatzung Dora', 'The Dora Crew')
Karl Ritter — Germany, 1943
Ritter, who had earlier directed propaganda pieces like **Pour le Mérite** and **Stukas**, saw this flagwaver about a crack bomber crew denied release by Göbbels when the war in the east, featured in the film, took a turn for the worse. Moreover,

GALLIPOLI
Mark Lee and Mel Gibson rustle up some corned beef. Associated R&R Films/Paramount (courtesy KOBAL)

its star, Stelzer, is seen musing over his settling down in German-occupied Russia after the war. *Lebensraum* was definitely no longer top of Hitler's agenda.
With *Hannes Stelzer, Hubert Kiurina*

IL GATTOPARDO See **The Leopard**

GAWAIN AND THE GREEN KNIGHT
See **Knights of the Round Table**

GENBAKU NO KO See **Children of Hiroshima**

THE GENERAL
Clyde Bruckman/Buster Keaton — U.S., 1926 [80min]
Like Chaplin's **The Great Dictator**, there will be room in this encyclopedia for comedy, if the film also warrants inclusion as a war movie. Keaton's classic certainly does. It may take liberties with the Andrews Raid (the stealing of the *General* — a locomotive — by Union soldiers from the Confederates) when Keaton single-handedly recaptures the engine, and a Yankee officer to boot, but it scores well over its serious remake (Francis D. Lyon's 1956 offering from Disney, **The Great Locomotive Chase** [75min], with Fess Parker and Jeffrey Hunter), and many other Civil War pictures, because of its faithfulness to period detail through a sympathetic camera. It is also one of the most visually-funny pictures ever made.
With *Buster Keaton, Marion Mack, Glen Cavander*

GENERAL CRACK
Alan Crosland — U.S., 1929 [100min]
Taking liberties with the early 18th century history of Austria and its part in the War of the Spanish Succession (1701-14), this swashbuckler was Barrymore's first talkie — not that anything he said as the dashing general (actually Prince Christian) made much sense.
With *John Barrymore, Marion Nixon*

GENERAL DELLA ROVERE
Roberto Rossellini — France/Italy, 1959 [130min]
Rossellini hated back-tracking to former achievements (**Open City**, **Paisà**), but this was very much a consolidation film for him after his time with Ingrid Bergman seemed to have drained him of his considerable talent. Set in German-occupied Genoa in late 1943, he elicits a wonderful performance from de Sica as a local ne'er-do-well being forced to imitate a dead Italian general in order to infiltrate partisans. The 'general', of course, gradually adopts the moral and patriotic stance of those he is supposed to betray. Nominated for Best Foreign film and the Rossellini (*et al*) screenplay by the Academy, the film won the Golden Lion at Venice, too.
With *Vittorio de Sica, Hannes Messemer, Sandra Milo*

THE GENERAL DIED AT DAWN
Lewis Milestone — U.S., 1936 [95min]
Expert Milestone feature, set in Civil War-ravaged China in the early 20th century, with gun-running Cooper imposing his own values of morality by taking the side of the down-trodden against a powerful warlord. Coop, as usual, sweats integrity, while anyone would want to be conned by grifter-spy Carroll. Comparatively high-brow fare, it was nevertheless Paramount's biggest earner of 1935.
With *Gary Cooper, Madeleine Carroll, Akim Tamaroff*

GENERAL KATO'S FALCON FIGHTERS
See **Torpedo Squadrons Move Out**

GENERAL SUVOROV See **Suvorov**

GENERAL YAMASHITA
Satsuo Yamamoto — Japan, 1952
The story of Tomoyuki Yamashita — commander of Japan's land forces which kicked the British out of Malaya and resisted the American liberation of the Philippines — perhaps, understandably for the time, painted whiter than white. Former silent favourite Hayakawa's powerful portrayal led to his role as camp commandant Col Saito in Lean's **Bridge on the River Kwai**, for which he was recognized by the Academy with a supporting actor nomination.
With *Sessue Hayakawa*

A GENERATION (aka 'Pokolenie')
Andrzej Wajda — Poland, 1954 [90min]
The film that brought Wajda (and Polish cinema, generally) to the eyes of the world. Set in 1942 Warsaw, this first part of what was to be regarded as his WW2 trilogy (**Kanal** and **Ashes and Diamonds** were to follow) deals with youth resistance to the Nazi occupiers, albeit told through deeper than rose-coloured glasses. The party line is duly toed here, and even the style of the director is early-Soviet realist. However, Wajda's true politics would come out eventually in his immense 'Solidarity'-influencing and -influenced movies, *Man of Marble* and *Man of Iron*. Interesting cast-member.
With *Tadeusz Lomnicki, Ursula Modrzynska, Roman Polanski, Zbigniew Cybulski*

GENGHIS KHAN
Henry Levin — U.S., 1964 [125min]
Another medieval foray for Levin (**The Bandit of Sherwood Forest**, **Dark Avenger**) about the unification of Mongol tribes in the late 12th century, and the platform for their Asian domination over the next century. Dully played (Mason, as usual, excepted) and directed, it benefits from some splendid set pieces nevertheless, with Geoffrey Unsworth's camerawork its best feature.
With *Omar Sharif, Stephen Boyd, Françoise Dorléac, James Mason, Eli Wallach, Robert Morley, Telly Savalas*

THE GENTLE GUNMAN
Basil Dearden — GB, 1952 [90min]
Out of character Ealing production, which, if released a decade and a half or so later, might have been the spark for the modern troubles in Ireland. Appalling Irish stereotyping (Mills, Bogarde and Beatty are all feuding and philosophising IRA men!), from a studio rightly applauded for its evocation of post-war English life, suggests again that characterisation doesn't travel (a fact that should have been learned from Hollywood's idea of how England — London, that is — should look).
With *John Mills, Dirk Bogarde, Elizabeth Sellars, Robert Beatty*

THE GENTLE SEX
Leslie Howard/Maurice Elvey — GB, 1943 [95min]
Howard's penultimate film involvement before his tragic death was a useful propaganda piece for its time — focusing on a group of female ATS enrolees, and showing the women of WW2 Britain that they could do more than just till the land or

work in munitions factories. Howard's narration provided the last opportunity to hear him on screen.
With *Rosamund John, Joan Greenwood, Lilli Palmer*

GEORG ELSER See **Seven Minutes**

GERMAIN, ANNO ZERO See **Germany, Year Zero**

GERMANIN See **The Riders of German East Africa**

THE GERMAN STORY
(aka *'You and Other Comrades'*) See **The Hitler Gang**

GERMANY, PALE MOTHER
(aka 'Deutschland im Herbst')
Helma Sanders-Brahms — West Germany, 1979 [150min]
Autobiographical and heavily symbolic piece relating the life of a young girl and her mother in WW2 Germany and the trials of the post-war years.
With *Eva Mattes, Ernst Jacobi, Elisabeth Stepanek, Angelika Thomas*

GERMANY, YEAR ZERO (aka 'Germain, Anno Zero')
Roberto Rosselini — Germany/Italy, 1947 [75min]
The third part of Rossellini's end-of-war trilogy after **Open City** and **Paisà**. Whilst not quite a film of the same rank as the others (which dealt with Italian hope as well as reflection), it is still an important picture, painting a different complexion in a totally defeated and defeatist scenario. This is the horrific tale of Nazi influences still harboured by a 13-year-old boy, scrabbling for existence in bleak and realistic Berlin rubble in the early days after VE Day. Without any apparent hope.
With *Edmund Moeschke, Werner Pittschau*

GERONIMO (1939)
See **Geronimo: An American Legend**

GERONIMO (1962)
See **Geronimo: An American Legend**

GERONIMO (1994)
See **Geronimo: An American Legend**

GERONIMO: AN AMERICAN LEGEND
(aka 'Geronimo')
Walter Hill — U.S., 1994 [115min]
White man's duplicity until the end. Despite superficially painting an heroic, misunderstood character, John Milius' (and Larry Gross') script cannot help revealing a certain satisfaction in the way the American interior was won over by white settlers, and really, that the red man was now in the best place for him. It's a shame, really, because Hill's film looks good.
With *Wes Studi, Gene Hackman, Jason Patric, Robert Duvall, Matt Damon*

Perhaps the most even-handed approach to the Geronimo saga (with the broken promises receiving reasonable coverage) came from Roger Young's TV movie of the same date, with Joseph Running Fox. This, too, was imaginatively-titled *Geronimo*.

Other movies featuring Geronimo as a major character include:

Geronimo ★★ (Paul H. Sloane — U.S., 1939 — 90min) With *Preston Foster, Chief Thunder Cloud* (as Geronimo)
I Killed Geronimo ★ (Sam Neuman — U.S., 1950) With *Chief Thunder Cloud*
Indian Uprising (Ray Nazarro — U.S., 1952 — 75min) With *George Montgomery, Miguel Inclan* (as Geronimo)
Battle at Apache Pass See separate entry
Walk the Proud Land ★★ (Jesse Hibbs — U.S., 1956 — 90min) With *Audie Murphy, Jay Silverheels* (as Geronimo)
Geronimo ★★ (Arnold Laven — U.S., 1962 — 100min) With *Chuck Connors*

GESCHWADER FLEDERMAUS
See **The Bat Squadron**

GESTAPO See **Night Train to Munich**

GESUM E KAKO SHIPTA See **To the Starry Island**

GETTYSBURG
Ronald F. Maxwell — U.S., 1993
The epic film version of the epic three-day battle of the War of Secession in 1863, based on Michael Shaara's best-selling novel *The Killer Angels*. A theatre version of it at just over four hours long was released from the original TV mini-series for Ted Turner's company (he actually played a Confederate infantryman extra): the director's cut video runs for almost six hours. Certainly a film for buffs of military cinema, with the emphasis on action and strategy, and making very little allowance for such cinematic niceties as characterisation and sub-plot. It goes overboard for authenticity — even filming at the Gettysburg National Military Park.

Some of the acting in the line of fire, however, deserves reporting in despatches. Sheen gives his expected low-key, controlled performance as Lee, while Daniels is impressive as

GERONIMO
Chuck Connors and the cavalry in harmony before the great betrayal, in this 1962 version. UA

Chamberlain of the 20th Maine. Sadly, Jordan, in the role of General Armistead, died soon afterwards of a brain tumour. With *Tom Berenger, Martin Sheen, Jeff Daniels, Sam Elliott, Richard Jordan, Stephen Lang*

A silent version was also made in 1914, by the influential Thomas Ince, called **The Battle of Gettysburg ★★★**.

GHOST OF THE CHINA SEA
Fred F Sears — U.S., 1958 [80min]
The Japanese invade the Philippines in 1942, but this 'B' picture tells us nothing more about it.
With *David Brian, Lynn Bernay*

THE GIANT OF MARATHON
(aka 'La Battaglia di Maratona')
Jacques Tourneur — France/Italy, 1959
The first great decisive battle: in 490BC, 11,000 Greeks routed 21,000 Persians at Marathon before the invasion fleet of another 100,000 could land. Told rather patchily by international director Tourneur (*Cat People, The Night of the Living Dead*, etc), it nonetheless has lots of gusto when it comes to the plentiful action sequences. Mr Universe, Reeves (**Goliath and the Barbarians, The Trojan War,** *Hercules Unchained,*), was the darling of Italian cinema's TotalScope 'adventures in classic history' series (sword-and-sandal dramas in other words), which brought on directors such as Sergio Leone and Mario Bava (who was cinematographer here).
With *Steve Reeves, Mylene Demengeot, Sergio Fantoni*

THE GIRL AND THE GENERAL
Pasquale Festa Campanile — France/Italy, 1967 [115min]
Would-be epic comedy-drama from the Carlo Ponti stable, about an Austrian general escaping from capture in WW1, getting involved with an Italian partisan of the opposite sex.

Despite a willing cast, the outcome is awful.
With *Rod Steiger, Virna Lisi, Umberto Orsini*

THE GIRL FROM LENINGRAD
(aka 'Frontovyye Podrugi', 'Front-Line Girlfriends')
Victor Eisimont — USSR, 1941
Stalin invaded Finland in November 1939 as a prelude to his entering the Baltic states in the summer of 1940. This is the most important of the few pictures made by the Soviet Union of the event, telling the tale of front-line nurses (although the Finnish-German relationship is better shown in Yevgeni Schneider's **In the Rear of the Enemy ★★★** of the same year).
With *Zoya Fyodorova*

Remade, as **Three Russian Girls ★** [U.S., 80min — aka 'She Who Dares'] by Fedor Ozep and Henry Kesler in 1943, with Anna Sten, Mimi Forsythe and Kathy Frye, with not a Finn in sight!

THE GIRL WHO STAYED AT HOME
D.W. Griffith — U.S., 1919
WW1 romantic drama about Doughboys shipped out to France. Best remembered for Griffith's inclusion of some of the earliest aerial footage of the war.
With *Richard Barthelmess, Clarine Seymour, Robert Harron, Carol Dempster*

THE GIRL WITH THE RED HAIR
(aka 'Het Meisje met het Rode Haar')
Ben Verbong — Holland, 1981 [115min]
Understated, intelligent biopic of Dutch WW2 resistance

GLORY
Murderous artillery rips into Matthew Broderick's 54th on assailing Fort Wagner. Tri-Star (courtesy KOBAL)

heroine Hannie Schaft. Atmospherics, action and acting are all very good.
With *Renée Soutendijk, Peter Tuinman*

GLORY
Edward Zwick — U.S., 1989 [120min]
Excellent American Civil War drama about the first black outfit to fight for the Union — the 54th Regiment of Massachusetts Volunteers. It deals, somewhat melodramatically at times, with the predictable racism and bad treatment the unit suffers while on basic training, and pumps up the dramatic element further in the clashes between the two white officers, Broderick and Elwes. Freeman acts as umpire and general good guy representing his race, while Washington is the tear-away element.

The picture's great strength, however, is the director's attention to historical detail — factors apparent in his other pictures (**Legends of the Fall**, **Courage under Fire**), and when the unit do get a chance to prove themselves in battle — typically, a suicidal frontal assault on the ramparts of Fort Wagner — the depiction of the tactics and the waste of life is chillingly stark. Oscars for Washington (Best Supporting Actor) and Freddie Francis (Cinematography): further nominations for art direction and editing. James Horner's lush score is also memorable.
With *Matthew Broderick, Denzel Washington, Cary Elwes, Morgan Freeman*

THE GLORY BRIGADE
Robert D. Webb — U.S., 1953 [80min]
Racial tension on the same side in Korea. A Greek detachment, fighting alongside the Americans, don't exactly cover themselves with glory in their first action — leading to several U.S. observations about national traits. Otherwise, just a routine war story.
With *Victor Mature, Lee Marvin, Richard Egan*

THE GLORY GUYS
Arnold Laven — U.S., 1965 [110min]
The one where the Indians win. Contrary to the hundreds of Hollywood Westerns which have gone before, the final battle of this Sam Peckinpah-scripted horse opera (sadly not any better for that) goes to the Indians over the U.S. Cavalry for probably the first time outside of the Little Big Horn pictures.
With *Tom Tryon, Harve Presnell, Senta Berger, James Caan, Andrew Duggan, Slim Pickens*

G'MAR GIVIYA See **Cup Final**

GO FOR BROKE
Robert Pirosh — U.S., 1951 [95min]
Pirosh was nominated by the Academy for his script about the WW2 activities of the *Nisei* — the third-generation Japanese Americans who fought in the European theatre for the Allies in WW2. Interesting only for that.
With *Van Johnson, Lane Nikano, George Miki*

GO TELL THE SPARTANS
Ted Post — U.S., 1978 [115min]
Low-key Vietnam War drama about American cadres in trouble during the period when the U.S. Army was supposedly only present in an advisory capacity (1964). Trapped at Muc Wa, they come across a symbolic sign above a cemetery where

GO TELL THE SPARTANS
U.S. Army detachment comes under fire on its way to Muc Wa.
UA/Spartan Co

French fighters from a decade before are buried. It reads ' . . . go tell the Spartans we lie here obedient to their orders' — a corruption of the famous epitaph on **The 300 Spartans** who died at Thermopylae in 480BC, defending Greece from Xerxes' Persians.

Smothered by Vietnamania in 1978 (**The Deer Hunter**, **Coming Home**, **The Boys in Company C**), it perhaps deserves to be remembered for its reasonably good script 'foreshadowing' many of the specific problems and contradictions of America's later involvement.
With *Burt Lancaster, Craig Wasson, Marc Singer, Jonathan Goldsmith*

GOD IS MY CO-PILOT
Robert Florey — U.S., 1945 [90min]
The story of the '**Flying Tigers**' and their incorporation into the U.S. Army Air Corps in 1942 following America's entry into the hostilities after several years' combating the Japanese in a freelance capacity over China.

Great title — routine film.
With *Dennis Morgan, Dane Clark, Raymond Massey, Alan Hale*

GOLDEN EARRINGS
Mitchell Leisen — U.S., 1947 [95min]
Absolutely unbelievable storyline makes you wonder why the stars got involved with this glossy but totally vacuous behind-German-lines WW2 espionage clap-trap.
With *Ray Milland, Marlene Dietrich*

THE GOLDEN HORDE
(aka 'The Golden Horde of Genghis Khan')
George Sherman — U.S., 1951 [75min]
While **Genghis Khan** is laying siege to Samarkand (c1220), the brave citizens receive aid from an English knight, Sir Guy, who somehow missed his turning on his way to **The Crusades** and ended up on the Silk Road instead. Easily done — 13th century signposting was not up to much. Sounds like

a chunk of *Monty Python and the Holy Grail* without even striving to be funny. Despite some grace-saving battle sequences, the whole thing is ludicrous bilge.

With *David Farrar, Ann Blyth, George Macready, Richard Egan*

THE GOLDEN HORDE OF GENGHIS KHAN
See **The Golden Horde**

GOLIATH AND THE BARBARIANS
(aka 'Il Terrore dei Barbari', 'The Terror of the Barbarians')
Carlo Campogalliani — Italy/U.S., 1959 [90min]

It is 568AD, and the glory that was Rome is no more. That still doesn't stop all and sundry crossing the Alps to pillage the Italian hinterland. Verona is the latest city to be sacked — again (it had already come under German rule a century earlier) — by another wave of barbarians. This time it's the Longobards (Lombards), but they get a rough time from Goliath (or Emiliano when he's at home) until even he's appeased and integrated through marriage to the invaders. Colourful comic-book history.

With *Steve Reeves, Chelo Alonso, Bruce Cabot*

GONE WITH THE WIND
Victor Fleming and George Cukor/Sam Wood — U.S., 1939 [220min]

1939 was *the* year *par excellence* for Hollywood. When Cukor was sacked for cissifying this picture too much, David O Selznick brought in Fleming off the back of the *Wizard of Oz*, and when it all got too much for him, Sam Wood from *Goodbye Mr Chips* (both films would have picked up a Best Picture Oscar in most other years). That *GWTW* walked away with most of the Academy Awards this year of all years is testament to its immortality in that capacity — but even that benchmark cannot begin to qualify what this, of all movies, means to the history of film. That it's the greatest collaboration of all aspects of filmmaking — acting, writing (F. Scott Fitzgerald had a hand in the script, as did a dozen others!) photography, design, and so on — taken in the context of its time — there is no doubt.

There is also little competition to the Rhett Butler/Scarlett O'Hara claim to be cinema's greatest love story; and it is doubtful that any other film could have been released 40 years on and been almost as popular again; *et cetera, et cetera* — its greatness can be tested on so many levels. Suffice to say, this romantic drama of a well-to-do Southern family hit by the effects of the Civil War has never been bettered as pure classy, middle-brow soap opera. As a war movie, apart from the obvious scenes such as the burning of Atlanta, the impression is that the Civil War is as much a part of the props as any of Menzies' (**Things to Come**) production designs. It is just one part of a consummate whole.

Now those Oscars: Best Picture; Best Actress (Leigh); Best Supporting Actress (McDaniel); Best Director (Fleming); Best Screenplay (Sidney Howard); Best Cinematography (Ernest Haller, Ray Rennehan); art direction; editing; and a special award to William Cameron Menzies.

GONE WITH THE WIND
Scarlett (Vivien Leigh) is awakening to the horrors of the Civil War.
Selznick/MGM (courtesy KOBAL)

Nominations were: Best Actor (Gable); Best Supporting Actress (de Havilland); score; sound; visual effects.
With *Clark Gable, Vivien Leigh, Hattie McDaniel, Leslie Howard, Olivia de Havilland, Butterfly McQueen*

GOOD MORNING, VIETNAM
Barry Levinson — U.S., 1987 [120min]
Oscar-nominated bravura performance from Williams, as the snappy DJ with the habit of rubbing up the top brass the wrong way, saves this doleful saga of 1965 Vietnam. Action is limited, romance seems contrived, and when not extemporising, even the star returns to the sentimental over-player he often becomes when he is not genuinely comic.
With *Robin Williams, Forest Whitaker, Tung Thanh Tran*

THE GOOD, THE BAD AND THE UGLY
(aka 'Il Buono, il Brutto, il Cattivo')
Sergio Leone — Italy, 1966 [180min]
The brashest and best of Leone's 'Man with no Name' trilogy which rocketed Eastwood to superstardom. This time Clint has U.S. co-stars for the first time to constitute the shabby triumvirate who squabble over buried treasure, cutting directly across the divisions of the Civil War which just happens to be going on at the time. Direct reference to the conflict develops gradually as if the infernal triangle cannot escape it any more, until the mass slaughter of soldiers of both sides in the bridge scene puts their personal rivalry into proper perspective. Visually quite brilliant, this bloody celluloid landmark to the historic West was Leone's perfect stepping stone to his marvellous *Once Upon a Time in the West*.
With *Clint Eastwood, Lee Van Cleef, Eli Wallach*

GOOSE STEP See Beasts of Berlin

GOTTERDAMMERUNG See The Damned

LE GRAAL See Lancelot du Lac

THE GRAIL See Lancelot du Lac

LE GRAND CIRQUE See The Great Circus

LE GRAND JEU (1933) See Beau Geste (1939)

LE GRAND JEU (1953)
(aka 'Card of Fate') See Beau Geste (1939)

LE GRAND RENDEZ-VOUS
Jean Dréville — France, 1949 [105min]
French intrigue in Algeria prior to the American landings in 1942. Average.
With *Véra Norman, Paula Dehelly, François Patrice*

IL GRANDE APPELO See The Great Challenge

IL GRANDE ATTACCO See The Great Battle

LA GRANDE ILLUSION
Jean Renoir — France, 1937 [115min]
Renoir claimed this masterpiece of anti-war propaganda was a true story, as it happened to him in WW1. His depiction of the POW camp and its escapees is multi-layered, however, and the title can be read as being a dream for ending other aspects of mankind's problems — race, class, religion — the causes of conflict, as much as war itself. Needless to say Göbbels banned it and supposedly arranged for all the prints in occupied Europe to be destroyed. The Italians rewarded it though, at the Venice Film Festival, before ordering its withdrawal. Still worth watching today for Renoir's handling of the assured screenplay and the outstanding acting. Nominated for a Best Picture Oscar, it remains one of cinema's great films.
With *Jean Gabin, Pierre Fresnay, Erich von Stroheim*

LA GRANDE VADROUILLE
See **Don't Look Now — We're Being Shot At**

THE GREAT BATTLE (1971) See **Liberation**

THE GREAT BATTLE (aka 'Battle Force', 'Il Grande Attacco')
Umberto Lenzi as Humphrey Longan — Germany/Yugoslavia, 1978 [95min]
Dreadful WW2 mish-mash with actors who should have known better (or those who needed the work), right down to the almost-anticipated Orson Welles narration.
With *Henry Fonda, Helmut Berger, Samantha Eggar, John Huston, Stacy Keach*

THE GREAT CHALLENGE (aka 'Il Grande Appello')
Mario Camerini — Italy, 1936
Italy's first documentary on the Abyssinian campaign takes the 'moral justification' of the invasion as its theme. This was followed by a routine propaganda piece, *The Path of the Heroes* ** by Luciano de Feo in 1937, and, eventually, a less-enthusiastic view in Karmen's 1939 *Abyssinia*.

THE GREAT CIRCUS (aka 'Le Grand Cirque')
Georges Péclet — France, 1949 [100min]
Patriotic look back by French cinema to those Free French airmen who flew from Britain after the fall of France in 1940.
With *Pierre Cressoy, Pierre Larquey*

GREAT DAY IN THE MORNING
Jacques Tourneur — U.S., 1956 [90min]
The question for citizens of Denver in 1861 was where were they going to send Colorado-mined gold — to the North or the South — in the run-up to the War of Secession. There are plenty of advisers and connivers on hand in this intelligent Western with a difference. Action is confined to the boiling over of sentiments on both sides of the separatist issue.
With *Robert Stack, Ruth Roman, Virginia Mayo, Alex Nicol, Raymond Burr*

THE GREAT DICTATOR
Charles Chaplin — U.S., 1940 [130min]
Chaplin talks and many people wish he hadn't — especially in the cringe-making climactic speech. A picture to love or to hate, it is not quintessential Chaplin, neither does it prove totally that he had the harder edge to go on to became a great filmmaker in a more sophisticated world.
Having said that, Chaplin's metamorphosis from one of the most loveable characters of the century (the little tramp) to the most hated man of the century (Hitler — caricatured here as Adenoid Hynkel) works as parody, even if it falls short of Groucho Marx's sting in **Duck Soup**. The humour and the message combine to make it a worthy example of anti-war satire.
With *Charlie Chaplin, Paulette Goddard, Jack Oakie*

THE GREAT ESCAPE
Scots celebrating the 4th of July? UA/Mirisch

THE GREAT ESCAPE

John Sturges — U.S., 1963 [175min]
The title may allude to Paul Brickhill's true story of a mass breakout from a German POW camp in WW2, but Sturges' high adventure should be taken just as it says — as a great peace of escapism. At that level it is highly enjoyable, with brisk direction, excellent colour photography, a stirring theme, and a classy trans-Atlantic cast totally upstaged by McQueen's enigmatic performance as the ungovernable 'Cooler King'.

For nit-pickers, the film may be a shade too long, and cocks a snoot at the conventional POW movies of the '50s (**Stalag 17**, **The Colditz Story**, etc). On the contrary, it is the apotheosis of those sterling but austere memoirs, bringing together all their humour and pathos, national stereotypes (even down to a 4th of July celebration), as well as personal courage and sacrifice — but shot in the mood of the confident '60s. It created a template for war movies (along with the later **The Dirty Dozen**) for many other films over the next decade or so.
With *Steve McQueen, James Garner, Richard Attenborough, James Donald, Charles Bronson, John Leyton, Gordon Jackson, David McCallum, James Coburn, Donald Pleasence, Nigel Stock*

A spin-off TV movie was made in 1988 by Paul Wendkos called *The Great Escape II: The Untold Story*, with Pleasence reincarnated as an SS officer.

THE GREAT IMPERSONATION (1921)
See **The Great Impersonation** (1935)

THE GREAT IMPERSONATION

Alan Crosland — U.S., 1935 [80min]

The second, and easily the most important, screen adaptation of the novel by E. Phillips Oppenheim, following on from George Melford's 1921 ★★ silent with James Kirkwood.

The standard story of WW1 espionage (German doppelganger adopts the role of English aristo) is solidly told, with the creepy surroundings a decided bonus.
With *Edmund Lowe, Valerie Hobson*

Remade and updated to WW2 by John Rawlins in 1942 ★★ starring Ralph Bellamy. (Gregory Ratoff's 1937 picture [80min], **Lancer Spy** ★★ with George Sanders, Dolores del Rio and Peter Lorre, told a very similar tale, as did the WW2 version, **Nazi Agent** ★ [1942 — 85min] with Conrad Veidt, directed by Jules Dassin.)

THE GREAT KING
See **Fridericus**

THE GREAT LOCOMOTIVE CHASE See **The General**

THE GREAT LOVE See **Hearts of the World**

THE GREAT SIOUX MASSACRE
See **They Died with their Boots On**

THE GREAT SIOUX UPRISING
Lloyd Bacon — U.S., 1953 [80min]
Cavalry and Indians nonsense at Fort Laramie — historical veracity nil.
With *Jeff Chandler*

THE GREAT SPY MISSION See **Operation Crossbow**

THE GREAT TURNING POINT (aka 'The Turning Point')
Friedrich Ermler — USSR, 1946
Superb re-enactment of the strategic drama that was **The Battle of Stalingrad**. Short on action, but scores top marks for atmosphere.
With *Mikhail Derxhavin, Pavel Andrievsky*

THE GREAT WALDO PEPPER
George Roy Hill — U.S., 1976 [110min]
The story of just one of the WW1 flyers who turned to stunt or flying circus work after the hostilities. John Erman's 1973 picture, **Ace Eli and Rodger of the Skies** ★★ [90min] with Cliff Robertson, was an earlier attempt to portray the same theme, but Hill's teaming up again with Redford (*Butch Cassidy and the Sundance Kid, The Sting*) makes for much better cinema. Thrilling aerial sequences, plus a telling segment involving a character closely based on Ernst Udet.
With *Robert Redford, Susan Sarandon*

A similar theme was also done way back in 1932 with George Archainbaud's all-star **The Lost Squadron** (80min — Richard Dix, Mary Astor, Erich von Stroheim, Joel McCrea).

THE GREAT WAR
Mario Monicelli — France/Italy, 1959 [120min]
What Price Glory?, Italian-style. Nothing like the class of the original though, as two Italian buddies shirk and scam their way through WW1.
With *Vittorio Gassman, Alberto Sordi*

THE GREATER GLORY
Curt Rehfeld — U.S., 1926
Life in WW1 Vienna. This lavish epic is more soap opera than war film — but even so, the conflict pervades every reel.
With *Conway Tearle, Anna Q. Nillson, Jean Hersholt*

THE GREATEST THING IN LIFE
D. W. Griffith — U.S., 1918
Another treatise on how war can change some people for the good. Otherwise the standard love sub-plot and trench battle sequences typical of WW1 Hollywood.
With *Robert Harron, Lillian Gish*

THE GREEN BERETS
Ray Kellogg/John Wayne — U.S., 1968 [140min]
Despite its box-office success, Wayne tried to superimpose WW2 and Korean War flagwaving propaganda on a theatre of war (Vietnam) he didn't understand, and serve it up for an audience he didn't understand (the younger movie-goers of the late '60s) — losing their support and sympathy into the bargain.

1968 was a watershed year in the Western world, with huge student riots in Europe and the USA, Russian tanks in Prague, and the assassinations of Bobby Kennedy and Martin Luther King. But Wayne's kind of nationalistic, jingoistic, racist heroism down the years, in countless pictures from *Stagecoach*, **The Sands of Iwo Jima**, through **The Searchers** to **The Alamo**, would not be moved an inch by such contemporary sentiments. Besides all that, the picture is not up to much as a straight actioner.
With *John Wayne, David Janssen, Jim Hutton, Aldo Ray, Bruce Cabot*

GREEN FOR DANGER
Sidney Gilliat — GB, 1946 [95min]
Classic murder mystery, with Gilliat's and Claude Guerney's script deliciously funny at times, while all the while V1 rockets are raining down on London. An indication of how normal life can be in the most extraordinary of war-time circumstances. Sim, and almost everybody else, is excellent.
With *Alastair Sim, Sally Gray, Trevor Howard, Rosamund John, Megs Jenkins, Leo Genn*

THE GREEN GODDESS (1923)
See **The Green Goddess** (1930)

THE GREEN GODDESS
Alfred E. Green — U.S., 1930 [80min]
Arliss was nominated for his role (he played it previously in the 1923 ★★ silent version) as an Indian ruler holding Brits hostage during the Raj.
With *George Arliss, Alice Joyce, H.B. Warner*

THE GREEN BERETS
Confusion in Vietnam for Aldo Ray and his group. WB/Batjac

Updated (but no more topical), as **Adventure in Iraq ★** by D. Ross Lederman in 1942, with Paul Cavanagh.

GRIEF AND PITY (aka 'La Chagrin et la Pitie')
André Harris/Marcel Ophuls — France, 1971
Damning documentary from Harris and Ophuls (son of Max), opening up a can of worms on French collaboration, even zealous anti-Semitism, during the German occupation of WW2. Banned by French TV, it found a cinema outlet and played to packed houses of '70s' generation audiences anxious to know the truth.

GUADALCANAL DIARY
Lewis Seiler — U.S., 1943 [95min]
Swift, and well-thought of, record of America's first substantial gain in WW2 — the driving out of the Japanese from Guadalcanal in 1942-43.

Strong cast (including a debut for career-long U.S. actor-soldier Jaeckel) and realistic action make it one of the better propaganda pieces emanating from Hollywood on the Pacific war.
With *Preston Foster, Lloyd Nolan, William Bendix, Richard Conte, Anthony Quinn, Richard Jaeckel*

See also **The Flying Leathernecks, The Thin Red Line (1998).**

GUERNICA
Alain Resnais — France, 1950
Resnais' famous Guernica abstract short documentary, inter-cutting newsreel of the Spanish Civil War bombings with the works of Picasso.

LA GUERRA DI TROIA See **The Trojan War**

LA GUERRE D'ALGERIE See **La Guerre sans Nom**

LA GUERRE DES BOUTONS
(aka 'The War of the Buttons')
Yves Robert — France, 1962 [90min]
War reduced to its purest form — street urchins snipping off buttons of a rival gang, with the situation escalating. All tactics and strategy — a charming little film with a grown-up message.
With *André Treton, Michel Isella*

Remade in an Irish [not sectarian] setting by John Roberts in 1993 ★★★ [90min], reuniting *Chariots of Fire* producer-writer team David Puttnam and Colin Welland and starring Gregg Fitzgerald and John Coffey). Jon Avnet's **The War** ★★ (1994, 125min) with Kevin Costner and Mare Winningham, takes the children/war allegory to a fight over a tree house.

LA GUERRE EST FINIE (aka 'The War is Over')
Alain Resnais — France/Sweden, 1966 [120min]
Unusually straightforward for Resnais, this is also his least-effective and affecting film. Montand, in exile after the Civil War in Spain, plots to overthrow Franco from Paris.
With *Yves Montand, Ingrid Thulin, Genevieve Bujold*

LA GUERRE SANS NOM (aka 'The Undeclared War')
Bertrand Tavernier — France, 1992
Over four hours long, feature filmmaker and screenwriter Tavernier has come up with the definitive documentary on the French-Algerian War (a shorter, less well-balanced newsreel with interviews was released in 1971 by Yves Courrière, called *La Guerre d'Algerie* ★★).
The nine-year 'police action' is told through the testimony of 28 French veterans and their families; although action footage is at a minimum, the human drama and the French authorities' intransigence are obvious, and the personal recollections and confessions are very moving.

LA GUERRILLA
Pierre Kast — France, 1981
Peninsular War adventure with a French aspect about a colonel of Napoleon's army in Portugal ordered to escort two ladies through the dangers of Spain. Slight plot.
With *Jean-Pierre Cassel, Agostina Belli, Alexandra Stewart*

GUERRILLA GIRL
John Christian — U.S., 1953
The Greek Civil War, which began after the Nazis were expelled in 1944, is aired for the first time by Hollywood (see also **Eleni**). An escapee from German occupation becomes a target for the communists, but — as the title suggests — the film's not up to much.
With *Helmut Dantine, Marianna*

LES GUICHETS DU LOUVRE
See **The Louvre Ticket Office**

GUILLAUME TELL See **William Tell**

THE GUN RUNNER See **Santiago**

THE GUN RUNNERS See **To Have and Have Not**

THE GUN THAT WON THE WEST
William Castle — U.S., 1955 [70min]
Not the Winchester, but the Springfield, that is. Hokey tale of Indian scout Jim Bridger, Chief Red Cloud's Sioux and the Cavalry with their new toys.
With *Dennis Morgan*

GUNG HO!
Ray Enright — U.S., 1943 [90min]
Time for the Marines to do their bit in this training and action flagwaver which takes place up to and including the U.S. raid on Makin Island (Gilbert Islands) in August 1942. Scott plays the colonel who commanded the raid — Evans F. Carlson — who apparently based his training for the new 2nd Marine Raider Battalion on the Royal Marine Commandos, and acted as advisor on the film. This was Mitchum's 17th and last acting credit in 1943-released pictures — his first year in the movies! Little wonder he always looks burned out.
With *Randolph Scott, Grace MacDonald, Alan Curtis, Noah Beery Jr, J. Carroll Naish, Robert Mitchum*

GUNGA DIN
George Stevens — U.S., 1939 [115min]
One of the best action adventure yarns to hit the screen — ever. Based on the water-carrier of Kipling's poem, Ben Hecht and others developed the story into one of heroism and loyalty (condescending and racially-biased, actually) to the British Raj, as things begin to turn bad on the North-West Frontier.
Wonderful performances from the three rogue NCOs who seem to be enjoying themselves immensely (unlike the *over*-indulgence of Messrs Sinatra, Lawford and Martin in John Sturges' shoddy 1961 remake, **Sergeants Three** ★★ [110min], set in the U.S. Army shortly after the Civil War), and Stevens' handling of the battle shots is exemplary. A real ripping yarn!
With *Cary Grant, Victor MacLaglen, Douglas Fairbanks Jr, Joan Fontaine, Sam Jaffe*

THE GUNS AND THE FURY
Tony Zarindast — U.S., 1981 [100min]
A travesty of history and of cinema. With a promising scenario of the Brits and Russians squabbling over oil rights in 1908 Persia (which they did, albeit diplomatically), the film introduces all kinds of laughable outside elements — U.S. mercenaries, a Raj overspill and marauding Cossacks. One for the shredder.
With *Peter Graves, Albert Salmi, Cameron Mitchell*

THE GUNS OF FORT PETTICOAT
George Marshall — U.S., 1957 [80min]
Murphy vehicle where, during the Civil War, he trains the women of a Texas town, drained by the war of its menfolk, to fight off a band of outraged Cheyenne and Arapaho who were somewhat miffed at being massacred at Sand Creek in 1864. A sort of 'package' Western, which hopes it will have something of interest for everyone — except that it doesn't.
With *Audie Murphy, Kathryn Grant*

THE GUNS OF LOOS
See **The Burgomaster of Stilemonde**

THE GUNS OF NAVARONE
J. Lee(-) Thompson — GB/U.S., 1961 [155min]
Without doubt the highlight of Thompson's directorial career; he works wonders with Carl Foreman's worthy but wordy

GUNGA DIN
'Play it again, Sam', says Sgt Cutter (Grant) to Gunga (Jaffe)! RKO

script, which sometimes seems to slow down the action like a dropped anchor. As it is, there is action to spare in this fantastic (in the proper sense of the word) WW2 adventure based on an Alistair MacLean best-seller.

British commandos and Greek patriots must knock out a giant pair of guns which dominate that part of the Aegean where British troopships will shortly have to pass. It was to preface a series of MacLean adaptations in the '60s and '70s (**Where Eagles Dare**, *Ice Station Zebra, Bear Island*, etc). Won an Oscar for Best Visual Effects and nominations for picture; Thompson; Foreman; Dimitri Tiomkin (score); editing; and sound.
With *Gregory Peck, David Niven, Anthony Quinn, Anthony Quayle, Stanley Baker, Irene Papas, James Darren, James Robertson Justice, Richard Harris*

Crudely sequelled in 1978 as **Force Ten from Navarone ★** by Guy Hamilton (120min — Starring Harrison Ford, with Robert Shaw as Peck's character, Capt Mallory, and Edward Fox — its only highlight — as the reincarnation of Niven's Cpl Miller). Vastly inferior fare involving duplicitous Chetniks and the destruction of a bridge in German-occupied Yugoslavia.

A GUY NAMED JOE
Victor Fleming — U.S., 1944 [120min]
A big box-office hit of its day (Spielberg redid it with fire-fighters in *Always* [1989], with Richard Dreyfuss and Holly Hunter), this story of a WW2 pilot who is shot down and dies, but returns as a ghost to inspire Johnson, brings the wrong sort of lump to one's throat today. Dripping with sentimentality and oozing with pro-American propaganda (the war was just about being won), the picture can only be worth watching (through narrowly-splayed fingers) for some of Dalton's wittier dialogue spoken by the phantasmal Tracy. David Boehm and Chandler Sprague were nominated for the original story.
With *Spencer Tracy, Irene Dunne, Van Johnson, Ward Bond, Lionel Barrymore, James Gleason*

HAIL THE CONQUERING HERO
Preston Sturges — U.S., 1944 [100min]
One of Sturges' last top-notch gentle satires, and one of WW2's favourite pictures. Poking fun at all that small-town America holds dear, he tells the tale of an army failure who, unable to face his folks, makes up a story that he is, in fact, a hero.

A typical Sturges admixture of verbal and visual gags, the satire blending into farce and back, with his stock company of actors creating controlled chaos, he proves once again (after *The Great McGinty, Sullivan's Travels, The Miracle of Morgan's Creek* and others) that he was definitely one of a kind.
With *Eddie Bracken, Ella Raines, William Demarest, Raymond Walburn, Franklin Pangborn, Bill Edwards, Elizabeth Patterson*

HALFWAY TO SHANGHAI
John Rawlins — U.S., 1942 [60min]
Spy-on-a-train suspenser trundles through pre-Pearl Harbor Burma. Weak.
With *Kent Tyler, Irene Hervey*

THE HALLS OF MONTEZUMA
Lewis Milestone — U.S., 1950 [115min]
The enigmatic Milestone, to this time, had made several excellent war pictures — from the sublime **All Quiet on the Western Front** to the thoughtful **A Walk in the Sun**. Intermingled with these have been poor efforts — **Arch of Triumph** and **The North Star** being two. Although not as bad as the latter two, this brutal movie of the Marines trying to discover the whereabouts of a Japanese rocket site in the Pacific does not belong to the top group either.

Thankfully it does have the steady Widmark in the lead (helped here by some pill-popping), as Palance goes bananas and everyone else has varying degrees of the heebie-jeebies. At this date filmmakers benefited from the availability of plentiful authentic WW2 hardware.
With *Richard Widmark, Jack Palance, Robert Wagner, Karl Malden, Richard Boone, Jack Webb, Neville Brand*

HAMBURGER HILL
John Irvin — U.S., 1987 [110min]
Evoking memories of Milestone's **Pork Chop Hill** (not just for the barbecue-type titles!), Irvin tells his true story of the attack on Ap Bia hill in Vietnam's notorious A Shau valley in May 1969 in the style of 30 years before.

Without the extra dimensions offered by pictures such as **Apocalypse Now** or **The Deer Hunter**, or the near-contemporaneous **Platoon** and **Full Metal Jacket** (which, some may argue, is no bad thing) this is still a powerful war movie, getting under the skin of the combatants as they inch excruciatingly to the target's summit. Little reference is made to the socio-political background, or if it is, it is drowned by its most infuriating fault — the jargon- and obscenity-littered dialogue. Good job done by an ensemble cast of unknowns, all the same.
With *Anthony Barrile, Michael Boatman, Don Cheadle*

HANGMEN ALSO DIE! (aka 'Lest We Forget')
Fritz Lang — U.S., 1943 [130min]
Bertold Brecht was bitterly disappointed with the outcome of this picture after working on the script originally with Lang. It tells the story of the assassination of Hitler's governor in Prague, Reinhard Heydrich, in May 1942, and the reprisal atrocities in the city (and, although not covered by this film, in the village of Lidice the following month).

Lang probably felt somewhat dissatisfied too, when comparing it with some of his impressive œuvre to date (*Metropolis*, **Man Hunt**, etc) but the dialogue is far better than the normal WW2 propaganda fare usually throws up, with typically Brechtian interludes of pedantry, and James Wong Howe's cinematography is broodingly magnificent.
With *Brian Donlevy, Walter Brennan, Anna Lee, Gene Lockhart, Hans von Twardowski*

Other pictures featuring the assassination of Heydrich and its repercussions include:
Hitler's Hangman ★★ (aka 'Hitler's Madman') (Douglas Sirk — U.S., 1943, 185min) With *Patricia Morrison, John Carradine*
The Silent Village See separate entry
Hostages ★ (Frank Tuttle — U.S., 1943, 190min) With *Arturo de Cordova, Luise Rainer*
A Higher Principle ★★★ (aka 'Vyssi Princip') (Jirí Krejcík — Czechoslovakia, 1960) With *Frantisek Smolik*
Assassination ★★★ (aka 'Atentat') (Jiri Sequens — Czechoslovakia, 1964*)* With *Radoslav Brzobohaty, Jirí Kodet*
Operation Daybreak ★★ (Lewis Gilbert — U.S., 1975, 120min) With *Timothy Bottoms, Martin Shaw*

HANNA'S WAR
Menahem Golan — U.S., 1988 [150min]
Routinely heavy and hammy Golan-Globus production, which is a shame, for the true story of Hanna Senesh — a Jewess working for British intelligence, dropping into the Balkans, getting caught, tortured and executed — is surely one worth telling. Good performances by Detmers and Pleasence's now typecast nasty-Nazi leave a talented cast scrabbling for scraps.
With *Maruschka Detmers, Ellen Burstyn, Anthony Andrews, Donald Pleasence, David Warner*

HANNIBAL
Carlo Ludovico Bragaglia — Italy, 1959 [105min]
Sword-and-sandal nonsense with little to do with the Punic Wars, apart from Hannibal crossing the Alps.
With *Victor Mature, Rita Gam*

The equally-unappealing **Carthage in Flames ★** (Carmine Gallone, 1960, with Anne Heywood) didn't even get Mature. Gallone did release one remarkable propagandist picture on Rome's African conquest, however — see **Scipio Africanus**.

HANNIBAL BROOKS
Michael Winner — GB, 1968 [100min]
Silly nonsense of allied POWs escaping over the Alps from Germany with an elephant from Munich Zoo. Talented director and stars on their way to careers of mediocrity.
With *Oliver Reed, Michael J. Pollard*

THE HANOI HILTON
Lionel Chetwynd — U.S., 1987 [130min]
One of a clutch of Vietnam War films to be released, seemingly after the success of **Platoon**, in the late '80s. This is a standard POW-picture stuff, though, with only the sophistication of the torturing giving a clue as to which war we're actually in.
With *Michael Moriarty, Jeffrey Jones, Paul La Mat, Lawrence Pressman*

HANOVER STREET
Peter Hyams — GB, 1979 [110min]
Ford, uncertainly between his first Han Solo and Indiana Jones parts, tried to keep his options open by playing the Robert Taylor role in almost another remake of **Waterloo Bridge**. He was certainly happy to know George Lucas at the time, because this diversion was *not* a good choice — a farrago of a brief encounter in war-torn, spy-ridden London in 1943 — but the Empire was just about to strike back, and **Raiders of the Lost Ark** would soon put him on the straight and narrow.
With *Harrison Ford, Lesley-Anne Down, Christopher Plummer, Alec McCowen*

HANS WESTMAR
Franz Wenzler — Germany, 1933
The best of the Nazism v Communism propaganda vehicles of the new Third Reich released in 1933 (Franz Seitz's **SA-Mann Brandt ★★** and Hans Steinhoff's **Hitlerjunge Quex ★★** — glorifying the Hitler Youth — were others). It begins by telling the story of Horst Wessel, the composer whose name stuck to the Nazi anthem *Die Fahne Hoch*, then focuses on Westmar, who becomes a martyr to the cause, having been gunned down by the pernicious communists.
With *Emil Lohkamp, Carla Bartheel*

HANUSSEN See **Colonel Redl**

HARA KIRI See **The Battle**

HAVANA
Sydney Pollack — U.S., 1990 [145min]
Richard Lester's **Cuba**, in long-winded '90s-style, but no more relevant to events in 1959 than the Connery vehicle. Redford plays a gambler in the last hours of decadence before Castro kicks them all out. Nominated for Dave Grusin's score.
With *Robert Redford, Lina Olin, Alan Arkin, Raul Julia*

HE RIJUN ZAI LAI
See **Au Revoir, Mon Amour**

HEART OF A HERO
Emile Chautard — U.S., 1916
The tale of American patriot Nathan Hale, who spied for the rebels and was hanged by the British in 1776. Patriotic fervour whipped up in readiness for what most Americans saw was inevitable — their entry into WW1.
With *Robert Warwick*

HEART OF A NATION (aka 'Untel Père et Fils')
Julien Duvivier — France, 1940 [110min]
Historical drama centring on a Paris family from the Franco-Prussian War, through WW1, to 1939. Banned by the occupying Germans who walked in just as the film was finished, it was later released out of America. Pays some attention to the historical detail as well as conveying the sense of foreboding the French must have felt entering WW2.
With *Louis Jouvet, Michèle Morgan, Raimu*

HEART OF HIROSHIMA
(aka 'Ai to Shi no Kioku') See **Hiroshima**

HEART OF HUMANITY
Allen Holubar — U.S., 1918
Holubar's respected anti-war tract may be best remembered for von Stroheim's portrayal of the archetypal cinema Hun of WW1, in this story of a Canadian husband (flyer) and wife (nurse), witnessing atrocities in France.
With *Dorothy Phillips, William Stowell, Walt Whitman, Erich von Stroheim*

HEARTBREAK
Alfred Werker — U.S., 1931
Far-fetched flying drama from WW1, involving a U.S. pilot's love for an Austrian aristocrat, his desertion of duty to be with her, and the predictable consequences.
With *Charles Farrell, Madge Evans*

HEARTBREAK RIDGE
Clint Eastwood — U.S., 1986 [130min]
Grizzly Vietnam vet Eastwood trains up a motley crew of disaffected American youth and gets an unexpected chance for a last piece of action when they invade Grenada. Very short on originality (see **The Dirty Dozen**), it is also devoid of any perceivable message (Eastwood seems ambivalent over America's stance on Grenada). That may not be a bad thing — and anyway, it is an Eastwood film, and as always the human character is to the fore. Despite the embarrassingly feeble opposition in the one-sided Grenada operation, Clint brings to his own role (his best performance in years) the double-edged sword of macho heroism and ageing vulnerability. Oscar-nominated for sound, not even close for anything else.
With *Clint Eastwood, Marsha Mason, Everett McGill*

HEARTS AND ARMOUR
Giacomo Battiato — Italy, 1982 [100min]
Huge liberties are taken with Ariosto's 1516 epic poem *Orlando Furioso*, ending up with no more than a sword-and-sorcery vehicle for Amazon Roberts, for whom this genre was quite kind in the early '80s (eg *Beastmaster*).

Battles form part of Charlemagne's campaign against the Moors in the late 8th century. See also **La Chanson de Roland**.
With *Tanya Roberts, Barbara de Rossi, Rick Edwards, Leigh McCloskey*

HEARTS AND MINDS
Peter Davis — U.S., 1974
Simplistic Vietnam War documentary with the messages coming from old Hollywood war pics as much as newsreel and narration. Rather surprisingly collected an Oscar.

HEARTS IN BONDAGE
Lew Ayres — U.S., 1936
Weak romantic drama against a canvas of the American Civil War's first naval battle (Hampton Roads). Taking a sunken wooden steamship, the *Merrimac*, the Confederates renamed her *Virginia*, clad her with iron and rigged her with guns and sent her into Chesapeake Bay. On 8-9 March 1862 she rammed and sank the *Cumberland* and confronted the *Monitor*, an iron-clad turret ship, before retiring with honours more than even (just 10 dead to the Yankees' 260). Ayres, who will always be best remembered for his starring role in **All Quiet on the Western Front** six years earlier, re-enacted the battle with models.
With *James Dunn, Mae Clarke, David Manners*

Remade for TV by Ted Turner's company in 1991 as *Ironsides* — directed by Delbert Mann and starring Virginia Madsen, E.G. Marshall and Alex Hyde-White — it was an equal yawn, though with the higher production values of the '90s.

HEARTS OF THE WORLD
D.W. Griffith — GB/U.S., 1918 [80min]
In London for the British premiere of **Intolerance**, Griffith was approached by the War Office to produce a WW1 propaganda drama in Britain. In the end he did better than that, for this tale of romance against the harsh environment of the front line was shot mostly on location close to the Front in France. Sadly, the sentimentality of the personal relationship swamps a promising project.
With *Lillian Gish, Robert Harron, Dorothy Gish*

HEARTBEAK RIDGE
Team photo after the biggest mis-match in U.S. military history.
WB/Malpaso

Griffith went on to make a further 'British' production (using much of the same, or unused, footage) later that year in **The Great Love,** with L. Gish and Harron again, and was even more sugary.

HEAVEN AND EARTH
Oliver Stone — U.S., 1993 [140min]

Stone ended his ambitious Vietnam trilogy (**Platoon, Born on the Fourth of July**) on a low note. The concept is laudable (taking the life of a young girl [Hiep Thi Le] in the French Indochina of 1953; through American involvement in Vietnam in the mid-60s; to marrying a Marine and leaving for a new life in America), but the execution is overlong and over-sentimental. As if there wasn't enough storyline, Stone builds in another plot — that of the war-affected GI (where have we heard that before?) — which actually takes over the second half of the movie, and leaves the audience wondering whether the peasant girl story was not just an extended prologue.

With *Tommy Lee Jones, Joan Cheng, Haing S. Ngor, Hiep Thi Le*

HEAVEN, HELL AND HOBOKEN
See **I Was Monty's Double**

HEAVEN KNOWS, MR ALLISON
John Huston — U.S., 1957 [105min]

Inadvertently left behind on a Pacific island, a nun first bumps into a Marine washed up when his submarine fails to rendezvous, then into a bunch of Japanese intent on invasion. This daft story was well-liked at the time and earned Kerr a nomination, and — yes — also for Huston's and John Lee Mahin's screenplay.

With *Robert Mitchum, Deborah Kerr*

HEDD WYN
Paul Turner — GB, 1992 [125min]

Trivia question: What is the only British film to be nominated for a Best Foreign Language Film Oscar? Yes, *Hedd Wyn*. It's the pseudonym of Welsh WW1 poet Ellis Evans, who was killed on the first day of Passchendale (9 October 1917), and whose poem of life and death in the trenches posthumously won him his lifetime ambition — the (bardic) Chair at the Welsh National Eisteddfod. (See also **Regeneration**.)

With *Huw Garmon, Sue Roderick, Catrin Fychan, Judith Humphreys*

HEIMAT (aka 'Homeland')
Edgar Reitz — West Germany, 1984 [925min]

Made as a serial for TV, this also had a 15-hour theatre release. Sometimes you *do* wonder whether you are watching in real time as this epic soap opera wanders oh-so-slowly from 1919 to 1980, but at other times it is riveting.

   The period detail is beautifully captured as the story stops off at the rise of Hitler, and then WW2, before revving up again to jump a few more years. One to dip into from time to time but an effort to sit right through.

With *Marita Breuer, Dieter Schaad, Michael Lesch, Karin Kienzler*

HEIMKEHR (aka 'Homecoming')
Gustav Ucicky — Germany/Austria, 1941

Providing the propaganda for the invasion of Poland, Ucicky (**Morgenrot**) tells of atrocities carried out in Poland before the War on German nationals.

With *Paula Wesseley, Peter Retersen*

HEAVEN AND EARTH
Le Ly (Hiep Thi Le) is blindfolded and led away.
WB/Regency/Canal/Alcor

HELD BY THE ENEMY
Donald Crisp — U.S., 1920

Crisp as a director dabbled in a few silents, notably **The Mark of Zorro** in 1922, but it was as a character actor in such classics as **The Birth of a Nation, The Dawn Patrol**, *Wuthering Heights* and especially *How Green was my Valley* that he will be best remembered. Nevertheless this Civil War picture is well-blessed with quality action sequences and is an interesting study of the conflict.

With *Lewis Stone, Jack Holt*

HELEN OF TROY See **The Trojan War**

HELL AND HIGH WATER
Samuel Fuller — U.S., 1954 [105min]

Always quick into action, Fuller is very fast on to a potential WW3 scenario here with a Chinese submarine being tracked to the Arctic by a maverick international crew and prevented from shooting down a nuke-bearing U.S. bomber in the Korean War.

   Lots of trademark Fuller camera work (his use of Cinemascope in the confines of a sweaty sub says it all), but the net effect is a bleak, pessimistic picture.

With *Richard Widmark, Bella Darvi, Cameron Mitchell, Victor Francen, David Wayne*

HELL BELOW
Jack Conway — U.S., 1933 [105min]

WW1 submarine heroics in the Mediterranean — better than many of WW2 and later vintage undersea drama-adventures, with a solid cast.

With *Robert Montgomery, Water Huston, Madge Evans, Jimmy Durante, Robert Young*

HELL BENT FOR GLORY
See **Lafayette Escadrille**

HELL BOATS
Paul Wendkos — GB, 1970
Late addition to films of the WW2 Mediterranean War theatre, but **The Malta Story** had already been told, and compared to **Patton** of the same cinematic vintage, this was not in the same class as the George C. Scott *tour-de-force*.
With *James Franciscus, Elizabeth Shepherd, Ronald Allen*

HELL IN KOREA
See **A Hill in Korea**

HELL IN THE HEAVENS
John Blystone — U.S., 1934 [80min]
A surplus-to-requirements WW1 air war drama based in France before the Americans came in. Baxter joins the French Flying Corps as a volunteer and routinely gets the girl and the Prussian star fighter-pilot.
With *Warner Baxter*

HELL IN THE PACIFIC
John Boorman — U.S., 1968 [105min]
Only Boorman's third film after *Catch Us If You Can* (with the Dave Clark Five — remember them?) and a (then) seemingly incongruous follow-up, the classic *Point Blank*, where he first teamed up with Marvin. Here real life Pacific veteran Marvin pits his acting and character against the marvellous Mifune, and like the picture, he comes out even.

The two-hander is based, except for the aforementioned American and Japanese antagonists, on a deserted island in WW2. From the originality of the scenario, with its built-in conventions of suspicion and curiosity, the film gradually descends into allegory, and there is a sense of unfulfilment — especially with the unsatisfactory ending.
With *Lee Marvin, Toshiro Mifune*

HELL IS FOR HEROES
Don Siegel — U.S., 1962 [90min]
Tough anti-war picture with McQueen giving the best acting performance of his career as the recalcitrant GI busted back to private. Basically a one-set drama (until the last brutal action scene) airing the tensions and belly-aching that go on when seemingly all the odds are against survival: a few men have been left to defend a section of the Siegfried Line — usually the role of a full company. Despite all the vitriol, McQueen and the rest die like heroes.
With *Steve McQueen, Bobby Darin, Fess Parker, Bob Newhart, James Coburn*

HELL BOATS
German E-Boat patrolling off Malta. UA/Oakmont

HELL TO ETERNITY
Hand-to-hand combat at Saipan in 1944. Allied Artists/Atlantic

HELL SQUAD
Bert Topper — U.S., 1958
Second-feature actioner taking place between U.S. and German troops in WW2 North Africa. Poor.
With *Wally Campo, Brendon Carroll*

HELL TO ETERNITY
Phil Karlson — U.S., 1960 [130min]
Good action scenes, including landings on Saipan during WW2, rescue this true-story morality drama. Hunter is the orphan kid brought up by Japanese-Americans (*Nisei*), only to be called upon by his country to use his knowledge of Japanese as a war weapon.
With *Jeffrey Hunter, David Janssen, Vic Damone*

HELLCATS OF THE NAVY
Nathan Juran — U.S., 1957 [80min]
This cliché-riddled submarine drama in the Pacific during WW2 is pretty dire fare. Remembered only as the sole professional outing for Mr and Mrs Reagan together.
With *Ronald Reagan, Nancy Davis, Arthur Franz, Robert Arthur*

HELL'S ANGELS
Howard Hughes — U.S., 1930 [135min]
Forget the plot — whatever there is of one. Just sit back and watch one of the most exciting aerial war pictures ever made. Hughes was no doubt miffed that Bill Wellman had beaten him to the punch with **Wings** when he began work on the picture as a silent in 1927. He then spent, for the time, a veritable fortune (some say $4m) to upgrade it to a talkie and was rewarded with a movie which has action scenes which will probably, of their type, never be beaten. Set in WW1, the RFC takes on Zeppelins, von Richthofen and anything else the Hun can throw at them in excitingly-staged dogfights and bombing raids (especially the ones over London). And, of course, it has the dazzling debut of the 18 year-old Harlow. Unsurprisingly, the camerawork of Tony Gaudio, Harry Perry and E. Burton Steene received an Academy Award nomination.
With *Ben Lyon, Jean Harlow, James Hall, John Darrow, Lucien Prival*

HELL'S HORIZON
Tom Gries — U.S., 1955 [80min]
Standard action drama of a single bomber raid in the Korean conflict, with no redeeming features.
With *John Ireland*

HELL'S ISLAND See **Beau Geste** (1939)

HENNESSY (aka 'The 5th of November')
Don Sharp — GB, 1975 [105min]
Shameful exploitation of the Irish troubles. Steiger loses his family in the crossfire during an ambush in Northern Ireland, but we are not allowed to know the whys and wherefores. He then plots to blow up the State Opening of Parliament (hence the alternate title), when of course the Queen would be present, and is pursued by both Special Branch and the IRA. Not even exciting, and a criminal misuse of top acting talent.
With *Rod Steiger, Lee Remick, Richard Johnson, Trevor Howard, Eric Porter, Peter Egan*

HENRY V
Laurence Olivier — GB, 1944 [135min]
One of only a few pictures made in Britain in 1944, this more than made up for the lack of quantity. As blousy and as subtle a piece of propaganda as was ever devised, Olivier's directorial debut in literally delivering the Bard's most heroic work to the screen (he moves it from a 1603 Globe Theatre performance, through gradually more-realistic scenes, to the crescendo of the Agincourt killing fields) is an unqualified triumph.

The 1415 battle scene itself is superbly staged, William Walton's music unforgettable, and the cast, made up of classical and movie actors, all do their bit. Olivier was nominated for his acting, along with the score and art direction. The picture was also nominated, but as if to say to Olivier, 'You haven't won anything, but we think you ought to have', the Academy presented him with a Special Oscar. It is still considered one of the best translations of Shakespeare's works onto the big screen.
With *Laurence Olivier, Robert Newton, Leslie Banks, Esmond Knight, George Robey, Leo Genn, Renée Asherson, Valentine Dyall, John Laurie*

In 1989 [135min], Kenneth Branagh took on the Olivier director/star mantle for his decidedly anti-war remake. While not trying to emulate the pomp and pageant of the original, he manages to produce a brutal, but equally-intelligent picture.

By using flashbacks to *Henry IV, Part 1*, we see the young prince gradually growing into the role of Warrior King, and the whole concept is more personal and less grandiose a venture. Again, the cast here is outstanding.
With *Kenneth Branagh, Brian Blessed, Richard Briers, Robbie Coltrane, Judi Dench, Ian Holm, Derek Jacobi, Paul Scofield, Robert Stephens, Emma Thompson*

HENRY V (1989) See **Henry V** (1944)

THE HEROES
Duccio Tessari — France/Italy/Spain, 1972 [110min]
Appalling sub-**Kelly's Heroes** bunk set in the North African desert in WW2. A truce between the Allies and the Germans is called to look for a missing £2m. Steiger and others in free-fall.
With *Rod Steiger, Rosanna Schiaffino, Rod Taylor, Terry-Thomas*

THE HEROES OF TELEMARK
Anthony Mann — GB, 1965 [130min]
Mann's earnest and often exciting story of Norwegian partisans and Allied commandos attacking a Nazi 'heavy water' plant in WW2 is a worthy dramatisation of a true event. It still cannot compete, however, with the Franco-German semi-documentary on the same subject, **The Battle for Heavy Water**.
With *Kirk Douglas, Richard Harris, Ulla Jacobsen, Roy Dotrice, Michael Redgrave, Anton Diffring*

THE HEROES OF THE ALAMO see **The Alamo**

HEROISM See **Eroica**

HET MEISJE MET HET RODE HAAR
See **The Girl with the Red Hair**

HIAWATHA
Kurt Neumann — U.S., 1952 [80min]
Semi-legendary story (there is enough historical evidence to suggest that Hiawatha existed) of the late 16th century Native American who united the Iroquois tribes, which were, individually, easy pickings for the powerful Algonquin nation. Low-budget and it shows.
With *Vince(nt) Edwards*

HIDDEN AGENDA
Ken Loach — GB, 1990 [110min]
Loach (temporarily) leaves a quarter of a century of social turmoil in England to impose his impressive, if sometimes lecturing, documentary-style of filmmaking on the Ulster troubles — a very suitable subject. What comes out is typically thought-provoking stuff, as Cox (John Stalker-like) leads an enquiry into the Security Forces' killing of an American observer. Whatever else, Loach puts his finger on one thing — making a film about the troubles is as complex as the troubles itself. Powerful drama, based on shreds of fact, it picked up the Jury Prize at Cannes.
With *Frances MacDormand, Brian Cox, Brad Dourif, Mai Zetterling, Maurice Roëves*

THE HIDDEN FORTRESS
(aka 'Kakushi Toride no San-Akunin')
Akira Kurosawa — Japan, 1958 [125min]
Finding the exact historical context for many Japanese feudal war dramas is not always possible, the political and cultural homogeneity of the millennium between 900 and 1900 sees to that. But this Kurosawa traditional (yet almost Fordian in its sweep) samurai action drama is definitely 16th century — the 'Epoch of a Warring Country', as Japanese history describes it. It was the time of civil war between the Ashikaga shoguns, who virtually controlled the emperors and their succession, and upstart feudal lords (daimyo). The faithful samurai Mifune, he of most of Kurosawa's middle-period masterpieces (*Rashomon, Seven Samurai*, **Throne of Blood**), chaperones an

THE HEROES OF TELEMARK
Much off-piste trouble for Kirk Dougla. Rank/Benton

imperial princess across enemy country confronting all kinds of hazards along the way. Sparkling work from the director — if not quite up there with his absolute best.
With *Toshiro Mifune, Misa Uehara, Takashi Shimura*

HIDEG NAPOK See **Cold Days**

THE HIDING PLACE
James F. Collier — U.S., 1974 [145min]
Limp biopic of Corrie and Betsy ten Boss, sisters who helped Jews escape from German-occupied Holland in WW2, and were sent to a concentration camp for their pains.
With *Julie Harris, Eileen Heckart, Arthur O'Connell, Jeannette Clift*

HIGH BOOT BENNY
Joe Comerford — Ireland, 1993 [80min]
Unusual, but no less pessimistic, insight into the Irish troubles. Set on the border between north and south in the present day, a social outcast youth, pacified by his non-aligned school surroundings, erupts on the death of the caretaker.
　The allegorical outcome means that the 'outsider' has no idea of who's to blame so, to find out, he questions everybody from the IRA to the Loyalist paramilitaries along the spectrum including the British Army and the RUC along the way. Dark and disturbing.
With *Frances Tomelty, Alan Devlin*

THE HIGH BRIGHT SUN (aka 'McGuire Go Home')
Ralph Thomas — GB, 1965 [115min]
Love amongst the politics of 1957 Cyprus makes a mockery of a sad period in history for the island and Britain. Bogarde is the British officer trying to stop the EOKA guerillas, but romance gets in the way. A shabby way to treat a serious subject.
With *Dirk Bogarde, Susan Strasberg, George Chakiris, Denholm Elliott*

HIGH BRIGHT SUN
George Chakiris (right) makes a break from EOKA gunmen to save
Susan Strasberg. Rank

HIGH TREASON

Maurice Elvey — GB, 1929 [90min]
At the time when filmmakers were pausing for breath and considering pacification and international brotherhood, Gaumont's first full talkie was not a startling piece of cinema — in fact, technically, it was quite amateurish — but it is interesting nonetheless. Projecting forward to 1940, it predicts another world war (c/f **Things to Come**), predicting attempts by women to stop wars, and the building of the Channel Tunnel (among other things).
With *Jameson Thomas, Benita Hume*

A HIGHER PRINCIPLE

(aka 'Vyssi Princip') See **Hangmen also Die**

THE HIGHEST HONOUR — A TRUE STORY

See **Southern Cross**

THE HILL

Sidney Lumet — GB, 1965 [120min]
A POW movie with a difference. Set in a British detention camp for errant squaddies in the North African desert in WW2, this was Lumet's third thought-provoking war movie within a year or so (**Fail Safe**, **The Pawnbroker**). The title refers to the ordeal of climbing the artificial 'hill' of sand for the slightest of misdemeanours, this symbol of punishment becoming more demoralizing and dehumanising each time it's tackled. Shot in stark monochrome by Oswald Morris (who won a BAFTA award for it). Sadistic guards and a rough, tough, unlovable bunch of inmates make it a sometimes distasteful, but entirely watchable, film.

With *Sean Connery, Harry Andrews, Michael Redgrave, Ian Hendry, Alfred Lynch, Ian Bannen, Roy Kinnear, Ossie Davis, Jack Watson*

A HILL IN KOREA

(aka 'Hell in Korea')
Julian Amyes — GB, 1956 [80min]
Low-budget picture whose title, and alternative title, say it all, and about as exciting. Almost an apology from the British film industry for its general non-participation in the Korean War film genre.

Interesting for an early appearance by Michael Caine, who in real life had fought in Korea as an infantryman with the Royal Fusiliers. Couple of good Bakers on set though!
With *George Baker, Stanley Baker, Harry Andrews, Michael Medwin*

HILL OF DEATH (aka 'Kozara')

Veljko Bulajic — Yugoslavia, 1962
Action-packed resistance drama of WW2, with Tito's partisans defending the mountain village of Kozara from a large force of Germans. Exciting.
With *Bert Sotlar, Olivera Markovic, Milena Dravic*

HILL 24 DOESN'T ANSWER

Thorold Dickinson — Israel, 1954 [100min]
British director Dickinson (*The Arsenal Stadium Mystery, Gaslight,* etc) was at the helm for what was to be the first feature film to be produced by the fledgling Israel. Centring on the story of four soldiers during the 1948 Arab War, it recounts (not always convincingly) the historic events leading to the formation of the Jewish state.
With *Edward Mulhare, Haya Harareet, Michael Wager*

HIROSHIMA

Hideo Sekigawa — Japan, 1953
A spectacular and vitriolic anti-American piece of propaganda centred on the dropping, and the after-effects on Japan and its people, of the atomic bomb. (Supported by the Japanese Teachers' Union after their sponsored project. **Children of Hiroshima** [*see below*], (didn't have the political teeth they desired.)
With *Yoshi Katch, Eiji Okada, Isuzu Yamada*

There have been several pictures, both feature films and documentaries made about the dropping of the first A-Bomb and/or its effects: Some others include:
Children of Hiroshima ★★ (aka 'Genbaku No Ko', 'Children of the Atom Bomb' — Kaneto Shindo, Japan, 1953)
With *Mobuko Otowa and Niwa Saito*
Shadow of Hiroshima ★★ (Hiroshi Teshigahara — Japan, 1956)
Hiroshima, Mon Amour See separate entry
A Night to Remember ★★★ (aka 'Sono yo wa Wasurenai',

'Hiroshima Heartache' — Kozaburo Yoshimura, Japan, 1962)
Heart of Hiroshima ** (aka 'Ai to Shi no Kiruko' — Koreyoshi Kurahara, Japan, 1966) With *Tetsuya Watari, Sayuri Yoshinaga*
Hiroshima — Remembering and Repressing *** (aka 'Hiroshima — Erinnern und Verdrängen' — Erwin Leiser, Switzerland, 1986)
Hiroshima: Out of the Ashes ** (Peter Werner — U.S., 1990, 100min) With *Max von Sydow, Judd Nelson.* Initially for TV.

HIROSHIMA — ERINNERN UND VERDRÄNGEN
See **Hiroshima — Remembering and Repressing**

HIROSHIMA HEARTACHE See **A Night to Remember**

HIROSHIMA, MON AMOUR
Alain Resnais — France/Japan, 1959 [90min]
A cinematic experience — and a half. Resnais' first dramatic feature following on from such landmark documentaries as **Guernica** and **Nuit et Brouillard** given extra impetus by an Oscar-nominated Margarite Duras script, and is not everyone's cup of tea: it's complex, and at times convolutedly so. But the intertwining themes, involving French actress Riva in a flashback love story, and fraternisation with the Germans in WW2 occupied France; the short, torrid romance she has in Hiroshima just after the war; and the symbolism of the bomb, will reward audience patience on a second, and even a third, viewing. (See also **Hiroshima**.)
With *Emmanuele Riva, Eiji Okada*

HIROSHIMA: OUT OF THE ASHES See **Hiroshima**

HIROSHIMA — REMEMBERING AND REPRESSING
(aka 'Hiroshima — Erinnern und Verdrängen')
See **Hiroshima**

HITLER See **The Hitler Gang**

HITLER, A FILM FROM GERMANY (aka 'Our Hitler')
Hans-Jurgen Syberberg — France/GB/West Germany, 1977 [360min]
A six-hour drama-documentary bringing to an end the director's introspective trilogy on Germany's thorniest historical characters (**Ludwig — Requiem for a Virgin King** *** [of Bavaria] kicks off with the kook who took the Prussian side in the Franco-Prussian War; and writer *Karl May* were the others). A film for historians and analysts of history — as well as lovers of filmmaking technique — it is physically and mentally draining to take it all at once. Originally in bite-sized chunks for TV. See also **Ludwig**.
With *Heinz Schubert, André Heller, Harry Baer*

HITLER — BEAST of BERLIN See **Beasts of Berlin**

HITLER — DEAD OR ALIVE
Nick Grinde — U.S., 1942 [70min]
Satirical farce about three ex-Alcatraz cons plotting to kill Hitler on a contract for Uncle Sam. Feeble, interesting only for the continuing impersonation of Hitler by Robert (Bob) Watson. The even-worse **The Devil with Hitler** (Gordon Douglas, U.S., 145min — co-starring Alan Mowbray) earlier that year saw his debut; and further tongue-in-cheek, screen performances occurred in **That Nazty Nuisance** ** (Glenn

Tryon — U.S., 1943 — with Joe Devlin) and Preston Sturges' marvellous *The Miracle of Morgan's Creek*, in the same year. He also came up with a convincingly serious portrayal in **The Hitler Gang**.
With *Ward Bond, Warren Heimer, Paul Fix, Robert Watson*

THE HITLER GANG
John Farrow — U.S., 1944 [100min]
As classic a piece of Hollywood anti-German propaganda as there ever was, Farrow takes Hitler from WW1 through his rise to power, and in the best feature of the film, develops the other major Nazi characters — Hess, Göring, Göbbels and Himmler — through the outstanding impersonation skills of his actors. Watson plays Hitler straight this time. (see **Hitler — Dead or Alive**).
With *Robert Watson, Martin Kosleck, Victor Varconi, Luis van Rooten, Alexander Pope*

Other films which describe Hitler's rise to power include:
Hitler's Reign of Terror * (Samuel Cummins/Mike Mindlin — U.S., 1934) With *Cornelius Vanderbilt Jr*
The German Story *** (aka 'You and Other Comrades') (Annelie and Andrew Thorndike — East Germany, 1956)
Mein Kampf *** (aka 'The Bloody Years') (Erwin Leiser — Sweden, 1960)
The Life of Adolf Hitler ** (Paul Rotha — West Germany, 1961)
Hitler (Stuart Heisler — U.S., 1961, 105min) With *Richard Baseheart*
The Black Fox See separate entry
Ordinary Fascism *** (aka 'Obyknovennyi Fashizm') (Mikhail Romm — USSR, 1965)
The Double-Headed Eagle (1973) See separate entry
Swastika (1973) See entry for **The Double-Headed Eagle**
For the story of Hitler's last days, see **Ten Days to Die**.

HITLER — THE BEAST OF BERLIN
See **Beasts of Berlin**

HITLER — THE LAST TEN DAYS See **Ten Days to Die**

HITLERJUNGE QUEX See **Hans Westmar**

HITLER'S CHILDREN
Edward Dmytryk — U.S., 1942 [85min]
Huge in the propaganda stakes, this is the 'true' story of the Hitler Youth! Despite its blatant stance, Dmytryk's direction and Emmet Lavery's adaptation of the book with the best title all — *Education for Death*, by Gregor Ziemer — is surprisingly intelligent for such a theme.
With *Tim Holt, Bonita Granville, Otto Kruger*

HITLER'S HANGMAN
(aka 'Hitler's Madman') See **Hangmen also Die!**

HITLER'S MADMAN See **Hitler's Hangman**

HITLER'S REIGN OF TERROR See **The Hitler Gang**

HOLD BACK THE NIGHT
Allan Dwan — U.S., 1956 [80min]
Dreadful Korean War drama with origins back in WW2.
With *John Payne, Peter Graves, Chuck Connors, Mona Freeman*

HOME OF THE BRAVE

★ *Mark Robson — U.S., 1949* [85min]

★ Early venture into racism among WW2 GIs in the Pacific. Produced by that preacher and moraliser Stanley Kramer (he of the future **The Men**, **The Caine Mutiny**, *The Defiant Ones*, **Judgment at Nuremberg**, etc, etc), you know you are in for a sermonising ear-bashing, but can't get out of it.

With *James Edwards, Douglas Dick, Steve Brodie, Lloyd Bridges, Frank Lovejoy, Jeff Corey*

HOMECOMING (1941) See **Heimkehr**

HOMECOMING

★ *Mervyn Le Roy — U.S., 1948* [115min]

WW2 Army doctor and nurse stuff, with Gable and Turner illicit lovers from Tunisia to the Ardennes. Sadly, there is no cure for this.

With *Clark Gable, Lana Turner, Anne Baxter, John Hodiak*

HOMELAND See **Heimat**

THE HONEST COURTESAN (aka 'Dangerous Beauty')

★ *Marshall Herskovitz — U.S., 1997* [110min]

★ Despite the title and the sexual undercurrents of the first part
★ of the film, this is little more then a good old-fashioned swashbuckler. What is more, it uses as its unusual backdrop the 16th century war between Venice and the Turks; which, of course, had as its centrepiece the great sea battle of Lepanto in 1571 (See also **In the Palace of the King** [1923]). Good performances from the leads too.

With *Catherine McCormack, Rufus Sewell, Oliver Platt, Fred Ward, Jeroen Krabbé, Joanna Cassidy*

L'HONNEURE D'UN CAPITAINE

★ (aka 'A Captain's Honour')

★ *Pierre Schoendoerffer — France, 1982* [120min]

Years after the Algerian conflict, a dead French army veteran is accused on a TV chat show of atrocities to prisoners, and his widow takes up his case. Schoendoerffer's least-effective look at the tribulations of French colonialism (**317e Section**, **Dien Bien Phu**) still makes powerful drama.

With *Jacques Perrin, Nicole Garcia*

HONG GAOLIANG See **Red Sorghum**

THE HONOURABLE ANGELINA

(aka 'L'Onorovole Angelina') See **Living in Peace**

THE HOOK

★ *George Seaton — U.S., 1962* [100min]

The Korean War is all but over, and three U.S. soldiers are making a getaway on board ship with a communist Korean they have orders to shoot. He escapes below, the cessation of hostilities is announced, but they can't make the fugitive understand. He is then predictably killed in the final struggle to overcome him. Big yawn.

With *Kirk Douglas, Robert Walker, Nick Adams*

HOPE AND GLORY

★ *John Boorman — GB, 1987* [115min]

★ Semi-autobiographical reflections through the eyes of a young
★ boy in London during the Blitz. Boorman's ability to ally his
★ wonderful visual touch to the effect on close groups of people

HOPE AND GLORY
Bill (Sebastian Rice-Edwards) and Sue (Geraldine Muir) have adventures during an air raid. Columbia

of outside factors (*Deliverance, The Emerald Forest*) is again present here. A warm, funny — but totally without schmaltz — soap opera set amongst the rubble and the bombings, he evokes a fine sense of period and exactly captures the Londoners' ability to carry on normally in totally abnormal conditions. He (as director and as writer) and his picture received Oscar nominations, as did Philippe Rousselot's camerawork and art direction. Wooldridge won a BAFTA for supporting actress.

With *Sebastian Rice-Edwards, Geraldine Muir, Sarah Miles, Sammi Davis, Ian Bannen, Susan Wooldridge*

HORNET'S NEST

Phil Karlson — U.S., 1970 [110min] ★

Completely far-fetched WW2 vehicle for Hudson who parachutes behind the lines in Italy and blows up a dam with the help of a gang of urchins.

With *Rock Hudson, Sylvia Koscina, Sergio Fantoni*

HORS LA VIE (aka 'Out of Life')

Maroun Bagdadi — France/Germany/Italy, 1991 [95min] ★

Intensive and coherent study of some of the complexities of ★
the Lebanese Civil War, as seen through the eyes of a photog- ★
rapher taken hostage in Beirut. The terrorists are portrayed as sympathetic captors. Based on the true experiences of Pierre Auque.

With *Hippolyte Giradot, Rafiq Ali Ahmad, Hussein Sbeity*

THE HORSE SOLDIERS

John Ford — U.S., 1959 [120min] ★

There's just enough John Ford in this rambling epic to make ★
it work, but the master's only full length picture on the Civil ★

War (see **How the West Was Won**) is not one of his best. The huge canvas is there, together with the romantic heroes of the late '40s vintage Ford, but the script is poor — surprisingly so, as the plot is based on one of the war's most exciting incidents. Grant attempts to stop Southern supplies reaching Vicksburg in 1863, by assigning Col Wayne to take his men some 300 miles into Confederate territory to cut off the route.

Still contains one of the most poignant of scenes from any war film, however, when a Southern military academy sends its child cadets marching off to fight. The 1957 Wimbledon Ladies Champion, Althea Gibson, plays the slave girl Lukey.
With *John Wayne, William Holden, Constance Towers, Althea Gibson*

THE HORSEMAN ON THE ROOF
(aka 'Le Hussard sur le Toit')
Jean-Paul Rappeneau — France, 1995 [135min]
Beautifully presented costume drama by Rappeneau on the back of his *Cyrano de Bergerac*, but the historic and military promise of the picture is eventually swamped by the sumptuous production values. The hussar is an Italian officer in exile in Provence during an Austrian purge and a cholera epidemic in 1832, and naturally he falls for Binoche.
With *Olivier Martinez, Juliette Binoche, Gérard Depardieu*

HOSTAGES See **Hitler's Hangman**

HOTEL BERLIN
Peter Godfrey — U.S., 1945 [100min]
Melodramatic fare supposedly painting the real decline of the Third Reich as a once great, classy hotel, now half bombed out, with once important people reduced to scurrying rats among the ruins. Inevitable defeat hangs over the place like a pall — and also sums up the picture's fate.
With *Helmut Dantine, Raymond Massey, Peter Lorre, Andrea King, Faye Emerson, Alan Hale*

HOTEL IMPERIAL (1926) See **Hotel Imperial** (1939)

HOTEL IMPERIAL
Robert Florey — U.S., 1939 [80min]
Remake of the 1926 ★★ silent directed by Mauritz Stiller, starring Pola Negri — and not much better, either. In 1916, the forces of Russia and Austria-Hungary took and retook the same pieces of the Balkans over and over again. Hardly surprising that a hotel on this mobile front becomes a haven of spies, soldiers and various other ne'er-do-wells. Collapses into melodrama before it becomes interesting enough.
With *Isa Miranda, Ray Milland, Reginald Owen, Gene Lockhart, J. Carroll Naish*

HOTEL SAHARA
Ken Annakin — GB, 1951 [95min]
Sub-**Casablanca**, but without the romance, suspense, action — in fact, this very frail farce, based in a WW2 North African hotel which switches its allegiance to whichever tide of soldiery should wash over it, is not left with much going for it at all.
With *Peter Ustinov, Yvonne de Carlo, Davis Tomlinson, Roland Culver, Anton Diffring*

THE HOUR BEFORE THE DAWN
Frank Tuttle — U.S., 1944 [75min]
Tuttle-tosh about pacifist Brit being taken for a ride by a Nazi spy and then doing the right thing. Apparently — amazingly — based on a Somerset Maugham short story.
With *Franchot Tone, Veronica Lake*

THE HOUSE ON 92ND STREET
Henry Hathaway — U.S., 1945 [90min]
For Nazis, read Reds in this J. Edgar Hoover-sponsored espionage treatise. Produced by Louis de Rochemont — he of the **March of Time** documentaries — it has its own brand of 'on-location' realism as it superficially tells a tale of German spies rounded up before they can make off with A-bomb secrets. Before WW2 was over, Hollywood was getting prepared for the Cold War.
With *William Eythe, Lloyd Nolan, Signe Hasso, Leo G. Carroll, Gene Lockhart*

HOW I WON THE WAR
Richard Lester — GB, 1967 [110min]
A film of the '60s from a director of the '60s (*A Hard Day's Night, Help!, The Knack*), Lester's bleak, black comedy set in North Africa and France in WW2 intermittently impresses, but the overall effect leaves you scratching your head.

The satire is dated, the jokes don't always come off. But the concept of a rag-bag British detachment, led by the idealistic Crawford, setting up a cricket pitch (towing a heavy roller and other equipment) behind German lines is a priceless anti-war statement if ever there was. The very surrealism of the project, and its dippy direction are maybe facets worth revisiting from time to time.
With *Michael Crawford, John Lennon, Roy Kinnear, Michael Hordern, Jack McGowran, Lee Montague, Jack Hedley*

HOW THE STEEL WAS TEMPERED
(aka 'Kak Zakalyalas Stal')
Mark Donskoi — USSR, 1942
A rare war picture from the Soviet Union at this time, it harks back to the 1918 Civil War and partisans fighting the Whites and the German Army in the Ukraine. Donskoi had to take his production unit out of Kiev back into the hinterland following the advance of German forces after Operation 'Barbarossa'.
With *V. Perist Petrensk*

HOW THE WEST WAS WON
John Ford/Henry Hathaway/George Marshall — U.S., 1962 [160min]
We only need to pay attention to the middle sequence of this sprawling, incoherent, made-for-Cinerama epic — Ford's directing of the history through the War of Secession.

The action is quite spectacular and the overall bigness is what you would expect of this director, but like the others, he had difficulty telling a human story above the overpowering scale of the physical geography which acts as the canvas on which the action takes place.

Spencer Tracy narrated — and just look at that cast. Oscars were won for James R. Webb's narrative, for editing and for sound. Further nominations were: the picture; the mob-handed photography team; the score; art direction; and costume design.
With *Henry Fonda, James Stewart, John Wayne, Richard Widmark, Gregory Peck, Robert Preston, Lee J. Cobb, George Peppard, Carroll Baker, Debbie Reynolds, Karl Malden, Eli Wallach, Carolyn Jones, Walter Brennan, Andy Devine, Raymond Massey, Russ Tamblyn*

HOW THE WEST WAS WON
Civil War action from John Ford's bit. MGM/Cinerama

THE HOWARDS OF VIRGINIA
★ (aka 'The Tree of Liberty')
★ *Frank Lloyd — U.S., 1940* [115min]
Over-long to maintain anything but sporadic excitement, this story of a colonial family caught up in the American Revolution has the rare distinction of Grant being miscast. Too urbane to be your average grizzly backwoodsman, he strives in vain to put one over on the oppressive British. Insensitive timing too, for 1940. Richard Hageman's score was nominated for an Oscar.
With *Cary Grant, Martha Scott, Cedric Hardwicke.*

HSIMENG RENSHENG See **The Puppetmaster**

THE HUMAN COMEDY
★ *Clarence Brown — U.S., 1943* [115min]
★ Sentimental home-front melodrama which went down big in the States at the time. Not for butch types. An Oscar went to William Saroyan for his original story, while the picture, the producer-director, Rooney and cinematographer Harry Stradling all picked up nominations.
With *Mickey Rooney, Van Johnson, Donna Reed*

THE HUMAN CONDITION
★ (aka 'Ningen no Joken: Parts 1, 2 and 3')
★ *Masaki Kobayashi — Japan, 1961*
★ Kobayashi's amazing nine-hour-long pacifistic plea — told as
★ a trilogy — starts with **No Greater Love** in 1930s Japanese-occupied Manchuria; with the hero trying to improve the lot of the Chinese labourers in his care at an iron ore mine. In Part 2 — **Road to Eternity** — he joins the Japanese army and

fights against the harsh treatment of the recruits. Finally, in **A Soldier's Prayer** in the summer of 1945, he becomes a Russian POW, only to escape and eventually perish in the harsh landscape.

The director's power is in his ability to drive forward the narrative without faltering; and he produces both a humanist plea from the heart and a powerful landmark document of the Japanese at war, in the process. Excellent performances from the leads.
With *Tatsuya Nakadai, Michiyo Aramata, So Yamamura, Keiji Sada, Hideko Takamine*

THE HUN WITHIN
Chester Withey — U.S., 1918
Not as cheesy as the title suggests, this is quite a neat but meaty tale of a German-American fighting for the Germans in WW1, and a spy-ring sub-plot back in the U.S. Written and produced by D.W. Griffith. ★ ★ ★
With *George Fawcett, Dorothy Gish*

HUNDE, WOLLT IHR EWIG LEBEN
See **Battle Inferno**

THE HUNT FOR RED OCTOBER
See **The Bedford Incident**

THE HUNTERS
Dick Powell — U.S., 1958 [110min] ★
Superior action in this Sabre jet-fighter propaganda piece ★
from the Korean War, but not too much else. ★
With *Robert Mitchum, Robert Wagner, Richard Egan, May Britt*

LE HUSSARD SUR LE TOIT
See **The Horseman on the Roof**

I AIM AT THE STARS
★ *J Lee(-)Thompson — U.S., 1960* [105min]
★ Fictionalised biopic of Nazi V2 rocket scientist Wernher von Braun, with most of the action happening after WW2 and his 'defection' to proto-NASA. Not as interesting as it sounds.
With *Curt Jurgens, Herbert Lom*

I COVER THE WAR
★ *Arthur Lubin — U.S., 1937* [70min]
★ An early Eastern-Western for Wayne (see **The Conqueror**): in this film he does play an American. As a journalist covering the problems of artificially-created nationhood and oil exploration in the inter-war Middle East, he gets involved in an uprising of Mesopotamian Arabs against the British-influenced government of the newly-founded kingdom of Iraq. Very low budget — but then so was the Duke in pre-*Stagecoach* days.
With *John Wayne, Gwen Gaze, Don Barclay*

I ESCAPED FROM THE GESTAPO (aka 'No Escape')
Harold Young — U.S., 1943 [75min]
U.S. counterfeiter breaks out of jail, courtesy of Nazi spies intent on dabbling with the dollar, and becomes a patriot when he finds out what their little game is. Rubbish.
With *Dean Jagger, John Carradine*

I KILLED GERONIMO
See **Geronimo: An American Legend**

I KILLED RASPUTIN See **Rasputin and the Empress**

I MARRIED A NAZI See **The Man I Married**

I SEE A DARK STRANGER (aka 'The Adventuress')
★ *Frank Launder — GB, 1945* [110min]
★ It wouldn't happen today. This Launder and Sidney Gilliat tale of a female IRA activist coming to England as a Nazi spy in WW2 is played for laughs; and it is quite funny.
With *Deborah Kerr, Trevor Howard, Raymond Huntley*

I SHALL RETURN
See **An American Guerrilla in the Philippines**

I WANT YOU
★ *Mark Robson — U.S., 1951* [100min]
★ Tepid Korean War home-front drama, with three generations of the same family reflecting over war three times over (WW1, WW2 and the then-present conflict), and its effect on them.
With *Dana Andrews, Dorothy McGuire, Farley Granger*

I WAS A FIREMAN See **Fires Were Started**

I WAS A MALE WAR BRIDE
★ *Howard Hawks — U.S., 1949* [105min]
★ The one where Grant is the most unconvincing French officer ever portrayed, marrying U.S. WAC Sheridan, and yet still manages to steal the picture. It may not be one of the Hawks-Grant classic farces in the mould of *Bringing up Baby*, *His Girl Friday* or even the later *Monkey Business*, but it is still very funny in parts — and its inclusion here is mostly for the evocative backcloth of war-torn Europe in 1945.
With *Cary Grant, Ann Sheridan*

I WAS A SPY
Victor Saville — GB, 1933 [85min]
Superior WW1 espionage story with Carroll as a deliciously-duplicitous nurse in Flanders and Veidt as, well, Veidt. Steadily slumps into melodrama, but the cast is always spot on.
With *Madeleine Carroll, Conrad Veidt, Herbert Marshall, Edward Gwenn, Nigel Bruce, Martita Hunt*

I WAS AN AMERICAN SPY
Lesley Selander — U.S., 1951 [85min]
The true story of Claire Phillips in Japanese-occupied Philippines during WW2, given the Selander pulp treatment.
With *Ann Dvorak, Gene Evans*

I WAS MONTY'S DOUBLE
(aka as 'Heaven, Hell and Hoboken')
John Guillermin — GB, 1958 [100min]
Clifton James, the actor (not the baccy-spitting Southern sheriff from the Bond pictures, *Live and Let Die* and *The Man with the Golden Gun*), so resembled General Montgomery that he was offered the role of his life to create a diversion by 'playing' the British commander in public appearances during WW2. Clifton James, the actor, then was offered the role of his life to play Clifton James, the actor, impersonating Montgomery. True — but how does the U.S. title fit in? The film is itself interesting without all the trivia asides, with Bryan Forbes' screenplay from, yes, Clifton James, the actor's, book, amusingly played by a stalwart cast.
With *John Mills, Cecil Parker, (M.E.) Clifton(-)James, Michael Hordern, Leslie Phillips, Patrick Allen*

ICE-COLD IN ALEX (aka 'Desert Attack')
J. Lee(-)Thompson — GB, 1958 [130min]
A Danish lager company obtained the neatest piece of advertising here, as Johnny Mills and chums slake a desert thirst more convincingly than in any other cinema scene before or since. The picture itself is over-long (probably the reason we're all so thirsty by the time *that* scene comes around), but is punctuated by good action sequences and plenty of suspense among the minefields and German patrols, as a motor ambulance limps back from Tobruk to Alexandria during the North African campaign in 1942.
With *John Mills, Sylvia Sims, Anthony Quayle, Harry Andrews*

IDI I SMOTRI See **Come and See**

IF I WERE KING
Frank Lloyd — U.S., 1938 [100min]
Hokey remake of J. Gordon Edwards' 1920 ★★ silent about the 15th century French semi-legendary poet and folk-hero, François Villon; also filmed in 1928 as **The Beloved Rogue** ★ by Alan Crosland [100min], with John Barrymore and Conrad Veidt, and twice reincarnated as the operetta, *The Vagabond King* (1930 and 1956). The historical context is France's Louis XI v Burgundy's Charles the Bad ('The War of the

Public Good'), and the film alludes to Villon's involvement in the Battle of Montlhéry in July 1465 — unfortunately, some two years after Villon's reputed death. Close.

This version does benefit from a spirited Preston Sturges script, however, some fine acting (Rathbone got nominated), and recognition was also given to Richard Hageman's score, and for art direction.

With *Ronald Colman, Basil Rathbone, Ellen Drew, Henry Wilcoxson, Frances Dee*

ILL MET BY MOONLIGHT (aka 'Night Ambush')
Michael Powell — GB, 1956 [105min]

Wish the moonlight had been a bit brighter — it is often too difficult to follow visually the proceedings here. This true but slow story, set in Crete during WW2 with Resistance and British Military Intelligence battling Germans, and out to abduct a senior Nazi officer, is not out of the Powell-Pressburger top draw (see **49th Parallel**, **The Life and Death of Colonel Blimp**, **A Matter of Life and Death**).

With *Dirk Bogarde, Marius Goring, Cyril Cusack, Michael Gough*

IMITATION GENERAL
George Marshall — U.S., 1958 [90min]

Unfunny sergeant-impersonating-general-and-leading-his-troops-to-victory scenario. Set in post D-Day France, it seemed that the WW2 movie had finally run its course with this effort.

With *Glenn Ford, Red Buttons, Dean Jones*

IMMORTAL BATTALION See **The Way Ahead**

THE IMMORTAL SERGEANT
John M. Stahl — U.S., 1943 [90min]

The first U.S. picture on the war in the desert in late 1942/early 1943 is a real emotional roller-coaster. Fonda takes over from Sergeant Mitchell, when he is killed, the command of a lost patrol — and finds himself, and the others, comparing himself against his mentor. Thankfully, decent battle scenes break up the psychological over-indulgences.

With *Henry Fonda, Thomas Mitchell, Maureen O'Hara*

THE IMPERIAL TRAGEDY
See **Rasputine** (1938)

THE IMPOSTOR
Julien Duvivier — U.S., 1944 [90min]

Exiled director and star fail to make this propaganda exercise for the Free French fighting Germans in North Africa any better than the many other programmers spewed out by Hollywood during WW2.

With *Jean Gabin, Ellen Drew*

IN ENEMY COUNTRY
Harry Keller — U.S., 1968 [105min]

Totally naive WW2 spy story set in 1940 France with the Maquis already in place to help the British (plus the token American 'observer') find out about some Nazi super torpedo that's playing havoc with shipping.

With *Tony Franciosa, Anjanette Comer, Guy Stockwell, Tom Bell*

IN FORMER DAYS
See **In Those Days**

IN HARM'S WAY
Otto Preminger — U.S., 1965 [165min]

Life in the U.S. Navy in the aftermath of Pearl Harbor. Shot, somewhat incongruously, in black and white with a starry cast, it sees (among other things) Wayne indirectly dabbling in PT (MTB) boats again 20 years after **They Were Expendable**. His son (de Wilde) is killed on one, and the Duke slugs it out with his chain of command again (see **The Flying Leathernecks**). Too much romancing and model-making, though. Too much of nothing really, when it's nearly three hours long. Lloyd Griggs received an Oscar nomination for photography, while Neal picked up a BAFTA.

With *John Wayne, Kirk Douglas, Patricia Neal, Henry Fonda, Tom Tryon, Paula Prentice, Dana Andrews, Stanley Holloway, Burgess Meredith, Franchot Tone, George Kennedy, Hugh O'Brian, Larry Hagman*

IN JENEN TAGEN See **In Those Days**

IN LOVE AND WAR
Philip Dunne — U.S., 1958 [110min]

Standard Hollywood WW2 Pacific theatre stuff, banging the drum — and U.S. Marines blasting the Japs — while thinking of the gals back home. When the action arrives, it's not bad.

With *Robert Wagner, Dana Wynter, Jeffrey Hunter, Hope Lange, Bradford Dillman, Sheree North, France Nuyen*

IN LOVE AND WAR
Richard Attenborough — U.S., 1996 [115min]

Attempt to show how Hemingway's plot for **A Farewell to Arms** was derived, as Attenborough, somewhat unconvincingly, tells the tale of the author's WW1 fling with an Army nurse in Italy. When he focuses on battles on the Austro-Italian Front the director is at his substantial best (as in **A Bridge Too Far**), but the central theme is the ill-conceived romance, and here he doesn't have, say, the Anthony Hopkins-Debra Winger chemistry of his earlier *Shadowlands* to make it work.

With *Sandra Bullock, Chris O'Donnell*

IMITATION GENERAL
Interesting vehicle as Glenn Ford (driving) and Dean Jones attack. MGM

IN OUR TIME

Vincent Sherman — U.S., 1944 [110min]

Earnest attempt to consider the break-up of class systems in Europe since WW1. Lupino, a girl from a British lower-class background, marries a Polish count — more a gentleman farmer, really — against his family's wishes. But status counts for nought when the blitzkrieg of 1939 comes.

With *Ida Lupino, Paul Henreid, Nancy Coleman, Alla Nazimova*

IN THE NAME OF THE FATHER

Jim Sheridan — GB/Ireland, 1993 [135min]

Sheridan's study of one of the greatest miscarriages of justice in British judicial history bears no grudges (except perhaps in the fictionalisation of the Court of Appeal scene), but paints a sad picture of the Irish troubles and the frustrations of the security forces, trying to plug too many holes in too many dykes.

The relationship between father and son forms the central, personal hub to an otherwise mainstream account of events leading up to the infamous pub bombing, and the now equally-infamous 'fit-up', albeit beautifully played by some of Britain's best. Actor Oscar nominations, in fact, were awarded to Day-Lewis, Postlethwaite and Thompson, whilst Sheridan received both a direction nomination, and along with Terry George, one for the screenplay. The editing was similarly recognized.

With *Daniel Day-Lewis, Pete Postlethwaite, Emma Thompson, Corin Redgrave, John Lynch*

IN THE NAME OF THE PEOPLE

Frank Christopher — U.S., 1984

Straightforward 'fly-on-the-wall' documentary about guerrilla rebel life in early-80s El Salvador. Restrained commentary by Martin Sheen.

IN THE PALACE OF THE KING (1915)

See **In the Palace of the King** (1923)

IN THE PALACE OF THE KING

Emmett Flynn — U.S., 1923

Already made by Fred E. Wright in 1915 ★★ this story of Don John of Austria and intrigue in the Spanish court of Philip II at the time of the Battle of Lepanto (1571) is more of an off-field drama than a blood and thunder action movie (although some early Christian-Moor skirmishes are used to set the scene). The famous battle gets short shrift, which is a shame for the first major sea battle since Actium in 31BC (see **Cleopatra**, 1963), and the last ever fought by oar-propelled galleys: the interesting one-off allegiance between the Papal States and Spain and her allies is hardly considered.

With *Edmund Lowe, Blanche Sweet, Hobart Bosworth*

IN THE REAR OF THE ENEMY

See **The Girl from Leningrad**

IN THOSE DAYS (aka 'In Jenen Tagen', 'In Former Days')

Helmut Kautner — Germany (British Zone), 1947

Some vivid and harrowing photography of the panic in Berlin in the snows of early 1945 stand out, but this product of the young post-war German cinema argues that the majority of Germans were anti-Nazi and decent folk.

With *Winnie Markus, Werner Hinz, Karl John*

IN WHICH WE SERVE

Noël Coward/David Lean — GB, 1942 [115min]

The *original* stiff upper lip movie of WW2. Hugely successful and influential on both sides of the Atlantic, this is a loose adaptation of the true sinking of Lord Louis Mountbatten's ship, HMS *Kelly* (here called the *Torrin*), after coming off second best to Stuka dive bombers off Crete in 1941. But the flashback memories of the stricken survivors is now so dated, it is difficult to take it all seriously today. The class-ridden pre-war stereotypes are all there, from the almost sub-human articulation of the men, to the patronising, suave, sophisticated drawling of the officers — all Coward trademarks.

As he produced, wrote, starred in and directed it (although Lean took over the [cinematic] helm part-way through), it is what can only be expected. Hollywood loved it, nominating the picture and Coward's script for Oscars, whilst bestowing on him a Special Award for such an all-round achievement. It also marked the film debuts of Attenborough and Johnson, as well as launching Lean as one of the all-time great war film directors — and of other types, too (*Brief Encounter*, **Great Expectations**, **Bridge on the River Kwai**, **Lawrence of Arabia**, *A Passage to India*, and many more).

With *Noël Coward, John Mills, Bernard Miles, Celia Johnson, Richard Attenborough, Michael Wilding, Kay Walsh, James Donald*

INCHON

Terence Young — U.S., 1981 [140min]

Arguably the worst war picture made in the last quarter of the 20th century; with a risible script (MacArthur's conducting of the Korean campaign underpinned by religious zeal — the film was financed by the Unification Church, the Moonies, after all); hammy acting (Olivier, Mifune and Roundtree are typical of the eccentric casting); but surprisingly passable action sequences.

With *Laurence Olivier, Jacqueline Bisset, Ben Gazzara, Toshiro Mifune, Richard Roundtree, David Janssen*

INCIDENT AT PHANTOM HILL

Earl Bellamy — U.S., 1966 [90min]

Stolen gold, North v South, and a smattering of Indians — it all adds up to a standard Western with a Civil War base.

With *Robert Fuller, Jocelyn Lane, Dan Duryea*

THE INDIAN FIGHTER

André de Toth — U.S., 1955 [90min]

Wagon train heads for an Army stockade on the Oregon Trail only to be attacked *en route* and stormed by Red Cloud's Sioux when they get there. OK.

With *Kirk Douglas, Elsa Martinelli, Walter Matthau*

THE INDIAN SCOUT See **Davy Crockett, Indian Scout**

INDIAN UPRISING See **Geronimo**

INDIANA JONES AND THE LAST CRUSADE See **Raiders of the Lost Ark**

THE INFORMER (1929) See **The Informer** (1935)

THE INFORMER

John Ford — U.S., 1935 [90min]

Ford magically creates an unbelievable atmosphere from the simplest of backgrounds. Set in the Irish troubles of the '20s (it had already been made as an early talkie in Britain by Arthur Robison in 1929 ★★), the story of betrayal and the

conscience that follows is wonderfully played, and the same directing, writing and acting triumvirate which produced the previous year's **The Lost Patrol** (Ford, Dudley Nichols and McLaglen) all won Oscars — as did Max Steiner for his music. It was also nominated for Best Picture and the editing.
With *Victor McLaglen, Heather Angel, Preston Foster, Wallace Ford, Margot Grahame*

INGLORIOUS BASTARDS
(aka 'Counterfeit Commandos')
Enzo G. Castellari — Italy, 1978 [100min]
Consummate character actor Bannen didn't get many lead roles, and perhaps he should have reconsidered taking this thinly-plotted WW2 exploitation piece. It's about soldiers awaiting court martial in post-D-Day France, escaping, and their adventures thereafter.
With *Ian Bannen, Bo Svenson, Fred Williamson*

THE INN OF THE SIXTH HAPPINESS
Mark Robson — GB, 1958 [160min]
Occasionally sentimental, but sometimes inspirational biopic of British missionary Gladys Aylward, leading over 100 children to safety over the mountains in 1938 during the Sino-Japanese War. Bergman, after Rossellini, would never be the same actress again, but this was one of her better performances as her stellar career started to wane. Poignantly, this was also the last screen performance of Donat (**The Thirty-Nine Steps**, *Goodbye Mr Chips*) — playing a feuding Chinese war-lord in love with Aylward. He died of chronic asthma some weeks after finishing the picture. Robson's direction was recognized with an Oscar nomination.
With *Ingrid Bergman, Robert Donat, Curt Jurgens*

INNOCENCE UNPROTECTED
(aka 'Nevinost Bez Zastite')
Dusan Makavejev — Yugoslavia, 1968 [80min]
Infamous filmmaker Makavejev (*WR — Mysteries of the Organism*) lends his experimental approach to this earlier piece about life in German-occupied Belgrade in 1942. Using footage from a German film stolen by partisans, interwoven with updated clips of the same characters (and often the same actors), he creates a melodrama both wistful and funny.
With *Dragoljub Aleksic, Ana Milosavljevic, Vera Jovanovic*

LA INSURRECCION
Peter Lilienthal — Nicaragua/Costa Rica, 1981 [95min]
Moving drama set at the time of the Somoza government in Nicaragua, with a family split either side of the divide. The son is a member of the National Guard while his father and sister join the rebels.
With *Augustin Pereira, Carlos Catania, Maria Lourdes*

THE INSURRECTION OF THE BOURGEOISIE
See *The Battle of Chile*

INTERNATIONAL LADY
Tim Whelan — U.S., 1941 [100min]
Routine WW2 spy drama with the FBI chasing a female *agent provocateur* working for the Axis powers.
With *George Brent, Basil Rathbone, Ilona Massey, Gene Lockhart*

INTERNATIONAL SETTLEMENT
Eugene Ford — U.S., 1938 [75min]
Quite exciting gun-running adventure of the Sino-Japanese War, as the action takes place during the bombing of Shanghai.
With *Dolores del Rio, George Sanders, John Carradine*

INTERNATIONAL SQUADRON
Lothar Mendes — U.S., 1941 [85min]
Updating Hawks' 1935 *Ceiling Zero*, with James Cagney, Mendes sends Reagan across the Atlantic to join the RAF. Samey flagwaver. See also **Eagle Squadron.**
With *Ronald Reagan, Olympe Bradna, James Stephenson*

INTOLERANCE
D. W. Griffith — U.S., 1916 [115min]
Hugely influential in its thematic and inter-cutting techniques, Griffith's immensely experimental (and one has to say, sometimes downright pretentious) attempt to enunciate 'intolerance' among people down the years is a definite curate's egg of a film. Available in versions from just under two hours to an almost indigestible four, we see man's inhumanity to man through four different period pieces — ancient Babylon, the Judea of Christ, the 1572 St Bartholomew's Day massacre in Paris, and 20th century industrial relations. The apocalyptic finale of a war to end all wars left a message even the dimmest cinema-goer could understand at the time.
With *Mae Marsh, Robert Harron, Lillian Gish, Fred Turner, Bessie Love, Constance Talmadge, Eugene Pallett, Elmo Lincoln*

INTRODUCTION TO THE ENEMY
Jane Fonda/Tom Hayden — U.S., 1975
Husband and wife team seeing how the land lies in North Vietnam at the end of the conflict; this realised a long-time ambition for Fonda. As one who wears her liberal politics-heart on her sleeve, this, unsurprisingly, is not a very pro-U.S. documentary. What *is* surprising is the couples' appraisal of the issues is only skin-deep .

THE INVADERS See **49th Parallel**

THE INVASION OF BRITAIN
(aka 'Victory and Peace') See **War Brides**

INVASION QUARTET
Jay Lewis — GB, 1961 [85min]
Unfunny farce about a British team attempting to knock out a German cross-channel gun.
With *Bill Travers, Spike Milligan, John Le Mesurier*

IRGENDWO IN BERLIN See **Somewhere in Berlin**

THE IRON TRIANGLE
Eric Weston — U.S., 1988 [90min]
Quiet and efficient 'humanity' film about the relationship between a U.S. soldier and his Viet Cong captor. Message comes across quite naturally.
With *Beau Bridges, Haing S Ngor, Johnny Hallyday*

THE IROQUOIS TRAIL See **The Last of the Mohicans**

IS PARIS BURNING? (aka 'Paris, Brûle-est-il?')
René Clément — France/U.S., 1965 [165min]
A determined attempt to produce an epic about the liberation of Paris in 1944; director Clément's real forte, though, is in

making the great *little* film (**Bataille du Rail, Les Jeux Interdits**). Heavyweight writers (Francis Ford Coppola and Gore Vidal) and a super-heavyweight cast just about sink the project. Marcel Grignon received an Academy Award nomination for making some photographic sense of it all.
With *Jean-Paul Belmondo, Charles Boyer, Leslie Caron, Kirk Douglas, Glenn Ford, Orson Welles, Alain Delon, Gert Frobe, Anthony Perkins, Jean-Pierre Cassel, Yves Montand, Robert Stack, George Chakiris, Simone Signoret*

ISLAND ESCAPE See **No Man is an Island**

ISLAND RESCUE See **Appointment with Venus**

ISN'T LIFE WONDERFUL?
D.W. Griffith — U.S., 1924 [100min]
Griffith was leading an attempt to build bridges here in a sympathetic look at life in post-WW1 Germany, but the U.S. public were not yet ready to forgive. It did become a watershed sentiment, however, with more even-handed considerations of the Great War being released during the second half of the decade and in the early 30s, the most famous embodiment of which was, of course, **All Quiet on the Western Front** in 1930.
With *Carol Dempster, Neil Hamilton*

IT HAPPENED HERE
Kevin Brownlow/Andrew Mollo — GB, 1963 [100min]
An unique picture. Taking seven years to complete by military enthusiasts and amateur filmmakers Brownlow and Mollo, it recreates a realistic post-WW2 Britain under Nazi occupation. It takes no position — indeed it balances repression with the German common-sense to allow the British to develop their own right-wing agenda. It anticipates the natural corollary of the victor and defeated lining up together in the inevitable war of dogma against the Soviet Union — there are cunning throwaway references to British Waffen-SS units convincingly titled 'Black Prince' and 'Richard Cœur de Lion' — but it is not anti-communist, either. Murray, as a nurse working for the government, joins the underground when she sees Eastern European war patients being killed. Effective use of (faked) Nazi propaganda newsreels give the documentary style its authentic feel.
With *Pauline Murray, Sebastian Shaw, Fiona Leland, Honor Fehrson, Percy Binns*

IT HAPPENED ON THE 20TH JULY
See **Jackboot Mutiny**

ITALIANO BRAVA GENTE
(aka 'Attack and Retreat')
Giuseppe de Santis — Italy, 1965
An Italian epic, providing American character actors with rare top-billing, which records the part played by Mussolini's doomed 8th Army in Operation Barbarossa. The picture tells the story of soldiers of various rank — and the civilians they affect — from the helter-skelter drive to Stalingrad to the Army's final annihilation in November-December 1942. One of very few films to touch upon Italian involvement on the Russian Front.
With *Arthur Kennedy, Peter Falk, Tatyana Samoilova, Rafaelle Pisu, Andrea Checchi*

IVAN GROSNYI
See **Ivan the Terrible**

IVAN THE TERRIBLE, Parts 1 and 2 (aka 'Ivan Grosnyi')
Sergei Eisenstein — USSR, 1942-46 [100min and 90min]
As Eisenstein was thwarted by Stalin in the release of the second part of this flawed masterpiece (it was only released in 1958), it was too late for the ailing genius to complete the third part of an originally-planned trilogy. He died in 1948.

Part 1 (completed in 1945) deals with Ivan's accession, his struggle to curtail the powers of the boyars and the securing of his eastern borders. Part 2 (subtitled 'The Revolt of the Boyars') considers his thoughts on abdication and return to power in the 1560s, while the uncompleted Part 3 ('Ivan's Battles') would have covered the sacking of Novgorod in 1570 and his repulsing of the Crimean Tartars, and — the sub-title suggests — his own inner battles, which were to rage for the rest of his life. Eisenstein's history is deeply flawed, but in many ways 'Ivan' is probably his most accessible work.
With *Nikolai Cherkassov, Ludmilla Tselikovskaya, Serafina Birman, Mikhail Nazvanov*

IVAN THE TERRIBLE
The incomparable Cherkassov. Mosfilm (courtesy KOBAL)

IVANHOE
See **The Adventures of Robin Hood**

IVANOVO DETSTVO See **Ivan's Childhood**

IVAN'S CHILDHOOD
(aka 'Ivanovo Detstvo', 'My Name is Ivan', 'The Youngest Spy')
Andrei Tarkovsky — USSR, 1962 [95min]
Tarkovsky's first important feature collected the Golden Lion award at the Venice Film Festival. Visually striking and imaginatively framed, the film works as both a parable of lost youth and high-class cinematic art.

Ivan, not yet in his teens, has seen his family progressively wiped out by the occupying Germans in WW2. Escaping from a concentration camp, he retaliates by performing behind-the-line spy missions for the Soviet forces, until he takes on one action too many. The war has effectively turned him from a young boy into a man overnight, then cruelly robbed him of his future.
With *Kolya Burlyaev, Valentin Zubkov, Irma Takovskaya*

IVAN'S CHILDHOOD
Ivan (Kolya Burlaev) accompanying Russians soldiers. The film is consistently visually striking and was awarded at the Venice Film Festival with the Golden Lion award. Mosfilm

J'ACCUSE
Abel Gance — France, 1939 [120min and 95min]
This powerful anti-war picture first surfaced in 1919 as a reaction to the horrors of WW1 — and such was its effect that some commentators suggested that if it had been made six years earlier there might have been no Great War. The picture was then remade in sound by the same director in the late '30s as a pacification plea to French and German governments caught up in the militaristic posturing of the time. (Göbbels actually banned it from German cinemas.)

Drawing on the harrowing imagery of the dead of previous wars rising to continue the endless conflict, the allegory convinces governments to end all war. Gance's aspirations were cruelly shattered, however — within 12 months of the remake, Paris was occupied by the Nazis.
With (in 1919) *Séverin Mars, Blaise Cendrars, Maryse Dauvray, Romuald Joubé*: (in 1939) *Victor Francen, Jean Max, Renée Devilliers, Delaitre, Line Noro, Marie Lou*

JACK LONDON

Alfred Santell — U.S., 1943 [95min]

Chance to turn a biopic of the *Call of the Wild* and *White Fang* author into some anti-Japanese propaganda. The picture, among other things, records Japanese 'atrocities' in the Russo-Japanese War of 1904-05 as seen through war correspondent London's eyes. Nominated for Frederic E. Rich's music.

With *Michael O'Shea, Susan Hayward, Osa Massen, Virginia Mayo, Harry Davenport*

Few pictures make any mention of the distant Russo-Japanese War of 1904-5. Only an obscure silent, **The Breath of the Gods ★★** made in 1920, and the various French and American versions of **La Bataille** pay it some attention — although **The Battleship Potemkin** spins off from the war, while Abraham Polonsky's Yugoslav/U.S. 1971 production, **Romance of a Horse Thief ★★** [100min], with Yul Brynner and Eli Wallach, uses it as backdrop.

JACKBOOT MUTINY

(aka 'Es Geschah am 20 Juli', 'It Happened on the 20th July')

G.W. Pabst — West Germany, 1955

20 July 1944, Wolfsschanze — the tale of the unsuccessful attempt to blow up Hitler is told, documentary-style, from the German point of view, by the director who first dramatised the demise of Hitler in **Ten Days to Die** the year before.

Apart from the historical interest, and a good performance from Wicki, there is little else to commend the picture. Pabst's power was on the wane.

With *Bernhard Wicki, Karl Ludwig Diehl, Carl Wery*

JACKNIFE

David Jones — U.S., 1989 [105min]

This Vietnam vet picture — depicting the psychologically-affected army buddies, the problems of rehabilitation and rejection by their own people, the mandatory disturbing flashbacks — is representative of the sub-genre in this remake of a work originally set for the stage.

The emphasis here is on the interaction between de Niro and Harris and Harris' sister (Baker) — the coming together of de Niro and Baker at the expense of Harris' fear of being squeezed out and having to face life alone. The acting is top-notch and it is this that sets it above the par for such movies.

With *Robert de Niro, Ed Harris, Kathy Baker, Charles Dutton, Elizabeth Franz, Loudon Wainwright III*

JEANNE LA POUCELLE, Parts I and II

(aka 'Joan of Arc') See **Joan of Arc**

THE JERUSALEM FILE

John Flynn — U.S./Israel, 1971 [95min]

Basically a political thriller, this lightweight effort covers, in a somewhat baffling series of events, the intrigues of the Middle East in the aftermath of the Six Day War of 1967.

Davison is the American archaeology student innocently caught up in Arab-Israeli terrorism — with a cast of stalwart British actors who should have known better and have been much better elsewhere.

With *Bruce Davison, Nicol Williamson, Donald Pleasence, Ian Hendry, Daria Halprin*

JESSE JAMES (1927)
See **Quantrill's Raiders**

JET ATTACK

Edward L. Cahn — U.S., 1958 [70min]

Typical, but inferior, Hollywood anti-communist picture of the '50s, with the Korean War as its backdrop.

With *John Agar, Audrey Totter, Gregory Walcott, James Dobson*

(LES) JEUX INTERDITS

(aka 'Forbidden Games', 'Secret Games')

René Clément — France, 1952 [85min]

Hailed at the time as one of the most famous anti-war pictures ever made, Clément's best picture now seems just a little diluted in its effect. The simple story of two children in war-torn France, performing their own funeral rituals for animals, parallels the wider agony of World War 2; but the sentiment intended to evoke poignancy in 1952 now seems almost maudlin in more world-weary times. It retains its powerful messages, however.

The animal cemetery, adorned with crosses the children have removed from the resting-places of human war dead, is a staggering metaphor for the perversion of war — especially when such desecration is perpetuated by innocents. The children acting out this tale of morality take their parts superbly, particularly the amazing five year-old Fossey as the Parisienne refugee, orphaned by the strafing Luftwaffe in the opening scenes. Academy Award winner for Best Foreign Film (BAFTA Best Film), and nominated for François Boyer's original story.

With *Brigitte Fossey, Georges Poujouly, Lucien Hubert, Amédée, Jacques Marin, Laurence Badie*

JEW SUSS (1934) See **Jew Suss** (1940)

JEW SUSS

Veit Harlan — Germany, 1940

An outrageous piece of overt anti-Semitism, rubber-stamped by Josef Göbbels and 'recommended for young people'! Turning around Leon Feuchtwanger's anti-racist fable (itself filmed in Britain in 1934 ★★ by Lothar Mendes [110min] for Michael Balcon, starring Conrad Veidt; but for diametrically-opposed propagandist reasons), this infamous tract portrays the Jew as a defiler of Aryan women, and as the epitome of evil.

With *Ferdinand Marian, Werner Krauss, Heinrich George, Kristina Soderbaum*

JOAN OF ARC

Victor Fleming — U.S., 1948 [145min]

Not the epic expected from Hollywood to match de Mille's first gargantuan stab at the story in 1916; nor Dreyer's master-piece with the amazing Falconetti (see below). This is a lack-lustre, studio-bound version of a play which itself was rather wordy. The familiar plot of the Maid answering a saintly call to lead France against the occupying English during the Hundred Years' War is duly trotted out. Fleming (**Gone with the Wind**, *The Wizard of Oz*) directs his last film as if it mirrors his own 'end-of-term' disposition; and Bergman, while as freshly original as ever, could have injected just a little more of her **Casablanca** vulnerability into the title role. Joe Valentine picked up an Oscar for cinematography, while producer Walter Wanger was given a special award. Other nominations were Bergman and Ferrer, and Hugo Friedhofer's score.

With *Ingrid Bergman, Jose Ferrer , Francis L. Sullivan, J. Carrol Naish, Ward Bond, George Colouris, John Ireland, Cecil Kellaway, Gene Lockhart*

Other pictures specifically dealing with 'The Maid of Orleans' include:

Joan the Woman ★★★ (Cecil B. de Mille — U.S., 1916, 125min) With *Geraldine Farrar*

La Passion de Jeanne d'Arc ★★★★ (Carl Dreyer — France, 1928, 175min) With *Renée Falconetti*

Saint Joan ★★ (Otto Preminger — GB, 1957, 110min) With *Jean Seberg, Anton Walbrook, Richard Widmark, John Gielgud, Richard Todd, Harry Andrews*

Stiff reconstruction of the Shavian play.

The Trial of Joan of Arc ★★★ (aka 'Procès de Jeanne d'Arc') (Robert Bresson — France, 1962, 165min) With *Florence Carrez*

Jeanne la Poucelle, Parts I and **II** ★★★ (aka 'Joan of Arc') (Jacques Rivette — France, 1994, 115min and 120min) With *Sandrine Bonnaire*

Modern interpretation with some views on feminism and the church.

JOAN OF ARC (1992)
See **Jeanne la Poucelle,** Parts I and II

JOAN OF PARIS
Robert Stevenson — U.S., 1942 [95min]

A French Resistance yarn all the better for a strong script and an interesting cast (Hollywood's European debutantes Morgan and Henreid teaming up with veteran Mitchell — and Ladd just about to make it big in *This Gun For Hire*). Morgan plays an underground leader who turns herself in to the Gestapo so that a group of Allied pilots can escape back to England.

With *Michèle Morgan, Paul Henreid, Thomas Mitchell, May Robson, Alan Ladd*

JOAN THE WOMAN See **Joan of Arc**

JOHN PAUL JONES
John Farrow — U.S., 1959 [125min]

American Revolutionary War hero biopic turned into a swash-buckling epic. It fails on both fronts. Stack is no Errol Flynn, and certainly doesn't convince as a Scotsman only recently residing in the colonies.

A catalogue of cameos (with Davis as **Catherine the Great**) really can't save the plod through Jones' adventures from America and France to Russia. The director's daughter, Mia, made her debut, aged 14.

With *Robert Stack, Charles Coburn, Bette Davis, Marisa Pavan, Peter Cushing, Bruce Cabot, Jean-Pierre Aumont*

JOHNNY GOT HIS GUN
Dalton Trumbo — U.S., 1971 [110min]

Trumbo's own novel, written at the beginning of WW2, took some 30 years to make it on to film. In that time a succession of directors — including first-choice Luis Buñuel — turned it down. It seems, therefore, almost in sheer frustration that the author took it upon himself to portray on the screen what many believed to be unfilmable.

The story is the worst-case scenario for any combatant: horrific injuries sustained in WW1 battle, leaving him without limbs, face, sight, hearing or speech. Through painstaking Morse Code he communicates with his doctors, pleading for the end of his life — which is repeatedly denied. Despite some inevitable sentimentality, Trumbo's only directorial venture is

a qualified success. A really harrowing, thought-provoking film.

With *Timothy Bottoms, Jason Robards, Marsha Hunt, Kathy Fields, Donald Sutherland, Diane Varsi, David Soul*

JOHNNY IN THE CLOUDS See **The Way to the Stars**

JOHNNY TREMAIN
Robert Stevenson — U.S., 1957 [80min]

A history lesson from Disney, about an American colonist joining in the fight for rights against George III's continuing neglect. He takes part in the Boston Tea Party and eventually lines up at Lexington. The blend of fact and fiction, taken superficially, works OK.

With *Hal Stalmaster, Luana Patten, Jeff York, Sebastian Cabot, Richard Beymer*

THE JOURNEY
Anatole Litvak — U.S., 1959 [125min]

Tedious melodrama done better 20 years before in films like **The Lady Vanishes**. It sets out to be noble and topical enough, in dealing with the Hungarian Uprising of 1956 and how a bus-load of Westerners are trying to flee to the Austrian border, but Litvak has definitely done much better (**Confessions of a Nazi Spy**, *The Snake Pit*, etc).

With *Deborah Kerr, Yul Brynner, Robert Morley, E.G. Marshall, Jason Robards (Jr), Anouk Aimée, David Kossoff*

JOURNEY FOR MARGARET
WS Van Dyke — U.S., 1942 [80min]

WW2 Blitz sniffler with the amazing five-year-old O'Brien as a distraught orphan whisked away from bombed-out London to the safety of America by correspondent Young.

With *Robert Young, Margaret O'Brien, Laraine Day, Billy Severn, Fay Bainter, Nigel Bruce*

JOURNEY INTO FEAR
Norman Foster — U.S., 1942 [70min]

Following *Citizen Kane* and *The Magnificent Ambersons*, this should rightly be regarded as Welles' third film at the helm, if only jointly. That Norman Foster can have the sole directorial credit can only be put down to some Wellesian eccentricity; as Welles not only directed all his own scenes, he produced, co-wrote and co-starred in a picture which carries his hallmarks of unconventionality as much as any other.

This tale of espionage, gun-running into Turkey, fleeing Americans, pursuing Gestapo, etc, in (pre-U.S.) WW2 Istanbul, is told in a brooding atmosphere, full of confusion and nightmare. Cotten, who co-wrote the screenplay with Welles, is wonderful in an understated way, and Moss as the hit-man has a truly spooky presence.

With *Joseph Cotten, Dolores del Rio, Ruth Warrick, Jack Moss, Orson Welles, Agnes Moorhead, Jack Durant, Everett Sloane*

It was remade, not too successfully, in 1975 by Daniel Mann, starring Sam Waterston and Zero Mostel.

JOURNEY INTO FEAR (1975)
See **Journey into Fear** (1942)

JOURNEY TO SHILOH
William Hale — U.S., 1967 [100min]

Would-be American Civil War epic that fails to convince.

Seven young men from Texas, caught up in the perceived romance and adventure of war, are keen to take on the Union forces in 1861, but their eagerness is short-lived. Interesting only for an early appearance by Harrison Ford.

With *James Caan, Michael Sarrazin, Don Stroud, Harrison Ford, Brenda Scott, Paul Peterson, Noah Beery Jr, Rex Ingram, John Doucette*

JOURNEY TOGETHER

John Boulting — GB, 1944 [95min]

This documentary-style propaganda feature was made in Britain by the RAF Film Unit; and was blessed by a tight Terence Rattigan script, good action sequences and a happy mixture of talented actors, old and new.

Set in WW2, both in Britain and the States, the film outlines the training needed by pilots to make long-distance bombing raids on Germany, and in doing so comes up with a very well made example of its type. The casting of Robinson, though, is certainly not to type.

With *Richard Attenborough, Jack Watling, Edward G. Robinson, David Tomlinson, Bessie Love*

JOURNEY'S END

James Whale — GB/U.S., 1930 [120min]

Quintessential British World War 1 drama, which became the first-ever Anglo-American production due to the need to use the superior sound facilities of Hollywood. The trip to California meant no turning back for the director and the star, who were to combine over the next few years in the groundbreaking early *Frankenstein* movies.

Set in the trenches in 1917, the picture addresses the tensions of war, and how men react to one another when their comrades around them are dying. Despite a brave attempt to bring it to the screen from the West End stage, it will always unfortunately suffer in comparison to that other WW1 picture — **All Quiet on the Western Front** — also from 1930.

With *Colin Clive, Ian MacLaren, David Manners*

JUAREZ

William Dieterlie — U.S., 1939 [130min]

Thanks to a distinctly pedestrian performance from Warners' main man Muni, what could have been an interesting marriage of historical fact and Hollywood munificence, is reduced to a plodding ramble.

The story of Napoleon III's puppet emperor, Maximilian of Austria, failing to bring the peasantry into line, develops into wholesale revolution in 1860s Mexico. The action is fine, however, and, Muni apart, the acting is first class — with Aherne as Maximilian collecting a Best Supporting Actor Oscar nomination.

JUAREZ
Juarez (Paul Muni) leads the Mexican people in revolt against the French puppet monarchy. Warner Bros (courtesy KOBAL)

With *Paul Muni, Bette Davis, Brian Aherne, Gale Sondergaard, Claude Rains, Donald Crisp, John Garfield*

JUDGMENT AT NUREMBURG

Stanley Kramer — U.S., 1961 [190min]

This multi-nominated, extended court-room drama has two definite advantages: a successful TV play as source, and a starry cast that for once earns its corn. The first Hollywood attempt at addressing the subject of Nazi war crimes possesses an atmosphere of doom and pessimism which comes straight from the director's tortured soul. But if he was going to suffer, should we all suffer too? Thankfully, the catalogue of high-class performances (sublime from Tracy as the judge, dignified by Dietrich, emotional from Clift — and Garland in her last meaningful film) maintains sufficient interest to reward the patient.

Out of 11 Oscar nominations, including picture, director, camera (Ernest Laszlo) — and Tracy, Garland and Clift — it picked up just two Academy Awards: Abby Mann's adaptation of his TV play, and Schell.

With *Spencer Tracy, Burt Lancaster, Maximilian Schell, Marlene Dietrich, Richard Widmark, Montgomery Clift, Judy Garland, William Shatner*

THE JUDGMENT HOUSE

J. Stuart Blackton — U.S., 1915

Blackton, an émigré Lancastrian, produced this well-timed piece of pro-British propaganda, by screening the victorious British in the Boer War — ignoring the case, or even the feats of the Boers, who, of course, really held out for a draw.

JUDITH
Daniel Mann — U.S., 1965 [110min]
Passable, but at times confusing story of Israel's fight for an independent state: with, as a cross-plot, concentration camp victim Loren hunting her husband, who happens to be a Nazi war criminal, aided by the Haganah.
With *Sophia Loren, Peter Finch, Jack Hawkins*

JULIUS CAESAR (1953) See **Cleopatra** (1963)

JULIUS CAESAR (1969) See **Cleopatra** (1963)

JUMP INTO HELL
David Butler — U.S., 1955 [95min]
Hollywood's first attempt to focus on a contemporary, hardly U.S.-involved (for the time being) theatre of war, in the French Indochina of 1954 is somewhat half-hearted: you can almost count the 10,000 French troops holed up at **Dien Bien Phu** on one hand.

Sam Fuller did much better in portraying the war with his low key **China Gate**; but Schoendoerffer's **317e Section** and his above-mentioned eponymous title are really the only ones to watch out for on this conflict.
With *Jacques Sernas, Kurt Kasznar, Arnold Moss, Peter van Eyck*

JUNGLE FIGHTERS
See **The Long and the Short and the Tall**

JUNGLE PATROL
Joseph Newman — U.S., 1948
Pacific heroics from a small group of U.S. flyers against superior Japanese odds. Definitely second-rate.
With *Arthur Franz, Ross Ford, Kristine Miller*

JUNO AND THE PAYCOCK
(aka 'The Shame of Mary Boyle')
Alfred Hitchcock — GB, 1930 [85min]
Sean O'Casey's play about a poor family caught up in the Irish troubles of the '20s is not really done justice by this early Hitchcock effort. The master had not developed his genius with single-set pieces yet (c/f **Lifeboat**, *Rope, Rear Window, Dial M for Murder*).
With *Sara Allgood, Edward Chapman, Maire O'Neill*

KAGEMUSHA
Destiny is about to change for Takeda (Tatsuya Nakadai) in Kurosawa's return to form. 20CF/Toho

KAFR KASSEM
Borhan Alaouïé — Libya/Syria, 1974 [100min]
Vitriolic Palestinian propaganda dramatising an alleged Israeli atrocity in a Palestinian village during the second Arab-Israeli War in October 1956. It describes the massacre of the villagers as the Israeli Army was pushing into the Sinai as a prologue to the Suez invasion (and the subsequent international incident involving France and Britain).
With *Abdallah Abbassi, Ahmed Ayoud*

KAGEMUSHA (aka 'Kakushi Toride no San-Akunin')
Akira Kurosawa — Japan, 1980 [180min]
Kurosawa's emergence from several years' hibernation was partly financed by aficionados — particularly Francis Coppola and George Lucas. The result is an almost vintage performance from the master, ending with a BAFTA award for his direction, as well an Oscar nomination in the foreign film category and art direction. The 16th century is secure and familiar ground for Kurosawa (**The Hidden Fortress)** and the civil wars amongst the shoguns and the daimyo are in full flow.

The plot involves an **I Was Monty's Double**-type scenario when a sneak thief is coerced into playing a warlord in order to create a diversion. Spectacular colour permeates the court scenes and splendid battle sequences.
With *Tatsuya Nakadai, Tsutomi Yamazaki, Kenichi Hagiwara*

KAISER, THE BEAST OF BERLIN
Rupert Julian — U.S., 1918
It was 1918, and it was relatively safe now to assassinate (at least the character of) Wilhelm II in this outrageous piece of gutter propaganda. As the billboard said, 'Any person throwing mud at this poster will not be prosecuted'.
With *Rupert Julian, Allan Sears, Lon Chaney (Sr)*

The 1918 'let's rubbish the Kaiser' theme also included another cheap side-swipe in **The Kaiser's Finish** ★ from John Joseph Harvey, starring Earl Schenck, where the goal *was* the physical assassination.

THE KAISER'S FINISH
See **Kaiser, The Beast of Berlin**

KAK ZAKALYALAS STAL
See **How the Steel was Tempered**

KAKUSHI TORIDE NO SAN-AKUNIN
See **The Hidden Fortress**

KAMERADSCHAFT See **Westfront 1918**

KAMPFGESCHWADER LUTZOW
See **Bomber Squadron (Wing) Lutzow**

KANAL
Andrzej Wajda — Poland, 1956 [95min]
This was the second of three influential pieces of WW2 cinema to come from Wadja (see also **A Generation** and **Ashes and Diamonds**) and is a hugely pessimistic tragedy. Polish Home Army fighters going underground into the city's sewer system during the 1944 Uprising, only to see their last hopes of freedom and life dashed.

Arguably the most powerful of the three: if **A Generation** brought the director to Western audiences, this was the work that cemented his position as the (perceived) best filmmaker behind the Iron Curtain at the time.
With *Teresa Izewska, Tadeusz Janczar, Vladek Sheybal*

KANSAS PACIFIC
Ray Nazarro — U.S., 1953 [75min]
Weak Western drama on the eve of the Civil War, with Southern interests attempting to block Union moves to extend the railroad to their military outposts.
With *Sterling Hayden, Eve Miller*

KANSAS RAIDERS See **Quantrill's Raiders**

KHARTOUM
The Mahdi's soldiers run past for the cameras! This is one of the great films for war movie buffs. UA

KAPO
Gillo Pontecorvo — France/Italy, 1960 [115min]
Deeply-flawed study of what a human being will do to survive — and then what she might do once guilt sets in. Pontecorvo, whose superb **The Battle of Algiers** was still some time away at this point, gets his character and emotional threads in a bit of a muddle as he leads Strasberg into a Nazi concentration camp; 'elevates' her to *kapo* where she thrives at the expense of her peers; before realising the only way to final redemption is through self-sacrifice. Still achieved a nomination for Best Foreign Film at the Oscars.
With *Susan Strasberg, Laurent Terzieff, Emmanuelle Riva*

KAVKAZSKI PLENNIK See **Prisoner of the Mountain**

KAWASHIMA YOSHIKO
See **The Last Princess of Manchuria**

THE KEEP
Michael Mann — U.S., 1983 [95min]
Similar setting (chateau) and a similar fantasy-based story to **Castle Keep**, but this time it's the Germans who take over the castle (in the Romanian Carpathians — just up the road from Transylvania) to defend a pass during WW2, and succumb to the strange legacy of their temporary billet.

Lots of spiritual mumbo-jumbo, but appealing to those who like their war films slightly out of kilter.
With *Scott Glenn, Alberta Watson, Jurgen Prochnow, Ian McKellen, Gabriel Byrne, Robert Prosky*

KELLY'S HEROES
Brian G. Hutton — U.S./Yugoslavia, 1970 [145min]
Easily the best war-caper movie (for what that's worth), it sees Kelly (Eastwood) organising a motley gang of scammers, skivers and psychos to cross a Rhine bridge behind German lines in WW2 and blow a bank with $16m worth of gold bars. Some funny moments, with type-cast performances from Sutherland and Savalas, and reasonable action scenes (with impressive Tiger tank replicas built over T-34/85s), but where does such an exploitative theme end up? Clint looks suitably unimpressed throughout.
With *Clint Eastwood, Telly Savalas, Don Rickles, Donald Sutherland*

LA KERMESSE HEROIQUE (aka 'Carnival in Flanders')
Jacques Feyder — France, 1935 [115min]
Charming comedy, which is also interesting historically in that it involves a fracas between Spain and the Flemish people during the 12 Years' Truce (the pause which punctuated the seemingly never-ending Netherlands War of Independence). The War began in 1571, and was finally put to rest with the Spanish defeat at Rocroi in 1643 during the complexities of the Thirty Years' War, with independence recognized only through the Peace of Westphalia five years later. Then the old Holy Roman Empire ruled by the Spanish branch of the Hapsburgs was partially dismantled, losing its European hegemony for ever.

These wider political issues, of course, are not covered by Feyder's picture, but the question of collaboration — or otherwise — with an occupying force is addressed rather earlier in the decade than some 'preparedness' propaganda films — if it is to be read other than as just a piece of costume comedy-drama, however good.
With *Françoise Rosay, Luis Jouvet*

THE KEY
Michael Curtiz — U.S., 1934 [70min]
Curtiz beat Ford (**The Informer**) to the punch on the Irish troubles, but this is an inferior picture — concerned primarily with a love story involving the Black and Tans, with the conflict as background.
With *William Powell, Edna Best, Colin Clive, Donald Crisp, Arthur Treacher*

THE KEY
Carol Reed — GB, 1958 [135min]
Hum-drum WW2 drama made worse by its unnecessary length. 'The key' is passed amongst merchant navy personnel about to cross the U-boat infested Atlantic, and unlocks the door to some pre-voyage creature comforts. Decent action at sea — when it comes. Howard's performance earned him a BAFTA Award.
With *William Holden, Trevor Howard, Sophia Loren*

KHARTOUM
Basil Dearden — GB, 1966 [135min]
Fine attention to detail makes this plodding historical drama of the British governance of Anglo-Egyptian Sudan work, especially for war movie buffs. Robert Ardrey's (Oscar-nominated) script is intelligent, but doesn't fully explain the historical context. It is left to the quality battle sequences at the 1885 Battle of Khartoum, and the death of Gordon at the hands of the Mahdi's army, to give the film its high spots. Good performance by Heston as Gordon, but surpassed by an idiosyncratic portrayal of the Mahdi by Olivier.
With *Charlton Heston, Laurence Olivier, Ralph Richardson, Richard Johnson, Michael Hordern*

KHYBER PATROL
Seymour Friedman — U.S., 1954 [70min]
It's the Khyber Pass in the 1890s and the Russians are supplying the Afghans with weapons to fight the British. Average.
With *Richard Egan, Dawn Addams, Raymond Burr*

THE KILLING FIELDS
Roland Joffe — GB, 1984 [140min]
Chris Menges' amazing photography was a most worthy Oscar winner from a most worthy film. The massacre of millions by Pol Pot's Khmer Rouge during the Cambodian Civil War is exposed through the autobiographical story of Pulitzer Prize-winning journalist Sidney Schanberg and his Cambodian interpreter. Very moving, it perhaps dwells too much on the personal relationship, but all-in-all it captures the harrowing bestiality of war as much as any picture on the terrible tragedy that once was French Indochina.

Further Oscars went to startling debutante Ngor for Best Supporting Actor (this was also Malkovitch's first film), and for editing: nominees included the picture, direction — again a debut picture — for Joffe (**The Mission** followed, but little else to date), Bruce Robinson's adapted screenplay, and the understated Waterston. BAFTAs for the picture, screenplay and Ngor.
With *Sam Waterston, Haing S. Ngor, John Malkovitch, Julian Sands, Craig T. Nelson, Bill Paterson*

KIM
Victor Saville — U.S., 1950 [110min]
Kipling's famous yarn of a young orphan taken up by a British

THE KILLING FIELDS
The Khmer Rouge enter Phnom Penh. The stunning cinematography only emphasises the heartless atrocities perpetrated by the Khmer Rouge. Enigma/Goldcrest

intelligence agent in mufti (Flynn) during the British Raj late in the 19th century, is a bit tired and out-moded. It may be, during the Cold War, a timely telling of the tale by Hollywood as Russian spies are perceived to be rife; but it is not in the same class as the pre-war 'empire' films (**Gunga Din**, **The Four Feathers**, etc). Has its few moments of high action when Flynn gets involved.
With *Erroll Flynn, Dean Stockwell, Paul Lukas*

KING AND COUNTRY
Joseph Losey — GB, 1964 [85min]
John Wilson's melancholy play, *Hamp*, is brought commendably to the screen by Losey; and Courtenay gives his usual top-class performance (Best Actor Award — Venice Film Festival) as the misunderstood WW1 deserter at a one-sided court martial.

An appraisal of the English class structure is apparent here, as much as the effects of war on its participants, and Bogarde too, gives a thoughtful performance as the soldier's advocate — a man from the establishment, who for the first time begins to question the Army's attitudes.
With *Dirk Bogarde, Tom Courtenay, Leo McKern, Barry Foster*

KING OF THE KHYBER RIFLES
Henry King — U.S., 1953 [100min]
One more foray into the North-West Frontier (a virtual remake of **Black Watch**), this time set during the Indian Mutiny in 1857. Tyrone Power is half-Indian, half-British, and leads the Khyber Rifles against Afghan enemies. Not over-exciting.
With *Tyrone Power, Terry Moore, Michael Rennie*

KING RAT
Bryan Forbes — U.S./GB, 1965 [135min]
The Holden-Garner 'scrounger' of earlier WW2 POW dramas is given that cynical '60s edge by Segal as he survives while other 'honourable' inmates don't at the hands of the Japanese. Burnett Guffey's camerawork earned an Academy nomination.

It's a small world, the one of POW stories on film. From this film alone there is an impressive list of connections. Writer-director Forbes acted in **The Wooden Horse** and **The Colditz Story**; original author James (**Shogun**) Clavell adapted the screenplay for **The Great Escape**; and James Donald has featured in no less than four POW films — two German, two Japanese (**Bridge on the River Kwai**, **The Great Escape**, this picture and **Hannibal Brooks**).
With *George Segal, John Mills, Tom Courtenay, James Fox, Denholm Elliott, Patrick O'Neal, James Donald*

KING RICHARD AND THE CRUSADERS
See **The Crusades**

KINGS GO FORTH
Delmer Daves — U.S., 1958 [110min]
Melodramatic tale of love and racial tension in the liberated Paris of August 1944, with Wood as the half-caste ditched by GI Curtis when he discovers the awful truth, but then romanced by GI Sinatra. Of course, Curtis then dies on a mission. Not much action here.
With *Frank Sinatra, Tony Curtis, Natalie Wood*

KINGS OF THE SUN
J. Lee(-)Thompson — U.S., 1963 [110min]
Pre-Conquistadores Mexico, and some peace-loving Mayans are ejected from their lands by a tribe of blood-thirsty cut-throats. They cross the Rio Grande (although of course it wasn't named that then) into Texas, and are, unlikely as it may seem, welcomed by Brynner's Red Indians, and given land to settle. However, the bad guys return. As simple as it sounds.
With *Yul Brynner, George Chakiris, Shirley Anne Field, Richard Basehart.*

THE KING'S PIRATE See **Against All Flags**

KIT CARSON
George B. Seitz — U.S., 1940 [95min]
The legendary frontiersman is historical reality, and features either directly or indirectly in pictures made about that most important of all wars to Hollywood — the wresting of Spanish California from Mexico in the Mexican War of 1846-48.

None of the films are particularly worth watching as pure cinema, but it is worth noting that but for Hollywood, events like this and **The Alamo** would not have become familiar to non-U.S. audiences. And it does set **Zorro** in its historical and geographical context!
With *Jon Hall, Dana Andrews, Lynn Bari, Ward Bond*

There was also a silent biopic, **Kit Carson Over the Great Divide ★★** released in 1925.
Other movies concerning the war in California include:
A California Romance ★ (Jerome Stern — U.S., 1923) With *John Gilbert*
California ★★ (WS Van Dyke — U.S., 1927) With *Tim McCoy*
Pirates of Monterey ★★ (Alfred Werker — U.S., 1947, 170min) With *Maria Montez*

California Conquest ★ (Lew Landers — U.S., 1952, 180min) With *Cornel Wilde*
The Man Behind the Gun ★★ (Felix Feist — U.S., 1952, 180min) With *Randolph Scott*

KIT CARSON OVER THE GREAT DIVIDE
See **Kit Carson**

THE KITCHEN TOTO
★ *Harry Hook — GB, 1987* [95min]
★ Drama — one of only a few films embracing the Mau-Mau
★ uprising in Kenya in the early 1950s. This piece just pre-dates the 1952 rebellion following which 11,000 Kikuyu tribes people were killed over a four-year period. The Mau Mau, a secret order of the Kikuyu, took bloody direct action after attempts to rectify land claims were being addressed too slowly, or not at all.

Here, a white policeman takes in a black orphan as kitchen helper, and watches him change over the ensuing months as he struggles with his allegiances and the killings on both sides mount up. Quite well done.
With *Bob Peck, Edwin Mahinda, Phyllis Logan*

KNIGHT WITHOUT ARMOUR
★ *Jacques Feyder — GB, 1937* [105min]
★ Popular romantic adventure involving Donat and Dietrich
★ (she stood by him when producer Korda took umbrage at the amount of time her asthmatic co-star was away from the set) escaping from Revolutionary Russia in 1918. Classy all round, but not much of a plot.
With *Marlene Dietrich, Robert Donat*

KNIGHTS OF THE ROUND TABLE
★ *Richard Thorpe — GB, 1953* [115min]
★ Stripping off the **Excalibur, Lancelot and Guinevere**, Holy
★ Grail and Lyonesse stuff, there is little doubt historically that a Romano-British chieftain out there somewhere gave rise to the legend which Malory, Tennyson and others have taken into the realms of fantasy. Cinema much prefers the later medieval (Malory) folk-lore king of Camelot, with its greater opportunity for pageant, than to delve into the early Dark Ages for something resembling the gritty truth. Not for them the Battles of Badon Hill and Camlann (the possible start- and end-points of Arthur's public life, some time between c490 and 530 AD), nor the post-Roman grot and mysticism (Bresson's **Lancelot du Lac** and Boorman's **Excalibur**, as you might expect, come closest); but the romantic legends of the Knights of the Round Table; the crafty Celt Merlin and the villainous Mordred and Morgana.

This is roughly what we have here (with director and star teaming up again after their adventure as **Ivanhoe** the previous year; and it's set at very much the same time — not half a millennium earlier), for which, surprise, surprise, the Academy nominated it for an art direction Oscar.
With *Robert Taylor, Mel Ferrer, Ava Gardner, Stanley Baker*

Other versions of the Arthurian and/or Holy Grail legends (invariably comic-strip in style — those mentioned in dispatches, above, excepted) include:
Prince Valiant ★★ (Henry Hathaway — U.S., 1954, 100min) With *Robert Wagner, James Mason*
Siege of the Saxons ★ (Nathan Juran — GB, 1963, 185min) With *Ronald Lewis, Janette Scott*

KITCHEN TOTO
Phyllis Logan lies dying after a Mau Mau assault.
Cannon/Skreba/British Screen/Film Four

Excalibur ★★★★ (John Boorman — U.S., 1981, 140min) With *Nigel Terry, Helen Mirren*
Brutal realism, sumptuously shot.
Lancelot and Guinevere ★★ (aka 'The Sword of Lancelot') (Cornel Wilde — GB, 1962, 115min) With *Cornel Wilde, Jean Wallace, George Baker*
Gawain and the Green Knight ★ (Anthony Woollard — GB, 1973, 195min) With *Murray Head*
Lancelot du Lac ★★★★ (aka 'Le Graal', 'The Grail') (Robert Bresson — France/Italy, 1974, 185min) With *Luc Simon, Laura Duke Condominas*
Typically sparse Bresson. A medieval mercenary binge.
Sword of the Valiant ★★ (Stephen Weeks — GB, 1984, 100min) With *Miles O'Keefe, Sean Connery*
More on Gawain and the supernatural.
Indiana Jones and the Last Crusade See separate entry
Price Valiant ★ (Anthony Hickox — Ger/GB/Ire/U.S., 1994, 190min) With *Stephen Moyer, Katherine Heigl*
Loose remake of the 54 swashbuckler.
First Knight ★★★ (Jerry Zucker — U.S., 1995) With *Sean Connery, Richard Gere*
Sensible and sensitive. One for the ladies.
Then, of course, there are:
The Serial — Spencer Bennet's *Adventures of Sir Galahad* (15 eps, U.S., 1949);
The Satirical Comedy — Terry Gilliam's and Terry Jones' *Monty Python and the Holy Grail* (GB, 1975);
The Musical — Alan Jay Lerner's *Camelot* (Joshua Logan — U.S., 1967);
The Cartoons — Disney's *The Sword in the Stone* (U.S., 1963); and *The Magic Sword: Quest for Camelot* (Frederick du Chau — U.S., 1998); and, finally —
The Opera — Wagner's *Parsifal* (filmed by Armin Jordan — West Germany, 1982).

KNIGHTS OF THE TEUTONIC ORDER
(aka 'Krzyzacy')
Aleksander Ford — Poland, 1960 [180min]
Having been established in Jerusalem in 1190, the Knights spent the best part of the 13th century trying to convert (coerce) the Baltic, roughly Polish, pagans to Christianity. The defeat by **Alexander Nevsky** at Lake Peipus in 1242 is well-

documented, but here Ford looks at other events in Poland/Lithuania in a mesmeric sweep of an epic — constructed not unlike a Hollywood blockbuster of its time from someone like Anthony Mann (**The Fall of the Roman Empire**, **El Cid**). Worth seeing.
With *Urszula Modrzynska, Andrzej Szalawski, Grazyna Staniszewska*

KNOW YOUR ALLY: BRITAIN See *Why We Fight*

KNOW YOUR ENEMY: GERMANY See *Why We Fight*

KNOW YOUR ENEMY: JAPAN See *Why We Fight*

KONYETS SANKT-PETERBURGA
See **The End of St Petersburg**

KORCZAK
Andrzej Wajda — France/GB/Germany/Poland, 1990 [120min]
Wadja's (surprisingly) straightforward account of the life of Janusz Korczak, heroic Jewish doctor of the Warsaw Ghetto in WW2 occupied Poland, who time and again defied the Nazis. Should be uplifting, but it's not.
With *Wotjek Pszoniak, Ewa Dalkowska*

KOREA PATROL
Max Nosseck — U.S., 1951
Early Korean War actioner — its smartness out of the trap is all that can be said about it.
With *Richard Emory*

KOZARA See **Hill of Death**

KRZYZACY See **Knights of the Teutonic Order**

KULTUR
Edward J. Le Saint — U.S., 1918
Re-enactment of the episodes that lead to the opening of WW1 — with no little dramatic licence — covering events between Vienna and Sarajevo, as well as a love story.
With *Gladys Brockwell, William Scott*

KUMONOSU-JO See **Throne of Blood**

KUNDUN
Martin Scorsese — U.S., 1997 [135min]
Scorsese inexplicably leaves the *Mean Streets* for the wide-open (tell that to the local populace) spaces of Tibet — actually Morocco and British Columbia — and, good for him, gets away with it. He tells the story, albeit in very rudimentary terms, of the 14th reincarnation of the Dalai Lama, Tensin Gyamtsho, at the time of the Chinese occupation in the 1950s, and the local uprising in 1959 when the Dalai Lama escaped to India. Using Asian amateur actors and visual skills heretofore unexpected from this director, Scorsese turns out a minor masterpiece of cinema. Oscar nominations for Dante Ferretti in both art direction and costume design.
With *Tenzin Thuthob Tsarong, Sonam Phunstok, Gyatso Lukhang, Robert Lin*

KUROI AME See **Black Rain**

DER KURIER DES ZAREN See **The Soldier and the Lady**

LACOMBE, LUCIEN
Louis Malle — France, 1974 [140min]
Malle moved to Hollywood (directing *Atlantic City*, among other things) after howls of criticism at home for taking a Resistance outcast and making him a collaborator — at a time when France was not yet fully on terms with the awful truth (see **Grief and Pity**). As usual, Malle's pictures are never as simple as that, and the way he maps out the confused boy's transformation from would-be patriot to compromised stooge of the local Vichy authorities, and his involvement with a Jewish father and daughter, is both moving and thought-provoking. Nominated for a Best Foreign Film Oscar, it walked away with the BAFTA Best Film Award. Malle was to return to France later to make the slightly-more conciliatory **Au Revoir, les Enfants**.
With *Pierre Blaise, Aurore Clément, Holger Lowenadler*

LADY FROM CHUNGKING
William Nigh — U.S., 1942 [65min]
Anti-Japanese fodder with cardboard action from the Sino-Japanese War.
With *Harold Huber, Anna May Wong, Mae Clarke*

LADY HAMILTON See **That Hamilton Woman**

THE LADY HAS PLANS See **The Conspirators**

THE LADY IN ERMINE
James Flood — U.S., 1927
Not to be confused with the 1948 Ernst Lubitsch musical *That Lady in Ermine*, this romantic adventure uses the Italian states v Austria conflicts of the Italian *Risorgimento*, during the 1860s, purely for background. It's not entirely happy with its history.
With *Corinne Griffith, Einar Hansen*

THE LADY VANISHES
Alfred Hitchcock — GB, 1938 [95min]
Released at a time when appeasement of Hitler's storm-trooping through *Mittel Europa* was the done thing, Hitch's dig at the Nazis still reflected some chance that war might never happen in this, his last British classic before moving to Hollywood (and becoming a little more vitriolic by the time he made **Foreign Correspondent**).
  The basic story of a dear old lady disappearing on a continental train and defying the seemingly limited number of hidey-holes available, is turned by the master into fast-paced, suspenseful and funny mystery-adventure, with the first appearance of the cricket-loving bumblers Charters (Radford) and Caldicott (Wayne) — see also **Night Train to Munich, Crook's Tours** — and Lockwood as a bemused heroine. The allusion to Nazi spies is now less sinister than it must have seemed to 1938 audiences.
With *Margaret Lockwood, Michael Redgrave, Paul Lukas, Dame May Whitty, Cecil Parker, Naunton Wayne, Basil Radford*

Inadvisably remade in 1979 *** by Anthony Page, starring Cybill Shepherd, Elliott Gould, Angela Lansbury, Herbert Lom; with Arthur Lowe and Ian Carmichael as C. and C.

Charters and Caldicott made a BBC TV appearance as a series in 1985 with Robin Bailey and Michael Aldridge.

LAFAYETTE
Jean Dréville — France/Italy, 1961 [160min]
The story of the Marquis de Lafayette — the French Army captain who was appointed major-general in the Continental Army when he offered the U.S. Congress his services against the British in 1777 — is told as the often-vacuous pan-European epic productions are: never mind the narrative, get as many (fading) star cameos in as possible.
With *Michel le Royer, Orson Welles, Jack Hawkins, Vittorio de Sica, Edmund Purdom, Howard St John*

LAFAYETTE ESCADRILLE (aka 'Hell Bent for Glory')
William A Wellman — U.S., 1957 [95min]
The aerial master (**Wings**, *Men with Wings, The High and the Mighty*) made one last visit to the genre. It was Wellman's intended retrospective on his own years as a WW1 flyer with Vanderbilt's U.S. squadron fighting over France before 1917 (a theme he first covered in **Legion of the Condemned** 30 years before). But it became his movie swan-song as a furious bust-up with producer Jack Warner saw him leave the set before shooting had finished, never to make another film. Perhaps the wrangling, or the lightweight (but interesting) cast, or Wellman's ambivalence to the project once it was under way, are the reasons why he didn't go out on a high note.
With *Tab Hunter, David Janssen, Clint Eastwood, Will Hutchins, Etchika Choureau, Bill Wellman Jr, Jody McCrea*

Captain Swagger ★ (Edward H. Griffith — U.S., 1928) with Rod La Roque, also dealt with the same subject.

LANCELOT AND GUINEVERE
(aka 'The Sword of Lancelot') See **Knights of the Round Table**

LANCELOT DU LAC (aka 'Le Graal', 'The Grail')
See **Knights of the Round Table**

LANCER SPY See **The Great Impersonation**

LAND AND FREEDOM
Ken Loach — GB/Germany/Spain, 1995 [110min]
Loach's second and best of his three 'foreign' ventures in latter years (ignoring the purely-political *Fatherland*), after **Hidden Agenda** and before **Carla's Song**, tells of a young Liverpudlian joining the Republican side in the Spanish Civil War, only to find that his brand of socialism doesn't square with that of the other international and home-based anti-fascist factions.

  Jim Allen's most rounded script allows Loach to create, equally well, a war drama, with the action sequences in the trenches a revelation. The hero's courageous but inept Anarchist unit is brought into convincing confrontation with the more rigidly centralised communist Popular Army. The ensemble acting from an international cast is uniformly excellent. One of the very best pictures made on the conflict.
With *Ian Hart, Rosana Pastor, Iciar Bollain, Ton Gilroy, Eoin McCarthy, Marc Martinez, Suzanne Maddock, Frederic Pierrot*

LAND GIRLS
David Leland — France/GB, 1997 [110min]
Supposedly a serious look at Britain's Women's Land Army during WW2, this lovingly recreated — but wholly too nostalgic — view from Leland misses the mark. The three Land Girls represent a cross-section of women trying to do their bit on the farms and still get on with one another — however they only succeed in lusting after a bit of rustic rough or a Canadian flier.
With *Catherine McCormack, Rachel Weisz, Anna Friel, Steven Mackintosh, Tom Georgeson*

LASSITER
Roger Young — U.S., 1984 [100min]
Shallow attempt to make a movie star of Selleck, after, for contractual (*Magnum, PI*) reasons, he couldn't take the role of Indiana Jones in **Raiders of the Lost Ark**. Chasing Nazi spies in the London of 1939, he comes up against some of Scotland Yard's less than finest in a concoction of overworked clichés, both verbal and visual.
With *Tom Selleck, Jane Seymour, Lauren Hutton, Bob Hoskins*

THE LAST ACT (aka 'Der Letzte Akt') See **Ten Days to Die**

THE LAST BLITZKRIEG
Arthur Dreifuss — U.S., 1958 [85min]
Over-the-top anti-war tract based on the English-speaking German commandos who created acts of sabotage behind American lines before **The Battle of the Bulge**.
With *Van Johnson, Keratin Matthews*

THE LAST BRIDGE
Helmut Canter — Austria/Yugoslavia, 1953 [95min]
A film for Germans, by Germans, that the German cinema could not make itself at the time. Schell plays a nurse captured by Yugoslav partisans during WW2, only to realise over time that her captors are right and Nazism and this crazy war are all wrong. It co-stars Wicki, who was to go on and direct one

LAND AND FREEDOM
The ranks of the International Brigade come under fire. Parallax (courtesy KOBAL)

116

of the most compelling of anti-war pictures, **The Bridge**, later in the decade.
With *Catherine Schell, Bernhard Wicki*

THE LAST CHANCE
Leopold Lindtberg — Switzerland, 1945 [105min]
Neutral Switzerland speaks out after the hostilities have ended in this tale of an American and a British POW escaping from Italy in 1943 under cover of a symbolically multi-national shield, to the safety of Switzerland.
With *E.G. Morrison, Ray Reagan*

THE LAST COMMAND
Josef Von Sternberg — U.S., 1928 [100min]
Jannings won the last silent Best Actor Oscar in Hollywood for this, before being unable to cope with talking pictures in English and returning to his native Germany. There he starred in such stomach-churning Nazi propaganda films as **Ohm Kruger** later in life. This first real masterpiece from Sternberg is an ingenious piece of cinema, with the story of a defeated aristocrat general driven out of Russia in 1917 to find, ten years later, that he is acting out the same role in a Hollywood film directed by his ex-Bolshevik opponent.

Amazingly futuristic techniques and the scale of the flash-back sequences to the Revolution is ambitious, but it worked well enough to impress the fledgling Academy to nominate both the picture and Lajos Biro's script for Awards.
With *Emil Jannings, William Powell, Evelyn Brent*

THE LAST COMMAND (1955) See **The Alamo**

THE LAST DAY OF THE WAR
Juan Antonio Bardem — Spain/U.S., 1969 [95min]
Little-known and little-respected end-of-WW2 chase picture with both the Americans and fading Nazis pursuing an escaped German scientist. Little wonder.
With *George Maharis, Maria Perschey*

THE LAST DAYS
Ken Lipper/James Moll — U.S., 1998
Executive-produced by Steven Spielberg, one might expect a populist approach to this documentary, but Spielberg has become a more mature filmmaker and relates the narrative without demeaning the intellectual or psychological effect of a subject matter close to his heart — the Holocaust.

Simply hearing the tales of five Hungarian Jews (now naturalised Americans) incarcerated by the Nazis in 1944, makes one wonder what else is to come out of the closet after half a century. Being Spielberg, too, it won the Best Documentary (feature) at the 1998 Academy Awards.

THE LAST EMPEROR
Bernardo Bertolucci — GB/Hong Kong/Italy, 1987 [160min]
From emperor of the world's most populous nation to a parks gardener — Bertolucci's visual banquet of images covers the life of China since the end of the Manchu (Chi'ing) Dynasty with the Civil War of 1912; and Emperor Pu Yi's passive response. It tells episodically of the Forbidden City imprisonment period, his puppet 'emperorship' during the Sino-Japanese War and his eventual release as a common citizen into Mao's 'Great Leap Forward' in 1959.

Bertolucci's handling of political matters is well-proven (see **The Conformist**), but the overwhelming memories of such a multi-layered classic must be his astonishing use of colour and light; particularly in illustrating the lavishness of the imperial palace and the sumptuous costumes of its inhabitants.

Deservedly the winner of the Best Picture Oscar — it scooped the pool, winning all nine out of nine nominated categories — Bertolucci won two more (for direction, and adapted screenplay with Mark Peploe); Vittorio Stotato (cinematography); Ryuichi Sakamoto (**Merry Christmas Mr Lawrence**) and Talking Heads' David Byrne for the score; and for editing; sound; and, unsurprisingly, for art direction and costume design. The picture was also recognized by BAFTA and raked in awards world-wide.
With *John Lone, Peter O'Toole, Joan Chen, Ryuichi Sakamoto*

THE LAST ESCAPE
Walter Grauman — GB, 1970 [90min]
Another of the 'American rescuing German scientist from the clutch of the Nazis' scenarios — and not a very good one at that.
With *Stuart Whitman, Martin Jarvis*

THE LAST FLIGHT
William Dieterlie — U.S., 1931 [80min]
WW1 psychological action-drama involving U.S. flyers in France — quite effectively putting across its anti-war message through the traumas of veterans who cannot face going home. Breakthrough picture for slick director Dieterlie (*The Life of Emil Zola*, **Juarez**, etc).
With *Richard Barthelmess, Elliott Nugent, John Mack Brown, Helen Chandler, David Manners*

THE LAST FRONTIER (aka 'The Savage Wilderness')
Anthony Mann — U.S., 1955 [100min]
Early, and relatively low-key, run-out for writer-director partnership of Philip Yordan and Mann (**El Cid**, **The Fall of the Roman Empire**). Set after the end of the Civil War, it deals routinely with revolting Indians and a Cavalry outpost.
With *Victor Mature, Guy Madison, Robert Preston, James Whitmore, Anne Bancroft*

THE LAST GRENADE See **The Mercenaries**

THE LAST LIEUTENANT (aka 'Secondvoitnanten')
Hans Petter Moland — Norway, 1993 [100min]
After several WW2 pictures about occupied Norway (**Edge of Darkness**, **The Heroes of Telemark**, etc) a rather late entry into the field from Norwegian cinema, which unfortunately says no more about the resistance/Quislings situation than the sum total of the others.
With *Espen Sjonberg, Lars Andreaslarsen*

THE LAST METRO (aka 'La Dernier Métro')
François Truffaut — France, 1980 [130min]
Truffaut's only war film — indeed the only one with any real kind of political comment — deals with the tensions between the hiders and the hidden in WW2 German-occupied Paris. Jewish theatre manager Bennett hides in his own theatre and can only look on as his wife (Deneuve) gets closer to actor Depardieu. The concentration on interiors and personal dramas minimises the director's attempt to capture the street atmosphere of the occupation. Nominated for Best Foreign Film Oscar, all the same.
With *Catherine Deneuve, Gérard Depardieu, Heinz Bennett, Jean Poiret*

THE LAST OF THE BUCCANEERS
See **The Buccaneer**

THE LAST OF THE COMANCHES See **Comanche**

THE LAST OF THE MOHICANS (1920)
See **The Last of the Mohicans** (1992)

THE LAST OF THE MOHICANS (1936)
See **The Last of the Mohicans** (1992)

THE LAST OF THE MOHICANS
Michael Mann — U.S., 1992

None of the three major versions of this picture (Maurice Tourneur's 1920 ★★ silent with Harry Lorraine and Wallace Beery; George B. Seitz's 1936 ★ [90 min], travesty, starring Randolph Scott and Bruce Cabot, being the other two) have done justice to James Fennemore Cooper's French and Indian War saga. The two British sisters, the Mohicans, Uncas and his father Chingachgook, and of course the trapper Hawkeye, and their to-dos with Magua's Hurons (who are in league with the French) are conventionally treated even in Mann's vastly more intelligent 1992 version — which, incidentally, was nominated for sound.

The sweeping cinematography is seductive; and — thanks to a huge crew of stuntmen — the ambush of the retreating garrison of Fort William Henry is convincingly terrifying. (The part of Magua made Wes Studi's career.)
With *Daniel Day-Lewis, Madeleine Stowe, Russell Means, Eric Schweig, Jodhi May, Steven Waddington, Wes Studi, Maurice Roeves*

A dreadful alternative, entitled **The Last of the Redmen (skins)**, directed by George Sherman, with Jon Hall and Michael O'Shea, was released in 1947 [80min]. Other films in a similar vein include:

The Iroquois Trail ★ [Phil Carlson — U.S., 1950] featuring B-movie king George Montgomery, is just exploitative mishmash on a similar theme.
Canadian TV brought out the successful *Hawkeye and the Last of the Mohicans* in 1957, with *The Lone Ranger* stand-in for Clayton Moore, John Hall, as Hawkeye, and Lon Chaney Jr as Chingachgook: an unsuccessful U.S. attempt was made to put *Hawkeye* back on the TV during the '80s, this time with Lee Horsley and Lynda Carter.

A miserable film version of Fennemore Cooper's **The Pathfinder** [80min], covering another tale of the French and Indian Wars, was made by Sidney Salkow in 1952, and starring Montgomery again.

LAST OF THE REDMEN
(aka 'Last of the Redskins') See **The Last of the Mohicans**

LAST OF THE REDSKINS See **Last of the Redmen**

THE LAST OUTPOST
Charles Barton/Louis Gasnier — U.S., 1935 [75min]
WW1 *Boys' Own* adventure with Grant and Rains as two Britons against what seems to be the whole Kurdish nation. Good, boisterous fun in parts.
With *Cary Grant, Claude Rains*

THE LAST OUTPOST (aka 'Cavalry Attack')
Lewis R. Foster — U.S., 1951 [90min]
Foster uses the above's title, but nothing else, not even the wit, in this very routine Civil War drama where the Blues and the Grays join forces to become the Whites v the Reds for a while. With *Ronald Reagan, Rhonda Fleming, Bruce Bennett, Noah Beery Jr*

THE LAST PLANE OUT
David Nelson — U.S., 1983 [90min]
Drama-documentary of the lowest order based on a journalist's (partially-narrated) memoirs from the Nicaraguan Civil War. With *Jan-Michael Vincent*

THE LAST PRINCESS OF MANCHURIA
(aka 'Kawashima Yoshiko')
Eddie Fong — Hong Kong, 1990 [110min]
(Probably) intended as an antidote to Bertolucci's **The Last Emperor**, Fong's highly stylized, yet highly original portrayal of Yoshiko's espionage adventures during the Sino-Japanese war is exhilarating cinema — the bisexuality symbolising her double-agent enigma.
With *Anita Mui, Andy Lau*

THE LAST SHOT
John Ferno — Holland/GB, 1946
With British finance and equipment, Dutchman Ferno's moving documentary on the devastation of the war in his homeland is particularly striking when it shows how much the physical landscape has been altered — polders awash with seawater again due to the breaching of the dykes, the blighted cities and the smashed infrastructure.

THE LAST STAGE (aka 'Ostatni Etap', 'The Last Stop')
Wanda Jakubowska — Poland, 1947 [110min]
Jakubowska and fellow internee Gerda Schneider recreate the horrors of Auschwitz (actually filmed there) from their combined consciences. A powerful and immensely saddening picture, if sometimes driven by an obsession to put the record straight, coming so soon after the event.
With *Huguette Faget*

THE LAST STOP See **The Last Stage**

LAST TRAIN (aka 'Le Train')
Pierre Garnier-DeFerre — France/Italy, 1973 [100min]
Dull and depressing illicit love story of French married man who has become separated from his family, and a German-Jewish refugee, as they both flee the invading Nazis.
With *Jean-Louis Trintignant, Romy Schneider*

THE LAST TRAIN FROM MADRID
James Hogan — U.S., 1937 [85min]
Gutless, spineless Hollywood cop-out on the Spanish Civil War, with all involved contracting haemorrhoids through so much fence-sitting. See **Blockade**.
With *Dorothy Lamour, Lew Ayres, Gilbert Roland, Anthony Quinn*

THE LAST VALLEY
James Clavell — GB, 1970 [130min]
Ambitious attempt by writer Clavell (**The Great Escape** — adapted; *Shogun* — original story) to write and direct a picture on a conflict which has never figured too highly in the English-

speaking (especially filmmaking) consciousness — the Thirty Year's War, 1618-48. Taking an incident in 1641, Caine's mercenaries arrive at a peaceful valley hitherto untouched by the conflict. Here the pillaging stops, however, due to an 'understanding' between local philosopher Sharif and Caine — who, for the first time, recognises the futility of it all.

A great idea and location for a rattling good yarn is smothered by its pervading pretentiousness. However, it has its visual highpoints, among them the stunning animated title sequence, and a brief but impressive night battle at a city gate — shades of Hieronymus Bosch.

With *Michael Caine, Omar Sharif, Florinda Bolkan, Nigel Davenport, Per Oscgrsson, Brian Blessed, Arthur O'Connell*

THE LAST WILL OF DR MABUSE
See **The Testament of Dr Mabuse**

LATINO
Haskell Wexler — U.S., 1985 [110min]
Incisive anti-U.S. look into the Nicaraguan War through the eyes of a 'Latino' Green Beret sent by Uncle Sam to train Contras in the jungles of Honduras. Pulls no punches in the depiction of the U.S. stance to help defeat the Sandinistas at all cost.
With *Robert Beltran, Annette Cardona*

LAWRENCE OF ARABIA
David Lean — GB, 1962 [220min]
Arguably Lean's greatest cinematic achievement, in which he

THE LAST VALLEY
Michael Caine's mercenaries descend on an unsuspecting community during the Thirty Years War. Cinerama (courtesy KOBAL)

combines an under-the-skin biopic of the almost mystical Lawrence with the epic sweep of a great adventure story; which, if it wasn't based on fact, could have been purpose-built for the big (and wide) screen. The British Intelligence officer, whose derring-do unites the Arabs against the Turks in WW1 at times seems the prototype Indiana Jones.

The acting — spearheaded by an amazing performance by O'Toole in his first starring role, and newcomer Sharif (introduced as a speck on the desert horizon) — is wonderful, and the set pieces (especially the storming of Aqaba) are excitingly handled. Most memorable of all is the beautifully photographed pale canvas of sand — panning out to even more sand, seemingly on to infinity.

Littered with Oscar nominations, it won seven out of nine — including picture, director, Robert Bolt's adapted screenplay, Freddie Young's lensing, Maurice Jarre's score, and for editing, art direction and sound. Only O'Toole and Sharif, in the acting categories, of the film's nominees missed out. BAFTAs for picture, Bolt and O'Toole.
With *Peter O'Toole, Alec Guinness, Anthony Quinn, Jack Hawkins, José Ferrer, Anthony Quayle, Omar Sharif, Claude Rains, Donald Wolfit, Arthur Kennedy*

THE LEATHERNECKS HAVE LANDED
Howard Bretherton — U.S., 1936 [70min]
Low budget hi-jinks as U.S. Marines rescue stranded Americans caught up in the Chinese civil war of the 1930s. Pretty shoddy.
With *Lew Ayres, J. Carroll Naish*

LEAVE ON WORD OF HONOUR See **Pour le Mérite**

THE LEGEND OF TOM DOOLEY
Ted Post — U.S., 1959 [75min]
The story of Rebel youths not accepting the ceasefire and attacking Northern troops at the end of the American Civil War. The folk song upon which it was based became a hit for the Kingston Trio and Lonnie Donegan.
With *Michael Landon, Jo Morrow*

LEGENDS OF THE FALL
Edward Zwick — U.S., 1994 [135min]
Monumental saga of a close Western family built on an epic scale but, of course, subject to some nasty sibling rivalry when the 'family' is affected by external factors (the girl, WW1, etc). Zwick, who directed the impressive **Glory**, goes for scale again, and indeed, John Toll won an Oscar for his camerawork; and Lilly Kilvert was nominated as production designer.

Father Hopkins is an Indian Wars vet who retires from the Army, appalled at the government's handling of the Indian position, to a spread in Montana. His three sons are like male equivalents of *Little Women*, with all the spark and spirit injected into Pitt's character (the 'Jo' persona) and of course with it, all the best scenes. He fights with Quinn over Ormond after seeing youngest brother, Thomas, killed in the WW1 barbed wire. After the war he, and the film, head for oblivion. Ambition and over-confidence, for both character and director, coincide.
With *Brad Pitt, Anthony Hopkins, Aidan Quinn, Julia Ormond, Henry Thomas*

THE LEGION JUMPS ON KOLWEZI
(aka 'La Légion Saute sur Kolwezi')
Raoul Coutard — France, 1980 [100min]
Re-enaction of the incident when French paratroopers took

LATINO
All looks up for Robert Beltran, embroiled between the Contras and Sandinistas in Nicaragua. Lucasfilm/ICA

out a band of terrorists and rescued hostages in Zaire's mining belt in 1978.
With *Bruno Crémer, Giuliano Gemma*

LEGION OF THE CONDEMNED
William Wellman — U.S., 1928
Wellman's first excursion into the world of **Lafayette Escadrille** involved scriptwriter Jean de Lemur, who flew with the director in the squadron in WW1 France. Wellman reused much of the footage that made **Wings** so successful the previous year.
With *Gary Cooper, Fay Wray*

THE LEGION OF THE DAMNED
See **The Battle of the Commandos**

LEGION OF THE DOOMED See **Beau Geste** (1939)

LA LEGION SAUTE SUR KOLWEZI
See **The Legion Jumps on Kolwezi**

LE LEGIONI DI CLEOPATRA
See **The Legions of Cleopatra**

THE LEGION'S LAST PATROL
(aka 'Commando', 'March or Die')
Frank Wisbar — Italy, 1964 [90min]
Standard ageing Granger-type actioner which takes him and his Foreign Legionnaires into war-torn Algeria in 1961.
With *Stewart Granger, Dorian Gray, Fausto Tozzi*

Not to be confused with the 1984 Schwarzenegger CIA block-buster of the same name; or **Commandos** ★ directed in Italy by Armando Crispino in 1968 [90min], with Lee Van Cleef and Jack Kelly, about WW2 Italian commandos in the North African desert; or Dick Richards' **March or Die** (1977). For other Legion pictures see **Beau Geste** (1939).

THE LEGIONS OF CLEOPATRA
(aka 'Le Legioni di Cleopatra')
See **Cleopatra** (1963)

LEKTIONEN IN FINSTERNIS See **Lessons in Darkness**

LENIN IN 1918 See **Lenin in October**

LENIN IN OCTOBER
Mikhail Romm — USSR, 1937 ★
[110min] ★
Stalin approved pictures which ★ almost deified Lenin, as they also showed his protégé in a very good light. Shuchkin plays Lenin and his part in events of the Revolution — a role he reprised two years later for the sequel — **Lenin in 1918** ★★, again directed by Romm — about the leadership of the Bolsheviks during the Civil War.
With *Boris Shuchkin, Nicolai Cherkassov*

LÉON MORIN, PRÊTRE See **Léon Morin, Priest**

LÉON MORIN, PRIEST (aka 'Léon Morin, Prêtre')
Jean-Pierre Melville — France/Italy, 1961 [115min] ★
Melville evokes a painful yet almost nostalgic picture of ★ emotions set in a French country town during the German ★ occupation in WW2. Lovely performances from Belmondo and Riva.
With *Jean-Paul Belmondo, Emmanuelle Riva*

THE LEOPARD (aka 'Il Gattopardo')
Luchino Visconti — Italy, 1962 [205min] ★
Visconti's masterpiece of fading style and grandeur in Italy ★ during the climax of the *Risorgimento* under Garibaldi in Sicily ★ in the early 1860s only fully saw the light of day in 1983. When ★ the picture was released, 20th Century Fox, who had allowed Lancaster to star in the picture subject to reciprocal distribu-tion rights, hacked it to pieces, dubbed it, and wondered why no-one particularly liked it. However Lancaster got rave reviews for his role as the once all-powerful aristo who is coming to terms with the new order (the picture is more concerned with reflection than with the revolution going on outside), and the lavish hour-long ball-room scene at the finale became rightly famous. Then, some 20 years later, the picture was restored to all its intended greatness. Winner of the 1963 *Palme d'Or* at Cannes.
With *Burt Lancaster, Alain Delon, Claudia Cardinale*

LEPA SELA LEPO GORE
See **Pretty Village, Pretty Flame**

LESSONS IN DARKNESS (aka 'Lektionen in Finsternis')
Werner Herzog — France/Germany, 1992 ★
Striking Herzog documentary visualizing the chaos that was ★ Kuwait at the end of the Gulf War. The apocalyptic scenario of ★ grotesquely-billowing flame and smoke, courtesy of Saddam's ★ spite, would seem unreal in fiction.

LEST WE FORGET
Leonce Perret — U.S., 1918
(Once more) over the top WW1 revenge picture as Doughboys fight in the trenches attempting to avenge the *Lusitania* atrocity. Flagwaver with a capital 'F'. Jolivet actually survived the sinking (of the ship, but not necessarily the film).
With *Hamilton Reville, Rita Jolivet*

LEST WE FORGET (1943) See **Hangmen Also Die!**

LETTERS TO AN UNKNOWN LOVER
(aka 'Les Louves') See **The Beguiled**

LETYAT ZHURAVLI See **The Cranes are Flying**

DER LETZTE AKT See **The Last Act**

LIBERATION (aka 'Osvobozhdenie')
Yuri Ozerov — E. Germany/Italy/Poland/USSR/Yugoslavia, 1969
Not to be confused with Dovzhenko's pro-German film made at the time of the Russo-German Non-Aggression Pact (1939-40), this massive co-operative venture recounts, documentary-style, the unfolding of WW2 on the Eastern Front between 1943 and 1945. Made up of four full-length feature films: **The Flaming Bulge**, **The Breakthrough**, **The Direction of the Main Blow** and **The Battle for Berlin**, it was edited down to a two-hour feature, dubbed into English as **The Great Battle ★★★** and re-released in 1971.
With *Nikolai Olyalin, Larisa Golubkina, Boris Zaidenberg*

LIBERTARIAS
Vicente Aranda — Belgium/Spain, 1996 [125min]
1990s female propaganda set against the '30s socialist struggle in Spain. Not too convincing as a Spanish Civil War movie, although there's plenty of blood and gore at the end, but the message is heavy.
With *Anna Belén, Victoria Abril*

EINE LIEBE IN DEUTSCHLAND
See **A Love in Germany**

THE LIFE AND DEATH OF COLONEL BLIMP
Michael Powell/Emeric Pressburger — GB, 1943 [165min]
Up there with the best of the Powell-Pressburger collaborations — many believe it is the best, and perhaps even the best British film of all time. The history of Clive Candy, VC, is told through three wars. Beginning in turn-of-the-century South Africa, he is a dashing young officer; by the time WW1 arrives he learns all there is to know about chivalry in warfare through a Prussian duelling opponent — a sentiment totally dashed by 1943, when he's living through the London Blitz.

The name was taken from David Low's *Evening Standard* cartoon character (satirising the British top brass' pomposity and obsolescence of thought). Attempts by Churchill to stop overseas marketing of this perceived dig at the armed forces (which, of course, it wasn't), at a time when thousands were laying down their lives for their country, failed completely — and UK audiences loved it.
With *Roger Livesey, Deborah Kerr, Anton Walbrook, Roland Culver*

LIFE AND NOTHING BUT (aka 'La Vie et Rien d'Autre')
Bertrand Tavernier — France, 1989 [135min]
Set two years after the Armistice, a French officer is painstak-ingly still trying to identify corpses from WW1. Two Parisian society ladies are attempting to find the graves of their loved ones, but time is running out as the French government wants to glorify a tomb to the Unknown Soldier.

A pacifist tract to stand with the best of them; Noiret beautifully brings out the humanism of the officer, but without a tinge of sentiment, and Tavernier combines all the threads of a complex narrative to come up with a compelling film — winner of a BAFTA Award for Best Foreign Picture.
With *Philippe Noiret, Sabine Azéma, Pascale Vignal*

LIFE IS BEAUTIFUL (aka 'La Vita è Bella')
Roberto Benigni — Italy, 1997 [115min]
Benigni tries the impossible here and for many gets away with it. Although distinctly falling into two parts — a comic idyll set in 1939 Umbria, followed by a tragic story of the Holocaust. The question must be asked, is comedy suitable in any part of the same picture? Undeniably beautifully made with Benigni writing and directing as well as playing the clown-hero, the picture had the unusual recognition of being nominated for Best Picture at the Academy Awards as well as Best Foreign Language Film (which it won). Benigni became the second (non-anglicised) Italian to win the top acting award after Sophia Loren in *Two Women* (1961); the picture also took the top award for Nicola Piovani's score. Benigni's direction was nominated, as was his script (written with Vincenzo Cerami) and a nomination was made for editing (Simona Paggi).
With *Roberto Benigni, Nicoletta Braschi, Giustino Durano, Sergio Bustric, Giorgio Cantarini, Horst Buccholz*

THE LIFE OF ADOLF HITLER See **The Hitler Gang**

THE LIFE OF GENERAL VILLA See **Viva Villa**

LIFEBOAT
Alfred Hitchcock — U.S., 1944 [95min]
Hitch's first totally single-set drama is as close to experimental cinema as mainstream Hollywood would ever get around that time. The confines of the set; the carefully picked cast and characters; the deliberate, even convoluted, spiky script with its purposely-provoking *contretemps* — you get the impression that the director is thinking, 'suck it and see'.

In the end, this blatantly propagandist piece about the lifeboat full of stereotypes, both Allied and German after a passenger ship is sunk by a U-boat in the Atlantic, is cinema to study, not a war picture necessarily to enjoy.
With *Tallulah Bankhead, Walter Slezak, John Hodiak, William Bendix, Hume Cronyn, Canada Lee, Henry Hull, Mary Anderson, Heather Angel*

Hitch was well-bedded down in Hollywood by now, but it is not generally known that he returned to Britain in 1944-45 — immediately following this picture — and made two 30 minute French-language tributes to the Resistance fighters [**Aventure Malgache ★★★** and **Bon Voyage ★★**], before returning and picking up the pieces, and an Oscar nomination for *Spellbound.*

THE LIGHT THAT FAILED (1916)
See **The Light That Failed** (1939)

THE LIGHT THAT FAILED (1923)
See **The Light That Failed** (1939)

THE LIGHT THAT FAILED

William A Wellman — U.S., 1939 [95min]

The third, and marginally the best version of a Kipling story which by 1939 was really past its 'sell-by' date. In 1916, the tale of the British soldier and artist returning from the Sudanese revolt in the 1880s, losing his sight and with it his love, and returning to take on the Mahdi again — knowing that this time he'll not be coming back — was made by Edward Jose, with Robert Edeson ★★★; and in 1923 ★★ by George Melford, starring Percy Marmount. At least Wellman stuck to the original story.

With *Ronald Colman, Walter Huston, Ida Lupino*

LIGHT UP THE SKY

Lewis Gilbert — GB, 1960 [90min]

Sentimental WW2 comedy about life on a searchlight battery during the Blitz. Has its tragic moments — one of which was the day of its release.

With *Ian Carmichael, Tommy Steele, Benny Hill, Sydney Tafler, Dick Emery, Johnny Briggs, Victor Maddern*

THE LIGHTHORSEMEN

Simon Wincer — Australia, 1988 [110min]

Meticulous account of the Aussie cavalry at Beersheba in 1917, charging the German and Turkish artillery. Ruined for the war movie purist by a silly sub-plot and the inevitable love interest. The Australian Lighthorse's Palestine adventures in WW1 were first covered in 1940, with **Forty Thousand Horsemen ★★★**.

With *Peter Phelps, Tony Bonner, Gary Sweet, Bill Kerr, Anthony Andrews*

LILAC TIME (aka 'Love Never Dies')

George Fitzmaurice — U.S., 1928 [90min]

WW1 aviation adventure-cum-melodrama involving RFC airships and German fighter planes over France. Good aerial sequences, but too much romance. No longer the attraction it once was.

With *Gary Cooper, Colleen Moore*

LILI MARLEEN

Rainer Werner Fassbinder — Germany, 1980 [115min]

Fassbinder really went too far with this mythification of the birth of the song (first made famous in Germany by Lale Anderson in 1938). He attempts to elicit a political drama from the supposed story of the song, through pre-war Nazi hysteria and then as an accompaniment for German atrocity during the war itself. The great irony is that *Lili Marlene* (the German spelling) became *the* song of WW2 — with versions in English, French and Italian — and was adopted at first by the British 8th Army in Africa, from the German original.

With *Hanna Schygulla, Giancarlo Giannini*

British documentary maker, Humphrey Jennings [**London Can Take It**, **Fires were Started**], investigated the story on screen in **Lili Marlene** in 1944

LILI MARLENE See **Lili Marleen**

THE LION HAS WINGS

Adrian Brunel/Brian Desmond Hurst/Michael Powell — GB, 1939 [75min]

Plenty of talent was involved in this dawn of the war flagwaver, which actually came out in November 1939, within weeks of the RAF raid on the Kiel Canal and before the Phoney War was seen to be phoney. Audiences would not have believed what they were seeing six months on.

With *Merle Oberon, Ralph Richardson*

LION OF THE DESERT

Moustapha Akkad — U.S./GB/Libya, 1980 [160min]

1929 — Mussolini wants his Carthage back as part of Greater Italy — and anyway, wouldn't Libya serve as a gentle warm-up for Ethiopia? In his way is Bedouin chieftain Omar Mukhtar (Quinn), but Graziani's legions eventually flush him out and hang him. Intriguing cast and lots of reasonable action amongst the *longeurs*, straightforwardly related, about an interesting prelude to the next decade's main spheres of action.

With *Anthony Quinn, Oliver Reed, Rod Steiger, Irene Papas, Raf Vallone, John Gielgud, Andrew Keir*

THE LION'S DEN (aka 'La Boca del Lobo')

Francisco J. Lombardi — Peru/Spain, 1988 [115min]

Peruvian government troops are holed up in a remote Andean village, some time in the late 1980s, being picked off one-by-one by the unseen *Sendero Luminoso* — the communist guerrilla group, the Shining Path.

With the film also considering the abuse of the local Native Americans, Lombardi has not only produced an intelligent anti-war movie, comparative with contemporary U.S. efforts on Vietnam; it is also a serious treatise on human rights in Latin America.

With *Gustavo Bueno, Toña Vega, Gilberto Torres, Bertha Pagaza*

THE LISBON STORY See **The Conspirators**

LITEN IDA See **Little Ida**

THE LITTLE AMERICAN

Cecil B. De Mille — U.S., 1917

One of America's biggest box-office propaganda pictures, hitting theatres just months before the U.S. entered the War. Using the embodiment of the symbol of virtue in Pickford — the object of the evil Hun's animal lust — was a masterstroke which the recruiting offices themselves could not have bettered. She eventually becomes a nurse in France following the German invasion — after going through the standard torpedoing by a U-boat along the way.

With *Mary Pickford, Jack Holt, Husband Bosworth*

LITTLE BIG HORN (1927)
See **They Died with Their Boots On**

LITTLE BIG HORN (1951)
See **They Died with Their Boots On**

LITTLE BIG MAN See **They Died with Their Boots On**

THE LITTLE DRUMMER GIRL

George Roy Hill — U.S., 1984 [130min]

Uneasy piece of political mumbo-jumbo between Arabs and Israelis, based on a lesser Le Carré novel. Too much plotting, too little action, as actress Keaton is used by Mossad agents to infiltrate PLO terrorists.

With *Diane Keaton, Yorgo Voyagis, Klaus Kinski, Anna Massey, David Suchet*

LION OF THE DESERT
Mussoliniis troops disembark in Libya, 1929. Falcon International

LITTLE IDA
Laila Mikkelsen — Norway/Sweden, 1981 [80min]
The end of the German occupation in Norway as seen through the eyes of a little girl, whose mother has been fraternising with a German soldier. Nicely done with a dramatic, colourful finale.
With *Sunniva Lindekliev, Howard Halvorsen, Lise Fjeldstadt*

THE LITTLE SOLDIER See **Le Petit Soldat**

LIVES OF A BENGAL LANCER
Henry Hathaway — U.S., 1934 [120min]
One of the first 'empire' films made in Hollywood, and good enough to encourage the development of the genre through **The Charge of the Light Brigade** and **Gunga Din** later in the decade (although also, it must be said, some pretty routine fare too; eg Sidney Salkow's bare-faced copy, **Storm Over Bengal **** in 1938, which even reuses Cromwell and Dumbrille in similar officer and native roles).

A mite faded now, the tale of father and son in the same command on the North-West Frontier of India is rather woolly, but the on-location action sequences are fine. Oscar nominations for the picture; for the multi-handed adaptation of Francis Yates-Brown's adventure yarn; direction; art direction; and editing — but no statuettes.
With *Gary Cooper, Franchot Tone, Richard Cromwell, Sir Guy Standing, Kathleen Burke, Monte Blue, Douglas Dumbrille, C. Aubrey Smith, Akim Tamaroff, J. Carroll Naish*

LIVING IN PEACE (aka 'Vivere in Pace')
Luigi Zampa — Italy, 1946
One of three popular farces which Zampa, between 1946 and 1948, used to illustrate the absurdity of war — using the conflict's finale in Italy as his canvas. Followed by **The Honourable Angelina *** (with Anna Magnani) in 1947, and **The Difficult Years *** in 1948 and starring Umberto

Spadaro, the works come as a welcome relief from the heavy realism of Rossellini (**Paisà**, **Open City**) from the same period — but they are not without pathos.
With *Aldo Fabrizi*

LOLA See **The Marriage of Maria Braun**

LONDON CAN TAKE IT (aka '*Britain Can Take It*')
Humphrey Jennings/Harry Watt — GB, 1940
The short documentary on the Blitz and the Battle of Britain that really opened up the eyes of the Free World — viz America — to the plight of Britain and the might of Germany. It was, in fact, slightly revised for the U.S. market and released as **Britain Can Take It**.

THE LONE EAGLE
Emory Johnson — U.S., 1927
WW1 flying drama, featuring the RFC, which stuttered in the shadow of Wellman's **Wings** in the same year.
With *Raymond Keane*

LONE STAR See **The Alamo**

THE LONG AND THE SHORT AND THE TALL
(aka 'Jungle Fighters')
Leslie Norman — GB, 1960 [105min]
Britain's new realistic cinema of the turn of the decade (*Room at the Top, Saturday Night and Sunday Morning*, etc) introduced a tough edge to all genres — and, although it seems very mild now, this was heavy drama at the time. The story of a British patrol in the Burmese jungle during WW2, becoming more and more paranoiac and divided over what to do with their Japanese captive, started life as a successful play with a young Peter O'Toole in the lead and Lindsay Anderson (*This Sporting Life, If, O! Lucky Man*) directing — but both were untried cineastes. Norman (**Dunkirk**) took over, and although his direction is taut, he is hamstrung by the stagey sets.
With *Laurence Harvey, Richard Todd, David McCallum, Richard Harris, Ronald Fraser, John Meillon, Kenji Takaki*

THE LONG DAY'S DYING
Peter Collinson — GB, 1968 [95min]
Poorly constructed film from Alan White's perceptive novel about the apparent paradox of professional soldiery happily harbouring pacifist beliefs. The three lost Tommies and their German prisoner go through the motions of dying in WW2 without the film hitting the right nail on the head.
With *David Hemmings, Tom Bell, Alan Dobie, Tony Beckley*

THE LONG DUEL
Ken Annakin — GB, 1967 [115min]
Superfluous tosh. This attempt to revive the British Raj picture was at least 15 years too late, and at least in the early '50s you knew what rubbish to expect. Much barking and posturing from the leads as the North-West Frontier gets stirred up again.
With *Trevor Howard, Yul Brynner, Harry Andrews*

THE LONG GOOD FRIDAY
John Mackenzie — GB, 1979 [105min]
The one jewel in the director's crown — albeit a little tarnished. McKenzie takes the complex action at a fair lick as East End hoodlum boss Hoskins (in the role that made him a star),

cock-a-hoop after thinking he's put one over on the Chicago mafia, bites off more than he can chew when he takes on the IRA as well. Very violent, and not too politically convincing, but Hoskins is worth the admission fee alone — and look out for Brosnan's debut as an Irish hit-man.

With *Bob Hoskins, Helen Mirren, Dave King, Derek Thompson, Brian Marshall, Eddie Constantine, Pierce Brosnan*

THE LONG RIDE See **Brady's Escape**

THE LONG RIDE HOME See **A Time for Killing**

THE LONG SHIPS See **The Vikings**

THE LONG VOYAGE HOME
John Ford — U.S., 1940 [105min]

Restrained Ford adaptation of the Eugene O'Neill play about life at sea and the interrelationships of the men, updated to take in the drama of WW2, when a merchantman is attacked by a German plane.

With *John Wayne, Thomas Mitchell, Ward Bond, Ian Hunter, Wilfrid Lawson, Barry Fitzgerald*

THE LONGEST DAY
Ken Annakin/Andrew Marton/Bernhard Wicki — U.S., 1962 [170min]

A triumphant marriage between cinema and one of the greatest days in all history (D-Day) — but like all good marriages, some wrinkles along the way. A war movie in the traditional sense (so many of the 40-odd stars cut their teeth on '40s, and particularly '50s, vintages, they probably couldn't play it any other way), it is full of individual heroics, national stereotypes and verbal clichés — it only (thankfully!) lacks the love story.

The use of international directors to deal with the different approaches to the U.S. and British-Canadian landing beaches (Annakin the British, Marton the American) and the German defence (Wicki, he of the **Bridge**), and with some linking (interfering?) work by Darryl F. Zanuck, one of the producers, works out well . . . on the whole.

The story, based on Cornelius Ryan's blockbuster book, is adapted by a clutch of Hollywood screenwriters and one can see the seams every now and again. However, the action is realistic and plentiful, with one scene particularly memorable — the horizon shot of the 'armada' as seen from a German pill-box above Omaha Beach.

The bevy of cinematographers picked up the Oscar for their monochrome filming and it was nominated for best picture — a rarity for such a mob-handed production. All concerned should be congratulated on a pretty satisfactory outcome.(PS: 'Red Buttons' is still hooked on to the church roof at Ste Maire Eglise by his parachute, the last time I looked!)

With *John Wayne, Robert Mitchum, Henry Fonda, Richard Todd, Richard Burton, Curt Jurgens, Robert Ryan, Rod Steiger, Kenneth More, Robert Wagner, Gert Frobe, Richard Beymer, Bourvil, Mel Ferrer, Jeffrey Hunter, Peter Lawford, Christian Marquand, Edmond O'Brien, Leo Genn, Red Buttons, Donald Houston, Sean Connery, Christopher Lee, Paul Anka*

LOOKING FOR RICHARD See **Richard III**

LOST COMMAND
Mark Robson — U.S., 1966 [130min]

Looking for topicality, and issued, coincidentally or not, at a

THE LONGEST DAY
A brave attempt to emphasize the scale of the D-Day landings. 20CF

time of deepening U.S. involvement in Vietnam, the film traces a unit of French paratroopers from honourable defeat in Indochina to — well — further defeat in Algeria; although the film's *dénouement* doesn't make that clear.

The film encapsulates all the tribulations of colonial war, has plenty of action, and pauses for some anti-war contemplation — but as a picture it doesn't inspire. Jean Larteguy's original novel *Les Centurions* really needed a French script and production to capture its true flavour.

With *Anthony Quinn, Alain Delon, George Segal, Michèle Morgan, Claudia Cardinale*

THE LOST PATROL (1929) See **The Lost Patrol** (1934)

THE LOST PATROL
John Ford — U.S., 1934 [75min]

Regarded now as something of a classic, if only for the number of copy-cat pictures it spawned (see **Bataan**, **Sahara**, for instance), Ford's first critical and box-office success now looks decidedly creaky.

A group of British soldiers, lost in the Meso-potamian desert during WW1, are picked off one by one by hostile tribesmen. MacLaglen's brother, Cyril, appeared in the original (British) version, directed by Walter Summers in 1929.

With *Victor MacLaglen, Boris Karloff, Wallace Ford, Alan Hale*

An Italian film of the same title [aka 'La Pattuglia Sperduta'], made in 1954 ★★ by Pierri Nelli and starring Sando Isola, is not a remake. It deals with the rumbling *Risorgimento* conflict, here Sardinia helping Lombardy against the occupying Austrians who were in turmoil after the 1848 revolution in Vienna.

THE LOST PATROL (1954)
(aka 'La Pattuglia Sperduta') See **The Lost Patrol** (1934)

THE LOST SQUADRON See **The Great Waldo Pepper**

LOTNA

Andrzej Wajda — Poland, 1959

Wajda turns his attention to the Polish cavalry, and the eponymous pony in particular, who in 1939 attempted to blunt the Blitzkrieg. Hopeless heroics simply related by the now new master of Polish cinema. (With *Jerzy Pichelski, Adam Pawlokowski, Jerzy Moes*

Channel Four TV's *A Flame to the Phoenix* dealt with the same subject.

LES LOUVES See **Letters to an Unknown Lover**

THE LOUVRE TICKET OFFICE

(aka 'Les Guichets du Louvre')

Michel Mitrani — France, 1974 [100min]

Stark WW2 drama of 16,000 French Jews rounded up in July 1942 and awaiting transportation in Paris to concentration camps. One of several French pictures in the early '70s at last acknowledging that collaboration and general non-involvement was as prominent as the Resistance during the German occupation. With *Michel Auclair, Christine Pascal*

LOVE AND ANARCHY (aka 'Film d'Amore e d'Anarchia')

Lina Wertmuller — Italy, 1973 [110min]

Wertmuller came to attention of mainstream audiences with this tale of politics and romance in fascist Italy in the '30s. Giannini plays the simpleton who attempts to assassinate Mussolini, Melato the soft-hearted whore. Giannini won the Best Actor award at Cannes. With *Giancarlo Giannini, Mariangela Melato*

LOVE AND DEATH

Woody Allen — U.S., 1975 [85min]

The last and best of Allen's early films, here Allen's sight gags are as common as the social insecurities which were to dominate in his later films. Using every cinematic style imaginable — from Eisenstein to Groucho Marx via Bob Hope and Ingmar Bergman — through the vehicle of his standard arch-coward character (loosely based on Tolstoy's Pierre Bezhukov from **War and Peace**), Allen proceeds to send up Napoleon's 1812 campaign. The assassination attempt on the Emperor, the Battle of Borodino — they're all there somewhere. The satire hardens into anti-war propaganda at a time when 'I told you so's' were rife in post-Vietnam America. With *Woody Allen, Diane Keaton*

LOVE AND GLORY

Rupert Julian — U.S., 1924

Itself a remake of the 1916 picture, **The Bugler of Algiers**, this silent deals with the colonial uprising in 1860s Algeria, involving two French soldiers and the girl they love. Interesting only for the scenario. With *Charles de Roche, Madge Bellamy, Wallace MacDonald*

LOVE AND SACRIFICE See **America**

LOVE IN A FALLEN CITY (aka Qingchengzhi Lian')

Ann Hui — Hong Kong, 1984 [95min]

Highly stylized romantic history of the Japanese invasion and occupation of Hong Kong in 1941. Good period feel, but the metaphors don't work. With *Cora Miao, Chow Yun Fat*

A LOVE IN GERMANY (aka 'Eine Liebe in Deutschland')

Andrzej Wajda — France/West Germany, 1983 [105min]

Wajda attempts to get under the skin of Nazism in this depressing tale of a German woman falling for a Polish POW while the neighbours and the Gestapo tut-tut and peek behind their curtains.

Not his best by any means. With *Hanna Schygulla, Armin Mueller-Stahl, Daniel Olbrychski, Bernhard Wicki*

LOVE NEVER DIES See **Lilac Time**

THE LOVE THIEF See **Viva Villa**

LOVE UNDER FIRE

George Marshall — U.S., 1937 [75min]

Comedy adventure with a backdrop of the Spanish Civil War. This sort of exploitative rubbish was typical of Hollywood's contribution to the conflict (see **Blockade**, **Last Train from Madrid**). With *Loretta Young, Don Ameche*

LUCIA

Humberto Solas — Cuba, 1969 [160min]

The story of three of Cuba's revolutions (1895, 1933 and 1958), told through the lives of three women, is probably just about the most informative picture about the history of that country since Spanish rule. Furthermore, an early stab at female emancipation, too. With *Raquel Revuelta, Eslinda Nuñez, Adela Legra*

LUCIE AUBRAC

Claude Berri — France, 1998 [115min]

Moving, if sometimes sentimental true story of Lucie and her Jewish husband Raymond, who both fought with the Maquis in WW2. With *Carole Bouquet, Daniel Auteuil*

LUCKY JORDAN

Frank Tuttle — U.S., 1942 [85min]

A con-man turns spy to infiltrate Nazi plotting in 1941 America. Run-of-the-mill espionage drama. With *Alan Ladd, Helen Walker*

THE LUCKY STAR

Max Fischer — Canada, 1980 [110min]

Not to be confused with the 1938 Sonja Henie skating extravaganza (!), this likeable film has developed minor cult status. A Dutch-Jewish youth wreaks revenge on the occupying forces during WW2 after his parents are hauled off to concentration camps. With *Rod Steiger, Louise Fletcher, Brett Marx*

LUDWIG

Luchino Visconti — France/Germany/Italy, 1972 [185min]

Typically Visconti in its historical pageantry and detail (**The Leopard**, **The Damned**), this picture loses interest in the world outside (Bavaria's siding with Prussia against France in 1870) to develop Mad Ludwig's passion for young boys and Wagner. It's a pity, as too few pictures, since the heyday of German nationalistic cinema of the 1930s, have concentrated on the Franco-Prussian War. With *Helmut Berger, Romy Schneider, Trevor Howard, Gert Frobe*

LUDWIG — REQUIEM FOR A VIRGIN KING
See **Hitler, a Film from Germany**

LYDIA BAILEY
★ *Jean Negulesco — U.S., 1952* [90min]
★ Interesting background subject — the 13-year revolt of slaves against the French colonial power on Saint-Domingue (Hispaniola) between 1791 and 1804, which resulted in the world's first independent black state — Haiti. Shame about the picture.
With *Dale Robertson, Anne Francis.*

MAARAKAT ALGER See **The Battle of Algiers**

MacARTHUR (aka 'MacArthur the Rebel General')
Joseph Sargent — U.S., 1977 [130min] ★ ★
Duly respectful biopic, bordering on deification — though it doesn't flinch from MacArthur's lust for publicity and the rewards of victory. Everybody is trying to keep the rig on an objective path, but the steering mechanism's failed, as the general is reluctantly plucked out of **Corregidor**, returns as promised to take the Japanese surrender, and then finds that he's no match for political expediency come the Korean conflict. At least he is played by Peck, who oozes dignity like a latter day Cooper or Fonda, as Sargent tugs at the great man's spiritual intestines rather more than the rationed action sequences.
With *Gregory Peck, Dan O'Herlihy, Ed Flanders*

MacARTHUR THE REBEL GENERAL See **MacArthur**

MACBETH
Orson Welles — U.S., 1948 [90min] ★
Welles is again out to prove the impossible can be done — ★
well, almost. He shot this adventurous yet tin-pot, version of ★
the Scottish Play in just three weeks. Don't look at the flaws, ★
just marvel at filmmaking on the very edge.
  During the Scottish civil wars of the 11th century, King Duncan is murdered by his general Macbeth (and his wife, of course), following a fortune-telling experience on some blasted heath. Macbeth takes an uneasy throne, riddled with guilt and the ghost of fellow general Banquo (also murdered), before being killed by MacDuff who is leading the army of revenge on behalf of Duncan's son, Malcolm.
With *Orson Welles, Jeanette Nolan, Dan O'Herlihy, Roddy McDowall*

A particularly gory version by Roman Polanski in 1971 ★★★ [140min] — made shortly after the murder of his wife, Sharon Tate, by Manson's gang — starred Jon Finch and Francesca Annis; whilst an impoverished 130-minute British version was released somewhat embarrassingly in 1997 ★★ by Jeremy Freeston, with Jason Connery and Helen Baxendale.

Kurosawa's production, **Throne of Blood**, ★★★★★ released in 1957 [105min], with Toshiro Mifune and Isuzu Yamada, takes the action to medieval Japan where he directs probably *the* definitive adaptation of a Shakespeare work for the cinema, in one of the most beautifully-filmed of movies.

MACBETH (1971) See **Macbeth** (1948)

MACBETH (1997) See **Macbeth** (1948)

THE McCONNELL STORY
Gordon Douglas — U.S., 1955 [105min] ★
Limp biopic of WW2 and Korean War U.S. pilot Capt Joseph

WAR FILMS – M

McConnell, who was killed testing a new jet fighter.
With *Alan Ladd, June Allyson, James Whitmore*

McGUIRE GO HOME See **The High Bright Sun**

THE McKENZIE BREAK
Lamont Johnson — GB, 1970 [105min]
Seemed like a good idea to turn the tables, a quarter of a century after the event, and show German POWs incarcerated in a British (Scottish) prison camp. It works pretty well, too, with hard men like Hendry (**The Hill**) among the MPs, and an Irish maverick played in character by Keith as an Army investigator, until the anti-Nazi propaganda sets in.

Whereas in the POW dramas of the '50s and '60s, Allied officers are all jolly good chaps and the well-being of the men is paramount, here Griem plays a stereotypical Nazi whose men are to sacrifice themselves for the good of their officer. A disappointing cop-out in an otherwise interesting and exciting movie partly based on truth — there really were cases of Nazi POWs murdering fellow prisoners after holding a 'court of honour', and of a U-boat attempting a pre-arranged pick-up of German escapees.
With *Brian Keith, Helmut Griem, Ian Hendry*

MADAME PIMPERNEL See **Paris Underground**

MADAM SPY (1918) See **Madame Spy** (1942)

MADAME SPY (1934) See **Madame Spy** (1942)

MADAME SPY
Roy William Neill — U.S., 1942 [65min]
The second film of this title issued by Universal in eight years, but dealing with different scenarios. Karl Freund's 70-min 1934 ★ edition (with Fay Wray and Nils Asther) considered romance among Austrian and Russian spies during the Great War, while Neill turns his attention to WW2 and the subject of double agents.
With *Constance Bennett, Don Porte*

LE MAHABARATA
Warfare 3,500 years ago. Virgin/Les Productions du 3Ème Etage

To add to the confusion, a third picture, **Madam Spy** — a 1918 silent — sees Jack Mulhall cross-dressing to foil a WW1 German spy ring.
None of the three is worth the admission money.

MADEMOISELLE DOCTEUR
Edmond Greville — GB, 1937 [85min]
Fact-based spy melodrama based on WW1 romance between a German **Mata Hari**-type and a British Intelligence officer.
With *Dita Parlow, John Loder, Erich von Stroheim, Clifford Evans*

Originally, with a slightly varied plot, **Stamboul Quest ★★★** made in 1934 [88min] by Sam Wood, with Myrna Loy, George Brent and Lionel Atwill: remade, with somewhat less panache, by Alberto Lattuada as **Fräulein Doktor ★** in 1968 [105min], with Suzy Kendall, Kenneth More and James Booth.

MADEMOISELLE FIFI
Robert Wise — U.S., 1944 [70min]
Pseudo-allegorical (hints at German ruthlessness and French collaboration?) adaptation of two de Maupassant short stories about honour and patriotism during the Franco-Prussian War. Stripped of its didacticism, it is more than a half-interesting melodrama, neatly played.
With *Simone Simon, Kurt Kreuger, John Emery, Jason Robards Sr*

MADEMOISELLE FRANCE See **Reunion in France**

MADEMOISELLE FROM ARMENTIERES
Maurice Elvey — GB, 1926
Elvey's second hit of the year, after his acclaimed version of the **Flag Lieutenant**, deals with the famous story-in-song of the brave French girl who helps British Tommies escape from the Germans in WW1. Good action scenes of trench warfare.
With *Estelle Brody*

MAGNIFICENT DOLL See **The Buccaneer**

LE MAHABHARATA
Peter Brook — France, 1989 [170min]
Hacked down from nine hours (even longer in its TV version), the expanse and grandeur, not to say the narrative, of the original, is lost in the theatre version. The 3,500-year-old epic poem about the Indian clans of the Pandavas and Kauravas was first put on stage — Brook's first home (RSC, ROH Covent Garden, etc) — but the film version shows that the decision to screen it, at least in its long incarnation, was justified. The colours are memorable and the music helps the narrative bound along; the action sequences are plentiful and dynamic. Despite the essential fantasy of warfare set back in the cradle of civilization, the message is there for all to see.
With *Urs Bihler, Ryszard Cieslak, Georges Corraface*

MAJOR DUNDEE
Sam Peckinpah — U.S., 1964 [135min]
As if touching his forelock to the conventional (Fordian?) Western when he paired Hollywood vets Joel McCrea and Randolph Scott two years before in *Ride the High Country* (aka *Guns in the Afternoon*), Peckinpah starts to paint *his* portrait of U.S. history in this rough, gory, yet eloquent film. Building into the plot a cross-section of events occurring in America during the 1860s (Civil War, marauding Apache, French intervention and revolution in Mexico) together with strong

personal character-drawing (especially Heston's jaundiced Federal zealot of the title role) the footings of the Pekinpah cinematic edifice of the next decade and more are established.
With *Charlton Heston, Richard Harris, Jim Hutton, Senta Berger, James Coburn, Warren Oates*

MALAYA (aka 'East of the Rising Sun')
Richard Thorpe — U.S., 1949 [95min]
Despite a strong cast, with Greenstreet, in particular, in good form, this based-on-fact adventure tale of two ex-cons contracted to Uncle Sam to free up some Malayan rubber from underneath the noses of the occupying Japanese, is something of a flat tyre.
With *Spencer Tracy, James Stewart, Sydney Greenstreet, John Hodiak, Valentina Cortesa, Gilbert Roland, Lionel Barrymore*

THE MALTA STORY
Brian Desmond Hurst — GB, 1953 [105min]
Disappointing drama about an under-represented campaign of WW2, which resulted in the presentation of the George Cross to the island and its people for courage in the face of incessant German and Italian bombing in 1942.
With *Alec Guinness, Anthony Steel, Jack Hawkins, Flora Robson*

MAMBA
Al Rogell — U.S., 1930 [75min]
Piffly action adventure set in East Africa in 1914 with the brouhaha just about to begin — Germans v Brits v Zulus(?)!
With *Jean Hersholt, Eleanor Boardman, Ralph Forbes*

THE MAN AT THE GATE
Norman Walker — GB, 1941 [50min]
Morale booster about how Cornish fishermen go about their business avoiding U-boats in WW2. Not top-notch.
With *Wilfred Lawson*

THE MAN BEHIND THE GUN See **Kit Carson**

A MAN ESCAPED
(aka 'Un Condamné à Mort s'est Echappé)
Robert Bresson — France, 1956 [100min]
Probably the most joyous film to come from distant director Bresson — but of course that doesn't mean it's at all happy. He tells the true tale of a French Resistance POW escaping from the Nazis in Lyon, in a spirit-lifting, quasi-religious atmosphere sublimated by the heavenly Mozart Great Mass in C Minor. A definite experience!
With *François Leterrier*

THE MAN FROM DAKOTA
Leslie Fenton — U.S., 1940 [75min]
Hokey Civil War drama as two Yankees escape from a Rebel POW camp. Saved by some spirited acting by Beery.
With *Wallace Beery, John Howard, Dolores del Rio*

THE MAN FROM MOROCCO
Max Greene — GB, 1944 [115min]
Nonsense about a Vichy-sponsored rail venture in WW2 North Africa and the (reluctant) hero who escapes to Britain with the gen.
With *Anton Walbrook, Margaretta Scott*

THE MAN FROM THE ALAMO See **The Alamo**

A MAN FROM WYOMING
Rowland V. Lee — U.S., 1930
WW1 romantic drama with Cooper as the Doughboy dumped by his wife. Coop though should have been the one to do the dumping — when he read the script.
With *Gary Cooper, June Collyer*

MAN HUNT
Fritz Lang — U.S., 1941 [100min]
Great fun as Lang (*Metropolis, You Only Live Once*) lightens up and shows that he can make a fast-paced thriller with the best of them. In fact, the story is downright corny — a British big-game hunter fancies a trophy to top the lot, so he tries to assassinate Hitler. Caught at Berchtesgaden by the Gestapo, he's tortured before escaping back to England, where he's chased in an exciting climax through the Hollywood equivalent of Surrey, or Dorset — or does it matter.
With *Walter Pidgeon, Joan Bennett, George Sanders, John Carridine, Roddy McDowall*

Remade for BBC TV by Clive Donner in 1976 under novelist Geoffrey Household's original title of *Rogue Male*, with an interesting cast including Peter O'Toole (in the Pidgeon role of Thorndike), playwright Harold Pinter, and — in his last role anywhere — the great Alastair Sim.

THE MAN I KILLED (aka 'Broken Lullaby')
Ernst Lubistch — U.S., 1932 [75min]
Highly rated at the time, this intelligent drama complemented the pacifist movie output at the beginning of the '30s (**All Quiet . . .**, **Journey's End**, **Kameradschaft**, etc), in its tale of a French soldier visiting the parents of a German adversary he had shot during WW1. Just descends into melodrama, unfortunately.
With *Lionel Barrymore, Nancy Carroll*

THE MAN I MARRIED (aka 'I Married a Nazi')
Irving Pichel — U.S., 1940 [80min]
Panic in the States as people everywhere were double-checking the backgrounds of their spouses, when Bennett discovers that Lederer, a German-American, just can't help being a Nazi. Funny now, but back then . . .
With *Joan Bennett, Francis Lederer, Lloyd Nolan, Maria Ouspenskaya*

THE MAN IN THE MIDDLE
Guy Hamilton — GB, 1964 [95min]
Political shenanigans during a WW2 murder court-martial of a U.S. lieutenant in India. Absorbing for the most part, but decidedly stagey.
With *Robert Mitchum, France Nuyen, Barry Sullivan, Trevor Howard, Keenan Wynn*

MAN OF CONQUEST See **The Alamo**

MAN OF THE CROSS (aka 'L'Uomo della Croce')
Roberto Rossellini — Italy, 1943
The last of three Rossellini propaganda films for the Italian fascists, after **The White Navy ★★** (1941) which concentrated on the work of hospital ships; and **A Pilot Returns ★★★★** (1942) when a flyer rejoins his unit after a period as a POW in Greece. This picture looks at the Italian deeds of derring-do on the Eastern Front, but through the eyes of an army priest,

leading some commentators to whiff a scent of pacifism permeating through the superficial heroics.
With *Alberto Tavazzi*

THE MAN WHO NEVER WAS
Ronald Neame — GB, 1955 [100min]
British Military Intelligence went in for all kinds of games and wheezes during WW2. **I Was Monty's Double** was one, and this plot to fit up a dead body with false documents and toss him into the sea where the Germans could find him was another. The rest of the picture deviates from the actual event for the sake of dramatic enhancement, with some success — Nazi spy Boyd's effort to check the dead man's background gives Grahame a memorably tense scene. Nigel Balchin collected a BAFTA for his adapted script.
With *Clifton Webb, Robert Flemyng, Gloria Grahame, Stephen Boyd*

THE MAN WHO RECLAIMED HIS HEAD
Edward Ludwig — U.S., 1934 [80min]
Anti-war tract involving double standards and highly dubious armament deals; as well as front-line heroics and domestic duplicity in WW1 France. Curious.
With *Claude Rains, Lionel Atwill, Joan Bennett*

THE MAN WHO WOULD BE KING
John Huston — GB, 1975 [130min]
Huston's dream come true. After planning to film the Kipling fable about greed and adventure on the 1880s Indian-Afghan border (Kafiristan) using dream-pairs of actors of different generations (Gable and Bogart, then Burton and O'Toole), he elicits vibrant performances from '70s icons Connery and Caine. They play British Raj NCOs with a nose for a scam, who are tempted by delusions of grandeur, with Connery subsequently being made ruler of an isolated mountain kingdom.

The picture goes over the top in parts, but it bowls along with great verve and humour and is sprinkled with good action set pieces, as the soldiers train the tribesmen in the arts of British soldiering. Huston finally got his bookend characters to complement Bogart's in *The Treasure of the Sierra Madre*.
With *Michael Caine, Sean Connery, Christopher Plummer*

THE MAN WITHOUT A COUNTRY (1917)
See **The Barbary Pirate**

THE MAN WITHOUT A COUNTRY (1925)
See **The Barbary Pirate**

THE MANCHURIAN CANDIDATE
John Frankenheimer — U.S., 1962 [125min]
From a director with his fair share of 'what might have been' scenarios (*Seven Days in May*,

Prophecy, **The Fourth War**) this picture was too topical for its own good. Dealing with the hitherto only rumoured effects of Korean War POW brainwashing programmes — in this scenario designed to make repatriated guinea pigs assassins of prominent political targets — it was withdrawn in the States after John Kennedy's killing, and not re-released until 1988.

Harvey, as the 'zombie', and Sinatra are excellent; and Lansbury was nominated for her role as the brainwashed victim's mother. Most of the kudos, however, must go to Frankenheimer, for tying up all the strings in this intelligent and haunting film. Unfortunately he was never able to match this in his later movies.
With *Laurence Harvey, Frank Sinatra, Janet Leigh, Angela Lansbury*

MANILA CALLING
Herbert I. Leeds — U.S., 1942 [80min]
Routine flagwaver involving U.S.-Filipino irregulars at the time of the Japanese invasion in WW2. Heavy on action, light on sense.
With *Lloyd Nolan, Cornel Wilde*

MANON
Henri-Georges Clouzot — France, 1949 [95min]
It says much about Abbé Prévost's tale of the 18th century coquette, that this was the first-ever straight film version (Jean Aurel's *Manon 70*, with Catherine Deneuve, came two decades later); yet Massenet (*Manon*) and Puccini (*Manon Lescaut*) had made operas from it in the 19th century. Clouzot, incomprehensibly, transplants the story into post-Liberation France, where the tease has moved from collaboration to

THE MAN WHO WOULD BE KING
A pause in the fighting to allow the priests to cross the battlefield.
Columbia/Allied Artists/Persky-Bright/Devon

black-marketing before she gets her final come-uppance.
With *Cécile Aubry, Michel Auclair*

Carmine Gallone (**Scipio Africanus**) filmed Puccini's opera in 1939.

MAN'S HOPE See (L')Espoir

THE MAP OF THE HUMAN HEART
Vincent Ward — Austria/Canada/France/GB, 1992 [110min]
Sprawling, often misguided, historical saga, set partly in Inuit Canada and partly in Europe. The film is devoted mainly to romantic matters, but includes WW2 aerial scenes as the old Eskimo who recounts the tale tells of his days in RAF Bomber Command.
With *Jason Scott Lee, Patrick Bergin, Jeanne Moreau, Anne Parillaud, John Cusack*

THE MARCH OF TIME
Louis de Rochemont (prod) — U.S., 1935-54
15-minute information documentaries which brought cinema-goers in America up to date on world events for nearly 20 years. It was, however, in the period leading up to WW2 and during the conflict itself that the series came into its own and did much to 'prepare' the population for hostilities as much as recruit and propagandise.
Some of the most evocative titles were:
U.S.A — Rehearsal for War (1937); *Inside Nazi Germany* (1938); *Inside the Maginot Line* (1938); *Crisis in the Pacific* (1940); *The Republic of Finland* (1940); *Britain's RAF* (1940); *America Prepares* (1941); *Peace — by Adolf Hitler* (1941); *Crisis in the Atlantic* (1941); *China Fights Back* (1941); *Australia at War* (1941); *Men of Norway* (1941); *G-Men Combat Saboteurs* (1941); *Battlefields of the Pacific* (1942); *America at War* (1942); *The Ramparts We Watch* (extended) (1942); *The Fighting French* (1942); *Prelude to Victory* (1943); *Food and War* (1943); *Preparation for Invasion* (1943); *Underground Report* (1944); *Back Door to Tokyo* (1944); *What to do with Germany* (1944); *The Returning Veterans* (1945)

MARCH OR DIE (1964) See The Legion's Last Patrol

MARCH OR DIE (1977) See Beau Geste (1939)

MARE NOSTRUM
Rex Ingram — U.S., 1925 [110min]
Famous fated love story from the pen of Vicente Blasco Ibáñez (**The Four Horsemen of the Apocalypse**), again put on the screen by Ingram, between a Spanish sea captain and a beautiful German spy in WW1. Action sequences include a German submarine being sunk by the hero's vessel. Big box office at the time.
With *Alice Terry, Antonio Moreno*

MARIE ANTOINETTE
W.S. Van Dyke — U.S., 1938 [160min]
Expensive, lavish costume drama dealing with the life of the monarchy before, and just after, the French Revolution. Has virtually no historical interest; neither did the 1955 ★★ French remake by Jean Delannoy [95min], with Michèle Morgan, Jacques Morel and Richard Todd. The 1938 version got Oscar nominations for Shearer, Morley and Herbert Stothard's music.
With *Norma Shearer, Tyrone Power, John Barrymore, Robert Morley*

MARIE ANTOINETTE (1955)
See **Marie Antoinette** (1938)

MARIE WALEWSKA See Conquest

MARINE RAIDERS
Harold Schuster — U.S., 1944 [90min]
One of the lesser contributions to the story of the U.S. Marines at Guadalcanal in WW2. See **Guadalcanal Diary**.
With *Pat O'Brien, Robert Ryan, Ruth Hussey*

THE MARINES ARE COMING See Flight

THE MARINES FLY HIGH See Flight

MARINES LET'S GO
Raoul Walsh — U.S., 1961 [105min]
Walsh redeems himself with some sparkling action in what is otherwise, for him, a pretty disappointing foray into the Korean War.
With *Tom Tryon, David Hedison*

THE MARK OF ZORRO
Douglas Fairbanks — U.S., 1920 [90min]
The first of two pictures with the same name, and generally speaking, along with **The Mask of Zorro** (see below) the three best films concerning the black-clad Don Diego de Vega. Set usually (although some incarnations take huge historical liberties) in 1840s California amid Spanish colonialism and the clamour for independence. Johnston McCulley's cartoon character was a huge success from the start, giving Californians in the 1920s their own period **Robin Hood**.
With *Douglas Fairbanks, Marguerite de la Motte, Noah Beery*

In 1940 ★★★ a classy Rouben Mamoulian version [95min], starred Tyrone Power, Basil Rathbone, J. Edward Bromberg and Linda Darnell, and Alfred Newman's score was nominated.

Other 'Zorro' pictures include:
Zorro Rides Again ★ (*William Witney/John English, U.S., 1937*, 70min) with John Carroll, Helen Christian.
Serial stitched together.
The Sign of Zorro (Norman Foster/Lewis R. Foster, U.S., 1960, 190min) with Guy Williams and Lewis R. Foster
One of several Disney concoctions originally seen on TV — and also the title two years later of an appalling vehicle for Sean Flynn.
Zorro ★★ (Duccio Tessari, Fr/It, 1975, 100min) with Alain Delon and Stanley Baker
For some reason set in South America.
Zorro the Gay Blade ★★ (Peter Medak, US, 1982, 195min) with George Hamilton, Lauren Hutton.
Spoof homophile version, predictable for its release date.
The Mask of Zorro ★★★ (Martin Campbell, US, 1998, 135min) Enjoyable romp which sees Anthony Hopkins pass over the Zorro mantle to Antonio Banderas; with Catherine Zeta Jones. This version received two Oscar nominations: for sound and sound effects editing.

THE MARRIAGE OF MARIA BRAUN
(aka 'Die Ehe der Maria Braun')
Rainer Werner Fassbinder — Germany, 1978 [120min]
The first of Fassbinder's loose triptych on Germany at the end

MATA HARI
As if butter wouldn't melt in her mouth. Sylvia Krystel playing (against type) the innocent with some suitably stereotypical Hun. Cannon

of WW2. Although this first story has its beginnings in 1943 Berlin under Allied bombing, and Maria's husband is fighting on the Russian Front, this, and the following **Lola ★★★** (1982, 115min) with Barbara Sukowa (in an update of the *Blue Angel* story); and **Veronika Voss ★★★** with Rosel Zech (his last picture, in the same year [105min], about a has-been actress who appeared in Third Reich extravaganzas), are really commentaries on the state of post-war Germany. The devastation, lack of morality, corruption and pessimism for the future, despite reconstruction, all take their toll on the audience.
With *Hanna Schygulla*

LA MARSEILLAISE
Jean Renoir — France, 1938 [145min]
Classic, romanticised retelling of how it was in 1789, with the decadent aristos losing out to the upright commoners, and all get their just deserts. Heroism and human rights pervade the picture, made within months of the master's **La Grande Illusion**, at the time of the Popular Front, and unlike the out-and-out anti-war stance of that picture, the message here is as much 'Frenchmen — fight for your rights'.
With *Pierre Renoir, Lise Delamare, Louis Jouvet*

THE MARTYRDOM OF NURSE CAVELL
See **Nurse Edith Cavell**

THE MARTYRS OF THE ALAMO See **The Alamo**

M★A★S★H★
Robert Altman — U.S., 1970 [115min]
Battle Circus with real blood, guts and total irreverence. Altman's cutting war satire, both literally and metaphorically, follows the edge-of-paranoia antics of two wise-cracking surgeons at a U.S. mobile hospital in Korea. Apart from the war, Altman digs at authority, sexual mores and the church, in a maelstrom of gags, set pieces and continuous mayhem. The fact that this was 1970 suggests that the military barbs were

not unconnected to another Asian war. The film won an Oscar for Ring Lardner Jr's adapted script (from Richard Hooker's acerbic novel), and nominations for picture, director, and ('Hot Lips') Kellerman for supporting actress.
With *Donald Sutherland, Elliott Gould, Tom Skerritt, Sally Kellerman, Robert Duvall, Gary Burghoff, Jo Ann Pflug*

A TV spin-off (with Burghoff the only cross-over actor as Radar O'Reilly) ran for 12 years; mainly through the writing of Larry Gelbart and its faithful star, Alan Alda, who plays Sutherland's Hawkeye Pierce much like Groucho Marx in Bilko's motor pool.

THE MASK OF ZORRO See **The Mark of Zorro** (1920)

MASSACRE IN ROME (aka 'Rappresaglia')
George Pan Cosmatos — France/Italy, 1973 [105min]
Filmed in English with a mostly British tinge to the top of the cast list, this is pretty routine WW2 fare about German reprisals in Rome, based on the actual Ardeatine Tunnels massacre of March 1944 led by SS Colonel Hubert Kappler.
With *Richard Burton, Marcello Mastroianni, Leo McKern, John Steiner, Robert Harris, Delia Boccardo, Peter Vaughan, Anthony Steel*

THE MASTER OF BALLANTRAE
William Keighley — GB, 1953 [90min]
Stevenson's classic novel about support and otherwise for the Young Pretender's, Bonnie Prince Charlie's, 1745 rebellion against the House of Hanover, deserved a better fate than this dull adaptation — its star not-withstanding.
With *Errol Flynn, Anthony Steel, Roger Livesey*

Douglas Hickox brought out a TV version in 1984, featuring Richard Thomas, Michael York, Timothy Dalton, and John Gielgud, no less. It was also quite a yawn.

THE MASTER RACE
Herbert J. Biberman — U.S., 1944 [95min]
It all looks up for the Nazis, so the time has come to cut the losses, disappear for a while, and then hit the world with the Fourth Reich. This cheaply-made second feature set when the Germans were retreating before the Allies after D-Day — gets full marks for the concept.
With *George Coulouris*

MASTERS OF MEN
David Smith — U.S., 1923
Romantic tosh, set at the outbreak of the Spanish-American War of 1898. Some decent naval action, nevertheless.
With *Earle Williams, Cullen Landis*

MATA HARI
George Fitzmaurice — U.S., 1931 [90min]
Released shortly after Dietrich had portrayed Agent X-27 in **Dishonored**, Garbo seemed the obvious choice for WW1's semi-legendary slinky spy. But she was not the only good thing on show in a picture where you get more because you somehow expect less.
With *Greta Garbo, Ramon Navarro, Lionel Barrymore, Lewis Stone*

A desperately bad version was brought out as late as 1985 [110min], by Curtis Harrington and starring Sylvia Kristel —

so you can guess where most of the action takes place. **Mata Hari, Agent H21** — also pap — was released in Italy in 1964 by Jean-Louis Richard [100min], with Jeanne Moreau, who should have known better. **Mata Hari's Daughter** (updated to WW2 Java) from Renzo Meruis (1954, 100min), and featuring Ludmilla Tcherina, defies description.

MATA HARI (1985) See **Mata Hari** (1931)

MATA HARI, AGENT H21 See **Mata Hari** (1931)

MATA HARI'S DAUGHTER
(aka 'The Daughter of Mata Hari') See **Mata Hari** (1931)

A MATTER OF LIFE AND DEATH
(aka 'Stairway to Heaven')
Michael Powell/Emeric Pressberger — GB, 1946 [105min]
P and P's wonderful fantasy of love overcoming death. An RAF bomber pilot during WW2, Niven is shot down and mistakenly allowed to live by the heavenly court that makes such judgements. He appeals against his number being up, because he fell in love with a woman *after* his appointed fatality should have taken place (during his perceived fight for life). The film gets away with murder (as well as reversing euthanasia), but just proves that no medium other than cinema could have made such a dog's breakfast of ideas work.

Produced as an attempt by the Ministry of Information to foster GB-U.S. post-war goodwill, it works when you know it shouldn't: a surreal charabanc of ideas, witticism, production and performances. Did it work as propaganda? Well, the title had to be changed for U.S. markets, so the two nations weren't on the same wavelength, at least there.
With *David Niven, Kim Hunter, Roger Livesey, Robert Coote, Marius Goring, Raymond Massey, Richard Attenborough*

LES MAUDITS (aka 'The Damned')
René Clément — France, 1947 [105min]
Important early exposure of prominent Nazis escaping 1945 Germany and attempting to set up the means to fight on in South America. Sort of **Ship of Fools** six years on, as the rats, literally, leave the sinking ship this time as they squabble amongst themselves, instead of fleeing oppression as in the other picture. The ship on this occasion is a U-boat. Provocative.
With *Henry Vidal, Dalio, Michel Auclair*

MEDITERRANEO
Gabriele Salvatores — Italy, 1991 [90min]
Lost and forgotten on an Aegean island in 1941 when their ship is sunk offshore, eight Italian military misfits eke out a Lotus-eating existence, seemingly for the duration.

An old-fashioned whimsical comedy with the modern cinematic distractions of sex and nudity, supposedly with a pacifist message, it won the Best Foreign Film Oscar — proving that it needn't be a metaphysical challenge to win an award.
With *Diego Abatantuono, Claudio Bigaglio*

MEIN KAMPF See **The Hitler Gang**

MEIN LEBEN FUR IRLAND See **My Life for Ireland**

THE MEMPHIS BELLE
William Wyler — U.S., 1944
Celebrated colour documentary from Col Wyler, on the lines

of *Target for Tonight*, looking at the life aboard a Flying Fortress operating from England on bombing raids over Germany in 1943-44.

A feature film of the same name by Michael Caton-Jones in 1990 *** [105min], and starring Matthew Modine, Eric Stoltz, Billy Zane, Jane Horrocks and Harry Connick Jr, was inspired by the Wyler documentary. The *Belle* was the first 8th USAAF B-17 to complete 25 daylight missions, and the 1990 version supposedly tells the story of the crew immediately before and during their final operation. It benefits from modern production values, and offers good aerial combat sequences; but although the cast are more convincingly young than in most war movies, some of the character stereotyping is still cringe-making, and the relentless piling-on of incident after incident destroys credibility.

MEMPHIS BELLE (1990) See **Memphis Belle** (1944)

THE MEN (aka 'Battle Stripe')
Fred Zinnemann — U.S., 1950 [85min]
Remembered for Brando's screen debut, it was equally ground-breaking in its honesty concerning problems affecting paraplegic WW2 vets — especially opening up the question of sex and paralysis. Brando is, of course, immense, and Carl Foreman's Oscar-nominated script continued his impressive Hollywood start (he was nominated the previous year for *Champion*), before his credits on *High Noon*, **Bridge on the River Kwai**, **The Guns of Navarone**, **The Victors**, etc. He was blacklisted by HUAC — hence his association with the later British titles. Zinnemann was warming up nicely, too, for *High Noon*, before **From Here to Eternity** — and would continue to direct with flair and insight for many years to come (*A Man for All Seasons, The Day of the Jackal, Julia*, and many others).
With *Marlon Brando, Teresa Wright, Everett Sloane, Jack Webb*

MEN IN WAR
Anthony Mann — U.S., 1957 [105min]
Low-key Korean War effort for Mann and his favourite scripter, Philip Yordan, with the inevitable hill to be captured by U.S. soldiers fighting their way back to HQ. Still quietly effective, with its underlying theme of blind loyalty, and, of course, Mann's complete control over his actors in their hostile environment.
With *Robert Ryan, Aldo Ray, Vic Morrow*

MEN MUST FIGHT
Edgar Selwyn — U.S., 1933 [75min]
Anti-war fantasy echoing H.G. Wells' *The Shape of Things to Come*, but pre-empting the filmed version **Things to Come** by some three years. It predicts friction among Americans some time towards the end of that decade, between isolationism and involvement; but when New York is bombed by the 'enemy', all pacifist leanings are dispelled. One for the archive — but to be taken out and looked at from time to time.
With *Diana Wynyard, Lewis Stone, Robert Young*

MEN OF SHERWOOD FOREST
See **The Adventures of Robin Hood**

MEN OF THE FIGHTING LADY
Andrew Marton — U.S., 1954 [80min]

Not the WW2 carrier made famous in de Rochemont's documentary **The Fighting Lady** ★★★ but Korean War exploitation — with routine plot and 'borrowed' footage — about a carrier and its jet fighter complement.
With *Van Johnson, Walter Pidgeon*

MEPHISTO
Istvan Szabo — Hungary, 1981 [145min]
Based on the novel by Thomas Mann's son Klaus, the Faustian legend is updated to inter-war Germany. Brandauer is thrilling as the actor selling his art (Brechtian theatre) to the Nazis (Göthe readings, for example) in order to become someone; his contemporaries, meanwhile, leave Germany (as Mann and his father did) in droves.

Deserved Oscar in the foreign language film category.
With *Klaus-Maria Brandauer, Krystyna Janda*

The combination of director and star was realised again, with almost the same magic, in **Colonel Redl** and **Hanussen**.

THE MERCENARIES (aka 'Dark of the Sun')
Jack Cardiff — GB, 1968 [100min]
Expert lenser Cardiff (**The Four Feathers, A Matter of Life and Death**, *Black Narcissus*, **War and Peace**) never had quite the same ability at the helm, and this turns out to be a turgid tale of **Dogs of War** in the Belgian Congo, c1960. Based on a Wilbur Smith novel.
With *Rod Taylor, Yvette Mimieux, Kenneth More, Peter Carsten, Jim Brown, André Morrell*

Other films which concern mercenary activity in post-colonial Africa (with most countries in question remaining entirely anonymous, or just downright fictitious), include:
The Last Grenade ★★ (Gordon Flemyng — GB, 1969) With *Stanley Baker, Richard Attenborough, Honor Blackman, John Thaw*
The Wild Geese ★★★ (Andrew V MacLaglen — GB, 1978) With *Richard Burton, Roger Moore, Richard Harris, Stewart Granger*

More like Frederick Forsyth's *The Dogs of War* than **The Dogs of War**!
The Dogs of War ★ (John Irvin — GB, 1980) With *Christopher Walken, Colin Blakely, Tom Berenger*. Amateurish adaptation of Frederick Forsyth's least-effective novel.

IL MERCENARIO (aka 'A Professional Gun') See **Bandido**

MERRILL'S MARAUDERS
Samuel Fuller — U.S., 1962 [100min]
As with much of Fuller, when you leave your local Roxy you think you've sweated as much blood as the exhausted cast, so involving is the every-day, bread-and-butter, grunt-and-fart soldiering. In this, a dry run for his *magnum opus* **The Big Red One**, we fight our way through the Burmese jungle as a squad of tough-nuts trying to help the Brits against the Japs; using every method in the book to kill the enemy, and many more that aren't.

Based on the true exploits of Brig-Gen Frank D. Merrill's version of Orde Wingate's Chindits, doing their bit to stop the Japanese progressing to India: although it didn't cause as much anti-American stir in British cinemas as Walsh's provocative **Objective Burma!** did. Ironic casting of clean-cut TV cowboy heroes, Hardin (*Bronco*) and Hutchins (*Sugarfoot/Tenderfoot*) in gritty roles: but one of the grittiest of them all, Chandler, died before the film was released.
With *Jeff Chandler, Ty Hardin, Will Hutchins, Claude Akins*

MERRY CHRISTMAS, MR LAWRENCE
Nagasia Oshima — GB, 1982 [125min]
One to love or to hate. This film, based on a semi-autobiographical novel by Laurens van der Post, and set in a Japanese POW camp in 1942 Java, is not for the purist fan of POW dramas. With its overt homosexual references and its difficult ethos-balance between Japanese and Western cultures, it is definitely not **The Great Escape**. It is, nevertheless, a prickly experience, with the much underrated Conti (as Lawrence) excellent, and the rest of the cast, especially Takeshi and the BAFTA recipient Sakamoto, nearly up there with him. There are echoes of **Bridge on the River Kwai**, but the first western picture by controversial director Oshima (*Ai No Corrida*) can be the product of no-one else.
With *David Bowie, Tom Conti, Ryuichi Sakamoto, Takeshi, Jack Thompson*

THE MESSAGE See **Mohammad, Messenger of God**

A MESSAGE TO GARCIA
George Marshall — U.S., 1936 [85min]
Good acting elevates this spy drama from the hum-drum. Based in Cuba during this offshoot branch of the Spanish-American War.
With *Wallace Beery, Barbara Stanwyck*

MICHAEL COLLINS
Neil Jordan — U.S., 1996 [130min]
Reasonably satisfying biopic of one of the founders of the Irish

MERRY CHRISTMAS, MR LAWRENCE
More Japanese POW camp monstrosities, but more-eloquently aired in Bridge on the River Kwai.
Recorded Picture/Cineventure TV/Oshima

Republican Army, after the collapse of the Easter Rising in 1916. Jordan seems to be getting closer to the mark with each successive film on the subject (**Angel**, **The Crying Game**), although the historical purist would like to have seen more of Collins' negotiations with the British which led to the compromise of the Irish Free State and his eventual death at the hands of the irreconcilable IRA faction during the Irish Civil War.

Good action shots and super acting throughout, especially by Neeson (as Collins), Rea, and Rickman's slightly-affected De Valera. Neeson won the Venice Acting Prize and the picture the Golden Lion, while the outstanding atmospheric photography of Chris Menges (**The Killing Fields**, **The Mission**) collected an Oscar nomination, as did Elliot Goldenthal's score. With *Liam Neeson, Stephen Rea, Aidan Quinn, Julia Roberts, Alan Rickman*

MICHAEL STROGOFF See **The Soldier and the Lady**

A MIDNIGHT CLEAR
Keith Gordon — U.S., 1992 [105min]
Arguably the most intelligent film made with the **Battle of the Bulge** as backdrop, Gordon's own script from William Wharton's autobiography uses humour and pathos in equal degree to enunciate the futility of war. Sent by their martinet CO to set up an OP in a gutted house, a U.S. Intelligence unit meet German soldiers wishing to express some Yuletide good will (they even have a snowball fight).

Christmas card settings in the snowy Ardennes forest seem to sum up the mood, before the counter-attack takes place with devastating results.
With *Peter Berg, Kevin Dillon, Arye Gross, Ethan Hawke*

MIDWAY (aka 'The Battle of Midway')
Jack Smight — U.S., 1976 [130min]
Big stars and reused footage summarise the incongruity of this dinosaur. Setting out, no doubt, to make the definitive movie of the battle that changed the war in the Pacific in 1942, Smight has reduced the picture to a series of cameos stitched together by newsreel and some genuinely fine action shots by Harry Stradling Jr (*Hello Dolly*, **Go Tell the Spartans**). An opportunity missed. Fonda plays Nimitz; Mitchum, Halsey; and Mifune is Yamamoto.
With *Charlton Heston, Henry Fonda, Robert Mitchum, Toshiro Mifune, Glenn Ford, James Coburn, Hal Holbrook, Robert Wagner, Edward Albert*

MILLE OTTOCENTO SESSANTA See **1860**

MILLIONS LIKE US
Frank Launder/Sidney Gilliat — GB, 1943 [105min]
Launder gets a direction credit for the only time with his scriptwriting partner, in this dour but popular picture of Britain's home front during WW2. It waves the flag vigorously, highlighting the sterling work achieved through female workers in an aircraft factory.
With *Patricia Roc, Gordon Jackson, Moore Marriott, Eric Portman, Basil Radford, Anne Crawford*

It unintentionally preceded a similar type of U.S. picture in **Rosie the Riveter** *** (Joseph Santley, 1944, 175min) with Jane Frazee and Frank Albertson — itself providing the background inspiration for Jonathan Demme's 1982 romantic

wartime drama, **Swing Shift** ** [100min], which brought together Goldie Hawn and Kurt Russell for the first time.

MINISTRY OF FEAR
Fritz Lang — U.S., 1944 [85min]
Clever Lang suspenser set amongst spies in WW2 London (read Paramount sets). Full of dark humour and characteristically heavy atmosphere, it takes great liberties with Graham Greene's original novel, but produces well above-average cinema.
With *Ray Milland, Marjorie Reynolds, Carl Esmond*

LES MISERABLES (pre-1935 versions)
See **Les Misérables** (1935)

LES MISERABLES
Richard Boleslawski — U.S., 1935 [110min]
Victor Hugo's sprawling slice of humanity, bridging the French Revolution and the Battle of Waterloo and beyond, through the perennial misfortunes of Jean Valjean — *The Fugitive* of Napoleonic Europe — has been documented on film more often than most works of literature. Boleslawski's is easily the best English-language version, but look to France — particularly the 1933 Bernard version — for the most faithful adaptations.
With *Frederic March, Charles Laughton, Cedric Hardwicke*

Some other versions are:
Les Misérables ** (J. Stuart Blackton — U.S., 09) With *Maurice Costello*
Les Misérables * (Albert Capellani — France, 13) With *Mistinguett, Marie Ventura*
Les Misérables ** (Frank Lloyd — U.S., 1917) With *William Farnum*
Les Misérables ** (Henri Fescourt — France, 1925) With *Gabriel Gabrio*
The Bishop's Candlesticks (U.S., 1929) With *Walter Huston*
Les Misérables **** (Raymond Bernard — France, 1933, 205min) With *Harry Baur*
Originally in three parts (*Tempête sous un Crane; Les Thénardiers; Liberté, Liberté, Chérie*) totalling over five hours: then edited into two 100+ minute sections — *Jean Valjean* and *Cosette*.
Les Misérables * (Riccardo Freda — Italy, 1946) With *Gino Cervi*
Les Misérables ** (Lewis Milestone — U.S., 1952, 106min) With *Michael Rennie*
Skimmed-over version: more of the Milestone enigma
Les Misérables de Victor Hugo *** (aka 'Les Misérables') (Jean-Paul Le Chanois — France/Italy/East Germany, 1958, 210min) With *Jean Gabin*
This can also be seen in two parts, or its over 3-hour entirety.
Les Misérables *** (Robert Hossein — France, 1982, 185min) With *Lino Ventura*
Les Misérables **** (Claude Lelouch — France, 1995, 175min) With *Jean-Paul Belmondo*
Valjean is memorably updated to Nazi-occupied France in WW2.
Il Miserabli ** (Riccardo Freda — Italy, 1997) With *Gino Cervi, Valentina Cortese*
Les Misérables ** (Billie August — U.S., 1998) With Liam Neeson, Uma Thurman, Geoffrey Rush
Unnecessary umpteenth remake — with only Neeson to look out for to make it interesting.

There are also two particularly good TV movies of the same name came from France (by Marcel Bluwal in 1972, with Georges Géret); and the other from the U.S. (made in 1978 by Glenn Jordan and starring Richard Jordan and Anthony Perkins, as the hunted and the hunter): and, of course, *that* stage musical from Alain Bourbil and Claude-Michel Schönberg.

LES MISERABLES (post-1935 versions)
See **Les Misérables** (1935)

LES MISERABLES DE VICTOR HUGO
See **Les Misérables** (1935)

IL MISERABLI See **Les Misérables** (1935)

THE MISFIT BRIGADE (aka 'Wheels of Terror')
Gordon Hessler — GB/U.S., 1987 [100min]
The Dirty Dozen in reverse, as German convicts are shanghaied into the crumbling army. Why bother to return to an overworked theme, which was itself exploitational anyway? And is the title descriptive of the cast?
With *Bruce Davison, David Carridine, Oliver Reed*

MISSILES FROM HELL See **The Battle of the V1**

MISSING
Costa-Gavras — U.S., 1982 [120min]
Powerful and frightening, Costa-Gavras' first English-language film (*Z*, **State of Siege**) gets right into the psyche of a military

MISSING
Tension on the streets of Santiago during the Pinochet coup. Universal

coup — Allende's Chile at the time of the Pinochet take-over in 1973. The story of Lemmon looking for his lost son in Santiago is secondary to the political structuring which is paramount to this director. With Donald Stewart, the director collected the Oscar (and BAFTA) for adapting Thomas Hauser's book, while the picture and the stars were nominated. With *Jack Lemmon, Sissy Spacek*

MISSING IN ACTION
Joseph Zito — U.S., 1984 [100 min]
This breast-beating box-office blockbuster even preceded **Rambo** in its heroic springing of U.S. POWs by U.S. Special Forces from Vietnam, years after the cessation of the war. Crude, violent and pathetically shallow, it went on to a prequel, directed by Lance Hool the following year, called **Missing in Action 2 — The Beginning** [95min]; and a sequel, Aaron Norris' **Braddock: Missing in Action 3**, in 1988 [100min]. Aaron's brother starred in all three.
With *Chuck Norris*

MISSING IN ACTION 2 — THE BEGINNING
See **Missing in Action**

THE MISSION
Roland Joffe — GB, 1986 [130min]
The David Puttnam/Roland Joffe combination that made **The Killing Fields** doesn't quite produce such a memorable piece of cinema here, interesting though it is. Two centuries on from Cortés and Pizarro, Europeans (this time Spanish and Portuguese) are still squabbling over the hinterland of South America, aided and abetted by whichever church faction you support. The upshot: it's only the Native American who really suffers.

Hampered by a muddled script from the erstwhile master, Robert Bolt (**Lawrence of Arabia**, **Dr Zhivago**, *A Man for All Seasons*); the action however is well done, with the director having the classy Chris Menges on top cinematographic form. Indeed Menges won the film's only Oscar.

De Niro looks a little out of place plucked from his New York habitat, but Irons, and especially McAnally (BAFTA Award) are very good. Further Academy Award nominations were for the picture and the director, for Ennio Morricone's score (he also won a BAFTA), and for editing, art direction, costumes and sound.
With *Robert de Niro, Jeremy Irons, Ray McAnally, Aidan Quinn, Cherie Lunghi, Ronald Pickup*

MISSION OVER KOREA
Fred F Sears — U.S., 1953 [85min]
Oh dear — more flagwaving claptrap with a title that says

far more than the whole film does in its 85 minutes.
With *John Hodiak, John Derek, Maureen O'Sullivan*

MISSION TO MOSCOW
Michael Curtiz — U.S., 1943 [110min]

Another Hollywoodized travelogue of some other place imposed on an audience who, presumably, didn't want to know any different. The story of U.S. Ambassador Joseph E. Davies, true-life diplomat: his relationship with the wartime Soviets is so blatantly chummy that before the decade was out all involved were worried about side-stepping HUAC. The Oscar nomination for art direction was probably recognizing the camouflage.
With *Walter Huston, Ann Harding, Oscar Homolka*

MISTER ROBERTS
John Ford/Mervyn Le Roy — U.S., 1955 [125min]

Shambolic adaptation of an immense Broadway hit, with Fonda and Ford's long-time love affair coming to an end. Exit Ford for Le Roy, and its stage director Joshua Logan, who finished the thing off.

The story of glory-bound First Officer Fonda aboard irascible skipper Cagney's U.S. Navy transport in WW2 gets bogged down; and the whole shebang only works thanks to the all-round performances, especially the Oscar-winning (as supporting actor) film debut of Lemmon as **Ensign Pulver**. The 1955 film was nominated, somehow, in the Best Picture category.
With *Henry Fonda, James Cagney, William Powell, Jack Lemmon*

In Logan's eponymous spin-off in 1964 [105min], Pulver is played, unfortunately, in the wake of the Lemmon characterization, by Robert Walker.

MISTER V See **Pimpernel Smith**

MR WINKLE GOES TO WAR (aka 'Arms and the Woman')
Alfred E. Green — U.S., 1944 [80min]

Star-vehicle propaganda picture for bank clerk-turned-WW2 hero Robinson. Amusing in parts.
With *Edward G. Robinson, Ruth Warrick*

MRS MINIVER
William Wyler — U.S., 1942 [135min]

Blytonesque England with a background straight out of Aunt Fanny's cottage in the Famous Five stories. Totally twee, sickeningly sentimental, and Churchill's favourite morale-boosting weapon during the darkest days of WW2. Hollywood's plea — 'we must save dear old England, how they must be suffering' — is set in an easier-to-stomach countryside at war rather than the totally unromantic London Blitz, which would have demanded an heretical reality in Tinsel Town. Despite the asides of stray Luftwaffe bombing and token death in the village and the armada of little boats setting off to save those brave boys at **Dunkirk**, **Millions Like Us**, **Went the Day Well?** (both released in the middle of the War), and even the more-considered comedy **Dad's Army**, evoked the feel and feelings of 1942 England far more accurately.

The film was huge box-office on both sides of the Atlantic, however, with British audiences obviously in it for the escapism and optimism, and that intangible pride in adversity that Hitler could never understand. Nominated for 12 Oscars, six were awarded, for: the picture, the many-fingered screenplay (the team included *Lost Horizon* author James Hilton),

the director, Garson (actress), Teresa Wright (supporting actress), and Joseph Ruttenberg (cinematography). The unlucky nominees included Pidgeon and Travers in the acting categories, and Whitty, uncommonly a second nominee from the same picture, for supporting actress.
With *Greer Garson, Walter Pidgeon, Teresa Wright, Henry Travers, Dame May Whitty*

A post-war sequel, *The Miniver Story*, also starring Garson and Pidgeon, and directed by H.C. Potter, appeared in 1950, and shouldn't have.

MOERU OZORA See **The Burning Sky**

MOHAMMED, MESSENGER OF GOD
(aka 'Al-Risalah', 'The Message')
Moustapha Akkad — Lebanon, 1976 [180min]

Huge historical pageant, almost rivalling Hollywood's halcyon days, about the rise of Islam during the 7th century AD; interesting in that, for obvious religious reasons, the Prophet never appears on screen. Over-the-top religious propaganda, but no more so than any of a number of Western films on Christianity since de Mille's *The Sign of the Cross*. One or two terrific Dark Age desert battles, however.
With *Anthony Quinn, Irene Papas*

MOHAWK See **Drums Along the Mohawk**

MONS
See ***The Battles of the Coronel and the Falkland Islands***

THE MOON IS DOWN
Irving Pichel — U.S., 1943 [90min]

Without doubt the most intelligent of the war-time Hollywood propaganda dramas on the German occupation of Norway (see also **The Commandos Strike at Dawn**, **Edge of Darkness**, **First Comes Courage**, etc) — probably because the original play was written by John Steinbeck. The Norwegian struggle becomes a metaphor for all occupied nations, with some good performances and a snow-covered set adapted from *How Green Was My Valley*.
With *Henry Travers, Cedric Hardwicke, Lee J. Cobb, Peter van Eyck*

THE MOONRAKER
David MacDonald — GB, 1957 [80min]

Not to be confused with the Bond movie, *Moonraker*, this is Ruth Rendell's cuddly Chief Inspector Wexford in a swashbuckling incarnation. An adventure picture set during the English Civil War is a rarity indeed, with our hero rescuing Royals and defying Roundheads before the Restoration of the monarchy, and Charles II, in 1660. Entertaining guff.
With *George Baker, Sylvia Sims, Peter Arne, Marius Goring, John Le Mesurier, Patrick Troughton*

MORGAN'S LAST RAID
Nick Grinde — U.S., 1929

One of several movies to appear during the early days of Hollywood dealing with the exploits of a real-life bunch of behind-the-lines Confederate marauders during the War of Secession. **Morgan's Raiders** ★★ (1918) by Wilfred Lucas, with Edward Burns as General John Morgan, was the best of the others. Here Morgan is played by McCoy.
With *Tim McCoy, Dorothy Sebastian*

MORGAN'S RAIDERS See **Morgan's Last Raid**

MORGENROT (aka 'Dawn')
Gustav Ucicky — Germany, 1933
Strictly speaking a non-Nazi anti-British propaganda film. This particularly well-made picture of a stricken WW1 U-boat was made before Hitler came to power, and managed to combine the anti-war sentiments preponderant in war films world-wide for several years, with strong nationalistic themes. The British are the villans as it was a Royal Navy destroyer which sank the submarine, seemingly unmercifully. The peril of the trapped submarine crew was taken up, ironically, by the British picture **Morning Departure**.
With *Rudolf Forster, Adele Sandrock, Fritz Genschow*

MORITURI See **The Saboteur, Code Name Morituri**

MORNING DEPARTURE (aka 'Operation Disaster')
Roy Baker — GB, 1950 [100min]
The predicament of the submariners first covered in **Morgenrot**, who are trapped on the sea-bed with only enough oxygen for eight people. Baker, in his WW2 update about a British sub, allows the psychological drama and the reminiscing to unfold, while the suspense mounts to the inevitable, yet still tragic *dénouement*.
With *John Mills, Richard Attenborough*

MOROCCO See **Beau Geste** (1939)

THE MORTAL STORM
Frank Borzage — U.S., 1940 [100min]
Vicious propaganda tract, showing the Nazification of a German family and their friends in 1930s Germany. It moved Göbbels to ban MGM's complete output.
With *James Stewart, Margaret Sullavan, Robert Young, Robert Stack*

MOSQUITO SQUADRON See **633 Squadron**

MOTHER NIGHT
Keith Gordon — U.S., 1996 [110min]
Those late '30s/early '40s spy dramas updated and sophisticated, with Nolte the spy (or is he?) passing intelligence encoded in seemingly blatant anti-Semitic broadcasts out of pre-WW2 Germany. The post-war interest in his activities from a variety of curious factions (including the Israelis) add an exciting postscript to a picture which holds a certain fascination.
With *Nick Nolte, Sheryl Lee, Alan Arkin, John Goodman*

THE MOUNTAIN ROAD
Daniel Mann — U.S., 1960 [100min]
Sabotage is the order of the day for an American demolition team ahead of encroaching Japanese in 1944 China, but they find the Chinese refugees as much of a problem. OK heroics with a semblance of understanding of the Chinese situation.
With *James Stewart, Lisa Lu, Frank Morgan*

THE MOUSE THAT ROARED
Jack Arnold — GB, 1959 [85min]
Initially, this is a sharp satire on America's world position and how support, through initiatives such as the Marshall Plan, can actually benefit countries defeated in conflict: or is it just British whinging? This adaptation of Leonard Wibberley's tales from the duchy of Grand Fenwick, which declares war on the U.S. as a wheeze to qualify for aid, tumbles into farce, however. Sellers does his best with three roles, but the plot hasn't enough variety to sustain it for too long.
With *Peter Sellers, Jean Seberg*

MURDER BY SIGNATURE
See **Eichmann and the Third Reich**

MURPHY'S WAR
Peter Yates — GB, 1971 [110min]
Lusty vehicle for O'Toole in a kind of **African Queen** environment, but this is WW2 Venezuela and the Orinoco River, and instead of the coaster, O'Toole fights the German U-boat with his home-made kamikaze plane. Although the picture has superior action sequences, the message here is the psychosis of revenge: O'Toole single-mindedly goes about wreaking retribution for the death of all his shipmates at the hands of the sub, even though the German nation has now surrendered and the war is over.
With *Peter O'Toole, Sian Phillips, Phillipe Noiret, Horst Janson*

MUTINY See **The Buccaneer**

MY ENGLISH GRANDFATHER (aka 'Robinsonada anu Chemi Ingliseli Papa', 'Robinson Crusoe in Georgia')
Nana Djordjadze — USSR, 1986 [75min]
A great glasnost guffaw — well, perhaps a Georgian jibe. Daft storyline of an English engineer caught up in Russia's 1917 Revolution, who creates a national island of three metres radius from the telegraph pole he's been erecting — claiming it as part of Britain — and is therefore neutral.
With *Zhanri Lolashvili, Nineli Chankvetadze*

MY FOUR YEARS IN GERMANY
William Nigh — U.S., 1918
Based on the memoirs of Ambassador James W. Gerrad, sorry tale of sour grapes and the Kaiser's duplicity involving so-called friendly states prior to the U.S.'s entry into WW1.
With *Halbert Brown*

MY LIFE FOR IRELAND
(aka 'Mein Leben für Irland') See **The Fox of Glenarvon**

MY NAME IS IVAN See **Ivan's Childhood**

MYSTERY SEA RAIDER
Edward Dmytryk — U.S., 1940 [75min]
A German crew takes over a cargo ship and terrorizes the Caribbean in this WW2 programmer of little note.
With *Carole Landis, Henry Wilcoxson, Onslow Stevens*

MYSTERY SUBMARINE (1950)
See **Mystery Submarine** (1962)

MYSTERY SUBMARINE (aka 'Decoy')
CM Pennington-Richards — GB, 1962 [90min]
Not to be confused with Douglas Sirk's nonsense picture of 1950 [80min], with Macdonald Carey, where a U-boat skipper has some extra-mural activities following VE-Day; this is Pennington-Richards' nonsense picture about a British crew taking over a U-boat during WW2, and getting caught by the British! Perhaps someday the title will spawn a decent movie.
With *Edward Judd, James Robertson Justice*

N

THE NAKED AND THE DEAD
Raoul Walsh — U.S., 1958 [130min]
Mailer's book would probably be adapted more faithfully for the screen today without the expletives deleted; but because of the tendency now to insert foul language instead of a script the shock value of Mailer's work would be negligible four decades on. Anyway, Walsh had been directing pictures since WW1, so his conventions were not going to be sacrificed for the sake of a few four-letter words. The story, stripped of its notoriety, turns out to be a routine (and over-long) yarn of a U.S. reconnaissance patrol somewhere in the Pacific theatre during WW2; lifted by some good performances from 'soldiers' who have often appeared in pressure situations.
With *Aldo Ray, Cliff Robertson, Raymond Massey, Richard Jaeckel, Joey Bishop, L. Q. Jones*

THE NAKED BRIGADE
Maury Dexter — U.S., 1965 [100min]
The defence of Crete on the cheap. Guerrillas and Eaton (the Bond girl gilded in *Goldfinger*) fight an uphill battle against the Nazi invasion in 1941. Desperate stuff for the Cretans, and audiences.
With *Shirley Eaton, Ken Scott*

NAPOLEON
Abel Gance — France, 1927 [380min]
Sandwiched between his immensely influential versions of **J'Accuse**, Gance took the silent movie, in visual techniques and sophistication of storyline, as far as anyone had by the time of its on-coming demise in 1926-7. This picture, outlining the majestic sweep of Bonaparte's early successes in Italy, was always on the 'must see' list; but with historical film expert Kevin Brownlow (**It Happened Here, Winstanley**) rebuilding a five-hour version of it during the '70s, and Carl Davis' Beethoven-biased score added, it is now symphonic cinema on its grandest scale. (Claude Lelouch also tinkered with it in 1982.) Politically unimportant, it does however depict Bonaparte's activities as moving from revolutionary zeal to almost fascist fervour. This was a point noted by Beethoven himself in 1803, when he withdrew the dedication to Napoleon from his Third Symphony, and simply called it the 'Eroica'; championing the universal freedoms the composer once associated with his fallen icon.

It's the visual combination, with its later accoutrements, which now make it one of *the* great cinematic experiences.
With *Albert Dieudonné, Harry Krimer, Antonin Artaud*

An all-star, yet lack-lustre, French remake of the same title came out in 1953 ** [185min]; directed by and starring Sacha Guitry, with Jean Gabin, Danielle Darrieux, Yves Montand, Michèle Morgan and Erich von Stroheim.

NAPOLEON (1953) See **Napoleon** (1927)

LA NAVE BIANCA See **The White Navy**

THE NAVY COMES THROUGH
Edward Sutherland — U.S., 1942 [80min]
Timely tribute to the merchant marine of the U.S. Navy, for their transatlantic gauntlet-running of war materiel during WW2.
With *Pat O'Brien*

NAZI AGENT See **The Great Impersonation**

THE NAZIS STRIKE See *Why We Fight*

THE NELSON AFFAIR See **Bequest to the Nation**

THE NELSON TOUCH See **Corvette K225**

NEUTRAL PORT
Marcel Varnel — GB, 1940 [90min]
Wooden propaganda yarn of merchantmen and U-boats in the early months of WW2.
With *Will Fyffe, Phyllis Calvert, Leslie Banks*

NEVER SO FEW
John Sturges — U.S., 1959 [125min]
WW2 adventure set in Burma which is high on star-, low on plot- and action-ratios. Unusually for a director already known for his movement (*Gunfight at the OK Coral* — he would direct *The Magnificent Seven* and **The Great Escape** over the next four years), the picture is punctuated with too many *longeurs* (usually involving La Lollo) and pauses for reflection and buddydom. Sturges' protégés, McQueen and Bronson, get small parts.
With *Frank Sinatra, Gina Lollobrigida, Peter Lawford, Paul Henreid, Richard Johnson, Steve McQueen, Brian Donlevy, Charles Bronson*

NEVINOST BEZ ZASTITE See **Innocence Unprotected**

THE NEW BABYLON (aka 'Novyi Vavilon')
Grigori Kozintsev/Leonid Trauberg — USSR, 1929 [80min]
Eisensteinian structures dominate this Marxist-tinged history of the Paris Commune, set up in 1871 after the French defeat in the Franco-Prussian War. The events are recalled by a shop assistant.
With *Yelena Kuzmina, Pyotr Sobelevsky*

NEW MEXICO
Irving Reis — U.S., 1952 [80min]
Following in the trend of **Broken Arrow**, this was another liberal Western about Cavalry and Indians scuffling down Mexico way. OK.
With *Lew Ayres, Andy Devine, Raymond Burr*

THE NEXT OF KIN
Thorold Dickinson — GB, 1942 [100min]
Expertly crafted 'careless talk' instructional film, involving a British commando raid in WW2, which did very well commercially.
With *Mervyn Johns, Nova Pilbeam, Basil Radford, Naunton Wayne*

NICHOLAS AND ALEXANDRA
Franklin Schaffner — GB, 1971 [190min]
Colourful mix of Sirk-style costume drama and reasonably

accurate history make up most of this enjoyable version of the **Fall of the Romanov Dynasty**. Jayston and Suzman are excellent, while *Doctor Who* Baker is a suitably frenzied **Rasputin**.

The narrative covers the unrest due to huge losses in WW1; but pays lip service to the characterization of the revolutionaries like Lenin (Bryant) and Trotsky (Cox), even during the deposition and executions. This apart, the action scenes are very good and the tragic family saga is expertly told.

The picture was nominated for an Oscar, as were Suzman, Freddie Young for his camerawork and Richard Rodney Bennett's music. Statuettes were awarded for art direction and costume design. Imperial cast.

With *Michael Jayston, Janet Suzman, Harry Andrews, Tom Baker, Timothy West, Jack Hawkins, Laurence Olivier, Michael Redgrave, Michael Bryant, Ian Holm, Curt Jurgens, Brian Cox*

NIGHT AMBUSH See **Ill Met by Moonlight**

NIGHT AND FOG See *Nuit et Brouillard*

THE NIGHT FIGHTERS See **A Terrible Beauty**

A NIGHT IN CASABLANCA See **Duck Soup**

NIGHT IN ROME See **Era Notte a Roma**

THE NIGHT IS ENDING See **Paris After Dark**

THE NIGHT OF SAN LORENZO
(aka 'La Notte di San Lorenzo', 'The Night of the Shooting Stars')
Paolo Taviani/Vittorio Taviani — Italy, 1981 [105min]
Good stuff from the Taviani brothers as they convert the shooting stars of the night in question to a full-blown WW2 adventure; including a group of Tuscans fleeing the retreating Germans under a welter of aerial shelling (the stars). The retelling takes place through the eyes of a little girl, who eventually rejoices in their liberation by American soldiers.
With *Omero Antonutti, Margarita Lozano*

THE NIGHT OF THE GENERALS
Anatole Litvak — GB, 1967 [150min]
Clumsy adaptation of Hans Helmut Kirst's WW2 murder thriller, which interweaves the main theme with the abortive assassination attempt by von Stauffenberg and others on Hitler in July 1944. Acting-wise, O'Toole is O'Toole, but the others are fine — especially Courtenay.
With *Peter O'Toole, Omar Sharif, Tom Courtenay, Donald Pleasence, Joanna Pettet, Phillipe Noiret, Harry Andrews, Christopher Plummer*

THE NIGHT OF THE SHOOTING STARS
See **The Night of San Lorenzo**

NIGHT PLANE FROM CHUNGKING
Ralph Murphy — U.S., 1942 [70min]
Just another variant on **Shanghai Express**, this time in the air, with a Nazi spy on board a flight of all-sorts fleeing Shanghai during the Sino-Japanese War.
With *Ellen Drew, Robert Preston*

THE NIGHT PORTER
(aka 'Il Portiere di Notte') See **The Damned**

A NIGHT TO REMEMBER (aka 'Sono yo wa Wasurenai', 'Hiroshima Heartache') See **Hiroshima**

NIGHT TRAIN See **Night Train to Munich**

NIGHT TRAIN TO MUNICH (aka 'Night Train', 'Gestapo')
Carol Reed — GB, 1940 [95min]
Almost a repeat of Hitchcock's **The Lady Vanishes**, complete with Charters and Caldicott (Radford and Wayne), and Lockwood again; this time involved in the escape from a Nazi concentration camp of a Czech inventor's daughter.

Thunders along with bursts of propagandist prattle and humour from the same writing team of Launder and Gilliat (from Gordon Wellesley's nominated original novel *Report on a Fugitive*). The only thing that's missing is Hitch — but Reed's picture is pretty well thought of in any case.
With *Margaret Lockwood, Rex Harrison, Basil Radford, Naunton Wayne, Paul Henreid*

Radford and Wayne came together one more time in the light comedy spy spoof, **Crooks' Tour ★★** (John Baxter — also 1940), when they come across Nazis in Baghdad.

THE NIGHT WATCH
See **The Woman from Monte Carlo**

NIGHTMARE
Tim Whelan — U.S., 1942 [80min]
Limited espionage piece set in WW2 London with Donlevy as a gambler helping Barrymore flee from Nazi spies.
With *Brian Donlevy, Diana Barrymore, Gavin Muir, Henry Daniell*

NIGHTS OF RASPUTIN See **Rasputin and the Empress**

NINE MEN
Harry Watt — GB, 1943 [70min]
Good early recapturing of events in the Libyan desert when a small detached outfit of **Desert Rats** defend an old fortification against the Italians. A flag-waver simply and straightforwardly told.
With *Jack Lambert, Gordon Jackson*

1941
Steven Spielberg — U.S., 1979 [120min]
Spielberg's first attempt at grown-up cinema badly misfires, in this intended satire of West Coast panic after Pearl Harbor (based, presumably, on the true incident of a Japanese submarine surfacing off Los Angeles). Some sight gags are good but there is no cohesive plot of any sort to link the set pieces together — especially over two hours.
With *Dan Aykroyd, Ned Beattie, John Belushi, Lorraine Gary, Christopher Lee, Toshiro Mifune, Robert Stack, Warren Oates, Treat Williams, Slim Pickens*

1914 See **The Outrage**

1900 (aka 'Novocento')
Bernardo Bertolucci — France/Germany/Italy, 1976 [320min]
After hitting the nail on the head with his articulate **The Conformist**, Bertolucci now splats his target of fascism throughout the baroque historical sweep of Italy in the first half of the 20th century. His approach to the familial saga is

more Cookson than Tolstoy, leaving any middle-brow aspirations well below stairs. Both major wars, linked by the Mussolini era, are in there somewhere, but this is a definite blip from the master — despite a cast to die for.
With *Burt Lancaster, Robert de Niro, Gérard Depardieu, Donald Sutherland*

NIPPON'S YOUNG EAGLES See **The Burning Sky**

NO DRUMS, NO BUGLES
Clyde Ware — U.S., 1971 [85min]
Virtual one-hander for Sheen as Confederate Ashby Gantrell, who, legend has it, sat out the whole of the American Civil War in a cave. The ultimate pacifist tract is pretty boring cinema, though, the excellent star apart.
With *Martin Sheen*

NO ESCAPE See **I Escaped from the Gestapo**

NO GREATER GLORY
Frank Borzage — U.S., 1934 [80min]
Borzage takes Ferenc Molnar's *The Paul Street Boys* from 1914 Budapest; but he doesn't capture the author's sense of the absurd in this anti-war allegory, where the strategy and tactics of warfare are viewed at schoolboy level. Similar themes occur in the various versions of **Le Guerre des Boutons**.
With *George Breakston, Jimmy Butler*

NO GREATER LOVE
(aka 'Ningen no Joken: Part 1') See **The Human Condition**

NO MAN IS AN ISLAND (aka 'Island Escape')
John Monk Jr — U.S., 1962 [115min]
Hunter stars as wireless operator George Tweed, in this biopic of the man who stayed behind after the fall of Guam in 1942, hiding from the Japanese and sending signals back to U.S. commanders. May have been exceptional heroism, but not cinematically so.
With *Jeffrey Hunter, Marshall Thompson*

NO TIME TO DIE (aka 'Tank Force')
Terence Young — GB, 1958 [80min]
Below-par WW2 yarn of multifarious Brits escaping from a POW camp in the Libyan desert.
With *Victor Mature, Leo Genn, Anthony Newley*

NOAH'S ARK
Michael Curtiz — U.S., 1929 [135min]
Curtiz, not long off the boat himself from his native Hungary, just about comes out on top (on points) in this confusing, but always fascinating part-talkie parallel between the Great Flood and the onset of WW1. Actors double up for their Biblical and WW1 characters, and apart from the flood effect itself, no expense is spared on the battle sequences. Not sure if it all works, but it's a curio and a half.
With *Dolores Costello, Wallace Beery*

NOBI See **Fires on the Plain**

NORTH-WEST FRONTIER
Kenneth More (middle-ground) approaches the death train. Rank

NONE BUT THE BRAVE
Frank Sinatra — U.S., 1965 [105min]
Unhappy directorial experience for Sinatra (his first and last) in this anti-war parable of enemies living together (Japanese and American soldiers cut off on a deserted Pacific island in WW2) in reasonable harmony, until one side (the Americans) seek, and gain, an advantage. The rest is blood and gore — and to be fair to the director, the action shots are OK. It's the concept that's a little ambitious, as even talented director John Boorman found out when attempting something similar (**Hell in the Pacific**) three years later.
With *Frank Sinatra, Clint Walker, Tommy Sands, Brad Dexter*

NONE SHALL ESCAPE
André de Toth — U.S., 1944 [85min]
Tense propaganda piece about German WW1 vet returning home, becoming influenced by Nazism, then a local leader, before ending up in front of a war trials tribunal. Nominated for Alfred Neumann's and Joseph Thau's original story.
With *Alexander Knox, Marsha Hunt, Henry Travers*

NORMANDIE-NIEMEN
Jean Dréville — France/USSR, 1959 [120min]
The unusual story of the Free French fighter squadron which flew Russian Yaks against the Luftwaffe on the Eastern Front — and Western Front. Interesting for its frequent aerial clips.
With *Marc Cassot, Gianni Esposito, Pierre Trabaud*

THE NORTH STAR (aka 'Armored Attack')
Lewis Milestone — U.S., 1943 [105min]
There are certain projects that should never have been conceived, let alone allowed to come to fruition. This is one. Milestone's (I'm sure) genuine attempt to portray Russia's fight against the German invasion backfired a few years later in the McCarthy era when it was considered pro-communist. It is not as if it was a classical work of art. Lillian Hellman's Oscar nomination for the script (?) just proves how farcical

these awards are sometimes (perhaps because the Academy showered the picture with four such nominations it should have appeared *en bloc* before the HUAC a few years later): James Wong Howe (photography), Aaron Copland (score) and Perry Ferguson (art direction) were the others to be nominated. To cap the whole thing, Prokofiev (**Alexander Nevsky, Ivan the Terrible**) was scheduled to write the music, but in the end the job was given to that son of the Steppes, Copland — from Brooklyn (but of Russian parentage). **Armored Attack** was the name given to a 'cleaned-up' revision in the '50s.

With *Anne Baxter, Dana Andrews, Walter Huston, Farley Granger, Jane Withers*

NORTHERN PURSUIT
Raoul Walsh — U.S., 1943 [95min]
Flynn leaves the Canadian Mounties to spy on a Nazi plan to bomb the locks on the Great Lakes and cut off support to Britain. Interesting thought — especially the Germans' secret hideaway of aircraft parts to build the bomber! Great stuff, as long as you ride along with it.

With *Errol Flynn, Julie Bishop, Helmut Dantine*

NORTH-WEST FRONTIER (aka 'Flame Over India')
J. Lee(-)Thompson — GB, 1959 [130min]
Terrific adventure story set in early 20th century India, almost up to the best on offer two decades before. Thompson was coming into a bit of a purple patch (**Ice Cold in Alex**, *Tiger Bay* and, shortly, **The Guns of Navarone**) and here he lets the action rip, as a runaway train carrying a young Indian prince hurtles into troublesome territory. *Boys' Own* of the moving image.

With *Kenneth More, Lauren Bacall, Herbert Lom*

NORTHWEST PASSAGE (Part One, Rogers' Rangers)
King Vidor — U.S., 1940 [125min]
Part Two never got made, unfortunately: that would have been the bit where the story crosses the Northern Rockies and finds the Pacific Ocean. Part One, from Kenneth Robert's best-selling novel, deals with the French and Indian War in a most convincing fashion; recounting the part played by British Army-seconded Major Robert Rogers (Tracy) and his 160 'Rangers' against the Abenaki tribesmen in what is now upper New York State.

The Rangers were well-trained, hard-bitten colonials who knew their environment well and usually had some axe to grind against the natives. Their title, 'Rangers', would be used by special detachments of U.S. military down the years: through Texas Rangers and WW2's **Darby's Rangers** to the current commando-style U.S. Rangers.

The script realistically includes the hazards of long missions in the empty forest; the pace is brisk; and the whole thing looks good (though there is a 'howler' notorious among uniform buffs — the costume department thought the term 'Scots bonnet' meant a Glengarry!). The final battle before setting off in search of the Pacific is excitingly done.

With *Spencer Tracy, Robert Young, Walter Brennan, Ruth Hussey*

NOT QUITE JERUSALEM
Lewis Gilbert — GB, 1985 [115min]
Love and bullets among the kibbutzim, as veteran Gilbert (**Albert RN, Reach for the Sky**) fails to elicit much interest from anybody, whether it be Jewish youth or Arab guerrilla.

With *Joanna Pacula, Sam Robards, Kevin McNally*

NOTHING PERSONAL
Thaddeus O'Sullivan — GB/Ireland, 1995 [85min]
Neatly played, but ultimately purposeless look at the Irish troubles, c1975. It balances the good and bad aspects of both Nationalist and Loyalist terrorist groups so finely, you wonder whether any controversy has been pre-weighed to ensure equilibrium. Says nothing new.

With *Ian Hart, John Lynch, James Frain, Michael Gambon*

NOTORIOUS
Alfred Hitchcock — U.S., 1946 [100min]
If Hitchcock's **Foreign Correspondent** was the first word on the WW2 spy thriller genre at the beginning of the global conflict, then this even better tale of love and betrayal amongst the settlement of Nazi exiles in Brazil is surely the ultimate word at the end of it. A better pair of bookends one could not wish for.

As suspenseful a picture as you can get, this is superb film-making: Ben Hecht's Oscar-nominated script; Ted Tetzlaff's magical monochrome photography; the stars' dangerously-heated sexual chemistry; the memorable set pieces — remember the 'key' shot zooming in to Bergman's open palm from the top of the staircase? Bergman shows why she was just about the best, while Grant even surpasses his own exalted standards; and Rains, as the Nazi leader, received a deserved Supporting Actor Oscar nomination. Hitchcock, as per usual, received nothing — except the gratitude of his audiences and the envy of his directorial peers.

With *Cary Grant, Ingrid Bergman, Claude Rains, Louis Calhern*

NOTORIOUS GENTLEMAN See **The Rake's Progress**

LA NOTTE DI SAN LORENZO
See **The Night of San Lorenzo**

NOUS SOMMES TOUS DES ASSASSINS
See **Are We All Murderers?**

NOVEMBER 1828
Teguh Karya — Indonesia, 1979 [135min]
The Dutch, along with the Spanish, were among the earliest European states to experience rumblings in their colonies. This Indonesian picture, helpfully dated for context, is a quite well-produced and acted epic, and tells of one of the unsuccessful Javanese revolts of the 1820s; before Dutch supremacy reigned again — until the Japanese took over in March 1942.

With *Slamet Rahardjo, Jenny Rachman*

NOVOCENTO See **1900**

NOVYI VAVILON See **The New Babylon**

NUIT ET BROUILLARD (aka 'Night and Fog')
Alain Resnais — France, 1955
The first real attempt by any filmmaker to expose cinematically the scale of suffering that occurred in Nazi concentration camps. Resnais' poignant documentary is shot in the present at Auschwitz in the colours of a peaceful pastoral scene: interspersed are the harrowing black-and-white newsreel clips of events which happened only a decade or so before. Bound together as a whole by Hans Eisler's moving music and co-scripter Jean Cayrol's emotional narration, this is a lasting cinematic requiem to the Holocaust. A powerful 30 minutes.

THE NUN AND THE SERGEANT
Franklin Adreon — U.S., 1962 [75min]
Shabby tale of a **Dirty Dozen**-esque demolition gang blowing up a fuel dump in Korea; with a nun on the run, and her charges providing distractions for the lascivious ex-cons.
With *Robert Webber, Anna Sten*

THE NUN'S STORY
★ *Fred Zinnemann — U.S., 1959* [150min]
★ Oscar nominations galore as Hollywood gets a good mix of
★ pious popularity — but not quite good enough, as older
★ religion prevailed in **Ben-Hur** and swept the board in 1959.

    Very well made (it was a brave venture to set so much of the film's opening scenes behind the closed doors of a strict religious order), the story revolves around a nun who is not quite hacking it in the Belgian Congo of the 1930s; comes home to Belgium when WW2 breaks out; joins the resistance when her father (evacuating Jews) is killed by the Nazis; and leaves the order. Would that such simplicity sufficed! Nominations for picture, director, Robert Anderson's adapted screenplay, Hepburn, Franz Planer's lensing, Franz Waxman's score, and the editing.
With *Audrey Hepburn, Peter Finch, Edith Evans, Peggy Ashcroft, Dean Jagger*

NURSE EDITH CAVELL
★ *Herbert Wilcox — U.S., 1939* [100min]
★ Wilcox remade the silent version called **Dawn ★★** after the book upon which it was based, starring Sibyl Thorndike; with his wife Neagle this time taking over the mantle of the heroic nurse. The timing of the pacifist plea (the film shows Cavell treating Germans injured in WW1 as well as Allies) couldn't have been worse, as Germany invaded Poland in the week it went on release in America. An Academy Award nomination was given to Anthony Collins for his music.
With *Anna Neagle, George Sanders, May Robson, Edna May Oliver*

The first version of this true tale of Cavell's heroism which resulted in her execution in 1915, was made in 1918 under the title **The Woman the Germans Shot ★** — sums it up, I suppose: with Julia Arthur as the nurse, and directed by John G. Adolfi.
Other silent films on the subject included **Why Germany Must Pay** and **The Martyrdom of Nurse Cavell ★**.

OBCHOD NA KORZE See **The Shop on Main Street**

OBERST REDL See **Colonel Redl**

OBJECTIVE BURMA!
Raoul Walsh — U.S., 1945 [140min]
★
Withdrawn in Britain after just one week, and not shown again ★
until 1953 (with apology), this above-average action piece ★
about a special force of U.S. paratroopers (*à la* **Merrill's Marauders**) got the big UK thumbs down, because the impression was given that no British were fighting in Burma. That Gen Wingate's Chindits were mostly Indian, anyway, didn't seem to make a difference.

    Flynn is in his element, knocking off the enemy in droves — and in this kind of form, probably didn't want the Brits under his feet anyway. Typical Walsh blood-and-thunder stuff.
With *Errol Flynn, William Prince, James Brown, Henry Hull*

OBYKNOVENNYI FASHIZM See *Ordinary Fascism*

OCTOBER (aka 'Oktyabr', 'Ten Days that Shook the World')
Sergei Eisenstein — USSR, 1927 [95min]
★
Cinematic masterpiece in terms of style and influence ★
(abstract montage, intercutting, etc) which made Eisenstein ★
one of the great icons of cinema art; cementing his position ★ ★
after the monumental **The Battleship Potemkin** two years ★
earlier. Called upon to commemorate ten years of the Bolshevik Revolution and the overthrow of Kerensky's provisional government, this heavily fictionalized version of history is told in magnificent set pieces (the storming of the Winter Palace and the raising of the bridges in Petrograd are particularly memorable — and, indeed, mistaken by some to be actual newsreel), interspersed with obscure (for the audiences of the day) imagery and metaphor.

    Despite all this innovation, it is clear that Eisenstein was at this point firmly toeing the Party line — the exploits of Comrade Trotsky, for example, have been conveniently overlooked. The alternative title is taken from the book of the same name by American socialite turned socialist John Reed, who died in Russia in 1920, and was buried in the Kremlin (see **Reds, Reed: Mexico Insurgente**).
With *Vasili Nikandrov, Boris Livanov, Eduard Tissé*

THE ODD ANGRY SHOT
Tom Jeffrey — Australia, 1979 [90min]
★
Thoughtful, sometimes grim, and often funny excursion of ★
Australian cinema into the Vietnam War. Dealing with the ★
personal relationships rather more than the patchy action, the message screams out: 'What the hell are *we* doing here?'

    First opportunity of international recognition for Brown, seen also in **Breaker Morant** released the same year. Indeed, it seemed, especially with Mel Gibson breaking through with *Mad Max*, and the 1981 picture **Gallipoli**, that the mid-70s promise of Australian cinema, spearheaded by Peter Weir (*Picnic at Hanging Rock* and Gallipoli) and Bruce Beresford

(*The Getting of Wisdom* and **Morant**) was about to bring fruit. Instead it ironically foundered on the Australian diaspora (read everyone went to LA!) such internationalism demanded. With *John Hargeaves, Graham Kennedy, Bryan Brown, John Jarratt*

THE ODD MAN OUT (aka 'Gang War')
Carol Reed — GB, 1946 [115min]

Dry run for Reed's *The Third Man* — its post-war austerity atmospherics, and theme of using dark city streets as a place to hide, would be used to great effect later. Mason is the IRA gunman wounded in a shooting, being hunted by the RUC in Belfast, and finding help from no-one. As usual, his performance is immaculate as the haunted fugitive, and, indeed, the acting is first-rate all through. But don't look for any political pointers — there are none. Winner of the Best British Film at the first-ever BAFTA Awards in 1947 (then the BFA, with the award nicknamed a 'Stella'), and an Oscar nomination for editing.

With *James Mason, Robert Newton, Kathleen Ryan, Robert Beatty, Cyril Cusack, FJ McCormick, Dan O'Herlihy, Fay Compton*

THE ODESSA FILE
Ronald Neame — GB, 1974 [130min]

Frederick Forsyth's second novel (after *The Day of the Jackal*) is faithfully adhered to in this suspenseful tale of idealist-journalist v secret society Nazis in 1963 Germany. Voight is good as the young journo trying to unravel the legacy of an old Jew; which leads him to a *dénouement* facing his quarry, a war criminal now turned influential businessman — and an appointment with his own past. Even Simon Wiesenthal is brought into the plot, and flashbacks to WW2 heighten the action. Music by a relatively pubescent Andrew Lloyd Webber.
With *Jon Voight, Maria Schell, Maximilian Schell, Mary Tamm, Derek Jacobi*

ODD ANGRY SHOT
Foreground (l-to-r), Graeme Blundell, John Jarratt, Graham Kennedy: Bryan Brown (background left) comes to link with them. Australia, Samson Productions/Tedderwick

ODETTE
Herbert Wilcox — GB, 1950 [125min]

After being shot by the Germans in WW1 as **Nurse Edith Cavell**, director Wilcox puts wife Neagle through it all over again in WW2. Was he trying to tell her something?

This true-life SOE heroine, Odette Churchill, a Frenchwoman with an English husband, is tortured by the Nazis. She survives and gains the George Cross — the highest honour given for civilian gallantry. It's packaged patriotism of gut-churning consistency.
With *Anna Neagle, Trevor Howard, Peter Ustinov, Marius Goring*

OFF LIMITS (aka 'Saigon')
Christopher Crowe — U.S., 1988 [100min]

Unusual setting for a crime thriller — the Vietnam War. Two U.S. forces MPs, investigate what is evetually an army cover-up. Not too exciting for all that.
With *Willem Dafoe, Gregory Hines, Fred Ward, Amanda Pays, Scott Glenn*

OH! WHAT A LOVELY WAR
Richard Attenborough — GB, 1969 [145min]

Ambitious, hit-or-miss WW1 satire; sending up the inept leadership and the pan-European, royal-familial infighting at the bottom of it all; told in sketches as an end-of-the-pier entertainment.

Equally admired as innovative and disliked as pretentious, Attenborough could have cut his directorial teeth on something less controversial than this tricky screen treatment of Joan Littlewood's successful stage production. The vast cast of cameos (many of them knighted thesps) are wheeled on and off-stage, and continuous interest is only engaged by the cinematic sequences — which are all too infrequent. On balance, a glorious failure — might this just be a metaphor for WW1?
With *John Gielgud, Ralph Richardson, Laurence Olivier, John Mills, Michael Redgrave, Maggie Smith, Vanessa Redgrave, Dirk Bogarde, Kenneth More, Corin Redgrave, Susannah York, Phyllis Calvert, Jack Hawkins, Ian Holm*

OHM KRUGER (aka 'Uncle Krüger')
Hans Steinhoff — Germany, 1941

The most famous anti-British picture to come out of Germany in the period up to and during WW2, tells of atrocities and double dealings of British forces against the Dutch settlers in Southern Africa, which led to the Boer Wars. Portraying Kitchener and Churchill as sadistic British officers, the visual attack went all the way through to the uncaring Royal Family.

Throwing back the Allied charges of inhuman behaviour in German WW2 concentration camps, Steinhoff was quick to point out that during the Second Boer War thousands of Afrikaaner families died of neglect in British concentration camps. Jannings, an Oscar-winning actor in the last year of silent films (see **The Last Patrol**), returned to Germany as a standard-bearer, willingly or unwillingly, for the Third Reich, and plays the eponymous Boer hero.
With *Emil Jannings*

OHMS (aka 'You're in the Army Now')
Raoul Walsh — GB, 1936 [85min]

American gangster flees the States, comes to Britain and, intimating he's a Canadian, joins HM Forces and is promptly shipped to China to meddle in the civil war. He goes from wrongly-accused murderer to war hero, through a process of

OH! WHAT A LOVELY WAR
No-Man's Land during a Christmas truce. Paramount/Accord

(Chinese) laundering as contrived as can be. Not the director's best. The alternate title is not to be confused with the 1941 service comedy of the same name, starring Phil Silvers and Jimmy Durante.
With *Wallace Ford, John Mills, Anna Lee*

OKINAWA
Leigh Jackson — U.S., 1952 [65min]
Another routine attempt to wave a flag by using one war as a substitute for another. Not so concerned with the land battle (see **The Battle of Okinawa**), this stroll down memory lane concentrates on the activities aboard a U.S. destroyer, in particular dealing with Japanese (newsreel) kamikaze tactics; while at the same time displaying the naval might at the country's disposal during the contemporaneous Korean War.
With *Pat O'Brien, Cameron Mitchell, Rhys Williams*

OKTYABR See October

OLD GRINGO
Luis Puenzo — U.S., 1989 [120min]
The speculative destiny of American short-story writer Ambrose Bierce (many considered him the natural successor to Edgar Allan Poe), who disappeared in the Mexico troubles of 1913. Puenzo takes Carlos Fuentes' novel quite literally, which means that the subtleties of the cross-plots don't always come through; but good performances from veteran Peck, in only his third cinema outing of the decade; and Smits as a rebel officer — together with a good feel for a country in turmoil — make it watchable.
With *Gregory Peck, Jane Fonda, Jimmy Smits*

OLD IRONSIDES See The Barbary Pirate

ONCE BEFORE I DIE
John Derek — U.S., 1965 [95min]
Before John knew Bo, there was Ursula. Risible vehicle for the sexy new star (*Dr No, She*) with a background of Japanese bombings in the Philippines during WW2.
With *Ursula Andress, John Derek, Richard Jaeckel*

ONCE UPON A TIME IN CHINA, Parts 1 and 2
(aka 'Wong Fei Hung')
Tsui Hark — Hong Kong, 1991and '92 [135min and 125min]
Tsui's attempt to make a Leone-type *Once Upon a Time . . .* movie is well-worth seeing. Well over four hours in length (in two parts, the second released in 1992), it covers three decades at the end of the 19th century, in and around Hong Kong. Focusing on one man's view of events — involving the beginnings of civil war (Sen-Yat-Sen) and the Boxer rumblings against the British — the first part outlines the history, while Part 2 is chock-a-block with outstanding action. With *Jet Li*

ONE AGAINST SEVEN See Counter-Attack

100 RIFLES
Tom Gries — U.S., 1969 [110min]
Gratuitous action hides a little-covered area of conflict — the Yaqui Indian revolt in Mexico in 1912. Attempts at originality stop at Brown's black sheriff and Welch's Amazonian Indian leader.
With *Jim Brown, Raquel Welch, Burt Reynolds*

ONE MAN MUTINY
See **The Court Martial of Billy Mitchell**

ONE MINUTE TO ZERO
Tay Garnett — U.S., 1952 [105min]
Routine Korean War picture, of interest only because it looks at one specific incident, which most fictionalized movies of this war do not. Here it deals with the communist invasion south of the 38th Parallel in 1950; and the UN's (America's) attempts to repel them from the Pusan perimeter, before MacArthur's landing at **Inchon**. It also concerns itself — unconvincingly — with the morality of mortar-bombing North Korean civilians who are sheltering communist soldiers.
With *Robert Mitchum, Ann Blyth*

ONE NIGHT IN LISBON See The Conspirators

ONE OF OUR AIRCRAFT IS MISSING
Michael Powell/Emeric Pressburger — GB, 1941 [100min]
Following hard on the heels of their Oscar-winning screenplay for **49th Parallel**, the plot of which has some similarities (the 'who do we trust?' theme), the masters of British cinema at that time were again nominated for their writing. This is not on the same scale of the earlier film — neither is it the very best of Powell and Pressburger — but it's a terrific yarn anyway; with a shot-down RAF bomber crew having to pick their way home via a Holland riven with collaboration.
With *Godfrey Tearle, Eric Portman, Hugh Williams, Bernard Miles, Googie Withers, Peter Ustinov*

THE ONE THAT GOT AWAY
Roy Baker — GB, 1957 [110min]
Exciting drama-adventure based on the true story of Luftwaffe pilot Franz von Werra, who had a habit of escaping from British POW camps during WW2. Nice to see some semblance of equilibrium, and a terrific performance from Kruger.
With *Hardy Kruger, Alec McCowen, Michael Goodliffe*

THE ONE THOUSAND PLANE RAID
See **The Thousand Plane Raid**

ONLY THE VALIANT
Gordon Douglas — U.S., 1950 [105min]
Six U.S. Cavalry officers defend an isolated fort against some angry redskins, and make the first use of the Gatling Gun in the Indian Wars. Sort of odds better portrayed in **Beau Geste**, **The Alamo** and Custer films, but with the result of **Zulu**.
With *Gregory Peck, Ward Bond, Gig Young, Lon Chaney Jr, Neville Brand*

THE ONLY WAY See **A Tale of Two Cities** (1935)

L'ONOREVOLE ANGELINA
See **The Honourable Angelina**

OPEN CITY (aka 'Roma, Città Aperta', 'Rome, Open City')
Roberto Rossellini — Italy, 1945 [100min]
With an Oscar-nominated script from Sergio Amidei and none other than a young Federico Fellini, Rossellini makes a stark semi-documentary of life in Italy after the 1943 armistice. He highlights the underground's campaign against the crumbling Nazi occupation, and with it opens the door for a surge of neo-realism to infect post-war European cinema. Aided and abetted by the decay and detritus of war that was everywhere to be seen in 1945 Rome, the former fascist propagandist of earlier in the decade (**The White Navy**, **A Pilot Returns**) produces a powerful cry for peace; while at the same time saluting the untold heroism of those who defied Mussolini, and finally, Hitler too.
With *Aldo Fabrizzi, Anna Magnani*

OPERATION AMSTERDAM
Michael McCarthy — GB, 1958 [105min]
Realistic spy thriller of Allied agents seeking out the Dutch diamond stock in Amsterdam ahead of the Nazi blitzkrieg. Solid cast.
With *Peter Finch, Tony Britton, Eva Bartok, Alexander Knox*

OPERATION BIKINI
Anthony Carras — U.S., 1963 [85min]
Intermittently exciting yarn of submarine frogmen diving into a sunken U.S. sub to ensure the radar equipment doesn't fall into Japanese hands during the Pacific campaign in WW2.
With *Tab Hunter, Frankie Avalon, Jim Backus, Scott Brady*

OPERATION BOTTLENECK
Edward L. Cahn — U.S., 1961 [80min]
'B' movie WW2 action by **Merrill's Marauders**-types against the Japanese in Burma. Not much to recommend it.
With *Ron Foster, Miiku Taka*

OPERATION CIA
Christian Nyby — U.S., 1965 [90min]
Early U.S. insight into the politics of mid-60s Vietnam, through a company man sent in to thwart an assassination attempt. Quite good.
With *Burt Reynolds, Kieu Chinh*

OPERATION CROSS EAGLES
Richard Conte — U.S., 1969 [90min]
Pretty awful nonsense about a U.S. lieutenant dropped into WW2 Yugoslavia to rescue another U.S. officer, who then decides to capture a German one for good measure.
With *Richard Conte, Rory Calhoun*

OPERATION CROSSBOW (aka 'The Great Spy Mission')
Michael Anderson — GB/Italy, 1965 [115min]
Exciting, if shallow and glossy, attempt to tell the (fictionalized) story of the destruction of Peenemunde and with it the German V1/V2 rocket threat to Britain (and further afield). Commandos get into the test centre as supposed Dutch scientists, aided by the Polish resistance.
Starry cast add to the attractive vista but a tighter script would have been appreciated.
With *George Peppard, Sophia Loren, Tom Courtenay, Richard Johnson, Jeremy Kemp, John Mills, Trevor Howard, Richard Todd, Sylvia Sims, Anthony Quayle, Paul Henreid, Patrick Wymark*

OPERATION DAYBREAK See **Hangmen Also Die**

OPERATION DISASTER See **Morning Departure**

OPERATION EICHMANN
RG Springsteen — U.S., 1961 [95min]
Cheap and nasty exploitation piece released immediately after the infamous war criminal's sensational trial in Israel.
With *Werner Klemperer, Ruta Lee, Donald Buka*

Erwin Leiser's equally quick-off-the-mark documentary, ***Eichmann and the Third Reich*** ★ [aka '*Murder by Signature*'], also smacks of opportunism.
A glossier fictionalized version, *The Man who Captured Eichmann*, was made by Turner Television in 1996 by Irving Cummings, with Robert Duvall as producer and the eponymous star.

OPERATION PACIFIC
George Waggner — U.S., 1950 [110min]
Gung-ho Wayne vehicle, with submariner Duke torpedoing all the Japs in sight during this eminently forgetable WW2 flagwaver.
With *John Wayne, Patricia Neal, Ward Bond*

OPERATION PETTICOAT
Blake Edwards — U.S., 1959 [125min]
Weak comedy of WW2 submarine skipper trying to get his ailing craft back into action is saved by the terrific chemistry between the marvellous Grant and an equally-good Curtis. The advent of women on board does not raise the temperature as expected.
With *Cary Grant, Tony Curtis, Joan O'Brien, Dina Merrill*

OPERATION SECRET
Lewis Seiler — U.S., 1952 [110min]
Biopic of U.S. agent, Lt Col Peter Ortiz, who infiltrates the French underground, trying to unearth a traitor. Ho-hum stuff.
With *Cornel Wilde, Karl Malden*

OPERATION SWALLOW
See **The Battle for Heavy Water**

OPERATION THUNDERBOLT
(aka 'Entebbe: Operation Thunderbolt')
Menahem Golan — Israel, 1977 [115min]
Unsatisfactory account of the storming of Entebbe airport by Israeli commandos, to free the Jewish hostages hijacked by the PFLP in Idi Amin's back yard. Thanks to Kinski's presence, this is still better than the rushed-out TV versions (see over),

whose only rationale seemed to be, 'Who do you know that's not working for the next few weeks? OK, get him!' Golan's film was actually nominated for Best Foreign Film Oscar.
With *Klaus Kinski, Yehoram Geon, Assaf Dayan, Ori Levy, Sybil Danning, Mark Heath*

Those TV versions, rushed out for U.S. audiences within months of the operation in 1976, were star-studded non-events:
Raid on Entebbe (Marvin J Chomsky), with Kirk Douglas, Burt Lancaster, Helmut Berger, Anthony Hopkins, Richard Dreyfuss, Linda Blair, Julius Harris, Helen Hayes and Elizabeth Taylor; and *Victory at Entebbe* (Irving Kirschner), starring Peter Finch, Martin Balsam, Charles Bronson, John Saxon, Jack Warden, Horst Buccholtz, Sylvia Sidney, Yaphet Kotto, James Woods, Robert Loggia and Eddie Constantine.

ORDERS TO KILL
Anthony Asquith — GB, 1958 [110min]
Taut, conscience-wringing suspenser about the killing of a French Resistance leader considered by the Allies to be a double-agent. Massie picked up a BAFTA for Best Newcomer — pity he didn't get another role like this — and Worth the Best Actress, among an eclectic cast. Another BAFTA went to Paul Dehn for the slick script.
With *Paul Massie, Irene Worth, Lillian Gish, Eddie Albert, Leslie French, James Robertson Justice, John Crawford, Lionel Jeffries, Jacques Brunius*

ORDINARY FASCISM
(aka '*Obyknovennyi Fashizm*') See **The Hitler Gang**

OREGON PASSAGE
Paul Landres — U.S., 1958 [80min]
Western based on a true incident involving Black Eagle, a chief of the Shoshone tribe, in a fracas with the U.S. Cavalry in the Pacific Northwest.
With *John Ericson, Lola Albright*

ORLANDO E I PALADINI DI FRANCIA
See **Roland and the Paladins of France**

ORPHANS OF THE STORM
D.W. Griffith — U.S., 1921 [125min]
Griffith manages to tell the tale of the unfortunate sisters within the wider sweep of the French Revolution, without one detracting from the other. The Revolution scenes are particularly gripping, and the storming of the Bastille a wonderfully detailed, yet dynamic set piece. The master's historical sense (**The Birth of a Nation**, **Intolerance**) had not deserted him.
With *Lillian Gish, Dorothy Gish, Joseph Schildkraut, Monte Blue*

OSS
Irving Pichel — U.S., 1946 [105min]
Action behind the lines for officers of the proto-CIA — the Office of Strategic Services. Captured by the Gestapo, Ladd has to decide whether to free his colleagues or return with vital intelligence. Nice and lively.
With *Alan Ladd, Geraldine Fitzgerald*

A TV series of the same name ran for three years in the late 1950s — one of the producers being ex-OSS man, William Eliscu.

OSTATNI ETAP See **The Last Stage**

OSTRA SLEDOVANE VLAKY
See **Closely Observed Trains**

OSVOBOZHDENIE See **Liberation**

OUR HERITAGE See **This England**

OUR HITLER See **Hitler, a Film from Germany**

OURSELVES ALONE See **Beloved Enemy**

OUT OF LIFE See **Hors la Vie**

OUT OF THE DEPTHS
Ross Lederman — U.S., 1946
A U.S. submarine plays cat-and-mouse with a Japanese aircraft carrier stocked with kamikaze aircraft late in the Pacific campaign of WW2. Routine.
With *Jim Bannon, Ross Hunter*

OUTPOST IN MOROCCO See **Beau Geste** (1939)

THE OUTRAGE
Cecil Hepworth — GB, 1915
WW1 was well underway when Hepworth produced this blistering attack on the savage Hun. One theme adopted early on was the invading Germans' apparent propensity to rape; and it was to be developed *ad nauseam* when Hollywood eventually took up the cudgel. Hepworth's picture, and one produced by the London Film Company called **1914 ★★** did at least offer more than this one single thread.
With *Henry Ainley, Albert Taylor*

THE OUTSIDER
The misery of Ulster as seen through the eyes of an American idealist. Cinematic Arts

THE OUTRIDERS
★ *Roy Rowland — U.S., 1950*
Prison camp drama from the American Civil War, when the Rebels effect a breakout. Despite its star, there is very little spark.
With *Joel McCrea, Arlene Dahl, Eamon Navarro*

THE OUTSIDER
★ *Delbert Mann — U.S., 1961* [95min]
★ Biopic of Ira Hayes, the American Indian Marine who famously helped raise the Stars and Stripes on Iwo Jima's Mt Suribachi in February 1945; and who actually re-enacted the feat in Dwan's **The Sands of Iwo Jima**. Other than that, and its pro-Indian stance, there is very little to add.
With *Tony Curtis, James Franciscus*

THE OUTSIDER
★ *Tony Luraschi — U.S., 1979* [130min]
★ An attempt by American cinema to throw light on the contemporary Irish troubles, it turns out to look more like exploitation. Being scrupulously but naively (un)fair to both the IRA and the British Security Forces, Luraschi's interesting plot is about an Irish-American volunteering for the Provisional IRA, only to discover that he's set up by both sides of the divide as a stool pigeon, and returns home demoralized.

It seems like an excuse to air every dirty trick conceived from either side during the previous decade. I don't know what American audiences thought, but cineastes from across the Pond have generally given the subject a wide berth since.
With *Craig Wasson, Sterling Hayden, Patricia Quinn, Niall O'Brien*

OVER THE TOP
★ *Wilfred North — U.S., 1918*
★ Star Empey's own novel about a U.S. hero of the Mexican border skirmishes in 1914, leaving for London to volunteer on behalf of the British when WW1 began. Good action.
With *Arthur Guy Empey, Lois Morrison*

THE OVERLANDERS
★ *Harry Watt — Australia, 1946* [90min]
★ Ealing's on location in the Outback, where Rafferty drives a thousand head of cattle away from the coast under the threat of Japanese invasion in WW2. Interesting 'scorched earth' tactic provides an insight into an Aussie Home Front which was anticipating the worst (the Japanese had bombed Darwin as early as February 1942, and mini-subs would cause chaos in Sydney harbour in the last week in May); before *The Battle of Midway* turned the tide in early June.
With *Chips Rafferty, John Nugent Hayward, Daphne Campbell*

OVERLORD
★ *Stuart Cooper — GB, 1975* [85min]
Mix of dull narrative, concerning the training for inevitable death on D-Day; and loosely-edited, supposedly 'saying-something', newsreel of aerial bombing. Portentous, but pointless, anti-war tract: and delivered much too late to make any mark (See **Saving Private Ryan**.)
With *Brian Stirner, Davyd Harris, Nicholas Ball*

PADENIYE BERLINA See **The Fall of Berlin**

PAISA (aka 'Paisan')
Roberto Rossellini — Italy, 1946 [115min]
Following on from the acclaim of **Open City**, Rossellini extended his semi-documentary approach to a six-part segmented history of WW2 in Italy, from the Allied landings in Sicily to 1945. Reusing Fellini to help write the (Oscar-nominated once more) screenplay, each tale seems to get more interesting as the picture progresses — some highly suspenseful, others contemplative. All through it is the starkly neo-realistic scene-setting and the ambivalent characterization that involves its audience so completely; and sets standards for the future for even documentary and newsreel presentation on matters of war. The almost nihilistic **Germany, Year Zero** was to follow.
With *Maria Michi, Gar Moore, William Tubbs*

PAISAN See **Paisà**

PANCHO VILLA See **Viva Villa**

PARADISE ROAD
Bruce Beresford — U.S./Australia, 1997 [115min]
More TV's *Tenko* than **Three Came Home**, this story of life in a Japanese prison camp for women during WW2 tells how the inmates survive through the choral singing which lifts their spirits and gives them a sense of purpose. The treacly plot is saved by some outstanding acting, particularly from Collins.
With *Glenn Close, Frances McDormand, Pauline Collins*

PARATROOP COMMAND
William Witney — U.S., 1959
Run of the mill U.S. parachute action over North Africa and Italy during WW2, with very little, even the action itself, to commend it.
With *Richard Bakalyan, Ken Lynch*

PARATROOPER See **The Red Beret**

PARIS AFTER DARK (aka 'The Night is Ending)
Leonide Moguy — U.S., 1943 [85min]
Taut little thriller surrounding a Resistance fighter whose resistance is not what it should be after a visit to the Gestapo.
With *George Sanders, Philip Dorn, Brenda Marshall*

PARIS, BRULE-EST-IL? See **Is Paris Burning?**

PARIS CALLING
Edwin L. Marin — U.S., 1941 [95min]
Convoluted propaganda piece with a plot incorporating a well-to-do French woman joining the Resistance as Paris falls to the Germans in 1940; helping an American with the RAF; and killing her collaborating husband along the way. Where *do* loyalties lie?
With *Elisabeth Bergner, Randolph Scott, Basil Rathbone*

PARIS UNDERGROUND (aka 'Madame Pimpernel')
Gregory Ratoff — U.S., 1945 [95min]
Biopic of Etta Shiber, who, with her friend, smuggles some 250 Allied airmen out of France in WW2; and who are just rescued in time by the Liberation. Wooden. Academy Award nomination for Alexander Tansman's score.
With *Constance Bennett, Gracie Fields*

THE PASSAGE
J. Lee(-)Thompson — GB, 1978 [100min]
Uninteresting WW2 story of a Basque peasant (played to type by Quinn) helping a famous scientist (played to type by Mason) escape occupied France ahead of a completely over-the-top sadistic SS officer (played to type by McDowell).
With *Anthony Quinn, James Mason, Malcolm McDowell*

LE PASSAGE DU RHIN See **The Crossing of the Rhine**

PASSAGE TO MARSEILLES
Michael Curtiz — U.S., 1944 [110min]
With four of the same major stars, as well as Dantine and one or two others, plus director Curtiz, this story of wartime factionalism in France was surely intended to follow in the steps of **Casablanca.** It tries a bit too hard, however, and at times seems to go round in circles with flashbacks of flashbacks — and even one flashback of a flashback in a flashback! The plot takes in Devil's Island, Free French v Vichy, shipboard adventure, romance and war action — but lightning, unfortunately for this stock company, doesn't strike twice.
With *Humphrey Bogart, Michèle Morgan, Claude Rains, Sydney Greenstreet, Peter Lorre, Helmut Dantine*

LA PASSION DE JEANNE D'ARC see **Joan of Arc**

THE PASSWORD IS COURAGE
Andrew L. Stone — GB, 1962 [115min]
Coward has the courage (Sgt Maj Charles Coward, that is) in this biopic — told somewhat tongue-in-cheek (a play on the name alone would have been enough) — about a rascally NCO with a habit for breaking out of German POW camps in WW2. Not as good as it might have been.
With *Dirk Bogarde, Maria Perschy, Alfred Lynch, Nigel Stock*

PASTOR HALL
Roy and John Boulting — GB, 1940 [95min]
Withering propaganda attack on the Nazi regime and the first horrors of concentration camp life, with this one-sided, no-holds-barred biopic of Pastor Martin Niemöller's stand against Nazi brutality in 1934 Germany. Boulting would soon temporarily give up feature films and join up for his incisive war documentaries (see *Desert Victory*, *Burma Victory*).
With *Nova Pilbeam, Wilfred Lawson, Seymour Hicks, Marius Goring*

THE PATENT LEATHER KID See **The Slacker**

THE PATHFINDER See **The Last of the Mohicans**

PATHS OF GLORY
Stanley Kubrick — U.S., 1957 [85min]
Not so much anti-war as a vitriolic venting of the spleen on military authority itself — its hypocrisy and its blinkered obsolescence of thought. Although the French hierarchy in WW1 comes under attack from Kubrick's ground-breaking film (taken from Humphrey Cobb's novel), the sentiments could be levelled at all sides during the immense stupidity that was the Great War. Douglas is outstanding as the colonel, the one voice of reason among the senior officers, as he defends three infantrymen who are falsely, but conveniently, accused of cowardice.

Banned in many countries' military establishments, this is arguably the greatest cinematic testament to the folly of how the war was conducted, and a harrowing depiction of trench warfare itself (tracking camera working overtime) — yet it was not shown anywhere in France until 1975. In most military movie fans' Top Ten, and obviously not understood by the Academy at the time.
With *Kirk Douglas, Ralph Meeker, Adolphe Menjou, George Macready*

THE PATHS OF THE HEROES
See **The Great Challenge**

PATRIOTEN See **Pour le Mérite**

PATTON (aka 'Patton — Lust for Glory')
Franklin Schaffner — U.S., 1970 [170min]
Schaffner's study of a complex, hugely-flawed character tells us so much more than the outstanding WW2 record of 'Old Blood and Guts'. His eccentric behaviour, mood swings, uncaring objectivity and paternal consciousness, are all marvellously articulated by the Oscar-winning (although not receiving!) Scott. It works as a war spectacle, too, with tank divisions rampaging across Sicily, then northern France; and the childish rivalry between Patton and Montgomery is also well-documented.

But it's the character study put together by actor and director, including his knowledge and love of military history (at the ruins of Carthage), his anti-communist stance — and yes, the face-slapping incident, too — which make the picture special. Not so much a biopic, but a full pictorial biography.

Swept up most of the telling Oscars: apart from Scott's acting, awards also went to the film, the director, to Francis Coppola's and Edmund North's script (adapted from *Patton: Ordeal and Triumph* by Ladislas Farago and Patton's colleague, Gen Omar N. Bradley's *A Soldier's Story*); and for editing, art direction, and sound. Further nominees were Fred Koenkamps' cinematography, Jerry Goldsmith's score, and for visual effects.
With *George C. Scott, Karl Malden, Michael Bates*

PATTON — LUST FOR GLORY See **Patton**

LA PATTUGLIA SPERDUTA
See **The Lost Patrol** (1954)

THE PAWNBROKER
Sidney Lumet — U.S., 1965 [115min]
Lumet's characteristically grim and grainy (*Twelve Angry Men*, **The Hill** — he still preferred black and white photography to create an unpleasant atmosphere in his pictures at that time) portrait of an ex-concentration camp inmate, living amongst low-life in New York City but still haunted, through many harrowing flashbacks, by his experiences.

Steiger was nominated for his performance by the Academy, and went one step further at the BAFTAs.
With *Rod Steiger, Brock Peters, Geraldine Fitzgerald*

— particularly the ending of Sweden as a military power at Poltava in 1709; the subsequent control of much of the southern Baltic shore at the close of the Great Northern War; and, finally perhaps most important of all, the boyar-bashing that went on apace.
With *Nikolai Simonov, Nikolai Cherkassov*

LE PETIT SOLDAT
(aka 'The Little Soldier')
Jean-Luc Godard — France, 1960 [90min]
To define the works of Godard defies brevity. Suffice to say this is a reasonably accessible piece about a *Sureté* agent tracking down an Algerian terrorist in France during the French-Algerian War.
With *Michel Subor, Anna Karina*

PATTON
Squaring up to Rommel in North Africa. 20CF

PERFECT STRANGERS (aka 'Vacation from Marriage')
Alexander Korda — GB, 1945 [100min]
Clemence Dane received the Academy Award for his original screenplay in this very light British comedy, where a dowdy husband and wife enlist in WW2 (he to the Navy, she becomes a Wren) and come back as different people. Was well-received at the time, apparently.
With *Robert Donat, Deborah Kerr, Glynis Johns, Ann Todd, Roland Culver, Roger Moore* (as a walk-on, nine years before his first accredited role)

PÉTAIN
Jean Marboeuf — France, 1992 [135min]
Disappointing, stultified history lesson of how WW1 hero Pétain was duped by Laval and others into believing collaboration was the best avenue for the French people, so crushingly defeated by Germany in WW2. Set at Vichy's Hôtel du Parc (where the puppets played at politics — but did little more than arrange for one-way tickets out for French Jews), the turgid narrative is hard enough to take for a non-Frenchman, so it's little wonder that the unpalatable subject matter, plus the pedestrian pacing, went down like a lead balloon in France.
With *Jacques Dufilho, Jean Yanne*

PETER THE GREAT
Vladimir Petrov — USSR, 1937and39
Sanitized and hugely nationalistic historical extravaganza about the founder of modern Russia and his brand of autocracy in the early 18th century. Petrov's uninspired piece came in two bits, and as cinema it pales into insignificance when compared with the contemporaneous **Alexander Nevsky**. It does, however, cover ground the Party approved of

THE PIED PIPER
Irving Pichel — U.S., 1942 [85min]
The children's story updated to WW2 by novelist Neville Shute, with Woolley picking up all kinds of waifs and strays across France and getting them to Britain before the German invasion overwhelms them. Oozes sentimentality, but has its good moments, with Preminger a suitably nasty Nazi. Nominated for Best Picture, Best Cinematography (Edward Cronjager) and for Woolley's pleasing performance.
With *Monty Woolley, Ann Baxter, Roddy McDowall, Otto Preminger, J. Carroll Naish*

THE PIGEON THAT TOOK ROME
Melville Shavelson — U.S., 1962 [100min]
Uncharacteristic light comedy from Heston in this unfunny WW2 piece about a U.S. officer behind enemy lines in Rome, sending out misleading messages by carrier pigeon.
With *Charlton Heston, Elsa Martinelli, Harry Guardino, Brian Donlevy*

PILLARS OF THE SKY
(aka 'The Tomahawk and the Cross')
George Marshall — U.S., 1956 [95min]
Some good action rescues this otherwise pretty dim Cavalry v Indians fare. Chandler takes a break from Cochise (see **Broken Arrow**, etc) to play an Indian scout this time.
With *Jeff Chandler, Dorothy Malone , Ward Bond, Keith Andes, Lee Marvin*

PILOT NUMBER FIVE
George Sidney — U.S., 1943 [70min]
Pretty horrendous propaganda piece with an anti-communist political aide joining the USAF and finally sacrificing himself, kamikaze-style, to sink a Japanese aircraft carrier. Pretty prophetic, too, as it would be a year or two before the Japanese took to it themselves.
With *Franchot Tone, Marsha Hunt, Gene Kelly, Van Johnson*

A PILOT RETURNS
(aka 'Un Pilota Ritorna') See **Man of the Cross**

UN PILOTA RITORNA See **A Pilot Returns**

PIMPERNEL SMITH
(aka 'The Fighting Pimpernel', 'Mister V')
Leslie Howard — GB, 1941 [120min]
Anti-German archaeologist, but the antithesis of Indiana Jones — this one's English, and superficially absent-minded — helps free many non-Nazis across the German-Swiss border in the 1930s. Howard himself directs his own reincarnation of the **Scarlet Pimpernel** in a very effective update.
With *Leslie Howard, Francis L. Sullivan*

THE PIRATES OF CAPRI
Edgar Ulmer — U.S., 1949 [95min]
Swashbuckling skulduggery in the Neapolitan court of King Ferdinand IV and Maria Carolina, c1779, loosely prologuing the upheavals which were to occur over the next four decades: the Revolution in France and its subsequent wars; and the age of the Two Sicilies, over which the king would reign as Ferdinand I. I doubt whether the director knew so much, or even cared.
With *Louis Hayward, Binnie Barnes, Alan Curtis*

PIRATES OF MONTEREY See **Kit Carson**

THE PLAINSMAN
Cecil B. de Mille — U.S., 1936 [115min]
Sweeping saga of the West's semi-legends, Bills Cody and Hickcock, with Calamity Jane thrown in for good measure. Typically lurid; at least de Mille did challenge the Cheyenne objection that he was, as usual, making up history as he went along. He quoted the source of the climactic battle in 1868, when 48 Cavalrymen held off against almost 1,000 redmen in Colorado Territory.
With *Gary Cooper, Jean Arthur, Charles Bickford*

PLATOON
Oliver Stone — U.S., 1986 [120min]
The Vietnam movie was more or less dead in the water, sunk by the heavy hallucinogenics of **Apocalypse Now**, and numbed by the anti-war namby-pambyism of pictures like **Coming Home**. Then, more than half a decade later, comes a blistering, unshackled and totally uncompromising combat movie of immense power and influence (it was followed by **Hamburger Hill**, and only marginally-upstaged by Kubrick's awesome **Full Metal Jacket** the following year).

The story of a platoon of GIs going through hell reminds one of the better WW2 and Korean War movies, and is based on Stone's own recollections of his time in 'Nam. Indeed, it is the bloody first of a varied Vietnam trilogy by the director, with next being the disappointing **Heaven and Earth**, but followed by a return to form with the definitive Vietnam vet movie, **Born on the Fourth of July**.

Winner of the Best Picture Academy Award, it also gained an Oscar (and BAFTA) for Stone's direction, the best editing and best sound. Stone's script was also nominated, as were Dafoe and Berenger in supporting actor roles (symbolizing the oustanding ensemble acting), and Robert Richardson's photography.
With *Tom Berenger, Willem Dafoe, Charlie Sheen, Forest Whitaker*

PLATOON LEADER
Aaron Norris — U.S., 1988 [100min]
Undiluted cash-in on the above entry — shameful Vietnam exploitation of the type equally associated with the director's brother, Chuck.
With *Michael Dudikoff*

PLAY DIRTY
André De Toth — GB, 1969 [120min]
Another **Dirty Dozen** replica, with script co-written by Melvyn Bragg — perhaps that's why there are some lip-service references to the futility of war — about Caine's gang of cut-throats attempting to blow up a German fuel dump in North Africa during WW2. Lack of imagination apart, it's not too badly done; but the world it depicts is not that of the 1940s.
With *Michael Caine, Nigel Davenport, Nigel Green, Harry Andrews*

THE PLOT TO KILL ROOSEVELT See **Teheran**

THE PLOUGH AND THE STARS
John Ford — U.S., 1936 [70min]
Ford stays with the Irish troubles, after his big success with **The Informer** the previous year. The luck of the director/writer partnership (Ford/Dudley Nicholls), which, with the above and the 1934 classic **The Lost Patrol**, had brought them consecutive Oscars, stopped here, however. This is rather an unconvincing filming of Sean O'Casey's play set during the Easter Rising of 1916.
With *Barbara Stanwyck, Barry Fitzgerald, Preston Foster*

THE PLOUGHMAN'S LUNCH
Richard Eyre — GB, 1983 [105min]
BBC journo Pryce is writing a book about the Suez crisis whilst drawing parallels with the Falklands War, which is happening as he writes. Intelligent and often cynical, it is unfortunately just an oblique reference to two conflicts which warrant a more front-on approach.
With *Jonathan Pryce, Tim Curry, Rosemary Harris, Frank Finlay, Charlie Dore*

POKOLOENIE See **A Generation**

POPIOL I DIAMENT See **Ashes and Diamonds**

PORK CHOP HILL
Lewis Milestone — U.S., 1959 [95min]
The brilliant but oh-so-erratic Milestone is back to nearly his best in one of the defining pictures of the Korean War. It must be said, however, that this particular conflict has not thrown up many of quality. The pacifist sentiments so eloquently expressed in **All Quiet . . .** and **A Walk in the Sun** return to a more modern theatre; a more deeply cynical, more sophisti-cated and complex post A-bomb world.

The futility of the taking of a knoll of ground — just a few metres, just a few thousand lives — is graphically and movingly portrayed. Indeed, the action as men move forward into an unknown hell literally inch-by-inch, is one of the high-spots in any war movie (emulated in **Hamburger Hill**). A fine tribute to a true incident, which bought the UN just a few more negotiating points at the peace conference table.
With *Gregory Peck, Harry Guardino, Rip Torn, George Peppard, Robert Blake, Woody Strode*

IL PORTIERE DI NOTTE
See **The Night Porter**

POUR LE MERITE
Karl Ritter — Germany, 1938
One of several patriotic and pro-Nazi pictures brought out by probably the most prolific of Germany's filmmakers at the time (eg **Leave on Word of Honour ★★** and **Patrioten ★★** — both 1937). This picture is slightly more than propagandist preaching, however, dealing with German flyers in WW1 — the Richthofen Squadron (Ritter was a WW1 pilot), which, resisting all attempts to disband it during the Weimar years, came to be regarded as the beginnings of Göring's Luftwaffe. Some excellent aerial sequences, too. Ritter's flying movies continued after WW2 broke out (see **Stukas**).
With *Paul Hartmann, Albert Hehn, Fritz Kampers*

POVEST PLAMENNYKH LET
See **The Flaming Years**

POW: THE ESCAPE (aka 'Behind Enemy Lines')
Gideon Amir — U.S., 1986
Awful attempt to make a caper movie out of the Vietnam War. Camp commandant (Mako) wants to flee the successful communist North Vietnam as the war comes to an end, with a bundle of loot. The incarcerated Americans play the POW game by the book, however, and kill him.
With *David Carradine, Mako, Charles R. Floyd*

THE POWER OF THE PEOPLE
See *The Battle of Chile*

A PRAYER FOR THE DYING
Mike Hodges — GB, 1987 [105min]
Empty film version (disowned by the director) of an empty novel (by Jack Higgins) about a reformed IRA killer.
With *Mickey Rourke, Bob Hoskins, Alan Bates*

PRED DOZDOT See **Before the Rain**

PRELUDE TO WAR See **Why We Fight**

THE PRESIDENT VANISHES
William Wellman — U.S., 1934 [80min]
Anti-fascist political fantasy involving the U.S. President faking his kidnapping, and blaming it on the Nazi-style 'Gray Shirts'; trying not to involve America in another world war. Amazing the lengths some people will go to. Being Wellman, though, you get something interesting to watch, as you would expect.
With *Arthur Byron, Janet Beecher*

PRETTY VILLAGE, PRETTY FLAME
(aka 'Lepa Sela Lepo Gore')
Srdjan Dragojevic — (Former) Yugoslavia, 1995 [130min]
Important early film on the conflict in Bosnia to come out of the former Yugoslavia. Although it covers the most basic concepts of war in making enemies out of former friends (here a Moslem and a Serb who have grown up together), the sheer imagery of a war still not cold is somehow more demanding of the audience than a conflict even 20 or so years older. Some scenes are deeply affecting: have no doubt about it, this is a true war film you are watching.
With *Dragan Bjelogrlic, Nikola Koyo, Dragan Maksimovic*

THE PRIDE AND THE PASSION
Stanley Kramer — U.S., 1957 [130min]
C.S. Forester's novel *The Gun* provided the basis for this over-serious, over-long epic of the Peninsular War set in 1810. Sinatra is miscast as a Spanish guerrilla towing a huge siege gun halfway across Spain to try to turf the French out of the fortified city of Avila. Enter the British in the shape of one man (that they had in fact been battling out of Portugal since 1808, and had already beaten the French in a decisive battle at Talavera in 1809, is not mentioned); but that man is Grant, so you know there'll be a happy ending.
With *Frank Sinatra, Cary Grant, Sophia Loren, Theodore Bikel*

PRIDE OF THE MARINES (aka 'Forever in Love')
Delmer Daves — U.S., 1945 [120min]
End-of-WW2 weepie which drew good box-office and critical kudos, about the true story of a blinded Marine vet (Al Schmid). Gooey, but quick to bring out the point being made about disabled returnees. Albert Maltz was nominated for his script.
With *John Garfield, Eleanor Parker*

PRINCE OF THIEVES
See **The Adventures of Robin Hood**

PRINCE VALIANT (1954)
See **Knights of the Round Table**

PRINCE VALIANT (1994)
See **Knights of the Round Table**

PRISON SHIP
Arthur Dreifuss — U.S., 1945
Heavily over-the top in the propaganda stakes, this WW2 drama shows just how dastardly the Japanese could be. They use a merchant ship filled with civilian prisoners as bait to draw out U.S. submarines. Cads. (See also **Torpedo Run** for a similar tale.)
With *Nina Foch, Robert Lowery*

PRISONER OF THE MOUNTAIN
(aka 'Kavkazski Plennik')
Sergei Bodrov — Kazakhstan/Russia, 1996 [95min]
Liberated production giving quite a keen insight into the 1994-96 Chechen revolt against Russia. Quite unelaborate (simple tale of Russian soldiers captured by Chechen rebels and held hostage), yet perceptive in its views of both sides, in a rare theatre of war for cinema. Oscar-nominated for Best Foreign Film.
With *Oleg Menshikov, Sergei Bodrov Jr, Alexai Zharkov*

PRISONER OF WAR
Andrew Marton — U.S., 1954 [80min]
Rushed out at the end of the Korean War, Marton cashes in on the heavy rumours about communist maltreatment of U.S. POWs, and the first talk of 'brainwashing'. Starred a future president — hard to say whether he should have stuck to the day job.

Not the studied treatise on the subject (see **The Manchurian Candidate**), but encouraged others such as Arnold Laven's **The Rack ★★** in 1956 [100min], with Paul Newman, Walter Pidgeon and Lee Marvin.
With *Ronald Reagan, Steve Forrest, Oscar Homolka*

PRIVATE ANGELO

Peter Ustinov — GB, 1949 [105min]
Unfunny comedy about an Italian soldier who switches to the British when the Germans are on the retreat in Italy in WW2. With *Peter Ustinov, Robin Bailey, James Robertson Justice*

PRIVATE POTTER

Caspar Wrede — GB, 1962 [90min]
Courtenay is court-martialled (it would become almost habit-forming, see **For King and Country**) whilst on active service in the British Army in Cyprus during the 1950s, after a religious visitation. Not in the same class as the other film. With *Tom Courtenay, Ronald Fraser*

PRIVATES ON PARADE

Peter Nichols — GB, 1982 [115min]
Arch and arcane comedy drama of British Army concert party getting caught in real action in the Malayan troubles of 1948. Not much above TV's *It Ain't Half Hot, Mum*, apart from the maniacal Cleese and a consummate performance in cross-dressing from the outstanding Quilley.

Drawing comedy from service situations has been profitable for movie-makers down the years (*Buck Privates, Private's Progress*, **M★A★S★H**, *Private Benjamin*, etc), but the tawdry backwater conflicts like post-WW2 Malaya, Singapore, etc, hardly lend themselves to laughs. Somewhat better, yet still a travesty when compared to the original book, is John Dexter's adaptation of Leslie Thomas' **Virgin Soldiers**. With *John Cleese, Dennis Quilley, Michael Elphick, Nicola Pagett*

PROCES DE JEANNE D'ARC
See **The Trial of Joan of Arc**

A PROFESSIONAL GUN See **Il Mercenario**

THE PROFESSIONALS

Richard Brooks — U.S., 1966 [125min]
Pre-**The Wild Bunch**, tough-as-they-come Western involving mercenaries and the Mexican Revolution in 1916. The title sums up the picture — strong plot, professionally played and directed (nominations for writing and directing for Brooks), and professionally photographed (nomination for Conrad Hall); but it is so 'professional', it doesn't lighten up at all, and a little levity here and there might have helped. Terrific fight scenes though. With *Burt Lancaster, Lee Marvin, Robert Ryan, Jack Palance, Claudia Cardinale, Woody Strode, Ralph Bellamy*

PROFESSOR MAMLOCK

Adolph Minkin/Herbert Rappoport — USSR, 1938
Story of a Berlin doctor who wants to kill himself rather than be a Jew in Hitler's Germany. Powerful Soviet propaganda in a year when filmmakers everywhere were beginning to take their gloves off. With *Sergei Mezhinski*

THE PROUD AND PROFANE

George Seaton — U.S., 1956
Boring romance, sub-**From Here to Eternity** style; set on New Caledonia during WW2, with lots of melodrama and patchy action. Holden is the U.S. Marine colonel falling for nurse Kerr. Oscar-nominated for art direction. With *William Holden, Deborah Kerr, Thelma Ritter*

THE PRUSSIAN CUR

Raoul Walsh — U.S., 1918
Has to be included for the title of this WW1 spy drama alone. Walsh, never the most subtle of action directors, certainly nailed his colours to the mast with this one. With *Miriam Cooper, James Marcus*

PT 109

Leslie H. Martinson — U.S., 1963 [140min]
Thin storyline to stretch over such a long film, for this, a superficial tribute to the WW2 heroism of the then incumbent U.S. President, John F. Kennedy. We follow his exploits as a lieutenant in command of a torpedo patrol boat (see **They Were Expendable**), which is sunk by the Japanese. The rest is just dour character study. With *Cliff Robertson, Ty Hardin, Robert Culp*

THE PUPPETMASTER (aka 'Hsimeng Rensheng')

Hou Hsaio-Hsien — Thailand, 1993 [140min]
Painterly portrait of Formosan (Taiwanese) life under Japanese occupation, 1895-1945, narrated by its octogenarian author. Not everyone's cup of tea, but gives an important insight into a dark corner of the world over half a century of torment and oppression. With *Li Tienlu* (narrator), *Lim Giong*

THE PURPLE HEART

Lewis Milestone — U.S., 1944 [100min]
Moving from pacifism to shrieking racism, Milestone continued to baffle. Sandwiched between the sublime **All Quiet on the Western Front** and the contemplative **A Walk in the Sun,** he directed the heavily anti-German propagandist **Arch of Triumph** and **Edge of Darkness**: then this vitriolic Jap-basher about show trials and executions of U.S. bomber crews downed over Japan in 1942. It naturally caused an outrage at the time, but really, a more measured tenor would have achieved the same outcry, and perhaps made a film for posterity — not the knee-jerk spasm it actually is. With *Dana Andrews, Richard Conte, Farley Granger*

PURPLE HEARTS

Sidney J. Furie — U.S., 1984 [115min]
Filmic non-event in that Vietnam War cinema void of 1980-85, with silly love story diluting what action there is. With *Ken Wahl, Cheryl Ladd*

THE PURPLE MASK See **The Scarlet Pimpernel**

THE PURPLE PLAIN

Robert Parrish — GB, 1954 [100min]
Disappointing adaptation by Eric Ambler of an H.E. Bates novel (he of the Larkin family sagas) which still did decent box-office. Peck is an RAF Mosquito pilot shot down over Burma in WW2, and has to find his way home on foot through the physical and psychological nightmare of the jungle. With *Gregory Peck, Bernard Lee, Maurice Denham*

THE PURPLE V

George Sherman — U.S., 1943
American pilot escaping from Germany receives help and important information from an anti-Nazi German. Propagandist plod. With *John Archer*

THE PURSUIT OF HAPPINESS
★ *Alexander Hall — U.S., 1934* [75min]
Romance during the American Revolution with a young colonial girl falling for a Hessian mercenary fighting on the British side. Action is limited.
With *Francis Lederer, Joan Bennett*

PURSUIT OF THE GRAF SPEE
See **The Battle of the River Plate**

QINGCHENGZHI LIAN See **Love in a Fallen City**

QUANTRILL'S RAIDERS
Edward Bernds — U.S., 1958 [70min] ★
Fictitious story based on renegade Confederate William ★
Quantrill's infamous revenge attack on the town and towns-folk of Lawrence, Kansas, in August 1863. He and his 'Raiders', some 450 strong on occasion, achieved notoriety for their daring and ruthlessness in a series of guerrilla skirmishes across the Missouri-Kansas border in the American Civil War. At one time both the James and Younger brothers rode with Quantrill, and they actually survived the end of the war to become history in their own right.
With *Steve Cochran, Diane Brewster, Leo Gordon*

Other pictures portraying the adventures of Quantrill, or Quantrill-mimics, include:
Jesse James ** (Lloyd Ingham — U.S., 1927) With *Fred Thompson*
Not to be confused with Henry King's *Jesse James* (1939), with Tyrone Power and Henry Fonda, which makes no reference to Quantrill.
The Dark Command ** (Raoul Walsh — U.S., 1940, 1990min) With *John Wayne, Roy Rogers*
Kansas Raiders ** (Ray Enright — U.S., 1950, 1980min) With *Audie Murphy, Brian Donlevy*
Red Mountain * (William Dieterlie — U.S., 1951, 1985min) With *Alan Ladd*
Arizona Rangers * (Wiliiam Witney — U.S., 1965, 1990min) with *Audie Murphy*
The Desperados * (Henry Levin — U.S., 1969. 90min) With *Jack Palance, Vince Edwards*

QUEBEC
George Templeton — U.S., 1951 [85min] ★
Daft romantic drama which takes place at the time of the 'Patriotes' revolt in Quebec in 1837. Easily quashed by the British, it did, however, result in a degree of self-determination for the French, until the Confederation of Canada in 1867 led to a strait-jacketing of French-Canadians.
With *John Barrymore Jr, Corinne Calvert, Barbara Rush, Patric Knowles*

¿QUIEN SABE? See **A Bullet for a General**

QUENTIN DURWARD
Richard Thorpe — GB, 1955 [100min] ★
Scott's Scottish hero who gets involved between the French ★
and Burgundian factions during the War of the Public Good ★
(1465-77), proved Britain and its 'history' to be a rich vein for director and star in the early '50s (see also **Ivanhoe**, **Knights of the Round Table**). Good period romp, even if Taylor was getting a little long in the tooth to keep swashing that buckler.
With *Robert Taylor, Kay Kendall, Robert Morley, George Cole, Alec Clunes*

THE QUICK AND THE DEAD
★ *Robert Totten — U.S., 1963*
★ Not to be confused with Sam Raimi's 1995 Western parody starring Gene Hackman and Sharon Stone, this is WW2 bang-bang. Action-filled to the point of brain-deadening, this low-budget adventure-drama takes place in 1944 Italy, with partisans helping a diminishing group of GIs to overcome superior German odds.
With *Larry Mann, Victor French*

THE QUIET AMERICAN
Joseph L. Mankiewicz — U.S., 1957 [120min]
Graham Greene's novel experiences a change of emphasis here — his original ending is altered from cautious pro-nationalist to blatant pro-American. In this political intrigue based in French Indochina in 1952 when the French were struggling to maintain colonial control, Redgrave's cynically fence-sitting British journalist is duped by the Reds into betraying the naive American (Murphy).
With *Audie Murphy, Michael Redgrave, Claude Dauphin*

THE RACK See **Prisoner of War**

THE RAGGEDY RAWNEY
Bob Hoskins — GB, 1987 [105min] ★★
Odd, wandering comedy drama of a group of gypsies eking out a living criss-crossing the Eastern Front during WW2. Nice period feel, but a bit of a head-scratcher.
With *Bob Hoskins, Dexter Fletcher, Zoe Wanamaker, Ian Dury, Ian McNeice*

UNA RAGIONE PER VIVERE E UNA MORIRE
See **A Reason to Live, a Reason to Die**

THE RAID
Hugo Fregonese — U.S., 1954 [85min] ★★★
Based on a true incident when six Southern soldiers, who had escaped a Union prison and fled to Canada, raided a Vermont town 'through the back door' so to speak, and caused great uproar in the North. Nicely done with a cast that would be generally going somewhere.
With *Van Heflin, Anne Bancroft, Richard Boone, Lee Marvin, Peter Graves*

RAID ON ROMMEL See **Tobruk** ★

THE RAIDER See **Western Approaches**

RAIDERS OF LEYTE GULF
Eddie Romero — U.S., 1963 [80min] ★
Cheapie Filipino guerrilla saga in WW2 prior to MacArthur's return.
With *Jennings Sturgeon*

RAIDERS OF THE LOST ARK
Steven Spielberg — U.S., 1981 [115min] ★★★★
Rousing comic-strip adventures of a larger-than-life archaeologist: Spielberg's and producer George Lucas' incarnation is based on a childhood of Saturday morning serial heroes. Twice on the big screen Indie (Ford) comes into contact with the Nazis: in the third film of the series, **Indiana Jones and the Last Crusade ★★★★** (co-starring Sean Connery, Elliott and Rhys-Davies, 1989, 125min), he vies with the Germans (who are forever seeking a spiritual advantage to take into WW2) for the Holy Grail; here it's the Ark of the Covenant.

Oscars for editing and visual effects: nominations for picture, director, Douglas Slocombe's cinematography and John Williams' score. ('Last Crusade' won the Oscar for best sound, and was nominated for sound effects editing and Williams' music again.)
With *Harrison Ford, Denholm Elliott, Karen Allen, Paul Freeman, Ronald Lacey, John Rhys-Davies*

The second film in the series, *Indiana Jones and the Temple of Doom*, pre-dates the first in its storyline, and doesn't feature Nazis.

RAIGEKITAI SHUTSUDO
See **Torpedo Squadrons Move Out**

THE RAKE'S PROGRESS (aka 'Notorious Gentleman')
Sidney Gilliat — GB, 1945 [125min]
Light confection about upper-class pre-*Alfie* style playboy, who needs WW2 to make him see reason, and makes him a most undeserved hero. Doesn't sit right.

Allegory is based on Hogarth's engravings and in 1951 Stravinsky turned it into great opera, using a more traditional (non-topical) scenario, with the libretto partially written by W.H. Auden. Although not really comparing apples to apples, it puts the cinema piece to shame.
With *Rex Harrison, Lilli Palmer*

RAMBO: FIRST BLOOD PART TWO
George Pan Cosmatos — U.S., 1985 [95min]
John Rambo, the Vietnam war hero who first appeared as a misunderstood vet in Ted Kotcheff's **First Blood ★★★** in 1982 [95min], provided enough murder and mayhem to exploit two further (and progressively inferior) pictures. In this, the first sequel, the **Missing in Action** theme about U.S. POWs thought still to be held in Vietnam ten years after the ceasefire is the excuse.

Rambo goes back in, kicks some ass, brings home the boys, and the result is the second biggest box-office success of 1985 (after *Back to the Future*). More interesting in concept is **Rambo III ★★** (Peter MacDonald, 1988, 100min), but the involvement of our hero in the Soviet war in Afghanistan pays scant regard to the politics, and only provides a different land-scape for Stallone to strut his super-macho stuff. The stars appear in all three of what must be the most confusingly-titled trilogy ever to reach the screen.
With *Sylvester Stallone, Richard Crenna*

RAMBO III See **Rambo: First Blood Part Two**

RAN
Akira Kurosawa — Japan, 1985 [160min]
Nearly 30 years after **Throne of Blood**, and now well into his 70s, Kurosawa returned to Shakespeare and once again (this time transplanting *King Lear* into the turmoil of 16th century Japan), proves he is the sublime master when it comes to converting the Bard to cinema. Instead of three daughters, the warlord Hidetora divides his empire among his three sons — with the predictable consequences. Sibling rivalry spills over into war: a war that only the director could bring to the screen — loud, colourful, barbaric, yet poetic.

The imagery is stunning, but Kurosawa's trademark humanity is never far from the surface. The haul of one Oscar (costumes), three nominations (the director, cinematography and art direction), and the BAFTA for Best Foreign Film is a poor return for the crowning achievement of one of the undoubted 'greats' of cinema.
With *Tatsuya Nakadai, Satoshi Terao, Jinpachi Nezu*

THE RAPE OF MALAYA See **A Town Like Alice**

RAPPRESAGLIA See **Massacre in Rome**

RASPOUTINE (1954) See **Rasputin and the Empress**

RASPUTIN (1930) See **Rasputin and the Empress**

RASPUTIN (1975) See **Agony**

RASPUTIN AND THE EMPRESS
(aka 'Rasputin the Mad Monk')
Richard Boleslawski — U.S., 1932 [135min]
Hollywood's answer to a Dovzhenko or Eisenstein epic on events leading to the Russian Revolution ended in MGM being sued $1m by a Russian aristo (for mis-representation) on the one hand; and the picture being banned by Stalin on the other.

The suitably lavish sets are to be expected, but apart from that, the main item of interest is that this is the only occasion that the Barrymore offsprings appeared together on screen. (See also **The Fall of the Romanoffs**, **The Fall of the Romanov Dynasty**, **Nicholas and Alexandra**.)
With *John Barrymore, Ethyl Barrymore, Lionel Barrymore, Ralph Morgan, Diana Wynyard*

Other films devoted to the story of Rasputin include:
Rasputin ★ (Germany, 1930) With *Conrad Veidt*
Rasputine ★★ (aka 'The Imperial Tragedy', etc) (Marcel L'Herbier — France, 1938) With *Harry Baur*
Rasputine ★ (Georges Combret — France, 1954, 110min) With *Pierre Brasseur*
Nights of Rasputin (Italy, 1960, 1995min) With *Edmund Purdom*
Rasputin the Mad Monk ★★★ (Don Sharp — GB, 1966, 1990min) With *Christopher Lee*
I Killed Rasputin ★★ (Robert Hossein — France, 1967, 1990min) With *Gert Frobe*
Agony ★★★ (aka 'Agonia', 'Rasputin') (Elem Klimov — USSR, 1977, 150min) With *Alexei Petrenko*

RASPUTIN THE MAD MONK (1932)
See **Rasputin and the Empress**

RASPUTIN THE MAD MONK (1966)
See **Rasputin and the Empress**

RASPUTINE (1938) (aka 'La Tragédie Impériale', 'The Imperial Tragedy', 'La Fin des Romanoff', 'Le Diable de Sibérie') See **Rasputin and the Empress**

THE RAVAGERS
Eddie Romero — U.S., 1965 [80min]
More gung-ho action with Filipino guerrillas taking on the Japanese in WW2. Throwback to the WW2 film of the early '50s, and not quite as satisfying.
With *John Saxon*

RAVISHED ARMENIA See **Auction of Souls**

REACH FOR THE SKY
Lewis Gilbert — GB, 1956 [135min]
Big box-office hit in the UK: the biopic of Douglas Bader, who flew in the **Battle of Britain** with artificial legs — and then escaped three times from the Germans after being shot down.

More is annoyingly chirpy in the lead role and there is a rather 'superior' air to it today. In hindsight, actually, it is a preening, sentimental and outmoded film — full of stiff upper lips, public school dormitory humour and the supercilious supremacy of the true Brit over the bumbling Hun. It's not very palatable — but its power was right for the time and it

picked up a BAFTA for Best British Film.
With *Kenneth More, Muriel Pavlow*

THE REAL GLORY

Henry Hathaway — U.S., 1939 [95min]

Pacy action lifts this yarn of a Moro uprising in the Philippines in 1905 a few years after the Americans had removed the Spanish flag. Cooper, Niven and a bunch of Filipino irregulars are called into service.
With *Gary Cooper, David Niven, Broderick Crawford*

A REASON TO LIVE, A REASON TO DIE

(aka 'Una Ragione per Vivere e Una per Morire')
Tonino Valerii — France/Italy/Spain, 1972 [95min]

More of the **Dirty Dozen** mixture, even down to the inclusion of Savalas; this time it's a malevolent seven recruited from Union prison cells to take on a Southern fort in the American War of Secession. Inferior to even the most inferior of the **D-D** sequels.
With *Telly Savalas, James Coburn, Bud Spencer (Carlo Pedersoli)*

THE REBEL SON (aka 'Taras Bulba', 'The Barbarian and the Lady') See **Taras Bulba**

REBELLION IN CUBA

Albert C. Gannaway — U.S., 1961

Interesting exercise in U.S. paranoia over Castro's revolution. Released shortly after the Bay of Pigs disaster in April 1961, it was still considered worthwhile putting out this fictitious account of a (more successful) Cuban-exile invasion. (Co-star LaMotta, the former World Middleweight boxing champion, was himself portrayed on film by Robert de Niro in Martin Scorsese's legendary *Raging Bull* [1980]).
With *Bill Fletcher, Jake LaMotta, Lon Chaney Jr*

THE RED BADGE OF COURAGE

John Huston — U.S., 1951 [70min]

Harold Rosson's camerawork makes this a visually-telling picture, with the graphic battle scenes some of the best ever on film — and certainly on films of the American Civil War. Stephen Crane's powerful anti-war theme (about American waging war on American) has been totally dissipated here due to some Philistine editing at MGM while the director was away on his next project, **The African Queen**. The point is missed, therefore, and the original footage gone for ever.

Murphy — as everyone knows the most decorated American soldier of WW2 — acts out of his skin in the seemingly incongruous role of loud-mouth coward, who eventually comes good. Hard to believe that this potential milestone war movie ended up as a support feature, cut to barely 70 minutes length. Another WW2 vet famous in another context also did surprisingly well in a supporting role — cartoonist Bill Mauldin, creator of the archetypal GIs 'Willie and Joe'.
With *Audie Murphy, Bill Mauldin, Douglas Dick*

RED BALL EXPRESS

Budd Boetticher — U.S., 1952 [85min]

The title refers to the harum-scarum competition of truck drivers trying to be first to keep **Patton**'s tanks and troops supplied from the Normandy beachheads in 1944. Routine actioner, otherwise.
With *Jeff Chandler, Alex Nichol, Hugh O'Brian, Sidney Poitier, Jack Kelly*

THE RED BARON See **Von Richthofen and Brown**

THE RED BERET (aka 'Paratrooper')

Terence Young — GB, 1953 [90min]

Predictable WW2 drama with an American joining the British paras before the U.S. came into the war, redeemed by some half-decent action. Instructed a generation of enthralled small boys in a grislier meaning of the term 'Roman candle'.
With *Alan Ladd, Leo Genn, Harry Andrews, Donald Houston, Stanley Baker*

RED DAWN

John Milius — U.S., 1984 [115min]

Right-wing writer/director Milius (*Magnum Force*, **Apocalypse Now** — writing: *Conan the Barbarian*, **Farewell to the King** — writing/direction) wrote this nonsense with Kevin Reynolds (director, **The Beast**, **Robin Hood: Prince of Thieves**). Tactically unsound, the concept of a Soviet airborne division landing in the American interior is nothing more than Reagan-esque paranoia, and an excuse to show off modern warfare set pieces (quite well done), and how the flag can still be waved.
With *Patrick Swayze, C. Thomas Howell, Ron O'Neal, Charlie Sheen, Ben Johnson, Harry Dean Stanton, Vladek Sheybal, Jennifer Grey, Lea Thompson*

RED MOUNTAIN See **Quantrill's Raiders**

RED DAWN
McDonald's opening on the Afghan border is the more-likely

THE RED POSTER (aka 'L'Affiche Rouge')

Franck Cassenti — France, 1976 [90min]

The story of a group of Resistance fighters in occupied Paris in WW2. The title comes from the red poster bearing their names and displayed by the Germans around the city.
With *Roger Ibanez, Pierre Clémenti, Maia Wodeska, Laszlo Szabo*

RED SORGHUM (aka 'Hong Gaoliang')

Zhang Yimou — China, 1987 [90min]

Vast, sprawling family saga, full of bucolic bonhommie and wistful charm; the narrator tells of the turbulent lives of his grandparents through the Sino-Japanese War. Cinematographer

Zhang Yimou (*Yellow Earth*) takes the helm for the first time, and impressed so much that his picture won the Golden Bear at Berlin — no doubt aided by the excellent acting.
With *Gong Li, Jiang Weng*

RED TOMAHAWK
See **They Died with Their Boots On**

THE RED, WHITE AND BLACK
John Cardos — U.S., 1970
One of the few films about 'buffalo soldiers' — the men of the all-black 9th and 10th U.S. Cavalry who served in Indian country in the late 19th century. Not bad.

Johnson, the 1960 Olympic Decathlon champion, led the way for several black sportsmen to enter films, the most prominent of which were Jim Brown (**The Dirty Dozen**), Carl Weathers (the *Rocky* pictures, **Force Ten from Navarone**) and O.J. Simpson (*Naked Gun*, etc).
With *Robert DoQui, Janee Michelle, Rafer Johnson*

REDL EZREDES See **Colonel Redl**

REDS
Warren Beatty — U.S., 1981 [195min]
In a seemingly unusual project for producer, co-writer, as well as director and star, Beatty, this almost David Lean-type historical epic is also expert filmmaking in the more detailed cameos to be found within the dramatic sweep.

Focusing on the love affair of dissident American journalists, John Reed and Louise Bryant, and weaving in subtle sub-plots of American left-wing characters and activities, he also tells the story of the October Revolution (the title of Reed's *Ten Days That Shook the World* was given to the shortened version of Eisentstein's **October**).

Immensely detailed, too long for some, Beatty's *magnum opus* is an intelligent and moving film. Nominated 12 times, it collected only three Academy Awards — director, cinematographer (Vittorio Storaro) and Best Supporting Actress (Stapleton). Some of the unsuccessful nominees were: the picture; Beatty as actor and jointly with Trevor Griffiths, the script; Keaton (Best Actress); and Nicholson (Supporting Actor).
With *Warren Beatty, Diane Keaton, Edward Herrman, Jack Nicholson, Paul Sorvino, Maureen Stapleton*

Reed's early life, getting involved with revolution in Mexico from 1913, can be seen in Paul Leduc's excellent Mexican picture, **Reed: México Insurgente ★★★★** (1972, 105min), with Claudio Obregon.

REED: MEXICO INSURGENTE See **Reds**

REGENERATION
Gillies Mackinnon — Canada/GB, 1997 [110min]
Moving anti-war plea involving the recuperation of war poets Sigfried Sassoon and Wilfred Owen in a Scottish hospital in 1917. Psychiatrist Pryce sees his own position change through his involvement with these and other WW1 wounded.

An unusual film, based — via Pat Barker's acclaimed novel — on actuality, including the pioneering work of Dr Rivers (Pryce).
With *Jonathan Pryce, James Wilby, Jonny Lee Miller, Stuart Bunce*

LA REGLE DU JEU (aka 'The Rules of the Game')
Jean Renoir — France, 1939 [115min]
Renoir's classic farce/satirical comment on the state of the French landed classes — made as Hitler was taking Czechoslovakia — hit home so hard on the eve of the Western Blitzkrieg that it was banned on release until 1956.

The metaphors of the rabbit-shoot carnage and the constant *La Ronde* of decadent love triangles, the surreal ghost and skeleton sequences — they were all (deliberately?) misunderstood by French cinema-goers in 1939. Within 12 short months, the message may have been appreciated, if hardly acknowledged. Way ahead of its time.
With *Marcel Dalio, Nora Gregor, Jean Renoir*

THE REIGN OF TERROR See **The Black Book**

LA REINE MARGOT (1954)
See **La Reine Margot** (1994)

LA REINE MARGOT
Patrice Chéreau — France/Germany/Italy, 1994 [160min]
Chéreau's bloody, but intelligent and sumptuous, look at French politics in 1572 picked up an Oscar nomination for its costumes. Margot (Marguerite de Valois), sister of French King Charles IX, marries Protestant Henri de Navarre, in a typically manipulative de Medici arrangement (Margot's mother was the spider-like Catherine de Medici). It doesn't work, however, as Charles becomes more and more influenced by the Protestant court, so Catherine instigates the massacre of perhaps up to 50,000 Huguenots on St Bartholomew's Day.
With *Isabelle Adjani, Daniel Auteuil, Virna Lisi*

An earlier version by Jean Dréville in 1954 [120min], starred Françoise Rosay, and gave a first screen performance to Jeanne Moreau, as Margot.

REMEMBER PEARL HARBOR
Joseph Santley — U.S., 1942
Flagwaver smartly out of the blocks, which takes place in the Philippines at the time of, and after, the Pearl Harbor strike. Some retaliatory Jap-thumping which, in hindsight, was several months premature. Nothing more to report.
With *Donald Barry, Alan Curtis, Sig Rumann*

RENEGADES See **Beau Geste** (1939)

REQUIEM FUR DOMINIC
Robert Dorhelm — Austria, 1990 [90min]
Brilliantly suspenseful account of an incident in the aftermath of the Romanian revolution of 1989, told in a docu-drama style. Blends actual events into a political thriller in Pontecorvo (**The Battle of Algiers**) or Costa-Gavras (*Z*) style. The Transylvanian town of Timisoara is the setting where a local man is accused of ordering the death of 80 factory workers. Revolutionary revenge takes over, and the corollary is further bloodshed.
With *Felix Mitterer, Viktoria Schubert*

RESURRECTED
Paul Greengrass — GB, 1989 [90min]
Thewlis is excellent as the Falklands soldier who, believed dead and accorded full military honours, turns up alive, only to be tried by a kangaroo court of his peers. Based on a true

story, this bold polemic attacks the effects of war, but equally considers the effects of a man's actions on his comrades in battle. With *David Thewlis, Tom Bell, Rita Tushingham*

RESURRECTION MAN
Marc Evans — GB, 1997 [100min]

Sharp murder/political thriller about a gang of ruthless Loyalist terrorists set in 1970s Belfast. Following a fictitious story about the real-life so-called 'Shankhill Butchers', an investigative journalist ventures into Ulster's mean streets in search of the truth behind the gang. Taken as a thriller, the complex plot keeps the audience on its toes, but falls down on any political point-making. With *James Nesbitt, Stuart Townsend, John Hannah, Brenda Fricker*

LA RETOUR DE MARTIN GUERRE
(aka 'The Return of Martin Guerre')
Daniel Vigne — France, 1982 [125min]
Although oft-told in France this tale only arrived on the big screen in 1982. Martin is a universal soldier of 16th century Europe, who arrives in a French village claiming to be the husband who left for war eight years ago. Of course the conundrum is whether he's telling the truth or whether he's an impostor. Unfortunately, Vigne's direction is so pedestrian, no-one is bothered after a while.
With *Gérard Depardieu, Nathalie Baye*

Updated as **Sommersby ★★** by Jon Amiel in 1993 [115min], into an American Civil War context, with Richard Gere and Jodie Foster. Contains much the same faults.

RETREAT, HELL!
Joseph H. Lewis — U.S., 1952 [95min]
The boast was a little premature after the landing at Inchon in the Korean War. Within weeks of progressing to Pyongyang and the Yalu River, the UN forces were forced back down the length of South Korea by a massive force of Chinese. The film pays little more than lip service to the context of the U.S. Marines' retreat from Chosin.
With *Frank Lovejoy, Richard Carlson, Rusty (Russ) Tamblyn*

RETURN FROM THE RIVER KWAI
Andrew V McLaglen — GB, 1988 [100min]
Sacrilegiously stealing the name from one of the great war movies, McLaglen (who initially traded off his father's name, and the style of his Dad's favourite director, John Ford) has not made the obliquest reference to Lean's POW classic. Standard WW2 adventure is all we get, with the Japanese attempting to take POWs back to Japan. Why does an actor of Fox's quality demean himself so?
With *Edward Fox, Denholm Elliott, George Takei*

RETURN FROM THE RIVER KWAI
Prison camp lip-service paid to the great original.
Braveworld/Rank

THE RETURN OF MARTIN GUERRE
See **La Retour de Martin Guerre**

RETURN OF THE SCARLET PIMPERNEL
See **The Scarlet Pimpernel**

REUNION IN FRANCE (aka 'Mademoiselle France')
Jules Dassin — U.S., 1942 [105min]
Soppy melodrama about a Parisienne dress-designer helping Allied airmen escape back to Britain during WW2.
With *Joan Crawford, John Wayne, Philip Dorn*

REVOLT AT FORT LARAMIE
Lesley Selander — U.S., 1957 [75min]
Blues' n'Grays combine — not for the first time in Hollywood — to lick the Indians (Sioux, this time, under Red Cloud) in another Selander 'Fort' movie. Red Cloud did, in reality, trouble Fort Laramie and other army outposts in the Montana-South Dakota regions, but the earliest assault was in 1866 — one year after the Civil War cease fire! He also signed the Treaty of Fort Laramie in 1869, for what it was worth.
With *John Dehner, Gregg Palmer*

REVOLUTION
Hugh Hudson — GB/U.S., 1985 [125min]
Director Hudson's fall from favour after *Chariots of Fire* was partly due to mixed reviews on his follow-up, *Greystoke*, and this, his poorly-accepted epic of the American War of Independence. Whereas the director's background in TV commercials positively helped the style of *Chariots*, the scale of this project left him cruelly exposed. He may not have had too much say in the savage cutting that went on, but the obviously

untouched set pieces don't work. The miscast star adds to the disbelief, and after so many attempts to convey a Celtic fringe accent (**The Eagle has Landed**, etc) why continue to use Sutherland? Bad news all round except for John Mollo's costumes. With *Al Pacino, Donald Sutherland, Natassja Kinski, Joan Plowright*

RHODES See **Rhodes of Africa**

RHODES OF AFRICA (aka 'Rhodes')
Berthold Viertel — GB, 1936 [90min]
After seeing this whitewash of ace carpetbagger Rhodes, it's little wonder the Germans came up with **Ohm Kruger**, or why the Boer War was started. The treatment of the Dutch is similar to the poor Bantu, as Huston's glorified Empire-builder devours ever more of the Southern African hinterland. With *Walter Huston, Oscar Homolka, Basil Sydney, Peggy Ashcroft*

RICHARD THE LION-HEARTED See **The Crusades**

RICHARD III
Laurence Olivier — GB, 1955 [160min]
After the critical success of **Henry V** and *Hamlet*, Olivier produced, part-adapted, directed, and starred in probably his most famous Shakespearean portrayal; as the hump-backed last Yorkist King who, having (according to the Bard and the Tudor myth) murdered his way to the throne, dies, horseless, on Bosworth Field in 1485. His defeat by Henry Tudor (Henry VII) brings to an end the Wars of the Roses.

Cinematically rewarding without hitting the heights of a Kurosawa epic, the one disappointing feature is the rather ordinary climactic battle. Olivier was Oscar-nominated for his stylized (almost definitive now?) performance, while he and the picture won BAFTAs.
With *Laurence Olivier, Claire Bloom, Ralph Richardson, Cedric Hardwicke, John Gielgud, Stanley Baker*

Other recent versions include:
Richard III ★★★★ (Richard Loncraine — GB, 1995, 105min) With *Ian McKellen, Annette Bening, Jim Broadbent, Kristin Scott-Thomas, Robert Downey Jr, Maggie Smith, Nigel Hawthorne, Bill Paterson, Michael Elphick, Adrian Dunbar*
Transported to an 'alternative' 1930s Britain — a fantasy of which Oswald Mosley might have approved. McKellen is spellbinding as the 'fascist' ruler, and the grimy backdrop of London's crummiest locations (behind St Pancras Station, Battersea Power Station, etc) make for a visually-disquieting atmosphere. Compelling entertainment. With a shoestring budget, the vaguely 1930s/40s impression achieved with a mishmash of designed and available costumes, weapons and hardware generally works well — viz, Henry Tudor as a Lord Lovat-like commando officer in rollneck sweater and beret.
Looking for Richard ★★★★ (Al Pacino — U.S., 1996, 110min) With *Al Pacino, Kevin Spacey, Winona Ryder, Alec Baldwin, Aidan Quinn, John Gielgud, Vanessa Redgrave, Kevin Kline, Kenneth Branagh, James Earl Jones*
An ambitious directorial debut that pays off for Pacino as, just as if the two **RIII** entries above seem prove his point, he goes about exploring (by documentary interviewing, and through rehearsal and performance) how differently the Crookback can be articulated on screen. The final mini-performance and mini-Battle of Bosworth are quite remarkable.

THE RIDERS OF GERMAN EAST AFRICA
Herbert Selpin — Germany, 1934
Colonial rivalry in Africa was the basis of several anti-British films to come out of Germany in the period leading up to and during WW2. Hitler made it no secret that his expansionist policies were only a belated attempt for a great country to exert its influence in far-flung parts, just as the British had been doing for the past 200 years. This was quite a mild piece — withdrawn for being too pacifist (!) — but in 1941 Selpin produced more what the doctor (Göbbels, that is) ordered in **Carl Peters ★★★** also based in East Africa. The Propaganda Reichsminister's brother-in-law, Max Kimmich (**The Fox of Glenarvon**, etc), also produced some pretty salacious stuff from a similar background in **Germanin ★★** (1943).

THE RIFLEMEN See **Les Carabiniers**

RIKUGUN See **Army**

RIO GRANDE
John Ford — U.S., 1950 [105min]
More glorification from Ford of the Cavalry's ongoing war against the Indian. It's 1880 and ex-Civil War vet Wayne is now a colonel trying to quell the Apaches near the Mexican border; but whose private life disintegrated all those yeras ago during the war. The third in the director's loose Cavalry trilogy after **Fort Apache** and **She Wore a Yellow Ribbon** is more introspective than the others — even mawkish in parts. Still plenty of Fordisms for the fans, though.
With *John Wayne, Maureen O'Hara, Ben Johnson, Harry Carey Jr, Victor McLaglen*

THE RISE OF CATHERINE THE GREAT
See **Catherine the Great**

THE ROAD BACK
James Whale — U.S., 1937 [105min]
Erich Marie Remarque's sequel to **All Quiet on the Western Front** tells of life after the Great War in Germany — but starts with the final fighting before the Armistice.

Like the written version, the film suffers in comparison with the original; and although continuity is attempted (Summerville reprises the Tjaden character, for example), Whale, whose Hollywood career began with the anti-war classic **Journey's End**, cannot match Milestone's powerful touch. A plea for peace, nevertheless, which eventually went unheeded. With *John King, Richard Cromwell, Slim Summerville, Andy Devine*

THE ROAD TO ETERNITY
(aka 'Ningen no Joken: Part 2') See **The Human Condition**

THE ROAD TO GLORY
Howard Hawks — U.S., 1936 [105min]
Realistic and harrowing scenes of WW1 trench warfare marked this story of French soldiers as one of the most telling anti-war movies of the 1930s. Based on Raymond Bernard's 1932 French film **Les Croix de Bois ★★★** (Wooden Crosses) with Pierre Blanchar [110min], the scene where the Germans try to undermine the French trenches was also used in **The Doomed Battalion**, released in the same year, with less fortunate results for the Italian soldiers in that case. With *Frederic March, Lionel Barrymore*

ROAR OF THE DRAGON See **Shanghai Express**

ROB ROY
★ *Michael Caton-Jones — U.S., 1995* [140min]
★ Lusty chunk of historical hokum, which, to give it credit,
★ fairly captures the life of the downtrodden Scots at the time of
the first Jacobite Rebellion (1715).

Certainly the language is fruity, with Cox and Roth in the
van, and the highland scenery is travelogue-enticing, providing
a superb backdrop for scattered redcoats in the action scenes.
The fact that the oppressors were fellow Scots rather than
English is only lightly suggested. Neeson (accent apart) is
more believable as a non-20th century Scottish hero than Mel
Gibson's **Braveheart** William Wallace, and Lange sensibly,
and sensitively, underplays McGregor's wife. Roth picked up
an Oscar nomination for his caddish English aristocrat: it also
earned him a BAFTA.
With *Liam Neeson, Jessica Lange, John Hurt, Tim Roth, Brian
Cox, Eric Stolz*

Sir Walter Scott's hero had an earlier cinematic outing in the
depressingly ordinary **Rob Roy the Highland Rogue ★**
directed by Harold French in 1953 [80min], with Richard
Todd and Glynis Johns.

ROB ROY THE HIGHLAND ROGUE See **Rob Roy**

ROBIN AND MARION
See **The Adventures of Robin Hood**

ROBIN HOOD (1922)
See **The Adventures of Robin Hood**

ROBIN HOOD (1991)
See **The Adventures of Robin Hood**

ROBIN HOOD: PRINCE OF THIEVES
See **The Adventures of Robin Hood**

ROBINSON CRUSOE IN GEORGIA
See **My English Grandfather**

ROBINSONADA ANU CHEMI INGLISELI PAPA
See **My English Grandfather**

ROCKY MOUNTAIN
★ *William Keighley — U.S., 1950* [85min]
★ Fair Western with heroic Flynn as near to his best as the budget would allow. He leads his Confederate troops against a
horde of Indians to allow a Union lady to escape, but with
tragic consequences.
With *Errol Flynn, Patrice Wymore, Slim Pickens*

ROGUE'S MARCH
★ *Allan Davis — U.S., 1953* [85min]
Russian spies threaten Britain's Raj in 19th century India.
Poor replication of much that had gone before.
With *Peter Lawford, Richard Greene, Janice Rule, Leo G. Carroll*

ROGUES OF SHERWOOD FOREST
See **The Adventures of Robin Hood**

ROGUES' REGIMENT See **Beau Geste** (1939)

ROLAND AND THE PALADINS OF FRANCE
(aka 'Orlando e I paladini di Francia')
See **La Chanson de Roland**

ROMA, CITTA APERTA See **Open City**

ROMANCE OF A HORSE THIEF See **Jack London**

ROME, OPEN CITY See **Open City**

ROMMEL, DESERT FOX See **The Desert Fox**

ROSES NOIRES See **Black Roses**

ROSES OF PICARDY
Maurice Elvey — GB, 1927
Elvey's impressive films of WW1 trench warfare continued
with this, after **Mademoiselle from Armentières** the
previous year. He was easily the best of a pretty ordinary
bunch of British directors making films about the Great War.
With *John Stuart*

ROSIE THE RIVETER See **Millions Like Us**

THE ROUGH RIDERS
Victor Fleming — U.S., 1927
An account of the U.S. charge up San Juan Hill, Santiago,
Cuba, in the Spanish-American War in June 1898; led by
soon-to-be-president Theodore Roosevelt and his 1st U.S.
Volunteer Cavalry. Good close combat sequences.
With *Charles Emmett Mack, Mary Astor*

ROYAL AFRICAN RIFLES (aka 'Storm Over Africa')
Lesley Selander — U.S., 1954 [75min]
Comic strip heroics in British East Africa on the verge of
WW1. Some Germans are attempting to get the natives
restless, while our hero looks for a stolen consignment of guns.
No better, no worse, than Selander's usual pulped output.
With *Louis Hayward, Veronica Hurst*

THE ROYAL HUNT OF THE SUN
Irving Lerner — GB, 1969 [120min]
A too-literal adaptation of Peter Shaffer's play about Pizarro v
Atahualpa, the god-king of the Incas; which means there's
much deception and little soldiering for the Conquistadores.
With *Robert Shaw, Christopher Plummer, Nigel Davenport*

THE RULES OF THE GAME
See **Le Règle du Jeu**

RUN OF THE ARROW
Samuel Fuller — U.S., 1957 [85min]
On the surface a bloody Western: underneath a welter of social
comment. Fuller's tale of a defeated Johnny Reb going
through hell in a series of initiation tests to join the Sioux (so
as to get back at the hated Yankees in battle), is really
questioning where '50s America is going.

Post-Korea Cold War neuroses among Americans: the crisis
of identity, patriotism, guilt, prejudice — they're all here, if
you want to look that deeply. However, it still works very well
simply as a tough Western.
With *Rod Steiger, Brian Keith, Srita Montiel, Ralph Meeker,
Charles Bronson*

RUN SILENT, RUN DEEP

Robert Wise — U.S., 1958 [95min]

Questions of revenge and cowardice are raised against Gable's character, a martinet skipper of a U.S. submarine, hunting one Japanese destroyer in particular, during WW2. Pity the script and plot are not strong enough for the above-average cast.

With *Clark Gable, Burt Lancaster, Jack Warden, Brad Dexter, Don Rickles*

The idea was closely followed in 1959 by Spencer G. Bennet in his ultra low-budget **Submarine Seahawk**, with John Bentley and Brett Halsey.

RUNNING OUT OF TIME (aka 'Dias Contados')

Imanol Uribe — Spain, 1994 [95min]

Disappointing as an opportunity to consider the world of ETA, the Basque separatists, this is a political thriller which loses its way. The age-old love story dominates, and the political situation is exploited as backdrop.

With *Carmelo Gomez, Ruth Gabriel*

RYAN'S DAUGHTER

David Lean — GB, 1970 [205min]

Unlike the pure sweep of **Lawrence of Arabia**, Lean seems to get bogged down with the minutiae of love and dishonour in 1916 Ireland. Robert Bolt again provides the script, but this time it's not as effective, as the director's sense of scale (and time, at almost four hours) swamps it as comprehensively as the waves do the wrecked gunrunner in the film's best scene. It's the love affair between local colleen Miles (ostracized by the village for her adultery) and shell-shocked British Army officer Jones that takes centre stage; when the huge budget, having created the scenario, might have been used to say so much more about German-IRA liaisons during the latter part of WW1.

Long-overdue Academy recognition for Mills (Best Supporting Actor), while Miles was nominated for Best Actress. An Oscar also went to Freddie Francis' cinematography for the third time on a Lean film, after **Lawrence** and **Dr Zhivago.**

With *Sarah Miles, Robert Mitchum, Christopher Jones, John Mills, Trevor Howard, Leo McKern*

SABOTEUR

Alfred Hitchcock — U.S., 1942 [110min]

The one with the climax atop the Statue of Liberty, this was one of Hitch's pause-for-breath pictures, after hitting Hollywood with *Rebecca* and **Foreign Correspondent** within three years; and before hitting even harder with **Lifeboat,** *Spellbound* and **Notorious** over the next three.

In many ways similar to **The Thirty-Nine Steps** and his earlier British pictures, the frenetic chase motif was perfected by the time the master reached *North by Northwest*, but it's still mighty exciting here. Cummings, as the munitions worker suspected of sabotage, fleeing the FBI and at the same time trying to find the Nazis who set him up, is somewhat disappointing for a Hitchcock lead (Gary Cooper was first choice).

With *Robert Cummings, Priscilla Lane, Otto Kruger, Norman Lloyd*

THE SABOTEUR (1965)
See **The Saboteur, Code Name Morituri**

THE SABOTEUR, CODE NAME MORITURI
(aka 'Morituri', 'The Saboteur')

Bernhard Wicki — U.S., 1965 [120min]

Fairly dull tale of a German spy aboard ship in WW2 gives a quality cast little to do. Nominated for Conrad Hall's camerawork.

With *Marlon Brando, Yul Brynner, Trevor Howard, Janet Margolin*

THE SABRE AND THE ARROW
See **The Last of the Comanches**

SAHARA
Afrika Korps digging in in the desert after Tobruk. Columbia

SABRE JET
Louis King — U.S., 1953 [95min]
Early Korean War flagwaver, featuring U.S. jet fighters in combat for the first time, dragged down by a soapy romance.
With *Robert Stack, Coleen Gray, Richard Arlen*

UN SAC DE BILLES See A Bag of Marbles

SAFARI
Terence Young — GB, 1956 [90min]
African actioner cashing in on the Mau Mau rebellion in Kenya. For a better appraisal of what the troubles are all about, see **The Kitchen Toto**.
With *Victor Mature, Janet Leigh, Roland Culver*

THE SAFECRACKER
Ray Milland — GB, 1958 [95min]
Reasonable premise of using a criminal to do some commando dirty work behind enemy lines in WW2, which was exploited fully by Robert Aldrich some years later in **The Dirty Dozen**. Quite suspenseful once it gets going.
With *Ray Milland, Barry Jones, Victor Maddern*

SAHARA
Zoltan Korda — U.S., 1943 [95min]
Straightforward action adventure in the Libyan Desert in WW2. Literally picking up the pieces after the defeat at Tobruk, Yank in the British Army tank corps (complete with tank), Bogart, collects a bunch of international flotsam — Brits, a South African, a Frenchman, etc — along the way, and therein lies the message of Allied brotherhood. As a confused Italian and a captured German pilot are also among them, we see the war in microcosm. The value of the '**Alamo**' spirit is evoked as well, as Bogie exhorts his comrades to stand and fight the force of 500 Germans approaching their waterhole.

Yes, the plot is ludicrous and the symbolism sledgehammer-subtle, but some of the action is top-notch and the characterization is actually very interesting.
With *Humphrey Bogart, Bruce Bennett, Lloyd Bridges, Rex Ingram, J. Carroll Naish, Dan Duryea*

Duff TV-film remake, by Brian Trenchard-Smith in 1995, with James Belushi in the Bogart role, and with sunlight so bright you need to turn the contrast buttons right down. If you could only say that about the movie.

SAIGON See Off Limits

SAILOR OF THE KING See Singlehanded

SAINT JOAN See Joan of Arc

ST QUENTIN See *The Battle of Arras*

SALADIN (aka 'An-Nasr Salah ad-Din') See The Crusades

SALUTE JOHN CITIZEN
Maurice Elvey — GB, 1942 [100min]
A piece of home-spun British propaganda telling Hitler that he can throw anything at London, but the Cockneys' spirit will remain indomitable.
With *Edward Rigby, Stanley Holloway, George Robey, Jimmy Hanley*

SALUTE TO THE MARINES
S. Sylvan Simon — U.S., 1943 [100min]
The Japanese invade the Philippines and 30-year vet Beery, now retired, springs back into action one more time. Energetic recruiter.
With *Wallace Beery, Fay Bainter*

SALVADOR
Oliver Stone — U.S., 1986 [125min]
Back-to-back with **Platoon**, Stone turns his attention to a more recent and more geographically-relevant civil war; that of El Salvador. Set in 1980 and co-written with real-life photo-journalist Richard Boyle (played by the Oscar-nominated Woods), Stone comes up with an action-packed, if politically-shallow polemic of U.S. interference in 'back-yard' politics; and the tragedy and senselessness of civil war is expertly captured. Boyle opens the door on the covert U.S. support for the right-wing junta with its notorious death squads, while at the same time finding his journalistic zeal once more.
With *James Woods, James Belushi, Michael Murphy, John Savage*

SALVADOR
John Savage (left) and James Woods, come under fire as journalists in San Salvador. Hemdale

EL SALVADOR: ANOTHER VIETNAM
Glenn Sliber/Tete Vascocellos — U.S., 1981
Salutary documentary with footage obtained from several countries and international news agencies, warning of the U.S.'s involvement in the politico-military situation within 'its own back yard'.

SA-MANN BRANDT See Hans Westmar

SAN DEMETRIO LONDON
Charles Frend — GB, 1943 [105min]
Low-key British propaganda vehicle celebrating the valiant running of the Atlantic U-boat gauntlet by an oil tanker. Now seems very outmoded, but very effective in its time.
With *Walter Fitzgerald, Mervyn Johns, Robert Beatty, Gordon Jackson*

THE SAND PEBBLES
Robert Wise — U.S., 1966 [195min]

Intelligent, if slow-moving insight into the plight of the small units of Western forces posted to protect our interests and enclaves in the civil war-torn China of 1926. The U.S. gun-boat, the *San Pablo*, is sniffing around in the Yangtse when it gets more than it bargains for. A nudge to the knowing on the follies of involvement with Asian countries, the film is also blessed with some realistic skirmishes.

McQueen (for the first and only time) and Mako get nominated for Oscars in the acting categories, whilst Joseph McDonald's evocative photography and Jerry Goldsmith's score — along with the picture itself — were also nominated. With *Steve McQueen, Richard Attenborough, Mako, Candice Bergen, Richard Crenna*

SANDS OF IWO JIMA
Allan Dwan — U.S., 1949 [110min]

Before his Oscar-winning role as Rooster Cogburn in *True Grit*, Wayne was only previously recognized by the Academy once — here playing a character simply made for him. As the martinet who trains his rookie Marines to beat the Japs in one of the last-gasp battles of the Pacific campaign, the portrayal seems the definitive Wayne, almost to the point of caricature, so intimately had it developed over nearly a decade of Hollywood flagwavers. Here he is, rough-tongued, heroic, sometimes compassionate, and always patently patriotic — an amalgam of everything you expect the Duke to be.

Dwan's handling of the action is a welcome return to form after some turkeys, and to cap it there is a totally over-the-top Mt Suribachi scene, where three of the leathernecks who hoisted the actual U.S. flag in 1945 were brought back to recreate the shot (see **The Outsider**). Harry Brown's original story was also nominated, as was the editing. In the '90s this film was still shown to USMC recruits to inculcate *esprit de corps*. With *John Wayne, John Agar, Adele Mara, Forrest Tucker, Richard Jaeckel*

SAVING PRIVATE RYAN
The hell that was Omaha Beach. DreamWorks LLC (courtesy KOBAL)

SANTA FE TRAIL
Michael Curtiz — U.S., 1940 [110min]

Exciting American Civil War *hors d'œuvres* hokum, concerning the exploits of abolitionist John Brown and his attempts to free Southern slaves by force during the late 1850s. A roll-call of Western and Civil War personnel ride through the film — including **Kit Carson**, and Robert E. Lee, who historically captured Brown after the latter had raided the U.S. Armory at Harper's Ferry in 1859. In this version, however, he is caught by future Rebel colonel Jeb Stuart (Flynn) and ably assisted by a certain George Armstrong Custer (Reagan!). The picture claims Custer had graduated from West Point in 1854 — which would have made him all of 15 years of age — but according to history didn't see action until Bull Run, after fast-track graduating in 1861 (See **They Died with Their Boots On**). With *Errol Flynn, Raymond Massey, Olivia de Havilland, Ronald Reagan, Alan Hale*

The John Brown story was repeated in 1955 in Charles Marquis Warren's inferior **Seven Angry Men ★** [90min], with Raymond Massey, Debra Paget and Jeffrey Hunter.

SANTIAGO (aka 'The Gun Runner')
Gordon Douglas — U.S., 1956 [90min]

The British title of this low-budget actioner is particularly confusing as it takes as its subject the running of arms into Cuba; as does **The Gun Runners**, the remake of **To Have and Have Not**. The plots are half a century apart though: Douglas' film deals with the Spanish-American War, while the Audie Murphy vehicle covers the then contemporary (1958) situation in Cuba before the fall of the Batista government. With *Alan Ladd, Rossana Podesta, Lloyd Nolan, Chill Wills*

THE SARACEN BLADE See **The Crusades**

SASKATCHEWAN See **They Died with Their Boots On**

THE SAVAGE
George Marshall — U.S., 1952 [95mins]

Question of loyalty as white boy (Heston in his third film appearance) brought up by the Sioux, chooses to fight on the side of the Cavalry. Good action climax. With *Charlton Heston*

THE SAVAGE WILDERNESS See **The Last Frontier**

SAVING PRIVATE RYAN
Steven Spielberg — U.S., 1998 [170min]

Widely predicted to clean up at the Oscars before the nominations were announced, Spielberg's WW2 epic in the event lost out to *Shakespeare in Love* as best picture, but still managed to collect several statuettes all the same. The director, after 20 years of neglect by his Hollywood peers, picked up his second award of the decade; and further Oscars were won by Janusz Kaminski (cinematography); editing; sound; and sound effects editing — testimony indeed to the power of the big screen to get across its story. Hanks missed a third Best Actor Oscar, and other unlucky nominees were in art direction, makeup and score (John Williams).

The picture has been widely regarded as the most potent action war movie ever made. It certainly leaves you somewhat shaken after the opening D-Day landing sequence, when the amazing camerawork throws the audience into the middle of the blood, bones, bombs and vomit. It also has a truly exciting endpiece in its hour-long conflict at the bridge, and comes as close as any picture ever has in realistically portraying battle scenes.

If, as a piece of cinema, it has to be faulted, it is in its attempts — largely through reused clichés — to portray the futility of war; this is particularly so through the middle section of the film. The tile itself begs the oft-asked question: in war who is chosen to be killed and who to be saved? Ryan (Damon) is the youngest of four Ryan brothers to hit the Normandy beaches: the Brass know that three have already been killed. They need to proect the fourth, if only from a PR point of view — hence Hanks' behind-the-lines mission to save him. See **The Sullivans**.
With *Tom Hanks, Tom Sizemore, Edward Burns, Matt Damon*

SAVIOR
Pedrag Antonijevic — U.S., 1998
Oliver Stone produced Hollywood's first attempt to comment on the wars in former Yugoslavia, and it is is reasonably well done. The story of an American mercenary witnessing atrocities perpetrated by Bosnian Moslems on Serbs (striving to show that such acts are not just down to Serbia), probably benefits from the eye of a non-American director, thus reducing the 'Hollywoodization' factor quite considerably. Quaid is good.
With *Dennis Quaid, Natasa Ninkovic*

SAYONARA
Joshua Logan — U.S., 1957 [145min]
Madama Butterfly updated to the Korean War, when the tricky question of U.S. servicemen with Japanese wives was topical and touchy. Not much action in this much acclaimed (at the time) film. Nominated for ten Oscars, it broadly lost out to **Bridge on the River Kwai**, winning only four (Buttons and Umeki in the supporting acting categories; art direction and sound). Other nominations: the picture; Brando; direction; adapted script, Paul Osborn for photography, Ellsworth Fredericks for editing.
With *Marlon Brando, Ricardo Montalban, Red Buttons, James Garner, Myoshi Umeki, Miiko Taka, Patricia Owens, Martha Scott*

SCARAMOUCHE (1923) See **The Scarlet Pimpernel**

SCARAMOUCHE (1952) See **The Scarlet Pimpernel**

THE SCARLET BLADE
(aka 'The Crimson Blade') *John Gilling — GB, 1963* [80min]
Apart from their jolly hammy horrors, Hammer Studios of this vintage turned out a few historical romps too. This rare swashbuckler of the English Civil War pits Roundhead Colonel Jeffries against Royalist Hedley, with Reed playing the joker in an over-used pack. The usual angle of love between members of the opposite camps is thankfully broken by bouts of swordplay and a nasty bit of torture (it is Hammer, after all). Could have been much better, though.
With *Lionel Jeffries, Oliver Reed, Jack Hedley, June Thorburn*

THE SCARLET COAT
John Sturges — U.S., 1955 [100min]
Set in the American War of Independence, this is the story of a Colonial double agent unearthing the duplicity of the notorious Benedict Arnold, who spied for the British. Unusually for this director, action is in short supply, giving way to some wordy intrigue and romance.
With *Cornel Wilde, Michael Wilding, George Sanders, Anne Francis*

SCARLET DAWN
William Dieterlie — U.S., 1932 [75min]
Heavy period romance that pays just lip service to the Russian Revolution. Elegantly staged, but little action.
With *Douglas Fairbanks Jr, Nancy Carroll*

THE SCARLET EMPRESS
Josef von Sternberg — U.S., 1934 [110min]
Paul Czinner's British film, **Catherine the Great ★★** [95min], starring Eisabeth Bergner, Douglas Fairbanks Jr and Flora Robson, was roundly beaten in both box-office and critical stakes when von Sternberg's extraordinary piece of indulgent cinema was released almost simultaneously.

The advantage of Dietrich is a massive one, but the almost ethereal sets and lavish production, plus the score and costumes, set this film apart. The Russian Empress who, after half a century of weak rule, picked up the pieces of **Peter the Great**'s lead, and set about the further westernizing of Russia. Both the 1934 pictures dwell on the ambitious Catherine's usurpation of mad husband Peter III in 1762; but unfortunately don't take it on into the historically-interesting Russo-Turkish Wars of the late 18th century.
With *Marlene Dietrich, Sam Jaffe, John Lodge, Louise Dresser*

THE SCARLET PIMPERNEL
Harold Young — GB, 1934 [100min]
Producer Alexander Korda, who had impressed Hollywood with *The Private Life of Henry VIII*, directed some scenes in this hugely-popular swashbuckler set during the French Revolution. Howard is splendid as the terribly English and oh-so dandy aristocrat who rescues his French counterparts from the guillotine in the nick of time. Much copied in its zest and humour, Howard brought the character up to date several years later in **Pimpernel Smith**.
With *Leslie Howard, Merle Oberon, Raymond Massey, Nigel Bruce*

Other swashbuckling adventures stories taking place in, or inspired by, the French Revolution and the associated wars include:
Scaramouche ★★ (Rex Ingram — U.S., 1923) With *Ramon Novarro*
The Return of the Scarlet Pimpernel (Hans Schwarz — GB, 1937, **1995**min) With *Barry K Barnes*
The Elusive Pimpernel ★★★ (Michael Powell/Emeric Pressburger — GB, 1950) With *David Niven, Margaret Leighton*
Scaramouche ★★★ (George Sidney — U.S., 1952, 115min) With *Stewart Granger*
Sea Devils ★★ (Raoul Walsh — GB, 1953, 190min) With *Rock Hudson, Yvonne de Carlo*
The Purple Mask ★ (Bruce Humberstone — U.S., 1955, 1980min) With *Tony Curtis*

THE SCARLET TUNIC
Stuart St Paul — GB, 1997
Forgetable adaptation of a Thomas Hardy short story, this

doomed romance is based in Napoleonic England, where a group of continental troops are billeted. As the Treaty of Amiens approaches, the disparate bunch are not interested in any more fighting and threaten to desert. One of the soldiers, a German (Barr) gets involved with the heroine (Fielding) and the the only action occurs in a shoot-out finale.
With *Jean-Marc Barr, Emma Fielding, Simon Callow, Jack Shepherd, John Sessions, Lynda Bellingham, Gareth Hale*

THE SCARLET WEST
See **They Died with Their Boots On**

SCHINDLER'S LIST
Steven Spielberg — U.S., 1993 [195min]
The unthinkable: the director of magically exciting adventure stories, which always seem to be seen through the wide eyes of children, is here the director of this wonderfully exciting adventure story (albeit just one of the many facets of such a beautifully-balanced picture); seen through the equally wide eyes of adults. Shades of Spielberg's monumental achievement were trailed in *The Color Purple* and **Empire of the Sun**, but his use of basically similar techniques to produce what many critics believe is the definitive dramatization of the Holocaust is quite extraordinary — and a lasting tribute to the director's remarkable craft.

Of course this is no Saturday morning serial: the pathos, horror and grainy monochrome see to that. But the Spielberg 'pace' is still there, as is the suspense and the unexpected. What he does, then, is to take his own art to a new plateau. The performances he extracts from the three main stars as gentile Schindler (Neeson); his Jewish conscience Stern (Kingsley); and the Nazi commandant with whom Schindler enters a Devil's pact (Fiennes); are all immense — and a skill perhaps not recognized in this director previously. Thomas Kenneally's novel, brilliantly adapted by Stephen Zaillian, of one man's war to free Polish Jews from the gas chambers, was thought unfilmable — until now. This is Spielberg-plus.

Winner of seven Academy Awards out of 12 nominations: the picture; Spielberg (amazingly his first Oscar); Zaillian; cinematography (Janusz Kaminski); score (John Williams); editing; and art direction. Among those who missed out on the ultimate award were Neeson and Fiennes in the two actor categories.
With *Liam Neeson, Ben Kingsley, Ralph Fiennes*

SCHOOL FOR SECRETS (aka 'Secret Fight')
Peter Ustinov — GB, 1946 [110min]
Light-hearted WW2 comedy-adventure which looks really lame now. Ustinov wrote the uninspired script as well.
With *Ralph Richardson, Raymond Huntley, Richard Attenborough, John Laurie, Marjorie Rhodes, David Tomlinson*

SCHWARTZE ROSEN See **Black Roses**

SCIPIO AFRICANUS
Carmine Gallone — Italy, 1937
Funded by the Mussolini government (it also won the Mussolini Cup at the Venice Film Festival for Best Italian Film!), this epic from Gallone, made to give the fascists some moral justification for their invasion of **Abyssinia**, sets out to remind Italians of their African empire in classical times.

The film traces Scipio's invasion of North Africa and the defeat of Hannibal at Zama in 202BC, which brought an end

SCHINDLER'S LIST
The fear of the 'showers'. Universal/Amblin

to the Second Punic War. Very exciting, and much better than his **Carthage in Flames** over 20 years later.
With *Annibale Ninchi, Isa Miranda*

SCIUSCIA See **Shoeshine**

SCOTLAND YARD
William K. Howard — U.S., 1930
Weak character-change plot after WW1 wounding in Flanders for British villain on the run.
With *Edmund Lowe, Joan Bennett, Donald Crisp*

A film of the same title and a similar theme, updated to the London of the Blitz, was made by Norman Foster in 1941 [70min], with Nancy Kelly, Edmund Gwenn and Henry Wilcoxson.

SCOTLAND YARD (1941) See **Scotland Yard** (1930)

SCREAMING EAGLES
Charles Haas — U.S., 1956 [80min]
D-Day, and U.S. paratroopers hold a strategic bridge. Routine WW2 fare.
With *Tom Tryon*

THE SEA CHASE
John Farrow — U.S., 1955 [115min]
Exactly as it says — all the way from Sydney, Australia to Germany — as Wayne tries to bring home his German merchantman, caught at sea when WW2 breaks out; and avoiding the Royal Navy on the way.

Not too exciting, with Wayne's attempt to play another non-American failing badly (see **The Conqueror**).
With *John Wayne, Lana Turner, David Farrar*

SEA DEVILS See **The Scarlet Pimpernel**

THE SEA HAWK (1924) See **The Sea Hawk** (1940)

THE SEA HAWK
Michael Curtiz — U.S., 1940 [120min]
A 1924 ★★★ Frank Lloyd silent of the same name, starring Wallace Beery, was based on an adventure yarn by Rafael Sabatini (he of **Scaramouche** fame), and set against conflicts between Spain and the Moors.

Here Warners pinched the title and took the Spanish-English tensions immediately prior to the construction of the Armada in the 1580s for this whiz-bang Flynn-Curtiz speciality — with perhaps just one eye on Hitler's adjacency to the English Channel at the time. They have able allies in Sol Polito (camera) and Erich Korngold (Oscar-nominated score), with Anton Grot's sets similarly acknowledged. Historical poppycock, but great fun.
With *Errol Flynn, Brenda Marshall, Claude Rains, Donald Crisp, Alan Hale, Una O'Connor*

SEA OF SAND (aka 'Desert Patrol')
Guy Green — GB, 1958 [100min]
Standard **Desert Rats** action based in the Libyan desert before **El Alamein**. British patrol attempts to blow up one of Rommel's supply dumps.
With *Richard Attenborough, John Gregson, Percy Herbert, Michael Craig, Barry Foster, Andrew Faulds, Dermot Walsh*

THE SEA SHALL NOT HAVE THEM
Lewis Gilbert — GB, 1954 [95min]
Glum tale of British bomber crew, solid chaps all, shot down, sitting it out in a dinghy awaiting rescue. Seen it all before somewhere.
With *Dirk Bogarde, Michael Redgrave, Jack Watling, Anthony Steel, Nigel Patrick*

THE SEA WOLVES
Andrew V. McLaglen — GB/Switzerland/U.S., 1980 [120min]
Fairly preposterous tale, by a director of increasingly preposterous movies. Some aged commandos — sons of the Empire, living in India during WW2 — assault a German communications ship in Goa.

Last lusty flings of manhood for most of the cast before their bus passes were issued — but I think they all enjoyed it. I did.
With *Gregory Peck, David Niven, Trevor Howard, Roger Moore, Patrick Macnee, Donald Houston, Glyn Houston, Bernard Archard, Allan Cuthbertson, Patrick Allen, Percy Herbert, John Standing, Michael Medwin, Barbara Kellerman, Kenneth Griffith*

SEALED CARGO
Alfred Werker — U.S., 1951 [90min]
A neat little suspenser about a fishing vessel off Newfoundland carrying German torpedoes in 1943. Some nice twists and genuinely explosive action involving U-boats.
With *Dana Andrews, Claude Rains, Carla Balenda, Philip Dorn*

THE SEARCHERS
John Ford — U.S., 1956 [120min]
Among almost everyone's Top Ten Westerns: in the history of Hollywood, this is so much more. This is Ford at the cross-roads. Before his informal acknowledgment that his career-long stamp of the red man as the not-so noble savage may have been misguided in **Cheyenne Autumn**, his 'repentance' to the Indian peoples starts here.

In a paradox of a film, the raw racism of Ethan Edwards (Wayne), in wanting to kill his neice who was abducted by the Comanche and is therefore tainted, is eventually tempered; but not before the Texas Rangers (seconded to the U.S. Cavalry) massacre the Indian village. Recounted through Wayne's most complex character, (where was Ethan for three years, between the Civil War ending and his riding to the homestead across Monument Valley, in that most elegaic of opening scenes?) and best-ever screen performance.

Ford tackles the American '50s' twin-paranoia of guilt and racism, whilst retaining the poetry (however hard-edged) of his best excursions into the genre. A Western never really looked better — the stark isolation of the landscape reflecting perfectly on its main character.

This seminal cinema release set standards for the time and for filmmakers to pursue in the future.
With *John Wayne, Jeffrey Hunter, Natalie Wood, Ward Bond, Vera Miles*

THE SEARCHING WIND
William Dieterlie — U.S., 1946 [105min]
Literary (based on Lillian Hellman's stage-play) rendition of the rise of fascism in Europe between the Wars, and of one man's failure to read what was happening. Pretty safe in 1946 — the message should have been screened a decade or so earlier.
With *Robert Young, Sylvia Sidney*

THE SEAS BENEATH
John Ford — U.S., 1931
Not very coherent early Ford vehicle involving U-boat bait in WW1 and the attendant romance and espionage.
With *George O'Brien*

SECONDVOITNANTEN See **The Last Lieutenant**

THE SECRET DOOR See **The Conspirators**

SECRET FIGHT See **School for Secrets**

SECRET GAMES See **(Les) Jeux Interdits**

THE SECRET INVASION
Roger Corman — U.S., 1964 [100min]
Cut-price Corman, except he's anticipating, not exploiting for once, in this sawn-off antecedent of the **Dirty Dozen**. Here five ne'er-do-wells are whipped into shape for a mission behind German lines in WW2 Yugoslavia. As usual with this director, there is a sneaking admiration for his ability to create something out of nothing.
With *Stewart Granger, Raf Vallone, Mickey Rooney, Henry Silva, Ed ('Kookie') Byrnes*

SECRET MISSION
Harold French — GB, 1942 [95min]
Very ordinary WW2 espionage stuff, with four daring Brits secreting themselves into occupied France, looking at Hitler's defensive capabilities.
With *Hugh Williams, James Mason, Roland Culver, Carla Lehmann, Michael Wilding*

THE SECRET OF BLOOD ISLAND
Quentin Lawrence — GB, 1964 [85min]
Some good Hammer styling in this WW2 POW hokum.

Imagine, if you can, a female agent parachuting into a Japanese POW camp in the Malayan jungle — then sneaking out again!
With *Barbara Shelley, Charles Tingwell, Patrick Wymark, Jack Hedley, Lee Montague, Bill Owen*

THE SECRET OF ST IVES
Phil Rosen — U.S., 1949 [75min]
Napoleonic War adventure, based on Robert Louis Stevenson's story of French POWs breaking out of Edinburgh Castle and traipsing down the length of England in search of a passage home. Weak actioner.
With *Richard Ney, Vanessa Brown, Henry Daniell*

THE SECRET OF SANTA VITTORIA
Stanley Kramer — U.S., 1969 [140min]
Silly WW2 story of Germans advancing on an Italian village sitting on a million bottles of wine. Lots of babble, arm-waving and standard Italian peasant stereotyping — but at least the director shows he can lighten up if he wants to. 140 minutes long, though? Music nomination for Ernest Gold.
With *Anthony Quinn, Anna Magnani, Virna Lisi, Hardy Kruger, Sergio Franchi*

SECRET SERVICE (1919) See **Secret Service** (1931)

SECRET SERVICE
J. Walter Ruben — U.S., 1931 [65min]
Espionage in the American Civil War, which leads to the taking of Richmond, Virginia by Grant in April 1865. Based on a renowned play by William Gillette, and first filmed in 1919 ** by Hugh Ford, starring Robert Warwick. Both film versions are somewhat stodgy fare.
With *Richard Dix*

THE SECRET WAR OF HARRY FRIGG
Jack Smight — U.S., 1967 [110min]
Pathetically weak comedy drama about a dopey GI who rescues some top brass from the Germans in WW2. The star surely disownes it.
With *Paul Newman, Sylva Koscina, John Williams, Tom Bosley*

SECRETS OF G32 See **Fly by Night**

SECRETS OF SCOTLAND YARD
George Blair — U.S., 1944 [70min]
More spy-comedy based in Hollywood's fantasy London — this time involving identical twins: one spying for the British, the other for the Nazis. Some imagination.
With *C. Aubrey Smith, Lionel Atwill*

SECRETS OF THE UNDERGROUND
William Morgan — U.S., 1943 [70min]
During WW2, a cool fashion-shop owner spies for the Germans. 'B' movie of surprisingly good quality.
With *John Hubbard, Virginia Grey, Miles Mander*

SECTION SPECIALE
Costa-Gavras — France/Germany/Italy, 1975 [115min]
Hard-hitting, but ultimately disappointing, political piece from Costa-Gavras; yet this story of corruption and collaboration in the French Vichy government in WW2 is topical, hard on the heels of the 'realization' pictures starting to sprout in France during the '70s. The latter half of the film is devoted to show-trials of innocent scapegoats, put on as 'entertainment' for the German authorities.
With *Louis Seigner, Mich(a)el Lonsdale, Jacques Perrin*

SEMINOLE
Bud Boetticher — U.S., 1953 [85min]
The Army attempt to take on the Seminole Indians in their inhospitable habitat of the Florida Everglades — with inevitable results. Chief Osceola (Quinn) rebelled against the Treaty of Paynes Landing in 1832; and the so-called Second Seminole War began in 1835, when this film was set. Boetticher's movie, however, is well up to his unambitious, but usually enjoyable, Western scratch, and has an interesting cast.
With *Rock Hudson, Barbara Hale, Richard Carlson, Anthony Quinn, Hugh O'Brian, Lee Marvin*

An inferior and less historically accurate picture about the Third Seminole War (1855-58), **Seminole Uprising ★** starring George Montgomery and directed by Earl Bellamy, came along in 1955 [75min]. The Seminoles have received poor coverage from Hollywood — George Sherman's **War Arrow ★★** in 1953 [80min], with Jeff Chandler; and Walsh's **Distant Drums** are just about the only other references to the Florida tribe.

SEMINOLE UPRISING See **Seminole**

SENSO (aka 'The Wanton Countess')
Luchino Visconti — Italy, 1953
Stylistically a forerunner to **The Leopard**, but historically set a few years later at the time of the Seven Weeks War; this sumptuous romantic drama of the *Risorgimento*, involving a Venetian countess and an officer of the Austrian occupying force, is early but defining Visconti. Action takes a back seat to the visual decadence of the director's lens.
With *Alida Valli, Farley Granger, Christian Marquand*

SERGEANT RYKER
Buzz Kulik — U.S., 1968 [85min]
Originally a TV film, *The Case Against Sergeant Ryker*, this version obtained theatre release. Concerns the court martial of alleged Korean War deserter. Stark, but standout performances from Marvin and his defence advocate, Dillman.
With *Lee Marvin, Vera Miles, Bradford Dillman, Peter Graves, Lloyd Nolan*

SERGEANT STEINER
(aka 'Breakthrough') See **Cross of Iron**

SERGEANT YORK
Howard Hawks — U.S., 1941 [135min]
Biopic of famous WW1 Doughboy hero who struggled with his religious feelings before capturing 132 Germans single-handedly during the Meuse-Argonne offensive late in 1918.
An important picture of its time, it was mighty propaganda for those Americans with pacifist leanings; although the timing of the film's release was more to do with the real-life Alvin York witholding permission for the picture to be made, until his choice of actor — Cooper — agreed to play him. Coop is terrific as the simple backswoodsman armed with homespun philosophy and buckets of integrity. He won the Best Actor Oscar, and editing also gained a statuette. Ten other nominees

were unsuccessful, and they included the picture; director; Brennan and Wycherly (supporting actor/actress); the screenplay by John Huston, Howard Koch and others; Sol Polito (camera); and Max Steiner's music.
With *Gary Cooper, Walter Brennan, Joan Leslie, George Tobias, Margaret Wycherly, Ward Bond, June Lockhart, Noah Beery Jr*

SERGEANTS THREE See **Gunga Din**

LE SERGENT X See **Beau Geste** (1939)

SERPENT OF THE NILE See **Cleopatra** (1963)

SEVEN ANGRY MEN See **The Santa Fe Trail**

SEVEN BEAUTIES
★ *Lina Wertmuller — Italy, 1975* [115min]
★ Striking but totally unpalatable satire-turned-farce, set in Italy
★ during WW2; where a disreputable *Candide*-type prostitutes himself to the Nazis, and anyone else it seems, in order that he and his coven of seven grotesque (in the Fellini/Pasolini sense) sisters survive. Were the Italians really like that during the war?

Ms Wertmuller was flavour of the month in Hollywood at this time, and was nominated for direction and script by the Academy, as was Giannini in the senior acting capacity, and the picture for Best Foreign Language Film.
With *Giancarlo Giannini, Fernando Rey, Shirley Stoler*

SEVEN MINUTES (aka 'Georg Elsor')
★ *Klaus Maria Brandauer — Germany/U.S., 1989* [90min]
★ Brandauer (**Mephisto**) turns his hands to directing as well as
★ taking the role of Georg Elsor, who wants to blow up Hitler when he visits a Munich beer-hall for a rally. Based on fact, it's a taut thriller with some periods of boredom, but Brandauer is as interesting as usual, ably supported by the reliable Dennehy.
With *Klaus-Maria Brandauer, Rebecca Miller, Brian Dennehy, Nigel Le Vaillant*

SEVEN SEAS TO CALAIS
★ *Rudolph Maté — Italy/U.S., 1962* [105min]
★ Robust swashbuckler telling the (somewhat fanciful) story of
★ Sir Francis Drake — bane of the Spanish treasure ships, and mastermind of the Armada's defeat. Full of the right clichés, it has a couple of Earls Court Aussies in the lead, but is thankfully more adept in the plentiful action sequences.
With *Rod Taylor, Keith Michell, Irene Worth*

SEVEN WOMEN
★ *John Ford — U.S., 1965* [100min]
★ '30s-style drama set in the Chinese Civil War, about a band of women captured by Mongolian bandits at their mission. Not a Ford classic, despite some good performances.
With *Anne Bancroft, Flora Robson, Sue Lyon, Margaret Leighton, Eddie Albert, Mildred Dunnock, Anna Lee, Woody Strode*

SEVENTH CAVALRY
See **They Died with Their Boots On**

THE SEVENTH CROSS
★ *Fred Zinnemann — U.S., 1944* [110min]
★ Heavy anti-Nazi propaganda as Hollywood recognized that
★ not all Germans were fascists. Set before WW2, Tracy leads seven anti-Nazi concentration camp prisoners to freedom. All

are caught and crucified, except for Tracy — for whom the seventh cross awaits. The anti-Christian values of the Nazis are also a target here; but the picture should not be overlooked as a tense thriller — its director would go on to become a master of time-ticking suspense (*High Noon, The Day of the Jackal*, etc). Cronyn was nominated for supporting actor (in one of several films with his wife Tandy, whom he married in 1942; after she and Jack Hawkins were divorced).
With *Spencer Tracy, Signe Hasso, Hume Cronyn, Jessica Tandy, Agnes Moorehead, George Macready*

SEVENTH HEAVEN
Frank Borzage — U.S., 1927 [95min]   ★
Famous romance with the backdrop of French mobilization   ★
and deployment on the Marne in 1914 (remade by Henry   ★
King, with James Stewart and Simone Simon ten years later in sound ★★★ [100min]).

Remembered cinematically because of the the first-ever Academy Awards (Borzage, Benjamin Glazer's script and Gaynor) and nominations (for film and art decoration).
With *Janet Gaynor, Charles Farrell*

SEVENTH HEAVEN (1937) See **Seventh Heaven** (1927)

SHADOW OF HIROSHIMA See **Hiroshima**

SHAKE HANDS WITH THE DEVIL
Michael Anderson — Ireland/U.S., 1959 [110min]   ★
Dodgy historical reference to the IRA violence of 1921   ★
Ireland, but quite a well-made piece all the same. Talk about a cast in transition!
With *James Cagney, Glynis Johns, Dana Wynter, Don Murray, Michael Redgrave, Sybil Thorndike, Cyril Cusack, Niall McGinnis, Richard Harris, Ray McAnally*

THE SHAME OF MARY DOYLE
See **Juno and the Paycock**

SHANGHAI BOUND
Luther Reed — U.S., 1927   ★
Early Hollywood look at the Chinese Civil War. Action-   ★
packed, it follows approximately the same timescale as the ★
Sand Pebbles, but this time it's an American merchant vessel, not warship, which sticks its nose in where it's not wanted.
With *Richard Dix, Mary Brian*

SHANGHAI EXPRESS
Josef von Sternberg — U.S., 1932 [85min]   ★
A picture with much to answer for. Not only did it spawn ★
innumerable train-set mysteries (really only surpassed by ★
Hitchcock's **The Lady Vanishes**); it was the first serious Hollywood attempt to understand what was going on in China in the two decades following the collapse of the Manchu dynasty in 1912. Filmed many times, Sternberg's is the original and best of its type — probably until **The Sand Pebbles**, 1930-odd years later.
With *Marlene Dietrich, Clive Brook, Warner Oland, Anna May Wong*

In other renditions, unfortunately for the purist, romance is often uppermost as in Wesley Ruggles' **Roar of the Dragon** ★★ with Richard Dix earlier that year [70min]; and the otherwise excellent **The Bitter Tea of General Yen** ★★★ (Frank

Capra, 1933 [90min], with Barbara Stanwyck and Nils Asther); and even **Shangahi Surprise ★★** (the Madonna, Sean Penn 1986 vehicle, directed by Jim Goddard).

SHANGHAI SURPRISE See **Shanghai Express**

SHATRANJ KE KHILARI See **The Chess Players**

SHCHORS
Alexander Dovzhenko — USSR, 1939
A straightforward dramatization of a Ukrainian hero of WW1, with undoubted deference to Stalin. Rather like the cinematic job done on **Chapayev**.
With *Yevgeni Samoilov*

SHE WHO DARES See **Three Russian Girls**

SHE WORE A YELLOW RIBBON
John Ford — U.S., 1949 [105min]
The old West is moving on as Capt Wayne, in one of his better, mellow roles, approaches retirement. The Red Indians, following the **Little Bighorn** massacre, are being hounded into eventual submission and one day there won't be any need for his type of soldiery.

In the second part of the trilogy in which, with **Fort Apache** and **Rio Grande**, Ford tells a poetic and glorious history of the white man's subduing of the Native American, the emphasis more than ever is on the rich spiritual mix of man and landscape. Momument Valley, Utah, (in Technicolor) never looked better, and Ford's coaxing of photographer Winton Hoch won the Oscar for his stunning deserts and dramatic skies. Characters and storyline once more lean heavily on James Warner Bellah's originals, and are all the better for it.
With *John Wayne, Joanne Dru, John Agar, Ben Johnson, Victor McLaglen, Harry Carey Jr, Mildred Natwick*

SHENANDOAH
Andrew V. McLaglen — U.S., 1965 [105min]
Victor's son, Andrew, began to echo John Ford's sweeping Western epics in his early movies. He'd just made *McLintock*, starring the Duke, and now employed half the master's stock company in this slightly off-beat but excellent Civil War drama. Stewart is the Virginian who's in a quandry about the war. Although a Southerner he's an abolitionist whose position changes in accordance with various events in his personal life. The director's early promise evaporated in a number of exploitative war movies in the decades to follow.
With *James Stewart, Doug McClure, Katharine Ross, Patrick Wayne, Harry Carey Jr, Warren Oates, George Kennedy, Strother Martin, Denver Pyle*

SHINING THROUGH
David Seltzer — U.S., 1992 [130min]
Very late, and none-too-distinguished entry into the WW2 spy genre. Glossy and probably more sophisticated than examples half a century older, this tale of a German-speaking secretary spying for her lawyer-employer is still just archaic tosh.
With *Michael Douglas, Melanie Griffith, Liam Neeson, Joely Richardson, John Gielgud*

SHIPS WITH WINGS
Sergei Nolbandov — GB, 1941 [105min]
Ealing WW2 flagwaver about the Fleet Air Arm, remembered not for its shots on board the aircraft carrier *Ark Royal*, but for its sub-*Blue Peter* model-making.
With *John Clements, Leslie Banks, Ann Todd, Basil Sydney, Michael Wilding*

SHOESHINE (aka 'Sciuscià)
Vittorio De Sica — Italy, 1946 [90min]
Released in the same year as Rosselini's **Open City**, de Sica's impressive portrayal of Rome's street urchins, running black market errands during the period between the Italian surrender and German withdrawal, is equally depressingly realistic in its approach. The four-handed script was nominated, and the Academy granted the film a special award in an era when there was no foreign film category.
With *Franco Interlenghi, Rinaldo Smordoni*

THE SHOP ON MAIN STREET
(aka 'Obchod na Korze', 'The Shop on the High Street')
Jan Kadar/Elmar Klos — Czechoslovakia, 1965 [130min]
Winner of the Best Foreign Film Award at the Oscars, Kaminska was nominated for her portrayal of an old Jewess, initially stripped of her shop by a fascist-conforming Slovak, but then looked after by the younger man. The tale ends tragically with the woman dying of shock when she is aware of a round-up by Nazis; and the man killing himself in shame.
With *Ida Kaminski, Jozef Kroner*

THE SHOP ON THE HIGH STREET
See **The Shop on Main Street**

SIEG IM WESTEN See **Victory in the West**

THE SIEGE AT RED RIVER
Rudolph Maté — U.S., 1954 [85min]
Routine Civil War Western, interesting because it involves the Confederates stealing one of the first Gatling guns (invented in 1862).
With *Van Johnson, Joanne Dru, Richard Boone*

THE SIEGE OF SYRACUSE
Pietro Francisci — Italy, 1959 [115min]
Superior sword-and-sandal stuff about Archimedes helping to defend his city from the Romans in the Second Punic War. Based on the acknowledged fact that the scientist built several war machines during his life (287-212BC), which coincided with his living in Syracuse at the time the Romans were knocking on the door.
With *Rossano Brazzi, Tina Louise, Sylva Koscina*

THE SIEGE OF THE SAXONS
See **Knights of the Round Table**

THE SIGN OF THE PAGAN See **Attila the Hun**

THE SILENT ENEMY
William Fairchild — GB, 1958 [110min]
WW2 Mediterranean underwater heroics, with British frogmen taking on the Italians. Sank without a trace — despite the strong (and never disproved) rumours at the time of its release that the film's real-life hero, Commander Crabb, had mysteriously died while diving to spy on a Soviet warship visiting Britain.
With *Laurence Harvey, John Clements, Michael Craig, Sidney James, Alec McCowen, Nigel Stock*

THE SILENT VILLAGE
Humphrey Jennings — GB, 1943

More documentary than drama, but using the villagers and location of Cwmgiedd in South Wales to replicate those of Lidice, in a heartfelt, if sentimental tribute to the victims of Hitler's vicious reprisals after the slaying of Heydrich in May 1942 (see **Hangman Also Die!**). A strange and disturbing film.

THE SILVER FLEET
Vernon Sewell/Gordon Wellesley — GB, 1943 [85min]

One of the better propaganda dramas to come out of Britain in WW2. A Dutch shipbuilder, forced to collaborate with the Germans, builds a U-boat, then sabotages it.
With *Ralph Richardson, Esmond Knight, Googie Withers*

SIMBA
Brian Desmond Hurst — GB, 1955 [100min]

Early, studio-bound attempt to dramatize events in Kenya at the time of the Mau Mau uprising during the early 1950s. Falls short of satisfactory. (See **The Kitchen Toto**.)
With *Dirk Bogarde, Donald Sinden, Virginia McKenna*

SINCE YOU WENT AWAY
John Cromwell — U.S., 1944 [170min]

One of the signal 'home front' movies of WW2, it brings the best out of Hollywood in technique and style, but it's definitely throwing-up time if you see it today. Winner of a single Oscar (Max Steiner's schmaltzy score), it was nominated for the picture; Colbert and Jones (both Best Actress) and Wooley (Supporting) in the acting stakes; art direction; and editing.
With *Claudette Colbert, Joseph Cotten, Jennifer Jones, Agnes Moorehead, Shirley Temple, Monty Woolley, Lionel Barrymore, Hattie McDaniel*

SINGLE-HANDED
(aka 'Sailor of the King') See **Brown on Resolution**

SINK THE BISMARK!
Lewis Gilbert — GB, 1960 [95min]

The last in a line of British sea war movies of WW2, which started with **In Which We Serve**. Once again the mannerisms and dialogue are pretty stereotyped on both sides, but where the film does score is in the clever intercutting between War Room planning and the action. The chase over 2,000 miles of Atlantic Ocean, after the sinking of HMS *Hood* and the damaging of the *Prince of Wales;* through the attacks by the *Ark Royal's* Swordfish torpedo bombers to the climactic confrontation with HMSs *King George V, Rodney* and the cruiser *Dorsetshire*; are fairly faithfully followed — even if the action is with models intercut with newsreel. Meanwhile, there's high tension back at the ranch, with Ops Director More plotting anew and waiting for news.
With *Kenneth More, Dana Wynter, Carl Mohner, Laurence Naismith, Geoffrey Keen, Karel Stepanek, Michael Hordern, Maurice Denham*

SIROCCO
Curtis Bernhardt — U.S., 1951 [100min]

Odd setting for a Bogart vehicle, but I suppose he got quite used to French colonial scenarios after **Casablanca** and **To Have and Have Not**. This time he's involved in gun-running in French-controlled Syria c1925, when the Druse Muslims are restless. Any attempt to recreate the feel of either of the other pictures dismally fails.
With *Humphrey Bogart, Marta Toren, Lee J. Cobb*

SITTING BULL See **They Died with Their Boots On**

633 SQUADRON
Walter Grauman — GB, 1964 [95min]

Don't let the fact that there was no such squadron get in the way of a good yarn. Old-fashioned, in the style of the **Dambusters**, the picture owes its slight popularity to the use of actual De Havilland Mosquito fighter/bombers.

Robertson leads the squadron on a bombing raid in a deep Norwegian fjord to stop German production of heavy water (see **The Battle for Heavy Water**). Pretty good action scenes, and Ron Goodwin's distinctive theme is always hummable; but it's obvious that Chakiris is still hankering for another, but only once-in-a-lifetime, *West Side Story* role.
With *Cliff Robertson, George Chakiris, Maria Perschy, Harry Andrews*

Another, totally derivative picture, **Mosquito Squadron** from Boris Sagal [90min], with David McCallum and Suzanne Neve, was released in 1968.

67 DAYS (aka 'Uziska Republika')
Zika Mitrovic — Yugoslavia, 1974 [175min]

Obviously a tribute to the then 82-year-old Tito, this historical reconstruction of events after the forming of the Yugoslav communist-dominated provisional government in 1942 goes on to glorify the opposition to both the occupying Germans, and to the royalist Chetnik Serbs. Quite good action scenes, if you strip away the propaganda.
With *Boris Buzancic, Bozidarka Fajit*

SKI PATROL See **The Doomed Battalion**

SKI TROOP ATTACK
Roger Corman — U.S., 1960 [65min]

Typical Corman lively programmer about ski-borne U.S. commandos blowing up a German bridge late in WW2.
With *Michael Forest, Frank Wolff*

A SKIRMISH WITH THE BOERS See **A Call to Arms**

SKY BANDITS
Zoran Perisic — GB, 1986 [95min]

WW1 flying antics — rather too late for even **The Blue Max/Aces High** mini-boom, and certainly not as good as either. Bill Wellman must have turned in his grave.
With *Scott McGinnis, Jeff Osterhage, Ronald Lacey*

SKY COMMANDO
Fred F. Sears — U.S., 1953

Routine Korean War drama, with despised flight commander Duryea gaining his men's respect only after they find out about his heroics over the Ploesti oilfields in Romania in 1943, during WW2.
With *Dan Duryea*

SKY HAWK
John Blystone — U.S., 1929

Flying action over London in WW1 when Garrick of the RFC

singlehandedly takes on a Zeppelin. Extensive use of models, but reasonably well done in an era and area of stiff competition. With *John Garrick, Helen Chandler*

THE SLACKER
Christy Cabanne — U.S., 1917
The title derived from the demeaning term given to American men who refused to volunteer for the forces in WW1. One of the most famous of the several films made to shame people into joining up was **The Patent Leather Kid ***** (Alfred Santell, 1927) with Richard Barthelmess. Cabanne's early exhortation was achieved with the love of a good woman (and a few patriotic prods, courtesy of some cinematic tricks). With *Emily Stevens, Walter Miller*

SLAUGHTERHOUSE FIVE
George Roy Hill — U.S., 1972 [105min]
Vonnegut's anti-war absurdity does not translate to the screen too readily. Hill's confusing odyssey of the 'time-tripper' Billy Pilgrim, takes him to the WW2 horrors of a Nazi POW camp and the Dresden bombing, before ending up on a mystery planet sometime in the future. The satire of the novel is totally lost. With *Michael Sacks, Ron Liebman, Valerie Perrine*

SLAVE WOMEN OF CORINTH
See **Aphrodite, Goddess of Love**

SMRT SIRIKA ENGELCHEN
See **Death is Called Engelchen**

SNIPERS RIDGE
John Bushelman — U.S., 1961 [60min]
OK end-of-Korean War saga, which despite its low budget has some tense moments. With *Jack Ging, John Goddard*

SO ENDS OUR NIGHT
John Cromwell — U.S., 1941 [120min]
One of several Remarque novels (this one called *Flotsam*) to be adapted for the screen after **All Quiet . . .** ; this story of stateless refugees tramping about pre-war Europe, trying to avoid the Nazi fog that was descending everywhere, is something of a let down.

Cromwell's really unsubtle references to German oppression and terror spoke volumes for Hollywood's discomfort with American isolationism, and the message it should give.

Amazingly Hitler's name is not even mentioned once. Louis Gruenberg was nominated for his score. With *Frederic March, Margaret Sullavan, Glenn Ford, Erich von Stroheim, Frances Dee, Anna Sten, Sig Rumann*

SO PROUDLY WE HAIL
Mark Sandrich — U.S., 1943 [125min]
Women's magazine approach to a war story which was well accepted at the time — picking up Oscar nominations for Goddard; writing by Allan Scott; and Charles Lang's camera work. Nurses at Bataan go through as much hell as the troops. Yucky now. With *Claudette Colbert, Paulette Goddard, Veronica Lake*

SO RED THE ROSE
King Vidor — U.S., 1935 [80min]
The reason why Paramount rejected **Gone with the Wind** — this Southern soap opera set during the Civil War failed badly at the box-office. The theme of the Southern patriarch who favours the policies of the Union was conveyed more convincingly in Andrew McLaglen's **Shenandoah**. With *Margaret Sullavan, Walter Connolly, Randolph Scott, Robert Cummings*

SOIOUZ VELIKSGO DELA See **Bloody Snow**

SOL ZIEMI CZARNEJ See **The Taste of the Black Earth**

THE SOLDIER AND THE LADY (aka 'Michael Strogoff', 'The Adventures of Michael Strogoff', 'Michel Strogoff')
George Nicholls — U.S., 1937 [85min]
Much-filmed Jules Verne adventure about Tsarist envoy Strogoff and his epic and eventful ride across the steppes of Asia during the Tartar troubles (which were an aside of the Russo-Turkish War of 1877-78). Walbrook's Hollywood debut was a rip-off of the previous year's Franco-German work by

SOLDIER BLUE
Tough action baptism for Peter Strauss. Avco

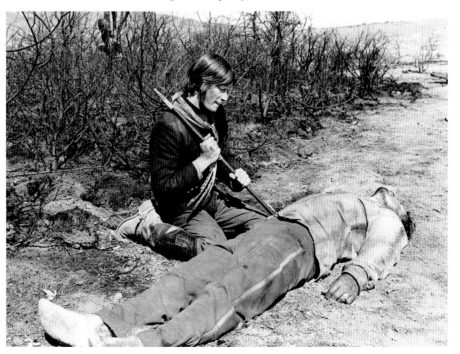

Jacques de Baroncelli, **Courier to the Tsar** ★★★ (aka 'Der Kurier des Zaren', 'Michel Strogoff' — 100min); with the same star listed as Adolf Wohlbrück. The same battle sequences, good though they are, are used in both pictures.
With *Anton Walbrook, Elizabeth Allan, Akim Tamiroff*

Other 'Michael Strogoff' pictures include:
Michael Strogoff (J. Searle Dawley — U.S., 10) With *Charles Ogle*
Michael Strogoff ★ (Lloyd B. Carleton — U.S., 1914) With *Jacob Adler*
Michael Strogoff ★★ (Carmine Gallone — France/Italy/Yugoslavia, 1956, 110min) With *Curt Jürgens*
Le Triomphe de Michel Strogoff ★ (Victor Tourjansky — France/Italy, 1961, 120min) With *Curt Jürgens, Capucine*
A reprise for Jürgens in a new adventure against the Tartars.

SOLDIER BLUE
★ *Ralph Nelson — U.S., 1970* [115min]
★ Taking Peckinpah's goriness in **The Wild Bunch** a stage
★ further, this, for a while, was the most realistically-bloody film
★ ever released. An important, if pretentious allegory coming shortly after the Vietnam My Lai revelations, it also did much to focus on the plight of the Native American, with a graphic and distasteful Cheyenne village massacre; based in part on the shameful Sand Creek action of 1864. It brought into popular focus the position of the Indian in modern times, and may have been influential in the 1973 siege of Wounded Knee, where, protesting for better conditions, two members of the American Indian Movement were killed by FBI agents. One trivial bonus: this was about the first Western to show U.S. Cavalry uniforms fairly accurately.
With *Candice Bergen, Peter Strauss, Donald Pleasence*

SOLDIER IN SKIRTS See **Triple Echo**

SOLDIER OF ORANGE
★ *Paul Verhoeven — Holland, 1977* [165min]
★ Before his Hollywood days, Verhoeven impressed with this
★ character study of a Dutch student reluctantly becoming an underground agent during WW2. The picture contains many tense action sequences, but it is the opening-out of Hauer's persona as Erik that brought international attention to both star (and his Dutch support) and director.
With *Rutger Hauer, Jeroen Krabbe, Derek de Lint, Edward Fox, Susan Penhaligan*

THE SOLDIERS See **Les Carabiniers**

THE SOLDIER'S RETURN See **The Call to Arms**

A SOLDIER'S PRAYER
(aka 'Ningen no Joken: Part 3') See **The Human Condition**

SOLDIERS THREE
★ *Tay Garnett — U.S., 1951* [85min]
★ A North-West Frontier romp that went badly wrong; the material for this adventure of rascally soldiers getting eventually involved in unlooked-for heroics (akin to the much sharper characters seen in **Gunga Din**), being far too weak to warrant such a relatively heavy-weight cast.
With *Stewart Granger, Walter Pidgeon, David Niven, Robert Newton, Cyril Cusack, Robert Coote, Dan O'Herlihy*

SOME MOTHER'S SON
Terry George — Ireland/U.S., 1996 [110min]   ★★★★
Fictionalization of the IRA hunger strikers of 1981 (Bobby Sands, *et al*), which views some of the saddest days of intransigence on both sides through the eyes of two different mothers. One of the deepest insights that cinema has so far made into the heart of the matter, sympathetically and even-handedly directed by George, with Mirren again superbly playing an Ulster role (see **Cal**) — but bleak, bleak watching.
With *Helen Mirren, Fionnula Flanagan, Aiden Gillen, John Lynck*

SOMETHING OF VALUE
Richard Brooks — U.S., 1957 [105min]   ★★
Attempt at a Hollywood objective stance on the Mau Mau rising in Kenya; with Tinsel Town's token black star playing a young Kikuyu initiated into the terror faction after trying to understand the British colonial position. Apart from some gratuitous hacking here and there, it's all a bit of a bore.
With *Rock Hudson, Sidney Poitier, Dana Wynter*

SOMEWHERE I'LL FIND YOU
Wesley Ruggles — U.S., 1942 [110min]   ★★
Another intended U.S. pre-war preparatory fable which was overtaken by events at the time of release. War correspondents Gable and Sterling fight over Turner, as (revised) action takes place from Indochina to the Philippines. The human story behind the film is stronger, however, with Gable's wife Carole Lombard killed in an air crash while he was filming.
With *Clark Gable, Lana Turner, Robert Sterling*

SOMEWHERE IN BERLIN (aka 'Irgendwo in Berlin')
Gerhard Lamprecht — Germany (Soviet Zone), 1946   ★★★
When Germany's best studios were overrun by the Russians in 1945, the prospects for filmmaking at the end of WW2 were not too promising. Among the first efforts of a batch of sociopolitical rehab pictures was this depressing tale of German soldiers coming home — but to what?
With *Harry Hindemith, Hedda Sarnow*

SOMEWHERE IN FRANCE
See **The Foreman went to France**

SOMMERSBY See **La Retour de Martin Guerre**

THE SON OF CAPTAIN BLOOD See **Captain Blood**

SON OF ROBIN HOOD
See **The Adventures of Robin Hood**

THE SONG OF LOVE See **The Dishonored Medal**

SONG OF RUSSIA
Gregory Ratoff — U.S., 1944 [105min]   ★
Ratoff's tribute to 'our Soviet allies' showed he didn't learn anything from Milestone's **The North Star** the previous year; and this ingenuous piece of anti-German propaganda rebounded in his face some years later when HUAC took some exception to its supposed pro-communist noises.
Considering just how much money was spent on it, it was a disaster of a movie — and one which Ratoff couldn't bury if he wanted.
With *Robert Taylor, Susan Peters, John Hodiak*

SPARTACUS
The eponymous hero (Kirk Douglas) leads the slaves in revolt. Bryna/Universal (courtesy KOBAL)

SONO YO WA WASURENAI See **A Night to Remember**

SOPHIE'S CHOICE
Alan J. Pakula — U.S., 1982 [155min]
Heavy story of the Holocaust, haunting Oscar-winning Streep well after her liberation from Auschwitz. Typically studied direction from Pakula (*Klute*, *All the President's Men*), who also wrote the adapted script (nominated), somehow still doesn't hit home as you feel it should; especially since Spielberg's **Schindler's List** makes all such pictures seem exploitative now. Oscar nominations also went to Nestor Almendros' cinematography, Marvin Hamlisch's music, and the costume design.
With *Meryl Streep, Kevin Kline*

SOROK PERVYI See **The Forty-First**

SOUTH SEA WOMAN
Arthur Lubin — U.S., 1953 [100min]
Unsatisfactory comedy drama concerning two Marines and a girl involved in unbargained-for heroics just after Pearl Harbor.
With *Burt Lancaster, Virginia Mayo, Chuck Connors*

SOUTH SEAS BOUQUET See **The Burning Sky**

SOUTHERN COMFORT
Walter Hill — U.S., 1981 [105min]
Exciting yet frightening, Hill shows his mettle as an action director (*The Driver*, *The Long Riders*, **Geronimo: An American Legend**, etc). Taking a story of National Guardsmen confronting Cajuns in the Louisiana bayou, it more than resembles a more sinister scenario somewhere in south-east Asia. Echoes, too, of Boorman's *Deliverance*.
With *Keith Carridine, Powers Boothe, Fred Ward*

SOUTHERN CROSS
(aka 'The Highest Honour — A True Story')
Peter Maxwell — Australia, 1982 [145min]
Friendship develops between an Australian POW and his Japanese captor after the fall of Singapore in 1942. A true story retold very flatly.
With *John Howard, Atsuo Nakamura, George Mallaby, Michael Aitkens*

SPANISH ABC
Thorold Dickinson — GB, 1938
A thoughtful British documentary superficially covering the efforts of the Republican government in Spain to improve education levels — but as the film was shot in a bombarded Barcelona during the Civil War, it emerges as a little more .

SPARTACUS
Stanley Kubrick — U.S., 1960 [195min]
Subdued spectacle set against the Third Servile (or Gladiators') War in Rome between 73 and 71 BC; it was originally going to be directed by Anthony Mann, who would soon indicate his penchant for historical epics with depth (**El Cid**, **Fall of the Roman Empire**).

Kubrick takes Dalton Trumbo's first script since leaving prison for not co-operating with HUAC, and on the back of his enormously influential **Paths of Glory**, interweaves similar themes here: of power — the struggle for it, and the abuse of it. Spartacus' insurrection of the gladiators was finally quelled by the praetor Crassus, who would gain the consulship of Rome in 70BC, before becoming, with Julius Caesar and Pompey, one of the First Triumvirate in 60BC. It is thought that Spartacus was actually killed in battle by Crassus' troops at Rhegium, northern Italy, in 71BC, not crucified like the survivors, as the film suggests.

The action scenes include a memorable sequence of a Roman army's geometrically exact deployment for battle — perhaps the cinema's only attempt to explain visually just what made the legions virtually invincible. Oscars for Russell Metty's dark camerawork, for Ustinov in a supporting role, and for art direction. Music (Alex North) and editing were also nominated.
With *Kirk Douglas, Laurence Olivier, Jean Simmons, Charles Laughton, Peter Ustinov, Tony Curtis, Herbert Lom, John Ireland*

An early sword-and-sandal entry to the genre, **Spartacus the Gladiator ★** surfaced in 1953 [105min], directed in rather nondescript fashion in Italy by Riccardo Greda, and starred Massimo Girotti.

SPARTACUS THE GLADIATOR See **Spartacus**

THE SPIDER'S STRATAGEM
(aka 'La Strategia del Ragno') See **The Conformist**

THE SPIRIT OF '76
Frank Montgomery — U.S., 1917
One of the most controversial (and costly for its producer/director) films ever made in Hollywood. Montgomery met wholesale opposition to his anti-British film (with scenes of baby-killing and torture during the American Revolution) just as the U.S. was entering WW1 as Britain's ally. He was fined $5,000 dollars under the Espionage Act, and imprisoned for 12 years! This was reduced by President

Wilson, eventually, and Montgomery left jail in 1921. The irony of all this is that the worst atrocities portrayed (the Wyoming Valley Massacre of 1778) were perpetrated by Americans — Loyalist colonials, known as Butler's Rangers.
With *Adda Gleason, Doris Pawn*

SPITFIRE See **The First of the Few**

SPRINGFIELD RIFLE
★ *André de Toth — U.S., 1952* [95min]
★ The rifle, introduced to Union forces in the 1850s, had very little to do with this routine Civil War actioner; which is all to do with the theft of Yankee horses.
With *Gary Cooper, Phyllis Thaxter, Lon Chaney Jr*

THE SPY IN BLACK (aka 'U-Boat 29')
★ *Michael Powell — GB, 1939* [80min]
★ Wonderfully atmospheric espionage classic of WW1, carrying
★ the most sinister sense of foreboding in 1939.
★   The first collaboration between writers Powell and Emeric Pressburger takes German agent Veidt across Scotland to the naval base at Scapa Flow, intriguing with the surprisingly-compatible Hobson, with whom he was to team up again in P and P's **Contraband** in 1940.
With *Conrad Veidt, Valerie Hobson*

SQUADRON See **Escuadrilla**

SQUADRON LEADER X
★ *Lance Comfort — GB, 1942* [100min]
Dubious WW2 tale of RAF man actually a German spy. Really not worth the effort.
With *Eric Portman, Ann Dvorak*

THE SQUARE OF VIOLENCE
★ *Leonardo Bercovici — U.S./*
★ *Yugoslavia, 1963*
★ WW2 hokum of German atrocities in Yugoslavia — although based on a true incident in Italy.
   After killing a group of German soldiers with a bomb, a partisan is forced to consider compromising his comrades, or seeing 300 civilians killed. The worst of both worlds happens when he gives himself up. Quite tense.
With *Broderick Crawford, Valentina Cortesa, Bibi Andersson*

STAB (aka 'Thong')
Chalong Pakdivijt — Thailand, 1975 [90min]
Strategic-Tactical Airborne Brigade — an early 'Nam exploitation piece years before Norris and Stallone.
   Behind-the-line commando work and a gold-for-opium scam makes for a pretty tawdry piece of tackiness, with the only surprising thing being the actual source of such drivel. Mission Improbable!
With *Greg Morris, Sombat Metanee*

STACHKA See **Strike**

STAIRWAY TO HEAVEN
See **A Matter of Life and Death**

STALAG 17
Billy Wilder — U.S., 1953 [120min]
Turned into a successful TV series, *Hogan's Heroes*, this is the archetypal cynical comedy based on war which was the forefather of next generation movies such as **The Dirty Dozen**, **M★A★S★H** and **Kelly's Heroes**. The German captors as characters are inhumanly treated by Wilder's own biting script, while Holden's brand of individual opportunism prefigures George Segal in **King Rat**.
   The U.S. POW camp scene seems somehow, at the same time, to be a more confident, if dog-eat-dog, environment than that of the plethora of British films on the subject which portray the POW as a plucky sort, but definitely a team player. Holden, nevertheless, is very good and picked up an Academy Award for his pains; and Strauss in a supporting role, and the director, were both nominated.
With *William Holden, Don Taylor, Otto Preminger, Robert Strauss, Peter Graves, Neville Brand, Sig Rumann*

STALINGRAD (1959) See **Battle Inferno**

STALINGRAD
Josef Vilsmaier — Germany, 1992 [140min]
Straight-laced, if graphically gory and thought-provoking account of the greatest battle of WW2 — as befits a director

STALAG 17
The 'harder' American style of prison camp drama is epitomized here.
Paramount

moving up from the photography department. The first hour offers convincing action; thereafter the characters' plight sometimes seems to be played out in real time, with endless dialogue and very little incident.

Stripped of any real sub-plot, the horrors of the battle are seen through a small group of German soldiers, suffering from the privations of the Russian winter as much as the enemy's fire, in as realistic and harrowing account of men in combat as you are likely to find. No human life is there. (See also Petrov's documentary, **The Battle of Stalingrad**.)
With *Dominique Horwitz, Thomas Kretschmann, Jochen Nickel*

STAMBOUL QUEST See **Mademoiselle Docteur**

THE STAND AT APACHE RIVER
Lee Sholem — U.S., 1953 [75min]
Lively shoot 'em up Western concerning those attention-seeking Apaches attacking a reservation to attract the Cavalry. In the days of our new-found 'understanding' for the red man, how else would you expect them to react?
With *Stephen McNally, Julia(e) Adams, Hugh O'Brian, Jack Kelly*

STAND BY FOR ACTION (aka 'Cargo of Innocents')
Robert Z. Leonard — U.S., 1943 [110min]
Flagwaving saga of an obsolete U.S. destroyer pressed into service in WW2. Routine.
With *Robert Taylor, Charles Laughton, Walter Brennan, Brian Donlevy*

STATE OF SIEGE (aka 'Etat de Siège')
Costa-Gavras, France/Germany/Italy, 1973 [120min]
After *Z* and before his U.S. debut with **Missing**, Costa-Gavras took his intrusive camera to several world trouble spots to create, with varying degrees of success, his political pot-boilers based on oppression and insurrection. Here he turns his attention, somewhat unsuccessfully, to the Tupamaros revolt in Uruguay in the late '60s-early '70s.

Some telling scenes, but unless the background is known fully, it is not always at all easy to follow exactly who's doing what to whom.
With *Yves Montand, Renato Salvatori*

THE STEEL BAYONET
Michael Carreras — GB, 1957 [85min]
You can usually tell it's a Hammer film when the suitably-named Ripper is somewhere down the cast list, and also when you see some of their earlier non-horror stuff in Hammerscope.

Dreadfully overworked plot of Tommies up against it in North Africa in WW2 — of interest only to see a young Caine as a German (if you're quick).
With *Leo Genn, Kieron Matthews, Michael Medwin, Michael Ripper, John Paul, Bernard Archard, Michael Caine*

THE STEEL CLAW
George Montgomery — U.S., 1961 [95min]
After years of starring in low-budget fillers, Montgomery has aspired here to direct his first low-budget filler. Progress of sorts perhaps, but he certainly hasn't broken out of that rut. Clichéd to the hilt, this Yank with Filipino guerrillas yarn is only OK.
With *George Montgomery, Charito Luna*

THE STEEL HELMET
Samuel Fuller — U.S., 1951 [85min]
Magical Fuller movie-making. Made on a shoe-string within weeks of the start of hostilities, this is *the* template for almost every Korean War picture. Whilst not eschewing the propagandist needs of his country at war, particularly at the start of the damn thing anyway, Fuller manages to evince the madness of fighting again so soon after the last affair — involving children and old sweats alike.

It's brutal, it's honest, it's very, very exciting. It is war without the romance or the glory. It should not be missed.
With *Gene Evans, William Chun, James Edwards*

STORM AT DAYBREAK
Richard Boleslawski — U.S., 1932 [80min]
Romantic melodrama using the assassination of Archduke Franz Ferdinand in Sarajevo in 1914 as the background. Some terse political point-scoring between the Serb and Hapsburg factions make it interesting historically.
With *Walter Huston, Kay Francis*

STORM OVER AFRICA See **Royal African Rifles**

STORM OVER BENGAL See **Lives of a Bengal Lancer**

STORM OVER LISBON See **The Conspirators**

STORM OVER THE ANDES
Christy Cabanne — U.S., 1935 [80min]
Exploitative piece for adventure and romance using the topical Bolivia-Paraguay (Chaco) War (1932-35) as its back-drop. Not even very good.
With *Jack Holt, Antonio Moreno, Mona Barrie*

STORM OVER THE NILE See **The Four Feathers**

THE STORY OF DR WASSELL
Cecil B. de Mille — U.S., 1944 [140min]
Dr Corydon M. Wassell was a hero tending the victims of conflict ranging from the wars in China during the '30s to the Pacific actions of WW2. As usual with de Mille, you get more than the simple truth, but no expense is spared on the sets.
With *Gary Cooper, Laraine Day, Signe Hasso*

THE STORY OF GI JOE
(aka 'War Correspondent') *William Wellman — U.S., 1945*
Maybe the model for Sam Fuller's films to follow, this is certainly no 1945 flagwaver. The plotless grind of a U.S. infantry platoon's day-to-day existence as seen through the eyes of a 'soldiers' own' correspondent — the real-life Ernie Pyle — who spells out what the man at the bottom of the military pile thought about it all. The action, when it comes, is non-heroic, matter-of-fact and disturbingly brutal.

At its time, both depressing and refreshing, it received some deserved recognition — if no Oscars — from the Academy. The multi-handed adaptation of Pyles' book; the music of Louis Applebaum; and the song from Ann Ronell all received nominations — and Mitchum, outstanding in a strong ensemble — was also nominated. Wellman unfairly went empty handed for one of the best films made during WW2 about WW2.
With *Burgess Meredith, Robert Mitchum, Freddie Steele, Willy Cassell*

THE STORY OF ROBIN HOOD AND HIS MERRIE MEN
See **The Adventures of Robin Hood**

STORY OF THE TURBULENT YEARS
See **The Flaming Years**

THE STRANGE DEATH OF ADOLF HITLER
James Hogan — U.S., 1943 [75min]
Daft and dangerous doppelganger plot, of Hitler's double being killed in an assassination attempt.
With *Ludwig Donath, Fritz Kortner, Gale Sondergaard*

THE STRANGLERS OF BOMBAY
See **The Bandit of Zhobe**

LA STRATEGIA DEL RAGNO
See **The Spider's Stratagem**

STRIKE (aka 'Stachka')
Sergei Eisenstein — USSR, 1924 [70min]
Eisenstein's first feature remains the most accessible of his early period, but trails the montage-style that would dominate his work later in the decade. It is also not exactly a war picture, but it is one of the mighty stepping stones that link the Russian Revolutions of 1905 and 1917 (in the director's case, **The Battleship Potemkin** and **October**), covering a protracted 1912 factory strike and its brutal and bloody crushing by the Imperial police.

Gross imagery, such as the intercutting of an abattoir scene with the massacre of the workers, lives long in the memory.
With *Maxim Straukh, Grigori Alexandrov, Mikhail Gomorov*

STRONGHOLD
Steve Sekely — U.S., 1952 [80min]
Weak romantic adventure set down Mexico way at the time of Maximilian's crumbling French control in the 1860s. All about ransom and silver mines and such.
With *Veronica Lake, Zachary Scott*

STUKAS
Karl Ritter — Germany, 1941
Once WW2 started, star German director Ritter turned his attention to applauding the exploits of the blitzkrieg advances east and west in 1939 and 1940; whilst at the same time plugging the message of personal and collective sacrifice. This picture employs graphic newsreel of Dunkirk and other German triumphs of the early years, when the Junkers JU87 dive bomber was the scourge of Europe.
With *Karl Raddatz*

SUBMARINE COMMAND
John Farrow — U.S., 1951 [85min]
Standard undersea adventure-drama about tough executive decisions taken in battle conditions, as Holden takes the sub down while his wounded commander is still on deck. Spread unconvincingly over WW2 and the Korean War.
With *William Holden, William Bendix, Don Taylor, Nancy Olsen*

SUBMARINE PATROL
John Ford — U.S., 1938 [95min]
Nicely-balanced comedy-drama with propagandist undertones, about WW1 sub-chasers — the specialist flotillas set up with the emphasis on quick response and manoeuvrability.

Starring 20-year-old Greene in his third Hollywood outing: his early promise would steadily fade and he returned to Britain to be eventually TV's **Robin Hood** (see **Sword of Sherwood Forest**).
With *Richard Greene, Nancy Kelly, Preston Foster*

SUBMARINE RAIDER See **Torpedo Run**

SUBMARINE SEAHAWK
See **Run Silent, Run Deep**

SUBMARINE X-1
William Graham — GB, 1967 [90min]
Obsolete WW2 sub film, which because of its content might have worked 10-15 years earlier. Midget subs are sent out to attack the *Lindendorf*. Action is only OK.
With *James Caan, Rupert Davies, Norman Bowler*

SUBMARINE ZONE See **Escape to Glory**

SUICIDE BATTALION
Edward L. Cahn — U.S., 1958 [80min]
Ho-hum adventure behind the lines for U.S. commandos in WW2 Philippines.
With *Michael Connors*

SUICIDE COMMANDO (aka 'Commando Suicida')
Camillo Bazzone — Italy, 1969 [95min]
Brawny, bulldozing yarn of British commando raid behind German lines during D-Day. Unsubtle but vibrant, with a star who's done it all before.
With *Aldo Ray, Pamela Tudor*

SUICIDE MISSION
Michael Forlong — Norway, 1956 [70min]
Norwegian underground heroics in WW2. Made in Norway, but could have been a Hollywood supporting feature.
With *Lief Larsen, Michael Aldridge*

SUICIDE SQUADRON See **Dangerous Moonlight**

THE SULLIVANS (aka 'The Fighting Sullivans')
Lloyd Bacon — U.S., 1944 [110min]
Heart-wrenching yet high propaganda true story of the five brothers who were killed at sea during the Pacific campaign in 1942.

Now overly sentimental, but with a new destroyer named in their honour, it was quite affecting at the time. It was nominated for the original story Oscar (Jules Schermer and Edward Doherty). May have had something to do with the underlying premise for the mission in **Saving Private Ryan**.
With *Anne Baxter, Thomas Mitchell*

SUNDOWN
Henry Hathaway — U.S., 1941 [90min]
Hollywood's tribute to battered Britain, before Pearl Harbor changed its focus somewhat, begins in an area where taunts of colonialism had been uttered in the past — British East Africa. It's the Germans, however, who come in for a bit of a pasting, both polemically and militarily, in this espionage adventure set in WW2's opening year.
With *Gene Tierney, Bruce Cabot, George Sanders, Harry Carey, Cedric Hardwicke*

SURRENDER
William K. Howard — U.S., 1931 [70min]
Odd WW1 POW drama set in Prussia in a castle setting more suited for the storyline of **La Grande Illusion**.
With *Warner Baxter, Leila Hyams, Ralph Bellamy, C Aubrey Smith*

SURRENDER — HELL!
John Barnwell — U.S., 1959 [85min]
Biopic of Lt Donald D. Blackburn, who fled the invading Japanese in the Philippines in WW2, and joined up with the local guerrillas to harass the occupiers until the return of **MacArthur**. As good as the title sounds.
With *Keith Andes, Susan Cabot*

SUVOROV (aka 'General Suvorov')
Vsevolod Pudovkin — USSR, 1938
At a time when Soviet cineastes were less politically fussy — nationalism meant more to the Russian people than dogma in the late '30s — there was a series of pictures about great national heroes of Russian history, Tsarist or otherwise. The greatest of these was undoubtedly **Alexander Nevsky**.

Suvorov was a great general of the late 18th century, winning his spurs in the Seven Years' War, before the heroism of the Russo-Turkish Wars of the early 1770s. He was elevated to Count Rimniksky (after his defeat of the Ottoman army on the River Rimnik in 1789) and also made commander of the Russo-Austrian forces. Ten years later he beat back French Revolutionary forces in Northern Italy, before finally failing in the Swiss Alps and going home in disgrace. Mighty performance from the magnificent Cherkassov.
With *Nikolai Cherkassov*

SUZY
George Fitzmaurice — U.S., 1936 [95min]
Over-used plot of husband shot, presumed dead, wife marries other chap, husband turns up, etc, in this WW1 spy comedy-drama — saved by the presence of Harlow and the goofy brilliance of Grant.
With *Jean Harlow, Cary Grant, Franchot Tone*

SWASTIKA See **The Double-Headed Eagle**

SWING SHIFT See **Millions Like Us**

SWORD IN THE DESERT
George Sherman — U.S., 1949 [100min]
Early Hollywood bash at the Jewish-Arab situation in the years after WW2. Customarily fence-sitting between the antagonists, it's the ref, like in some corny WWF catchweight bout, that takes the beating (for ref, read the British).
With *Dana Andrews, Marta Toren, Stephen McNally, Jeff Chandler*

THE SWORD OF LANCELOT
See **Lancelot and Guinevere**

THE SWORD OF SHERWOOD FOREST
See **The Adventures of Robin Hood**

SWORD OF THE VALIANT
See **Knights of the Round Table**

SZERENCSES DANIEL See **Daniel Takes a Train**

A TALE OF TWO CITIES (1911)
See **A Tale of Two Cities** (1935)

A TALE OF TWO CITIES (1917)
See **A Tale of Two Cities** (1935)

A TALE OF TWO CITIES
Jack Conway — U.S., 1935 [120min]
The pick of several screen adaptations of Dickens' famous tale of love and honour in the French Revolution. High production values commensurate with Hollywood epics of the period lend an urgency to the mob scenes, particularly, that the others cannot compete with.

Nominated for Academy Awards in the Best Picture and Editing categories.
With *Ronald Colman, Elizabeth Allan, Basil Rathbone, Edna May Oliver*

Some other versions (all with the same title, unless noted):
(J. Stuart Blackton/William Humphrey — U.S., 1911 ★★) With *Maurice Costello, Florence Turner*
(Frank Lloyd — U.S., 1917 ★★) With *William Farnum, Jewel Carmen*
The Only Way (Herbert Wilcox — GB, 1926 ★) With *John Martin-Harvey*
(Ralph Thomas — GB, 1958 ★★★ 115min) With *Dirk Bogarde, Dorothy Tutin*

TV versions of the same name — in 1980, directed by Jim Goddard, and starring Chris Sarandon, Peter Cushing, Kenneth More, Billie Whitelaw and Flora Robson; and 1989, by Philippe Monnier, with James Wilby, Jean-Pierre Aumont and John Mills — were both disappointments.

A TALE OF TWO CITIES
John Monck — GB, 1942
Nothing to do with the Carton tragedy, this is an interesting little documentary where the director compares London's Blitz with the German bombing of Moscow.

A TALE OF TWO CITIES (1958)
See **A Tale of Two Cities** (1935)

TAMPICO
Lothar Mendes — U.S., 1944 [75min]
Rather routine WW2 spy drama with Robinson, captain of a supply ship, picking up all kinds of flotsam from a torpedoed victim.
With *Edward G. Robinson, Lynn Bari, Victor McLaglen*

TANK BATTALION
Sherman A. Rose — U.S., 1958
Low-budget actioner about what it says in the title, in Korea. Why is it that the Korean War threw up so many turkeys?
With *Don Kelly, Edward G. Robinson*

TANK COMMANDOS
Burt Topper — U.S., 1959
U.S. soldiers blow up a bridge in Italy used by German tanks during WW2. Unpretentious, but also uninteresting.
With *Robert Barron, Maggie Lawrence*

TANK FORCE (1958) See **No Time to Die**

THE TANKS ARE COMING
Lewis Seiler — U.S., 1951 [90min]
Flagwaving nonentity as U.S. 3rd Armored Division breaks out of St Lô and make a dash across France in June 1944.
With *Steve Cochran, Philip Carey*

TAP ROOTS
George Marshall — U.S., 1948 [110min]
Love and politics in **Gone with the Wind** fashion, which concerns a Missouri family and their oppositon to Southern cessation. Not much action, but interesting casting of Karloff as a noble savage.
With *Van Heflin, Susan Hayward, Boris Karloff, Julie London*

TARAS BULBA (aka 'Tarass Boulba')
Alexis Granowsky — France, 1936 [105min]
Nikolai Gogol's story of life among the Ukrainian Cossacks in the early 17th century, was remade in English in 1939 (see below) using much of the original footage. The theme of love and loyalty issues in the battles against the Poles is one used in many war pictures; but as Gogol's novel was written in 1835 his claim, if not original, is at least earlier than anything on celluloid. Rousing battle sequences. (A rather more wooden remake came out in 1962 — see below.)
With *Harry Bauer, Danielle Darrieux*

Other versions about Taras Bulba include:
The Rebel Son *** (aka 'Taras Bulba', 'The Barbarian and the Lady') (Alexis Granowsky/Adrian Brunel — GB, 1939, 1990min) With *Harry Baur*
Taras Bulba ** (J. Lee(-)Thompson — U.S., 1962, 125min) With *Yul Brynner, Tony Curtis*

TARAS BULBA (1939) See **The Rebel Son**

TARAS BULBA (1962) See **Taras Bulba** (1936)

TARASS BOULBA See **Taras Bulba** (1936)

TARAWA BEACHHEAD
Paul Wendkos — U.S., 1958 [75min]
Ordinary account of U.S. Marines' very costly 1943 victory over the Japanese in the Gilbert Islands. Done to death.
With *Kerwin Mathews, Julie Adams, Ray Danton*

For the real thing try to see **With the Marines at Tarawa** **** which won the 1944 Oscar for Best Documentary. It was combat footage from Tarawa — and the high Marine casualties suffered in taking a couple of square miles of coral and sand — which first shocked the complacent U.S. public into some understanding of the squalor and the human cost of battle.

TARGET FOR TONIGHT
Harry Watt — GB, 1941
Britain's first real offensive (as against defensive) piece of documentary propaganda in WW2; as if the fuse had been lit by Watt's own (with Humphrey Jennings) *London Can Take It*. It follows the routine night-by-night sorties of a Wellington bomber crew making its way to and from targets in Germany and giving the audience a first-hand ride through the flak and the fires. The template for future bomber documentaries (see **The Memphis Belle**.)

TARGET UNKNOWN
George Sherman — U.S., 1951 [90min]
WW2 USAF bomber pilots are shot down over Germany and interrogated. Anti-Nazi propaganda, just a few years too late — and really not worth the effort.
With *Mark Stevens, Alex Nicol, Don Taylor, Gig Young*

TARGET ZERO
Harmon Jones — U.S., 1955 [95min]
Standard behind-the-lines Korean War action drama, with disappointingly average battle scenes from a normally bruising cast.
With *Richard Conte, Charles Bronson, Chuck Connors, L.Q. Jones, Strother Martin, Peggie Castle*

THE TARTARS See **The Vikings**

TARTU See **The Adventures of Tartu**

TASK FORCE
Delmer Daves — U.S., 1949 [115min]
WW2 action-drama, which involves kamikaze scenes and a vigorous portrayal of the **Battle of Midway**, seen through the pioneering adventures of U.S. Navy aircraft carriers, and their intrinsic value to the Pacific strategy.
Heavily-propagandized fare in 1949.
With *Gary Cooper, Walter Brennan, Jane Wyatt*

A TASTE OF HELL
Neil Yarema/Basil Bradbury — U.S., 1973
Gratuitous WW2 actioner, set in the Philippines but masquerading as an allegory for the Vietnam War. Completely transparent.
With *John Garwood, Lisa Lorena*

THE TASTE OF THE BLACK EARTH
(aka 'Sol Ziemi Czarnej')
Kazimierz Kutz — Poland, 1989
Accessible, visually breath-taking and genuinely exciting story of a neglected struggle. The post-Treaty of Versailles Silesian uprising in still German-held territory during the League of Nation plebiscites in 1920 is imaginatively told through the eyes of the youngest of seven brothers.
With *Olgierd Lucaszewicz*

TAZA, SON OF COCHISE
Douglas Sirk — U.S., 1954 [80min]
Another in the vogue of sympathetic Red Indian pictures generally attributed to **Broken Arrow** (this also has a cameo from Chandler playing Cochise again before exiting to the Happy Hunting Ground), and Sirk's only Western. Geronimo tries to persuade Taza to join his bellicose stance. Pretty tame stuff, despite all that arrow-averting exercise (it was originally released in 3-D).
With *Rock Hudson, Barbara Rush, Gregg Palmer, Jeff Chandler*

TEA WITH MUSSOLINI
Franco Zeffirelli — GB/Italy, 1998 [115min]

Based on the first three chapters of the director's autobiography (screenplay shared with *Rumpole*'s John Mortimer) this is undoubtedly a women's movie, but has a good deal to offer history buffs as well.

Set during the claustrophobic atmosphere of 1930s Tuscany (and later during the war and internment itself), it retells the adventures of a group of ageing English governesses who fancifully call themselves the 'Scorpioni'. Zeffirelli can be depended upon to make things look good, but here we have the added bonus of an excellent period feel, and a cast of matronly thesps who should be wheeled out more often.
With *Cher, Judi Dench, Joan Plowright, Maggie Smith, Lily Tomlin, Baird Wallace, Michael Williams*

TEARING DOWN THE SPANISH FLAG
J. Stuart Blackton/Albert E Smith — U.S., 1897

Probably the first 'war' movie — certainly the first propaganda film. Blackton re-enacted the scene of the lowering of Spanish colours in the Cuban arena of the Spanish-American War on the roof of his studio in New York City.

TEHERAN (aka 'The Plot to Kill Roosevelt')
William Freshman/Giacomo Gentilomo — GB, 1947 [85min]
One of very few immediate post-war British cinema revisitations to the WW2 espionage sub-genre, and you wonder why they bothered. The alternative title says all anyone needs to know about the plot — set around the summit in Iran in 1943 between Roosevelt, Stalin and Churchill.
With *Derek Farr, Marta Labarr, John Slater*

TELL ENGLAND (aka 'The Battle of Gallipoli')
Anthony Asquith/Gerald Barkas — GB, 1931 [90min]

After the impact and success of **Journey's End**, this wholly British production extends the 1930 vintage of classic, seminal anti-war movies into the following year. With characteristics of both **All Quiet on the Western Front** (comradeship and romanticism turned to dust) and **Westfront 1918** (the brutality and hopelessness), Asquith's portrayal of the class-riven British army of WW1 floundering against the Turks at **Gallipoli** in 1915 is a powerful reminder of England through the eyes of the silver-spooned. And, viewed somewhat askance, a totally dated caricature upon which — heroics apart — Richard Curtis' and Rowan Atkinson's TV *Blackadder Goes Forth* could have been modelled! Barkas' second unit direction brings home the futility of the battle — and all war — in the end.
With *Fay Compton, Tony Bruce, Carl Harbord*

TEN DAYS THAT SHOOK THE WORLD See October

TEN DAYS TO DIE (aka 'The Last Act', 'Der Letzte Akt')
G. W. Pabst — West Germany, 1954

Pabst (**Westfront 1918**) took the July 1944 assassination attempt on Hitler as his theme in **Jackboot Mutiny**: here he considers those claustrophobic last days in the Berlin bunker in April 1945, in a disappointingly shallow appraisal of Hitler's power over all his officers and staff right up to the end.
With *Albin Skoda, Oskar Werner*

Other films featuring Hitler's last days include:
Hitler — the Last Ten Days ** (Ennio de Concini —

GB/Italy, 1973) with Alec Guinness. A marginally better film (certainly performance-wise).

Naturally, being one of *the* roles to play, the story of his demise has attracted some heavyweight thesps to impersonate Hitler — albeit on TV. For instance, also in 1973, Frank Finlay played the Führer in *The Death of Hitler*; in 1981 it was Anthony Hopkins in *The Bunker*. In a broader portrayal, Derek Jacobi starred in *Inside the Third Reich* in 1982.

TEN GENTLEMEN FROM WEST POINT
Henry Hathaway — U.S., 1942 [105min]
Enjoyable, if historically-dubious story of the early days of West Point — the famous U.S. Military Academy founded in 1802. Trainees head off into Indian Territory and experience some hair-raising adventures. Treated in similar fashion to the *Boys' Own* 'empire' yarns like Hathaway's earlier **Lives of a Bengal Lancer**.
With *Laird Creggar, George Montgomery, Maureen O'Hara, Harry Davenport, Ward Bond, Douglas Dumbrille*

TEN TALL MEN See Beau Geste (1939)

A TERRIBLE BEAUTY (aka 'The Night Fighters')
Tay Garnett — GB/U.S., 1960 [90min]
Mitchum and O'Herlihy do their best with the blarney playing IRA men siding with the Germans in an attempt to rid Ireland of the Brits during WW2. Struggles to convince.
With *Robert Mitchum, Anne Heywood, Dan O'Herlihy, Cyril Cusack, Richard Harris.*

THE TERROR OF THE BARABARIANS
See **Goliath and the Barbarians**

IL TERRORE DEI BARBARI
See **Goliath and the Barbarians**

DAS TESTAMENT DES DR MABUSE
See **The Testament of Dr Mabuse**

THE TESTAMENT OF DR MABUSE
(aka 'Das Testament des Dr Mabuse', 'The Last Will of Dr Mabuse', 'The Crimes of Dr Mabuse')
Fritz Lang — Germany, 1932
Lang's supposed anti-Nazi sequel to his famous *Dr Mabuse — The Gambler*, of 1922, meant he had to high-tail it out of Nazi Germany especially after rumours that he based his deranged criminal mastermind on Adolf Hitler. Thea von Harbou, Lang's wife and his co-scripter here, enigmatically stayed in Germany during the War.
With *Rudolf Klein-Rogge*

A belated trilogy — probably the longest-spanning one involving the same director in cinema history — was completed in 1960 with *The Thousand Eyes of Dr Mabuse*.

DES TEUFELS GENERAL See The Devil's General

THAT HAMILTON WOMAN (aka 'Lady Hamilton')
Alexander Korda — U.S., 1941 [130min]
Popular pro-British propaganda widely acknowledged (and championed by Churchill) on this side of the Atlantic, about the romance of Admiral Lord Nelson and Lady Hamilton.

Suitably toned-down for the delicates of 1941, the tale is told, thankfully, with a fair sprinkling of Napoleonic sea engagements, including the climactic scenes at Trafalgar.

The combination of Nelson's heroism in the most adverse of conditions struck a chord at the time — and husband-and-wife stars Leigh (**Gone with the Wind**) and Olivier (*Rebecca*) were then just about the hottest pairing in Hollywood. Oscar nominations for Korda and cameraman Rudolph Maté.
With *Laurence Olivier, Vivien Leigh, Gladys Cooper*

The Divine Lady ★★ (Frank Lloyd — U.S., 1929, 100min) with Corinne Griffith and Victor Varconi, also looked into the affair; as did **Bequest to the Nation ★★** (James Cellan Jones, 1973, 115min) with the then starry Peter Finch and Glenda Jackson.

THAT NAZTY NUISANCE See **Hitler — Dead or Alive**

THAT SUMMER OF WHITE ROSES
Rajko Grlic — GB/Yugoslavia, 1989 [105min]
WW2 drama, set in Yugoslavia in 1945, about a mentally-slow life-guard who saves a German officer from drowning and is accused of collaboration. Sadly out of date and out of place. Shame for the interesting cast.
With *Tom Conti, Susan George, Rod Steiger, Alun Armstrong*

THEIRS IS THE GLORY See **A Bridge too Far**

THEY CAME TO BLOW UP AMERICA
Edward Ludwig — U.S., 1943 [75min]
Tame and dated WW2 espionage piece about Nazi agents trained for sabotage work in the U.S.
With *George Sanders, Anna Sten, Ward Bond, Sig Rumann*

THEY CAME TO CORDURA
Robert Rossen — U.S., 1959 [125min]
Coop was only to make three more features after this excursion south of the border, into the cauldron of 1916 Mexico in the wake of Black Jack Pershing's reprisal raids. Action unfortunately takes a back seat to the romance.
With *Gary Cooper, Rita Hayworth, Van Heflin, Tab Hunter, Richard Conte*

THEY DIED WITH THEIR BOOTS ON
Raoul Walsh — U.S., 1941
Flynn's eighth and last outing with de Havilland since **Captain Blood** all those years ago (actually only seven) is a fitting tribute to their joint impact on the historical adventure-swashbuckler genre. Telling the grossly mythical story of the West Point hi-jinks, fast track Civil War command and tragi-heroic climax at the Little Bighorn of George Armstrong

THEY DIED WITH THEIR BOOTS ON
Even Errol Flynn can't win this one. Warner Bros (courtesy KOBAL)

Custer; this is Hollywood at its best, and at its peak. Flynn is larger than life as the flamboyant hero in the series of vignettes that chart his progress to general. He is ably supported by a terrific cast, and Walsh's direction gallops along to the inevitable doom.
With *Errol Flynn, Olivia de Havilland, Arthur Kennedy, Charles Grapewind, Anthony Quinn, Sidney Greenstreet, Hattie McDaniel, Gene Lockhart*

Other accounts of the Battle of the Little Bighorn, or events surrounding it, occur in:
Britton of the Seventh ★★ (Lionel Belmore — U.S., 1916) With *Darwin Karr*
Bob Hampton of Placer ★ (Marshall Neilan — U.S., 1921) With *James Kirkwood*
The Flaming Frontier (Edward Sedgwick — U.S., 1926) With *Hoot Gibson*
The Scarlet West ★★ (John G. Adolfi — U.S., 1926) With *Robert Edeson, Clara Bow*
Little Big Horn ★ (Harry L. Fraser — U.S., 1927) With *Roy Stewart, John Beck* (as Custer)
Little Big Horn ★★ (Charles Marquis Warren — U.S., 1951, 185min) With *Lloyd Bridges*
Bugles in the Afternoon ★★★ (Roy Rowland — U.S., 1952, 185min) With *Ray Milland*
Sitting Bull ★ (Sidney Salkow — U.S., 1954, 105min) With *Dale Robertson, J. Carroll Naish*
Chief Crazy Horse ★★ (George Sherman — U.S., 1955, 1985min) With *Victor Mature*
Seventh Cavalry ★★★ (Joseph H. Lewis — U.S., 1956, 1975min) With *Randolph Scott*
Tonka ★ (Lewis R. Foster — U.S., 1958, 1995min) With *Sal Mineo, Phil Carey*
Disney's contribution: characteristically sentimental as it concentrates on the pony of the title.

The Great Sioux Massacre ★★ (Sidney Salkow — U.S., 1965, 195min) With *Joseph Cotten, Philip Carey* (as Custer)
Custer of the West ★★★ (Robert Siodmark — U.S., 1967, 145min) With *Robert Shaw*
Cinerama comes to the Little Big Horn
Red Tomahawk ★ (RG Springsteen — U.S., 1967, 180min) With *Howard Keel*
Deals with events in nearby Deadwood, after the massacre.
Little Big Man ★★★★ (Arthur Penn — U.S., 1970, 145min) With *Dustin Hoffman, Richard Mulligan* (as Custer)
Much more than the Little Bighorn massacre, this is an eloquent a voyage through the glory of the old West as was ever made — seen through the (often humorous) reminiscences of 120-year-old Jack Crabb.

After the battle, **Sitting Bull** escaped with his tribe to a refuge in Canada, which spawned at least three awful Westerns — Lesley Selander's **Fort Vengeance**, starring James Craig (1953 — 75min); an under-par 1954 Raoul Walsh picture called **Saskatchewan ★** (85min — with Alan Ladd and Shelley Winters); and Burt Kennedy's disappointing first feature, **The Canadians ★** in 1961 [85min], with Robert Ryan.

THEY RAID BY NIGHT
Spencer G. Bennet — U.S., 1942
Hollywood tribute to Britain's commando units, which made a big impression with reports of their derring-do during the early years of WW2. This is a cheapie routine yarn about a raid into occupied Norway to free a high-ranking Norwegian from German custody.
With *Lyle Talbot, June Duprez*

THEY WERE EXPENDABLE
John Ford — U.S., 1945 [135min]
Ford's first feature film after his war documentaries (see ***The Battle of Midway, December 7th***), and it shows in the sense of downbeat realism as much as in the technique he employs. This is no ordinary flagwaver — indeed it stoically accepts the U.S. defeats at **Bataan** and **Corrigedor**; acknowledging the need to retreat and regroup.
The story of real-life officers (Montgomery as Lt John Bulkeley — here named Brickley — and Wayne as his executive officer) warring with top brass over the need for motor torpedo boats, and with each other, is tautly told without nearly the rhetoric and jingoism usually imbued into the characters. An important film of, and for, its time. Nominated for sound and visual effects.
With *Robert Montgomery, John Wayne, Donna Reed, Ward Bond, Jack Holt*

THEY WERE NOT DIVIDED
Terence Young — GB, 1950 [100min]
Unusual and ultimately unsatisfactory drama, which despite its documentary-style realistic pre-tensions is overly-sentimental and rudderless. The story of an Englishman, a Welshman and an American in the same Welsh Guards regiment in WW2 reeks of unnecessary propaganda too.
With *Edward Underdown, Michael Brenna, Ralph Clanton, Helen Cherry*

THEY WHO DARE
Lewis Milestone — GB, 1953 [105min]
Middle-way Milestone — nowhere near his best — but quite a convincing actioner all the same, with British commandos dropping on a German airfield in occupied Rhodes. Buffs will appreciate the Italian SM79 bombers (from the Lebanese air force); and the script is a good deal more convincing for the 1940s — with tough-minded, unsentimental relationships between the ranks — than those of many artificially cynical 1960s attempts.
With *Dirk Bogarde, Denholm Elliott, Akim Tamaroff*

THE THIN RED LINE (1964)
See **The Thin Red Line** (1998)

THE THIN RED LINE
Terrence Malick — U.S., 1998 [170min]
Andrew Marton followed up his impressive work on the Omaha and Utah Beach sections of the **Longest Day** with a pretty flat adaptation of James Jones' **The Thin Red Line ★★** [U.S., 1964, 100min] — based on events at Guadalcanal, and starring Kier Dullea and Jack Warden (See also **Guadalcanal Diary**).
When Malick took hold of Jones' book however, we see a completely different picture. Malick's semi-arty background (*Badlands, Days of Heaven*) is virtually his total output as director, and he'd produced nothing for 20 years before this;

THE THIN RED LINE
(l-to-r): Ben Chaplin, John Cusack and Jim Caviezel at Guadalcanal in the 1998 version. 20th Century Fox (courtesy KOBAL)

but for the first half-hour the audience might think it's watching the first eco-war movie, with the hinterland of Guadalcanal filmed in travelogue-type detail. Then the first great land battle of the Pacific War kicks in, and the narrative flows almost normally. The characterization is still uppermost in Malick's mind, however, with newcomer James Caviezel's Witt living long in the memory.

Certainly not as bloody as the 1998 film **Saving Private Ryan** with which it will always be compared, it will hold its own with the very best of the genre. No Oscars, however, but it did receive a Best Picture nomination; Malick was nominated for direction and screenplay; John Toll for cinematography; Hans Zimmer for the score; and for editing and sound.
With *Sean Penn, Nick Nolte, John Cusack, George Clooney, James Caviezel, Ben Chaplin*

THINGS TO COME
William Cameron Menzies — GB, 1936 [115min]
Brilliant sci-fi cinema well ahead of its time, although undoubtedly influenced by Lang's *Metropolis*. Shot in the middle of an extremely nervous decade, with Nazi air power about to manifest itself in the skies over Spain, H.G. Wells' vision of London's Blitz in 1940 was not necessarily the stuff of Nostradamus, but it shocked Britain to the core and became influential in stepping up the rate of remobilization. Wells' screenplay was based on his 1933 novel *The Shape of Things to Come*.
With *Raymond Massey, Edward Chapman, Ralph Richardson, Cedric Hardwicke, Margaretta Scott*

THIRTEEN FIGHTING MEN
Harry Gerstad — U.S., 1960 [70min]
The Rebs are after Yankee gold again in the American Civil War. Shame the producer didn't use some to improve the appalling production values. Dexter, later that year, was to become the member of John Sturges' *The Magnificent Seven* that nobody can ever remember in quizzes.
With *Harry Gerstad, Grant Williams, Brad Dexter*

THE THIRTEENTH WARRIOR See **The Vikings**

13 RUE MADELEINE
Henry Hathaway — U.S., 1947 [95min]
Heavy spy drama based on an **OSS** operation to a missile site in German-occupied France in WW2. The semi-documentary style had already been used by Hathaway in his earlier **The House on 92nd Street**.
With *James Cagney, Annabella, Richard Conte*

THE THIRTY-NINE STEPS (1936)
See **The Thirty-Nine Steps** (1978)

THE THIRTY-NINE STEPS (1958)
See **The Thirty-Nine Steps** (1978)

THE THIRTY-NINE STEPS
Don Sharp — GB, 1978 [100min]
Despite not holding a candle to the marvellous Hitchcock 1936 version with Robert Donat and Madeleine Carroll [80min], this is infinitely better than Ralph Thomas' limp remake in 1958 [95min] with Kenneth More and Taina Elg; and, most relevantly, it adheres to the original 1914 setting that John Buchan intended, which the other versions are

disappointingly woolly about. The dashing but desperate Richard Hannay subverts a Prussian plot to invade Britain; but only after being chased the length and breadth of Britain by various agencies (including Scotland Yard for a murder he didn't commit), in what was a telling piece of propaganda when the novel was released in 1915. Powell went on to replay Hannay in a rather unsuccessful TV series.
With *Robert Powell, Karen Dotrice, John Mills, Eric Porter, David Warner, Timothy West, George Baker, Ronald Pickup*

THIRTY SECONDS OVER TOKYO
Mervyn Le Roy — U.S., 1944 [140min]
Excellent, detailed, documentary-influenced, fact-based film of the first U.S. bombing of the Japanese mainland in 1942 — the 'Doolittle raid' — just over three months after Pearl Harbor. Because of the problems of range, twin-engined B-25 Mitchell bombers were launched from aircraft carrier USS *Hornet*, but were too big to land on their return, so had to go on and play it by ear in Japanese-occupied China. Amazingly, some bombers got back to tell the tale.

Taut direction by Le Roy and Dalton Trumbo's intelligent script make it a very satisfactory experience. The camerawork of Harold Rosson and Robert Surtees gained an Academy Award nomination, and the visual effects went all the way to the Oscar.
With *Spencer Tracy, Van Johnson, Robert Walker, Phyllis Thaxter, Robert Mitchum*

THIRTY-SIX HOURS
George Seaton — U.S., 1964 [115min]
An American is captured and brainwashed by the Nazis in 1944, and thinks the war's over when he wakes up. Silly premise to obtain D-Day information, but strangely enjoyable, much due to its affable star.
With *James Garner, Rod Taylor, Eva Marie Saint*

THIS ABOVE ALL
Anatole Litvak — U.S., 1942 [110min]
Simplified adaptation of a thoughtful novel by Eric Knight, about men and war, class and war, Britain and war — all through American eyes. Not a **Mrs Miniver**, but having the same effect in allying U.S. minds to Britain's cause, it tells of a **Dunkirk** vet, mind and body shattered, who deserts to sort himself out. He then makes the kind of redemption demanded by Hollywood — he is seriously wounded rescuing a mother and child in an air raid, and, with the help of a good woman, is at one with himself again. Dated, but still rather good. It won an Oscar for art decoration, and nominations for Arthur Miller's camerawork and the editing.
With *Tyrone Power, Joan Fontaine, Thomas Mitchell, Henry Stevenson, Nigel Bruce, Gladys Cooper*

THIS ENGLAND (aka 'Our Heritage')
David MacDonald — GB, 1941 [85min]
Crass propaganda piece as a village unloads a pile of bilge on an American journo, avaricious for days-of-yore tradition. It convolutedly recounts the five attempts to invade England since 1066 (Norman, Armada, Napoleon, WW1 and Hitler's current threat) with the yokels playing the same character through the ages. It was renamed 'Our Heritage' for Scottish audiences: I don't suppose Northern Ireland and Wales even bothered to show it. Embarrassing.
With *Emlyn Williams, Constance Cummings, John Clements*

THIS LAND IS MINE
Jean Renoir — U.S., 1943 [105min]
Even a director as respected as Renoir (**La Grande Illusion, Le Règle du Jeu**), exiled to Hollywood during WW2, had to bow to the standardization of war output in 1942-43. This supposed homage to the brave French living under the heel of the jackboot is just another propaganda confection with the French-flavoured topping of national stereotype — just as **The Moon is Down** is the same with a Norwegian flavour, **The North Star** Russian, **Hitler's Hangman** and **Hangmen Also Die**, Czech; and of course, **Mrs Miniver**, British. Renoir never really recovered and was never quite the same assured director again.
With *Charles Laughton, Maureen O'Hara, George Sanders*

THIS MAN'S NAVY
William Wellman — U.S., 1945 [100min]
Wellman's **The Story of GI Joe**, issued in the same year, is vastly superior to this tale of old salts reminiscing about the number of subs they sank over two world wars.
With *Wallace Beery, Tom Drake, James Gleason, Noah Beery Sr*

THIS WAS PARIS
John Harlow — GB, 1941 [90min]
Unimaginative studio piece about Nazi spies in Paris early in 1940, before the invasion.
With *Ben Lyon, Ann Dvorak, Robert Morley, Griffith Jones*

THONG See STAB

THE THOUSAND PLANE RAID
(aka 'The One Thousand Plane Raid')
Boris Sagal — U.S., 1968 [95min]
High ambition, low budget, routine WW2 flying picture with the star doubting the morality of saturation daylight bombing of German cities. Seen better.
With *Christopher George, Laraine Stephens, Ben Murphy*

THREE CAME HOME
Jean Negulesco — U.S., 1950 [105min]
Poignant adaptation of the autobiography of Agnes Newton Keith, imprisoned by the Japanese along with other Anglo-American residents of Borneo in WW2. The depiction of the deprivation and atrocity is harrowing for Hollywood at that time.
With *Claudette Colbert, Patric Knowles, Sessue Hayakawa*

THREE COMRADES
Frank Borzage — U.S., 1938 [100min]
Popular romantic tear-jerker, but toothless as a propaganda exercise as F. Scott Fitzgerald's adaptation of yet another Remarque novel (**All Quiet on the Western Front**, etc), misses the required mark in 1938.

Set in post-WW1 Germany, it is fine in its reconstruction of the Weimar period — a time of hyper-inflation, destitution, guilt and disgrace — but fails to underline the quiet reference that the need for change is one of radical nationalism. Sullavan was nominated for her performance.
With *Margaret Sullavan, Robert, Taylor, Robert Young, Franchot Tone, Lionel Atwill*

THREE FACES EAST (1926)
See **Three Faces East** (1930)

THREE FACES EAST
Roy Del Ruth — U.S., 1930 [70min]
Remake of Rupert Julian's 1926 **★★★** film which relaunched the filming of WW1 spy stories (after a few quiet years) and starred Jetta Goudal. Here the melodrama is spread thick as we attempt to unravel the intrigues of a British Cabinet minister, his butler and a German nurse.
With *Constance Bennett, Erich von Stroheim*

Heavily propagandist second remake as **British Intelligence ★★** (aka 'Enemy Agent' — Terry Morse, 1940, 165min), starred Boris Karloff.

THE 300 SPARTANS
Rudolph Maté — U.S., 1962 [115min]
The events leading up to Battle of Thermopylae in 480BC — with Leonidas' 300 men holding the narrow pass (to cover for a larger force of escaping Greeks) against a Persian invasion force reputed to be 100,000-strong. Reasonably good effects when on location and the battle is vigorously enacted.
With *Richard Egan, Ralph Richardson, Davis Farrar, Donald Houston, Kieron Moore, Diane Baker*

317e SECTION
Pierre Schoendoerffer — France, 1964 [95min]
An early Schoendoerffer entry into the oppressive jungle warfare of the French-Indochina War, which he knew so well as a colonial soldier. French and Montagnard commandos are stranded behind enemy lines, and their path to freedom is littered with incident in this compelling picture, where the rains are as much an enemy as the Viet Minh, and the pervading atmosphere is one of fear.

The director was to return to the war in 1992 via **Dien Bien Phu**, having first considered the plight of the Americans in by then divided Vietnam after 1959 in his Oscar-winning documentary, ***The Anderson Section ★★★★***.
With *Jacques Perrin, Bruno Crémer*

THREE RUSSIAN GIRLS (aka 'She Who Dares')
See **The Girl from Leningrad**

THRONE OF BLOOD (aka 'Kumonosu-Jo') See **Macbeth**

THUNDER ACROSS THE PACIFIC
See **The Wild Blue Yonder**

THUNDER IN THE EAST See **The Battle**

THUNDER OF BATTLE
See **Coriolanus — Hero Without a Country**

A THUNDER OF DRUMS
Joseph Newman — U.S., 1961 [95min]
Intriguing late return to the original stories and characters of James Warner Bellah (see **Fort Apache, She Wore a Yellow Ribbon**), here with the dour Boone portraying a very different 'Captain Nathan Brittles' from John Wayne's typical creation.

Newman was no John Ford, but the Cavalry v Apache patrol and action scenes are quite tense and exciting. Several of the supporting cast went on to greater fame.
With *George Hamilton, Luana Patten, Richard Boone, Richard Chamberlain, Charles Bronson, Slim Pickens*

THUNDER ROCK

Roy Boulting — GB, 1942 [110min]

Strident anti-isolationist propaganda, told through an allegory of a British news reporter escaping the sycophantic appeasement-mongers in Europe; and retiring to an American lighthouse, where his hopes rise through a series of inspiring visions. Superb performances all round.

With *Michael Redgrave, Lilli Palmer, Barbara Mullen, James Mason*

TIGHT LITTLE ISLAND See **Whisky Galore**

TILL WE MEET AGAIN

Frank Borzage — U.S., 1944 [90min]

Nun helps Allied flyer escape from the Nazis in France in WW2. Ordinary tale given the Borzage moony-eyed treatment.

With *Ray Milland, Barbara Britton*

A TIME FOR KILLING (aka 'The Long Ride Home')

Phil Karlson — U.S., 1967 [85min]

Anti-war sentiments gently wash through this otherwise standard American Civil War hunter-and-hunted picture. Early roles for H. Ford, and Stanton when he wasn't Harry.

With *Glenn Ford, George Hamilton, Inger Stevens, Max Baer, (Harry) Dean Stanton, Harrison Ford*

TIME LIMIT

Karl Malden — U.S., 1957 [95min]

After this, it's surprising Malden didn't direct more. He keeps the momentum going admirably in this Widmark vehicle (he was co-producer) of a U.S. officer court-martialled in Korea for alleged collaboration. Suspenseful to the end.

With *Richard Widmark, Richard Basehart, Dolores Michaels, June Lockhart, Rip Torn, Martin Balsam*

A TIME TO LOVE AND A TIME TO DIE

Douglas Sirk — U.S., 1958 [130min]

Sirk's penultimate melodrama is based on a Remarque story of heavy romance in WW2. The author's usual trademark pacifist threads weave through the plot — as a German soldier returns to his doom on the Russian Front after his last leave — and he himself has a small role, too.

With *John Gavin, Lilo Pulver, Jock Mahoney, Keenan Wynn, Klaus Kinski, Erich Maria Remarque*

THE TIN DRUM (aka 'Die Blechtrommel')

Volker Schlöndorff — France/West Germany, 1979 [140min]

Gunther Grass' novel may be too much for some, but don't think this film version provides an easy cop-out, either. The deep-thinking is still there, but punctuated by visual impressions difficult to formulate from the print.

The savage satire of Germany's Nazification is told through the eyes of a child who refuses to grow up into a ridiculous adult, and whose normalcy is manifested in the playing of his drum. Winner of the Best Foreign Film Oscar, it also shared the top prize at Cannes with **Apocalypse Now**.

With *David Bennent, Mario Adorf, Angela Winkler*

TITANIC TOWN

Roger Mitchell — France/Germany/GB, 1998 [100min]

The *Titanic* was built at the Harland and Wolff shipyards in Belfast — hence the title. The setting is 1972 and Roger (*Notting Hill*) Mitchell's attempt to portray the first peace movement of the Ulster troubles (loosely based on the pacifist activities of Nobel Peace Prize winners, Mairead Corrigan and Betty Williams) is not convincing.

Whilst Walters gives energetically and from the heart, there is always a fair chunk of humour in her earthy incarnations. Unfortunately, some of the humour here is misplaced as the director doesn't seem sure how to play it. After an early skirmish between the IRA and British forces, the story becomes increasingly concerned with the domestic problems of living with the troubles, rather than concetrating on the political situation.

With *Julie Walters, Ciaran Hinds, Ciaran McMenamin, Nuala O'Neill, Lorcan Cranitch*

TO BE OR NOT TO BE

Ernst Lubitsch — U.S., 1942 [100min]

Murderously-funny satire of Nazi delusions of grandeur — played out through a Polish theatre group in occupied Warsaw, and which was misunderstood at the time. Lubitsch's slight of hand is brilliant as the gags come and go within what is a quite suspenseful plot; the cinematically-underused Benny and the tragic Lombard (she died in a plane crash before release) are hugely funny. Sadly, its only recognition was an Oscar nomination for Werner Heymann's score.

With *Jack Benny, Carole Lombard, Robert Stack, Lionel Atwill, Sig Rumann*

Remade in 1983 **★★** [105min] by Alan Johnson, with Mel Brooks and Anne Bancroft rather shoddily playing the Benny and Lombard roles.

TO BE OR NOT TO BE (1983)

See **To Be or Not to Be** (1942)

TO HAVE AND HAVE NOT

Howard Hawks — U.S., 1945 [100min]

Nearly the masterpiece to go alongside **Casablanca** for Bogart, this tale of Nazi spies, Free French intrigue and gun-running in Martinique, in WW2 before Pearl Harbor is based on Hemingway's novel.

Bogie is a fisherman who (like Rick) is caught up in something he considers has nothing to do with him. He is gradually shown that there are certain things he can't avoid. Hawks had a bonus when 19-year-old Bacall, in her first picture, fell for Bogart, and this added tangible emotion to their scenes together — quite uncharacteristic of the director.

With *Humphrey Bogart, Lauren Bacall, Walter Brennan, Hoagy Carmichael*

Remade as **The Gun Runners ★★** by Don Siegel in 1958, with Audie Murphy running the guns into Batista's Cuba.

TO HELL AND BACK

Jesse Hibbs — U.S., 1955 [105min]

After the measured performance he gave in the anti-heroic lead of **Red Badge of Courage**, Murphy was tipped in some quarters for super-stardom. That it didn't happen for the real-life war hero is down to unambitious type-casting, mainly, but this farrago couldn't have helped. It is vastly disappointing and cheapening to him that he not only allowed his autobiography to be filmed, but starred in it himself. The result is a gung-ho war movie glorifying his every heroic (but, no-one can deny, spectacular) set piece as his GI persona

WAR FILMS - T

progresses through Europe towards celluloid canonization.
With *Audie Murphy, Marshall Thompson, Jack Kelly*

TO THE SHORES OF HELL
Will Zens — U.S., 1966
Very early Vietnam picture, featuring a soldier's attempt to rescue his brother from the Vietcong, is distinguished in that it is one of only a few about that conflict to be shot on location in the country itself — and one of several supporting roles that silent star Arlen made late in life.
With *Marshall Thompson, Kiva Lawrence, Richard Arlen*

TO THE SHORES OF TRIPOLI
Bruce Humberstone — U.S., 1942 [80min]
Run-of-the-mill U.S. Marine training picture where the star dreams of being a hero in the up-coming North African campaign. One of those dreams you can never quite remember.
With *Maureen O'Hara, John Payne, Randolph Scott*

TO THE STARRY ISLAND (aka 'Gesom e Kako Shipta')
Park Kwang-Su — South Korea, 1993 [100min]
Harrowing yet fascinating insight into rural life in South Korea, with the legacy of the war in the '50s still plainly to be seen — and the action itself is witnessed in lengthy flashbacks.
With *An Song-Gi, Moon Sung-Kuen*

TO THE VICTOR
Delmer Daves — U.S., 1948 [100min]
Leaden drama concerning the trials of French collaborators after WW2. Woeful.
With *Dennis Morgan, Viveca Lindfors*

TOBRUK
Arthur Hiller — U.S., 1967 [110min]
Pretentious actioner set in the North African desert in WW2 loosely based on an actual raid — uses the title as a crutch. A commando unit comprising German Jews, led by a British major, blow up a German fuel dump — quite spectacularly — but oh, those wordy *longueurs*. Hiller's film picked up an Oscar nomination for its special effects.
With *Rock Hudson, George Peppard, Nigel Green, Guy Stockwell*

Henry Hathaway covered a similar theme (except he used POWs, not Jews) in the same location in his equally-nondescript **Raid on Rommel** ★ starring Richard Burton, released in 1972.

TODAY WE LIVE
Howard Hawks — U.S., 1933 [115min]
More romance than action as Crawford joins up with three sometime lovers on the Western Front in WW1. **Hells' Angels** again provides some aerial stock footage, but the melodrama is more clinging than the mud of the Marne.
With *Joan Crawford, Gary Cooper, Robert Young, Franchot Tone*

TOMAHAWK (aka 'The Battle for Powder River')
George Sherman — U.S., 1951 [80min]
Old-fashioned shoot 'em up Western involving the Sioux and the Cavalry. Bags of action.
With *Yvonne de Carlo, Van Heflin, Rock Hudson*

THE TOMAHAWK AND THE CROSS
See **Pillars of the Sky**

TOMAHAWK TRAIL
Lesley Selander — U.S., 1957
Selander's titles always seem more at home on the covers of those lurid action comics of the 1950s — from where he probably obtained most of his scripts anyway. If you're a Selander fan, this derivative mish-mash of Apache-Cavalry conflict will be right up your trail.
With *Chuck Connors, John Smith, Susan Cummings*

TOMORROW'S WARRIOR
Greek Cypriots captured by invading Turkish tanks. Cinegate

TOMORROW WE LIVE (aka 'At Dawn We Die')
George King — GB, 1942 [85min]
Insignificant chummy-Allies picture exhorting the bravery of the Maquis. Of curiosity if only for the most inapposite alternate title yet imagined.
With *John Clements, Greta Gynt*

TOMORROW'S WARRIOR (aka 'Avrianos Polemistis')
Michael Papas — Cyprus, 1974 [95min]
Somewhat subjective and overly-sentimental view of the Turkish invasion of Cyprus in 1974, as seen through the eyes of a Greek Cypriot boy. Could have been so interesting.
With *Christos Zannides, Aristodemos Fessas*

TONIGHT WE RAID CALAIS
John Bahm — U.S., 1943 [70min]
Ordinary, dropped-behind-the lines WW2 suspenser, with a British spy earmarking some decent bombing targets. Cheapie Channel crossing.
With *John Sutton, Annabella, Lee J. Cobb*

TONKA See **They Died with Their Boots On**

TOO LATE THE HERO
Robert Aldrich — U.S., 1969 [145min]
Rough, tough Aldrich, hot on his success of the **Dirty Dozen**. The rag-bag of war's human detritus is a reminder of the latter, as is the cynical humour of their verbal interplay. This

185

time the enemy is Japanese — complete with their savage jungle war techniques and morale-sapping Tannoys of terror. The ambivalent Allied force, full of life's flawed, is well characterized and often excellently acted (Elliott is the pick), whilst their at-odds leaders, Caine and Robertson, vent their mutual spleens in a running sore of petty nationalism.

Gutsy, chewy fare. Like so many knowing WW2 movies of the 1960s-70s, it really doesn't have anything to do with the actual War or the generation who fought it — see **Play Dirty**, etc.

With *Michael Caine, Cliff Robertson, Henry Fonda, Ian Bannen, Denholm Elliott, Harry Andrews, Ken Takakura, Ronald Fraser, Lance Percival*

TORA! TORA! TORA!

Richard Fleischer — U.S., 1970 [145min]

An epic account of the attack on Pearl Harbor, told as straightforward narrative, with both sides of the story getting equal time — intercut *à la* **The Longest Day**. A rare joint production (Japanese directors Kinji Fukasuku and Toshio Masuda took control of the Japanese sections), it was one of Hollywood's most expensive pictures to that time, as the production values (in reconstructing, then redestroying the U.S. base and its supine fleet) show only too well.

There is no time for characterization or philosophizing here — indeed there is scant footage given to the infamous top brass incompetence. It is flawed cinematically: because there are no heroes, no sub-plots, there are no hooks to hang your anxieties on. It's action all the way — one of the few big-budget war films which is just that — but almost reconstructed documentary, all the same.

TORA! TORA! TORA!
All hell breaks out at Pearl Harbor. 20CF

Deserved Oscar for the special effects: nominations for the Japanese-American cinematography led by Charles F. Wheeler, art direction, editing and sound.

With *Martin Balsam, Soh Yamamura, Jason Robards, Joseph Cotten, Tatsuya Mihashi, E.G. Marshall, James Whitmore, George Macready*

TORN ALLEGIANCE

Alan Nathanson — U.S., 1984

Pro-Dutch account of actions from the Boer War — itself a rare cinematic target, especially nearly a century on. The British are portrayed as butchers, rapists and torturers in this, one of the occasional digs American filmmakers have made from time to time against British imperialism and its implications.

With *Trevyn McDowell, Jonathan Morris*

TORPEDO ALLEY

Lew Landers — U.S., 1953 [85min]

Landers had the ability to rehash a superior film, or body of films, for next to no budget — so you always knew what you were getting. This tacky piece of regurgitation comes from the Korean War submarine sub-sub-genre (if you take the meaning).

With *Dorothy Malone, Mark Stevens, Charles Wininger*

TORPEDO BAY

Charles Frend — France/Italy, 1964 [90min]

Reasonably interesting Italian-British naval imbroglio during WW2, with a good cast, and with honours even.

With *James Mason, Lilli Palmer, Gabriele Ferzeti, Geoffrey Keen*

TORPEDO RUN

Joseph Pevney — U.S., 1958 [100min]

Ford looks for revenge after blowing up a prison ship carrying his own family, which was used as a shield for the Japanese aircraft carrier *Shinaru*. He eventually gets his chance in Tokyo Bay after a near nervous breakdown and a mutiny.

With *Glenn Ford, Ernest Borgnine, Diane Brewster, Dean Jones*

Similar themes were covered in earlier films like Lew Landers' **Submarine Raider ★★** (1942) with John Howard and Marguerite Chapman — probably the only time Landers influenced anyone else's movies!

TORPEDO SQUADRONS MOVE OUT

(aka 'Raigekitai Shutsudo')

Kajiro Yamamoto — Japan, 1944

The dramatized story of Japan's submarine equivalent to the kamikaze fighters of the air — the human torpedoes. Here a Japanese force sink a U.S. battleship in the Pacific.

Yamamoto was to the fore with back-slapping propaganda items throughout the war —

186

notably **The War at Sea from Hawaii to Malaya ★★★** issued on the anniversary of Pearl Harbor (using particularly effective model-work), and **General Kato's Falcon Flyers ★★** (1944), glorifying the heroics of the air force over Burma and Malaya.

TOWER OF LONDON
★ *Rowland V. Lee — U.S., 1939* [90min]
★ **Richard III** told as comic horror doesn't exactly work as history, although the intrigues and a vivid Bosworth Field are all there. Suitably pickled in Malmsey wine, Clarence (Price), is resurrected (and promoted) as Crookback himself for Roger Corman's cut-price remake in 1962 **★★** [80min].
With *Basil Rathbone, Boris Karloff, Barbara O'Neil, Ian Hunter, Vincent Price*

TOWER OF LONDON (1962)
See **Tower of London** (1939)

A TOWN CALLED BASTARD
★ *Robert Parrish — GB/Spain, 1971* [95min]
Bearing all the excesses of the spaghetti Western, this revenge actioner set in the Mexican revolution during the early 20th century, is a disturbing and gratuitous binge of violence, with nihilistic undertones. Unsavoury dish.
With *Robert Shaw, Stella Stevens, Telly Savalas, Michael Craig, Martin Landau, Fernando Rey*

A TOWN LIKE ALICE (aka 'The Rape of Malaya')
★ *Jack Lee — GB, 1956* [115min]
★ Neville Shute's hard-hitting novel delicately relayed on the
★ silver screen for audiences of the mid-50s. I daresay the book might be followed, especially in its context of overt brutality, much closer if it were filmed today. Set in a women's POW camp under the Japanese, the U.S. title says more than the plot provides for, but you get the gist.
  Popular at the box-office, it also won BAFTAs for Finch and McKenna, but the themes were far more grittily realized in the early-80s BBC TV series *Tenko*.
With *Virginia McKenna, Peter Finch, Tagaki, Marie Lohr*

LA TRAGEDIE IMPERIAL See **Rasputine** (1938)

LE TRAIN See **Last Train**

THE TRAIN
★ *John Frankenheimer — U.S., 1965* [105min]
★ Trainspotters' delight — a riveting (in more than one sense)
★ action drama with built-in locos, tracks, stations, signals and
★ other rail paraphernalia. Lancaster is the railways inspector who is persuaded by the French Resistance to stop a train carrying away priceless works of art to Germany during WW2.
  The train is covered from all angles (often with simultaneous split shots) as Frankenheimer goes for locational realism to back up the mounting suspense: Lancaster plays a game of chess with German colonel Scofield — and the rail network of north-eastern France forms the board. Highly enjoyable for train anoraks, war movie buffs and lovers of well-constructed cinema — and not necessarily in that order. The multi-handed script was deservedly Oscar-nominated.
With *Burt Lancaster, Paul Scofield, Jeanne Moreau, Michel Simon*

LA TRAVERSEE DE PARIS See **Crossing Paris**

THE TRAIN
Burt Lancaster leads the Nazis a merry dance courtesy of the French Railways. UA/Ariane

TREACHERY WITHIN
See **Double Crime on the Maginot Line**

THE TREASURE OF PANCHO VILLA see **Viva Villa**

THE TREE OF LIBERTY See **The Howards of Virginia**

THE TRENCH
William Boyd — France/GB 1995 [100min] ★
Low-budget psychological set-piece, which employs plentiful ★ symbolism (characters representing all corners of the British Isles, and its class stereotypes; the 'handful' of troops going over the top — shown meeting their individual fates) rather than Hollywood's commercial realism, to make its point (c/f **Saving Private Ryan**, **The Thin Red Line** of the same vintage). Which ever way it comes across, **Paths of Glory** more than adequately said it all back in 1957, making this and numerous other WW1 trench warfare pictures quite redundant.
With *Paul Nicholls, Daniel Craig, Julian Rhynd-Tutt, Danny Dyer, James D'Arcy*

THE TRIAL OF JOAN of ARC
(aka 'Procès de Jeanne d'Arc') See **Joan of Arc**

TRIPLE CROSS
Terence Young — GB, 1967 [140min] ★
Based on Frank Owen's *The Eddie Chapman Story*, this biopic ★ of a petty thief captured when the Germans occupied the Channel Islands, who later became a double-agent, is over-long and fairly uneventful.
With *Christopher Plummer, Yul Brynner, Romy Schneider, Trevor Howard, Gert Frobe, Claudine Auger*

TRIPLE ECHO (aka 'Soldier in Skirts')
Michael Apted — GB, 1972 [95min] ★
Whimsy from a novel by H.E. Bates, as a British soldier in ★

WW2 deserts and cross-dresses to hide out on a farm as Jackson's sister. Better than it sounds.
With *Glenda Jackson, Brian Deacon, Oliver Reed*

TRIPOLI
See **The Barbary Pirate**

TRIUMPH DES WILLENS
See *Triumph of the Will*

LE TRIOMPHE DE MICHEL STROGOFF
See **The Soldier and the Lady**

TRIUMPH OF THE SPIRIT
Robert M. Young — U.S., 1989 [120min]
Clichéd Nazi concentration camp drama, based on the true-life case of a Greek boxer who like some latter-day gladiator fights his co-internees for his life and better rations. Losers are sent to their deaths. Actually shot at Auschwitz.
With *Willem Dafoe, Wendy Gazelle, Robert Loggia*

TRIUMPH OF THE WILL
Leni Riefenstahl — Germany, 1935
Hitler's 'hymn of praise'. He titled and styled this study in mass hysteria when the Nazi party rally was 'staged' at Nuremburg in September 1934. Riefenstahl's work may be technically brilliant (as she was to prove with the amazing *Olympiad* in 1936), but this mesmeric, disturbing and prophetic picture of Aryan power is down to one man.

So hypnotic is the presence of the Führer deemed to be that the film was banned in Germany after WW2 for many years. Testimony, if any were needed then, that this is indeed the most terrifying — *ergo*, the greatest — propaganda picture ever made.

THE TROJAN WAR (aka 'La Guerra di Troia', 'The Trojan Horse', 'The Wooden Horse of Troy')
Giorgio Ferroni — France/Italy, 1961 [105min]
Routine sword-and-sandal stuff, albeit one of the better Reeves vehicles, but this adaptation, cobbling together some of Homer's *Iliad* and Virgil's *Aeneid* opens up the question of validity, or otherwise, of the Troy legend. Late Mycenean Greeks were known to be at odds with the Anatolian city states over Aegean trade, and many squabbles turned into full-scale conflicts. Historians and archaeologists argue there is proof of a battle and the sacking of Troy around the early 12th century BC; whilst acknowledging the additions of the Roman poets (Helen, the Ten Years' War, the Trojan Horse, etc) as fictitious.
With *Steve Reeves, John Drew Barrymore*

Other pictures which allude to the Trojan legend include:
Helen of Troy * (Robert Wise — U.S., 1955, 120min) With *Rossana Podesta, Stanley Baker*

THE TRIUMPH OF THE WILL
Hitler's will that is, transported through the lens of Reifensthal. NSDAP (courtesy KOBAL)

The Trojan Women ★★ (Michael Cacoyannis — U.S., 1971, 110min) With *Katharine Hepburn, Vanessa Redgrave*

THE TROJAN HORSE See **The Trojan War**

THE TROJAN WOMEN See **The Trojan War**

TROOPSHIP See **Farewell Again**

TROUBLE IN MOROCCO See **Beau Geste** (1939)

THE TRUE GLORY
Garson Kanin/Carol Reed — U.S./GB, 1945
Inevitably chest-thumping but genuinely impressive documentary of the D-Day landings and the months to follow, as Allied tanks sweep across north-west Europe in the race to the Rhine. Remarkable pairing of directors — shortly to be involved in *Adam's Rib* (Kanin, as writer) and *The Third Man* (Reed, director). Winner of the Oscar for Best Documentary.

TSAREUBIITSA See **Assassin of the Tsar**

TULIPAA See **Flame Top**

TUMULT IN DAMASCUS (aka 'Aufuhr in Damaskus')
Gustav Ucicky — Germany, 1939
Before any shots were fired in WW2, cinema representing all sides fired propaganda salvos. This anti-British feature deals with WW1 Jordan and the extrication of German troops from under the noses of British forces. Ucicky was also responsible for the ultra-nationalist **Morgenrot** and **Heimkehr**.

TUNISIAN VICTORY See *Desert Victory*

THE TURNING POINT See **The Great Turning Point**

TWELVE O'CLOCK HIGH
Henry King — U.S., 1949 [130min]
With WW2 receding, filmmakers were starting to review WW2 pictures with a degree of objective hindsight. King's intelligent picture takes the war as it affects individuals; and in this instance it is about Peck's human frailty as the CO of a U.S. bomber crew out of England, who eventually suffers a breakdown. Wonderfully acted by Peck and the others (Jagger won the Oscar for Best Supporting Actor). Nominations went to the picture and Peck.

The authenticity benefits not only from plentifully available B-17s, but from writers and a cast who had recently lived through the war, giving a real 1940s flavour apparently irretrievable by later generations (see the 1990 **Memphis Belle**). With *Gregory Peck, Hugh Marlowe, Gary Merrill, Millard Mitchell, Dean Jagger*

TWENTY DAYS WITHOUT WAR
(aka 'Dvadtsat Dnei bez Voini')
Alexei Gherman — USSR, 1976 [100min]
Banned by the Soviets for its anti-war stance (it was released in 1986, in more tolerant times), Gherman tells his story through a series of conversations between the hero (a WW2 war correspondent) and strangers on a train. OK it leaves one thoughful, but Hitchcock made much better cinema from similar. With *Yuri Nikulin, Ludmils Gurchenko*

TWO FLAGS WEST
Robert Wise — U.S., 1950 [90min]
A force of Southern POWs are released to fight Indians in this appallingly-scripted yarn of the War of Secession in America. Redeemed only by some goodish action shots and a good cast. With *Joseph Cotten, Linda Darnell, Jeff Chandler, Cornel Wilde, Dale Robertson, Noah Beery Jr*

THE TWO-HEADED SPY
André de Toth — GB, 1958 [95min]
Boring biopic of British Colonel Alex Schottland, who infiltrates the Wehrmacht and influences the Germans at quite a high level during WW2.
With *Jack Hawkins, Gia Scala, Alexander Knox, Donald Pleasence, Kenneth Griffith*

TWO MULES FOR SISTER SARA
Don Siegel — U.S., 1969 [115min]
A Budd Boetticher story for the Siegel-Eastwood team should have produced something better than this listless drifter movie set during the Villa Revolution in Mexico. Even MacLaine, as a whore in nun's clothing, can do little to raise the temperature. With *Clint Eastwood, Shirley MacLaine*

TWO THOUSAND WOMEN
Frank Launder — GB, 1944
Launder's blend of poignancy and schoolgirl boisterousness (he and Gilliat created the *St Trinians* series) makes for OK watching in this tale of a women's POW camp in WW2 France. With *Phyllis Calvert, Patricia Roc, Flora Robson, Renée Houston, Thora Hird, Dulcie Gray*

TWO RODE TOGETHER
John Ford — U.S., 1961 [110min]
Undemanding, almost uninteresting late Ford (apart from Stewart and some typical outdoor shots), about a sheriff and an Army officer negotiating with the Comanche for the return of white children abducted many years before. With *James Stewart, Richard Widmark, Shirley Jones, Linda Cristal*

TWO WOMEN (aka 'La Ciociara')
Vittorio De Sica — Italy, 1962 [110min]
Stand-out Oscar-winning performance from Loren in de Sica's bleak portrayal of Rome under Allied bombing in WW2. Fleeing south with her daughter, she hits more trouble from various soldiery, but she has the emotional strength to overcome her misfortunes. Loren won a BAFTA. With *Sophia Loren, Eleanora Brown, Jean-Paul Belmondo*

TYRANT OF THE SEA
Lew Landers — U.S., 1950 [70min]
Cheap and cheerful attempt to invade England in 1803 by Napoleon's forces. Sharp work by Williams' proto-commandos scupper Boneparte's plans. Historically-enervating tosh. With *Rhys Williams, Ron Randell*

TWENTY DAYS WITHOUT WAR
The old and the new on the Eastern Front. Lenfilm/The Other Cinema

U-BOAT PRISONER
Lew Landers — U.S., 1944
Cheapie WW2 biopic of U.S. sailor Archie Gibbs who, rather incredibly, posed as a spy on a U-Boat, and helped free further prisoners. Don't know whether to believe Landers or not.
With *Bruce Bennett, Erik Rolf*

U-BOAT 29 See The Spy in Black

UKRAINE IN FLAMES See Battle for the Ukraine

ULZANA'S RAID
Robert Aldrich — U.S., 1972 [105min]
Intelligent yet brutal Western from Aldrich which not too subtly parallels Americans and their involvement in Vietnam. Articulated by an excellent script from Alan Sharp, Lancaster's cynical old army scout interplays with Davison's bright-eyed-and-bushy-tailed Cavalry officer. The ingenuous West Point graduate witnesses the grossness of war for the first time (here Aldrich is characteritically graphic), and it is something he can't comprehend.

Not very pleasant, but certainly affecting. By this time the ever-reliable Jaeckel qualified — on grounds of age and long-service! — for the role of the grizzled veteran sergeant.
With *Burt Lancaster, Bruce Davison, Richard Jaeckel*

THE UNBEARABLE LIGHTNESS OF BEING
Philip Kaufman — U.S., 1987 [170min]
Arty and erotic love triangle which also shines as a realistic docu-drama of Soviet tanks entering Prague in 1968. The adaptation of Milan Kundera's ironic novel is sensitively played by an attractive cast, and Kaufman must be congratulated for keeping faith with a distinctly un-American style of filmmaking, which the source material surely demands. Sven Nykvist was nominated by the Academy, as were Kaufmann and Jean-Claude Carrièrre for the adapted script (recognition mirrored by BAFTA).
With *Daniel Day-Lewis, Juliette Binoche, Lena Olin*

UNCENSORED
Anthony Asquith — GB, 1942 [110min]
Pedestrian WW2 drama of a Dutch newspaper secretly supporting the underground. Quite tedious — not one of the director's best.
With *Eric Portman, Phyllis Calvert, Griffith Jones*

UNCERTAIN GLORY
Raoul Walsh — U.S., 1944 [100min]
Flynn is a French libertine forced to rethink his priorities when the Germans invade in 1940. Preachy *vieux jeu*, desperate for a bit more of its star's (and director's) penchant for heroics, not homilies.
With *Errol Flynn, Paul Lukas, Jean Sullivan*

UNCLE KRUGER See Ohm Krüger

UNCOMMON VALOR
Ted Kotcheff — U.S., 1983 [105min]
Sparked by his successful venture into Vietnam sub-culture the year before in **First Blood**, Kotcheff pioneered a mini-surge of 'Missing in Action' Vietnam movies, ahead of the eponymous Chuck Norris trail of exploitation, and, somewhat ironically, **Rambo: First Blood Part Two** — which he didn't direct.

Styled on the mission movies of previous wars, Kotcheff does move things along, however, and easily produces the best of a depressing bunch of macho comic-America clap-trap.
With *Gene Hackman, Robert Stack, Fred Ward, Patrick Swayze*

UNCONQUERED
Cecil B. de Mille — U.S., 1947 [145min]
Typically flabby de Mille engorgement of a slight historical incident, used as a backdrop for an interminable melodrama. Cooper is a Virginia militiaman during the French and Indian Wars who falls for British transportee Goddard.

Some action between the Redskins and the settlers, but the overall effect is one of the producer/director's worst excesses. Nominated for special effects.
With *Paulette Goddard, Gary Cooper, Howard da Silva, Boris Karloff, Cecil Kellaway, Ward Bond, Henry Wilcoxson*

THE UNDECLARED WAR See La Guerre sans Nom

UNDER FIRE
James B. Clark — U.S., 1957 [80min]
Uneventful programmer about desertion of U.S. soldiers during WW2. Desertion seems apt. Not to be confused with Roger Spottiswode's film on the Nicaraguan conflict.
With *Rex Reason, Harry Morgan*

UNDER FIRE
Roger Spottiswoode — U.S., 1983 [125min]
Rather superfluous in its polemic, but a gripping tale of the Somoza-Sandinista struggle in Nicaragua all the same. Nolte is good as the converted dispassionate photo-journo who sets the world alight with his (initially rigged) exposées of Somoza's excesses.

The scene of the killing of news anchor-man Hackman by government troops fictionalizes the actual broadcast murder of ABC's Bill Stewart in 1979 — and sets up the universal belief that the Sandinistas were the good guys. Not as deeply convincing as Stone's **Salvador**, but an important historical event more than satisfactorily covered by the medium of cinema.

An Oscar nomination for Jerry Goldsmith's score.
With *Nick Nolte, Gene Hackman, Joanna Cassidy, Jean-Louis Trintignant, Ed Harris*

UNDER TEN FLAGS
Duilio Coletti/Silvio Narizzano — U.S., 1960 [90min]
Lame WW2 actioner as seen from the German-Italian view-point, with a masquerading warship weaving in and out of Allied shipping, creating some havoc.
With *Van Heflin, Charles Laughton, Alex Nicol, Mylène Demongeot*

UNDER THE CLOCK See The Clock

UNDER TWO FLAGS (1916) See Beau Geste (1939)

UNDER TWO FLAGS (1922) See **Beau Geste** (1939)

UNDER TWO FLAGS (1936) See **Beau Geste** (1939)

UNDERCOVER
★ *Sergei Nolbandov — GB, 1943* [80min]
Pasty flagwaver of brave Yugoslavian partisans having a go at the occupying Nazis. Seems that anything Hollywood can do badly in 1943, then so can Ealing.
With *Michael Wilding, Tom Walls, John Clements*

UNDERGROUND
★ *Vincent Sherman — U.S., 1941* [95min]
★ One of three war films, all with different plots, to come out
★ under this title. This is an interesting account of the work of the German resistance during WW2 and the personal story of two brothers — one either side of the divide.
With *Philip Dorn, Jeffrey Lynn*

UNDERGROUND
★ *Arthur H. Nadel — U.S., 1970* [100min]
★ Acting vehicle for stiff singer-cabaret star Goulet; a film of a type which was done far better 20-25 years before. U.S. pilot behind enemy lines, joins forces with the French Resistance. Familiar storyline.
With *Robert Goulet, Danièle Gaubert*

UNDERGROUND
★ *Emir Kusturica — France/Germany/Hungary, 1995* [170min]
★ Head-scratching allegorical tale of two con-men, which is
★ really all about the life and death of Yugoslavia (what was it without Tito?). It meanders from German bombings of Belgrade in 1941, to the break-up of the ethnically-unreal federation during the '90s. Good action, but the message gets lost in the pretentious imagery.
With *Miki Manojlovic, Lazar Ristovski*

UNDERWATER WARRIOR
★ *Andrew Marton — U.S., 1958* [90min]
★ If undersea photography is your thing, then this is the film for you. Shot in the Philippines, it's a shame that the storyline of U.S. Navy frogmen training for action in 1945 is not as expansive as it should have been.
With *Dan Dailey, Claire Kelly, Ross Martin*

AN UNFORGETTABLE SUMMER
★ (aka 'Un Eté Inoubliable')
★ *Lucien Pintilie — France/Romania, 1994* [80min]
★ Striking piece of historical re-enactment with disturbing
★ echoes of the Balkans today, and early references to ethnic cleansing in the region. Set on the border between Romania and Bulgaria in 1925, it tells the tale of a massacre inflicted by displaced bandits and the reprisals taken against a Bulgarian village.
   The mid-1920s was a time of rewritten borders after the Balkan Wars and WW1. Bulgaria had lost much territory in the Dobrouja region to Romania, and there was a general displacement of peoples, with ethnic minorities everywhere. This picture tells of the heartache today through similar events of the past, coherently and without sentimentality.
With *Kristin Scott-Thomas, Claudio Beunt*

UNSEEN HEROES See **The Battle for the V1**

UNDER FIRE
Nick Nolte runs for it in troubled Nicaragua. Orion/Lion's Gate

UNTEL PERE ET FILS See **Heart of a Nation**

L'UOMO DELLA CROCE See **Man of the Cross**

UP FROM THE BEACH
Robert Parrish — U.S., 1965 [100min]   ★
After D-Day a U.S. sergeant becomes involved in the life of a   ★
French village, while the Army is still trying to break through   ★
in Normandy. Action is lively, despite the sub-plot.
With *Cliff Robertson, Red Buttons, Françoise Rosay, Irena Demick, Marius Goring, Broderick Crawford, James Robertson Justice, Slim Pickens*

UP PERISCOPE
Gordon Douglas — U.S., 1959 [110min]   ★
Naval Intelligence officer Garner is landed behind enemy lines   ★
by submarine in order to steal Japanese secrets in this adequate WW2 actioner.
With *James Garner, Edmond O'Brien*

URANUS
Claude Berri — France, 1990 [100min]   ★
Attempt by Berri to tackle that perennial French 'under the   ★
carpet' issue of WW2 collaboration during the German   ★
occupation.
   The tale of a guilt and vengeance-riven town liberated in 1944 is told in a boisterous narrative peppered with enthusiastic, if sometimes over-the-top performances. The dilemma is addressed with all due seriousness, however, which has to be welcomed.
With *Philippe Noiret, Gérard Depardieu, Jean-Pierre Marielle, Michel Blanc*

USS TEAKETTLE See **You're in the Navy Now**

UTU
★ *Geoff Murphy — New Zealand, 1983* [120min]
★ The British atrocities in New Zealand against the Maori
★ people in the 19th century get a rare airing here — in the style
★ of a Western revenge movie. A Maori guide for the Army
embarks on a journey of retribution when he discovers the
British have massacred his village. This is a film which manages to combine the message of imperialist oppression, grand-
scale brutal action and the wonderful scenery of New Zealand
— itself a metaphor for the European's greed for more and
more of the planet's space. A landmark film in New Zealand
cinema.
With *Anzac Wallace, Bruno Lawrence*

UZISKA REPUBLIKA See **67 Days**

VACATION FROM MARRIAGE See **Perfect Strangers**

THE VALIANT ★
Roy Baker — GB/Italy, 1961 [90min]
Uninspired WW2 drama of British warship mined off
Alexandria, and the consciences of the people who have to
deal with the saboteurs. Quite ordinary.
With *John Mills, Ettore Manni, Robert Shaw*

¡VAMOS A MATAR, CAMPANEROS! See **Campañeros**

THE VANISHING CORPORAL
See **The Elusive Corporal**

VERA CRUZ ★
Robert Aldrich — U.S., 1954 [95min] ★
When Aldrich and Lancaster get together there's usually ★
something a bit better than average on show (see the contemporaneous **Apache**, and **Ulzana's Raid**). This is no different,
and really wouldn't have been out of place a decade or so later
among **The Professionals** and **The Wild Bunch**, with which
it has a certain commonality and scope.
   Lancaster and Cooper are a mis-matched pair of post-Civil
War vets headed for Mexico and **Juarez**'s revolution in 1866.
The former plays a misogynous con-man out to work for
whichever side pays best, while Coop is Coop — over-serious,
over-gallant and not quite over *High Noon*. The action is
tremendous when the pair are employed to escort gold to
Maximillian's stronghold of Vera Cruz — but the *dénouement*
is disappointingly predictable.
With *Gary Cooper, Burt Lancaster, Denise Darcell, Cesar Romero,
Sarita Montiel, George Macready, Ernest Borgnine, Charles
Bronson*

VERONIKA VOSS See **The Marriage of Maria Braun**

VERY IMPORTANT PERSON
(aka 'A Coming Out Party') ★
Ken Annakin — GB, 1961 [100min]
Very dated, the puerile parochial humour ruins the OK plot
concept of a WW2 German POW satire; as a louder-than-loud
VIP scientist (JRJ) is prepared for escape by his colleagues.
With *James Robertson Justice, Stanley Baxter, Leslie Phillips, Eric
Sykes, Richard Wattis, John Le Mesurier*

THE VICAR OF BRAY ★
Henry Edwards — GB, 1937 [70min]
Empty, light-headed romp through the English Civil Wars, as
a man of the cloth survives the violent Catholic-Protestant
swings from Charles I to the Restoration, via Cromwell's
Commonwealth. Few historical points are made.
With *Stanley Holloway, Felix Aylmer, Hugh Miller*

LA VICTOIRE EN CHANTANTE
See **Black and White in Colour**

THE VICTORS
Carl Foreman — GB, 1963 [175min]
This over-long, tedious drama of Allied troops fighting and groping their way across Europe after D-Day was a sorry comedown for Carl Foreman, after the heights of **Bridge on the River Kwai** (writer) and **The Guns of Navarone** (producer/ writer). George Peppard is the pick of a workmanlike cast, which fights manfully with a rambling, episodic script.

Foreman partly redeems himself with some good action sequences, and, opting for monochrome to emphasise the reality of war, Christopher Challis' cinematography is a plus point. The overall sprawl, however, resulted in the 175-minute Panavison original being eventually cut to 156 minutes for American audiences.
With *George Peppard, George Hamilton, Vince Edwards, Albert Finney, Melina Mercouri, Eli Wallach, Elke Sommer, Jeanne Moreau, Senta Berger*

VICTORY (aka 'Escape to Victory')
John Huston — U.S., 1981 [115min]
Several world stars, including Pelé, Ardiles, Deyna and Moore, plus half of Ipswich Town FC, helped soccer fans, at least, enjoy the staged 'match' between the Allied POW team and the German team. Unfortunately the ball sometimes arrived at the feet of the paunchy Caine (who was 48 at the time), or the unco-ordinated Stallone in goal.

THE VIKINGS
Einar (Kirk Douglas) navigating his longship through a fjord.
Bryna Prods/United Artists (courtesy KOBAL)

This story of POW breakouts from a German camp in France during a challenge football match must be Huston's silliest ever. A definite own-goal.
With *Michael Caine, Sylvester Stallone, Max von Sydow, Pelé, Bobby Moore*

VICTORY AND PEACE See **Invasion of Britain**

VICTORY IN THE UKRAINE See ***Battle for the Ukraine***

VICTORY IN THE WEST (aka '*Sieg im Westen*')
Fritz Hippler — Germany, 1940
Along with **Campaign in Poland** *** this was the second pat-on-the-back documentary to be fed to German cinema audiences in 1940 by Dr Hippler. Both are important for their newsreel footage of blitzkrieg warfare, and the demoralizing influence of the **Stukas**.

VICTORY THROUGH AIR POWER
H.C. Potter and others — U.S., 1943
The famous Disney studio WW2 propaganda picture-*cum*-documentary, concerning Major Alexander de Seversky's theories on aviation and its place in war is an interesting mix of live-action and stunning animation.

LA VIE ET RIEN D'AUTRE See **Life and Nothing But**

THE VIKING QUEEN See **The Vikings**
Don Chaffey — GB, 1967

THE VIKINGS
Richard Fleischer — U.S., 1958 [115min]
Beautifully photographed on location in the atmospheric Norwegian fjords with plenty of gory action, authentic craft and costumes; this rousing piece of medieval hokum at least proves that flat-bottomed longships could have crossed the North Sea and penetrated inland along the rivers of eastern England. The adventure of two warring brothers and the inevitable love interest generally bowls along energetically, making it a spectacular that was often copied over later years.
With *Kirk Douglas, Tony Curtis, Janet Leigh, Ernest Borgnine, Alexander Knox, James Donald, Maxine Audley, Frank Thring*

Other bandwagon movies (allegedly) concerning Viking life and conquests include:
Erik the Conqueror ** (Mario Bava — Italy, 1961, 180min) With *Cameron Mitchell, Alice* and *Ellen Kessler*
The Long Ships ** (Jack Cardiff — GB/Yugoslavia, 1963, 125min) With *Richard Widmark, Sidney Poitier*
Mediterranean flavour here — difficult to cast Poitier otherwise.
The Tartars * (Richard Thorpe — Italy, 1960, 105min) With *Orson Welles, Victor Mature*
Vikings stray on to the Asian steppes. Worth the grimaces for the delicious star pairing.
The Thirteenth Warrior ** (John McTiernan, U.S., 1999) With *Antonio Banderas, Diane Venora, Omar Sharif*
10th century meeting between Arab poet, Ahmed Ibn Fahdlan and Viking chief Buliwyf (Beowulf) from a silly Michael Crichton book. Some good action.
The Viking Queen (Don Chaffey — GB, 1967, 190min) With *Don Murray, Carita*
Actually about Icenii revolt against the Romans in 1st century Britain, some 800 years before!

VILLA RIDES See **Viva Villa**

THE VIOLENT ENEMY

★ *Don Sharp — GB, 1968* [100min]
★ Badly-timed IRA melodrama, when explosives man Bell escapes from jail on the British mainland and fights with his leaders over a bit of sabotage. The whole thing was to restart for real within a matter of months.
With *Tom Bell, Ed Begley, Susan Hampshire*

THE VIRGIN SOLDIERS

★ *John Dexter — GB, 1969* [95min]
★ Sometimes funny, sometimes crude, sometimes just boringly
★ clichéd barrack-room banter, this adaptation of Leslie Thomas' much funnier autobiographical novel is at least watchable, and in parts entertainingly so.

Set in Singapore in 1950, the film focuses on a bunch of green National Service conscripts up against Malayan terrorists — and any women they can find. Politically vacuous, at least the humour is up a notch on *Carry On Sergeant* — which is more than can be said about the deplorable 1977 sequel, *Stand Up Virgin Soldiers*.
With *Hywel Bennett, Lynn Redgrave, Nigel Patrick, Nigel Davenport*

VIVA VILLA!
The crowd attempt to prevent mass hangings. Paramount

VIRGINIA CITY

Michael Curtiz — U.S., 1940 [120min]   ★
★
Familiar theme of Union gold and how the Rebels plan to steal it — with the help of the glamorous female spy — in this under-par Civil War romp from the usually sparkling Curtiz-Flynn team (**Captain Blood**, **The Adventures of Robin Hood**). Cast is pretty solid, though.
With *Errol Flynn, Randolph Scott, Humphrey Bogart, Miriam Hopkins, Alan Hale*

LA VITA E BELLA See **Life is Beautiful**

VIVA VILLA!

Jack Conway — U.S., 1934 [110min]   ★
★
★
Hollywoodized history of Villa's part in the Mexican revolutions of 1911-19. Mucho misrepresentation, therefore, but terrific entertainment all the same. Conway was given a helping hand by Howard Hawks on the fast-paced direction and the many action set pieces are well handled. Beery gives one of his best performances as the multi-layered bandito-revolutionary-politician in what is without doubt the most enjoyable of many Villa biopics.

David O. Selzick's (**Gone With the Wind**) production was one of three Oscar nominations. Ben Hecht's adapted screenplay and Sound were the others. (See also **Viva Zapata!**)
With *Wallace Beery, Fay Wray, Leo Carrillo, Stuart Erwin, Donald Cook, Joseph Schildkraut, Henry B Wathall*

Other pictures covering the exploits of Pancho Villa include:
The Life of General Villa ★★ (Christy Cabanne — U.S., 1914) With *Raoul Walsh*
Behind the Lines ★★ (Henry McRae — U.S., 1916) With *Harry Carey Sr, Edith Johnson, Ruth Clifford*
The Brand of Cowardice ★ (John Noble — U.S., 1916) With *Lionel Barrymore, Grace Valentine, Robert Cummings*
The Love Thief (Richard Stanton — U.S., 1916) With *Alan Hale*
The Treasure of Pancho Villa ★ (George Sherman — U.S., 1955, 1995min) With *Rory Calhoun, Shelley Winters*
Villa Rides ★★ (Buzz Kulik — U.S., 1968, 125min) With *Yul Brynner, Robert Mitchum*
Pancho Villa ★ (Eugenio Martin — Spain, 1971, 1995min) With *Telly Savalas, Clint Walker*

VIVA ZAPATA
Elia Kazan — U.S., 1952
With Kazan at the helm (*A Tree Grows in Brooklyn*, *A Streetcar Named Desire*, *On the Waterfront*) and with John Steinbeck adapting the script, this is the thinking person's picture on the Mexican revolutions of the early 20th century. Yes, there are pregnant pauses when the moralizing and philosphizing take over, but basically this is an intelligent action-historical adventure story. Whereas **Pancho Villa** did his bit to support Madero from the north, Zapata did likewise in the Morelos region and other southerly provinces — although the film takes liberties here.

Kazan's Actors' Studio prodigy, Brando, is brooding as the heroic revolutionary, and was nominated for his 'method'; as were Quinn, in support; Steinbeck; Alex North (score); and art direction.
With *Marlon Brando, Jean Peters, Anthony Quinn, Joseph Wiseman*

VIVERE IN PACE See Living in Peace

THE VOLGA BOATMAN
Cecil B. De Mille — U.S., 1926
Which came first — the story or the song? De Mille's picture doesn't tell us, but instead it's a decent effort about a man of the waterways' part in the Russian Revolution, with the set-piece battles definitely the highlight.
With *William Boyd, Elinor Fair*

VON RICHTHOFEN AND BROWN
(aka 'The Red Baron')
Roger Corman — U.S., 1971 [95min]
Here, without any visible historical justification, the (actually Canadian) Brown (Stroud) is the modern U.S. war machine: the (actually coldly ruthless) Red Baron (Law), the dinosaur from the age of gentlemen jousters and duellists he's out to make extinct. Corman, coming of age — a good thing or bad? — enjoys much higher production values than normal. Indeed the effect might almost be described as glossy. The picture lacks spark, however, and is not as satisfying as the also-flawed 1966 WW1 aviation spectacular, **The Blue Max**.
With *John Phillip Law, Don Stroud, Corin Redgrave*

VON RYAN'S EXPRESS
Mark Robson — U.S., 1965 [115min]
Enjoyable WW2 POW adventure. Sinatra is the American in a great minority (and nicknamed 'von' for his perceived collaboration with the Italian commandant), and ranking officer over the major British contingent. Italy surrenders, and their captors abandon the camp. Aiming for Switzerland and safety, the erstwhile prisoners let the train take the strain and plan to side-step the Nazis in northern Italy in their hijacked rolling stock.

Lots of strafing and bombing ensues as well as internal irritations (from Howard, still miffed that Sinatra's in charge; and a captured German brass, and his bimbo) before the end is in sight. (Sadly for buffs, the planes are those horrible fat Messerschmitt Bf108s filmmakers used when they couldn't get hold of Spanish Bf109s — see also **The Longest Day**, etc.) The finale is unexpectedly downbeat. Nominated for its sound effects: more importantly, Carra had a 1978 UK Top Ten Hit with the memorable disco ditty, *Do It Do It Again*.
With *Frank Sinatra, Trevor Howard, Raffaella Carra, Brad Dexter, Sergio Fantoni, John Leyton, Adolfi Celi, James Brolin, Edward Mulhare*

VOSKHOZDHDENIE See The Ascent (1976)

VOYAGE OF THE DAMNED
Stuart Rosenberg — GB, 1976 [155min]
The story of Göbbels' expulsion of 937 Jews from Germany in 1939 — his defining line, I suppose, of Aryan purification of Germany. It backfires when the ship they are on is not allowed to land anywhere, and it returns to Hamburg.

Too obviously copying the superior soap opera techniques of the similarly-themed *Ship of Fools* (which, set in the early '30s, deals with all kinds of issues, not just Nazism), the plot gets bogged down by often irrelevant cameos and vignettes. Despite being Oscar-nominated for Steve Shagan's and David Butler's adapted screenplay; Grant as supporting actress; and Lalo Schifrin's music, Rosenburg has sadly bitten off more than he can chew.
With *Faye Dunaway, Osker Werner, Max von Sydow, Orson Welles, Malcolm McDowell, James Mason, Lee Grant, Wendy Hiller, José Ferrer, Katharine Ross, Sam Wanamaker, Denholm Elliott, Julie Harris, Maria Schell, Ben Gazzara*

VYSSI PRINCIP See A Higher Principle

THE W PLAN See **The Burgomaster of Stilemonde**

THE WACKIEST SHIP IN THE ARMY
Richard Murphy — U.S., 1960 [100min]
Although quite amusing, this tale of a scrap-bound U.S. sailing ship acting as a decoy in the WW2 Pacific theatre is not all pratfall, slapstick and farce as the title suggests. It can get quite exciting, but not that much.
With *Jack Lemmon, Rick(y) Nelson, Chips Rafferty*

WAKE ISLAND
John Farrow — U.S., 1942 [80min]
Important flagwaver so early in the American participation in WW2, just when news everywhere was so depressing. Although this high-octane fictionalization of the last days of leatherneck resistance to the Japanese on Wake couldn't portray a U.S. victory, it still had audiences and boot camps cheering on the defiant heroics of Donlevy and co.
The Academy liked it enough to nominate it in four categories: picture, director, Bendix as supporting actor, and the Frank Butler-WR Burnett script.
With *Brian Donlevy, William Bendix, Macdonald Carey*

A WALK IN THE SUN
Lewis Milestone — U.S., 1946 [115min]
A Milestone milestone. Unlike his jingoistic **The Purple Heart** (of the previous year,) the director moves from the glorification of war, to the hard grit and unremiting grind of men at war in an absorbing, depressing and provocative study of one action at Salerno after the landings in 1943; the picture is shot almost in real-time.
The action is all there; its very omnipresence pervades the picture in the way it affects the men. The stress of combat is strongly played out, but so too are the asides (the small-talk of the GIs is a constant under-current), in a rolling narrative of subdued yet powerful performances. Robert Rossen's adaptation of Harry Brown's compelling novel is spot on. Milestone explores the theme again, a little less successfully, in **The Halls of Montezuma** and **Pork Chop Hill**.
With *Dana Andrews, Richard Conte, John Ireland, Lloyd Bridges*

WALK THE PROUD LAND
See **Geronimo: an American Legend**

WALKER
Alex Cox — U.S., 1987 [95min]
One-time cult director Cox (*Sid and Nancy, The Repo Man*) applies absurdist techniques to what might otherwise have been an interesting piece of history if told more straightforwardly. The true story of U.S. mercenary William Walker raising an army to support the Liberals in the Nicaraguan Civil War of 1855; and becoming dictator until overthrown by an army of neighbouring nations two years later, is ruined by the director's cheap gimmicks.
With *Ed Harris, Peter Boyle*

THE WALLS OF HELL
Gerardo De Leon — U.S., 1964 [90min]
Poor WW2 actioner set in the Philippines, with absolutely nothing going for it.
With *Jock Mahoney*

THE WANNSEE CONFERENCE
(aka 'Die Wannseekonferenz')
Heinz Schirk — Germany/Austria, 1984 [85min]
Based on the written minutes taken at the infamous conference in 1942, this is a verbatim, minute-for-minute timed account of the planning of the 'final solution'. Chilling in its matter-of-factness.
With *Dietrich Mattausch, Gerd Bockmann, Friedrich Beckhaus, Robert Artzorn*

DIE WANNSEEKONFERENZ
See **The Wannsee Conference**

THE WANTON COUNTESS See **Senso**

THE WAR See **La Guerre des Boutons**

WAR AND PEACE (1956) See **War and Peace** (1967**)**

WAR AND PEACE
Sergei Bondarchuk — USSR, 1967 [505min]
At a mere three and a half hours, King Vidor and Mario Soldati's 1956 ★★★ version [210min], with Audrey Hepburn, Herbert Lom as Napoleon and a wildly miscast Henry Fonda as Pierre Bezukhov, emasculates Tolstoy's epic — all that is left is the husk with a Hollywood sheen**.** Vidor and lenser Jack Cardiff may have been nominated along with the costume designs — which in itself tells a story — but if any wholesale bowdlerization exercise is to be done on the project, then why not go the whole hog as Woody Allen does in **Love and Death**?
Going in completely the opposite direction is Bondarchuk's mighty eight hour monolith; where he attempts (and often fails) to capture every scene, every characteristic nuance, and, it seems, every bit of dialogue from the novel; and in doing so, he weakens the power of the medium of cinema. What this immense production does have, however, are some of the greatest battle scenes ever filmed — with some 20,000 extras at Borodino alone.
Bondarchuk's *magnum opus* took five years to make, but for all its majesty it is deeply flawed, with the acting and characterization sometimes unconvincing (American English dubbing is a matter of taste); and without the respite of the chapter-end of the original medium. Its sledgehammer effect on the Academy, however, resulted in Best Foreign Film Oscar.
With *Lyudmila Savelyeva, Sergei Bondarchuk, Vyacheslav Tikhonov*

For those who like their epics in bite-sized chunks and with first class performances, BBC TV serialised the novel in 1972 — Pierre being played with strength and sensitivity by a young Anthony Hopkins.

THE WAR AT HOME
Emilio Estevez — U.S., 1996
Estevez's follow-up to his dire directorial debut in *Men at Work*, is really not that auspicious either. For one thing, why

choose such a moribund subject as the misunderstood Vietnam war vet, especially when so much better has been done before? Dad (Sheen) is one of the only assets his son has in the picture, even if the character he plays does not seem so. Told with the obligatory war flashbacks.
With *Kathy Bates, Martin Sheen, Kimberley Williams, Emilio Estevez, Carla Gugino*

THE WAR AT SEA FROM HAWAII TO MALAYA
See **Torpedo Squadrons Move Out**

WAR ARROW See **Seminole**

WAR BRIDES
Herbert Brenon — U.S., 1916
Articulate and influential anti-war picture which, along with Ince's **Civilization** in the same year, fuelled the U.S. isolationist lobby to the point that it was eventually governmentally suppressed. A latter-day *Lysistrata*, it hits upon a theme which makes grown men flinch — women of the world will bear no more children until all war is stopped.
With *Alla Nazimova*

Brenon, although Irish, accepted a British invitation along with D.W. Griffith to come over and direct a propaganda piece in 1918; the result being **The Invasion of Britain** (aka 'Victory and Peace'), with Matheson Lang and Ellen Terry, and which, as events overtook it, was never shown.

WAR COMES TO AMERICA See **Why We Fight**

WAR CORRESPONDENT See **The Story of GI Joe**

WAR AND PEACE
Russian cannon in action at Borodino in the 1956 version, with Henry Fonda's Pierre Bezukhov surveying the carnage. Ponti/DEG

WAR DRUMS
Reginald Le Borg — U.S., 1957 [75min]
Action-packed programmer with a half-decent cast and killings galore in a tale of gold miners harassed by Indians during the American Civil War.
With *Lex Barker, Joan Taylor, Ben Johnson, Stuart Whitman*

WAR HUNT
Denis Sanders — U.S., 1961 [80min]
Standard Korean War action drama about a hard-bitten GI who uncharacteristically takes a shine to an orphan boy. Distinguished only by the film debut of one R. Redford.
With *John Saxon, Robert Redford, Sidney Pollack*

WAR IS HELL
Burt Topper — U.S., 1963 [80min]
Grossly over-the-top Korean War blood-fest, masquerading as psychological drama. After wrongly taking credit for the destruction of an enemy pill-box, Russel goes on a killing orgy. Made even tackier by a voice-over introduction by Audie Murphy — which did little for his esteem as a war hero.
With *Tony Russel, Baynes Barron, Burt Topper*

THE WAR IS OVER See **La Guerre est Finie**

WAR, ITALIAN STYLE
Luigi Scattini — Italy, 1967 [85min]
Dumb WW2 espionage adventure, played for laughs, but it's stretching a point too much to call it satire. A tired and rather sad farewell to the movie world from Keaton, one of its undoubted greats.
With *Buster Keaton, Martha Hyer, Fred Clark*

THE WAR LORD
Franklin Schaffner — U.S., 1965 [120min]
Put Heston into historical costume and images of **Ben-Hur** and **El Cid** are conjured — vast epics of war, romance and religion. Not so here, in a tale of magic and mystery set — perhaps uniquely? — in 11th century Normandy. Heston is a stern liege-man of the Duke entrusted with an isolated tower, where he is plagued by pre-Christian magic, Friesian raiders, sibling rivalry and sexual obsession in this adaptation of Leslie Stevens' play *The Lovers*. He also invokes the little-known law of *droit de siegneur* — his right to sleep with another man's bride on the night of their wedding. Curious, aloof — it begs the question, what would John Boorman have done with it? The action is OK, and the supporting cast solid.
With *Charlton Heston, Richard Boone, Rosemary Forsyth*

THE WAR LOVER
Philip Leacock — GB, 1962 [105min]
McQueen dies twice in 1962 —

here, and in **Hell is for Heroes**. In this solemn picture about a cynical B-17 pilot flying missions out of East Anglia, he is the height of cool — totally dispassionate in anything he does until he falls for Field. Then the title (from the original novel by John Hershey) takes on its *double entendre* — he's as much in love with the war as he can be with any woman. This is where we came in.

Wagner and Field are relentlessly unexciting. From the aviation buff's viewpoint this monochrome production falls between two stools. It lacks both the authenticity of plentiful wartime equipment (see **Twelve O'Clock High**), and the expertise of modern special effects to overcome the shortage (see **Memphis Belle**, 1990).
With *Steve McQueen, Shirley Anne Field, Robert Wagner, Michael Crawford*

WAR OF THE BUTTONS (1962)
See **La Guerre des Boutons**

THE WAR OF THE BUTTONS (1993)
See **La Guerre des Boutons**

WAR PAINT (1926) See **War Paint** (1953)

WAR PAINT
Lesley Selander — U.S., 1953 [90min]
Pacy Selander bang-bang stuff with the Cavalry and the Indians going at it hammer and tongs, Winchesters and arrows, sabres and tomahawks. Take plenty of popcorn.
With *Robert Stack, Peter Graves*

Has nothing to do with W.S. Van Dyke's more cultured silent Western of the same title in 1926.

WAR PARTY (1965) See **War Party** (1989)

WAR PARTY
Franc Roddam — U.S., 1989 [95min]
Not to be confused with a 1965 cowboys v Indians trifle by the master of production-line pictures and crass titles, Lesley Selander, this subtly-titled attempt to draw attention to the plight of the present-day Native American does not quite come off for former whiz-kid Roddam (*Quadrophenia*).

In a re-enactment of a Blackfoot massacre to mark the centenary of an atrocity, an Indian is killed by a white youth, sparking off a real reprise of the event. Shame — the concept is fine. (See also **Soldier Blue**.)
With *Billy Wirth, Kevin Dillon, Tim Sampson*

WAR REQUIEM
Derek Jarman — GB, 1989 [95min]
Doyen of British experimental homophile cinema in the '70s and '80s, this is nevertheless a striking anti-war movie from Jarman. He melds newsreel and drama into Benjamin Britten's oratorio of the title. The images seen through the poetry of Wilfred Owen about death in the trenches in WW1 are often excruciating and always powerful. The actors do a fine job in mime, and this will always be remembered as Olivier's screen swansong.
With *Nathaniel Parker, Tilda Swinton, Laurence Olivier, Patricia Hayes, Nigel Terry, Sean Bean, Alex Jennings*

WAR ZONE See **Circle of Deceit**

THE WARRENS OF VIRGINIA
Cecil B. de Mille — U.S., 1915
Based upon his brother William's play and screenplay, here we have a de Mille without the usual excesses. The story is a common one — Northern officer is a guest at his belle's home in Virginia before the War of Secession: they then become enemies during the conflict, only to reunite after the War. Reasonable action scenes.
With *Blanche Sweet, House Peters*

Inappropriately remade by Elmer Clifton in 1924, with himself and George Backus.

THE WARRENS OF VIRGINIA (1924)
See **The Warrens of Virginia** (1915)

THE WARRIORS See **The Dark Avenger**

WARRIORS FIVE
Leopoldo Savona — Italy, 1962 [85min]
Palance on European duty again in this eminently forgettable story of courage behind German lines in WW2 Italy.
With *Jack Palance, Giovanna Ralli*

WARSHOTS
Heiner Stadler — Germany, 1995 [95min]
A war photo-journalist wins a press award for his filming of the British killing an IRA gunman in Belfast; meets a sniper when he covers the 1992 Somalian civil war — and considers the similarity in their professions. Promises much, but doesn't deliver.
With *Herbert Knaup, Peter Francke*

WASHINGTON AT VALLEY FORGE
Grace Cunard/Francis Ford — U.S., 1914
This early four-reeler, by the starring directors, packs in as much about the American Revolution as it can, as well as the famous 1777-78 winter encampment of the title. Looking at events surrounding its central character, it considers the causes of the conflict with Britain before devoting time to the battles; the rise of the Minutemen; and the parts played by others, such as Paul Revere and **Lafayette**.
With *Grace Cunard, Francis Ford*

Vitagraph brought out an historical re-enactment called **Washington Under the British Flag ★★** in 1916, showing the part played by the first president in the earlier French and Indian Wars.

WASHINGTON UNDER THE BRITISH FLAG
See **Washington at Valley Forge**

WATCH ON THE RHINE
Herman Shumlin — U.S., 1943 [115min]
Important early 'philosophizing' war picture for Hollywood, exposing the cancerous effect of Nazism. Based on Lillian Helman's play (the script is from companion Dashiell Hammett), this middle-brow entertainment of Nazi spies' tentacles crossing the Atlantic and infiltrating U.S. business and diplomatic circles was filmed as the director helmed the stage play, thereby losing any potential cinematic advantages.

A prestigious film for the studio (WB), however, and recognized as such by the Academy, in a Best Actor Oscar for Lukas

as the German refugee; with further nominations for the picture, Watson as supporting actress, and Hammett.
With *Bette Davis, Paul Lukas, Geraldine Fitzgerald, Lucile Watson*

WATERLOO
Sergei Bondarchuk — Italy/USSR, 1970 [130min]
Having pushed back Napoleon from Moscow in **War and Peace**, Bondarchuk goes for the jugular. As with his 1967 *tour de force*, the director's strength lies in his handling of the battle scenes — here *the* battle comprises almost one thrilling hour of colour, smoke, blood and thunder.

The original Russian print is nearly four hours long, which may explain the muddled plot of the Western edition: the first half of the English version makes little sense of the Hundred Days of 1815; Steiger's Bonaparte is also way off the mark and something of a distraction; and Plummer's too-humourous Wellington is apparently given every one of his lifetime of quotable epigrams to speak in one day. Even with its odd gaps (we see the Scots Greys charge, but at what?) the battle itself, however, is worth the price of the admission alone. Production designer, Mario Garbuglia, won a BAFTA Award.
With *Rod Steiger, Christopher Plummer, Orson Welles, Jack Hawkins, Virginia McKenna*

WATERLOO BRIDGE (1931)
See **Waterloo Bridge** (1940)

WATERLOO BRIDGE
Mervyn Le Roy — U.S., 1940
Robert E. Sherwood's play about a dancer-turned-(WW1 London) prostitute was first filmed in 1931 ★★ by James Whale [70min], and starred Mae Clarke and Kent Douglass (Montgomery). The reason for the heroine's transition is the age-old format of lover reported missing in action, and the need for self-deprecation: then hero turns up again . . . In the 1940 version the lover is a brooding Taylor — albeit an English officer with a Nebraskan accent — who set female audiences aquiver in one of his best performances. With Leigh as the female lead immediately on the back of **Gone With the Wind**, and with the action told in fashionable flashback (including that fatal first air raid), it meant the picture couldn't fail in 1940. Oscar nominations for Joseph Ruttenberg (cinematography) and Herbert Stothart (score).
With *Vivien Leigh, Robert Taylor, Lucile Watson, C Aubrey Smith*

Badly remade as **Gaby** ★ (Curtis Berhardt, 1956, 95min), with Leslie Caron, John Kerr and Cedric Hardwicke.

WATERLOO ROAD
Sidney Gilliat — GB, 1944 [75min]
Following on from their influential **Millions Like Us**, Gilliat and co-writer Frank Launder, again in a documentary style, tell the story of a Tommy going AWOL to sort out his marital problems during the Blitz. Very dated now, but a stepping stone to Britain's post war cinema realism.
With *John Mills, Stewart Granger, Joy Shelton, Alastair Sim*

THE WAY AHEAD (aka 'Immortal Battalion')
Carol Reed — GB, 1944 [115min]
Released at about the same time as the above entry, director Reed (*The Third Man* was quite imminent) endorses the semi-documentary approach of Launder and Gilliat, and also Asquith, the Boulting Brothers and others, in this well-remembered comedy-drama about a disparate bunch of late call-up recruits; their training; and their subsequent action at **El Alamein**. Clever script by Eric Ambler and 23-year-old Peter Ustinov, and smashing ensemble acting (including Howard's debut).
With *David Niven, Stanley Holloway, Raymond Huntley, William Hartnell, James Donald, Trevor Howard, John Laurie*

THE WAY TO THE STARS (aka 'Johnny in the Clouds')
Anthony Asquith — GB, 1945 [110min]
On alphabetical cue, it is appropriate that Asquith's best-ever film follows the last two entries, as they were all building blocks to the development of the style of British filmmaking in the austere world of the late 1940s.

The story of Anglo-American rivalries, both in the air and with the ladies, in a bomber squadron before the U.S. entered the war, realistically evokes the atmosphere of the times more than most WW2 pictures. Taken by producer Anatole de Grunwald and Terence Rattigan from a poem by John Pudney called *Johnny Head-in-the-Air*, the intelligent script focuses on the personal relationships interwoven into the action with a balance rarely experienced; and all is tied up neatly by Asquith.
With *John Mills, Michael Redgrave, Douglass Montgomery, Rosamund John, Stanley Holloway, Trevor Howard, Basil Radford, Jean Simmons*

WE DIVE AT DAWN
Anthony Asquith — GB, 1943 [100min]
Splendid action adventure of the British submarine *Sea Tiger* torpedoing the new German battleship *Brandenburg* in this fictitious and often propagandist effort from Asquith. Although still retaining much of his earlier style, there are signs, particularly in the closely-confined atmosphere of the sub, that the tide of documentary realism was about to wash over him (see **The Way to the Stars**). Super acting from Mills, in particular, and very exciting.
With *John Mills, Eric Portman, Niall McGinnis*

WEE WILLIE WINKIE
John Ford — U.S., 1937 [100min]
Yucky Temple vehicle based on a Kipling yarn of the British Raj. Some action between the British and the rebels of Khoda Khan, but you can't escape the gooey sentimentality of this 'made for middle America' menu. Shame on Ford: shame on McLaglen.
With *Shirley Temple, Victor McLaglen, C. Aubrey Smith, Cesar Romero*

WEEK-END A ZUYDCOOTE See **Weekend at Dunkirk**

WEEKEND AT DUNKIRK
(aka 'Week-end à Zuydcoote') See **Dunkirk**

WELCOME IN VIENNA
Axel Corti — Austria/West Germany, 1986 [125min]
Interesting look at German and Austrian emigrés from the Third Reich fighting in an American battalion in late 1944. The story jumps on to the end of the war and studies the lives of the combatants in their old habitats — or what's left of them. Filmed in grainy black-and-white for a newsreel effect.
With *Gabriel Barylli, Nicolas Bridler, Claudia Messner, Karlheinz Hacki*

WELCOME TO SARAJEVO
Michael Winterbottom — GB, 1997 [100min]

Winterbottom's film — the first in English about the Bosnian Civil War of the 1990s — is loosely based on ITN reporter Michael Nicholson's interest in a Sarajevo orphanage, and the bringing to Britain of one little girl out of the madness.

Unsentimental in approach, Winterbottom is, however, critical of the European Union's stance of non-involvement. The jerky action is mostly made up of newsreel footage.

With *Stephen Dillane, Woody Harrelson, Kerry Fox, Marisa Tomei, Emily Lloyd*

WENT THE DAY WELL? (aka 'Forty-Eight Hours')
Alberto Cavalcanti — GB, 1942 [90min]

Evocative, frightening scenario of a German parachute unit taking over a sleepy English village in 1942. This Ealing production from Brazilian Cavalcanti (who had produced **The Big Blockade** and **The Foreman Went to France** earlier in the war) sees the village unite in resistance — all except the quisling squire; thereby adding fuel to the contemporary fire that some of Britain's upper classes might collaborate with the Germans (as their French counterparts reputedly did) should Britain be invaded.

The story, devised by none other than Graham Greene, was developed into a full invasion fantasy in Mollo and Brownlow's remarkable **It Happened Here**.

With *Leslie Banks, Elizabeth Allan, Basil Sydney, Frank Lawton, Mervyn Johns, Thora Hird, Harry Fowler, John Slater*

WEST BEIRUT (aka 'West Beyrouth')
Ziad Doueiri — Belgium/France/Lebanon/Norway 1998

Rare fictionalization around the breakout of the Christian-Moslem Lebanese Civil War in 1975. Using the innocence of children as did Clément in **Les Jeux Interdits**, and to an extent, Boorman in **Hope and Glory**, Tarantino lenser Doueiri builds up an impressive picture of a war zone and the cross-culture unrest in the city where he was brought up. In particular, the bleak rubble of the No Man's Land streets are strikingly evocative.

The concurrent 'rites-of-passage' parable does not detract from what is a welcome addition to the genre.

With *Rami Doueiri, Mohammad Chamas, Rola Al Amin, Leila Karam*

WEST BEYROUTH See **West Beirut**

WESTERN APPROACHES
(aka 'The Raider') *Pat Jackson — GB, 1944*

Another in the gritty documentary/realistic style that British cinema was adopting towards the end of WW2 — this is in fact a re-enactment of an event involving merchantmen decoying U-boats in the Atlantic, with every part played by a seaman involved in the action. The colour photography of Jack Cardiff is still a marvel today.

WESTFRONT 1918
G.W. Pabst — Germany, 1930 [95min]

No film at the time, including the contemporaneous **All Quiet on the Western Front**, depicts the horrors of trench warfare more graphically than Pabst's harrowing masterpiece. Indeed it is diametrically opposite to the poetic stance taken by the Milestone classic, whilst still arriving at the same heavy anti-war message.

With limited dialogue and no soundtrack to the action sequences, the Western Front is eerily real: the tracking shots across no-man's land reinforce the nonsense of it all, with the foreground and middle distance littered with corpses; mud is everywhere.

Using many French and German veterans as extras, this remarkable and always disturbing film stays in the memory, and is as eloquent a piece of polemic today as it was in 1930. With *Gustav Diessl, Fritz Kampers, Claus Clausen*

One year later the director released the almost as powerful **Kameradschaft ★★★★** (aka 'Comradeship'), with Ernst Busch and Alexander Granach [90min]; the story of Germans helping French miners trapped under ground in the Saarland — an anti-nationalist image too dangerous for the emerging Third Reich, who promptly banned it on gaining power in 1933.

WE'VE NEVER BEEN LICKED
(aka 'From Texas to Tokyo')
John Rawlins — U.S., 1943 [105min]

Blatantly chauvinistic, this unsavoury propaganda piece tells the story of an American who was brought up in Japan, and episodes after Pearl Harbor.

With *Richard Quine*

WHAT DID YOU DO IN THE WAR, DADDY?
Blake Edwards — U.S., 1966 [115min]

After his successes with *The Pink Panther* and its sequel, *A Shot in the Dark*, Edwards tries woefully to transfer the formula to WW2 Italy, and the shenanigans going on in a village just taken by the Americans.

Unfortunately there's no Peter Sellers to hang the limp jokes on, and one wonders whether any war scenario warrants almost two hours of second-rate humour.

With *James Coburn, Dick Shawn, Sergio Fantoni, Giovanna Ralli, Aldo Ray*

WHAT PRICE GLORY?
Raoul Walsh — U.S., 1926 [120min]

The 'buddy' movie was probably born with the transference of the Capt Flagg and Sgt Quirt characters from Maxwell Anderson's and Laurence Stallings' anti-war play to the big screen. In Walsh's film version, however, pacifist sentiments take a back seat to the love-hate in-fighting of the main characters, and the hurly-burly WW1 action sequences are reminiscent of the slightly earlier **The Big Parade**.

With *Victor McLaglen, Edmund Lowe, Dolores del Rio*

John Ford's 1952 remake of the 1926 **★★** original [110min], with James Cagney as Flagg and Dan Dailey as Quirt, is both unworthy and irrelevant.

On demobilization, Walsh directed McLaglen and Lowe in three Flagg and Quirt non-war sequels — *The Cock-Eyed World* (1929), *Women of All Nations* (1931) and *Under Pressure* (1935).

WHAT PRICE GLORY? (1952)
See **What Price Glory?** (1926)

WHEELS OF TERROR See **The Misfit Brigade**

WHEN HELL BROKE LOOSE
Kenneth G. Crane — U.S., 1958 [80min]

WHAT PRICE GLORY?
A poignant peace. Fox

Grating WW2 melodrama about a GI who thwarts an assassination attempt on Eisenhower.
With *Charles Bronson, Richard Jaeckel*

WHEN THE LIGHTS GO ON AGAIN
William K. Howard — U.S., 1944 [70min]
Ground-breaking WW2 drama in dealing with shell-shock victims while the war was still being fought — it is, nonetheless, done on too modest a budget and plot to make its intended mark.
With *James Lydon*

WHEN THE REDSKINS RODE
Lew Landers — U.S., 1951 [80min]
Poor, even for Landers, this sorry Western uses a Seven Years' War (French and Indian Wars) canvas to scribble on.
With *Jon Hall, Mary Castle*

WHEN WILLIE COMES MARCHING HOME
John Ford — U.S., 1950 [80min]
'Local boy makes good' theme in middle America, with much confusion, mistrust and some action along the way. Reminiscent in theme to Preston Sturges' hilarious **Hail the Conquering Hero**, but with nothing of the style or panache, Dailey's wartime instructor persona changes for a few days when he stumbles on to a bomber; then is stranded in occupied France before returning home with important secrets. Resuming his instructor role again, no-one knows anything different until he's decorated by the president. Amusing in parts.
With *Dan Dailey, Corinne Calvert, William Demarest*

WHERE EAGLES DARE
Brian G. Hutton — GB, 1969 [155min]
Alistair MacLean's brand of high-octane but totally vacuous, adventure stories do not happily convert to the screen — but this, along with **The Guns of Navarone** and the underrated *Ice Station Zebra*, is a definite exception to the rule.
  Excellent photography, some remarkable action set-pieces (especially the ones on the cable-cars and the bus) and a starry twosome backed up by a stalwart cast, make this utterly preposterous WW2 espionage yarn enjoyable.
  Of course the Germans can't shoot straight, Eastwood's only missing his cheroot and poncho, and you always really knew who the double agents are amongst Burton's troop of middle-aged parachutists (really?) — but since when did you have such exhilarating fun? Is the helicopter a Focke?
With *Richard Burton, Clint Eastwood, Mary Ure, Patrick Wymark, Michael Hordern, Donald Houston, Peter Barkworth, Robert Beatty, Anton Diffring, Derren Nesbitt, Ingrid Pitt*

WHISKY GALORE
(aka 'Tight Little Island') *Alexander Mackendrick — GB, 1948*
One of the first Ealing comedies — and still one of the best — is a gentle satire on war shortages, bureaucracy, and even empire. Some wily Hebridean Scots put one over on the 'English' authorities by stashing away a valuable cargo of Scotch whisky relieved from a stricken merchant ship during WW2. Wonderfully funny in that understated Ealing fashion. Stands the test of time surprisingly well.
With *Basil Radford, Joan Greenwood, Jean Cadell, Gordon Jackson, James Robertson Justice, Wylie Watson, John Gregson, Duncan Macrae, Catherine Lacey, Bruce Seton, Compton Mackenzie, A.E. Matthews*

THE WHITE ANGEL
William Dieterlie — U.S., 1936 [90min]
Flat biopic of Florence Nightingale and her life up to and including her achievements in the Crimean War. Little action.
With *Kay Francis, Ian Hunter, Nigel Bruce, Donald Woods, Donald Crisp*

THE WHITE CLIFFS OF DOVER
Clarence Brown — U.S., 1944 [125min]
Soppy propaganda piece about American woman marrying into British society, then carelessly losing her husband in WW1, and son in WW2. With Yanks marching to the rescue at the close, there is no more Hollywood could have done for the cause. Boasts most of Hollywood's English stock company, young and old.
With *Irene Dunne, Alan Marshal, Frank Morgan, Roddy McDowall, Peter Lawford, Dame May Whitty, C. Aubrey Smith, Gladys Cooper, Van Johnson, Elizabeth Taylor*

WHITE FEATHER
Robert Webb — U.S., 1955 [100min]
Another in the trend of Westerns sympathetic to the Indian as the Cavalry try to persuade Cheyennes to move on so that slavering gold prospectors can move in. OK.
With *Robert Wagner, Jeffrey Hunter, Debra Paget, John Lund, Noah Beery Jr, Hugh O'Brian*

THE WHITE NAVY
(aka 'La Nave Bianca') See **Man of the Cross**

THE WHITE SQUADRON (aka 'Lo Squadrone Bianco')
Augusto Genina — Italy, 1936
Italian expansionist propaganda, told in the fashion of British 'empire' films like **Lives of a Bengal Lancer**, where Italian occupiers in North Africa — with the help of the collaborators — put down rebel attacks.

WHO GOES NEXT? See **Captured**

WHY GERMANY MUST PAY See **Nurse Edith Cavell**

WHY WE FIGHT
Frank Capra and others — U.S., 1942-45
Celebrated series of feature-length 'orientation' documentaries aimed primarily at American audiences; the style and content were admired by both British and Russian cineastes and influenced the work of even the great Dovzhenko. More importantly, because of their palpably predisposed stance, they were accepted as great flagwavers by Allied servicemen and cinema audiences.

Using Allied and captured newsreel along with their own footage and intercut with diagrams, maps, etc, the pictures were put together with the skill you would expect from a team of movie heavyweights. Capra volunteered in December 1941 and the U.S. War Department had no hesitation in getting him to head the film department with the rank of major. The writer of most of the seven main features which made up the series, and some-time director, was Capt (then major) Anthony Veiller, whilst voice-overs were usually supplied by Walter Huston and the music by Dmitri Tiomkin. Some of the series, particularly the first, stand out in their own right as superb records of a global conflict. The seven main titles were:
Prelude to the War (Frank Capra, 1942)
Background to the Axis' political and territorial ambitions. Nominated for Best Documentary.
The Nazis Strike (Frank Capra/Anatole Litvak, 1942)
Early German aggression in late-1930s Europe.
Divide and Conquer (Frank Capra/Anatole Litvak, 1943)
Blitzkrieg, the German wedge between east and west, Dunkirk and de Gaulle.
The Battle of Britain (Anthony Veiller, 1943)
The preparation for the proposed German invasion of Britain.
The Battle of Russia (Anatole Litvak, 1943)
Excerpts from such great Soviet epics as Eisenstein's **Alexander Nevsky** and Petrov's **Peter the Great** embellish the eulogy to the Russian people. Nominated for Best Documentary.
The Battle of China (Frank Capra/Anatole Litvak, 1944)
Politically naive — the weakest of the series.
War Comes to America (Anatole Litvak, 1945)
How the war has changed American outlooks and attitudes.
Capra, leaving Litvak in charge in 1943, also produced a series of instructional documentaries on the other major players:
Know Your Ally: Britain (Anthony Veiller, 1943)
Know Your Enemy: Japan (Frank Capra/Joris Ivens, 1945)
Not released.
Know Your Enemy: Germany (Gottfried Reinhardt, 1945)

THE WIFE TAKES A FLYER (aka 'A Yank in Dutch')
Richard Wallace — U.S., 1942 [85min]
Unfunny WW2 farce of U.S. flyer shot down in Holland assuming the role of Bennett's institutionalized husband under the nose of a Nazi officer.
With *Joan Bennett, Franchot Tone*

THE WILD BLUE YONDER
(aka 'Thunder Across the Pacific')
Allan Dwan — U.S., 1952 [100min]
Tame tribute to the B-29 bomber undergoing routine heroics against the Japanese in WW2.
With *Wendell Corey, Forrest Tucker, Vera Ralston, Phil Harris, Walter Huston, Ruth Donnelly*

THE WILD BUNCH
Sam Peckinpah — U.S., 1969 [145min]
The one that closed the door on the Western of Ford and Hathaway, Walsh and Hawks — some say on the genre for ever. It would take another two decades for a 'new' type of Western to emerge with Kostner's environmentally-friendly **Dances with Wolves**. Arguably this is Peckinpah's best, and certainly most famous film, it is a violently poetic end-of-an-era homage to the ruthlessness of the period which would end with WW1.

Set in and around the Tex-Mex border of 1913, and with the Mexican Revolution in full swing, Holden's ageing gang of cut-throat robbers are being hunted for their bounties by Ryan and his rag-bag vermin in the pay of the railroad. Getting involved with gun-running, one of their number persuades Holden to skim off a case to defend his village against bandits and the German-influenced government forces. The effect is predictable, with the bloodiest finale of any film to that date (including *Bonnie and Clyde*), as the Federales wipe out the gang (as they did not in *Butch Cassidy and the Sundance Kid*, the up-beat Western classic of the same year).

Nominated for its script, in which the director also had a hand, and its Jerry Fielding score, the film is best remembered for Lucien Ballard's moving photography of a landscape half-forgotten, and the tired, bickering anti-heroes who belong to another age.
With *William Holden, Ernest Borgnine, Robert Ryan, Edmond O'Brien, Warren Oates, Ben Johnson, Jaime Sanchez, Strother Martin, L.Q. Jones*

THE WILD GEESE
See **The Mercenaries**

THE WILD WESTERNERS
Oscar Rudolph — U.S., 1962 [70min]
Another sub-standard U.S. Civil War adventure which involves bringing gold back East for the benefit of the Union — or at least for two fringe country/pop stars.
With *James Philbrook, Nancy Kovak, Duane Eddy, Guy Mitchell*

WILLIAM TELL (aka 'Guillaume Tell', 'Flammende Berge')
Michael Dickoff — Switzerland, 1960
Basic retelling of the famous half-legend — the so-called catalyst of Swiss nationhood, apple-splitting and all. Tradition has it that Tell refused to acknowledge the suzerainty of the Austrian occupiers (through the governor, Gessler) of his canton in 1291, escaped on his way to prison, ambushed Gessler and killed him.

Just like **Robin Hood** in English folklore, the legend developed a few centuries later: just as in England, the folk-hero became a figurehead of the people against injustice and oppression, and in this case led a national uprising.
With *Robert Freitag, Wolfgang Rott Sieper*

Other airings for William Tell include:
Schiller put the legend on stage in 1804: it was the subject of Rossini's 37th and last opera in 1829 — both incarnations coming at a time of great national upheaval in Europe.
British TV produced a series of adventures in the late 1950s, starring Conrad Phillips and Willoughby Goddard, *The Adventures of William Tell*, for no other motive than to provide companion series for the above-mentioned Earl of Loxley and his chum **Ivanhoe**.

THE WIND AND THE LION
★
★ *John Milius — U.S., 1975*
[120min]
Early piece of Milius sabre-rattling — and over-dramatizing the truth behind an incident so small it's hardly worth mentioning let alone filming.

In reality, U.S. finger-wagging, — no more — resulted in the release of hostages held by Riff rebels in 1904 Morocco. Milius, however, depicts hero-President Teddy Roosevelt sending a Marine landing force to North Africa to crack Connery's Berber nut. A force of German vultures are also on hand and the inevitable fire fight takes place, with you know who winning. Nominations for sound and Jerry Goldsmith (score).
With *Sean Connery, Candice Bergen, Brian Keith, John Huston*

THE WIND CANNOT READ
Ralph Thomas — GB, 1958
[115min]
Dreadful WW2 weepie involving an RAF officer who falls for a Japanese girl out Burma way. He gets incarcerated and tortured — rather like unsuspecting cinema audiences.
With *Dirk Bogarde, Yoko Tani, Ronald Lewis*

THE WINDING STAR See **Beau Geste** (1939)

WINDOM'S WAY
★
★ *Ronald Neame — GB, 1957* [110min]
Earnest attempt to say something intelligent about the 'Domino Principle' of one country falling to communism after another in South East Asia during the 1950s. Unfortunately it just comes across as another British colonial piece of melodramatic propaganda. Finch's doctor tries to show Malayan natives the error of communist ways and ends up attempting to stop an uprising.
With *Peter Finch, Mary Ure, Michael Hordern, Natasha Parry*

WING AND A PRAYER
★
★ *Henry Hathaway — U.S., 1944* [95min]
Sub-standard Hathaway actioner set aboard WW2 aircraft carrier. Cast do well with a distinctly ropey script.
With *Don Ameche, Dana Andrews, Richard Jaeckel, Charles Bickford, Cedric Hardwicke, Harry Morgan*

WINGED VICTORY
★
★ *George Cukor — U.S., 1944* [130min]
Unusual foray for 'women's director' Cukor (*Little Women, The Philadelphia Story, A Star is Born, My Fair Lady,* etc) into a WW2 action picture.

A competent account of young air force crews during training and into action.
With *Lon McCallister, Jeanne Crain, Edmond O'Brien, Jane Ball, Don Taylor, Lee J. Cobb, Red Buttons, Judy Holliday, Karl Malden, Martin Ritt*

WINGS
Panic among German troops when planes swoop in WW1 France.
Paramount (courtesy KOBAL)

WINGS
★
William Wellman — U.S., 1927 [135min] ★
Wellman's seminal WW1 air-war movie was raped and pillaged ★
by all and sundry over the following few years, but still stood ★
head and shoulders above its copies and competition. Its epic ★
scope and intuitive story-telling, combining with technically-unheard of stunts (the director flew with the **Lafayette Escadrille**), was a huge breakthrough for Hollywood.

Already **The Big Parade** and **What Price Glory?** had re-established the big war movie as box-office. Wellman's picture took the genre to another level. It won the Best Picture Oscar at the inaugural Academy Awards (and Best Engineering Effects, as it was called); showed that the 'It' girl Bow was more than a sex siren; and provided a career-making cameo for Cooper.

The slight story of two friends fighting with the U.S. air corps in 1918 France merely provides the thread which holds the aerial and ground battle set pieces together, until Rogers tragically downs Arlen by mistake.

Innovative at so many levels, this was Wellman's early, but most indelible mark on an industry he was to grace for another 30 years; paradoxically, it was also the last (but lasting) memorial to the great silent epic.
With *Clara Bow, Richard Arlen, Charles (Buddy) Rogers, Gary Cooper*

WINGS FOR THE EAGLE
Lloyd Bacon — U.S., 1942 [85min] ★
Stilted tribute to U.S. aircraft workers, which was more convincingly told in **Millions Like US** the following year.
With *Ann Sheridan, Dennis Morgan, Jack Carson*

WINGS OF THE HAWK
★ *Budd Boetticher — U.S., 1953* [80min]
★ 3-D bang-bang masquerading as an historical actioner based at the beginning of the troubles in Mexico in 1911. Not one of the director's best from a usually effective œuvre of Westerns. With *Van Heflin, Julie Adams*

WINSTANLEY
★ *Kevin Brownlow/Andrew Mollo — GB, 1975* [95min]
★ The team that made the WW2 invasion fantasy picture, **It Happened Here**, have gone in for straight historical reconstruction here. It's a re-enactment of Winstanley's proto-communist Diggers, objecting to private land-ownership in the middle of the English Civil War — until their 'commune' is dispersed by Roundhead troops. A lack-lustre attempt to portray the pioneer of a kind of radical thought that was to infect the whole world a century or so later. With *Miles Halliwell, Jerome Willis, Terry Higgins*

WIPING SOMETHING OFF THE SLATE
See **The Call to Arms**

WITCHFINDER GENERAL (aka 'The Conqueror Worm')
★ *Michael Reeves — GB, 1968* [85min]
★ Reeves died within two years of making this well-studied
★ historical narrative, aged only 25; and shows enough talent
★ here for us to mourn such an early death.

   The film depicts the infamous Matthew Hopkins riding across a bleak landscape during the English Civil War. He preys on the superstitions of the common men and women, whose brains have been manipulated by five years of family-against-family, neighbour-versus-neighbour conflict. In some ways, it is a minor classic of the British horror genre — and no less a valid insight into the religio-sadistic sideshows of war. With *Vincent Price, Ian Ogilvy, Rupert Davies, Patrick Wymark, Wilfrid Brambell*

WITH THE MARINES AT TARAWA
See *Tarawa Beachhead*

THE WOMAN BETWEEN
See **The Woman I Love**

THE WOMAN FROM MONTE CARLO
★ *Michael Curtiz — U.S., 1932* [70min]
★ Remade from Alexander Korda's silent **The Night Watch ★** (1928), with Billie Dove and Paul Lukas, about love aboard ship before it is sunk by Germans in WW1, and the resulting trial for negligence of the captain. Not really worth one version, never mind two. With *Lil Dagova, Walter Huston*

THE WOMAN I LOVE
★ (aka 'L'Equipage', 'The Woman Between')
★ *Anatole Litvak — U.S., 1937* [85min]
Remake by Litvak of his own French update, **L'Equipage ★★** (1935 — with Charles Vanel and Jean-Pierre Aumont) of Maurice Tourneur's 1927 ★★ original starring Georges Charlia and Claire de Lorez. Eccentrically remade for the fourth time by Alexandre Mitta, with Giorgiu Jionov and Anatoli Vassiliev, in 1980, in Russian, did this mawkish WW1 weepie involving French flyers warrant so much celluloid? With *Paul Muni, Miriam Hopkins, Louis Hayward*

THE WOMAN THE GERMANS SHOT
See **Nurse Edith Cavell**

WOMEN IN BONDAGE
Steve Sekely — U.S., 1943 [70min]
Risible exploitation piece about the Nazis' abuse of women in subjugated nations during WW2. With *Gail Patrick, Nancy Kelly*

WOMEN IN WAR
John H. Auer — U.S., 1942 [70min]
Utter rubbish about socialite female doing her bit as a nurse for Uncle Sam. Early U.S. flagwaver strictly for Americans. With *Elsie Janis, Wendy Barrie, Patric Knowles, Mae Clarke*

WONG FEI HUNG See **Once upon a Time in China**

WOODEN CROSSES See **Les Croix de Bois**

THE WOODEN HORSE
Jack Lee — GB, 1950 [100min] ★
The near-classic British escape picture; moving on from the ★
more strictly documentary approach of the **Captive Heart**, to ★
set the trend for the POW dramas of the next decade and a bit, ★
and culminating in **The Great Escape**.

   Here the public school dorm replaces the unpalatable squalor and degradation of the reality of POW life, and the whole thing is treated rather like a sporting event — anything to put one over on (the always mentally sub-normal) 'Fritz'.

   The famous vaulting horse exercise scenes camouflaging the escape attempt, although in themselves quite tense at times, dominate the picture; its failing is that there aren't enough sub-plot diversions, and the stereotypes are too rigid to make it a truly great war film. With *Leo Genn, David Tomlinson, Anthony Steel, Bryan Forbes, Bill Travers*

THE WOODEN HORSE OF TROY See **The Trojan War**

THE WOODEN HORSE
Leo Genn (centre) co-ordinating escape plans. British Lion/London/Wessex

YANGTSE INCIDENT
(aka 'Battle Hell', 'Escape of the *Amethyst*')
Michael Anderson — GB, 1957 [115min]
Dull exposition of an interesting incident, about the frigate HMS *Amethyst* bombarded by Mao's communist forces when supposedly minding its own business on the Yangtse River in 1949.
With *Richard Todd, William Hartnell, Akim Tamiroff, Donald Houston*

A YANK IN DUTCH See **The Wife Takes a Flyer**

A YANK IN INDO-CHINA
Wallace A. Grissell — U.S., 1952 [65min]
American mercenary pilots, not having had enough of recent conflicts, go in against the Viet Minh. Pretty desperate stuff.
With *John Archer, Douglas Dick*

A YANK IN KOREA
Lew Landers — U.S., 1951 [75min]
What we have come to expect from Landers: borrowed plot, borrowed script, borrowed sets, borrowed footage; to sum up — the original Korean War stinker.
With *Lon McCallister, William Phillips*

A YANK IN THE RAF
Henry King — U.S., 1941 [100min]
British-influenced flagwaver sees Power join the RAF after bumping into old flame Grable in London in 1940. Adventures include the evacuation at **Dunkirk**, and upper lips were never stiffer. Amusing yet hollow entertainment.
With *Tyrone Power, Betty Grable, John Sutton*

A YANK IN VIET-NAM (aka 'Year of the Tiger')
Marshall Thompson — U.S., 1964 [80min]
Set in the days when the country was hyphenated — both geo-politically and apparently grammatically — and the U.S. were in Saigon in an 'advisory' capacity. Here a major from the Green Berets, whose helicopter is downed by the Vietcong, joins South Vietnamese guerrillas in a particularly grubby exploitation piece from a conflict which, in time, would throw up more than its fair share.
With *Marshall Thompson, Enrique Magalona*

A YANK ON THE BURMA ROAD
(aka 'China Caravan') *George B. Seitz — U.S., 1942* [65min]
Dreadful cornball of WW2 heroics when a driver of medical supplies witnesses Japanese atrocities in China. One of the first films released after Pearl Harbor.
With *Barry Nelson, Laraine Day*

YANKEE PASHA See **The Barbary Pirate**

YANKS
John Schlesinger — GB, 1979 [140min]

Schlesinger's attention to period detail helps hold together this tedious tale of WW2 romances between north of England girls, and GIs stationed in Britain awaiting Operation Overlord. Roberts won a BAFTA as supporting actress.
With *Vanessa Redgrave, Richard Gere, William Devane, Rachel Roberts, Lisa Eichhorn*

THE YEAR OF LIVING DANGEROUSLY
Peter Weir — Australia, 1982 [115min]
Rescuing Gibson from almost certain death in **Gallipoli**, Weir now dumps him as a war correspondent in 1965 Indonesia, and into the middle of a coup against Sukarno. Superficial in its politics, the film works quite well as a romantic adventure, but no deeper. Hunt won the Best Supporting Actress Oscar — in a male role.
With *Mel Gibson, Sigourney Weaver, Linda Hunt, Michael Murphy, Bill Kerr*

YANKS
A new batch of GIs arrive in industrial Lancashire. UA/CIP

YEAR OF THE TIGER See **A Yank in Viet-Nam**

YELLOW CANARY
Herbert Wilcox — GB, 1943 [95min]
Better-than-average WW2 espionage drama, with some tense moments, as English socialite Neagle, in probably her least-saintly role, does her bit (allusions of some nooky with the Führer, no less!) for Britain.
With *Anna Neagle, Richard Greene, Nova Pilbeam, Cyril Fletcher, Margaret Rutherford*

YESTERDAY'S ENEMY
Val Guest — GB, 1959 [95min]
In this unjustly-overlooked film version of a TV play, Baker perpetrates the unthinkable un-British act — a war crime. In 1942 Burma, a British patrol discover some Japanese plans,

but no code for them. Baker carries out his threat to kill two villagers when his Japanese prisoner refuses to convey it. Baker's conscience is articulated by the talk and actions of his squad, until they themselves are captured, and die withholding the same kind of information. Baker is outstanding at the head of an impressive ensemble, and although the whole thing is studio-bound the menace of the jungle is omnipresent.
With *Stanley Baker, Guy Rolfe, Leo McKern, Gordon Jackson, Bryan Forbes*

YOU AND OTHER COMRADES
See **The German Story**

YOU, ME AND MARLEY
Graham Veevers — GB, 1992 [90min]
BBC film shown as a theatre release at the Edinburgh Festival — a reasonably assured attempt to deal with the Irish troubles in microcosm, as a group of joy-riding youths irritate the IRA.
With *Marc O'Shea, Bronagh Gallagher, Michael Liebmann*

YOUNG DANIEL BOONE See **Daniel Boone**

YOUNG EAGLES
William Wellman — U.S., 1930 [70min]
Using some used and unused stock from **Wings**, Wellman tried to repeat the success in sound. By 1930, however, the world had already seen **Hell's Angels**, **Dawn Patrol**, **Sky Hawk**, **Lilac Time** and Wellman's own **Legion of the Condemned**; the effect of this WW1 war-in-the-air-action-espionage-romantic drama was thus somewhat diluted, and convoluted.
With *Charles (Buddy) Rogers, Jean Arthur, Paul Lukas*

THE YOUNG LIONS
Edward Dmytryk — U.S., 1958 [165min]
A slow-moving but always absorbing adaptation of Irwin Shaw's book about three soldiers — two American, one German — who take up arms against each other in WW2.

At just under three hours the episodic, interwoven triptych manages to hold attention, particularly in the Brando (German) action scenes in North Africa (could there have been a more stereotypical Panzer commander with that short-cropped blond hair?). Brando's and Martin's characters knew each other from skiing before the war; and the fusion of the three is complete when Clift, a Jew, is drafted alongside Martin, and they become firm friends. The paths of all three eventually cross near a concentration camp in 1945, when the irony is finally played out. Oscar nominations for cinematography (Joe MacDonald), score (Hugo Friedhofer), and sound.
With *Marlon Brando, Montgomery Clift, Barbara Rush, Lee van Cleef, Maximilian Schell, Dean Martin, Hope Lange, Mae Britt,*

THE YOUNG MR PITT
Carol Reed — GB, 1942 [120min]
WW2 propaganda piece in the sheep's clothing of the Napoleonic invasion threat some 140 years earlier. Script lacks the structure one would expect from Launder and Gilliat. Interesting in its concept of a primeval Churchillian character and its cast — with Lom at 25 having his first stab at Bonaparte (see **War and Peace**).
With *Robert Donat, Robert Morley, Phyllis Calvert, John Mills, Max Adrian, Felix Aylmer, Raymond Lovell, Stephen Haggard, Herbert Lom*

YOUNG WINSTON
Richard Attenborough — GB, 1972 [155min]
Straightforward approach by Attenborough, after **Oh! What a Lovely War**, to this biopic of Churchill's early career as soldier, then war reporter: before he stood for Parliament for the first time, he was already a public figure at 25. Having served in India, we pick up his African adventures in the Sudan; then on to South Africa, and his escape from the Boers.

The battle scenes are well done, particularly the charge of the 21st Lancers at Omdurman, and are the best parts of what is a disappointingly superficial look at an already extraordinary human being. Starry cast again turned out for Dickie.
With *Simon Ward, John Mills, Anne Bancroft, Robert Shaw, Jack Hawkins, Ian Holm, Anthony Hopkins, Edward Woodward, Peter Cellier, Ronald Hines, Dino Shafeek, Pat Heywood, Laurence Naismith, Patrick Magee*

THE YOUNGEST SPY See **Ivan's Childhood**

YOU'RE IN THE ARMY NOW See **OHMS**

YOU'RE IN THE NAVY NOW (aka 'USS Teakettle')
Henry Hathaway — U.S., 1951 [95min]
Stewed brew of USN patrol vessel having steam turbines installed (hence the nick-name); and Cooper is uneasy in this creaky WW2 comedy-adventure. Of interest for the debuts of Marvin and Bronson.
With *Gary Cooper, Jane Greer, Millard Mitchell, Eddie Albert, John McIntyre, Ray Collins, Jack Webb, Lee Marvin, Charles Buchinski (Bronson)*

YPRES
See *The Battles of the Coronel and the Falkland Islands*

YUKI YUKITE SHINGUN
See *The Emperor's Naked Army Marches On*

ZARAK
Terence Young — GB, 1956 [100min]
A reasonable rehash of the 1930s 'empire' pictures, but unforgivable in spawning a mini-revival which produced much mindless guff (**The Bandit of Zhobe** and **The Stranglers of Bombay**, for example). North-West frontier action is OK.
With *Victor Mature, Michael Wilding, Anita Eckberg, Bernard Miles*

ZBEHOVIA A POUTNICI
See **The Deserter and the Nomads**

ZEEBRUGGE See **The Battle of Jutland**

ZEPPELIN
Etienne Perier — GB, 1971 [95min]
Goodish action and novel effects spark this somewhat old-fashioned WW1 espionage drama. York is the German-born British flyer with mixed emotions, as secrets are stolen from the Zeppelin factory at Friedrichshafen.
With *Michael York, Elke Sommer, Peter Carsten, Marius Goring, Anton Diffring, Rupert Davies*

THE ZEPPELIN'S LAST RAID
Thomas Ince — U.S., 1917
A German flyer of Zeppelins refuses to bomb 'a city' as

ordered, then joins the Legion of Liberty in this, another piece of pacifistic propaganda from Ince (see **Civilization**). With *Howatrd Hickman*

ZHONGHUA NUER See **Daughters of China**

ZORRO (and a list of variants)
See **The Mark of Zorro** (1920)

ZULU
Cy Endfield — GB, 1964 [135min]
War-movie buffs' treat, as the savagely staged Battle of Rorke's Drift — surely just about the most tension-filled 20 minutes or so of cinema action ever filmed before **Saving Private Ryan** — leaves the audience (even after multiple viewings) limp and in a cold sweat. Co-producers Endfield and Baker had the dickens of a job to explain to the native extras what they were trying to achieve — a feat they actually managed only through showing them an old Western. They then made up for lost time.

The attack on the tiny mission station and hospital at Rorke's Drift immediately followed Zulu chief Cetawayo's massacre of British troops at Isandlwana in January 1879 — when some 20,000 warriors overwhelmed about 1,300 British troops and African irregulars, including most of the 24th Regiment — a sort of 'afters' to complement the Zulus' main course. In several sorties some 400 Zulus were killed by the stout defence of 139 men, mostly South Wales Borderers, who

had 25 causalties, and they were eventually repelled. 11 VCs were awarded — still the greatest number for any one action.

Baker shares the acting honours with Caine (in his first leading role), as the lieutenants who mastermind the defence; and with Green, in a definitive portrait of the old-time British regular NCO.
With *Stanley Baker, Michael Caine, Jack Hawkins, Ulla Jacobsson, James Booth, Nigel Green, Ivor Emmanuel, Paul Daneman, Glynn Edwards, Neil McCarthy*

The Battle of Isandlwana is the high spot of Douglas Hickox's otherwise disappointing 1978 prequel, **Zulu Dawn ★★** — co-written again by Enfield — with Burt Lancaster, Denholm Elliott, Peter O'Toole, John Mills and Simon Ward.

ZULU DAWN See **Zulu**

ZULU
Do I feel 'Men of Harlech' coming on? Ivor Emmanuel (left) gets ready to lead the chorus. Paramount/Diamond

Note: an asterisk in front of a film title — eg *Intolerance — indicates
that the film is covered in the first, A–Z section of this book.

PRE-CLASSICAL ANTIQUITY FROM 3500BC
David and Goliath   *Richard Pottier — ITA, 1961*
The Emperor's Shadow   *Zhou Xia Owen — CHI/HK, 1996*
*Intolerance   *D. W. Griffith — U.S., 1916*
Land of the Pharaohs   *Howard Hawks — US, 1955*
*Le Mahabharata   *Peter Brook — FRA, 1989*
The Pharaoh   *Jerzy Kawalerowicz — POL, 1966*
Solomon and Sheba   *King Vidor — U.S., 1959*

ANCIENT GREEK   C1300BC–350BC
*Alexander the Great   *Robert Rossen — U.S., 1956*
*The Colossus of Rhodes   *Sergio Leone — ITA, 1960*
*The Giant of Marathon   *Jacques Tourneur — FRA/ITA, 1959*
*Helen of Troy   *Robert Wise — U.S., 1955*
*The 300 Spartans   *Rudolph Mate — U.S., 1962*
*The Trojan War   *Georgio Ferroni — FRA/ITA, 1961*
*The Trojan Women   *Michael Cacoyannis — U.S., 1971*

JULIUS CAESAR
Action from the Battle of Philippi in the 1953 version. MGM

ROMAN   C350BC–450AD
*Antony and Cleopatra   *Charlton Heston — GB/SPA/SWI, 1972*
*Aphrodite, Goddess of Love   *Mario Bonnard — ITA, 1958*
*Attila the Hun   *Pietro Fancisci — FRA/ITA, 1954*
*The Battle of Corinth   *Mario Costa — ITA, 1962*
*Ben-Hur   *Fred Niblo — U.S., 1926*
*Ben-Hur   *William Wyler — U.S., 1959*
*Carthage in Flames   *Carmine Gallone — ITA, 1960*
*Cleopatra   *Cecil B. De Mille — U.S., 1934*
*Cleopatra   *Joseph L. Mankiewicz — U.S., 1963*
*Coriolanus — Hero Without a Country   *Georgio Ferroni —
    FRA/ITA, 1965*
*The Fall of the Roman Empire   *Anthony Mann — U.S., 1964*
*Hannibal   *Carlo Ludivico Bragaglia/Edgar G. Ulmer — ITA,
    1959*
*Julius Caesar   *Joseph L. Mankiewicz — U.S., 1953*
*Julius Caesar   *Stuart Burge — GB, 1969*
*The Legions of Cleopatra   *Vittorio Cottafavi — ITA, 1959*
The Revolt of the Praetorians   *Alfonso Brescia — ITA, 1964*
Rome Against Rome   *Giuseppe Vari — ITA, 1963*
*Scipio Africanus   *Carmine Gallone — ITA, 1937*
Sebastiane   *Paul Humfress/Derek Jarman — GB, 1976*
*Serpent of the Nile   *William Castle — U.S., 1953*
*The Siege of Syracuse   *Pietro Francisci — ITA, 1959*
Sign of the Gladiator   *Guido Brignone /Riccardo Freda —
    FRA/FRG/ITA, 1959*
*The Sign of the Pagan   *Douglas Sirk — U.S., 1954*
Son of Spartacus   *Sergio Corbucci — ITA, 1963*
*Spartacus   *Stanley Kubrick — U.S., 1960*
*Spartacus the Gladiator   *Riccardo Freda — ITA, 1953*
*The Viking Queen   *Don Chaffey — GB, 1967*

THE DARK AGES   C450–1000AD
*Alfred the Great   *Clive Donner — GB, 1969*
*La Chanson De Roland   *Frank Cassenti — FRA, 1978*
*Erik the Conqueror   *Mario Bava — ITA, 1963*
*Excalibur   *John Boorman — U.S., 1981*
*First Knight   *Jerry Zucker — U.S., 1995*
*Goliath and the Barbarians   *Carlo Campogalliani — ITA/U.S.,
    1959*
*Knights of the Round Table   *Richard Thorpe — U.S., 1953*
*Lancelot and Guinevere   *Cornel Wolde — GB, 1962*
*Lancelot Du Lac   *Robert Bresson — FRA/ITA, 1974*
*Mohammed, Messenger of God   *Moustapha Akkad — LEB,
    1976*
The Paladins   *Giacomo Battiato — ITA, 1983*
*Prince Valiant   *Henry Hathaway — U.S., 1954*
*Prince Valiant   *Anthony Hickox — GER/GB/IRE/U.S. 1994*
Roland and the Paladins of France   *Pietri Francisci — ITA,
    1956*

*Siege of the Saxons   *Nathan Juran — GB, 1963*
*The Thirteenth Warrior   *John McTiernan — U.S., 1999*
*The Vikings   *Richard Fleischer — U.S., 1958*

THE MIDDLE AGES   C1000–1500

*The Adventures of Robin Hood   *Michael Curtiz/William Keighley — U.S., 1938*
*Alexander Nevsky   *Sergei Eisenstein — USSR, 1938*
*The Bandit of Sherwood Forest   *George Sherman/Henry Levin — U.S., 1946*
*The Black Arrow   *Gordon Douglas — U.S., 1948*
*The Black Shield of Falworth   *Rudolph Mate — U.S., 1954*
*The Beloved Vagabond   *Alan Crosland — U.S., 1928*
*Braveheart   *Mel Gibson — U.S., 1995*
*Chimes at Midnight   *Orson Welles — SPA/SWI, 1966*
*El Cid   *Anthony Mann — Ita/U.S., 1961*
*The Conqueror   *Dick Powell — U.S., 1955*
*The Conquest of Albania   *Alfonso Ungria — SPA, 1982*
*The Crusades   *Cecil B. De Mille — U.S., 1935*
*The Dark Avenger   *Henry Levin — GB, 1955*
The Fate of Lee Khan   *King Hu — HK, 1973*
*The Flame and the Arrow   *Jacques Tourneur — U.S., 1950*
Flavia the Heretic   *Gianfranco Mingozzi — FRA/ITA, 1974*
*1492: Conquest of Paradise   *Ridley Scott — U.S., 1992*
Gate of Hell   *Teinosuke Kinugasa — JAP, 1953*
*Genghis Khan   *Henry Levin — U.S., 1964*
*The Golden Horde   *George Sherman — U.S., 1951*
*Henry V   *Laurence Olivier — GB, 1944*
*Henry V   *Kenneth Branagh — GB, 1989*
*If I Were King   *J. Gordon Edwards — U.S., 1920*
*If I Were King   *Frank Lloyd — U.S., 1938*
*Ivanhoe   *Richard Thorpe — GB/U.S., 1952*
*Jeanne La Pucelle: Parts I and II   *Jacques Rivette — FRA, 1994*
*Joan of Arc   *Victor Fleming — U.S., 1948*
*Joan the Woman   *Cecil B. De Mille — U.S., 1916*
*King Richard and the Crusaders   *David Butler — U.S., 1954*
*Kings of the Sun   *J. Lee Thompson — U.S., 1963*
*Knights of the Teutonic Order   *Aleksander Ford — POL, 1960*
Kuroneko   *Kaneto Shindo — JAP, 1968*
*Lionheart   *Franklin J. Schaffner — U.S., 1987*
*The Long Ships   *Jack Cardiff — GB/YUG, 1963*
*Looking for Richard   *Al Pacino — U.S., 1996*
Lucrezia Borgia   *Abel Gance — FRA, 1935*
*Macbeth   *Orson Welles — U.S., 1948*
*Macbeth   *Roman Polanski — GB, 1972*
*Men of Sherwood Forest   *Val Guest — GB, 1954*
The Miracle of the Wolves   *Andre Hunebelle — FRA, 1962*
Our Lady of the Turks   *Carmelo Bene — ITA, 1968*
*La Passion De Jeanne D'Arc   *Carl Dreyer — FRA, 1928*
*Prince of Thieves   *Howard Bretherton — U.S., 1948*
Princess of the Nile   *Harmon Jones — U.S., 1954*
*Quentin Durward   *Richard Thorpe — GB, 1955*
*Richard the Lionhearted   *Chet Webey — U.S., 1923*
*Richard III   *Laurence Olivier — GB, 1955*
*Richard III   *Richard Loncraine — GB, 1995*
*Robin and Marion   *Richard Lester — U.S., 1976*
*Robin Hood   *Allan Dwan — U.S., 1922*
*Robin Hood   *John Irvin — U.S., 1991*
*Robin Hood: Prince of Thieves   *Kevin Reynolds — U.S., 1991*
*Rogues of Sherwood Forest   *Gordon Douglas — U.S., 1950*
*Saint Joan   *Otto Preminger — GB, 1957*
*Saladin   *Youssef Chahine — EGY, 1963*

Sansho the Bailiff   *Kenji Mizoguchi — JAP, 1954*
*The Saracen Blade   *William Castle — U.S., 1954*
The Seventh Seal   *Ingmar Bergman — SWE, 1956*
*Son of Robin Hood   *George Sherman — GB, 1958*
*The Story of Robin Hood and His Merrie Men   *Ken Annakin — GB, 1952*
The Sword of El Cid   *Miguel Iglesias — SPA, 1962*
*The Sword of Sherwood Forest   *Terence Fisher — GB, 1961*
*The Tartars   *Richard Thorpe — ITA, 1960*
*This England   *David Macdonald — GB, 1941*
*Throne of Blood   *Akira Kurosawa — JAP, 1957*
Le Tournoi   *Jean Renoir — FRA, 1928*
*Tower of London   *Rowland V. Lee — U.S., 1939*
*Tower of London   *Roger Corman — U.S., 1962*
*The Trial of Joan of Arc   *Robert Bresson — FRA, 1962*
A Walk With Love and Death   *John Huston — U.S., 1969*
*The War Lord   *Franklin Schaffner — U.S., 1965*
*William Tell   *Michel Dickoff — SWI, 1960*
Yojimbo   *Akira Kurosawa — JAP, 1961 Toho*

THE HUNDRED YEARS' WAR, 1337–1457

*Chimes at Midnight   *Orson Welles — SPA/SWI, 1966*
*Henry V   *Laurence Olivier — GB, 1944*
*Henry V   *Kenneth Branagh — GB, 1989*
*Jeanne La Pucelle: Parts I and II   *Jacques Rivette — FRA, 1994*
*Joan of Arc   *Victor Fleming — U.S., 1948*
*Joan the Woman   *Cecil B. De Mille — U.S., 1916*
Love, Soldiers and Women   *FRA/ITA, 1953*

CHIMES AT MIDNIGHT

The aftermath of the bloody Battle of Shrewsbury; and time for contemplation for the future Henry V, Prince Hal (Keith Baxter). Int Films Espanola-Alpine Prods (courtesy KOBAL)

AGUIRRE, WRATH OF GOD
Jungle horrors for those seeking El Dorado. Hessicher Rundfunk

*La Passion De Jeanne D'Arc   *Carl Dreyer — FRA, 1928*
*Saint Joan   *Otto Preminger — GB, 1957*
*The Trial of Joan of Arc   *Robert Bresson — FRA, 1962*
A Walk With Love and Death   *John Huston — U.S., 1969*

THE WARS OF THE ROSES, 1455–85
*The Black Arrow   *Gordon Douglas — U.S., 1948*
*The Dark Avenger   *Henry Levin — GB, 1955*
*Looking for Richard   *Al Pacino — U.S., 1996*
*Quentin Durward   *Richard Thorpe — GB, 1955*
*Richard III   *Laurence Olivier — GB, 1955*
*Richard III   *Richard Loncraine — GB, 1995*
*Tower of London   *Rowland V. Lee — U.S., 1939*
*Tower of London   *Roger Corman — U.S., 1962*

THE 16TH CENTURY
*Aguirre, Wrath of God   *Werner Hertzog — FRG, 1972*
*Les Aventures De Till L'Espiegle   *Gerard Phillipe — FRA,
1956*
*Cabeza De Vaca   *Nicolas Echevarria — MEX/SPA, 1990*
*Captain From Castile   *Henry King — U.S., 1947*
The Captive God   *Charles Swickard — U.S., 1916*
Cervantes   *Vincent Sherman — FRA/ITA/SPA, 1968*
*El Dorado   *Carlos Saura — FRA/SPA, 1988*
*Drake of England   *Arthur Woods — GB, 1935*
*The Fighting Prince of Donegal   *Michael O'Herlihy — GB,
1966*
*Fire Over England   *William K. Howard — GB, 1936*
*1492: Conquest of Paradise   *Ridley Scott — U.S., 1992*
*Hearts and Armour   *Giacomo Battiato — ITA, 1982*
*Hiawatha   *Kurt Neumann — U.S., 1952*
*The Hidden Fortress   *Akira Kurosawa — JAP, 1958*
Homeland   *Louis Daquin — FRA, 1945*
*In the Palace of the King   *Fred E. Wright — U.S., 1915*
*In the Palace of the King   *Emmett Flynn — U.S., 1923*
*Ivan the Terrible, Parts I and II   *Sergei Eisenstein — USSR,
1945, 1958*
*Kagemusha   *Akira Kurasawa — JAP, 1980*

*La Kermesse Heroique   *Jacques Feyder — FRA, 1935*
Lucrezia Borgia   *Abel Gance — FRA, 1935*
Prince of Foxes   *Henry King — U.S., 1949*
Quilombo   *Carlos Diegues — BRA, 1984*
*Ran   *Akiro Kurosawa — JAP, 1985*
*The Rebel Son   *Alexis Granowsky/Adrian Brunel — GB, 1939*
*La Reine Margot   *Jean Dreville — FRA, 1954*
*La Reine Margot   *Patrice Chereau — FRA/GER/ITA, 1994*
*La Retour De Martin Guerre   *Daniel Vigne — FRA, 1982*
*The Royal Hunt of the Sun   *Irving Lerner — GB, 1969*
*The Sea Hawk   *Frank Lloyd — U.S., 1924*
*The Sea Hawk   *Michael Curtiz — U.S., 1940*
*Seven Seas To Calais   *Rudolph Mate — ITA/U.S., 1962*
Suleman the Magnificent   *Mario Tota — ITA, 1961*
The Swordsman of Siena   *Etienne Perier — ITA, 1961*
*Taras Bulba   *Alexis Granowsky — FRA, 1936*
*Taras Bulba   *J. Lee Thompson — U.S., 1962 UA*
*This England   *David Macdonald — GB, 1941*
Ugetsu Monogatari   *Kenji Mizoguchi — JAP, 1953*
The Virgin Queen   *Henry Koster — U.S., 1955*
The Woman God Forgot   *Cecil B. De Mille — U.S., 1917*

THE 17TH CENTURY
*Against All Flags   *Gerorge Marshall — U.S., 1952*
*Beach of the War Gods   *Wang Yu — HK, 1972*
*Les Camisards   *Rene Allio — FRA, 1972*
*Captain Blood   *David Smith — U.S., 1924*
*Captain Blood   *Michael Curtiz — U.S., 1935*
Cardinal Richelieu   *Rowland V. Lee — U.S., 1935*
*Cromwell   *Ken Hughes — GB, 1970*
Dangerous Maid   *Victor Heerman — U.S., 1923*
The Deluge   *Jerzy Hoffman — POL, 1974*
*The Exile   *Max Ophuls — U.S., 1947*
*The Gallant Blade   *Henry Levin — U.S., 1948*
Georgi Saakhadze   *Mikhail Chiaureli — USSR, 1942*
The Golden Hawk   *Sidney Salkow — U.S., 1952*
*La Kermesse Heroique   *Jacques Feyder — FRA, 1935*
*The Last Valley   *James Clavell — GB, 1970*
*The Moonraker   *David Macdonald — GB, 1957*
*Peter the Great   *Vladimir Petrov — USSR, 1937*
    *Scaramouche   *Rex Ingram — U.S., 1923*
*Scaramouche   *George Sidney — U.S., 1952*
*The Scarlet Blade   *John Gilling — GB, 1963*
Seven Cities of Gold   *Robert D. Webb — U.S., 1955*
Stronger Than the Storm   *Jerzy Hoffman — POL, 1974*
A Touch of Zen   *King Hu — TAI, 1969*
Under the Red Robe   *Victor Sjostrom — U.S., 1937*
Ursus and the Tartar Princess   *Remigo Del Grosso — FRA/ITA,
1961*
The Valiant Ones   *King Hu — HK, 1974*
*The Vicar of Bray   *Henry Edwards — GB, 1937*
*Winstanley   *Kevin Brownlow — GB, 1975*
*Witchfinder General   *Michael Reeves — GB, 1968*

THE THIRTY YEARS' WAR, 1618–48
*Cardinal Richelieu   *Rowland V. Lee — U.S., 1935*
The Deluge   *Jerzy Hoffman — POL, 1974*
*The Gallant Blade   *Henry Levin — U.S., 1948*
*The Last Valley   *James Clavell — GB, 1970*
Stronger Than the Storm   *Jerzy Hoffman — POL, 1974*
Under the Red Robe   *Victor Sjostrom — U.S., 1937*

THE ENGLISH CIVIL WARS, 1642–92
*Captain Blood   *David Smith* — U.S., 1924
*Captain Blood   *Michael Curtiz* — U.S., 1935
*Cromwell   *Ken Hughes* — GB, 1970
Dangerous Maid   *Victor Heerman* — U.S., 1923
*The Exile   *Max Ophuls* — U.S., 1947
*The Moonraker   *David Macdonald* — GB, 1957
*The Scarlet Blade   *John Gilling* — GB, 1963
*The Vicar of Bray   *Henry Edwards* — GB, 1937
*Winstanley   *Kevin Brownlow* — GB, 1975
*Witchfinder General   *Michael Reeves* — GB, 1968

THE 18TH CENTURY
THE WAR OF THE SPANISH SUCCESSION, 1701–14
*The Fortunes of Captain Blood   *Gordon Douglas* — U.S., 1950
*General Crack   *Alan Crosland* — U.S., 1929
Me and Marlborough   *Victor Saville* — GB, 1935
*The Son of Captain Blood   *Tulio Demicheli* — ITA/SPA, 1961

RUSSIA IN THE 18TH CENTURY
*Catherine the Great   *Paul Czinner* — GB, 1934
*Peter the Great   *Vladimir Petrov* — USSR, 1937
*The Scarlet Empress   *Josef Von Sternberg* — U.S., 1934

THE JACOBITE REBELLIONS, 1715 AND 1745
*Bonnie Prince Charlie   *Anthony Kimmins* — GB, 1948
*Chasing the Deer   *Graham Holloway* — GB, 1994
The Iron Glove   *William Castle* — U.S., 1954
*The Master of Ballantrae   *William Keighley* — GB, 1953
*Rob Roy   *Michael Caton-Jones* — U.S., 1995
*Rob Roy the Highland Rogue   *Harold French* — GB, 1953

THE WAR OF THE AUSTRIAN SUCCESSION, 1740–48
*The Adventures of Casanova   *Roberto Gavaldon* — U.S., 1948
*A Celebrated Case   *George Melford* — U.S., 1914

THE SEVEN YEARS' WAR, FRENCH AND INDIAN WARS, THIRD SILESIAN WAR, 1754–63
*Allegheny Uprising   *William A. Seiter* — U.S., 1939
*Barry Lyndon   *Stanley Kubrick* — GB, 1975
*The Battles of Chief Pontiac   *Felix Feist* — U.S., 1952
*Cardigan   *John W. Noble* — U.S., 1922
*The Chorale of Leuthen   *Carl Froelich* — GER, 1933
*Clive of India   *Richard Boleslawski* — U.S., 1934
*Daniel Boone   *David Howard* — U.S., 1936
*Daniel Boone, Trail Blazer   *Albert C. Gannaway/Ismael Rodriguez* — U.S., 1956
*Drums Along the Mohawk   *John Ford* — U.S., 1939
Fanfan the Tulip   *Christian-Jaque* — FRA, 1952
*The Flame of Calcutta   *Seymour Friedman* — U.S., 1953
*Fort Ti   *William Castle* — U.S., 1953
*Fridericus   *Johannes Meyer* — GER, 1936
*The Great King   *Veit Harlan* — GER, 1942
*The Iroquois Trail   *Phil Karlson* — U.S., 1950
*The Last of the Mohicans   *Maurice Tourneur* — U.S., 1920
*The Last of the Mohicans   *George B. Seitz* — U.S., 1936
*The Last of the Mohicans   *Michael Mann* — U.S., 1992
*Last of the Redmen   *George Sherman* — U.S., 1947
*Mohawk   *Kurt Neumann* — U.S., 1956
*Northwest Passage   *King Vidor* — U.S., 1940
*The Pathfinder   *Sidney Salkow* — U.S., 1952

*Unconquered   *Cecil B. De Mille* — U.S., 1947
*Washington Under the British Flag — U.S., 1916
*When the Redskins Rode   *Lew Landers* — U.S., 1951
Winners of the Wilderness   *W. S. Van Dyke* — U.S., 1927
*Young Daniel Boone   *Reginald Leborg* — U.S., 1950

AMERICAN REVOLUTIONARY WAR, 1775–81
*America   *D. W. Griffith* — U.S., 1924
Beaumarchais   *Edouard Molinaro* — FRA, 1996
Betsy Ross   *George Cowl/Travers Yale* — U.S., 1917
*Cardigan   *John W. Noble* — U.S., 1922
*Daniel Boone, Trail Blazer   *Albert C. Gannaway/Ismael Rodriguez* — U.S., 1957
*The Devil's Disciple   *Guy Hamilton* — GB, 1959
*Drums Along the Mohawk   *John Ford* — U.S., 1939
*Heart of a Hero   *Emile Chautard* — U.S., 1916
*The Howards of Virginia   *Frank Lloyd* — U.S., 1940
Janice Meredith   *Mason Hopper* — U.S., 1924
Jefferson in Paris   *James Ivory* — U.S., 1995
*John Paul Jones   *John Farrow* — U.S., 1959
*Johnny Tremain   *Robert Stevenson* — U.S., 1957
*Lafayette   *Jean Dreville* — FRA/ITA, 1961
My Own United States   *John W. Noble* — U.S., 1918
*The Pursuit of Happiness   *Alexander Hall* — U.S., 1934
*Revolution   *Hugh Hudson* — GB/U.S., 1985
*The Scarlet Coat   *John Sturges* — U.S., 1955
1776   *Peter Hunt* — U.S., 1972
*The Spirit of '76   *Frank Montgomery* — U.S., 1918
The Spy   *Otis Turner* — U.S., 1914
*Washington at Valley Forge   *Grace Cunard/Francis Ford* — U.S., 1914

THE FRENCH REVOLUTION AND REVOLUTIONARY WARS, 1789–1802
*Adieu Bonaparte   *Youssef Chahine* — EGY/FRA, 1984
*L'affaire du Courrier de Lyon   *Claude Autant-Lara/Maurice Lehmann* — FRA, 1937
Beaumarchais   *Edouard Molinaro* — FRA, 1996
*Bequest to the Nation   *James Cellan Jones* — GB, 1973
*Billy Budd   *Peter Ustinov* — GB/U.S., 1962
*The Black Book   *Anthony Mann* — U.S., 1949
Captain of the Guard   *John S. Robertson* — U.S., 1930
Caroline Cherie   *Richard Pottier* — FRA, 1950
Caroline Cherie   *Denys De La Patelliere* — FRA, 1967
Dangerous Exile   *Brian Desmond Hurst* — GB, 1958
*Danton   *Various* — See Encyclopedia
Darling Caroline's Fancy   *Jean Devaivre* — FRA, 1952
*Le Dialogue Des Carmalites   *Phillipe Agostini/R. l. Bruckberger* — FRA/ITA, 1959
*The Divine Lady   *Frank Lloyd* — U.S., 1929
*The Elusive Pimpernel   *Michael Powell/Emeric Pressburger* — GB, 1950
*The Fighting Guardsman   *Henry Levin* — U.S., 1945
Hms Defiant   *Lewis Gilbert* — GB, 1962
Jefferson in Paris   *James Ivory* — U.S., 1995
The King's Pirate   *Don Weis* — U.S., 1967
The Lame Devil   *Sacha Guitry* — FRA, 1948
Madame Sans-Gene   *Leonce Perret* — U.S., 1925
Madame Sans-Gene   *Roger Richebe* — FRA, 1941
Madame Sans-Gene   *Christian-Jaque* — FRA/ITA/SPA, 1962
Mam'zelle Bonaparte   *Maurice Tourneur* — FRA, 1941
*Marie Antoinette   *W. S. Van Dyke* — U.S., 1938

*Marie Antoinette   *Jean Delannoy* — FRA, 1955
Marquis   *Henri Xhonneux* — FRA, 1989
The Marquise of O   *Eric Rohmer* — FRA/FRG, 1976
The Marriage of Corbal   *Karl Grune* — GB, 1936
*La Marseillaise   *Jean Renoir* — FRA, 1938
*Les Miserables   *Various* — See Encyclopedia
*Napoleon   *Abel Gance* — FRA, 1927
*Napoleon   *Sacha Guitry* — FRA, 1953
La Nuit De Varennes   *Ettore Scola* — FRA /ITA, 1982
*Orphans of the Storm   *D. W. Griffith* — U.S., 1921
*The Purple Mask   *Bruce Humberstone* — U.S., 1955
*Return of the Scarlet Pimpernel   *Hans Schwarz* — GB, 1937
The Rover   *Terence Young* — ITA, 1967
*Scaramouche   *Rex Ingram* — U.S., 1923
*Scaramouche   *George Sidney* — U.S., 1952
*The Scarlet Pimpernel   *Harold Young* — GB, 1934
*The Scarlet Tunic   *Stuart St Paul* — GB, 1997
The Scoundrel   *Jean-Paul Rappeneau* — FRA/ITA/ROM, 1971
*A Tale of Two Cities   *Various* — See Encyclopedia
*That Hamilton Woman   *Alexander Korda* — U.S., 1941
The Three Drums   *Maurice De Canonge* — FRA, 1939
*The Young Mr Pitt   *Carol Reed* — GB, 1942

THE 19TH CENTURY
U.S.-TRIPOLI WARS, 1800–05
*The Barbary Pirate   *Lew Landers* — U.S., 1949
*The Man Without a Country   *Ernest C. Warde* — U.S., 1917
*The Man Without a Country   *Rowland V. Lee* — U.S., 1925
*Old Ironsides   *James Cruze* — U.S., 1926
*Tripoli   *Will Price* — U.S., 1950
*Yankee Pasha   *Joseph Pevney* — U.S., 1954

NAPOLEONIC WARS, 1803–15
INCLUDING THE PENINSULAR WAR, 1808–14;
UNITED STATES-BRITISH WAR [THE WAR OF 1812] 1812–15
*The Adventures of Gerard   *Jerzy Skolimowski* — GB, 1970
*Austerlitz   *Abel Gance* — FRA/ITA/LEICH/YUG, 1959
*Bequest to the Nation   *James Cellan Jones* — GB, 1973
*Brave Warrior   *Spencer G. Bennet* — U.S., 1952
*The Buccaneer   *Cecil B. De Mille* — U.S., 1938
*The Buccaneer   *Anthony Quinn* — U.S., 1958
*Captain Caution   *Richard Wallace* — U.S., 1940
*Captain Horatio Hornblower, RN   *Raoul Walsh* — GB, 1951
*Captain Lightfoot   *Douglas Sirk* — U.S., 1955
Carlota Joaquina, Princess of Brazil   *Carla Camurati* — BRA, 1995
*La Chartreuse De Parme   *Christian-Jaque* — FRA, 1948
Le Colonel Chabert   *Yves Angelo* — FRA, 1994
*Conquest   *Clarence Brown* — U.S., 1937
The Death Throes of the Eagles   *Jean-Alden Delos* — FRA, 1951
*Desiree   *Henry Koster* — U.S., 1954
*The Divine Lady   *Frank Lloyd* — U.S., 1929
*The Duellists   *Ridley Scott* — GB, 1977
*Eagle in a Cage   *Fielder Cook* — GB, 1970
*1812   *Vassili Goncharov/Kai Hansen/Alexander Vralsky* — RUS, 1912
The Fabulous Destiny of Desiree Clary   *Sacha Guitry* — FRA, 1942
*The Fighting Kentuckian   *George Waggner* — U.S., 1949
*The Fighting O'flynn   *Arthur Pierson* — U.S., 1949
Fiorile   *Paolo Taviani/Vittorio Taviani* — FRA/GER/ITA, 1993

*Forever and a Day   *R. Clair /C. Hardwicke /V. Saville / H. Wilcox, etc* — U.S., 1942
From Man To Man   *Christian-Jaque* — FRA, 1948
*The Frontiersman   *Reginald Barker* — U.S., 1927
*La Guerilla   *Pierre Kast* — FRA, 1981
The Hundred Days   *Giovaccino Forzano* — ITA, 1935
The Iron Duke   *Victor Saville* — GB, 1934
*The King's Pirate   *Don Weis* — U.S., 1967
Kolberg   *Veit Harlan* — GER, 1944
Kutuzov   *Vladimir Petrov* — USSR, 1944
The Lame Devil   *Sacha Guitry* — FRA, 1948
*The Last of the Buccaneers   *Lew Landers* — U.S., 1950
*Love and Death   *Woody Allen* — U.S., 1975
*Lydia Bailey   *Jean Negulesco* — U.S., 1952
*Magnificent Doll   *Frank Borzage* — U.S., 1946
Mam'zelle Bonaparte   *Maurice Tourneur* — FRA, 1941
The Marquise of O   *Eric Rohmer* — FRA/FRG, 1976
The Miracle   *Irving Rapper* — U.S., 1959
*Les Miserables   *Various* — See Encyclopedia
*Mutiny   *Edward Dmytryk* — U.S., 1952
*Napoleon   *Abel Gance* — FRA, 1927
*Napoleon   *Sacha Guitry* — FRA, 1953
Nez De Cuir   *Yves Allegret* — FRA, 1951
*The Pride and the Passion   *Stanley Kramer* — U.S., 1957
Prince of Homberg   *Marco Bellocchi* — ITA, 1997
The Reluctant Widow   *Bernard Knowles* — GB, 1950
A Royal Divorce   *Jack Raymond* — GB, 1938
The Saragossa Manuscript   *Wojciech Has* — POL, 1964
*Sea Devils   *Raoul Walsh* — GB, 1953
*The Secret of St Ives   *Phil Rosen* — U.S., 1949
Suvorov   *Vsevolod Pudovkin* — USSR, 1938
*That Hamilton Woman   *Alexander Korda* — U.S., 1941
*This England   *David Macdonald* — GB, 1941
*Tyrant of the Sea   *Lew Landers* — U.S., 1950
*War and Peace   *King Vidor with Mario Soldati* — ITA/U.S., 1956
*War and Peace   *Sergei Bondarchuk* — USSR, 1967
*Waterloo   *Sergei Bondarchuk* — ITA/USSR, 1971

WARS OF ITALIAN INDEPENDENCE
RISORGIMENTO, 1821–70
Bride of the Regiment   *John Francis Dillon* — U.S., 1930
The Brigand of the Wolf Cave   *Pietro Germi* — ITA, 1952
Cavalcade of Heroes   — ITA, 1949
Il Condotteri   — ITA, 1937
*1860   *Alexander Blasetti* — ITA, 1934
Fiorile   *Paolo Taviani/Vittorio Taviani* — FRA/GER/ITA, 1993
*The Horseman on the Roof   *Jean-Paul Rappeneau* — FRA, 1995
*The Lady in Ermine   *James Flood* — U.S., 1927
*The Leopard   *Luchino Visconti* — ITA, 1962
Long Live Italy   *Roberto Rossellini* — ITA, 1960
*The Lost Patrol   *Pierro Nelli* — ITA, 1954
Mask of the Avenger   *Phil Karlson* — U.S., 1951
The Old Guards   *Alexander Blasetti* — ITA, 1934
Passione d'Amore   *Ettore Scola* — ITA, 1981
The Red Shirts   *G. Prandi* — ITA, 1952
*Senso   *Luchino Visconti* — ITA, 1953
Villafranca   — ITA, 1933

TEXAS-MEXICO WAR, 1836
*The Alamo   *John Wayne* — U.S., 1960

THE BRIGAND OF KANDAHAR
Sepoys and their charges come under fire from bandits. EMI/Hammer

*Davy Crockett   *Norman Foster — U.S., 1955*
Deaf Smith and Johnny Ears   *Paolo Cavara — ITA, 1972*
*The First Texan   *Byron Haskin — U.S., 1956*
*The Heroes of the Alamo   *Harry Fraser — U.S., 1938*
*The Last Command   *Frank Lloyd — U.S., 1955*
*Lone Star   *Vincent Sherman — U.S., 1952*
*The Man from the Alamo   *Budd Boetticher — U.S., 1953*
*Man of Conquest   *George Nicholls — U.S., 1939*
*The Martyrs of the Alamo   *Christy Cabanne — U.S.,1915*
Viva Max   *Jerry Paris — U.S., 1969*

ALGERIAN UNREST FROM C1840
*The Bugler of Algiers   U.S., 1916
*The Dishonored Medal   *Christy Cabanne — U.S., 1914*
*Love and Glory   *Rupert Julian — U.S., 1924*
*The Song of Love   *Chester Franklin — U.S., 1924*

UNITED STATES-MEXICO WAR, 1846–48
*California   *W. S. Van Dyke — U.S., 1927*
*California Conquest   *Lew Landers — U.S., 1952*
*A California Romance   *Jerome Storm — U.S., 1923*
*Kit Carson   *George B. Seitz — U.S., 1940*
*Kit Carson Over the Great Divide   — U.S., 1925
The Lash   — U.S., 1931
*The Man Behind the Gun   *Felix Feist — U.S., 1952*
*The Mark of Zorro   *Douglas Fairbanks — U.S., 1920*
*The Mark of Zorro   *Rouben Mamoulian — U.S., 1940*
*The Mask of Zorro   *Martin Campbell — U.S., 1998*
*Pirates of Monterey   *Alfred Werker — U.S., 1947*
*The Sign of Zorro   *Norman Foster/Lewis R. Foster — U.S., 1960*
*Zorro Rides Again   *William Witney/John English — U.S., 1937*
*Zorro the Gay Blade   *Peter Medak — U.S., 1982*

CRIMEAN WAR, 1853–56
*The Charge of the Lancers   *William Castle — U.S., 1953*
*The Charge of the Light Brigade   *Michael Curtiz — U.S., 1936*
*The Charge of the Light Brigade   *Tony Richardson — GB, 1968*
*The Cossacks   *Giorgio Rivalta — ITA, 1959*
*Forever and a Day   *R. Clair/C. Hardwicke/V. Saville/H. Wilcox — U.S., 1942*
*The White Angel   *William Dieterlie — U.S., 1936*

19TH CENTURY BRITISH WARS IN INDIA AND THE INDIAN MUTINY, 1856–58
*The Bandit of Zhobe   *John Gilling — GB, 1959*
*The Beggar of Cawnpore   *Charles Swickard — U.S., 1916*
*Bengal Brigade   *Laslo Benedek — U.S., 1954*
*The Brigand of Kandahar   *John Gilling — GB, 1965*
*The Campbells Are Coming   *Francis Ford — U.S.,1915*
*The Charge of the Light Brigade   *Michael Curtiz — U.S., 1936*
*The Chess Players   *Satyajit Ray — IND, 1977*
*The Drum   *Zoltan Korda — GB, 1938*
Four Men and a Prayer   *John Ford — U.S., 1938*
*The Green Goddess   U.S., 1923
*The Green Goddess   *Alfred E. Green — U.S., 1930*
*Gunga Din   *George Stevens — U.S., 1939*
*Khyber Patrol   *Seymour Friedman — U.S., 1954*
*Kim   *Victor Saville — U.S., 1950*
*King of the Khyber Rifles   *Henry King — U.S., 1953*
*Lives of a Bengal Lancer   *Henry Hathaway — U.S., 1934*
*The Long Duel   *Ken Annakin — GB, 1967*
*The Man Who Would Be King   *John Huston — GB, 1975*
*North-West Frontier   *J. Lee Thompson — GB, 1959*
*Rogue's March   *Allan Davis — U.S., 1953 MGM*
Rose of the World   *Maurice Tourneur — U.S., 1918*
*Soldiers Three   *Tay Garnett — U.S., 1951 MGM*
*Storm Over Bengal   *Sidney Salkow — U.S., 1938*
*The Stranglers of Bombay   *Terence Fisher — GB, 1959*
*Wee Willie Winkie   John Ford — U.S., 1937
*Zarak   *Terence Young — GB, 1956*

MEXICAN REVOLUTIONS, 1855–67
Blue   *Silvio Narizzano — ITA/U.S., 1968*
*Border River   *George Sherman — U.S., 1954*
*The Eagle and the Hawk   *Lewis R. Foster — U.S., 1949*
*1871   *Kenneth Macmillan — GB, 1989*
*Juarez   *William Dieterlie — U.S., 1939*
My Name is Alleluia   *Anthony Ascott — ITA, 1971*
*Stronghold   *Steve Sekely — U.S., 1952*
The Undefeated   *Andrew V. Maclaglen — U.S., 1969*
*Vera Cruz   *Robert Aldrich — U.S., 1953*
Woman in Love   *Emilio Fernandez — MEX, 1946*

AMERICAN CIVIL WAR, 1861–65
*Abraham Lincoln   *D.W. Griffith — U.S., 1930*
*According to the Code   *Charles Michelson — U.S., 1916*
*Advance to the Rear   *George Marshall — U.S., 1964*
*Alvarez Kelly   *Edward Dmytryk — U.S., 1966*
*Arizona Bushwackers   *Lesley Selander — U.S., 1968*
*Arizona Raiders   *William Witney — U.S., 1965*
*Bad Company   *Robert Benton — U.S., 1972*
*The Battle of Gettysburg   *Thomas Ince — U.S., 1914*

*The Beguiled   *Don Siegel — U.S., 1971*
*The Birth of a Nation   *D.W. Griffith — U.S., 1915*
The Black Dakotas   *Ray Nazarro — U.S., 1954*
*Border River   *George Sherman — U.S., 1954*
*Charley One-Eye   *Don Chaffey — GB, 1972*
*Column South   *Frederick De Cordova — U.S., 1953*
The Copperhead   *Charles Maigne — U.S., 1920*
Court Martial   *George B. Seitz — U.S., 1928*
*The Coward   *Reginald Barker — U.S., 1915*
*The Crisis   *Colin Campbell — U.S., 1915*
Dan   *— U.S., 1914*
*The Dark Command   *Raoul Walsh — U.S., 1940*
*The Desperados   *Henry Levin — U.S., 1969*
*Devil's Doorway   *Anthony Mann — U.S., 1950*
*Drums in the Deep South   *William Cameron Menzies — U.S., 1951*
*Escape from Fort Bravo   *John Sturges — U.S., 1953*
The Field of Honor   *Allen Holubar — U.S., 1917*
*Fort Defiance   *John Rawlins — U.S., 1951*
*Friendly Persuasion   *William Wyler — U.S., 1956*
*The General   *Clyde Bruckman/Buster Keaton — U.S., 1926*
*Gettysburg   *Ronald F. Maxwell — U.S., 1993*
*Glory   *Edward Zwick — U.S., 1989*
*Gone with the Wind   *Victor Fleming and George Cukor/Sam Wood — U.S., 1939*
*The Good, the Bad and the Ugly   *Sergio Leone — ITA, 1966*
*Great Day in the Morning   *Jacques Tourneur — U.S., 1956*
*The Great Locomotive Chase   *Francis D. Lyon — U.S., 1956*
*The Guns of Fort Petticoat   *George Marshall — U.S., 1957*
The Heart of Maryland   *Herbert Brenon — U.S., 1915*
The Heart of Maryland   *Lloyd Bacon — U.S., 1927*
*Hearts in Bondage   *Lew Ayres — U.S., 1936*
*Held by the Enemy   *Donald Crisp — U.S., 1920*
Her Father's Son   *William Desmond Taylor — U.S., 1916*
The Highest Law   *Ralph Ince — U.S., 1921*
*The Horse Soldiers   *John Ford — U.S., 1959*
*How the West Was Won   *John Ford/Henry Hathaway/George Marshall — U.S., 1962*
Incident at Owl Creek   *Jean Boffety — FRA, 1961*
*Incident at Phantom Hill   *Earl Bellamy — U.S., 1966 L*
*Jesse James   *Lloyd Ingaham — U.S., 1927*
Jesse James   *Henry King — U.S., 1939*
Jesse James Under the Black Flag   *— U.S., 1921*
Jim Bludso   *Tod Browning — U.S., 1917*
Johnny Ring and the Captain's Sword   *Norman L. Stevens — U.S., 1921*
*Journey to Shiloh   *William Hale — U.S., 1967*
*Kansas Pacific   *Ray Nazarro — U.S., 1953*
*Kansas Raiders   *Ray Enright — U.S., 1951*
The Killing Box   *George Hickenlooper — U.S., 1992*
*The Last Outpost   *Lewis R. Foster — U.S., 1951*
*The Legend of Tom Dooley   *Ted Post — U.S., 1959*
Madam Who?   *Reginald Barker — U.S., 1918*
*Major Dundee   *Sam Peckinpah — U.S., 1964*
The Man from Colorado   *Henry Levin — U.S., 1948*
*The Man from Dakota   *Leslie Fenton — U.S., 1940*
May Blossom   *Allan Dwan — U.S., 1915*
*Morgan's Last Raid   *Nick Grinde — U.S., 1929*
*Morgan's Raiders   *Wilfred Lucas — U.S., 1918*
My Own United States   *John W. Noble — U.S., 1918*
*No Drums, No Bugles   *Clyde Ware — U.S., 1971*
Operator 13   *Richard Boleslawski — U.S., 1934*

BROKEN ARROW
(l-to-r) Debra Paget, Jeff Chandler (as Cochise) and James Stewart.
20th Century Fox (courtesy KOBAL)

The Outlaw   *— U.S., 1921*
*The Outriders   *Roy Rowland — U.S., 1950*
*Quantrill's Raiders   *Edward Bernds — U.S., 1958*
Quincannon, Frontier Scout   *Lesley Selander — U.S., 1956*
*The Raid   *Hugo Fregonese — U.S., 1954*
*A Reason To Live, a Reason To Die   *Tonino Valerii — FRA/ITA/SPA, 1972*
Rebel City   *Thomas Carr — U.S., 1953*
Rebel Love   *Milton Bagby Jr — U.S., 1984*
*The Red Badge of Courage   *John Huston — U.S., 1951*
*Red Mountain   *William Dieterlie — U.S., 1951*
The Redhead and the Cowboy   *Leslie Fenton — U.S., 1950*
*Revolt at Fort Laramie   *Lesley Selander — U.S., 1957*
Rio Conchos   *Gordon Douglas — U.S., 1964*
Rio Lobo   *Howard Hawks — U.S., 1970*
*Rocky Mountain   *William Keighley — U.S., 1950*
Rose of the South   *Robert Scardon — U.S., 1916*
*Run of the Arrow   *Samuel Fuller — U.S., 1957*
San Antone   *Joe Kane — U.S., 1952*
*Santa Fe Trail   *Michael Curtiz — U.S., 1940*
*Secret Service   *Hugh Ford — U.S., 1919*
*Secret Service   *J. Walter Ruben — U.S., 1931*
*Seven Angry Men   *Charles Marquis Warren — U.S., 1955*
*Shenandoah   *Andrew V. Maclaglen — U.S., 1965*
*The Siege at Red River   *Rudolph Mate — U.S., 1954*
Smoke in the Wind   *Joseph Kane — U.S., 1975*
*So Red the Rose   *King Vidor — U.S., 1935*
*Sommersby   *Jon Amiel — FRA/U.S., 1993*
South of St Louis   *Ray Enright — U.S., 1948*
A Southern Yankee   *Edward Sedgwick — U.S., 1948*
*Springfield Rifle   *Andre De Toth — U.S., 1952*
The Supernaturals   *Armand Mastroianni — U.S., 1986*
*Tap Roots   *George Marshall — U.S., 1948*
*Thirteen Fighting Men   *Harry Gerstad — U.S., 1960*
Those Without Sin   *Marshall Neilan — U.S., 1917*
*A Time for Killing   *Phil Karlson — U.S., 1967*
The True Story of Jesse James   *Nicholas Ray — U.S., 1956*

*War Party   *Lesley Selander — U.S., 1965*
*War Party   *Franc Roddam — U.S., 1989*
Warpath   *Byron Haskin — U.S., 1951*
*White Feather   *Robert Webb — U.S., 1955*
Wyoming   *W. S. Van Dyke — U.S., 1928*
The Yellow Tomahawk   *Lesley Selander — U.S., 1954*

FRANCO-PRUSSIAN WAR, 1870–71
*Bismark   *Wolfgang Liebeneiner — GER, 1940*
*Colonel Redl   *Istvan Szabo — AUST/HUN/FRG, 1984*
*1871   *Kenneth Macmillan — GB, 1989*
The Four Horsemen of the Apocalypse   *Rex Ingram — U.S., 1921*
*Heart of a Nation   *Julien Duvivier — FRA, 1940*
Horrors of War   *— FRA, 1914*
*Ludwig   *Luchino Visconti — FRA/FRG/ITA, 1972*
*Ludwig — Requiem for a Virgin King   *Hans Jurgen Syberberg — FRG, 1972*
*Mademoiselle Fifi   *Robert Wise — U.S., 1944*
*The New Babylon   *Grigori Kozintsev/Leonid Trauberg — USSR, 1929*
Royal Flash   *Richard Lester — GB, 1975*

RUSSO-TURKISH WAR AND THE TARTAR CAMPAIGNS, 1877–78
*Courier to the Tsar   *GER, 1936*
*Michael Strogoff   *Various — See Encyclopedia*
*Michel Strogoff   *Jacques de Baroncelli — FRA, 1936*
*The Soldier and the Lady   *George Nicholls — U.S., 1937*
*The Triumph of Michael Strogoff   *Victor Tourjansky — FRA/ITA, 1961*

BRITISH-ZULU WAR, 1879
*Zulu   *Cy Endfield — GB, 1964*
*Zulu Dawn   *Douglas Hickox — HOL/U.S., 1979*

YOUNG WINSTON
Churchill sees action in the Sudan. Columbia (courtesy KOBAL)

BRITISH CAMPAIGNS — EGYPT/SUDAN, 1882–98
*East of Sudan   *Nathan Juran — GB, 1964*
*The Four Feathers   *Various — See Encyclopedia*
*Khartoum   *Basil Dearden — GB, 1966*
*The Light that Failed   *Various — See Encyclopedia*
*Storm Over the Nile   *Terence Young — GB, 1955*
*Young Winston   *Richard Attenborough — GB, 1972*

VARIOUS LATIN AMERICAN CONFLICTS OF THE 19TH CENTURY
*Americano   *John Emerson — U.S., 1916 Patagonia*
*Lucia   *Humberto Solas — CUB, 1969 Cuba*
*Walker   *Alex Cox — U.S., 1987 Nicaragua*

VARIOUS COLONIAL DISPUTES OF THE 19TH CENTURY
*Captain Fury   *Hal Roach — U.S., 1939 Britain/Australia*
*November 1828   *Teguh Karia — INDO, 1979 Holland/Java*
*Quebec   *George Templeton — U.S., 1951 Britain/Quebec*
*Utu   *Geoff Murphy — NZ, 1983 Britain/Maoris*

SPANISH-AMERICAN WAR, 1898
*Across the Pacific   *Roy Del Ruth — U.S., 1926*
The Denial   *Hobart Henley — U.S., 1925*
The Last Man   *William Wolbert — U.S., 1916*
*Masters of Men   *David Smith — U.S., 1923*
*A Message To Garcia   *George Marshall — U.S., 1936*
Posse   *Mario Van Peebles — GB/U.S., 1993*
*The Real Glory   *Henry Hathaway — U.S., 1939*
*The Rough Riders   *Victor Fleming — U.S., 1927*
*Santiago   *Gordon Douglas — U.S., 1956*
The Tangle   *Harry Lambart — U.S., 1914*
*Tearing Down the Spanish Flag   *J. Stuart Blackton — U.S., 1898*

THE 20TH CENTURY
BOER WAR, 1899–1902
*The Boer War   *George Melford — U.S., 1914*
*Breaker Morant   *Bruce Beresford — AUS, 1980*
*The Call to Arms   *Cecil Hepworth — GB, 1902*
*Cavalcade   *Frank Lloyd — U.S., 1932*
*Forever and a Day   *R. Clair/C. Hardwicke/V. Saville/H. Wilcox — U.S., 1942*
*The Judgment House   *J. Stuart Blackton — U.S., 1915*
The Life and Death of Colonel Blimp   *Michael Powell/Emeric Pressburger — GB, 1943*
*Ohm Kruger   *Hans Steinhoff — GER, 1941*
*Rhodes of Africa   *Berthold Viertel — GB, 1936*
The Second in Command   *William J. Bowman — U.S., 1915*
*A Skirmish with the Boers . . .   *Joseph Rosenthal — GB, 1899*
Spoor   *Howard Rennie — SA, 1975*
The Stick   *Darrell Roodt — SA, 1988*
*Torn Allegiance   *Alan Nathanson — U.S., 1984*
*Young Winston   *Richard Attenborough — GB, 1972*

EARLY 20TH CENTURY CHINESE UNREST AND CIVIL WARS, 1900–49
*Accidental Legend   *Wang Shaudi — TAI, 1996*
*The Bitter Tea of General Yen   *Frank Capra — U.S., 1933*
*Barricade   *Gregory Ratoff — U.S., 1939*
*Boxer Rebellion   *Chag Che — HK, 1979*
Buddha's Lock   *Yim Ho — HK/CHI, 1987*
*A City of Sadness   *Hou Xiaoxian — TAI, 1989*

THE BATTLESHIP POTEMKIN
Bloodshed on the Odessa Steps — one of cinema's most memorable scenes. Goskino (courtesy KOBAL)

Little Red Devils   *Ivan Perestiani — USSR, 1923*
The Love of Jeanne Ney   *GW Pabst — GER, 1927*
The Man with the Gun   *Sergei Yutkevich — USSR, 1938*
Mirror   *Andrei Tarkovsky — USSR, 1974*
Mockery   *Benjamin Christensen — U.S., 1927*
Moscow Nights   *Anthony Asquith — GB, 1935*
Mother   *Vsevolod Pudovkin — USSR, 1926*
*My English Grandfather   *Nana Djordjadze — USSR, 1986*
The Mysterious Lady   *Fred Niblo — U.S., 1928*
*Nicholas and Alexandra   *Franklin Schaffner — GB, 1971*
*Nights of Rasputin   *— ITA, 1960*
*October   *Sergei Eisenstein — USSR, 1927*
The Rainbow   *Mark Donskoi — USSR, 1944*
*Raspoutine   *Georges Combret — FRA, 1954*
*Rasputin and the Empress   *Richard Boleslawski — U.S., 1932*
*Rasputin the Mad Monk   *Don Sharp — GB, 1966*
Le Rebelle   *Adelqui Millar — FRA, 1930*
The Red and the White   *Miklos Jancso — HUN/USSR, 1967*
The Red Dance   *Raoul Walsh — U.S., 1928*
*Reds   *Warren Beatty — U.S., 1981*
Russian Guerrillas   *Ivan Pyriev — USSR, 1942*
*Scarlet Dawn   *William Dieterlie — U.S., 1932*
*Shchors   *Alexander Dovzhenko — USSR, 1939*
A Slave of Love   *Nikita Mikhalkov — USSR, 1976*
Storm Over Asia   *Vsevolod Pudovkin — USSR, 1928*
*Strike   *Sergei Eisenstein — USSR, 1924*
Surrender   *Edward Sloman — U.S., 1927*
Tempest   *Sam Taylor — U.S., 1928*
Tovarich   *Anatole Litvak — U.S., 1937*
Under False Colors   *Emile Chautard — U.S., 1917*
Vassa   *Gleb Panfilov — USSR, 1983*
*The Volga Boatman   *Cecil B. De Mille — U.S., 1926*
The Vow   *Mikhail Chiaureli — USSR, 1946*
We from Kronstadt   *Yefim Dzigan — USSR, 1936*
The Youth of Maxim   *Grogori Koznitzev/Leonid Trauberg — USSR, 1935*

THE WILD BUNCH
Borgnine, Oates and Holden (l-to-r) about to do some serious banking.
WB/Seven Arts

MEXICAN REVOLUTIONS, 1910–21
*Bandido   *Richard Fleischer — U.S., 1956*
*Behind the Lines   *Henry Mcrae — U.S., 1916*
Blazing Guns   *Anthony Ascott — ITA/SPA, 1972*
*The Brand of Cowardice   *John Noble — U.S., 1916*
*A Bullet for the General   *Damiano Damiani — ITA, 1966*
Cannon for Cordoba   *Paul Wendkos — U.S., 1970*
*Companeros   *Sergio Corbucci — ITA/SPA/FRG, 1971*
*The Fighter   *Herbert Kline — U.S., 1952*
A Fistful of Dynamite   *Sergio Leone — ITA, 1971*
*Five Man Army   *Don Taylor — U.S., 1970*
*The Fugitive   *John Ford — U.S., 1947*
*The Life of General Villa   *Christy Cabanne — U.S., 1914*
Like Water for Chocolate   *Alfonso Arau — MEX, 1991*
*The Love Thief   *Richard Stanton — U.S., 1916*
The Man Who Was Afraid   *Fred E. Wright — U.S., 1917*
*Il Mercenario   *Sergio Corbucci — ITA/SPA, 1968*
*Old Gringo   *Luis Puenzo — U.S., 1989*
*100 Rifles   *Tom Gries — U.S., 1969*
*Over the Top   *Wilfred North — U.S., 1918*
*Pancho Villa   *Eugenio Martin — SPA, 1971*
The Patriot   *William S. Hart — U.S., 1916*
*The Professionals   *Richard Brooks — U.S., 1966*
*Reed — Mexico Insurgente   *Paul Leduc — MEX, 1971*
Soldiers of Fortune   *Allan Dwan — U.S., (date unknown)*
*They Came To Cordura   *Robert Rossen — U.S., 1959*
A Town Called Bastard   *Robert Parrish — GB/SPA, 1971*
*The Treasure of Pancho Villa   *George Sherman — U.S., 1955*
*Two Mules for Sister Sara   *Don Siegel — U.S., 1969*
*Villa Rides   *Buzz Kulik — U.S., 1968*
*Viva Villa!   *Jack Conway — U.S., 1934*
*Viva Zapata   *Elia Kazan — U.S., 1952*
*The Wild Bunch   *Sam Peckinpah — U.S., 1969*
*Wings of the Hawk   *Budd Boetticher — U.S., 1953*

BALKAN WARS, 1912–13
*The Captive   *Cecil B. De Mille — U.S., 1915*
Isle of the Dead   *Mark Robson — U.S., 1945*
Pascali's Island   *James Dearden — GB, 1988*

WORLD WAR I, 1914–18
WESTERN FRONT AND HOME FRONT
*An Alien Enemy   *Wallace Worsley — U.S., 1918*
*All Quiet on the Western Front   *Lewis Milestone — U.S., 1930*
*Barbed Wire   *Erich Pommer/Rowland V. Lee — U.S., 1927*
*The Battle of Ancre   *Geoffrey Malins/J. B. Mcdowell — GB, 1917*
*The Battle of Arras   *Geoffrey Malins/J. B. Mcdowell — GB, 1917*
*The Battle of the Somme   *Geoffrey Malins/J. B. Mcdowell — GB, 1916*
Behind the Front   *Edward Sutherland — U.S., 1926*
The Bells of Rheims   *Maurice Elvey — GB, 1915*
*Berlin Via America   *Francis Ford — U.S., 1918*
Beyond Victory   *John Robertson — U.S., 1931*
*The Big Parade   *King Vidor — U.S., 1925*
*The Birth of a Race   *John W. Noble — U.S., 1919*
*The Black Watch   *John Ford — U.S., 1929*
*The Blue Max   *John Guillermin — U.S., 1966*
*Body and Soul   *Alfred Santell — U.S., 1931*
*The Burgomaster of Stilemonde   *George J. Banfield — GB, 1928*

The Razor's Edge   *John Byrum* — U.S., 1984

Red Clay   *Ernst Laemmle* — U.S., 1927

*Regeneration   *Gillies Mackinnon* — CAN/GB, 1997

Remembrance   *Rex Davis* — GB, 1915

Rendezvous   *William K. Howard* — U.S., 1935

Rendezvous at Bray   *Andre Delvaux* — BEL/FRA/FRG, 1971

The Road Through the Dark   *Edmund Mortimer* — U.S., 1918

*The Road Back   *James Whale* — U.S., 1937

*The Road To Glory   *Howard Hawks* — U.S., 1936

The Roaring Twenties   *Anatole Litvak/Raoul Walsh* — U.S., 1939

Romance in Flanders   *Maurice Elvey* — GB, 1937

A Romance of the Air   *Harry Revier* — U.S., 1918

*Roses of Picardy   *Maurice Elvey* — GB, 1927

A Sacred Love   — FRA, 1915

*St Quentin   *Geoffrey Malins/J. B. Mcdowell* — GB, 1917

*Scotland Yard   *William K. Howard* — U.S., 1930

*Sergeant York   *Howard Hawks* — U.S., 1941

*Seventh Heaven   *Frank Borzage* — U.S., 1927

*Seventh Heaven   *Henry King* — U.S., 1937

Shell 42   *Reginald Barker* — U.S., 1916

Shock   *Roy J. Pomeroy* — U.S., 1934

Shocktroop 1917   *Hans Zoberlein* — GER, 1934

Shopworn Angel   *H. C. Potter* — U.S., 1938

Shoulder Arms   *Charles Chaplin* — U.S., 1918

The Silver Car   *David Smith* — U.S., 1921

*The Slacker   *Christy Cabanne*   — U.S., 1917

Smilin' Through   *Sidney A. Franklin* — U.S., 1922

Smilin' Through   *Sidney A. Franklin* — U.S., 1932

Smilin' Through   *Frank Borzage* — U.S., 1941

The Somme   *Ma Wetherell* — GB, 1927

Sonny   *Henry King* — U.S., 1922

Thomas l'Imposteur   *Georges Franju* — FRA, 1964

*Three Comrades   *Frank Borzage* — U.S., 1938

To Hell with the Kaiser   *George Irving* — U.S., 1918

*Today We Live   *Howard Hawks* — U.S., 1933

Treason   *Allen Holubar* — U.S., 1917

*The Trench   *William Boyd* — FRA/GB, 1999

*The Unbeliever   *Alan Crosland* — U.S., 1918

Uncle Sam of Freedom Ridge   *George A. Beranger* — U.S., 1920

The Unknown Soldier   *Renaud Hoffmann* — U.S., 1926

The Unpardonable Sin   *Marshall Neilan* — U.S., c. 1919

The Vanishing American   *George B. Seitz* — U.S., 1925

*War Brides   *Herbert Brenon* — U.S., 1916

War Nurse   *Edgar Selwyn* — U.S., 1930

*Waterloo Bridge   *James Whale* — GB, 1931

*Waterloo Bridge   *Mervyn Le Roy* — U.S., 1940

*Westfront 1918   *Gw Pabst* — GER, 1930

*What Price Glory?   *Raoul Walsh* — U.S., 1926

*What Price Glory?   *John Ford* — U.S., 1952

*The White Cliffs of Dover   *Clarence Brown* — U.S., 1944

*Who Goes There?   *William P. S. Earle* — U.S., 1917

*The Woman I Love   *Anatole Litvak* — U.S., 1937

*The Woman the Germans Shot   *J. G. Adolphi* — U.S., 1918

*Ypres   *Walter Summers/H. Bruce Woolfe* — GB, 1925

EASTERN FRONT, ITALY, THE BALKANS, THE MIDDLE EAST AND AFRICA

*The African Queen   *John Huston* — GB, 1951

*Archangel   *Guy Maddin* — CAN, 1990

*Armageddon   *H. Bruce Woolfe* — GB, 1923

*Arsenal   *Alexander Dovzhenko* — USSR, 1929

*Assassination at Sarajevo   *Veljko Bulajic* — YUG/CZE, 1975

*Auction of Souls   *Oscar Apfel* — U.S., 1919

*The Battle and Fall of Przemsyl   *American Correspondent Film Co* — U.S., 1915

*The Battles of a Nation   *Albert K. Dawson* — U.S., 1915

*Beau Geste   *Various* — See Encyclopedia

*Black and White in Color   *Jean-Jacques Annaud* — IVC/FRA/SWI, 1976

*Burning Sands   *George Melford* — U.S., 1922

*Carl Peters   *Herbert Selpin* — GER, 1941

*The Case of Sergeant Grisha   *Herbert Brenon* — U.S., 1930

*The Crouching Beast   *W.Victor Hanbury* — GB, 1935

*The Deserter and the Nomads   *Juro Jakubisco* — CZE/ITA, 1968

*The Doomed Battalion   *Cyril Gardner* — GER/U.S., 1932

*A Farewell To Arms   *Frank Borzage* — U.S., 1932

*The Fifth Day of Peace   *Giuliano Montaldo* — ITA, 1972

*The First World War   *Laurence Stallings* — U.S., 1934

*The Flag Lieutenant   *Maurice Elvey* — GB, 1926

*The Flame of the Desert   *Reginald Barker* — U.S., 1919

The Forest of the Hanged   *Liviu Ciulei* — Rom, 1965

*Forty Thousand Horsemen   *Charles Chauvel* — AUS, 1940

Fragment of An Empire   *Friedrich Ermler* — USSR, 1929

*From Mayerling To Sarajevo   *Max Ophuls* — FRA, 1940

*Fugitive Road   *Frank Strayer* — U.S., 1934

*Gallipoli   *Peter Weir* — AUS, 1981

*Germanin   *Max Kimmich* — GER, 1943

*The Girl and the General   *Pasquale Festa Campanile* — ITA, 1967

Golden Dawn   *Ray Enright* — U.S., 1930

*The Great War   *Mario Monicelli* — FRA/ITA, 1959

*The Greater Glory   *Curt Rehfeld* — U.S., 1926

*Hotel Imperial   *Mauritz Stiller* — U.S., 1926

*Hotel Imperial   *Robert Florey* — U.S., 1939

*Kultur   *Edward J. Le Saint* — U.S., 1918

*In Love and War   *Richard Attenborough* — U.S., 1996

*The Last Outpost   *Charles Barton/Louis Gasnier* — U.S., 1935

*The Last Outpost   *Charles Barton/Louis Gasnier* — U.S., 1935

*Lawrence of Arabia   *David Lean* — GB, 1962

*The Lighthorsemen   *Simon Wincer* — AUS, 1988

*The Lost Patrol   *John Ford* — U.S., 1934

*Madame Spy   *Karl Freund* — U.S., 1934

*Mamba   *Al Rogell* — U.S., 1930

The Mysterious Lady   *Fred Niblo* — U.S., 1928

*Noah's Ark   *Michael Curtiz* — U.S., 1929

Patriots   *Boris Barnet* — USSR, 1933

*The Riders of German East Africa   *Herbert Selpin* — GER, 1934

*Royal African Rifles   *Lesley Selander* — U.S., 1954

*Shchors   *Alexander Dovzhenko* — USSR, 1939

The Silent Battle   *Herbert Mason* — GB, 1939

Shout at the Devil   *Peter Hunt* — GB, 1976

*Storm at Daybreak   *Richard Boleslawski* — U.S., 1932

   *Surrender   *Edward Sloman* — U.S., 1927

*Tell England   *Anthony Asquith* — GB, 1931

Tempest   *Sam Taylor* — U.S., 1928 MGM

*Tumult in Damascus   *Gustav Ucicky* — GER, 1939

Two Arabian Nights   *Lewis Milestone* — U.S., 1927

Ultimatum   *Robert Wiene* — FRA, 1938

The White Black Sheep   *Sidney Olcott* — U.S., 1926

The Winding Stair   *John Griffith Wray* — U.S., 1926

*The W Plan   *Victor Savile* — GB, 1930
Who Goes There?   *William Ps Earle* — U.S., 1917
*The Woman the Germans Shot   *John G. Adolfi* — U.S., 1918
*Zeppelin   *Etienne Perier* — GB, 1971

THE IRISH TROUBLES, 1916–98
*Acceptable Levels   *John Davies* — GB, 1983
*Angel   *Neil Jordan* — IRE, 1982
*Ascendancy   *Edward Bennett* — GB, 1982
*Beloved Enemy   *H. C. Potter* — U.S., 1936
Blown Away   *Stephen Hopkins* — U.S., 1994
Born for Hell   *Denis Heroux* — CAN/FRA/GER, 1978
*The Boxer   *Jim Sheridan* — GB/IRE, 1997
*Boy Soldier   *Karl Francis* — GB, 1986
*The Brylcreem Boys   *Terence Ryan* — GB, 1995
*Cal   *Pat O'Connor* — GB, 1984
*The Crying Game   *Neil Jordan* — GB, 1992
*The Dawning   *Robert Knights* — GB, 1988
*The Devil's Own   *Alan J. Pakula* — U.S., 1997
*Fools of Fortune   *Pat O'Connor* — GB, 1990
Four Days in July   *Mike Leigh* — GB, 1985
*The Fox of Glenarvon   *Max Kimmich* — GER, 1940
*The Gentle Gunman   *Basil Dearden* — GB, 1952
*Hennessy   *Don Sharp* — GB, 1975
*Hidden Agenda   *Ken Loach* — GB, 1990

BOY SOLDIER
Welsh squaddies and Celtic anti-English undertones in troubled Ulster. GB, Cine Cymru/The Other Cinema

*High Boot Benny   *Joe Comerford* — IRE, 1993
Hush-A-Bye Baby   *Margo Harkin* — IRE, 1989
*I See a Dark Stranger   *Frank Launder* — GB, 1945
*In the Name of the Father   *Jim Sheridan* — GB/IRE, 1993
*The Informer   *Arthur Robison* — GB, 1929
*The Informer   *John Ford* — U.S., 1935
*Juno and the Paycock   *Alfred Hitchcock* — GB, 1930
*The Key   *Michael Curtiz* — U.S., 1934
*The Long Good Friday   *John Mackenzie* — GB, 1979
Maeve   *John Davies/Pat Murphy* — GB, 1981
*Michael Collins   *Neil Jordan* — U.S., 1996
*My Life for Ireland   *Max W Kimmich* — GER, 1941
*Nothing Personal   *Thaddeus O'Sullivan* — GB/IRE, 1995
*The Odd Man Out   *Carol Reed* — GB, 1946
*Ourselves Alone   *Brian Desmond Hurst* — GB, 1936
*The Outsider   *Tony Luraschi* — U.S., 1979
Patriot Games   *Phillip Noyce* — U.S., 1992
*The Plough and the Stars   *John Ford* — U.S., 1936
*A Prayer for the Dying   *Mike Hodges* — GB, 1987
Reefer and the Model   *Joe Comerford* — IRE, 1988
*Resurrection Man   *Marc Evans* — GB, 1998
The Rising of the Moon   *John Ford* — IRE, 1957
The Run of the Country   *Peter Yates* — GB/IRE, 1995
*Ryan's Daughter   *David Lean* — GB, 1970
Secret People   *Thorold Dickinson* — GB, 1951
*Shake Hands with the Devil   *Michael Anderson* — IRE /U.S., 1959
*Some Mother's Son   *Terry George* — IRE /U.S., 1996
*A Terrible Beauty   *Tay Garnett* — GB/U.S., 1960
This Other Eden   *Muriel Box* — GB, 1960
*Titanic Town   *Roger Mitchell* — FRA/GER/GB, 1998
Traveller   *Joe Comerford* — GB, 1981
Vendetta   *Stuart Margolin* — ITA, 1990
*The Violent Enemy   *Don Sharp* — GB, 1968
*Warshots   *Heiner Stadler* — GER, 1995
Whom the Gods Destroy   *William P. S. Earle* — U.S., 1916
The Writing on the Wall   *Armand Gatti* — BEL/FRA, 1982
*You, Me and Marley   *Graham Veevers* — GB, 1992

NICARAGUAN CIVIL WAR, 1926–27
*Flight   *Frank Capra* — U.S., 1929
*The Marines Are Coming   *David Howard* — U.S., 1935
*The Marines Fly High   *George Nicholls Jr/Ben Stoloff* — U.S., 1940

JAPAN IN MANCHURIA FROM 1931 AND THE SINO-JAPANESE WAR, 1937–45
*Aerograd   *Alexander Dovzhenko* — USSR, 1935
*The Attack Lasted Five Days   *Ting Shan-Si* — CHI/JAP, 1977
*Au Revoir, Mon Amour   *Tony Au* — HK, 1991
*The Battle of China   *Frank Capra/Anatole Litvak* — U.S., 1943
*Behind the Rising Sun   *Edward Dmytryk* — U.S., 1943
*Burma Convoy   *Noel Smith* — U.S., 1941
*The Burning Sky   *Yutaka Abe* — JAP, 1940
*Chocolate and Soldiers   *Take Sado* — JAP, 1941
*A City of Sadness   *Hou Xiaoxian* — Tai, 1989
*Daughters of China   *Ti-Chang/Ling Tsu-Feng* — CHI, 1949
*Dragon Seed   *Harold Bucquet/Jack Conway* — U.S., 1944
*Farewell My Concubine   *Chen Kaige* — CHI /HK, 1993
The Fisherman's Song   *Tsai Choseng* — CHI, 1938
Five Scouts   *Tomotaka Tasaka* — JAP, 1938

*Flying Tigers   *David Miller — U.S., 1942*
Girls of China   *Ling Tse-Feng/Chai Chiang — CHI, 1949*
*God Is My Co-Pilot   *Robert Florey — U.S., 1945*
*The Human Condition   *Masaki Kobayashi — JAP, 1961*
Incident in Shanghai   *John Paddy Carstairs — GB, 1938*
*The Inn of the Sixth Happiness   *Mark Robson — GB, 1958*
*International Settlement   *Eugene Ford — U.S., 1938*
*Lady from Chungking   *William Nigh — U.S., 1942*
*The Last Emperor   *Bernardo Bertolucci — GB/HK/ITA, 1987*
*The Last Princess of Manchuria   *Eddie Fong — HK, 1990*
Men and War   *Satauo Yamamoto — JAP, 1972*
*The Mountain Road   *Daniel Mann — U.S., 1960*
Mud and Soldiers   *Tomotaka Tasaka — JAP, 1938*
*Night Plane from Chungking   *Ralph Murphy — U.S., 1942*
*Nippon's Young Eagles   *Yutaka Abe — JAP, 1941*
Prayer To Mother Earth   *Takeo Murato — JAP, 1941*
*The Puppetmaster   *Hou Hsaio-Hsien — TAI, 1993*
*Red Sorghum   *Zhang Yimou — CHI, 1987*
The Road To Life   *Sun Yu — CHI, 1937*
Shadows Over Shanghai   *— U.S., 1938*
Shanghai   *Akira Iwasaki — JAP, 1937*
Shanghai Blues   *Tsui Hark — HK, 1984*
*Shanghai Surprise   *Jim Goddard — GB, 1986*
*The Story of Dr Wassell   *Cecil B. De Mille — U.S., 1944*
The Story of Tank Commander Nishizumi   *Kimisaburo
    Yoshimura — JAP, 1940*
Street Angel   *Yuan Muzhi — CHI, 1937*
Too Hot To Handle   *Jack Conway — U.S., 1938*
Twenty-Eight Pupils   *Keisuke Kinoshita — JAP, 1954*
Victory Symphony   *T. S. Shih — Chi, 1940*
Who Are You , Monsieur Sorge?   *Yves Ciampi —
    FRA/ITA/JAP, 1961*
*A Yank on the Burma Road   *George B. Seitz — U.S., 1942*
Yellow Earth   *Chen Kaige — CHI, 1984*

The Spanish Civil War, 1936–39

*The Angel Wore Red   *Nunnally Johnson — U.S., 1960*
*L'Arbre De Guernica   *Fernando Arrabal — FRA/SPA, 1975*
*Arise, My Love   *Mitchell Leisen — U.S., 1940*
*Ay, Carmela!   *Carlos Saura — ITA/SPA, 1990*
*Behold a Pale Horse   *Fred Zinnemann — U.S., 1964*
*Blockade   *William Dieterlie — U.S., 1938*
*Confidential Agent   *Herman Shumlin — U.S., 1945*
Cows   *Julio Medem — SPA, 1992*
*Escuadrilla   *Antonio Roman — SPA, 1941*
*L'Espoir   *Andre Malraux — FRA, 1939*
*The Fallen Sparrow   *Richard Wallace — U.S., 1943*
*For Whom the Bell Tolls   *Sam Wood — U.S., 1943*
*Guernica   *Alain Resnais — FRA, 1950*
*La Guerre Est Finie   *Alain Resnais — FRA/SWE, 1966*
Heroes of the Air   *— SPA, 1957*
The Hunt   *Carlos Saura — SPA, 1965*
*Land and Freedom   *Ken Loach — GB/GER/SPA, 1995*
The Last Barricade   *Alex Bryce — GB, 1938*
*The Last Train from Madrid   *James Hogan — U.S., 1937*
*Libertarias   *Vicente Aranda — BEL/SPA, 1996*
The Long Holidays of 1936   *Jaime Camino — SPA, 1976*
*Love Under Fire   *George Marshall — U.S., 1937*
Pascual Duarte   *Ricardo Franco — SPA, 1977*
The Roads to the South   *Joseph Losey — FRA, 1978*
The Searching Wind   *William Dieterlie — U.S., 1946*
The Siege of Alcazar   *Augusto Genina — ITA, 1940*

*Spanish ABC   *Thorold Dickinson/Sidney Cole — GB, 1938*
Spanish Earth   *Joris Ivens — U.S., 1937*
The Snows of Kilimanjaro   *Henry King — U.S., 1952*
The Spirit of the Beehive   *Victor Erice — SPA, 1973*

WORLD WAR II, 1939–45
Atlantic Theatre
*Above Us the Waves   *Ralph Thomas — GB, 1955*
*Action in the North Atlantic   *Lloyd Bacon — U.S., 1943*
*Atlantic Convoy   *Lew Landers — U.S., 1942*
*Battle of the River Plate   *Michael Powell/Emeric Pressburger —
    GB, 1956*
*The Big Blockade   *Charles Frend — GB, 1941*
*The Boat   *Wolfgang Petersen — FRG, 1981*
*Convoy   *Pen Tennyson — GB, 1940*
*Corvette K-225   *Richard Rosson — U.S., 1943*
*Crash Dive   *Archie Mayo — U.S., 1943*
*The Cruel Sea   *Charles Frend — GB, 1952*
*The Enemy Below   *Dick Powell — U.S., 1957*
*Escape To Glory   *John Brahm — U.S., 1940*
*For Freedom   *Maurice Elvey/Castleton Knight — GB, 1940*
*For Those in Peril   *Charles Crichton — GB, 1944*
*The Key   *Carol Reed — GB, 1958*
*Lifeboat   *Alfred Hitchcock — U.S., 1944*
The Lightship   *Jerzy Skolimowski — U.S., 1985*
*The Long Voyage Home   *John Ford — U.S., 1940*
*Les Maudits   *Rene Clement — FRA, 1947*
*Mystery Submarine   *Douglas Sirk — U.S., 1950*
*Mystery Submarine   *C. M. Pennington-Richards — GB, 1962*
*The Navy Comes Through   *Edward Sutherland — U.S., 1942*
*Neutral Port   *Marcel Varnel — GB, 1940*
*Sink the Bismark!   *Lewis Gilbert — GB, 1960*
*Submarine X-1   *William Graham — GB, 1967*
Submarines Head West   *— GER, 1941*
*U-Boat Prisoner   *Lew Landers — U.S., 1944*
*Under Ten Flags   *Duilio Coletti/Silvio Narizzano — U.S., 1960*
*Voyage of the Damned   *Stuart Rosenberg — GB, 1976*
*Western Approaches   *Pat Jackson — GB, 1944*

Germany including the Rise of Nazism
*Address Unknown   *William Cameron Menzies — U.S., 1944*
*The Ballad of Berlin   *Robert Stemmle — GER, 1948*
*Beasts of Berlin   *Sherman Scott — U.S., 1939*
*Berlin   *Yuli Raizman — USSR, 1945*
*Berlin Correspondent   *Eugene Forde — U.S., 1942*
*The Big Red One   *Samuel Fuller — U.S., 1980*
*The Black Fox   *Louis Clyde Stoumen — U.S., 1961*
*The Bridge   *Bernhard Wicki — FRG, 1959*
*The Bridge at Remagen   *John Guillermin — U.S., 1968*
*Cabaret   *Bob Fosse — U.S., 1972*
*Canaris   *Alfred Wiedenmann — FRG, 1954*
Council of the Gods   *Kurt Maetzig — FRG, 1950*
*The Crossing of the Rhine   *Andre Cayatte — FRA/FRG/ITA,
    1960*
*The Damned   *Luchino Visconti — FRG/ITA, 1969*
*David   *Peter Lilienthal — FRG, 1979*
*Death Is My Trade   *Theodor Kotulla — FRG, 1977*
*The Devil's General   *Helmut Kautner — FRG, 1955*
*The Double-Headed Eagle   *Lutz Becker/Philippe Mora —
    FRG, 1972*
*Duped Till Doomsday   *Kurt Jung-Alsen — DDR, 1957*
*Eichmann and the Third Reich   *Erwin Leiser — SWI, 1961*

*England Made Me   *Peter Duffell — GB, 1972*

*Escape   *Mervyn Leroy — U.S., 1940*

Europa   *Lars Von Trier — DEN, 1991*

*Europa, Europa   *Agnieska Holland — FRA/GER, 1991*

*Forbidden   *Anthony Page — GB/FRG, 1984*

Genghis Cohn   *Elijah Moshinsky — GB, 1993*

*Four Sons   *Archie Mayo — U.S., 1940*

*Fraulein   *Henry Koster — U.S., 1958*

*Friendly Enemies   *Allan Dwan — U.S., 1942*

*The German Story   *Annelie and Andrew Thorndike — DDR, 1956*

*Germany, Pale Mother   *Helma Sanders-Brahms — FRG, 1979*

*Germany, Year Zero   *Roberto Rosselini — GER/ITA, 1947*

Gorilla Bathes at Noon   *Dusan Makavejev — GER, 1993*

*The Great Dictator   *Charles Chaplin — U.S., 1940*

*Hans Westmar   *Franz Wenzler — GER, 1933*

*Hanussen   *Istvan Szabo — HUN/FRG, 1988*

*Heimat   *Edgar Reitz — FRG, 1984*

Held for Questioning   *Frank Beyer — GER, 1983*

*Hell is for Heroes   *Don Siegel — U.S., 1962*

*Hitler   *Stuart Heisler — U.S., 1961*

*Hitler, a Film from Germany   *Hans-Jurgen Syberberg — FRA/GB/FRG, 1977*

*Hitler — Dead Or Alive   *Nick Grinde — U.S., 1942*

*The Hitler Gang   *John Farrow — U.S., 1944*

*Hilterjunge Quex   *Hans Steinhoff — GER, 1933*

*Hitler — The Last Ten Days   *Ennio de Concini — GB/ITA, 1973*

*Hitler's Children   *Edward Dmytryk — U.S., 1942*

*Hitler's Reign of Terror   *Samuel Cummins/Mike Mindin — U.S., 1934*

*Hotel Berlin   *Peter Godfrey — U.S., 1945*

Ich Klage Un   *Wolfgang Liebeneiner — GER, 1941*

*In Those Days   *Helmet Kautner — GER, 1947*

*Indiana Jones and the Last Crusade   *Steven Spielberg — U.S., 1989*

Inside Out   *Peter Duffell — GB/GER, 1975*

*Jackboot Mutiny   *G. W. Pabst — GER, 1955*

Jakko   *Fritz Peter Buch — GER, 1941*

*Jew Suss   *Lothar Mendes — GB, 1934*

*Jew Suss   *Veit Harlan — GER, 1940*

*Judgment at Nuremburg   *Stanley Kramer — U.S., 1961*

*Kapo   *Gillo Pontecorvo — FRA/ITA, 1960*

*Know Your Enemy: Germany   *Gottfried Reinhardt — U.S., 1945*

*Leave On Word of Honour   *Karl Ritter — U.S., 1937*

*Lili Marleen   *Rainer Werner Fassbinder — FRG, 1980*

*The Long Day's Dying   *Peter Collinson — GB, 1968*

*Man Hunt   *Fritz Lang — U.S., 1941*

*The Man I Married   *Irving Pichel — U.S., 1940*

*The Marriage of Maria Braun   *Rainer Werner Fassbinder — FRG, 1978*

*The Master Race   *Herbert J. Biberman — U.S., 1944*

*Mephisto   *Istvan Szabo — HUN, 1981*

*The Misfit Brigade   *Gordon Hessler — GB/U.S., 1987*

*The Mortal Storm   *Frank Borzage — U.S., 1940*

*Mother Night   *Keith Gordon — U.S., 1996*

Murderers Are Among Us   *Wolfgang Staudte — GER, 1946*

*The Night of the Generals   *Anatole Litvak — GB, 1967*

*The One Thousand Plane Raid   *Boris Sagal — U.S., 1969*

*Operation Crossbow   *Michael Anderson — GB/ITA, 1965*

*Ordinary Fascism   *Mikhail Romm — USSR, 1965*

Over Everyone in the World   *Karl Ritter — GER, 1941*

*Pastor Hall   *Roy and John Boulting — GB, 1940*

*Patrioten   *Karl Ritter — GER, 1937*

Peace to the Newcomer   *Aleksander Alov/Vladimir Naumov — USSR, 1961*

*Pimpernel Smith   *Leslie Howard — GB, 1941*

Portrait from Life   *Terence Fisher — GB, 1948*

*Prelude to the War   *Frank Capra/Anatole Litvak — U.S., 1942*

The Producers   *Mel Brooks — U.S., 1968*

*Professor Mamlock   *Adolf Minkin/Herbert Rappaport — USSR, 1938*

Romance in a Minor Key   *Helmut Kautner — GER, 1943*

*Sa-Mann Brandt   *Franz Seitz — GER, 1933*

Schtonk!   *Helmut Dietl — GER, 1992*

Sealed Verdict   *Lewis Allen — U.S., 1948*

The Search   *Fred Zinnemann — SWI/U.S., 1948*

*Seven Minutes   *Klaus-Maria Brandauer — FRG, 1989*

*Ski Troop Attack   *Roger Corman — U.S., 1960*

*So Ends Our Night   *John Cromwell — U.S., 1941*

*Somewhere in Berlin   *Gerhard Lamprecht — GER, 1946*

*The Strange Death of Adolf Hitler   *James Hogan — U.S., 1943*

Stronger Than the Night   *Slatan Dudow — FRG, 1954*

*The Tanks Are Coming   *Lewis Seiler — U.S., 1951*

*Ten Days To Die   *Gw Pabst — AUST, 1954*

Ten Seconds To Hell   *Robert Aldrich — GB/U.S., 1958*

*The Testament of Dr Mabuse   *Fritz Lang — GER, 1932*

Thou Shalt Not Kill   *Claude Autant-Lara — ITA/YUG, 1961*

*Three Comrades   *Frank Borzage — U.S., 1938*

*The Tin Drum   *Volker Schlondorff — FRG/FRA, 1979*

*To Hell and Back   *Jesse Hibbs — U.S., 1955*

*Triumph of the Will   *Leni Riefenstahl — GER, 1935*

*Underground   *Vincent Sherman — U.S., 1941*

Verboten!   *Samuel Fuller — U.S., 1959*

*The Victors   *Carl Foreman — GB, 1963*

*Voyage of the Damned   *Stuart Rosenberg — GB, 1976*

*The Wannsee Conference   *Heinz Schirk — GER/AUST, 1984*

*Where Eagles Dare   *Brian G. Hutton — GB, 1969*

*Women in Bondage   *Steve Sekely — U.S., 1943*

*The Young Lions   *Edward Dmytryk — U.S., 1958*

*Yellow Canary   *Herbert Wilcox — GB, 1943*

Zero-Eight-Fifteen   *Paul May — GER, 1954*

LOW COUNTRIES

*The Assault   *Fons Rademakers — HOL, 1986*

*A Bridge Too Far   *Richard Attenborough — GB/U.S., 1977*

*Castle Keep   *Sydney Pollack — U.S., 1969*

*The Diary of Anne Frank   *George Stevens — U.S., 1959*

*Dirty Heroes   *Alberto Demartino — ITA, 1969*

*The Flemish Farm   *Jeffrey Dell — GB, 1943*

*The Girl with the Red Hair   *Ben Verbong — HOL, 1981*

*The Hiding Place   *James F. Collier — U.S., 1974*

*The Last Shot   *John Ferno — HOL/GB, 1946*

*The Lucky Star   *Max Fischer — CAN, 1980*

*The Nun's Story   *Fred Zinnemann — U.S., 1959*

*Operation Amsterdam   *Michael Mccarthy — GB, 1958*

*The Silver Fleet   *Vernon Sewell/Gordon Wellesley — GB, 1943*

So Little Time   *Compton Bennett — GB, 1952*

*Soldier of Orange   *Paul Verhoeven — HOL, 1977*

*Theirs Is the Glory   *Brian Desmond Hurst — GB, 1946*

*Uncensored   *Anthony Asquith — GB, 1942*

*Victory in the West   *Fritz Hippler — GER, 1940*

MEPHISTO
Nazi decadence and the swagger of 1930s Germany. Mafilm

FRANCE

*The Accompanist   *Claude Miller — FRA, 1992*
*Arch of Triumph   *Lewis Milestone — U.S., 1948*
*Are We All Murderers?   *Andre Cayatte — FRA, 1948*
*The Army in the Shadows   *Jean-Pierre Melville — FRA/ITA,*
    1969
*Attack on the Iron Coast   *Paul Wendkos — GB, 1967*
*Au Revoir, Les Enfants   *Louis Malle — FRA, 1987*
*Babette Goes To War   *Christian-Jaque — FRA, 1959*
*A Bag of Marbles   *Jacques Doillon — FRA, 1975*
A Balcony in the Forest   *Michel Mitrani — FRA, 1979*
*La Bataille Du Feu   *Maurice De Canogne — FRA, 1948*
*La Bataille Du Rail   *Rene Clement — FRA, 1945*
Behind these Walls   *— FRA, 1945*
A Child in the Crowd   *Gerard Blain — FRA, 1975*
*Counter-Attack   *Zoltan Korda — U.S., 1945*
*Crossing Paris   *Claude Autant-Lara — FRA, 1956*
*The Demons of the Dawn   *Yves Allegret — FRA, 1945*
*The Dirty Dozen   *Robert Aldrich — GB/U.S., 1967*
*Divide and Conquer   *Frank Capra/Anatole Litvak — U.S.,*
    1943
*Dr Petoit   *Christian de Chalonge — FRA, 1990*
*Dunkirk   *Leslie Norman — GB, 1958*
*The Americanization of Emily   *Arthur Hiller — U.S., 1966*
Firing Squad   *Andre Bethomieu — FRA, 1945*
*The Foreman Went To France   *Charles Frend — GB, 1941*
*The Four Horsemen of the Apocalypse   *Vincente Minelli —*
    U.S., 1961
A Friend Will Come This Evening   *Raymond Bernard — FRA,*
    1945
*Grief and Pity   *Andre Harris/Marcel Ophuls — FRA, 1971*
*Hiroshima, Mon Amour   *Alain Resnais — FRA/JAP, 1959*
*I Was a Male War Bride   *Howard Hawks — U.S., 1949*
*Imitation General   *George Marshall — U.S., 1958*
*In Enemy Country   *Harry Keller — U.S., 1968*
*Inglorious Bastards   *Enzo G. Castellari — ITA, 1978*

Irony of Fate   *Edouard Molinaro — FRA, 1974*
*Is Paris Burning?   *Rene Clement — FRA/U.S., 1965*
*J'accuse   *Abel Gance — FRA, 1939*
*Les Jeux Interdits   *Rene Clement — FRA, 1952*
*Joan of Paris   *Robert Stevenson — U.S., 1942*
*Kings Go Forth   *Delmer Daves — U.S., 1958*
*Lacombe, Lucien   *Louis Malle — FRA, 1974*
*The Last Metro   *Francois Truffaut — FRA, 1980*
*The Last Train   *Pierre Garnier-Deferre — FRA/ITA, 1973*
*Leon Morin, Priest   *Jean-Pierre Melville — FRA/ITA, 1961*
*The Longest Day   *Ken Annakin, Andrew Marton, Bernard*
    Wicki — U.S., 1962
The Lost People   *Bernard Knowles — GB, 1949*
*The Louvre Ticket Office   *Michel Mitrani — FRA, 1974*
*Lucie Aubrac   *Claude Berri — FRA, 1998*
*Manon   *Henri-Georges Clouzot — FRA, 1949*
Marie Octobre   *Julien Duvivier — FRA, 1958*
Menaces   *Edmond T. Greville — FRA, 1939*
Mercie La Vie   *Bertrand Blier — FRA, 1991*
*Les Miserables   *Claude Lelouch — FRA, 1995*
Monsieur Klein   *Joseph Losey — FRA/ITA, 1976*
Novembermond   *Alexandra Von Grote — FRG, 1984*
*Odette   *Herbert Wilcox — GB, 1950*
The Old Rifle   *Robert Enrico — FRA, 1975*
*Operation Secret   *Lewis Seiler — U.S., 1952*
*Orders To Kill   *Anthony Asquith — GB, 1958*
Orphee   *Jean Cocteau — FRA, 1949*
The Other Side of Midnight   *Charles Jarrott — U.S., 1977*
Our Miss Fred   *Bob Kellett — GB, 1972*
*Paris After Dark   *Leonide Moguy — U.S., 1943*
*Paris Calling   *Edwin L. Marin — U.S., 1941*
*Paris Underground   *Gregory Ratoff — U.S., 1945*
*The Passage   *J. Lee Thompson — GB, 1978*
*Passage To Marseilles   *Michael Curtiz — U.S., 1944*
*Patton   *Franklin Schaffer — U.S., 1970*
Le Père Tranquille   *Rene Clement — FRA, 1946*
*Petain   *Jean Marboeuf — FRA, 1992*
Le Petit Matin   *Jean-Gabriel Albicocco — FRA, 1970*
*The Pied Piper   *Irving Pichel — U.S., 1942*
Plenty   *Fred Schepsi — U.S., 1985*
The Raven   *Henri-Georges Clouzot — FRA, 1943*
*The Red Poster   *Franck Cassenti — FRA, 1976*
*La Regle Du Jeu   *Jean Renoir — FRA, 1939*
Rene La Canne   *Francis Girod — FRA/ITA, 1977*
Retour à La Vie   *Andre Cayette/H. G. Clouzot/Jean Dreville/Geo*
    Lampin — FRA, 1949
*Reunion in France   *Jules Dassin — U.S., 1942*
*The Safecracker   *Ray Milland — GB, 1958*
Saving Private Ryan   *Steven Spielberg — U.S. 1998*
The Saviour   *Michel Mardore — FRA, 1971*
*Secret Mission   *Harold French — GB, 1942*
*Section Speciale   *Costa-Gavras — FRA/FRG/ITA, 1975*
A Self-Made Hero   *Jacques Audiard — FRA, 1995*
La Sentence   *Jean Valere — FRA, 1979*
Le Silence De La Mer   *Jean-Pierre Melville — FRA, 1947*
Soft Beds, Hard Battles   *Roy Boulting — GB, 1973*
Sons of France   *Pierre Blondy — FRA, 1945*
Souvenir   *Geoffrey Reeve — GB, 1987*
*13 Rue Madeleine   *Henry Hathaway — U.S., 1947*
*This Land Is Mine   *Jean Renoir — U.S., 1943*
*This Was Paris   *John Harlow — GB, 1941*
*Till We Meet Again   *Frank Borzage — U.S., 1944*

*To Hell and Back   *Jesse Hibbs* — U.S., 1955
*To the Victor   *Delmer Daves* — U.S., 1948
*Tomorrow We Live   *George King* — GB, 1942
*Tonight We Raid Calais   *John Bahm* — U.S., 1943
*The Train   *John Frankenheimer* — U.S., 1965
Le Train   *Pierre Granier-Deferre* — FRA, 1974
The Two of Us   *Claude Berri* — FRA, 1966
*Uncertain Glory   *Raoul Walsh* — U.S., 1944
Under the Sign of Monte Christo   *Andre Hunebelle* — FRA, 1947
*Underground   *Arthur H. Nadel* — U.S., 1970
*Up from the Beach   *Robert Parrish* — U.S., 1965
*Uranus   *Claude Berri* — FRA, 1990
*Victory in the West   *Fritz Hippler* — GER, 1940
Les Violons Du Bal?   *Michel Drach* — FRA, 1974
Les Visiteurs Du Soir   *Marcel Carne* — FRA, 1942
Vive La Liberte   *Jeff Musso* — FRA, 1944
We Were One Man   *Phillipe Vallois* — FRA, 1978
*Victory   *John Huston* — U.S., 1981
*Weekend at Dunkirk   *Henri Verneuil* — FRA/ITA, 1965
The Wheel   *Andre Haguet* — FRA, 1956

BRITAIN

*Adolf Hitler — My Part in His Downfall   *Norman Cohen* — GB, 1972
*The Affair   *Paul Seed* — GB, 1995
*Another Time, Another Place   *Lewis Allen* — GB, 1958
*Another Time, Another Place   *Michael Radford* — GB, 1983
*Appointment With Venus   *Ralph Thomas* — GB, 1951
*Battle of Britain   *Anthony Veiller* — U.S., 1943
*The Battle of Britain   *Guy Hamilton* — GB, 1969
Behind the Guns   *Montgomery Tully* — GB, 1940
*The Bells Go Down   *Basil Dearden* — GB, 1943
*Chicago Joe and the Showgirl   *Bernard Rose* — GB, 1989
*Confirm or Deny   *Archie Mayo* — U.S., 1941
*Cottage To Let   *Anthony Asquith* — GB, 1941
*Count Five and Die   *Victor Vicas* — GB, 1959
*Dad's Army   *Norman Cohen* — GB, 1971
*The Dressmaker   *Jim O'Brien* — GB, 1988
*Dunkirk   *Leslie Norman* — GB, 1958
*The Eagle Has Landed   *John Sturges* — GB, 1976
*Elenya   *Steve Gough* — GB, 1992
The End of the Affair   *Edward Dmytryk* — GB, 1954
*Fires Were Started   *Humphrey Jennings* — GB, 1943
*Foreign Correspondent   *Alfred Hitchcock* — U.S., 1940
*Forever and a Day   *R. Clair/C. Hardwicke/V. Saville/H. Wilcox* — U.S., 1942
Frieda   *Basil Dearden* — GB, 1947
*Gaby   *Curtis Bernhardt* — U.S., 1956
*The Gentle Sex   *Leslie Howard* — GB, 1943
*Green for Danger   *Sidney Gilliat* — GB, 1946
*Hanover Street   *Peter Hyams* — GB, 1979
*Hope and Glory   *John Boorman* — GB, 1987
*I Aim at the Stars   *J. Lee Thompson* — U.S., 1960
I Live in Grosvenor Square   *Hebert Wilcox* — GB, 1945
*International Squadron   *Lothar Mendes* — U.S., 1941
Invasion Quartet   *Jay Lewis* — GB, 1961
*It Happened Here   *Kevin Brownlow/Andrew Mollo* — GB, 1963
John Smith Wakes Up   *Jiri Weiss* — GB, 1940
Johnny Frenchman   *Charles Frend* — GB, 1945
*Journey for Margaret   *W. S. Van Dyke* — U.S., 1942

*Know Your Ally: Britain   *Anthony Veiller* — U.S., 1943
*The Land Girls   *David Leland* — FRA/GB, 1997
*Lassiter   *Roger Young* — U.S., 1984
*Light Up the Sky   *Lewis Gilbert* — GB, 1960
Lilacs in the Spring   *Herbert Wilcox* — GB, 1954
*The Lion Has Wings   *Adrian Brunel/Brian Desmond Hurst/Michael Powell* — GB, 1939
*London Can Take It   *Humphrey Jennings/Harry Watt* — GB, 1940
*The Mckenzie Break   *Lamont Johnson* — GB, 1970
*The Man at the Gate   *Norman Walker* — GB, 1941
*Man Hunt   *Fritz Lang* — U.S., 1941
Medal for the General   *Maurice Elvey* — GB, 1944
*Millions Like Us   *Frank Launder/Sidney Gilliat* — GB, 1943
*Ministry of Fear   *Fritz Lang* — U.S., 1944
*Mrs Miniver   *William Wyler* — U.S., 1942
*The Next of Kin   *Thorold Dickinson* — GB, 1942
*Nightmare   *Tim Whelan* — U.S., 1942
*The One That Got Away   *Roy Baker* — GB, 1957
Piccadilly Incident   *Herbert Wilcox* — GB, 1946
*The Rake's Progress   *Sidney Gilliat* — GB, 1945
*Reach for the Sky   *Lewis Gilbert* — GB, 1956
*The Red Beret   *Terence Young* — GB, 1953
*Salute John Citizen   *Maurice Elvey* — GB, 1942
*Scotland Yard   *Norman Foster* — U.S., 1941
Secret Places   *Zelda Barron* — GB, 1984
*Secrets of Scotland Yard   *George Blair* — U.S., 1944
Sherlock Holmes and the Secret Weapon   *Roy William Neill* — U.S., 1942
Sherlock Holmes and the Voice of Terror   *John Rawlins* — U.S., 1942
The Small Back Room   *Michael Powell/Emeric Pressburger* — GB, 1948
*The Spy in Black   *Michael Powell* — GB, 1939
*Target for Tonight   *Harry Watt* — GB, 1941
Tawny Pipit   *Bernard Miles* — GB, 1944
*This Above All   *Anatole Litvak* — U.S., 1942
*This England   *David Macdonald* — GB, 1941
To Each His Own   *Mitchell Leisen* — U.S., 1946
Tonight and Every Night   *Victor Savile* — U.S., 1945
*Triple Cross   *Terence Young* — GB, 1967
*Triple Echo   *Michael Apted* — GB, 1972
*Waterloo Bridge   *Mervyn Le Roy* — U.S., 1940
*Waterloo Road   *Sidney Gilliat* — GB, 1944
*The Way to the Stars   *Anthony Asquith* — GB, 1945
Welcome Mr Washington   *Leslie Hiscott* — GB, 1944
*Went the Day Well?   *Alberto Cavalcanti* — GB, 1942
While the Sun Shines   *Anthony Asquith* — GB, 1946
*Whisky Galore   *Alexander Mackendrick* — GB, 1948
*The White Cliffs of Dover   *Clarence Brown* —
*Yanks   *John Schlesinger* — GB, 1979
The Years Between   *Compton Bennett* — GB, 1946

ITALY, INCLUDING THE RISE OF FASCISM

*Abyssinia   *Roman Karmen* — USSR, 1939
*Anzio   *Edward Dmytryk* — ITA, 1968
*The Assissi Underground   *Alexander Ramati* — U.S., 1985
*The Battle of San Pietro   *John Huston* — U.S., 1944
*A Bell for Adano   *Henry King* — U.S., 1945
*The Bold and the Brave   *Lewis Foster* — U.S., 1956
*Catch-22   *Mike Nichols* — U.S., 1970
*The Cavern   *Edgar G. Ulmer* — ITA/U.S., 1966

Cinema Paradiso   *Giuseppe Tornatore — ITA, 1988*
*The Conformist   *Bernardo Bertolucci — FRA/FRG/ITA, 1969*
*Conspiracy of Hearts   *Ralph Thomas — GB, 1960*
*Darby's Rangers   *William Wellman — U.S., 1957*
*The Devil's Brigade   *Andrew V. Maclaglen — U.S., 1968*
*The Difficult Years   *Luigi Zampa — ITA, 1948*
Disobedience   *Aldo Lado — ITA, 1981*
*Eight Iron Men   *Edward Dmytryk — U.S., 1952*
*The English Patient   *Anthony Minghella — U.S., 1996*
*Era Notte a Roma   *Roberto Rossellini — FRA/ITA, 1960*
*A Face in the Rain   *Irvin Kershner — U.S., 1963*
*Five Men for Hell   *Frank Kramer — ITA, 1968*
*Force of Arms   *Michael Curtiz — U.S., 1951*
The Four Days of Naples   *Nanni Loy — ITA, 1962*
*The Garden of the Finzi-Continis   *Vittorio de Sica — FRG/ITA, 1970*
*General Della Rovere   *Roberto Rosselini — FRA/ITA, 1959*
The Great Challenge   *Mario Camineri — ITA, 1936*
A Handful of Rubbish?   *Enzo G. Castellari — ITA, 1978*
*The Honorable Angelina   *Luigi Zampa — ITA, 1947*
*Hornet's Nest   *Phil Karlson — U.S., 1970*
*The Last Chance   *Leopold Lindtberg — SWI, 1945*
*The Lion of the Desert   *Moustapha Akkad — U.S./GB/LIB, 1980*
*Life Is Beautiful   *Roberto Benigni — ITA, 1997*
*Living in Peace   *Luigi Zampa — ITA, 1946*
*Love and Anarchy   *Lina Wertmuller — ITA, 1973*
Love Letters   *William Dieterlie — U.S., 1945*
*Man of the Cross   *Roberto Rossellini — ITA, 1943*
*Massacre in Rome   *George Pan Cosmatos — FRA/ITA, 1973*
Monsignor   *Frank Perry — U.S., 1982*
*The Night of San Lorenzo   *Paolo Taviani/Vittorio Taviani — ITA, 1981*
*1900   *Bernardo Bertolucci — FRA/FRG/ITA, 1976*
120 Days of Sodom   *Pier Paolo Pasolini — ITA/FRA, 1975*
*Open City   *Roberto Rosselini — ITA, 1945*
*Paisa   *Roberto Rossellini — ITA, 1946*
*The Paths of the Heroes   *Luciano De Feo — ITA, 1937*
*Paratroop Command   *William Witney — U.S., 1959*
*The Pigeon That Took Rome   *Melville Shavelson — U.S., 1962*
*A Pilot Returns   *Roberto Rossellini — ITA, 1942*
*Private Angelo   *Peter Ustinov — GB, 1949*
*The Quick and the Dead   *Robert Totten — U.S., 1963*
The Reign of Naples   *Werner Schroeter — FRG/ITA, 1978*
Salon Kitty   *Tinto Brass — FRA/FRG/ITA, 1978*
*The Secret of Santa Vittoria   *Stanley Kramer — U.S., 1969*
*Seven Beauties   *Lina Wertmuller — ITA, 1975*
*Shoeshine   *Vittorio De Sica — ITA, 1946*
The Skin   *Liliana Cavani — ITA, 1981*
*The Spider's Stratagem   *Bernardo Bertolucci — ITA, 1970*
*The Story of GI Joe   *William Wellman — U.S., 1945*
The Sun Rises Again   *Aldo Vergano — ITA, 1946*
The Suspicion   *Francesco Maselli — ITA, 1975*
Tabor   *Georges Peclet — FRA, 1954*
*Tank Commandos   *Burt Topper — U.S., 1959*
*Tea With Mussolini   *Franco Zeffirelli — GB/ITA, 1998*
The Terrorist   *Gianfranco De Bosio — FRA/ITA, 1963*
Then There Were Three   *Alex Nicol — ITA, 1961*
A Time of Destiny   *Gregory Nava — U.S., 1988*
*To Hell and Back   *Jesse Hibbs — U.S., 1955*
The Tragic Chase   *Giuseppe De Santis — ITA, 1947*

The Trial of Verona   *Carlo Lizzani — ITA, 1962*
*Two Women   *Vittorio De Sica — ITA, 1962*
Up Front   *Alexander Hall — U.S., 1951*
*Von Ryan's Express   *Mark Robson — U.S., 1965*
*A Walk in the Sun   *Lewis Milestone — U.S., 1946*
*War, Italian Style   *Luigi Scattini — ITA, 1967*
*Warriors Five   *Leopoldo Savona — ITA, 1962*
*What Did You Do in the War, Daddy?   *Blake Edwards — U.S., 1966*
*The White Navy   *Roberto Rossellini — ITA, 1941*
*The White Squadron   *Augusto Genina — ITA, 1936*
Without Pity   *Alberto Lattuada — ITA, 1948*
Zone Troopers   *Danny Bilson — U.S., 1985*

NORWAY

*The Battle for Heavy Water   *Titus Wibe Muller — FRA/NOR, 1947*
*The Commandos Strike at Dawn   *John Farrow — U.S., 1942*
*The Day Will Dawn   *Harold French — GB, 1942*
*Edge of Darkness   *Lewis Milestone — U.S., 1943*
*First Comes Courage   *Dorothy Arzner — U.S., 1943*
*The Heroes of Telemark   *Anthony Mann — GB, 1965*
*The Last Lieutenant   *Hans Petter Moland — NOR, 1993*
*Little Ida   *Laila Mikkelsen — NOR, 1981*
*The Moon is Down   *Irving Pichel — U.S., 1943*
*Suicide Mission   *Michael Forlong — NOR, 1956*
*They Raid by Night   *Spencer G. Bennet — U.S., 1942*

DENMARK

*A Day in November   *Kenneth Madsen — DEN/U.S., 1990*
Once There Was a War   *Palle Kjaerulff-Schmidt — DEN, 1966*
The Red Earth   *Lau Lauritzen — DEN, 1945*

THE ASSISI UNDERGROUND
Rufino (Ben Cross), is made to watch the execution of Jewish prisoners.
Cannon

CZECHOSLOVAKIA

*The Adventures of Tartu   *Harold S. Bucquet* — GB, 1943
*Assassination   *Jiri Sequens* — CZE, 1964
Carriage To Vienna   *Karel Kachyna* — CZE, 1966
*Closely Observed Trains   *Jiri Menzel* — CZE, 1966
*Death Is Called Engelchin   *Jan Kadar/Elmar Klos* — CZE, 1963
*Diamonds of the Night   *Jan Nemec* — CZE, 1964
*Hangmen Also Die!   *Fritz Lang* — U.S., 1943
The Heroes Are Silent   *Miroslav Cikan* — CZE, 1946
*A Higher Principle   *Jiri Krejcik* — CZE, 1960
*Hitler's Hangman   *Douglas Sirk* — U.S., 1943
*Hostages   *Frank Tuttle* — U.S., 1943
The Last Days   *Jerzy Passendorfer* — CZE, 1968
Life Was at Stake   *Jiri Weiss* — CZE, 1956
Men Without Wings   *Frantisek Cap* — CZE, 1946
Midnight Mass   *Jiri Krejcik* — CZE, 1962
The Mountains Are Rumbling   *Vaclav Kubasek* — CZE, 1946
*The Nazis Strike   *Frank Capra/Anatole Litvak* — U.S., 1942
*On Our Own Soil   *France Stiglic* — CZE, 1948
*Operation Daybreak   *Lewis Gilbert* — U.S., 1975
Romeo and Juliet and Darkness   *Jiri Krejcik* — CZE, 1960
Schweik's New Adventures   *Karel Lamac* — GB, 1943
*The Shop On Main Street   *Jan Kadar/Elmar Klos* — CZE, 1965
The Silent Barricade   *Otakar Vavra* — CZE, 1949
A Silent Village   *Humphrey Jennings* — GB, 1943
Stolen Frontiers   *Jiri Weiss* — CZE, 1947
Supermen   *Vaclav Wasserman* — CZE, 1946
Two Peasants   *Zorz Skrigin* — CZE, 1954
A Voice in the Wind   *Arthur Ripley* — U.S., 1944
White Darkness   *Frantisek Cap* — CZE, 1948
Wolves' Lairs   *Palo Bielik* — CZE, 1948

POLAND

*Ashes and Diamonds   *Andrzej Wajda* — POL, 1958
*Border Street   *Aleksander Ford* — POL, 1948
*Campaign in Poland   *Fritz Hippler* — GER, 1940
*Divide and Conquer   *Frank Capra/Anatole Litvak* — U.S., 1943
Enemies   *Viktor Tourjansky* — GER, 1940
Forbidden Songs   *Leonard Buczkowski* — POL, 1947
*A Generation   *Andrzej Wajda* — POL, 1954
*Heimkehr   *Gustav Ucicky* — GER, 1941
The House of the Wastelands   *Jan Rybkowski* — POL, 1950
*In Our Time   *Vincent Sherman* — U.S., 1944
*Kanal   *Andrzej Wajda* — POL, 1956
Long Is the Road   *H. B. Fredersdorf/M. Goldstein* — GER, 1947
*Lotna   *Andrzej Wajda* — POL, 1959
*The Nazis Strike   *Frank Capra/Anatole Litvak* — U.S., 1942
*Nuit Et Brouillard   *Alain Resnais* — FRA, 1955
*The Odessa File   *Ronald Neame* — GB, 1974
Others Will Follow   *Antoni Bohdziewicz* — POL, 1949
The Road Home   *Jerzy Kaszubowski* — GB/POL, 1987
Samson   *Andrzej Wajda* — POL, 1961
*Schindler's List   *Steven Spielberg* — U.S. 1993
A Tear of the Ocean   *Henri Glaeser* — FRA, 1971
The Third Part of the Night   *Andrzej Zulawski* — POL, 1971
*To Be Or Not To Be   *Ernst Lubitsch* — U.S., 1942
*To Be Or Not To Be   *Mel Brooks* — U.S., 1983
Unvanquished City   *Jerzy Zarzycki* — POL, 1950
A Year of the Quiet Sun   *Krzysztof Zanussi* — FRG/POL/U.S., 1984

USSR

*The Adventures of Werner Holt   *Joachim Kunert* — GER, 1963
*The Ascent   *Larissa Shepitko* — USSR, 1976
*Ballad of a Soldier   *Grigori Chukrai* — USSR, 1959
*Battle for the Ukraine   *Yulia Solntseva* — USSR, 1943
*Battle Inferno   *Frank Wisbar* — FRG, 1959
*The Battle of Russia   *Anatole Litvak* — U.S., 1943
*The Battle of Stalingrad   *Vladimir Petrov* — USSR, 1950
*The Clear Skies   *Grigori Chukhrai* — USSR, 1961
*Come and See   *Elem Klimov* — USSR, 1985
*The Cranes Are Flying   *Mikhail Kalatozov* — USSR, 1957
*Cross of Iron   *Sam Peckinpah* — GB/FRG, 1977
*Days of Glory   *Jacques Tourneur* — U.S., 1944
Destiny of a Man   *Sergei Bondarchuck* — USSR, 1959
The Doctor of Stalingrad   *Geza Von Radvanyi* — HUN, 1958
Don't Move, Die and Rise Again   *Vitaly Kanevsky* — USSR, 1989
Eskadrilya Nr. 5   *Avram Room* — USSR, 1941
*Europa, Europa   *Agnieska Holland* — FRA/GER, 1991
*The Fall of Berlin   *Mikhail Chiaureli* — USSR, 1949
*The Flaming Years   *Yulia Solntseva* — USSR, 1961
Garrison Dora   *Karl Ritter* — GER, 1943
*The Girl from Leningrad   *Victor Eisimont* — USSR, 1941
Girl No 217   *Mikhail Romm* — USSR, 1944
The Great Earth   *Sergei Gerasimov* — USSR, 1944
The Great Patriotic War   *Roman Karmen* — USSR, 1965
*The Great Turning Point   *Friedrich Ermler* — USSR, 1946
Here Beneath The North Star   *Edvin Laine* — FIN, 1970
In The Name of the Fatherland   *Vsevolod Pudovkin/Georgi Vasiliev* — USSR, 1943
*In the Rear of the Enemy   *Yevgeni Schneider* — USSR, 1941
*Italiano Brava Gente   *Giuseppe De Santis* — ITA, 1965
*Ivan's Childhood   *Andrei Tarkovsky* — USSR, 1962
Letters from the East   *Andrew Grieve* — FIN/GB/GER/SWE, 1995
*Liberation   *Yuri Ozerov* — DDR/ITA/POL/USSR/YUG, 1969
The Life and Exciting Adventures of Private Ivan Chonkin   *J. Menzel* — CZE/FRA/GB/ITA/RUS — 1994
Life in the Citadel   *Herbert Rappaport* — USSR, 1947
The Longest Months   *Alexander Stolpev* — USSR, 1963
Mainland   *Sergei Gerasimov* — USSR, 1944
*Man of the Cross   *Roberto Rossellini* — ITA, 1943
Marite   *Vera Stroyevna* — USSR, 1947
*The Marriage of Maria Braun   *Rainer Werner Fassbinder* — GER, 1978
Masenka   *Yuli Raizman* — USSR, 1942
*Mission To Moscow   *Michael Curtiz* — U.S., 1943
Moscow Skies   *Yuli Raizman* — USSR, 1944
No Greater Love   *Frederick Ermler* — USSR, 1943
*Normandie-Niemen   *Jean Dreville* — FRA/USSR, 1959
*The North Star   *Lewis Milestone* — U.S., 1943
Once There Was a Girl   *Victor Eisimont* — USSR, 1944
The Patriot   *Alexander Kluge* — FRG, 1979
Radouga   *Mark Donskoi* — USSR, 1944
The Scout's Exploit   *Boris Barnet* — USSR, 1947
She Defends Her Country   *Friedrich Ermler* — USSR, 1943
6 pm   *Ivan Piriev* — USSR, 1944
Soldiers   *A. Ivanov* — USSR, 1956
A Soldier's Father   *Revaz Chkheidze* — USSR, 1965
Son of the Soviet East   *V. Pronin* — USSR, 1942
*Song of Russia   *Gregory Ratoff* — U.S., 1944
*Stalingrad   *Josef Vilsmaier* — GER, 1992

FORCE TEN FROM NAVERONE
Harrison Ford (left) and Robert Shaw running out of time after blowing up a dam. Columbia/American International

*In Which We Serve   *Noel Coward/David Lean* — GB, 1942
*The Malta Story   *Brian Desmond Hurst* — GB, 1953
*Mediterraneo   *Gabriele Salvatores* — ITA, 1991
*The Naked Brigade   *Maury Dexter* — U.S., 1965
Operation Snatch   *Robert Day* — GB, 1962
Signs of Life   *Werner Herzog* — FRG, 1968
The Silent Enemy   *Wlliam Fairchild* — GB, 1958
*They Who Dare   *Lewis Milestone* — GB, 1953
*Torpedo Bay   *Charles Frend* — FRA/ITA, 1964
Uomini Sul Fondo   *Francesco De Robertis* — ITA, 1940
*The White Navy   *Roberto Rossellini* — ITA, 1941
*The Valiant   *Roy Baker* — GB/ITA, 1961

NORTH AFRICA
*El Alamein   *Fred F. Sears* — U.S., 1953
*The Battle of El Alamein   *Giorgio Ferroni* — FRA/ITA, 1968
*The Big Red One   *Samuel Fuller* — U.S., 1980
*Bitter Victory   *Nicholas Ray* — U.S./FRA, 1957
The Black Tent   *Brian Desmond Hurst* — GB, 1956
*Cairo   *W. S. Van Dyke* — U.S., 1941
*Candlelight in Algeria   *George King* — GB, 1943
*Casablanca   *Michael Curtiz* — U.S., 1942
*Chronique Des Annees De Braise   *Mohamed Lakhdar Hamina* — ALG, 1975
*Commandos   *Armando Crispino* — FRG/ITA, 1968
*Darby's Rangers   *William Wellman* — U.S., 1957
*The Desert Fox   *Henry Hathaway* — U.S., 1951
Desert Mice   *Michael Relph* — GB, 1959
*The Desert Rats   *Robert Wise* — U.S., 1953
*Desert Victory   *Roy Boulting* — GB, 1943
*Five Graves To Cairo   *Billy Wilder* — U.S., 1943
*Foxhole in Cairo   *John Moxey* — GB, 1960
*Garrison Dora   *Karl Ritter* — GER, 1943
Gates of Fire   *Claude Bernard-Aubert* — FRA, 1974
Gli Eroi   *Duccio Tessari* — ITA, 1973

THE BIG RED ONE
Marvin, the shepherd with his flock. UA/Lorimar

*Le Grand Rendezvous   *Jean Dreville* — FRA, 1949
*Hell Squad   *Bert Topper* — U.S., 1958
*The Heroes   *Duccio Tessari* — FRA/ITA/SPA, 1972
*The Hill   *Sidney Lumet* — GB, 1965
*Homecoming   *Mervyn Leroy* — U.S., 1948
*Hotel Sahara   *Ken Annakin* — GB, 1951
*How I Won the War   *Richard Lester* — GB, 1967
*I Was Monty's Double   *John Guillermin* — GB, 1958
*Ice-Cold in Alex   *J. Lee Thompson* — GB, 1958
*The Immortal Sergeant   *John M. Stahl* — U.S., 1943
*The Impostor   *Julien Duvivier* — U.S., 1944
*The Man from Morocco   *Max Greene* — GB, 1944
Mission To Tangiers   *Andre Hunebelle* — FRA, 1949
*A Night in Casablanca   *Archie Mayo* — U.S., 1946
*Nine Men   *Harry Watt* — GB, 1943
*No Time To Die   *Terence Young* — GB, 1958
Operation Snafu   *Nanni Loy* — ITA/YUG, 1970
*Paratroop Command   *William Witney* — U.S., 1959
Passport To Suez   *Andre De Toth* — U.S., 1943
*Patton   *Franklin Schaffner* — U.S., 1970
*Play Dirty   *Andre De Toth* — GB, 1969
*Raid On Rommel   *Henry Hathaway* — U.S., 1971
Rats of Tobruk   *Charles Chauvel* — AUS, 1944
*Sahara   *Zoltan Korda* — U.S., 1943
*Sea of Sand   *Guy Green* — GB, 1958
Seven Men for Tobruk   *Mino Loy* — FRA/ITA, 1969
The Star of Africa   *Alfred Weidenmann* — GER, 1957
*The Steel Bayonet   *Michael Carreras* — GB, 1957
Taxi for Tobruk   *Denys De La Patelliere* — FRA, 1965
*Tobruk   *Arthur Hiller* — U.S., 1967
*Tunisian Victory   *Frank Capra/Roy Boulting* — U.S., 1944
*The Way Ahead   *Carol Reed* — GB, 1944
A Yank in Libya   *Albert Herman* — U.S., 1942
*The Young Lions   *Edward Dmytryk* — U.S., 1958

OTHER AFRICA
*The Ascent   *Donald Shebib* — U.S., 1994
*The Best of Enemies   *Guy Hamilton* — ITA/U.S., 1961
*Camp De Thiaroye   *Ousmane Sembene/Thierno Faty Sow* — ALG/SEN/TUN, 1988
*Emitai   *Ousmane Sembene* — SEN, 1972
*The Impostor   *Julien Duvivier* — U.S., 1944
Mr Kingstreet's War   *Percival Rubens* — U.S., 1970
The Sun Never Sets   *Rowland V. Lee* — U.S., 1939
*Sundown   *Henry Hathaway* — U.S., 1941
Tarzan Triumphs   *William Thiele* — U.S., 1943
Timbuktu   *Jacques Tourneur* — U.S., 1958

SOUTH AMERICA
*Battle of the River Plate   *Michael Powell/Emeric Pressburger* — GB, 1956
The Boys from Brazil   *Franklin Schaffner* — GB/U.S., 1978
The Holcroft Covenant   *John Frankenheimer* — GB, 1985
*Murphy's War   *Peter Yates* — GB, 1971
*Notorious   *Alfred Hitchcock* — U.S., 1946
*Operation Eichmann   *R. G. Springsteen* — U.S., 1961

UNITED STATES
*All Through the Night   *Vincent Sherman* — U.S., 1942
*The Best Years of Our Lives   *William Wyler* — U.S., 1946
*Betrayal from the East   *William Berke* — U.S., 1945
Careful, Soft Shoulder   *Oliver Hp Garrett* — U.S., 1942

*A Night To Remember   *Kozaburo Yoshimura — JAP, 1962*
No Regrets for My Youth   *Akiro Kurosawa — JAP, 1946*
*The Purple Heart   *Lewis Milestone — U.S., 1944*
A Record of My Love   *Shiro Toyoda — JAP, 1941*
The Saga of Anatahan   *Josef Von Sternberg — JAP, 1953*
*Shadow of Hiroshima   *Hiroshi Teshigahara — JAP, 1956*
The Teahouse of the August Moon   *Daniel Mann — U.S., 1956*
*Thirty Seconds Over Tokyo   *Mervyn Le Roy — U.S., 1944*
Tokyo Rose   *Lew Landers — U.S., 1945*
Tomoyuki Yamashita   *Kyoshi Saeki — JAP, 1955*
The Tower of Lilies   *Tadashi Imai — JAP, 1953*
Twenty-Eight Pupils   *Keisuke Kinoshita — JAP, 1954*
Vacuum Zone   *Kajiro Yamamoto — JAP, 1951*
War and Peace   *Fumio Kamei/Satsuo Yamamoto — JAP, 1947*
Weep, People of Japan   *Hiroshi Noguschi — JAP, 1956*
Who Are You, Monsieur Sorge?   *Yves Ciampi — FRA/ITA/JAP, 1961*

OTHER FAR EASTERN COUNTRIES

*All-Out Attack On Singapore   *Koji Shima — JAP, 1943*
*The Battle of China   *Frank Capra/Anatole Litvak — U.S., 1944*
*Bombs Over Burma   *Joseph H. Lewis — U. S., 1942*
*The Bridge on the River Kwai   *David Lean — GB, 1957*
Buddha's Lock   *Yim Ho — HK/CHI, 1987*
*Burma Victory   *Roy Boulting — GB, 1945*
*The Burmese Harp   *Kon Ichikawa — JAP, 1956*
*The Burning Sky   *Yutaka Abe — JAP, 1940*
*Bye Bye Blues   *Anne Wheeler — CAN, 1989*
*The Camp On Blood Island   *Val Guest — GB, 1958*
*China   *John Farrow — U.S., 1943*
China Doll   *Frank Borzage — U.S., 1958*
*China Girl   *Henry Hathaway — U.S., 1942*
*China Sky   *Ray Enright — U.S., 1945*
*China Venture   *Don Siegel — U.S., 1953*
*China's Little Devils   *Monta Bell — U.S., 1945*
*A City of Sadness   *Hou Xiaoxian — TAI, 1989*
*The Clay Pigeon   *Richard Fleischer — U.S., 1949*
*The Day England Fell   *Shigeo Tanaka — JAP, 1942*
*Destination Gobi   *Robert Wise — U.S., 1953*
*Empire of the Sun   *Steven Spielberg — U.S., 1987*
Escape at Dawn   *Senkichi Taniguchi — JAP, 1950*
*Farewell My Concubine   *Chen Kaige — CHI/HK, 1993*
Forward! Flag of Independence   *Teinosuke Kinugasa — JAP, 1943*
*General Kato's Falcon Fighters   *Kajiro Yamamoto — JAP, 1944*
*General Yamashita   *Satsuo Yamamoto — JAP, 1952*
Generals, Staff and Soldiers   *Tetson Taguchi — JAP, 1942*
*Halfway To Shanghai   *John Rawlins — U.S., 1942*
The Hasty Heart   *Vincent Sherman — GB, 1949*
*The Human Condition   *Masaki Kobayashi — JAP, 1961*
An Indecent Obsession   *Lex Marinos — AUS, 1985*
*King Rat   *Bryan Forbes — U.S., 1965*
The Left Hand of God   *Edward Dmytryk — U.S., 1955*
The List of Adrian Messenger   *John Huston — U.S., 1983*
*The Long and the Short and the Tall   *Leslie Norman — GB, 1960*
*Love in A Fallen City   *Ann Hui — HK, 1984*
*Malaya   *Richard Thorpe — U.S., 1949*
*The Man in the Middle   *Guy Hamilton — GB, 1964*
*Merrill's Marauders   *Samuel Fuller — U.S., 1962*

*Merry Christmas, Mr Lawrence   *Nagasia Oshima — GB, 1982*
*The Mountain Road   *Daniel Mann — U.S., 1960*
*Never So Few   *John Sturges — U.S., 1959*
*Nippon's Young Eagles   *Yutaka Abe — JAP, 1941*
*Objective Burma!   *Raoul Walsh — U.S., 1945*
*Operation Bottleneck   *Edward L. Cahn — U.S., 1961*
*Paradise Road   *Bruce Beresford — U.S./AUS, 1997*
*The Purple Plain   *Robert Parrish — GB, 1954*
Repatriation   *Kunio Watanabe — JAP, 1949*
*Return from the River Kwai   *Andrew V. Maclaglen — GB, 1988*
Samurai   *Raymond Cannon — U.S., 1945*
Sea Wife   *Bob Mcnaught — GB, 1957*
Secret Agent of Japan   *Irving Pichel — U.S., 1942*
*The Secret of Blood Island   *Quentin Lawrence — GB, 1964*
Seven Women from Hell   *Robert D. Webb — U.S., 1961*
Soaring Passion   *Eiichi Koishi — JAP, 1941*
*Somewhere I'll Find You   *Wesley Ruggles — U.S., 1942*
*The Southern Cross   *Peter Maxwell — AUS, 1982*
The Suicide Troops of the Watchtower   *Tadashi Imai — JAP, 1942*
They Met in Bombay   *Clarence Brown — U.S., 1941*
*Three Came Home   *Jean Negulesco — U.S., 1950*
*A Town Like Alice   *Jack Lee — GB, 1956*
*The Wind Cannot Read   *Ralph Thomas — GB, 1958*
Women in the Night   *William Rowland — U.S., 1948*
A Yank on the Burma Road   *George B. Seitz — U.S., 1942*
*Yesterday's Enemy   *Val Guest — GB, 1959*

AUSTRALASIA

*Attack Force Z   *Tim Burstall — AUS/TAI, 1981*
*Blood Oath   *Stephen Wallace — AUS, 1990*
*Death of a Soldier   *Phillipe Mora — AUS, 1985*
Emma's War   *Clytie Jessop — AUS, 1985*
An Indecent Obsession   *Lex Marinos — AUS, 1985*
*The Overlanders   *Harry Watt — AUS, 1946*
*The Sea Chase   *John Farrow — U.S., 1955*
*The Southern Cross   *Peter Maxwell — AUS, 1982*

PACIFIC THEATER

*Air Force   *Howard Hawks — U.S., 1943*
*Ambush Bay   *Ron Winston — U.S., 1966*
*An American Guerrilla in the Philippines   *Fritz Lang — U.S., 1950*
*Attack: Invasion of New Britain   *Frank Capra — U.S., 1944*
*Attack Force Z   *Tim Burstall — AUS/TAI, 1981*
*Away All Boats!   *Joseph Pevney — U.S., 1956*
*Back Door To Hell   *Monte Hellman — U.S., 1964*
*Back To Bataan   *Edward Dmytryk — U.S., 1945*
*Bataan   *Tay Garnett — U.S., 1943*
*Battle at Bloody Beach   *Herbert Coleman — U.S., 1961*
*Battle Cry   *Raoul Walsh — U.S., 1956*
*The Battle for the Marianas   *U.S. Marine Corps — U.S., 1944*
*The Battle of Blood Island   *Joel Rapp — U.S., 1960*
*The Battle of Midway   *John Ford — U.S., 1942*
*The Battle of Okinawa   *Kihachi Okamoto — JAP, 1971*
Battle of the Coral Sea   *Paul Wendkos — U.S., 1959*
*Battle Stations   *Lewis Seiler — U.S., 1956*
*Beach Red   *Cornel Wilde — U.S., 1967*
*Beachhead   *Stuart Heisler — U.S., 1953*
*Behind the Rising Sun   *Edward Dmytryk — U.S., 1943*
*Between Heaven and Hell   *Richard Fleischer — U.S., 1956*

*Blood and Steel   *Bernard L. Kowalski* — U.S., 1959
*Blood Oath   *Stephen Wallace* — AUS, 1990
*Bombardier   *Richard Wallace* — U.S., 1943
*Captive Hearts   *Paul Almond* — U.S., 1987
*Corregidor   *William Nigh* — U.S., 1943
*Cry Havoc   *Richard Thorpe* — U.S., 1943
*Cry of Battle   *Irving Lerner* — U.S., 1963
Dawn, 15 August   *Hideo Sekigawa* — JAP, 1954
*Death of a Soldier   *Phillipe Mora* — AUS, 1985
*The Deep Six   *Rudolph Mate* — U.S., 1958
*Destination Tokyo   *Delmer Daves* — U.S., 1943
*Destroyer   *William A. Seiter* — U.S., 1943
Eagle of the Pacific   *Inshiro Honda* — JAP, 1952
*The Emperor's Naked Army Marches On   *Kazuo Hara* — JAP, 1987
*Ensign Pulver   *Joshua Logan* — U.S., 1964
*The Eternal Sea   *John H. Auer* — U.S., 1955
*The Eve of St Mark   *John M. Stahl* — U.S., 1944
The Extraordinary Seaman   *John Frankenheimer* — U.S., 1968
*A Farewell to the King   *John Milius* — U.S., 1988
*Father Goose   *Ralph Nelson* — U.S., 1964
*The Fighting Lady   *Louis De Rochemont* — U.S., 1944
*The Fighting Seabees   *Edward Ludwig* — U.S., 1944
*The Final Countdown   *Don Taylor* — U.S., 1980
Fires on the Plain   *Kon Ichikawa* — JAP, 1959
*First to Fight   *Christian Nyby* — U.S., 1967
*First Yank into Tokyo   *Gordon Douglas* — U.S., 1945
*Flat Top   *Lesley Selander* — U.S., 1952
*Flight for Freedom   *Lothar Mendes* — U.S., 1943
*Flying Leathernecks   *Nicholas Ray* — U.S., 1951
*The Flying Missile   *Henry Levin* — U.S., 1950
*The Frogmen   *Lloyd Bacon* — U.S., 1951 20cf
*From Here to Eternity   *Fred Zinnemann* — U.S., 1953
*The Gallant Hours   *Robert Montgomery* — U.S., 1959
*General Yamashita   *Satsuo Yamamoto* — JAP, 1952
*Ghost of the China Sea   *Fred F. Sears* — U.S., 1958
The Girls of Pleasure Island   *Alvin Ganzer/F Hugh Herbert* — U.S., 1953
*God is My Co-Pilot   *Robert Florey* — U.S., 1945
*Guadalcanal Diary   *Lewis Seiler* — U.S., 1943
*Gung Ho!   *Ray Enright* — U.S., 1943
*The Halls of Montezuma   *Lewis Milestone* — U.S., 1950
*Heaven Knows, Mr Allison   *John Huston* — U.S., 1957
*Hell in the Pacific   *John Boorman* — U.S., 1968
*Hell to Eternity   *Phil Karlson* — U.S., 1960
*Hellcats of the Navy   *Nathan Juran* — U.S., 1957
High Barbaree   *Jack Conway* — U.S., 1947
*Home of the Brave   *Mark Robson* — U.S., 1949
*I Was an American Spy   *Lesley Selander* — U.S., 1951
If We Go to Sea   *Masanori Igayama* — JAP, 1943
*In Harm's Way   *Otto Preminger* — U.S., 1965
*In Love and War   *Philip Dunne* — U.S., 1958
*Jungle Patrol   *Joseph Newman* — U.S., 1948
Kiss Them for Me   *Stanley Donen* — U.S., 1957
Listen to the Roar of the Ocean   *Hideo Sekigawa* — JAP, 1950
*Macarthur   *Joseph Sargent* — U.S., 1977
*Manila Calling   *Herbert I. Leeds* — U.S., 1942
*Marine Raiders   *Harold Schuster* — U.S., 1944
*Midway   *Jack Smight* — U.S., 1976
Minesweeper   *William Berke* — U.S., 1943
Mission Batangas   *Keith Larsen* — U.S., 1969
*Mister Roberts   *John Ford/Mervyn Leroy* — U.S., 1955

BATTLE OF MIDWAY
Japanese carriers take some of their own medicine. Universal/Mirisch

*Mr Winkle Goes To War   *Alfred E. Green* — U.S., 1944
*The Naked and the Dead   *Raoul Walsh* — U.S., 1958
Navy   *Tomotaka Tasaka* — JAP, 1943
*No Man is an Island   *John Monk Jr* — U.S., 1962
*None But the Brave   *Frank Sinatra* — U.S., 1965
*Okinawa   *Leigh Jackson* — U.S., 1952
*Once Before I Die   *John Derek* — U.S., 1965
*Operation Bikini   *Anthony Carras* — U.S., 1963
*Operation Pacific   *George Waggner* — U.S., 1950
*Operation Petticoat   *Blake Edwards* — U.S., 1959
*Out of the Depths   *Ross Lederman* — U.S., 1946
*The Outsider   *Delbert Mann* — U.S., 1961
The Philadelphia Experiment   *Stewart Raffill* — U.S., 1984
*Pilot Number Five   *George Sidney* — U.S., 1943
*Pride of the Marines   *Delmer Daves* — U.S., 1945
*Prison Ship   *Arthur Dreifuss* — U.S., 1945
The Private Navy of Sgt O'Farrell   *Frank Tashlin* — U.S., 1968
*The Proud and the Profane   *George Seaton* — U.S., 1956
*PT 109   *Leslie H. Martinson* — U.S., 1963
*Raiders of Leyte Gulf   *Eddie Romero* — U.S., 1963
*The Ravagers   *Eddie Romero* — U.S., 1965
Rebel   *Michael Jenkins* — AUS, 1985
*Remember Pearl Harbor   *Joseph Santley* — U.S., 1942
Rough, Tough and Ready   *Del Lord* — U.S., 1945
*Run Silent, Run Deep   *Robert Wise* — U.S., 1958
The Saga of Anatahan   *Josef Von Sternberg* — JAP, 1953
*Salute to the Marines   *S. Sylvan Simon* — U.S., 1943
Samurai   *Raymond Cannon* — U.S., 1945
*Sands of Iwo Jima   *Allan Dwan* — U.S., 1949
Saturday Island   *Stuart Heisler* — GB, 1951
*So Proudly We Hail   *Mark Sandrich* — U.S., 1943
South Pacific   *Joshua Logan* — U.S., 1958
*South Sea Woman   *Arthur Lubin* — U.S., 1953
*South Seas Bouquet   *Yutaka Abe* — JAP, 1942
*Stand by for Action   *Robert Z. Leonard* — U.S., 1943
*The Steel Claw   *George Montgomery* — U.S., 1961
A Storm from the Sea   *Shue Matsubayashi* — JAP, 1961
*The Story of Dr Wassell   *Cecil B. De Mille* — U.S., 1944
*Submarine Raider   *Lew Landers* — U.S., 1942
*Submarine Seahawk   *Spencer G. Bennet* — U.S., 1959
*Suicide Battalion   *Edward L. Cahn* — U.S., 1958

*The Sullivans   *Lloyd Bacon — U.S., 1944*
*Surrender — Hell!   *John Barnwell — U.S., 1959*
*Tarawa Beachhead   *Paul Wendkos — U.S., 1958*
*A Taste of Hell   *Neil Yarema — U.S., 1973*
The Teahouse of the August Moon   *Daniel Mann — U.S., 1956*
*They Were Expendable   *John Ford — U.S., 1945*
*The Thin Red Line   *Andrew Marton — U.S., 1964*
*The Thin Red Line   *Terrence Malick — U.S., 1998*
*Thirty Seconds Over Tokyo   *Mervyn Le Roy — U.S., 1944*
*Too Late the Hero   *Robert Aldrich — U.S., 1969*
*Tora! Tora! Tora!   *Richard Fleischer — U.S., 1970*
*Torpedo Run   *Joseph Pevney — U.S., 1958*
*Torpedo Squadrons Move Out   *Kajiro Yamamoto — JAP, 1944*
Two-Man Submarine   *Lew Landers — U.S., 1944*
Until They Sail   *Robert Wise — U.S., 1957*
Up in Arms   *Elliott Nugent — U.S., 1944*
*Up Periscope   *Gordon Douglas — U.S., 1959*
*The Wackiest Ship in the Army   *Richard Murphy — U.S., 1960*
*Wake Island   *John Farrow — U.S., 1942*
*The Walls of Hell   *Gerardo De Leon — U.S., 1964*
*The War at Sea from Hawaii to Malaya   *Kajiro Yamamoto — JAP, 1942*
Warkill   *Ferde Grofe Jr — U.S., 1967*
Weep, People of Japan   *Hiroshi Noguschi — JAP, 1956*
*We've Never Been Licked   *John Rawlins — U.S., 1943*
*The Wild Blue Yonder   *Allan Dwan — U.S., 1952*
*Wing and a Prayer   *Henry Hathaway — U.S., 1944*
Wings of the Sea   *Shue Matsubayashi — JAP, 1962*
Wings Over the Pacific   *Phil Rosen — U.S., 1943*
With the Marines at Tarawa   — U.S., 1944
*You're in the Navy Now   *Henry Hathaway — U.S., 1951*
The Zero Fighter   *Toshio Masuda — JAP, 1961*

WORLD WAR II IN THE AIR

*Above and Beyond   *Melvin Frank/Norman Panama — U.S., 1952*
*Aerial Gunner   *William H. Pine — U.S., 1943*
*Air Force   *Howard Hawks — U.S., 1943*
*Angels One Five   *George More O'ferrall — GB, 1952*
*Appointment in London   *Philip Leacock — GB, 1952*
*Baptism of Fire   *Hans Bertram — GER, 1940*
*The Battle of Britain   *Frank Capra — U.S., 1943*
*The Battle of Britain   *Guy Hamilton — GB, 1969*
*Battle Squadron Lutzow   *Hans Bertram — GER, 1941*
*Battle Stations   *Lewis Seiler — U.S., 1956*
*Bomber's Moon   *Charles Fuhr — U.S., 1943*
*Bombs Over Burma   *Joseph H. Lewis — U.S., 1942*
*Captains of the Clouds   *Michael Curtiz — U.S., 1942*
China Doll   *Frank Borzage — U.S., 1958*
*China's Little Devils   *Monta Bell — U.S., 1945*
*The Clear Skies   *Grigori Chukhrai — USSR, 1961*
*Command Decision   *Sam Wood — U.S., 1948*
*Corvette K-225   *Richard Rosson — U.S., 1943*
*Diii   *Herbert Maisch — GER, 1939*
*The Dam Busters   *Michael Anderson — GB, 1954*
*Dangerous Moonlight   *Brian Desmond Hurst — GB, 1941*
*Desperate Journey   *Raoul Walsh — U.S., 1942*
*Destroyer   *William A. Seiter — U.S., 1943*
*Dive Bomber   *Michael Curtiz — U.S., 1941*
*Don't Look Now . . . We're Being Shot at   *Gerard Oury — FRA, 1966*

*During One Night   *Sidney J. Furie — GB, 1961*
*Eagle Squadron   *Arthur Lubin — U.S., 1942*
Eskadrilya Nr. 5   *Avram Room — USSR, 1941*
*The Eternal Sea   *John H. Auer — U.S., 1955*
*Every Time We Say Goodbye   *Moshe Mizrahi — U.S., 1996*
*Fighter Attack   *Lesley Selander — U.S., 1953*
*Fighter Squadron   *Raoul Walsh — U.S., 1948*
*The Fighting Lady   *Louis De Rochemont — U.S., 1944*
*The Final Countdown   *Don Taylor — U.S., 1980*
*The First of the Few   *Leslie Howard — GB, 1942*
*Flat Top   *Lesley Selander — U.S., 1952*
*Flight Command   *Frank Borzage — U.S., 1940*
*Flight for Freedom   *Lothar Mendes — U.S., 1943*
*Flight Lieutenant   *Sidney Salkow — U.S., 1942*
*Flying Fortress   *Walter Forde — GB, 1942*
*Flying Leathernecks   *Nicholas Ray — U.S., 1951*
*For Those in Peril   *Charles Crichton — GB, 1944*
*From Here To Eternity   *Fred Zinnemann — U.S., 1953*
*Garrison Dora   *Karl Ritter — GER, 1943*
*General Kato's Falcon Fighters   *Kajiro Yamamoto — JAP, 1944*
The Glass Mountain   *Henry Cass — GB, 1949*
The Glenn Miller Story   *Anthony Mann — U.S., 1953*
*God is My Co-Pilot   *Robert Florey — U.S., 1945*
*The Great Circus   *Georges Pecles — FRA, 1949*
*A Guy Named Joe   *Victor Fleming — U.S., 1943*
High Barbaree   *Jack Conway — U.S., 1947*
I Wanted Wings   *Mitchell Leisen — U.S., 1941*
*In Harm's Way   *Otto Preminger — U.S., 1965*
*In Which We Serve   *Noel Coward/David Lean — GB, 1942*
*International Squadron   *Lothar Mendes — U.S., 1941*
*(Les Jeux Interdits   *Rene Clement — FRA, 1952*
*Journey Together   *John Boulting — GB, 1944*
*Jungle Patrol   *Joseph Newman — U.S., 1948*
*The Key   *Carol Reed — GB, 1958*
Kiss Them for Me   *Stanley Donen — U.S., 1957*
Ladies Courageous   *John Rawlins — U.S., 1944*
*Light Up the Sky   *Lewis Gilbert — GB, 1960*
*The Lion Has Wings   *Adrian Brunel/Brian Desmond Hurst/Michael Powell — GB, 1939*
*The Longest Day   *Ken Annakin, Andrew Marton, Bernhard Wicki — U.S., 1962*
*The Mcconnell Story   *Gordon Douglas — U.S., 1955*
*The Malta Story   *Brian Desmond Hurst — GB, 1953*
The Map of the Human Heart   — AUS/CAN/FRA/GB, 1992
*A Matter of Life and Death   *Michael Powell/Emeric Pressburger — GB, 1946*
*Memphis Belle   *William Wyler — U.S., 1944*
*Memphis Belle   *Michael Caton-Jones — GB, 1990*
*Men Must Fight   *Edgar Selwyn — U.S., 1933*
*Midway   *Jack Smight — U.S., 1976*
Mission Batangas   *Keith Larsen — U.S., 1969*
*Mrs Miniver   *William Wyler — U.S., 1942*
Moscow Skies   *Yuli Raizman — USSR, 1944*
*Mosquito Squadron   *Boris Sagal — GB, 1968*
*Murphy's War   *Peter Yates — GB, 1971*
*1941   *Steven Spielberg — U.S., 1979*
*Nippon's Young Eagles   *Yutaka Abe — JAP, 1941*
*Normandie-Niemen   *Jean Dreville — FRA/USSR, 1959*
On the Fiddle   *Cyril Frankel — GB, 1961*
*One of Our Aircraft is Missing   *Michael Powell/Emeric Pressburger — GB, 1941*

*The One Thousand Plane Raid   *Boris Sagal* — U.S., 1968

*Operation Bikini   *Anthony Carras* — U.S., 1963

*Out of the Depths   *Ross Lederman* — U.S., 1946

*Pilot Number Five   *George Sidney* — U.S., 1943

*A Pilot Returns   *Roberto Rossellini* — ITA, 1942

*The Purple V   *George Sherman* — U.S., 1943

*Reach for the Sky   *Lewis Gilbert* — GB, 1956

*School for Secrets   *Peter Ustinov* — GB, 1946

*The Sea Shall Not Have Them   *Lewis Gilbert* — GB, 1954

*Ships With Wings   *Sergei Nolbandov* — GB, 1941

*633 Squadron   *Walter Grauman* — GB, 1964

*Sky Commando   *Fred F. Sears* — U.S., 1953

Soaring Passion   *Eiichi Koishi* — JAP, 1941

The Sons of Herr Gaspery   *Rolf Meyer* — GER, 1948

*South Seas Bouquet   *Yutaka Abe* — JAP, 1942

Spies of the Air   *David Macdonald* — GB, 1939

*Squadron Leader X   *Lance Comfort* — GB, 1942

The Star of Africa   *Alfred Weidenmann* — GER, 1957

A Storm from the Sea   *Shue Matsubayashi* — JAP, 1961

The Story of a Dive Bomber   — USSR, 1967

The Story of a Fighter Plane   *Hubert Drapella* — POL, 1958

*Stukas   *Karl Ritter* — GER, 1941

*Target for Tonight   *Harry Watt* — GB, 1941

*Target Unknown   *George Sherman* — U.S., 1951

*They Were Not Divided   *Terence Young* — GB, 1950

*Thirty Seconds Over Tokyo   *Mervyn Le Roy* — U.S., 1944

*Tonight We Raid Calais   *John Bahm* — U.S., 1943

*Tora! Tora! Tora!   *Richard Fleischer* — U.S., 1970

*Twelve O'clock High   *Henry King* — U.S., 1949

*Victory Through Air Power   *H. C. Potter, etc* — U.S., 1943

*The War Lover   *Philip Leacock* — GB, 1962

*The Way to the Stars   *Anthony Asquith* — GB, 1945

Weep, People of Japan   *Hiroshi Noguschi* — JAP, 1956

*When Willie Comes Marching Home   *John Ford* — U.S., 1950

*The Wife Takes a Flyer   *Richard Wallace* — U.S., 1942

TWELVE O CLOCK HIGH
'Glad to be back', thinks Gregory Peck. 20CF

*The Wild Blue Yonder   *Allan Dwan* — U.S., 1952

*Wing and a Prayer   *Henry Hathaway* — U.S., 1944

*Winged Victory   *George Cukor* — U.S., 1944

The Wings of Eagles   *John Ford* — U.S., 1957

Wings of the Navy   *Lloyd Bacon* — U.S., 1938

Wings of the Sea   *Shue Matsubayashi* — JAP, 1962

Wings Over the Pacific   *Phil Rosen* — U.S., 1943

The World Owes Me a Living   *Vernon Sewell* — GB, 1944

*A Yank in the RAF   *Henry King* — U.S., 1941

The Zero Fighter   *Toshio Masuda* — JAP, 1961

WORLD WAR II AT SEA

*Above Us the Waves   *Ralph Thomas* — GB, 1955

*Atlantic Convoy   *Lew Landers* — U.S., 1942

*Battle of the River Plate   *Michael Powell/Emeric Pressburger* — GB, 1956

*Battle Stations   *Lewis Seiler* — U.S., 1956

*The Big Blockade   *Charles Frend* — GB, 1941

*The Boat   *Wolfgang Petersen* — FRG, 1981

*The Burning Sky   *Yutaka Abe* — JAP, 1940

*The Caine Mutiny   *Edward Dmytryk* — U.S., 1954

*Casabianca   *Georges Peclet* — FRA, 1950

*Cockleshell Heroes   *Jose Ferrer* — GB, 1955

*Convoy   *Pen Tennyson* — GB, 1940

*Corvette K-225   *Richard Rosson* — U.S., 1943

*Crash Dive   *Archie Mayo* — U.S., 1943

*The Cruel Sea   *Charles Frend* — GB, 1952

Dark Waters   *Andre De Toth* — U.S., 1944

Death Ship   *Alvin Rakoff* — CAN/GB, 1980

*The Deep Six   *Rudolph Mate* — U.S., 1958

*The Demi-Paradise   *Anthony Asquith* — GB, 1943

*Destination Tokyo   *Delmer Daves* — U.S., 1943

*Destroyer   *William A. Seiter* — U.S., 1943

Eagle of the Pacific   *Inshiro Honda* — JAP, 1952

*The Enemy Below   *Dick Powell* — U.S., 1957

*Ensign Pulver   *Joshua Logan* — U.S., 1964

*Escape to Glory   *John Brahm* — U.S., 1940

*The Eternal Sea   *John H. Auer* — U.S., 1955

The Extraordinary Seaman   *John Frankenheimer* — U.S., 1968

*Father Goose   *Ralph Nelson* — U.S., 1964

*The Fighting Coast Guard   *Joseph Kane* — U.S., 1951

*The Fighting Lady   *Louis De Rochemont* — U.S., 1944

*The Final Countdown   *Don Taylor* — U.S., 1980

*Flat Top   *Lesley Selander* — U.S., 1952

*The Flying Missile   *Henry Levin* — U.S., 1950

*For Freedom   *Maurice Elvey/Castleton Knight* — GB, 1940

*For Those in Peril   *Charles Crichton* — GB, 1944

*The Frogmen   *Lloyd Bacon* — U.S., 1951

*From Here to Eternity   *Fred Zinnemann* — U.S., 1953

*The Gallant Hours   *Robert Montgomery* — U.S., 1959

*Ghost of the China Sea   *Fred F. Sears* — U.S., 1958

*Hell Boats   *Paul Wendkos* — GB, 1970

*Hellcats of the Navy   *Nathan Juran* — U.S., 1957

If We Go to Sea   *Masanori Igayama* — JAP, 1943

*In Harm's Way   *Otto Preminger* — U.S., 1965

*In Which We Serve   *Noel Coward/David Lean* — GB, 1942

Kiss Them for Me   *Stanley Donen* — U.S., 1957

*Lifeboat   *Alfred Hitchcock* — U.S., 1944

The Lightship   *Jerzy Skolimowski* — U.S., 1985

*The Long Voyage Home   *John Ford* — U.S., 1940

*The Longest Day   *Ken Annakin, Andrew Marton, Bernhard Wicki* — U.S., 1962

*Les Maudits   *Rene Clement — FRA, 1947*
Men of the Lightship   *David Macdonald — GB, 1940*
*Midway   *Jack Smight — U.S., 1976*
Minesweeper   *William Berke — U.S., 1943*
*Mister Roberts   *John Ford/Mervyn Leroy — U.S., 1955*
*Mrs Miniver   *William Wyler — U.S., 1942*
*Morning Departure   *Roy Baker — GB, 1950*
*Murphy's War   *Peter Yates — GB, 1971*
*Mystery Sea Raider   *Edward Dmytryk — U.S., 1940*
*Mystery Submarine   *Douglas Sirk — U.S., 1950*
*Mystery Submarine   *C. M. Pennington-Richards — GB, 1962*
Navy   *Tomotaka Tasaka — JAP, 1943*
*The Navy Comes Through   *Edward Sutherland — U.S., 1942*
*Neutral Port   *Marcel Varnel — GB, 1940*
*No Man is an Island   *John Monk Jr — U.S., 1962*
*Operation Bikini   *Anthony Carras — U.S., 1963*
*Operation Pacific   *George Waggner — U.S., 1950*
*Operation Petticoat   *Blake Edwards — U.S., 1959*
*Out of the Depths   *Ross Lederman — U.S., 1946*
*Prison Ship   *Arthur Dreifuss — U.S., 1945*
*Pt 109   *Leslie H. Martinson — U.S., 1963*
*Remember Pearl Harbor   *Joseph Santley — U.S., 1942*
*Run Silent, Run Deep   *Robert Wise — U.S., 1958*
*San Demetrio London   *Charles Frend — GB, 1943*
*The Sea Chase   *John Farrow — U.S., 1955*
*The Sea Shall Not Have Them   *Lewis Gilbert — GB, 1954*
Sea Wife   *Bob Mcnaught — GB, 1957*
*The Sea Wolves   *Andrew V. Maclaglen — GB/SWI/U.S., 1980*
*Sealed Cargo   *Alfred Werker — U.S., 1951*
*Ships With Wings   *Sergei Nolbandov — GB, 1941*
*The Silent Enemy   *Wlliam Fairchild — GB, 1958*
*The Silver Fleet   *Vernon Sewell/Gordon Wellesley — GB, 1943*
*Singlehanded   *Roy Boulting — U.S./GB, 1953*
*Sink the Bismark!   *Lewis Gilbert — GB, 1960*
*The Spy in Black   *Michael Powell — GB, 1939*
*Stand by for Action   *Robert Z. Leonard — U.S., 1943*
   *Submarine Command   *John Farrow — U.S., 1951*
*Submarine Raider   *Lew Landers — U.S., 1942*
*Submarine Seahawk   *Spencer G. Bennet — U.S., 1959*
*Submarine X-1   *William Graham — GB, 1967*
Submarines Head West   *— GER, 1941*
*The Sullivans   *Lloyd Bacon — U.S., 1944*
*Tampico   *Lothar Mendes — U.S., 1944*
*Task Force   *Delmer Daves — U.S., 1949*
*They Were Expendable   *John Ford — U.S., 1945*
*Thirty Seconds Over Tokyo   *Mervyn Le Roy — U.S., 1944*
*To Have and Have Not   *Howard Hawks — U.S., 1944*
*This Man's Navy   *William Wellman — U.S., 1945*
*Torpedo Bay   *Charles Frend — FRA/ITA, 1964*
*Torpedo Run   *Joseph Pevney — U.S., 1958*
*Torpedo Squadrons Move Out   *Kajiro Yamamoto — JAP, 1944*
Two-Man Submarine   *Lew Landers — U.S., 1944*
Two Yanks in Trinidad   *Gregory Ratoff — U.S., 1942*
*U-Boat Prisoner   *Lew Landers — U.S., 1944*
*Under Ten Flags   *Duilio Coletti/Silvio Narizzano — U.S., 1960*
*Underwater Warrior   *Andrew Marton — U.S., 1958*
Uomini Sul Fondo   *Francesco De Robertis — ITA, 1940*
*Up Periscope   *Gordon Douglas — U.S., 1959*
*The Valiant   *Roy Baker — GB/ITA, 1961*
*Voyage of the Damned   *Stuart Rosenberg — GB, 1976*
*The Wackiest Ship in the Army   *Richard Murphy — U.S., 1960*

*The War at Sea from Hawaii to Malaya   *Kajiro Yamamoto — JAP, 1942*
*We Dive at Dawn   *Anthony Asquith — GB, 1943*
*Western Approaches   *Pat Jackson — GB, 1944*
*The White Navy   *Roberto Rossellini — ITA, 1941*
*Wing and a Prayer   *Henry Hathaway — U.S., 1944*
Wings of the Navy   *Lloyd Bacon — U.S., 1938*
*You're in the Navy Now   *Henry Hathaway — U.S., 1951*

SUBMARINES

*Above Us the Waves   *Ralph Thomas — GB, 1955*
*Action in the North Atlantic   *Lloyd Bacon — U.S., 1943*
*Battle of the Coral Sea   *Paul Wendkos — U.S., 1959*
*The Boat   *Wolfgang Petersen — GER, 1981*
*Casabianca   *Georges Peclet — FRA, 1950*
*Crash Dive   *Archie Mayo — U.S., 1943*
*The Cruel Sea   *Charles Frend — GB, 1952*
*The Day Will Dawn   *Harold French — GB, 1942*
*Destination Tokyo   *Delmer Daves — U.S., 1943*
*The Enemy Below   *Dick Powell — U.S., 1957*
*Escape to Glory   *John Brahm — U.S., 1940*
*The Flying Missile   *Henry Levin — U.S., 1950*
*49th Parallel   *Michael Powell — GB, 1941*
*Hellcats of the Navy   *Nathan Juran — U.S., 1957*
*Lifeboat   *Alfred Hitchcock — U.S., 1944*
The Lightship   *Jerzy Skolimowski — U.S., 1985*
*Les Maudits   *Rene Clement — FRA, 1947*
*Morning Departure   *Roy Baker — GB, 1950*
*Murphy's War   *Peter Yates — GB, 1971*
*Mystery Submarine   *Douglas Sirk — U.S., 1950*
*Mystery Submarine   *C. M. Pennington-Richards — GB, 1962*
*The Navy Comes Through   *Edward Sutherland — U.S., 1942*
*Northern Pursuit   *Raoul Walsh — U.S., 1943*
*Operation Bikini   *Anthony Carras — U.S., 1963*
*Operation Pacific   *George Waggner — U.S., 1950*
*Operation Petticoat   *Blake Edwards — U.S., 1959*
*Out of the Depths   *Ross Lederman — U.S., 1946*
*Run Silent, Run Deep   *Robert Wise — U.S., 1958*
*The Silver Fleet   *Vernon Sewell/Gordon Wellesley — GB, 1943*
*Submarine Raider   *Lew Landers — U.S., 1942*
*Submarine Seahawk   *Spencer G. Bennet — U.S., 1959*
*Submarine X-1   *William Graham — GB, 1967*
Submarines Head West   *— GER, 1941*
*Torpedo Bay   *Charles Frend — FRA/ITA, 1964*
*Torpedo Run   *Joseph Pevney — U.S., 1958 Mgm*
Two-Man Submarine   *Lew Landers — U.S., 1944*
Two Tickets to London   *Edwin L. Marin — U.S., 1943*
*U-Boat Prisoner   *Lew Landers — U.S., 1944*
Uomini Sul Fondo   *Francesco De Robertis — ITA, 1940*
*Up Periscope   *Gordon Douglas — U.S., 1959*
*We Dive at Dawn   *Anthony Asquith — GB, 1943*
*Western Approaches   *Pat Jackson — GB, 1944*

ATOMIC BOMB

*Above and Beyond   *Melvin Frank/Norman Panama — U.S., 1952*
*The Battle for Heavy Water   *Titus Wibe Muller — FRA/NOR, 1947*
*The Beginning or the End   *Norman Taurog — U.S., 1947*
The Bell of Nagasaki   *— JAP, 1953*
*Black Rain   *Shohei Imamura — JAP, 1988*
*Children of Hiroshima   *Kaneto Shindo — JAP, 1952*

Dawn, 15 August   *Hideo Sekigawa — JAP, 1954*
*First Yank into Tokyo   *Gordon Douglas — U.S., 1945*
*Heart of Hiroshima   *Koreyoshi Kurahara — JAP, 1966*
*Hirosima   *Hideo Sekigawa — JAP, 1953*
*Hiroshima, Mon Amour   *Alain Resnais — FRA/JAP, 1959*
*Hiroshima: Out of the Ashes   *Peter Werner — U.S., 1990*
*Hiroshima — Remembering and Repressing   *Erwin Leiser —
   SWI, 1986*
*The House on 92nd Street   *Henry Hathaway — U.S., 1945*
I'll Not Forget the Song of Nagasaki   *— JAP, 1953*
Night Boat to Dublin   *Lawrence Huntington — GB, 1945*
Rendezvous 24   *James Tinling — U.S., 1946*
*Shadow of Hiroshima   *Hiroshi Teshigahara — JAP, 1956*
Shadow of Terror   *Lew Landers — U.S., 1945*
Twenty-Eight Pupils   *Keisuke Kinoshita — JAP, 1954*

WORLD WAR II ESPIONAGE

*Above Suspicion   *Richard Thorpe — U.S., 1943*
*Across the Pacific   *John Huston — U.S., 1942*
*Adventure in Iraq   *D. Ross Lederman — U.S., 1942*
*The Adventures of Tartu   *Harold S. Bucquet — GB, 1943*
*Against the Wind   *Charles Crichton — GB, 1947*
*All Through the Night   *Vincent Sherman — U.S., 1942*
*The Angry Hills   *Robert Aldrich — GB, 1959*
*Appointment in Berlin   *Alfred E. Green — U.S., 1943*
*Armored Command   *Byron Haskin — U.S., 1961*
*Assignment in Brittany   *Jack Conway — U.S., 1943*
*Atlantic Convoy   *Lew Landers — U.S., 1942*
*Background to Danger   *Raoul Walsh — U.S., 1943*
*The Battle of the V1   *Vernon Sewell — GB, 1958*
*Berlin Correspondent   *Eugene Forde — U.S., 1942*
*Betrayal from the East   *William Berke — U.S., 1945*
*Betrayed   *Gottfried Reinhardt — U.S., 1954*
The Black Parachute   *Lew Landers — U.S., 1944*
*Blood on the Sun   *Frank Lloyd — U.S., 1945*
*Bombs Over Burma   *Joseph H. Lewis — U.S. 1942*
Brass Target   *John Hough — U.S., 1978*
*Cairo   *W. S. Van Dyke — U.S., 1941*
*Canaris Master Spy   *Alfred Weidenmann — FRG, 1954*
*Candlelight in Algeria   *George King — GB, 1943*
Careful, Soft Shoulder   *Oliver Hp Garrett — U.S., 1942*
*Carve Her Name With Pride   *Lewis Gilbert — GB, 1958*
*Casablanca   *Michael Curtiz — U.S., 1942*
*Circle of Deception   *Jack Lee — GB, 1960*
*Cloak and Dagger   *Fritz Lang — U.S., 1946*
Code Name: Emerald   *Jonathan Sanger — U.S., 1985*
Code Name, Red Roses   *Fernando Di Leo — ITA, 1969*
*Confessions of a Nazi Spy   *Anatole Litvak — U.S., 1939*
*The Conspirators   *Jean Negulesco — U.S., 1944*
*Contraband   *Michael Powell — GB, 1940*
*Cottage to Let   *Anthony Asquith — GB, 1941*
*Count Five and Die   *Victor Vicas — GB, 1959*
Counterblast   *Paul Stein — GB, 1948*
*The Counterfeit Traitor   *George Seaton — U.S., 1962*
*Crooks' Tour   *John Baxter — GB, 1940*
*Crossroads of Passions   *Ettore Giannini — FRA, 1947*
*Dangerously They Live   *Robert Florey — U.S., 1941*
*Decision Before Dawn   *Anatole Litvak — U.S., 1944*
*Double Crime in the Maginot Line   *Felix Gandera — FRA,
   1939*
*The Eagle Has Landed   *John Sturges — GB, 1976*
*Enemy Agent   *Lew Landers — U.S., 1940*

*The Enemy General   *George Sherman — U.S., 1960*
Escape To Danger   *Lance Comfort — GB, 1943*
*Espionage Agent   *Lloyd Bacon — U.S., 1939*
*Eye of the Needle   *Richard Marquand — GB, 1981*
*A Face in the Rain   *Irvin Kershner — U.S., 1963*
*First Comes Courage   *Dorothy Arzner — U.S., 1943*
*First Yank into Tokyo   *Gordon Douglas — U.S., 1945*
*Five Fingers   *Joseph L. Mankiewicz — U.S., 1952*
*Five Graves to Cairo   *Billy Wilder — U.S., 1943*
*Flight for Freedom   *Lothar Mendes — U.S., 1943*
*Fly by Night   *Robert Siodmark — U.S., 1942*
*Foreign Correspondent   *Alfred Hitchcock — U.S., 1940*
Forward! Flag of Independence   *Teinosuke Kinugasa — JAP,
   1943*
The Four Just Men   *Walter Forde — GB, 1939*
*Foxhole in Cairo   *John Moxey — GB, 1960*
*Golden Earrings   *Mitchell Leisen — U.S., 1947*
The Goose Steps Out   *Basil Dearden/Will Hay — GB, 1942*
*The Great Impersonation   *John Rawlins — U.S., 1942*
*Halfway To Shanghai   *John Rawlins — U.S., 1942*
*Hanover Street   *Peter Hyams — GB, 1979*
Hotel Reserve   *Lance Comfort/Max Greene/Victor Hanbury —
   GB, 1944*
*The Hour Before the Dawn   *Frank Tuttle — U.S., 1944*
*The House on 92nd Street   *Henry Hathaway — U.S., 1945*
I Deal in Danger   *Walter Grauman — U.S., 1966*
*I Escaped from the Gestapo   *Harold Young — U.S., 1943*
*I See a Dark Stranger   *Frank Launder — GB, 1945*
*I Was an American Spy   *Lesley Selander — U.S., 1951*
*I Was Monty's Double   *John Guillermin — GB, 1958*
*In Enemy Country   *Harry Keller — U.S., 1968*
*International Lady   *Tim Whelan — U.S., 1941*
Jericho   *Henri Calef — FRA, 1945*
Joe Smith, American   *Richard Thorpe — U.S., 1942*
*Journey into Fear   *Norman Foster/Orson Welles — U.S., 1942*
*Journey into Fear   *Daniel Mann — U.S., 1976*
*The Lady Vanishes   *Alfred Hitchcock — GB, 1938*
*The Lady Vanishes   *Anthony Page — GB, 1979*
*Lassiter   *Roger Young — U.S., 1984*
*The Last Blitzkrieg   *Arthur Dreifuss — U.S., 1958*
*The Last Day of the War   *Juan Antonio Bardem — SPA/U.S.,
   1969*
*The Last Escape   *Walter Grauman — GB, 1970*
The Last Time I Saw Archie   *Jack Webb — U.S., 1961*
*The Lisbon Story   *Paul Stein — GB, 1946*
Little Tokyo Usa   *Otto Brower — U.S., 1942*
*Lucky Jordan   *Frank Tuttle — U.S., 1942*
*Madame Spy   *Roy William Neill — U.S., 1942*
The Magic Face   *Frank Tuttle — U.S., 1951*
*The Man from Morocco   *Max Greene — GB, 1944*
*Man Hunt   *Fritz Lang — U.S., 1941*
*The Man Who Never Was   *Ronald Neame — GB, 1955*
Margin for Error   *Otto Preminger — U.S., 1943*
*Mata Hari's Daughter   *Renzo Merius — ITA, 1954*
*Ministry of Fear   *Fritz Lang — U.S., 1944*
Miss V from Moscow   *Albert Herman — U.S., 1942*
Mission to Tangiers   *Andre Hunebelle — FRA, 1949*
*Mother Night   *Keith Gordon — U.S., 1996*
My Favorite Blonde   *Sidney Lanfield — U.S., 1942*
The Mysterious Doctor   *Ben Stoloff — U.S., 1942*
*Nazi Agent   *Jules Dassin — U.S., 1942*
*Never So Few   *John Sturges — U.S., 1959*

*The Next of Kin   *Thorold Dickinson — GB, 1942*
Nick Carter — Master Detective   *Jacques Tourneur — U.S., 1939*
Night Boat To Dublin   *Lawrence Huntington — GB, 1945*
The Night Invader   *Herbert Mason — GB, 1943*
*Night Train To Munich   *Carol Reed — GB, 1940*
*Nightmare   *Tim Whelan — U.S., 1942*
*No Man is an Island   *John Monk Jr — U.S., 1962*
*Northern Pursuit   *Raoul Walsh — U.S., 1943*
*Notorious   *Alfred Hitchcock — U.S., 1946*
*Odette   *Herbert Wilcox — GB, 1950*
On the Double   *Melville Shavelson — U.S., 1961*
*One Night in Lisbon   *Edward H. Griffith — U.S., 1941*
*Operation Amsterdam   *Michael McCarthy — GB, 1958*
*Operation Crossbow   *Michael Anderson — GB/ITA, 1965*
*Operation Secret   *Lewis Seiler — U.S., 1952*
*Orders to Kill   *Anthony Asquith — GB, 1958*
*Oss   *Irving Pichel — U.S., 1946*
Passport to Suez   *Andre De Toth — U.S., 1943*
*The Pigeon That Took Rome   *Melville Shavelson — U.S., 1962*
*Pimpernel Smith   *Leslie Howard — GB, 1941*
Private's Progress   *John Boulting — GB, 1956*
Quiet Please, Murder   *John Larkin — U.S., 1942*
*Raiders of the Lost Ark   *Steven Spielberg — U.S., 1981*
*Remember Pearl Harbor   *Joseph Santley — U.S., 1942*
Rendezvous 24   *James Tinling — U.S., 1946*
The Rocketeer   *Joe Johnston — U.S., 1991*
Rough Shoot   *Robert Parrish — GB, 1952*
*Saboteur   *Alfred Hitchcock — U.S., 1942*
*The Saboteur, Code Name Morituri   *Bernhard Wicki — U.S., 1965*
Salon Kitty   *Tinto Brass — FRA/FRG/ITA, 1978*
Samurai   *Raymond Cannon — U.S., 1945*
Secret Agent of Japan   *Irving Pichel — U.S., 1942*
Secret Command   *Eddie Sutherland — U.S., 1944*
*The Secret Door   *Gilbert Kay — GB, 1964*
*Secret Mission   *Harold French — GB, 1942*
*The Secret of Blood Island   *Quentin Lawrence — GB, 1964*
*Secrets of Scotland Yard   *George Blair — U.S., 1944*
*Secrets of the Underground   *William Morgan — U.S., 1943*
The Seventh Survivor   *Leslie Hiscott — GB, 1941*
Shadow of Terror   *Lew Landers — U.S., 1945*
Sherlock Holmes and the Secret Weapon   *Roy William Neill — U.S., 1942*
Sherlock Holmes and the Voice of Terror   *John Rawlins — U.S., 1942*
Sherlock Holmes in Washington   *Roy William Neill — U.S., 1943*
*Shining Through   *David Seltzer — U.S., 1992*
Spies of the Air   *David Macdonald — GB, 1939*
*The Spy In Black   *Michael Powell — GB, 1939*
*Squadron Leader X   *Lance Comfort — GB, 1942*
*Storm Over Lisbon   *George Sherman — U.S., 1944*
*The Southern Cross   *Peter Maxwell — AUS, 1982*
*Tampico   *Lothar Mendes — U.S., 1944*
Tangier   *George Waggner — U.S., 1946*
*Teheran   *William Freshman/Giacomo Gentilomo — GB, 1947*
Teheran 43   *Alexander Alov/Vladimir Naoumov — FRA/USSR, 1979*
*A Terrible Beauty   *Tay Garnett — GB/U.S., 1960*
*They Came To Blow Up America   *Edward Ludwig — U.S., 1943*

They Met in the Dark   *Karel Lamac — GB, 1943*
*13 Rue Madeleine   *Henry Hathaway — U.S., 1947*
*Thirty-Six Hours   *George Seaton — U.S., 1964*
This Gun for Hire   *Frank Tuttle — U.S., 1942*
*This Was Paris   *John Harlow — GB, 1941*
*To Have and Have Not   *Howard Hawks — U.S., 1945*
*Tomorrow We Live   *George King — GB, 1942*
*Tonight We Raid Calais   *John Bahm — U.S., 1943*
The Tower of Terror   *Lawrence Huntington — GB, 1941*
The Traitor   *Michael McCarthy — GB, 1957*
Traitor Spy   *Walter Summers — GB, 1939*
*Triple Cross   *Terence Young — GB, 1967*
*The Two-Headed Spy   *Andre De Toth — GB, 1958*
Two-Man Submarine   *Lew Landers — U.S., 1944*
Two Yanks in Trinidad   *Gregory Ratoff — U.S., 1942*
*U-Boat Prisoner   *Lew Landers — U.S., 1944*
Under the Rainbow   *Steve Rash — U.S., 1981*
*Underground   *Vincent Sherman — U.S., 1941*
*War, Italian Style   *Luigi Scattini — ITA, 1967*
*Watch on the Rhine   *Herman Shumlin — U.S., 1943*
Waterfront   *Steve Sekely — U.S., 1942*
*Went the Day Well?   *Alberto Cavalcanti — GB, 1942*
*When Hell Broke Loose   *Kenneth G. Crane — U.S., 1958*
*When Willie Comes Marching Home   *John Ford — U.S., 1950 20cf*
*Where Eagles Dare   *Brian G. Hutton — GB, 1969*
Who Are You, Monsieur Sorge?   *Yves Ciampi — FRA/ITA/JAP, 1961*
*Yellow Canary   *Herbert Wilcox — GB, 1943*

CONCENTRATION CAMPS
*The Adventures of Werner Holt   *Joachim Kunert — FRG, 1963*
*Bomb at 10.10   *Charles Damic — YUG, 1966*
The Boxer and Death   *Petr Solan — CZE, 1962*
*Death is My Trade   *Theodor Kotulla — FRG, 1977*
*Distant Journey   *Alfred Radok — CZE, 1949*
*Eichmann and the Third Reich   *Erwin Leiser — SWI, 1961*
*Empire of the Sun   *Steven Spielberg — U.S., 1987*
*Fragments of Isabella   *Ronan O'Leary — IRE, 1989*
Hours of Hope   *Jan Rybkowski — POL, 1955*
*Judith   *Daniel Mann — U.S., 1965*
*Kapo   *Gillo Pontecorvo — FRA/ITA, 1960*
*Korczak   *Andrzej Wajda — FRA/GB/GER/POL, 1990*
Landscape After Battle   *Andrzej Wajda — POL, 1970*
*The Last Days   *Ken Lipper/James Moll — U.S., 1998*
*The Last Stage   *Wanda Jakubowska — POL, 1947*
*Life is Beautiful   *Roberto Benigni — ITA, 1997*
The Long Journey   *Alfred Radok — CZE, 1949*
*The Louvre Ticket Office   *Michel Mitrani — FRA, 1974*
Madame Rosa   *Moshe Mizrahi — FRA, 1977*
*The Night Porter   *Liliana Cavani — ITA, 1973*
*Night Train to Munich   *Carol Reed — GB, 1940*
The Ninth Circle   *France Stiglic — YUG, 1960*
*None Shall Escape   *Andre De Toth — U.S., 1944*
*Nuit Et Brouillard   *Alain Resnais — FRA, 1955*
Once Upon a Honeymoon   *Leo Mccarey — U.S., 1942*
Passenger   *Andrzej Munk and Witold Lesiewicz — POL, 1963*
*Pastor Hall   *Roy and John Boulting — GB, 1940*
*The Pawnbroker   *Sidney Lumet — U.S., 1965*
The Prisoners   *Gustav Gavrin — CZE, 1949*
The Revolt of Job   *Imre Gyongyossi — HUN, 1983*

FOXHOLE IN CAIRO
Rommel (Albert Lieven, left) receives a coded message about the enemy spy. Omnia

*Schindler's List   Steven Spielberg — U.S., 1993
*The Seventh Cross   Fred Zinnemann — U.S., 1944
*Sophie's Choice   Alan J. Pakula — U.S., 1982
Sterne   Konrad Wolf — FRG, 1959
The Summer of Aviya   Eli Cohen — ISR, 1988
Transport from Paradise   Zbynek Brynych — CZE, 1962
*Triumph of the Spirit   Robert M. Young — U.S., 1989
The Truce   Francesco Rosi — FRA/GER/ITA, 1997
*Two Thousand Women   Frank Launder — GB, 1944
Women in the Night   William Rowland — U.S., 1948

POW CAMPS
*Albert, RN   Lewis Gilbert — GB, 1953
*The Bridge on the River Kwai   David Lean — GB, 1957
Brute Force   Jules Dassin — U.S., 1947
*The Brylcreem Boys   Terence Ryan — GB, 1995
*The Camp on Blood Island   Val Guest — GB, 1958
*The Captive Heart   Basil Dearden — GB, 1946
*Captive Hearts   Paul Almond — U.S., 1987
*The Colditz Story   Guy Hamilton — GB, 1954
Cornered   Edward Dmytryk — U.S., 1945
*Counterpoint   Ralph Nelson — U.S., 1967
*The Cross of Lorraine   Tay Garnett — U.S., 1943
*Danger Within   Don Chaffey — GB, 1959
The Doctor of Stalingrad   Geza Von Radvanyi — HUN, 1958
Don't Move, Die and Rise Again   Vitaly Kanevsky — USSR, 1989
*The Elusive Corporal   Jean Renoir — FRA, 1962
*Era Notte a Roma   Roberto Rossellini — FRA/ITA, 1960
*Eroica   Andrzej Munk — POL, 1957
*Escape in the Desert   Edward A. Blatt — U.S., 1945
*Escape to Athena   George P. Cosmatos — GB, 1979
*Une Femme Francaise   Regis Wargnier — FRA/GB/GER, 1994
*Fraulein   Henry Koster — U.S., 1958
*The Great Escape   John Sturges — U.S., 1963
Half-Time in Hell   Zoltan Fabri — HUN, 1961
*Hannibal Brooks   Michael Winner — GB, 1968

*The Human Condition   Masaki Kobayashi — JAP, 1961
*The Hill   Sidney Lumet — GB, 1965
*I Was a Siberian Pow   Kunio Watanabe — JAP, 1952
*King Rat   Bryan Forbes — U.S., 1965
*The Last Chance   Leopold Lindtberg — SWI, 1945
*Letters to an Unknown Lover   Peter Duffell — FRA/GB, 1985
Libel   Anthony Asquith — GB, 1959
The List of Adrian Messenger   John Huston — U.S., 1983
*A Love in Germany   Andrzej Wajda — GER/FRA, 1983
*The Mckenzie Break   Lamont Johnson — GB, 1970
*A Man Escaped   Robert Bresson — FRA, 1956
*Merry Christmas, Mr Lawrence   Nagasia Oshima — GB, 1982
Morituri   Arthur Brauner — GER, 1946
*No Time to Die   Terence Young — GB, 1958
One Man Too Many   Costa-Gavras — FRA/ITA, 1966
*The One That Got Away   Roy Baker — GB, 1957
Pacific Inferno   Rolf Bayer — U.S., 1981
*Paradise Road   Bruce Beresford — U.S./AUS, 1997
Pasqualino   Lina Wertmuller — ITA, 1975
*The Password is Courage   Andrew L. Stone — GB, 1962
Repatriation   Kunio Watanabe — JAP, 1949
*Return from the River Kwai   Andrew V. Maclaglen — GB, 1988
Road to Eternity   Masaki Kobayashi — JAP, 1959
*The Secret of Blood Island   Quentin Lawrence — GB, 1964
*The Secret War of Harry Frigg   Jack Smight — U.S., 1967
Seven Thunders   Hugo Fregonese — GB, 1957
Seven Women from Hell   Robert D. Webb — U.S., 1961
Situation Hopeless But Not Serious   Gottfried Reinhardt — U.S., 1944
*Slaughterhouse Five   George Roy Hill — U.S., 1972
*The Southern Cross   Peter Maxwell — AUS, 1982
Stalag 17   Billy Wilder — U.S., 1953
Taiga   Wolfgang Liebeneiner — FRG, 1961
Target Unknown   George Sherman — U.S., 1951
*Three Came Home   Jean Negulesco — U.S., 1950
Tokyo Rose   Lew Landers — U.S., 1945
*A Town Like Alice   Jack Lee — GB, 1956
Until Hell is Frozen   Leopold Lahola — FRG, 1960
*Very Important Person   Ken Annakin — GB, 1961
*Victory   John Huston — U.S., 1981
*Von Ryan's Express   Mark Robson — U.S., 1965
*The Wind Cannot Read   Ralph Thomas — GB, 1958
*The Wooden Horse   Jack Lee — GB, 1950

BATTLE OF BRITAIN
*Angels One Five   George More O'Ferrall — GB, 1952
*The Battle of Britain   Frank Capra — U.S., 1943
*The Battle of Britain   Guy Hamilton — GB, 1969
*Dangerous Moonlight   Brian Desmond Hurst — GB, 1941
*The First of the Few   Leslie Howard — GB, 1942
*Hope and Glory   John Boorman — GB, 1987
*London Can Take It   Humphrey Jennings/Harry Watt — GB, 1940
*Mrs Miniver   William Wyler — U.S., 1942
The Story of a Fighter Plane   Hubert Drapella — POL, 1958
*The Way to the Stars   Anthony Asquith — GB, 1945

PEARL HARBOR
*Across the Pacific   John Huston — U.S., 1942 WB
*Behind the Rising Sun   Edward Dmytryk — U.S., 1943
*Come See the Paradise   Alan Parker — U.S., 1990
December   Gabe Torres — U.S., 1991

*December 7th   *John Ford* — U.S., 1943
*The Final Countdown   *Don Taylor* — U.S., 1980
*From Here To Eternity   *Fred Zinnemann* — U.S., 1953
*In Harm's Way   *Otto Preminger* — U.S., 1965
Navy   *Tomotaka Tasaka* — JAP, 1943
*1941   *Steven Spielberg* — U.S., 1979
*Remember Pearl Harbor   *Joseph Santley* — U.S., 1942
A Storm from the Sea   *Shue Matsubayashi* — JAP, 1961
*Submarine Raider   *Lew Landers* — U.S., 1942
*Suicide Battalion   *Edward L. Cahn* — U.S., 1958
*To the Shores of Tripoli   *Bruce Humberstone* — U.S., 1942
*Tora! Tora! Tora!   *Richard Fleischer* — U.S., 1970
Two Yanks in Trinidad   *Gregory Ratoff* — U.S., 1942
*The War at Sea from Hawaii To Malaya   *Kajiro Yamamoto* — JAP, 1942
*We've Never Been Licked   *John Rawlins* — U.S., 1943

D-DAY
*The Americanization of Emily   *Arthur Hiller* — U.S., 1964
*The Battle of the Commandos   *Umberto Lenzi* — ITA, 1969
*Breakthrough   *Lewis Seiler* — U.S., 1950
*D-Day the Sixth of June   *Henry Koster* — U.S., 1956
*The Desert Fox   *Henry Hathaway* — U.S., 1951
*The Dirty Dozen   *Robert Aldrich* — GB/U.S., 1967
*From Hell To Victory   *Umberto Lenzi* — FRA/ITA/SPA, 1979
*The Longest Day   *Ken Annakin, Andrew Marton, Bernhard Wicki* — U.S., 1962
A Monkey in Winter   *Henri Verneuil* — FRA, 1962
*OSS   *Irving Pichel* — U.S., 1946
*Overlord   *Stuart Cooper* — GB, 1975
*Red Ball Express   *Budd Boetticher* — U.S., 1952
*Saving Private Ryan   *Steven Spielberg* — U.S. 1998
*Screaming Eagles   *Charles Haas* — U.S., 1956
*Sergeant Steiner   *Andrew V. Maclaglen* — FRG, 1979
*Suicide Commando   *Camillo Bazzone* — ITA, 1969
*The True Glory   *Garson Kanin/Carol Reed* — U.S./GB, 1945
*Up from the Beach   *Robert Parrish* — U.S., 1965
*The Victors   *Carl Foreman* — GB, 1963
La Vie De Chateau   *Jean-Paul Rappenau* — FRA, 1965
*Saving Private Ryan   *Steven Spielberg* — U.S., 1998
The Young Warriors   *John Peyser* — U.S., 1967

BATTLE OF THE BULGE
*Armored Command   *Byron Haskin* — U.S., 1961
*Attack!   *Robert Aldrich* — U.S., 1956 UA
*The Battle of the Bulge   *Ken Annakin* — U.S., 1965
*The Battle of the Bulge — The Brave Rifles   *Lawrence Mascott* — U.S., 1966
*Battleground   *William Wellman* — U.S., 1949
*Castle Keep   *Sydney Pollack* — U.S., 1969
*Counterpoint   *Ralph Nelson* — U.S., 1967
*Homecoming   *Mervyn Leroy* — U.S., 1948
*The Last Blitzkrieg   *Arthur Dreifuss* — U.S., 1958
*A Midnight Clear   *Keith Gordon* — U.S., 1992
*Patton   *Franklin Schaffner* — U.S., 1970

GREEK CIVIL WAR AND COUPS, 1944–70
The Captive City   — ITA, 1962
*Eleni   *Peter Yates* — U.S., 1985
*Guerrilla Girl   *John Christian* — U.S., 1953
The Travelling Players   *Theodor Angelopolous* — GRE, 1975
Z   *Costa-Gavras* — ALG/FRA, 1968

COLD WAR, 1945–91
*The Bed Sitting Room   *Richard Lester* — GB, 1969
*The Bedford Incident   *James B. Harris* — GB, 1965
Berlin Express   *Jacques Tourneur* — U.S., 1948
The Big Lift   *George Seaton* — U.S., 1950
*Crimson Tide   *Tony Scott* — U.S., 1995
*Dr Strangelove   *Stanley Kubrick* — GB, 1963
*Fail Safe   *Sidney Lumet* — U.S., 1964
Firefox   *Clint Eastwood* — U.S., 1982
*Hell and High Water   *Samuel Fuller* — U.S., 1954
*The Hunt for Red October   *John Mctiernan* — U.S., 1990
On the Beach   *Stanley Kramer* — U.S., 1959
Panic in Year Zero   *Ray Milland* — U.S., 1962
The Red Danube   *George Sidney* — U.S., 1949
*Red Dawn   *John Milius* — U.S., 1984
The Russians Are Coming, the Russians Are Coming   *Norman Jewison* — U.S., 1965

FRENCH-INDOCHINA WAR, 1946–54
*The Bat Squadron   *Erich Engel* — DDR, 1958
*China Gate   *Samuel Fuller* — U.S., 1957
Cobra   *Yves Boisset* — FRA, 1971
*Dien Bien Phu   *Pierre Schoendoerffer* — FRA, 1992
*Fort-Du-Fou   *Leo Joannon* — FRA, 1962
*Heaven and Earth   *Oliver Stone* — U.S., 1993
*Jump into Hell   *David Butler* — U.S., 1955
*Lost Command   *Mark Robson* — U.S., 1966
The Postman Goes To War   *Claude Bernard-Aubert* — FRA, 1966
*The Quiet American   *Joseph L. Mankiewicz* — U.S., 1952
Ramuntcho   *Pierre Schoendorfer* — FRA, 1958
*Rogues' Regiment   *Robert Florey* — U.S., 1948
*317 Section   *Pierre Schoendoerffer* — FRA, 1964
*A Yank in Indo-China   *Wallace A. Grissell* — U.S., 1952

ARAB-ISRAELI CONFLICTS, 1947–94
The Ambassador   *J. Lee Thompson* — U.S., 1984
*Avanti-Popolo   *Rafi Bukaee* — ISR, 1986

CASTLE KEEP
Winter 1944-45, and war-weary GIs stagger across Belgium.
Columbia/Filmways

Berlin Jerusalem   *Amos Gitai — FRA, 1989*
*Cast a Giant Shadow   *Melville Shavelson — U.S., 1966*
*Cup Final   *Eran Riklis — ISR, 1991*
*Every Bastard a King   *Uri Zohar — ISR, 1970*
*Exodus   *Otto Preminger — U.S., 1960*
*Friendship's Death   *Peter Wollen — GB, 1987*
Harvest of Hate   *Michael Thornhill — AUS, 1979*
*Hill 24 Doesn't Answer   *Thorold Dickinson — ISR, 1954*
The Inspector   *Mark Robson — GB, 1961*
*The Jerusalem File   *John Flynn — ISR /U.S., 1971*
*Judith   *Daniel Mann — U.S., 1965*
*Kafr Kassem   *Borhan Alaouie — LIB/SYR, 1974*
The Last Winter   *Riki Shelach Nissimoff — ISR, 1983*
*The Little Drummer Girl   *George Roy Hill — U.S., 1984*
Madame Rosa   *Moshe Mizrahi — FRA, 1977*
*Not Quite Jerusalem   *Lewis Gilbert — GB, 1985*
One of Us   *Uri Barbash — ISR, 1989*
*Operation Thunderbolt   *Menahem Golan — ISR, 1977*
Paratroopers   *Yehuda Judd Ne'eman — ISR, 1976*
Ricochets   *Eli Cohen — ISR, 1986*
Rosebud   *Otto Preminger — U.S., 1975*
*Sword in the Desert   *George Sherman — U.S., 1949*
Wedding in Galilee   *Michel Kleifi — BEL/FRA, 1987*

MALAYAN EMERGENCY, 1948–57
*Privates on Parade   *Peter Nichols — GB, 1982*
The Seventh Dawn   *Lewis Gilbert — GB/U.S., 1964*
Stand Up Virgin Soldiers   *Norman Cohen — GB, 1977*
*The Virgin Soldiers   *John Dexter — GB, 1969*
*Windom's Way   *Ronald Neame — GB, 1957*

KOREAN WAR, 1950–53
*All the Young Men   *Hall Bartlett — U.S., 1960*
*An Annapolis Story   *Don Siegel — U.S., 1955*
*The Bamboo Prison   *Lewis Seiler — U.S., 1954*
*Battle Circus   *Richard Brooks — U.S., 1952*
*Battle Flame   *R. G. Springsteen — U.S., 1959*
*Battle Hymn   *Douglas Sirk — U.S., 1957*
*Battle of the 38th Parallel   *Lin Kwon Taek — U.S./SKO, 1976*
*Battle Taxi   *Herbert L. Strock — U.S., 1954*
*Battle Zone   *Lesley Selander — U.S., 1952*
Bombers B-52   *Gordon Douglas — U.S., 1957*
*The Bridges at Toko-Ri   *Mark Robson — U.S., 1954*
*Captain Newman, MD   *David Miller — U.S., 1963*
Chattahoochee   *Mick Jackson — U.S., 1989*
*Combat Squad   *Cy Roth — U.S., 1953*
*Dragonfly Squadron   *Lesley Selander — U.S., 1954*
*The Eternal Sea   *John H. Auer — U.S., 1955*
The Fearmakers   *Jacques Tourneur — U.S., 1958*
*Fixed Bayonets   *Samuel Fuller — U.S., 1951*
*Flight Nurse   *Allan Dwan — U.S., 1953*
Glory Alley   *Raoul Walsh — U.S., 1952*
*The Glory Brigade   *Robert D. Webb — U.S., 1953*
*Hell and High Water   *Samuel Fuller — U.S., 1954*
*Hell's Horizon   *Tom Gries — U.S., 1955*
Here Come the Jets   *Gene Fowler — U.S., 1959*
*A Hill in Korea   *Julian Amyes — GB, 1956*
*Hold Back the Night   *Allan Dwan — U.S., 1956*
*The Hook   *George Seaton — U.S., 1962*
*The Hunters   *Dick Powell — U.S., 1958*
*I Want You   *Mark Robson — U.S., 1951*
*Inchon   *Terence Young — U.S., 1981*

*Jet Attack   *Edward L. Cahn — U.S., 1958*
Korea   *Cathal Black — IRE, 1995*
Korea Patrol   *Max Nosseck — U.S., 1951*
Love is a Many Splendored Thing   *Henry King — U.S., 1955*
*Macarthur   *Joseph Sargent — U.S., 1977*
*The Mcconnell Story   *Gordon Douglas — U.S., 1955*
*The Manchurian Candidate   *John Frankenheimer — U.S., 1962*
*Marines Let's Go   *Raoul Walsh — U.S., 1961*
*M*A*S*H*   *Robert Altman — U.S., 1970*
*Men in War   *Anthony Mann — U.S., 1957*
*Men of the Fighting Lady   *Andrew Marton — U.S., 1954*
Mission Over Korea   *Fred F. Sears — U.S., 1953*
Moranbong: Korean Chronicle   *Jean-Claude Bonnardot — FRA/SKO, 1959*
*The Nun and the Sergeant   *Franklin Adreon — U.S., 1962*
*One Minute to Zero   *Tay Garnett — U.S., 1952*
Operation Dames   *Louis Clyde Stoumen — U.S., 1959*
*Pork Chop Hill   *Lewis Milestone — U.S., 1959*
*Prisoner of War   *Andrew Marton — U.S., 1954*
*The Rack   *Arnold Laven — U.S., 1956*
*Retreat, Hell!   *Joseph H. Lewis — U.S., 1952*
*Sabre Jet   *Louis King — U.S., 1953*
*Sergeant Ryker   *Buzz Kulik — U.S., 1963*
*Sky Commando   *Fred F. Sears — U.S., 1953*
*Sniper's Ridge   *John Bushelman — U.S., 1961*
*The Steel Helmet   *Samuel Fuller — U.S., 1951*
*Submarine Command   *John Farrow — U.S., 1951*
The Taebaek Mountains   *Im Kwon-Taek — SKO, 1994*
*Tank Battalion   *Sherman A. Rose — U.S., 1958*
*Target Zero   *Harmon Jones — U.S., 1955*
*Time Limit   *Karl Malden — U.S., 1957*
*To the Starry Island   *Park Kwang-Su — SKO, 1993*
*Torpedo Alley   *Lew Landers — U.S., 1953*
Toward the Unknown   *Mervyn Leroy — U.S., 1956*
*War Hunt   *Denis Sanders — U.S., 1961*
*War is Hell   *Burt Topper — U.S., 1963*
*A Yank in Korea   *Lew Landers — U.S., 1951*
The Young and the Brave   *Francis D. Lyon — U.S., 1963*

KENYA — MAU MAU RISING, 1952–60
*The Kitchen Toto   *Harry Hook — GB, 1987*
*Safari   *Terence Young — GB, 1956*
*Simba   *Brian Desmond Hurst — GB, 1955*
*Something of Value   *Richard Brooks — U.S., 1957*

LAOS CIVIL WAR, 1953–73
*Air America   *Roger Spottiswoode — U.S., 1990*
Come Back   *Hal Bartlett — U.S., 1983*

CYPRUS, 1954–74
*Attila '74   *Michael Cacoyannis — GRE, 1975*
*The High Bright Sun   *Ralph Thomas — GB, 1965*
*Private Potter   *Caspar Wade — GB, 1962*
*Tomorrow's Warrior   *Michael Papas — CYP, 1974*

FRENCH-ALGERIAN WAR, 1954–62
*The Battle of Algiers   *Gillo Pontecorvo — ALG/ITA, 1965*
*Chronique Des Annees De Braise   *Mohamed Lakhdar Hamina — ALG, 1975*
*Le Coup De Sirocco   *Alexandre Arcady — FRA, 1979*
*La Guerre Sans Nom   *Bertrand Tavernier — FRA, 1992*

*L'honneur D'un Capitaine   *Pierre Schoendoerffer* — FRA, 1982
*The Legion's Last Patrol   *Frank Wisbar* — ITA, 1964
*Lost Command   *Mark Robson* — U.S., 1966
Madame Rosa   *Moshe Mizrahi* — FRA, 1977
Muriel   *Alain Resnais* — FRA, 1963
New Certainties   *Jacques Davila* — FRA, 1979
Noua   *Abdelaziz Tolbi* — ALG, 1973
Objective 500 Million   *Pierre Schoendorfer* — FRA, 1966
Les Parapluies De Cherbourg   *Jacques Demy* — FRA, 1964
*Le Petit Soldat   *Jean-Luc Godard* — FRA, 1960
La Question   *Laurent Heynemann* — FRA, 1977
Ras   *Yves Boisset* — FRA, 1973
The Rebel   *Alain Cavalier* — FRA, 1964
Les Roseaux Sauvages   *Andre Techne* — FRA, 1993
Les Sacrifices   *Okach Touita* — FRA, 1982
Le Vent Des Aure   *Mohammed Lakhdar* — ALG, 1966

HUNGARIAN UPRISING, 1956

*The Beast of Budapest   *Harmon C. Jones* — U.S., 1958
*Daniel Takes a Train   *Pal Sandor* — HUN, 1983
Diary for My Loves   *Marta Meszaros* — HUN, 1987
In Praise of Older Women   *George Kaczender* — CAN, 1977
*The Journey   *Anatole Litvak* — U.S., 1959
Red Psalm   *Miklos Jancso* — HUN, 1971
Silence and Cry   *Miklos Jancso* — HUN, 1967
The Valley   *Tamas Renyi* — HUN, 1969
Whooping Cough   *Peter Gardos* — HUN, 1987

SUEZ CRISIS, 1956

*Kafr Kassem   *Borhan Alaouie* — LIB/SYR, 1974
*The Ploughman's Lunch   *Richard Eyre* — GB, 1983

THE CUBAN REVOLUTION, 1958–59

*Che!   *Richard Fleischer* — U.S., 1969
*Cuba   *Richard Lester* — U.S., 1979
*Cuba Si!   *Chris Marker* — FRA, 1961
*Cuban Rebel Girls   *Barry Mahon* — U.S., 1959
Un Dia De Noviembre   *Humberto Solas* — CUB, 1976
The Godfather Part II   *Francis Ford Coppola* — U.S., 1974
*The Gun Runners   *Don Siegel* — U.S., 1958
*Havana   *Sydney Pollack* — U.S., 1990
*Lucia   *Humberto Solas* — CUB, 1969
*Rebellion in Cuba   *Albert C. Gannaway* — U.S., 1961

VIETNAM WAR, 1959–75

*Air America   *Roger Spottiswoode* — U.S., 1990
*The Anderson Section   *Pierre Schoendoerffer* — FRA, 1966
*Apocalypse Now   *Francis Ford Coppola* — U.S., 1979
*Baby Blue Marine   *John Hancock* — U.S., 1976
*Bat 21   *Peter Markle* — U.S., 1988
*Birdy   *Alan Parker* — U.S., 1984
Blind Fury   *Phillip Noyce* — U.S., 1989
Boat People — Passport To Hell   *Ann Hui* — HK, 1982
Born for Hell   *Denis Heroux* — CAN/FRA/FRG, 1978
*Born on the Fourth of July   *Oliver Stone* — U.S., 1989
*The Boys in Company C   *Sidney J. Furie* — U.S., 1978
*Braddock: Missing in Action III   *Aaron Norris* — U.S., 1988
Bullet in the Head   *John Woo* — HK, 1990
*Casualties of War   *Brian De Palma* — U.S., 1989
Cease Fire   *David Nutter* — U.S., 1985
*Coming Home   *Hal Ashby* — U.S., 1978
The Crazy World of Julius Vrooder   *Arthur Hiller* — U.S., 1974

*Dead Presidents   *Allen Hughes/Albert Hughes* — U.S., 1995
*Dear America: Letters Home from Vietnam   *Bill Coutourie* — U.S., 1987
*The Deer Hunter   *Michael Cimino* — U.S., 1978
Distant Thunder   *Rick Rosenthal* — CAN/U.S., 1988
*Don't Cry, It's Only Thunder   *Peter Werner*   U.S., 1982
*84 Charlie Mopic   *Patrick Duncan* — U.S., 1988
Firefox   *Clint Eastwood* — U.S., 1982
*First Blood   *Ted Kotcheff* — U.S., 1982
*Flight of the Intruder   *John Milius* — U.S., 1991
Forrest Gump   *Robert Zemeckis* — U.S., 1994
*Full Metal Jacket   *Stanley Kubrick* — GB/U.S., 1987
*Gardens of Stone   *Francis Coppola* — U.S., 1987
*Go Tell the Spartans   *Ted Post* — U.S., 1978
Good Guys Wear Black   *Ted Post* — U.S., 1978
*Good Morning, Vietnam   *Barry Levinson* — U.S., 1987
Gordon's War   *Ossie Davis* — U.S., 1973
*The Green Berets   *Ray Kellogg/John Wayne* — U.S., 1968
Hail, Hero!   *David Miller* — U.S., 1969
*Hamburger Hill   *John Irvin* — U.S., 1987
*The Hanoi Hilton   *Lionel Chetwynd* — U.S., 1987
*Hearts and Minds   *Peter Davis* — U.S., 1974
*Heaven and Earth   *Oliver Stone* — U.S., 1993
Heroes   *Jeremy Paul Kagan* — U.S., 1977
Hi, Mom!   *Brian De Palma* — U.S., 1969
In Country   *Norman Jewison* — U.S., 1989
*Introduction to the Enemy   *Jane Fonda/Tom Hayden* — U.S., 1975
*The Iron Triangle   *Eric Weston* — U.S., 1988
*Jacknife   *David Jones* — U.S., 1989
Jacob's Ladder   *Adrian Lyne* — U.S., 1990
Limbo   *Mark Robson* — U.S., 1972
The Line   *Robert J. Siegel* — U.S., 1980
The Losers   *Jack Starrett* — U.S., 1970
*Missing in Action   *Joseph Zito* — U.S., 1984
*Missing in Action 2 — the Beginning   *Lance Hool* — U.S., 1985
*The Odd Angry Shot   *Tom Jeffrey* — AUS, 1979
*Off Limits   *Christopher Crowe* — U.S., 1988
*Operation Cia   *Christian Nyby* — U.S., 1965
Operation Dumbo Drop   *Simon Wincer* — U.S., 1995
Ordinary Heroes   *Peter H. Cooper* — U.S., 1986
*Platoon   *Oliver Stone* — U.S., 1986
*Platoon Leader   *Aaron Norris* — U.S., 1988
*Pow: the Escape   *Gideon Amir* — U.S., 1986
*Purple Hearts   *Sidney J. Furie* — U.S., 1984
*Rambo: First Blood Part Two   *George Pan Cosmatos* — U.S., 1985
Rolling Thunder   *John Flynn* — U.S., 1977
Search and Destroy   *William Fruett* — U.S., 1981
Some Kind of Hero   *Michael Pressman* — U.S., 1981
Some May Live   *Vernon Sewell* — U.S., 1967
*STAB   *Chalong Pakdivijt* — THAI, 1975
The Story of Woo Viet   *Ann Hui* — HK, 1981
Streamers   *Robert Altman* — U.S., 1983
Summer Soldiers   *Hiroshi Teshigahara* — JAP, 1971
Summertree   *Anthony Newley* — U.S., 1971
Suspect   *Peter Yates* — U.S., 1987
There is No 13   *William Sachs* — U.S., 1974
*To the Shores of Hell   *Will Zens* — U.S., 1966
Tracks   *Henry Jaglom* — U.S., 1976
Turtle Beach   *Stephen Wallace* — AUS, 1992

Twilight's Last Gleaming   *Robert Aldrich — GER/U.S., 1977*
★Uncommon Valor   *Ted Kotcheff — U.S., 1983*
Universal Soldier   *Roland Emmerich — U.S., 1992*
★The War   *Jon Avnet — U.S., 1994*
Welcome Home   *Franklin Schaffner — U.S., 1989*
Welcome Home Soldier Boys   *Richard Crompton — U.S., 1972*
Who'll Stop the Rain?   *Karel Reisz — U.S., 1978*
★A Yank in Viet-Nam   *Marshall Thompson — U.S., 1964*

BASQUE SEPARATISTISM IN SPAIN, 1959–
★Running Out of Time   *Imanol Uribe — SPA, 1994*

CONGO CIVIL WARS, 1960–71
★The Last Grenade   *Gordon Flemyng — GB, 1969*
★The Legion Jumps On Kolwezi   *Raoul Coutard — FRA, 1980*
★The Mercenaries   *Jack Cardiff — GB, 1968*
★The Nun's Story   *Fred Zonnemann — U.S., 1959*
The Sins of Rachel Cade   *Gordon Douglas — U.S., 1961*

INDONESIA, 1965–66
★The Year of Living Dangerously   *Peter Weir — AUS, 1982*

CZECHOSLOVAKIA, 1968
The Unbearable Lightness of Being   *Philip Kaufman — U.S., 1987*

URUGUAY, TUPAMAROS MOVEMENT, 1968-72
★State of Siege   *Costa-Gavras — FRA/FRG/ITA, 1973*

CAMBODIA, 1971-86
Kampuchea Express   *Alex King — THA, 1982*
★The Killing Fields   *Roland Joffe — GB, 1984*
Rice People   *Rithy Panh — CAM/FRA, 1994*

CHILE, 1973
★Amnesia   *Gonzalo Justiniano — CHL, 1994*
★The Battle of Chile   *Patricio Guzman — CHL, 1978*
The House of the Spirits   *Bille August — DEN/GER/POR, 1993*
It Rains on Santiago   *Helvio Soto — BUL/FRA, 1975*
★Missing   *Costa-Gavras — U.S., 1982*

Lebanon Civil War, 1975–90
★Circle of Deceit   *Volker Schlondorff — FRA/FRG, 1981*
Deadline   *Nathaniel Gutman — FRG, 1987*
★Hors La Vie   *Maroun Bagdadi — FRA/GER/ITA, 1991*
Navy Seals   *Lewis Teague — U.S., 1990*
★War Zone   *Nathaniel Gutman — FRG, 1986*
★West Beirut   *Ziad Doueiri — BEL/FRA/LEB/NOR, 1998*

AFGHANISTAN, 1979-88
★The Beast   *Kevin Reynolds — U.S./ISR, 1988*
100 Days Before the Command   *Khusein Erkenov — RUS, 1990*
★Rambo III   *Peter Macdonald — U.S., 1988*

NICARAGUA, 1979-88
★Carla's Song   *Ken Loach — GB/GER/SPA, 1996*
★La Insurrecion   *Peter Lilienthal — NIC/CRCA, 1981*
★The Last Plane Out   *David Nelson — U.S., 1983*
★Latino   *Haskell Wexler — U.S., 1985*
★Under Fire   *Roger Spottiswoode — U.S., 1983*

THE YEAR OF LIVING DANGEROUSLY
Anti-American demonstration in Djakarta, 1965. MGM/UA

EL SALVADOR, 1980-94
★Diplomatic Immunity   *Sturla Gunnarsson — CAN, 1991*
★In the Name of the People   *Frank Christopher — U.S., 1984*
Romero   *John Duigan — U.S., 1989*
★Salvador   *Oliver Stone — U.S., 1986*
★El Slavador: Another Vietnam   *Glenn Sliber/Tete Vascocellos — U.S., 1981*
The SAS at San Salvador   *Raoul Coutard — FRA, 1982*

GUATEMALA, 1980–
El Norte   *Gregory Nava — U.S., 1983*

PERU, SHINING PATH INSURGENCY, 1980–
★The Lion's Den   *Francisco J. Lombardi — PER/SPA, 1988*

FALKLANDS/MALVINAS WAR, 1982
★Argie   *Jorge Blanco — GB, 1985*
Dream Demon   *Harley Cokliss — GB, 1988*
★For Queen and Country   *Martin Stellman — GB/U.S., 1988*
★The Ploughman's Lunch   *Richard Eyre — GB, 1983*
Remembrance   *Colin Gregg — GB, 1982*
★Resurrected   *Paul Greengrass — GB, 1989*
Veronico Cruz   *Wiguel Pereira — ARG/GB, 1987*

GRENADA, 1986
★Heartbreak Ridge   *Clint Eastwood — U.S., 1986*

BURMA/MYANMAR, 1988–
★Beyond Rangoon   *John Boorman — U.S., 1995*

ROMANIAN REVOLUTION, 1989
★Requiem for Dominic   *Robert Dorhelm — AUST, 1990*

PANAMA, 1989–90
★Dollar Mambo   *Paul Leduc — MEX, 1993*
Sniper   *Luis Lhosa — U.S., 1992*

GULF WAR OPERATION DESERT STORM, 1990–91
*Courage Under Fire   *Edward Zwick — U.S., 1996*
*The Finest Hour   *Shimon Dotan — U.S., 1991*
*Lessons in Darkness   *Werner Herzog — FRA/GER, 1992*
The Song of the Siren   *Eytan Fox — ISR, 1995*

YUGOSLAVIA, 1990–
*Beautiful People   *Jasmin Dizdar — GB, 1999*
*Before the Rain   *Milcho Manchevski — FRA/GB/MAC, 1994*
The Gaze of Ulysses   *Theo Angelopoulos — FRA/GRE/ITA, 1995*
*Pretty Village, Pretty Flame   *Srdjan Dragojevic —YUG, 1995*
*Savior   *Pedrag Antonijevic — U.S., 1998*
*Underground   *Emir Kusturica — FRA/GER/HUN, 1995*
*An Unforgettable Summer   *Lucien Pintilie — FRA/ROM, 1994*
*Welcome To Sarajevo   *Michael Winterbottom — GB, 1997*

CHECHNYA, 1991–
*Prisoner of the Mountain   *Sergei Bodrov — RUS/KAZ, 1996*

VARIOUS 20TH CENTURY DISPUTES
*Kundun   *Martin Scorsese — U.S., 1997 Tibet/China, 1959*
*Lucia   *Humbero Solas — CUB, 1969 Cuba, 1933*
*Sirocco   *Curtis Bernhardt — U.S., 1951 Syria, 1925*
*Storm Over the Andes   *Christy Cabanne — U.S., 1935*
Bolivia/Paraguay, 1932–35
*The Taste of the Black Earth   *Kazimierz Kutz — POL, 1989 Silesia, 1920*
*An Unforgettable Summer   *Lucien Pintilie — FRA/ROM, 1994 Bulgaria/Romania, 1925*
*The Wind and the Lion   *John Milius — U.S., 1975 U.S./Morocco, 1904*

WAR IN THE 20TH CENTURY —
ABSTRACT, FANTASY AND SATIRE
*The Battle Cry of Peace   *Wilfred North — U.S., 1915*
*Beautiful People   *Jasmin Dizdar — GB, 1999*
*The Bed Sitting Room   *Richard Lester — GB, 1969*
Beware!   *William Nigh — U.S., 1919*
Bullets and Brown Eyes   *Scott Sidney — U.S., 1916*
*Les Carabiniers   *Jean-Luc Godard — FRA/ITA, 1963*
*Castle Keep   *Sydney Pollack — U.S., 1969*
*Civilization   *Thomas Ince — U.S., 1916*
Death Ship   *Alvin Rakoff — CAN/GB, 1980*
Dream Demon   *Harley Cokliss — GB, 1988*
*Duck Soup   *Leo McCarey — U.S., 1933*
The Extraordinary Seaman   *John Frankenheimer — U.S., 1968*
*The Fall of a Nation   *Bartley Cushing — U.S., 1916*
*Fear and Desire   *Stanley Kubrick — U.S., 1953*
*Figures in a Landscape   *Joseph Losey — GB, 1970*
*The Fourth War   *John Frankenheimer — U.S., 1990*
*The Final Countdown   *Don Taylor — U.S., 1980*
Forrest Gump   *Robert Zemeckis — U.S., 1994*
*Friendship's Death   *Peter Wollen — GB, 1987*
Genghis Cohn   *Elijah Moshinsky — GB, 1993*
*The Great Dictator   *Charles Chaplin — U.S., 1940*
*La Guerre Des Boutons   *Yves Robert — FRA, 1962*
*A Guy Named Joe   *Victor Fleming — U.S., 1943*
High Barbaree   *Jack Conway — U.S., 1947*
*High Treason   *Maurice Elvey — GB, 1929*
*How I Won the War   *Richard Lester — GB, 1967*

*Indiana Jones and the Last Crusade   *Steven Spielberg — U.S., 1989*
*Intolerance   *D. W. Griffith — U.S., 1916*
*It Happened Here   *Kevin Brownlow/Andrew Mollo — GB, 1963*
*J'Accuse   *Abel Gance — FRA, 1939*
John Smith Wakes Up   *Jiri Weiss — GB, 1940*
*The Keep   *Michael Mann — U.S., 1983*
The Land That Time Forgot   *Kevin Connor — GB, 1974*
*A Matter of Life and Death   *Michael Powell/Emeric Pressburger — GB, 1946*
Meet John Doe   *Frank Capra — U.S., 1941*
*Men Must Fight   *Edgar Selwyn — U.S., 1933*
*Mercie La Vie   *Bertrand Blier — FRA, 1991*
*The Mouse That Roared   *Jack Arnold — GB, 1959*
*No Greater Glory   *Frank Borzage — U.S., 1934*
*Noah's Ark   *Michael Curtiz — U.S., 1929*
Not Reconciled   *Jean-Marie Straub — FRG, 1965*
On the Beach   *Stanley Kramer — U.S., 1959*
The Ordeal   *Edward M Roskam — U.S., 1914*
120 Days of Sodom   *Pier Paolo Pasolini — ITA, 1975*
Orphee   *Jean Cocteau — FRA, 1949*
The Patriot   *Alexander Kluge — FRG, 1979*
*The President Vanishes   *William Wellman — U.S., 1934*
*Raiders of the Lost Ark   *Steven Spielberg — U.S., 1981*
*Red Dawn   *John Milius — U.S., 1984*
Red Hot Romance   *Victor Fleming — U.S., 1922*
La Regle Du Jeu   *Jean Renoir — FRA, 1939*
Richard III   *Richard Loncraine — GB, 1995*
The Riddle of the Sands   *Tony Maylam — GB, 1978*
A Self-Made Hero   *Jacques Audiard — FRA, 1995*
Seven Days in May   *John Frankenheimer — U.S., 1964*
The Shame   *Ingmar Bergman — SWE, 1968*
*The Slacker   *Christy Cabanne — U.S., 1917*
*Slaughterhouse Five   *George Roy Hill — U.S., 1972*
*The Strange Death of Adolf Hitler   *James Hogan — U.S., 1943*
Strange Holiday   *Arch Oboler — U.S., 1945*
Testament   *Lynne Littman — U.S., 1983*
*Things To Come   *William Cameron Menzies — GB, 1936*
To Hell with the Kaiser   *George Irving — U.S., 1918*
*To the Starry Island   *Park Kwang-Su — SKO, 1993*
Under the Rainbow   *Steve Rash — U.S., 1981*
Under the Sign of Monte Christo   *Andre Hunebelle — FRA, 1947*
Universal Soldier   *Roland Emmerich — U.S., 1992*
Viva Maria!   *Louis Malle — FRA/ITA, 1965*
Viva Max   *Jerry Paris — U.S., 1969*
*The War   *Jon Avnet — U.S., 1994*
War Be Damned   *Alfred Machin — BEL/FRA, (date unknown)*
*War Brides   *Herbert Brenon — U.S., 1916*
*War of the Buttons   *John Roberts — FRA/GB, 1993*
*War Requiem   *Derek Jarman — GB, 1988*
*Went the Day Well?   *Alberto Cavalcanti — GB, 1942*
Zone Troopers   *Danny Bilson — U.S., 1985*

Note: all films covered in the first, A–Z section of this book.

Abe, Yutaka
The Burning Sky   *JAP, 1940*
Nippon's Young Eagles   *JAP, 1941*
South Seas Bouquet   *JAP, 1942*

Akkad, Moustapha
Lion Of The Desert   *U.S., 1980*
Mohammed, Messenger Of God
Lebanon, 1976

Aldrich, Robert
The Angry Hills   *GB, 1959*
Apache   *U.S., 1954*
Attack!   *U.S., 1956*
The Dirty Dozen   *GB/U.S., 1967*
Too Late The Hero   *U.S., 1969*
Ulzana's Raid   *U.S., 1972*
Vera Cruz   *U.S., 1954*

Allen, Woody
Love And Death   *U.S., 1975*

Altman, Robert
M*A*S*H   *U.S., 1970*

Anderson, Michael
The Dam Busters   *GB, 1954*
Operation Crossbow   *GB/ITA, 1965*
Shake Hands With The Devil
  IRE/U.S., 1959
Yangtse Incident   *GB, 1957*

Annakin, Ken
The Battle Of The Bulge   *U.S., 1965*
Hotel Sahara   *GB, 1951*
The Long Duel   *GB, 1967*
The Longest Day (+ Andrew
Marton/Bernhard Wicki)   *U.S., 1962*
The Story Of Robin Hood And His
Merrie Men   *GB, 1952*
Very Important Person   *GB, 1961*

Ashby, Hal
Coming Home   *U.S., 1978*

Asquith, Anthony
Cottage To Let   *GB, 1941*
The Demi-Paradise   *GB, 1943*
Freedom Radio   *GB, 1941*
Orders To Kill   *GB, 1958*
Tell England (+ Gerald Barkas)   *GB, 1931*
Uncensored   *GB, 1942*
The Way To The Stars   *GB, 1945*
We Dive At Dawn   *GB, 1943*

Attenborough, Richard
A Bridge Too Far   *GB/U.S., 1977*

In Love And War   *U.S., 1996*
Oh! What A Lovely War   *GB, 1969*
Young Winston   *GB, 1972*

Autant-Lara, Claude
L'affaire Du Courrier De Lyon
  (+ Maurice Lehmann) *FRA, 1937*
Crossing Paris   *FRA, 1956*
Le Diable Au Corps   *FRA, 1947*

Bacon, Lloyd
Action In The North Atlantic *U.S., 1943*
Captain Eddie   *U.S., 1945*
Espionage Agent   *U.S., 1939*
The Frogmen   *U.S., 1951*
The Great Sioux Uprising   *U.S., 1953*
The Sullivans   *U.S., 1944*
Wings For The Eagle   *U.S., 1942*

Baker, Roy
Morning Departure   *GB, 1950*
The One That Got Away   *GB, 1957*
The Valiant   *GB/ITA, 1961*

Barkas, Gerald See **Anthony Asquith**

Barker, Reginald
The Coward   *U.S., 1915*
Flame Of The Desert   *U.S., 1919*
The Frontiersman   *U.S., 1927*

Beatty, Warren
Reds   U.S., 1981

Benigni, Roberto
Life Is Beautiful   *ITA, 1997*

Benton, Robert
Bad Company   *U.S., 1972*

Beresford, Bruce
Breaker Morant   *Australia, 1980*
Paradise Road   *U.S./Australia, 1997*

Bernard, Raymond
Le Croix De Bois   *FRA, 1931*
Les Miserables   *FRA, 1933*

Berri, Claude
Lucie Aubrac   *FRA, 1998*
Uranus   *FRA, 1990*

Bertolucci, Bernardo
The Conformist   *FRA/FRG/ITA, 1969*
The Last Emperor   *GB/HK/ITA, 1987*
 1900   *FRA/FRG/ITA, 1976*
The Spider's Stratagem   *ITA, 1970*

Blackton, J. Stuart
The Judgment House   *U.S., 1915*
Les Miserables (+ William Humphrey)
  U.S., 1909
A Tale Of Two Cities   *U.S., 1911*
Tearing Down The Spanish Flag (+
Albert E. Smith) *U.S., 1898*

Blystone, John
Hell In The Heavens   *U.S., 1934*
Sky Hawk   *U.S., 1929*

Boetticher, Budd
The Man From The Alamo   *U.S., 1953*
Red Ball Express   *U.S., 1952*
Seminole   *U.S., 1953*
Wings Of The Hawk   *U.S., 1953*

Boleslawski, Richard
Clive Of India   *U.S., 1934*
Les Miserables   *U.S., 1935*
Rasputin And The Empress   *U.S., 1932*
Storm At Daybreak   *U.S., 1932*

Bondarchuk, Sergei
War And Peace   *USSR, 1967*
Waterloo   *ITA/USSR, 1971*

Boorman, John
Beyond Rangoon   *U.S., 1995*
Excalibur   *U.S., 1981*
Hell In The Pacific   *U.S., 1968*
Hope And Glory   *GB, 1987*

Borzage, Frank
A Farewell To Arms   *U.S., 1932*
Flight Command   *U.S., 1940*
Magnificent Doll   *U.S., 1946*
The Mortal Storm   *U.S., 1940*
No Greater Glory   *U.S., 1934*
Seventh Heaven   *U.S., 1927*
Three Comrades   *U.S., 1938*
Till We Meet Again   *U.S., 1944*

Boulting, John
Journey Together   *GB, 1944*
Pastor Hall (+ Roy Boulting)   *GB, 1940*
Private's Progress   *GB, 1956*

Boulting, Roy
Burma Victory   GB, 1945
Desert Victory   GB, 1943
Pastor Hall (+ John Boulting)   *GB, 1940*
Singlehanded   *U.S./GB, 1953*
Thunder Rock   *GB, 1942*
Tunisian Victory (+ Frank Capra)
  U.S., 1944

Branagh, Kenneth
Henry V   *GB, 1989*

Brenon, Herbert
Beau Geste   *U.S., 1926*
Beau Ideal   *U.S., 1931*
The Case Of Sergeant Grisha
    U.S., 1930
The Fall Of The Romanoffs   *U.S., 1917*
The Invasion Of Britain   *GB, 1918*

Bresson, Robert
Lancelot Du Lac   *FRA/ITA, 1974*
A Man Escaped   *FRA, 1956*
The Trial Of Joan Of Arc   *FRA, 1962*

Brook, Peter
Le Mahabharata   *FRA, 1989*

Brooks, Richard
Battle Circus   *U.S., 1952*
The Professionals   *U.S., 1966*
Something Of Value   *U.S., 1957*

Brown, Clarence
Conquest   *U.S., 1937*
The Human Comedy   *U.S., 1943*
The White Cliffs Of Dover   *U.S., 1944*

Brownlow, Kevin
It Happened Her (+ Andrew Mollo)
    GB, 1963
Winstanley (+ Andrew Mollo) *GB, 1975*

Bruckman, Clyde See **Buster Keaton**

Brunel, Adrian
The Lion Has Wings (+ Brian Desmond
Hurst/Michael Powell)   *GB, 1939*
The Rebel Son (+ Alexis Granowsky)
    GB, 1939

Bucquet, Harold S.
The Adventures Of Tartu   *GB, 1943*
Dragon Seed (+ Jack Conway)   *U.S., 1944*

Bulajic, Velijko
The Battle Of Neretva
    YUG/ITA/U.S./FRG, 1969
Hill Of Death   *YUG, 1962*

Butler, David
Jump into Hell   *U.S., 1955*
King Richard And The Crusaders
    U.S., 1954

Cabanne Christy
The Dishonored Medal   *U.S., 1914*
The Life Of General Villa   *U.S., 1914*
The Martyrs Of The Alamo   *U.S., 1915*
The Slacker   *U.S., 1917*
Storm Over The Andes   *U.S., 1935*

Cacoyannis, Michael
Attila '74   *Greece, 1975*
The Trojan Women   *U.S., 1971*

Cahn, Edward L.
Jet Attack   *U.S., 1958*

Operation Bottleneck   *U.S., 1961*
Suicide Battalion   *U.S., 1958*

Capra, Frank
Attack: Invasion Of New Britain
    U.S., 1944
The Bitter Tea Of General Yen
    U.S., 1933
Flight   *U.S., 1929*
Tunisian Victory (+ Roy Boulting)
    U.S., 1944
Why We Fight *(series)   U.S., 1942-45*

Cardiff, Jack
The Long Ships   *GB/YUG, 1963*
The Mercenaries   *GB, 1968*

Castle, William
The Charge Of The Lancers   *U.S., 1953*
Conquest Of Cochise   *U.S., 1953*
Fort Ti   *U.S., 1953*
The Gun That Won The West
    U.S., 1955
The Saracen Blade   *U.S., 1954*
Serpent Of The Nile   *U.S., 1953*

Caton-Jones, Michael
Memphis Belle   *U.S./GB, 1990*
Rob Roy   *U.S., 1995*

Cavalcanti, Alberto
Went The Day Well?   *GB, 1942*

Cayette, André
Are We All Murderers?   *FRA, 1948*
The Crossing Of The Rhine
    FRA/ITA/FRG, 1960

Chaffey, Don
Charley One-Eye   *GB, 1972*
Danger Within   *GB, 1959*
The Viking Queen   *GB, 1967*

Chahine, Youssef
Adieu Bonaparte   *EGY/FRA, 1984*
Saladin   *EGY, 1963*

Chaplin, Charles
The Great Dictator   *U.S., 1940*

Chukrai, Grigori
Ballad Of A Soldier   *USSR, 1959*
The Forty-First   *USSR, 1956*

Cimino Michael
The Deer Hunter   *U.S., 1978*

Clair, René
Forever And A Day (+ many others)
    U.S., 1942

Clavell, James
The Last Valley   *GB, 1970*

Clement, René
La Bataille Du Rail   *FRA, 1945*
Is Paris Burning?   *FRA/U.S., 1965*
Les Jeux Interdits   *FRA, 1952*
Les Maudits   *FRA, 1947*

Cohen, Norman
Adolf Hitler — My Part In His Downfall
    GB, 1972
Dad's Army   *GB, 1971*

Conway, Jack
Assignment In Brittany   *U.S., 1943*
Dragon Seed (+ Harold Bucquet)
    U.S., 1944
Hell Below   *U.S., 1933*
A Tale Of Two Cities   *U.S., 1935*
Viva Villa!   *U.S., 1934*

Cooper, Merian C.
The Four Feathers (+ Lothar
Mendes/Ernest Schoedsack)   *U.S., 1929*

Coppola, Francis Ford
Apocalypse Now   *U.S., 1979*
Gardens Of Stone   *U.S., 1987*

Corman, Roger
The Secret Invasion   *U.S., 1964*
Ski Troop Attack   *U.S., 1960*
Tower Of London   *U.S., 1962*
Von Richthofen And Brown   *U.S., 1971*

Cosmatos, George Pan
Escape To Athena   *GB, 1979*
Massacre In Rome   *FRA/ITA, 1973*
Rambo: First Blood Part Two
    U.S., 1985

Costa-Gavras
Missing   *U.S., 1982*
Section Speciale   *FRA/FRG/ITA, 1975*
State Of Siege   *FR/GER/ITA, 1973*

Costner, Kevin
Dances With Wolves   *U.S., 1990*
Robin Hood: Prince Of Thieves
    U.S., 1991

Coward, Nöel See **David Lean**

Crichton, Charles
Against The Wind   *GB, 1947*
For Those In Peril   *GB, 1944*

Cromwell, John
The Fountain   *U.S., 1934*
Since You Went Away   *U.S., 1944*
So Ends Our Night   *U.S., 1941*

Crosland, Alan
General Crack   *U.S., 1929*
The Great Impersonation   *U.S., 1935*

Cukor, George
Gone With The Wind (+ Victor
Fleming/Sam Wood)   *U.S., 1939*
Winged Victory   *U.S., 1944*

Curtiz, Michael
The Adventures Of Robin Hood
(+ William Keighley)   *U.S., 1938*
British Agent   *U.S., 1934*
Captain Blood   *U.S., 1935*
Captains Of The Clouds   *U.S., 1942*

Casablanca   *U.S., 1942*
The Charge Of The Light Brigade
   U.S., 1936
Dive Bomber   *U.S., 1941*
Force Of Arms   *U.S., 1951*
The Key   *U.S., 1934*
Mission To Moscow   *U.S., 1943*
Noah's Ark   *U.S., 1929*
Passage To Marseilles   *U.S., 1944*
Santa Fe Trail   *U.S., 1940*
The Sea Hawk   *U.S., 1940*
Virginia City   *U.S., 1940*
The Woman From Monte Carlo
   U.S., 1932

Dassin, Jules
Brute Force   *U.S., 1947*
Nazi Agent   *U.S., 1942*

Daves, Delmer
Broken Arrow   *U.S., 1950*
Destination Tokyo   *U.S., 1943*
Drum Beat   *U.S., 1954*
Kings Go Forth   *U.S., 1958*
Pride Of The Marines   *U.S., 1945*
Task Force   *U.S., 1949*
To The Victor   *U.S., 1948*

De Mille, Cecil B.
The Buccaneer   *U.S., 1938*
The Captive   *U.S., 1915*
Cleopatra   *U.S., 1934*
The Crusades   *U.S., 1935*
For Better, For Worse   *U.S., 1919*
Joan The Woman   *U.S., 1916*
The Little American   *U.S., 1917*
The Plainsman   *U.S., 1936*
The Story Of Dr Wassell   *U.S., 1944*
Unconquered   *U.S., 1947*
The Volga Boatman   *U.S., 1926*
The Warrens Of Virginia   *U.S., 1915*

De Palma, Brian
Casualties Of War   *U.S., 1989*

De Rochemont, Louis
The Fighting Lady   *U.S., 1944*
The March Of Time (series prod)
   U.S., 1934-54

De Sica, Vittorio
The Garden Of The Finzi-Continis
   FRG/ITA, 1970
Shoeshine   *ITA, 1946*
Two Women   *ITA, 1962*

De Toth, André
The Indian Fighter   *U.S., 1955*
The Last Of The Comanches
   U.S., 1952
None Shall Escape   *U.S., 1944*
Play Dirty   *GB, 1969*
Springfield Rifle   *U.S., 1952*
The Two-Headed Spy   *GB, 1958*

Dearden, Basil
The Bells Go Down   *GB, 1943*
The Captive Heart   *GB, 1946*
The Gentle Gunman   *GB, 1952*
Khartoum   *GB, 1966*

Del Ruth, Roy
Across The Pacific   *U.S., 1926*
Captured   *U.S., 1933*
Three Faces East   *U.S., 1930*

Dickinson, Thorold
Hill 24 Doesn't Answer   *ISR, 1954*
The Next Of Kin   *GB, 1942*

Dieterlie, William
Blockade   *U.S., 1938*
Juarez   *U.S., 1939*
The Last Flight   *U.S., 1931*
Red Mountain   *U.S., 1951*
Scarlet Dawn   *U.S., 1932*
The Searching Wind   *U.S., 1946*
The White Angel   *U.S., 1936*

Dmytryk, Edward
Alvarez Kelly   *U.S., 1966*
Anzio   *ITA, 1968*
Back To Bataan   *U.S., 1945*
Behind The Rising Sun   *U.S., 1943*
The Caine Mutiny   *U.S. 1954*
Eight Iron Men   *U.S., 1952*
Hitler's Children   *U.S., 1942*
Mutiny   *U.S., 1952*
Mystery Sea Raider   *U.S., 1940*
The Young Lions   *U.S., 1958*

Dorhelm, Robert
Requiem Fur Dominic   *Austria, 1990*

Douglas, Gordon
The Black Arrow   *U.S., 1948*
The Charge At Feather River   *U.S., 1953*
First Yank into Tokyo   *U.S., 1945*
The Fortunes Of Captain Blood
   U.S., 1950
The McConnell Story   *U.S., 1955*
Only The Valiant   *U.S., 1950*
Rogues Of Sherwood Forest   *U.S., 1950*
Santiago   *U.S., 1956*
Up Periscope   *U.S., 1959*

Dovzhenko, Alexander
Aerograd   *USSR, 1935*
Arsenal   *USSR, 1929*
Shchors   *USSR, 1939*

Dreville, Jean
The Battle For Heavy Water (prod)
   FRA/NOR, 1947
Le Grand Rendezvous   *FRA, 1949*
Lafayette   *FRA/ITA, 1961*
Normandie-Niemen   *FRA/USSR, 1959*
La Reine Margot   *FRA, 1954*

Duvivier, Julien
Heart Of A Nation   *FRA, 1940*
The Impostor   *U.S., 1944*

Dwan, Allan
Flight Nurse   *U.S., 1953*
Friendly Enemies   *U.S., 1942*
Hold Back The Night   *U.S., 1956*
Robin Hood   *U.S., 1922*
Sands Of Iwo Jima   *U.S., 1949*
The Wild Blue Yonder   *U.S., 1952*

Eastwood, Clint
Heartbreak Ridge   *U.S., 1986*

Edwards, Blake
Darling Lili   *U.S., 1969*
Operation Petticoat   *U.S., 1959*
What Did You Do In The War, Daddy?
   U.S., 1966

Eisenstein, Sergei
Alexander Nevsky   *USSR, 1938*
The Battleship Potemkin   *USSR, 1925*
Ivan The Terrible, Parts I and II
   USSR, 1945, 1958
October   *USSR, 1927*
Strike   *USSR, 1924*

Elvey, Maurice
The Flag Lieutenant   *GB, 1926*
For Freedom (+ Castleton Knight)
   GB, 1940
The Gentle Sex (+ Leslie Howard)
   GB, 1943
Mademoiselle From Armentieres
   GB, 1926
Roses Of Picardy   *GB, 1927*
Salute John Citizen   *GB, 1942*
Who Goes Next?   *GB, 1938*

Endfield, Cy
Zulu   *GB, 1964*

Enright, Ray
China Sky   *U.S., 1945*
Gung Ho!   *U.S., 1943*
Kansas Raiders   *U.S., 1951*

Ermler, Friedrich
The Great Turning Point   *USSR, 1946*

Estevez, Emilio
The War At Home   *U.S., 1996*

Farrow, John
China   *U.S., 1943*
The Commandos Strike At Dawn
   U.S., 1942
The Hitler Gang   *U.S., 1944*
John Paul Jones   *U.S., 1959*
The Sea Chase   *U.S., 1955*
Submarine Command
   U.S., 1951
Wake Island   *U.S., 1942*

Fassbinder, Rainer Werner
Lili Marleen   *FRG, 1980*
Lola   *FRG, 1982*
The Marriage Of Maria Braun
   FRG, 1978
Veronika Voss   *FRG, 1982*

Ferrer, José
Cockleshell Heroes,   *GB, 1955*

Ferroni, Georgio
The Battle Of El Alamein
   FRA/ITA, 1968
Coriolanus — Hero Without A Country
   FRA/ITA, 1965
The Trojan War   *FRA/ITA, 1961*

Feyder, Jacques
La Kermesse Heroique   *FRA, 1935*
Knight Without Armour   *GB, 1937*

Fitzmaurice, George
The Dark Angel   *U.S., 1925*
Lilac Time   *U.S., 1928*
Mata Hari   *U.S., 1931*
Suzy   *U.S., 1936*

Fleischer, Richard
Bandido   *U.S., 1956*
Between Heaven And Hell   *U.S., 1956*
Che!   *U.S., 1969*
The Clay Pigeon   *U.S., 1949*
Tora! Tora! Tora!   *U.S., 1970*
The Vikings   *U.S., 1958*

Fleming, Victor
Gone With The Wind (+ George
   Cukor/Sam Wood)   *U.S., 1939*
A Guy Named Joe   *U.S., 1943*
Joan Of Arc   *U.S., 1948*
Renegades   *U.S., 1930*

Florey, Robert
Dangerously They Live   *U.S., 1941*
God Is My Co-Pilot   *U.S., 1945*
Hotel Imperial   *U.S., 1939*
Outpost In Morocco   *U.S., 1949*
Rogues' Regiment   *U.S., 1948*

Forbes, Bryan
King Rat   *U.S./GB, 1965*

Ford, Aleksander
Border Street   *POL, 1948*
Knights Of The Teutonic Order *POL, 1960*

Ford, Eugene
Berlin Correspondent   *U.S., 1942*
International Settlement   *U.S., 1938*

Ford, John
The Battle Of Midway   *U.S., 1942*
The Black Watch   *U.S., 1929*
Cheyenne Autumn   *U.S., 1964*
December 7th   *U.S., 1942*
Drums Along The Mohawk   *U.S., 1939*
Fort Apache   *U.S., 1948*
Four Sons   *U.S., 1928*
The Fugitive   *U.S., 1947*
The Horse Soldiers   *U.S., 1959*
How The West Was Won (+ Henry
   Hathaway/George Marshall)   *U.S., 1962*
The Informer   *U.S., 1935*
The Long Voyage Home   *U.S., 1940*
The Lost Patrol   *U.S., 1934*
Mister Roberts (+ Mervyn Le Roy)
   U.S., 1955
The Plough And The Stars   *U.S., 1936*
Rio Grande   *U.S., 1950*
The Searchers   *U.S., 1956*
The Seas Beneath   *U.S., 1931*
Seven Women   *U.S., 1965*
She Wore A Yellow Ribbon   *U.S., 1949*
Submarine Patrol   *U.S., 1938*
They Were Expendable   *U.S., 1945*
Two Rode Together   *U.S., 1961*
Wee Willie Winkie   *U.S., 1937*

What Price Glory?   *U.S., 1952*
When Willie Comes Marching Home
   U.S., 1950

Forde, Walter
Brown On Resolution   *GB, 1935*
Flying Fortress   *GB, 1942*

Foreman, Carl
The Victors   *GB, 1963*

Foster, Lewis, R.
The Bold And The Brave   *U.S., 1956*
The Eagle And The Hawk   *U.S., 1949*
The Last Outpost   *U.S., 1951*
The Sign Of Zorro (+ Norman Foster)
   U.S., 1960

Foster, Norman
Davy Crockett   *U.S., 1955*
Journey into Fear (+ Orson Welles)
   U.S., 1942
Scotland Yard   *U.S., 1941*
The Sign Of Zorro (+ Lewis R. Foster)
   U.S., 1960

Francisci, Pietro
Attila The Hun   *ITA/FRA, 1954*
Roland — Paladin Of France   *ITA, 1956*
The Siege Of Syracuse   *ITA, 1959*

Frankenheimer, John
The Fourth War   *U.S., 1990*
The Manchurian Candidate   *U.S., 1962*
The Train   *U.S., 1965*

French, Harold
The Day Will Dawn   *GB, 1942*
Rob Roy The Highland Rogue
   GB, 1953
Secret Mission   *GB, 1942*

Frend, Charles
The Big Blockade   *GB, 1941*
The Cruel Sea   *GB, 1952*
The Foreman Went To France   *GB, 1941*
San Demetrio London   *GB, 1943*
Torpedo Bay   *FRA/ITA, 1964*

Fuller, Samuel
The Big Red One   *U.S., 1980*
China Gate   *U.S., 1957*
Fixed Bayonets   *U.S., 1951*
Hell And High Water   *U.S., 1954*
Merrill's Marauders   *U.S., 1962*
Run Of The Arrow   *U.S., 1957*
The Steel Helmet   *U.S., 1951*

Furie, Sidney J.
The Boys In Company C   *U.S., 1978*
During One Night   *GB, 1961*
Purple Hearts   *U.S., 1984*

Gallone, Carmine
Carthage In Flames   *ITA, 1960*
Michael Strogoff   *ITA, 1956*
Scipio Africanus   *ITA, 1937*

Gance, Abel
Austerlitz   *FRA/ITA/LEICH/YUG, 1959*

J'accuse   *FRA, 1939*
Napoleon   *FRA, 1927*

Garnett, Tay
Bataan   *U.S., 1943*
The Cross Of Lorraine   *U.S., 1943*
One Minute To Zero   *U.S., 1952*
Soldiers Three   *U.S., 1951*
A Terrible Beauty   *GB/U.S., 1960*

Gibson, Mel
Braveheart   *U.S., 1995*

Gilbert, Lewis
Albert, RN   *GB, 1953*
Carve Her Name With Pride   *GB, 1958*
Hms Defiant   *GB, 1962*
Light Up The Sky   *GB, 1960*
Not Quite Jerusalem   *GB, 1985*
Operation Daybreak   *U.S., 1975*
Reach For The Sky   *GB, 1956*
The Sea Shall Not Have Them   *GB, 1954*
Sink The Bismark!   *GB, 1960*

Gilliat, Sidney
Green For Danger   *GB, 1946*
Millions Like Us (+ Frank Launder)
   GB, 1943
The Rake's Progress   *GB, 1945*
Waterloo Road   *GB, 1944*

Gilling, John
The Bandit Of Zhobe   *GB, 1959*
The Brigand Of Kandahar   *GB, 1965*
The Scarlet Blade   *GB, 1963*

Godard, Jean-Luc
Les Carabiniers   *FRA/ITA, 1963*
Le Petit Soldat   *FRA, 1960*

Golan, Menahem
Hanna's War   *U.S., 1988*
Operation Thunderbolt   *ISR, 1977*

Gordon, Keith
A Midnight Clear   *U.S., 1992*
Mother Night   *U.S., 1996*

Goulding, Edmund
The Dawn Patrol   *U.S., 1938*
Forever And A Day (+ many others)
   U.S., 1942

Granowsky, Alexis
Taras Bulba   *FRA, 1936*
The Rebel Son (+ Adrian Brunel)
   GB, 1939

Grauman, Walter
The Last Escape   *GB, 1970*
633 Squadron   *GB, 1964*

Green, Alfred E.
Appointment In Berlin   *U.S., 1943*
The Green Goddess   *U.S., 1930*
Mr Winkle Goes To War   *U.S., 1944*

Griffith, D.W.
Abraham Lincoln   *U.S., 1930*
America   *U.S., 1924*

The Birth Of A Nation   *U.S., 1915*
The Girl Who Stayed At Home   *U.S., 1919*
The Great Love   *U.S., 1918*
The Greatest Thing In Life   *U.S., 1918*
Hearts Of The World   *U.S., 1918*
Intolerance   *U.S., 1916*
Isn't Life Wonderful?   *U.S., 1924*
Orphans Of The Storm   *U.S., 1921*

Guest, Val
The Camp On Blood Island   *GB, 1958*
Men Of Sherwood Forest   *GB, 1954*
Yesterday's Enemy   *GB, 1959*

Guillermin, John
The Blue Max   *U.S., 1966*
The Bridge At Remagen   *U.S., 1968*
I Was Monty's Double   *GB, 1958*

Hamilton, Guy
The Battle Of Britain   *GB, 1969*
The Best Of Enemies   *ITA/U.S., 1961*
The Colditz Story   *GB, 1954*
The Devil's Disciple   *GB, 1959*
Force Ten From Navarone   *GB, 1978*
The Man In The Middle   *GB, 1964*

Hardwicke, Cedric
Forever And A Day (+ many others)
   U.S., 1942

Harlan, Veit
The Great King   *GER, 1942*
Jew Suss   *GER, 1940*

Harris, André See **Marcel Ophuls**

Hathaway, Henry
China Girl   *U.S., 1942*
The Desert Fox   *U.S., 1951*
The House On 92nd Street   *U.S., 1945*
How The West Was Won (+ John
   Ford/George Marshal)   *U.S., 1962*
Lives Of A Bengal Lancer   *U.S., 1934*
Prince Valiant   *U.S., 1954*
Raid On Rommel   *U.S., 1971*
The Real Glory   *U.S., 1939*
Sundown   *U.S., 1941*
Ten Gentlemen From West Point
   U.S., 1942
13 Rue Madeleine   *U.S., 1947*
Wing And A Prayer   *U.S., 1944*
You're In The Navy Now   *U.S., 1951*

Hawks, Howard
Air Force   *U.S., 1943*
The Dawn Patrol   *U.S., 1930*
I Was A Male War Bride   *U.S., 1949*
The Road To Glory   *U.S., 1936*
Sergeant York   *U.S., 1941*
To Have And Have Not   *U.S., 1945*
Today We Live   *U.S., 1933*

Heisler, Stuart
Beachhead   *U.S., 1953*
Hitler   *U.S., 1961*

Hepworth, Cecil
The Call To Arms   *GB, 1902*
The Outrage   *GB, 1914*

Herzog, Werner
Aguirre, Wrath Of God   *FRG, 1972*
Lessons In Darkness   *FRA/GER, 1992*

Hill, George Roy
The Great Waldo Pepper   *U.S., 1975*
The Little Drummer Girl   *U.S., 1984*
Slaughterhouse Five   *U.S., 1972*

Hill, Walter
Geronimo: An American Legend
   U.S., 1994
Southern Comfort   *U.S., 1981*

Hiller, Arthur
The Americanization Of Emily
   U.S., 1964
Tobruk   *U.S., 1967*

Hitchcock, Alfred
Aventure Malgache   *GB, 1944*
Bon Voyage   *GB, 1944*
Foreign Correspondent   *U.S., 1940*
Juno And The Paycock   *GB, 1930*
The Lady Vanishes   *GB, 1938*
Lifeboat   *U.S., 1944*
Notorious   *U.S., 1946*
Saboteur   *U.S., 1942*
The Thirty-Nine Steps   *GB, 1936*

Hook, Harry
The Kitchen Toto   *GB, 1987*

Hoskins, Bob
The Raggedy Rawney   *GB, 1987*

Howard, David
Crimson Romance   *U.S., 1934*
Daniel Boone   *U.S., 1936*
The Marines Are Coming   *U.S., 1935*

Howard, Leslie
The First Of The Few   *GB, 1942*
The Gentle Sex (+ Maurice Elvey)
   GB, 1943
Pimpernel Smith   *GB, 1941*

Howard, William K.
Fire Over England   *GB, 1936*
Scotland Yard   *U.S., 1930*
Surrender   *U.S., 1931*

Hughes, Howard
Hell's Angels   *U.S., 1930*

Humphrey, William See **J. Stuart
Blackton**

Hurst, Brian Desmond
Dangerous Moonlight   *GB, 1941*
The Lion Has Wings (+ Adrian
   Brunel/Michael Powell)   *GB, 1939*
The Malta Story   *GB, 1953*
Ourselves Alone   *GB, 1936*
Simba   *GB, 1955*
Theirs Is The Glory   *GB, 1946*

Huston, John
Across The Pacific   *U.S., 1942*
The African Queen   *GB, 1951*

The Battle Of San Pietro   *U.S., 1944*
Heaven Knows, Mr Allison   *U.S., 1957*
The Man Who Would Be King
   GB, 1975
The Red Badge Of Courage   *U.S., 1951*
Victory   *U.S., 1981*

Hutton, Brian G.
Kelly's Heroes   *U.S./YUG, 1970*
Where Eagles Dare   *GB, 1969*

Ichikawa, Kon
The Burmese Harp   *JAP, 1956*
Fires On The Plain   *JAP, 1959*

Ince, Thomas H.
The Battle Of Gettysburg   *U.S., 1914*
Civilization   *U.S., 1916*
The Zeppelin's Last Raid   *U.S., 1917*

Ingram, Rex
The Four Horsemen Of The Apocalypse
   U.S., 1921
Mare Nostrum   *U.S., 1925*
Scaramouche   *U.S., 1923*

Irvin, John
The Dogs Of War   *GB, 1980*
Hamburger Hill   *U.S., 1987*
Robin Hood   *U.S., 1991*

Jarman, Derek
War Requiem   *GB, 1989*

Jennings, Humphrey
London Can Take It (+ Harry Watt)
   GB, 1940
Fires Were Started   *GB, 1943*
The Silent Village   *GB, 1943*

Joffe, Roland
The Killing Fields   *GB, 1984*
The Mission   *GB, 1986*

Johnson, Nunnally
The Angel Wore Red   *U.S., 1960*

Jordan, Neil
Angel   *IRE, 1982*
The Crying Game   *GB, 1992*
Michael Collins   *U.S., 1996*

Julian, Rupert
Kaiser, The Beast Of Berlin
   U.S., 1918
Love And Glory   *U.S., 1924*
Three Faces East   *U.S., 1926*

Justiniano, Gonzalo
Amnesia   *Chile, 1994*

Kadar, Jan
Death Is Called Engelchin
   (+ Elmar Klos)   *CZE, 1963*
The Shop On Main Street
   (+ Elmar Klos)   *CZE, 1965*

Kaige, Chen
Farewell My Concubine
   China/HK, 1993

Kalatozov, Mikhail
The Cranes Are Flying   *USSR, 1957*

Kanin, Garson See **Carol Reed**

Karlson, Phil
Hell To Eternity   *U.S., 1960*
Hornet's Nest   *U.S., 1970*
The Iroquois Trail   *U.S., 1950*
A Time For Killing   *U.S., 1967*

Karmen, Roman
Abyssinia   *USSR, 1939*

Kazan, Elia
Viva Zapata   *U.S., 1952*

Keaton, Buster
The General (+ Clyde Bruckman)
   U.S., 1926

Keighley, William
The Adventures Of Robin Hood
   (+ Michael Curtiz)   *U.S., 1938*
The Fighting 69th   *U.S., 1940*
The Master Of Ballantrae   *GB, 1953*
Rocky Mountain   *U.S., 1950*

Kimmich, Max
The Fox Of Glenarvon   *GER, 1940*
Germanin   *GER, 1943*
My Life For Ireland   *GER, 1941*

King, Henry
A Bell For Adano   *U.S., 1945*
Captain From Castile   *U.S., 1947*
King Of The Khyber Rifles   *U.S., 1953*
Seventh Heaven   *U.S., 1937*
Twelve O'Clock High   *U.S., 1949*
A Yank In The RAF   *U.S., 1941*

Klimov, Elim
Agony   *USSR, 1975*
Come And See   *USSR, 1985*

Klos, Elmar See **Jan Kadar**

Knight, Castleton See **Maurice Elvey**

Kobayashi, Masaki
The Human Condition   *JAP, 1961*
   1 No Greater Love
   2 Road To Eternity
   3 A Soldier's Prayer

Korda, Alexander
The Night Watch   *U.S., 1928*
Perfect Strangers   *GB, 1945*
That Hamilton Woman   *U.S., 1941*

Korda, Zoltan
Counter-Attack   *U.S., 1945*
The Drum   *GB, 1938*
The Four Feathers   *GB, 1939*
Sahara   *U.S., 1943*

Koster, Henry
D-Day The Sixth Of June   *U.S., 1956*
Desiree   *U.S., 1954*
Fraulein   *U.S., 1958*

Kotcheff, Ted
First Blood   *U.S., 1982*
Uncommon Valor   *U.S., 1983*

Kozintsev, Grigori
Bloody Snow   *USSR, 1929*
The New Babylon (+ Leonid Trauberg)
   USSR, 1929

Kramer, Stanley
Judgment At Nuremburg   *U.S., 1961*
The Pride And The Passion   *U.S., 1957*
The Secret Of Santa Vittoria   *U.S., 1969*

Kubrick, Stanley
Barry Lyndon   *GB, 1975*
Dr Strangelove   *GB, 1963*
Fear And Desire   *U.S., 1953*
Full Metal Jacket   *GB/U.S. 1987*
Paths Of Glory   *U.S., 1957*
Spartacus   *U.S., 1960*

Kurosawa, Akira
The Hidden Fortress   *JAP, 1958*
Kagemusha   *JAP, 1980*
Ran   *JAP, 1985*
Throne Of Blood   *JAP, 1957*

Landers, Lew
Atlantic Convoy   *U.S., 1942*
The Barbary Pirate   *U.S., 1949*
California Conquest   *U.S., 1952*
Davy Crockett, Indian Scout
   (+ Ford Beebe)   *U.S., 1950*
Enemy Agent   *U.S., 1940*
The Last Of The Buccaneers
   U.S., 1950
Ski Patrol   *U.S., 1940*
Submarine Raider   *U.S., 1942*
Torpedo Alley   *U.S., 1953*
Tyrant Of The Sea   *U.S., 1950*
U-Boat Prisoner   *U.S., 1944*
When The Redskins Rode   *U.S., 1951*
A Yank In Korea   *U.S., 1951*

Lang, Fritz
An American Guerrilla In The Philippines
   U.S., 1950
Cloak And Dagger   *U.S., 1946*
Hangmen Also Die!   *U.S., 1943*
Man Hunt   *U.S., 1941*
Ministry Of Fear   *U.S., 1944*
The Testament Of Dr Mabuse
   GER, 1932

Launder, Frank
I See A Dark Stranger   *GB, 1945*
Millions Like Us (+ Sidney Gilliat)
   GB, 1943
Two Thousand Women   *GB, 1944*

Laven, Arnold
Geronimo   *U.S., 1962*
The Glory Guys   *U.S., 1965*
The Rack   *U.S., 1956*

Leacock, Philip
Appointment In London   *GB, 1952*
The War Lover   *GB, 1962*

Lean, David
The Bridge On The River Kwai
   GB, 1957
Doctor Zhivago   *U.S., 1965*
In Which We Serve (+ Nöel Coward)
   GB, 1942
Lawrence Of Arabia   *GB, 1962*
Ryan's Daughter   *GB, 1970*

Lee, Jack
Circle Of Deception   *GB, 1960*
A Town Like Alice   *GB, 1956*
The Wooden Horse   *GB, 1950*

Lee, Rowland V
Barbed Wire (+ Erich Pommer)
   U.S., 1927
A Man From Wyoming   *U.S., 1930*
The Man Without A Country
   U.S., 1925
Tower Of London   *U.S., 1939*

Lee-Thompson, J.
see **Thompson, J. Lee**

Leisen, Mitchell
Arise My Love   *U.S., 1940*
Golden Earrings   *U.S., 1947*

Lenzi, Umberto
The Battle Of The Commandos
   ITA, 1969
From Hell To Victory
   FRA/ITA/SPA, 1979
The Great Battle   *FRG/YUG, 1978*

Leone, Sergio
The Colossus Of Rhodes   *ITA, 1960*
The Good, The Bad And The Ugly
   ITA, 1966

Le Roy, Mervyn
Escape   *U.S., 1940*
Homecoming   *U.S., 1948*
Mister Roberts (+ John Ford)
   U.S., 1955
Thirty Seconds Over Tokyo
   U.S., 1944
Waterloo Bridge   *U.S., 1940*

Lester, Richard
The Bed Sitting Room   *GB, 1969*
Cuba   *U.S., 1979*
How I Won The War   *GB, 1967*
Robin And Marion   *U.S., 1976*

Levin, Henry
The Bandit Of Sherwood Forest
   (+ George Sherman)   *U.S., 1946*
The Dark Avenger   *GB, 1955*
The Desperados   *U.S., 1969*
The Fighting Guardsman
   U.S., 1945
The Flying Missile   *U.S., 1950*
The Gallant Blade   *U.S., 1948*
Genghis Khan   *U.S., 1964*

Levinson, Barry
Good Morning, Vietnam
   U.S., 1987

Lewis, Joseph H.
Bombs Over Burma   *U.S., 1942*
Retreat, Hell!   *U.S., 1952*
Seventh Cavalry   *U.S., 1956*

Liebeneiner, Wolfgang
Bismark   *GER, 1940*
The Dismissal   *GER, 1942*

Lilienthal, Peter
David   *FRG, 1979*
La Insurreccion
   COSTA RICA/NIC, 1981

Litvak, Anatole
Confessions Of A Nazi Spy
   U.S., 1939
Decision Before Dawn   *U.S., 1944*
L'equipage   *FRA, 1935*
The Journey   *U.S., 1959*
The Night Of The Generals   *GB, 1967*
This Above All   *U.S., 1942*
Why We Fight   *U.S., 1942-45*
The Woman I Love   *U.S., 1937*

Lloyd, Frank
Blood On The Sun   *U.S., 1945*
Cavalcade   *U.S., 1932*
The Divine Lady   *U.S., 1929*
Forever And A Day
   (+ many others) *U.S., 1942*
The Howards Of Virginia   *U.S., 1940*
If I Were King   *U.S., 1938*
The Last Command   *U.S., 1955*
The Sea Hawk   *U.S., 1924*
A Tale Of Two Cities   *U.S., 1917*
Under Two Flags   *U.S., 1936*

Loach, Ken
Carla's Song   *GB/GER/SPA, 1996*
Hidden Agenda   *GB, 1990*
Land And Freedom
   GB/GER/SPA, 1995

Logan, Joshua
Ensign Pulver   *U.S., 1964*
Sayonara   *U.S., 1957*

Loncraine, Richard
Richard III   *GB, 1995*

Losey, Joseph
Figures In A Landscape   *GB, 1970*
King And Country   *GB, 1964*

Lubin, Arthur
Eagle Squadron   *U.S., 1942*
I Cover The War   *U.S., 1937*
South Sea Woman   *U.S., 1953*

Lubitsch, Ernst
The Man I Killed   *U.S., 1932*
To Be Or Not To Be   *U.S., 1942*

Ludwig, Edward
The Fighting Seabees   *U.S., 1944*
The Man Who Reclaimed His Head
   U.S., 1934
They Came To Blow Up America
   U.S., 1943

Lumet, Sidney
Fail Safe   *U.S., 1964*
The Hill   *GB, 1965*
The Pawnbroker   *U.S., 1965*

McCarey, Leo
Duck Soup   *U.S., 1933*

MacDonald, David
The Moonraker   *GB, 1957*
This England   *GB, 1941*

Mackendrick, Alexander
Whisky Galore   *GB, 1948*

McLaglen, Andrew V
The Devil's Brigade   *U.S., 1968*
Return From The River Kwai
   GB, 1988
The Sea Wolves   *GB/SWI/U.S., 1980*
Sergeant Steiner   *FRG, 1979*
Shenandoah   *U.S., 1965*
The Wild Geese   *GB, 1978*

McTiernan, John
The 13th Warrior   *U.S., 1999*

Malick, Terrence
The Thin Red Line   *U.S., 1998*

Malle, Louis
Au Revoir, Les Enfants   *FRA, 1987*
Lacombe, Lucien   *FRA, 1974*

Malins, Geoffrey/Mcdowell, J.B.
The Battle Of Ancre   *GB, 1917*
The Battle Of Arras   *GB, 1917*
The Battle Of The Somme
   GB, 1916
St Quentin   *GB, 1917*

Mamoulian, Rouben
The Mark Of Zorro   *U.S., 1940*

Mankiewicz, Joseph L.
Cleopatra   *U.S., 1963*
Five Fingers   *U.S., 1952*
Julius Caesar   *U.S., 1953*
The Quiet American   *U.S., 1952*

Mann, Anthony
The Black Book   *U.S., 1949*
El Cid   *ITA/U.S., 1961*
Devil's Doorway   *U.S., 1950*
The Fall Of The Roman Empire
   U.S., 1964
The Heroes Of Telemark   *GB, 1965*
The Last Frontier   *U.S., 1955*
Men In War   *U.S., 1957*

Mann, Daniel
Journey into Fear   *U.S., 1976*
Judith   *U.S., 1965*
The Mountain Road   *U.S., 1960*
The Teahouse Of The August Moon
   U.S., 1956

Mann, Michael
The Keep   *U.S., 1983*
The Last Of The Mohicans   *U.S., 1992*

Marshall, George
Advance To The Rear   *U.S., 1964*
Against All Flags   *U.S., 1952*
The Guns Of Fort Petticoat   *U.S., 1957*
How The West Was Won (+ John
   Ford/Henry Hathaway)   *U.S., 1962*
Imitation General   *U.S., 1958*
Love Under Fire   *U.S., 1937*
A Message To Garcia   *U.S., 1936*
Pillars Of The Sky   *U.S., 1956*
The Savage   *U.S., 1952*
Tap Roots   *U.S., 1948*

Marton, Andrew
The Longest Day (+ Ken
   Annakin/Bernhard Wicki)   *U.S., 1962*
Men Of The Fighting Lady   *U.S., 1954*
Prisoner Of War   *U.S., 1954*
The Thin Red Line   *U.S., 1964*
Underwater Warrior   *U.S., 1958*

Mate, Rudolph
The Black Shield Of Falworth
   U.S., 1954
The Deep Six   *U.S., 1958*
Seven Seas To Calais   *ITA/U.S., 1962*
The Siege At Red River   *U.S., 1954*
The 300 Spartans   *U.S., 1962*

Maxwell, Ronald F.
Gettysburg   *U.S., 1993*

Mayo, Archie
Confirm Or Deny   *U.S., 1941*
Crash Dive   *U.S., 1943*
Four Sons   *U.S., 1940*
A Night In Casablanca   *U.S., 1946*

Melford, George
The Boer War   *U.S., 1914*
A Celebrated Case   *U.S., 1914*
Burning Sands   *U.S., 1922*
Friendly Enemies   *U.S., 1925*
The Great Impersonation   *U.S., 1921*
The Light That Failed   *U.S., 1923*

Melville, Jean-Pierre
The Army In The Shadows
   FRA/ITA, 1969
Leon Morin, Priest   *FRA/ITA, 1961*

Mendes, Lothar
Flight For Freedom   *U.S., 1943*
The Four Feathers (+ Merian C.
   Cooper/Ernest Schoedsack)   *U.S., 1929*
International Squadron   *U.S., 1941*
Tampico   *U.S., 1944*

Menzel, Jiri
Closely Observed Trains   *CZE, 1966*

Menzies, William Cameron
Address Unknown   *U.S., 1944*
Drums In The Deep South   *U.S., 1951*
Things To Come   *GB, 1936*

Milestone, Lewis
All Quiet On The Western Front
   U.S., 1930
Arch Of Triumph   *U.S., 1948*

Edge Of Darkness   *U.S., 1943*
The General Died At Dawn   *U.S., 1936*
The Halls Of Montezuma   *U.S., 1950*
Les Miserables   *U.S., 1952*
The North Star   *U.S., 1943*
Pork Chop Hill   *U.S., 1959*
The Purple Heart   *U.S., 1944*
They Who Dare   *GB, 1953*
A Walk In The Sun   *U.S., 1946*

Milius, John
A Farewell To The King   *U.S., 1988*
Flight Of The Intruder   *U.S., 1991*
Red Dawn   *U.S., 1984*
The Wind And The Lion   *U.S., 1975*

Minelli, Vincente
The Clock   *U.S., 1945*
The Four Horsemen Of The Apocalypse
   U.S., 1961

Minghella, Anthony
The English Patient   *U.S., 1996*

Mollo, Andrew see **Kevin Brownlow**

Neame, Ronald
The Man Who Never Was
   GB, 1955
The Odessa File   *GB, 1974*
Windom's Way   *GB, 1957*

Negulesco, Jean
The Conspirators   *U.S., 1944*
Lydia Bailey   *U.S., 1952*
Three Came Home   *U.S., 1950*

Nelson, Ralph
Counterpoint   *U.S., 1967*
Duel At Diablo   *U.S., 1965*
Father Goose   *U.S., 1964*
Soldier Blue   *U.S., 1970*

Neumann, Kurt
Hiawatha   *U.S., 1952*
Mohawk   *U.S., 1956*

Newman, Joseph
Fort Massacre   *U.S., 1958*
Jungle Patrol   *U.S., 1948*
A Thunder Of Drums   *U.S., 1961*

Nicholls Jr, George
Man Of Conquest   *U.S., 1939*
The Marines Fly High (+ Ben Stoloff)
   U.S., 1940
The Soldier And The Lady   *U.S., 1937*

Nichols, Mike
Catch-22   *U.S., 1970*

Nigh, William
Corregidor   *U.S., 1943*
My Four Years In Germany   *U.S., 1918*

Noble, John W.
The Birth Of A Race   *U.S., 1919*
The Brand Of Cowardice
   U.S., 1916
Cardigan   *U.S., 1922*

Norman, Leslie
Dunkirk   *GB, 1958*
The Long And The Short And The Tall
   GB, 1960

North, Wilfred
The Battle Cry Of Peace   *U.S., 1915*
Over The Top   *U.S., 1918*

O'Connor, Pat
Cal   *GB, 1984*
Fools Of Fortune   *GB, 1990*

Olivier, Laurence
Henry V   *GB, 1944*
Richard III   *GB, 1955*

Ophuls, Marcel
Grief And Pity (+ André Harris) *FRA, 1971*

Ophuls, Max
The Exile   *U.S., 1947*
From Mayerling To Sarajevo   *FRA, 1940*

Oshima, Nagasia
Merry Christmas, Mr Lawrence
   GB, 1982

Pabst, G.W.
Jackboot Mutiny   *FRG, 1955*
Kameradschaft   *GER, 1931*
Ten Days To Die   *Austria, 1954*
Westfront 1918   *GER, 1930*

Pacino, Al
Looking For Richard   *U.S., 1996*

Pakula, Alan J.
The Devil's Own   *U.S., 1997*
Sophie's Choice   *U.S., 1982*

Parker, Alan
Birdy   *U.S., 1984*
Come See The Paradise   *U.S., 1990*

Parrish, Robert
The Purple Plain   *GB, 1954*
A Town Called Bastard   *GB/SPA, 1971*
Up From The Beach   *U.S., 1965*

Peckinpah, Sam
Cross Of Iron   *GB/FRG, 1977*
Major Dundee   *U.S., 1964*
The Wild Bunch   *U.S., 1969*

Petersen, Wolfgang
The Boat   *GER, 1981*

Petrov, Vladimir
The Battle Of Stalingrad   *USSR, 1950*
Peter The Great   *USSR, 1937*

Pevney, Joseph
Away All Boats!   *U.S., 1956*
Desert Legion   *U.S., 1953*
Torpedo Run   *U.S., 1958*
Yankee Pasha   *U.S., 1954*

Pichel, Irving
The Man I Married   *U.S., 1940*

The Moon Is Down   *U.S., 1943*
Oss   *U.S., 1946*
The Pied Piper   *U.S., 1942*

Pollack, Sydney
Castle Keep   *U.S., 1969*
Havana   *U.S., 1990*

Pontecorvo, Gillo
The Battle Of Algiers   *ALG/ITA, 1965*
Kapo   *FRA/ITA, 1960*

Post, Ted
Go Tell The Spartans   *U.S., 1978*
The Legend Of Tom Dooley   *U.S., 1959*

Powell, Dick
The Conqueror   *U.S., 1955*
The Enemy Below   *U.S., 1957*
The Hunters   *U.S., 1958*

Powell, Michael
Battle Of The River Plate
   (+ Emeric Pressburger)   *GB, 1956*
Contraband   *GB, 1940*
The Elusive Pimpernel
   (+ Emeric Pressburger)   *GB, 1950*
49th Parallel   *GB, 1941*
Ill Met By Moonlight   *GB, 1956*
The Life And Death Of Colonel Blimp
   (+ Emeric Pressburger)   *GB, 1943*
The Lion Has Wings (+ Adrian Brunel/
   Brian Desmond Hurst)   *GB, 1939*
A Matter Of Life And Death
   (+ Emeric Pressberger)   *GB, 1946*
One Of Our Aircraft Is Missing
   (+ Emeric Pressburger)   *GB, 1941*
The Spy In Black   *GB, 1939*

Preminger, Otto
The Court-Martial Of Billy Mitchell
   U.S., 1955
Exodus   *U.S., 1960*
In Harm's Way   *U.S., 1965*
Saint Joan   *GB, 1957*

Pressburger, Emeric See **Michael
Powell**

Pudovkin, Vsevolod
The End Of St Petersburg
   USSR, 1927
Suvurov   *USSR, 1938*

Ratoff, Gregory
Barricade   *U.S., 1939*
Lancer Spy   *U.S., 1937*
Paris Underground   *U.S., 1945*
Song Of Russia   *U.S., 1944*

Rawlins, John
Fort Defiance   *U.S., 1951*
The Great Impersonation   *U.S., 1942*
Halfway To Shanghai   *U.S., 1942*
We've Never Been Licked   *U.S., 1943*

Ray, Nicholas
Bitter Victory   *U.S./FRA, 1957*
55 Days At Peking   *SPA/U.S., 1963*
Flying Leathernecks   *U.S., 1951*

Ray, Satyajit
The Chess Players   *IND, 1977*

Reed, Carol
The Key   *GB, 1958*
Night Train To Munich   *GB, 1940*
The Odd Man Out   *GB, 1946*
The True Glory *(+ Garson Kanin)*
   U.S./GB, 1945
The Way Ahead   *GB, 1944*
The Young Mr Pitt   *GB, 1942*

Renoir, Jean
The Elusive Corporal   *FRA, 1962*
La Grande Illusion   *FRA, 1937*
La Marseillaise   *FRA, 1938*
La Regle Du Jeu   *FRA, 1939*
This Land Is Mine   *U.S., 1943*

Resnais, Alain
Guernica   *FRA, 1950*
La Guerre Est Finie   *FRA/SWE, 1966*
Hiroshima, Mon Amour   *FRA/JAP, 1959*
Nuit Et Brouillard   *FRA, 1955*

Reynolds, Kevin
The Beast   *U.S./ISR, 1988*
Robin Hood: Prince Of Thieves
   U.S., 1991

Richardson, Tony
The Charge Of The Light Brigade
   GB, 1968

Riefenstahl, Leni
Triumph Of The Will   *GER, 1935*

Ritt, Martin
5 Branded Women   *ITA/U.S., 1960*

Ritter, Karl
Garrison Dora   *GER, 1943*
Leave On Word Of Honour   *GER, 1937*
Patrioten   *GER, 1937*
Pour Le Merite   *GER, 1938*
Stukas   *GER, 1941*

Robson, Mark
The Bridges At Toko-Ri   *U.S., 1954*
Home Of The Brave   *U.S., 1949*
I Want You   *U.S., 1951*
The Inn Of The Sixth Happiness
   GB, 1958
Lost Command   *U.S., 1966*
Von Ryan's Express   *U.S., 1965*

Romm, Mikhail
Lenin In 1918   *USSR, 1939*
Lenin In October   *USSR, 1937*

Rossellini, Roberto
Era Notte A Roma   *FRA/ITA, 1960*
General Della Rovere   *FRA/ITA, 1959*
Germany, Year Zero   *FRG/ITA, 1947*
Long Live Italy   *ITA, 1960*
Man Of The Cross   *ITA, 1943*
Open City   *ITA, 1945*
Paisa   *ITA, 1946*
A Pilot Returns   *ITA, 1942*
The White Navy   *ITA, 1941*

Rossen, Robert
Alexander The Great   *U.S., 1956*
They Came To Cordura   *U.S., 1959*

Ruben, J. Walter
Ace Of Aces   *U.S., 1933*
Secret Service   *U.S., 1931*

Salkow, Sidney
Flight Lieutenant   *U.S., 1942*
The Great Sioux Massacre   *U.S., 1965*
The Pathfinder   *U.S., 1952*
Sitting Bull   *U.S., 1954*
Storm Over Bengal   *U.S., 1938*

Santell, Alfred
Body And Soul   *U.S., 1931*
Jack London   *U.S., 1943*
The Patent Leather Kid   *U.S., 1927*

Santley, Joseph
Remember Pearl Harbor   *U.S., 1942*
Rosie The Riveter   *U.S., 1944*

Saura, Carlos
Ay, Carmela!   *ITA/SPA, 1990*
El Dorado   *FRA/SPA, 1988*

Saville, Victor
Dark Journey   *GB, 1937*
Forever And A Day *(+ many others)*
   U.S., 1942
I Was A Spy   *GB, 1933*
Kim   *U.S., 1950*
The W Plan   *GB, 1930*

Schaffner, Franklin J.
Nicholas And Alexandra   *GB, 1971*
Patton   *U.S., 1970*
The War Lord   *U.S., 1965*
Lionheart   *U.S., 1987*

Schoedsack, Ernest
The Four Feathers *(+ Merian C.
   Cooper/Lothar Mendes) U.S., 1929*

Schlondorff, Volker
Circle Of Deceit   *FRA/FRG, 1981*
The Tin Drum   *FRG/FRA, 1979*

Schoendoerffer, Pierre
The Anderson Section   *FRA, 1967*
Dien Bien Phu   *FRA, 1992*
L'Honneur D'un Capitaine   *FRA, 1982*
317e Section   *FRA, 1964*

Scorsese, Martin
Kundun   *U.S., 1997*

Scott, Ridley
The Duellists   *GB, 1977*
1492: Conquest Of Paradise   *U.S., 1992*

Scott, Tony
Crimson Tide   *U.S., 1995*

Sears, Fred F.
El Alamein   *U.S., 1953*
Ghost Of The China Sea
   U.S., 1958

Mission Over Korea   *U.S., 1953*
Sky Commando   *U.S., 1953*

Seaton, George
The Counterfeit Traitor   *U.S., 1962*
The Hook   *U.S., 1962*
The Proud And The Profane   *U.S., 1956*
Thirty-Six Hours   *U.S., 1964*

Seiler, Lewis
The Bamboo Prison   *U.S., 1954*
Battle Stations   *U.S., 1956*
Breakthrough   *U.S., 1950*
Guadalcanal Diary   *U.S., 1943*
Operation Secret   *U.S., 1952*
The Tanks Are Coming   *U.S., 1951*

Seiter, William A.
An Alien Enemy   *U.S., 1918*
Allegheny Uprising   *U.S., 1939*
Destroyer   *U.S., 1943*

Seitz, George B.
Kit Carson   *U.S., 1940*
The Last Of The Mohicans   *U.S., 1936*
A Yank On The Burma Road   *U.S., 1942*

Selander, Lesley
Arizona Bushwackers   *U.S., 1968*
Battle Zone   *U.S., 1952*
Desert Sands   *U.S., 1955*
Dragonfly Squadron   *U.S., 1954*
Fighter Attack   *U.S., 1953*
Flat Top   *U.S., 1952*
Fort Algiers   *U.S., 1953*
Fort Courageous   *U.S., 1965*
Fort Osage   *U.S., 1952*
Fort Utah   *U.S., 1968*
Fort Yuma   *U.S., 1955*
I Was An American Spy   *U.S., 1951*
Revolt At Fort Laramie   *U.S., 1957*
Royal African Rifles   *U.S., 1954*
Tomahawk Trail   *U.S., 1957*
War Paint   *U.S., 1953*

Selpin, Herbert
Carl Peters   *GER, 1941*
The Riders Of German East Africa
   GER, 1934

Sembene, Ousmane
Camp De Thiaroye *(+ Thierno Faty Sow)*
   Algeria/Senegal/Tunisia, 1988
Emitai   *Senegal, 1972*

Sewell, Vernon
The Battle Of The V1   *GB, 1958*
The Silver Fleet
   (+ Gordon Wellesley) GB, 1943

Sharp, Don
Hennessy   *GB, 1975*
Rasputin The Mad Monk   *GB, 1966*
The Thirty-Nine Steps   *GB, 1978*
The Violent Enemy   *GB, 1968*

Sheridan, Jim
The Boxer   *GB/IRE, 1997*
In The Name Of The Father   *GB/IRE,
   1993*

Shavelson, Melville
Cast A Giant Shadow   *U.S., 1966*
The Pigeon That Took Rome   *U.S., 1962*

Sherman, George
The Bandit Of Sherwood Forest
  (+ Henry Levin)   *U.S., 1946*
Battle At Apache Pass   *U.S., 1952*
Border River   *U.S., 1954*
Chief Crazy Horse   *U.S., 1955*
Comanche   *U.S., 1956*
Comanche Territory   *U.S., 1950*
The Enemy General   *U.S., 1960*
The Golden Horde   *U.S., 1951*
Last Of The Redmen   *U.S., 1947*
The Purple V   *U.S., 1943*
Son Of Robin Hood   *GB, 1958*
Storm Over Lisbon   *U.S., 1944*
Sword In The Desert   *U.S., 1949*
Target Unknown   *U.S., 1951*
Tomahawk   *U.S., 1951*
The Treasure Of Pancho Villa
  U.S., 1955
War Arrow   *U.S., 1953*

Sherman, Vincent
All Through The Night   *U.S., 1942*
In Our Time   *U.S., 1944*
Lone Star   *U.S., 1952*
Underground   *U.S., 1941*

Shumlin, Herman
Confidential Agent   *U.S., 1945*
Watch On The Rhine   *U.S., 1943*

Siegel, Don
An Annapolis Story   *U.S., 1955*
The Beguiled   *U.S., 1971*
China Venture   *U.S., 1953*
The Gun Runners   *U.S., 1958*
Hell Is For Heroes   *U.S., 1962*
Two Mules For Sister Sara   *U.S., 1969*

Sinatra, Frank
None But The Brave   *U.S., 1965*

Sirk, Douglas
Battle Hymn   *U.S., 1957*
Captain Lightfoot   *U.S., 1955*
Hitler's Hangman   *U.S., 1943*
Mystery Submarine   *U.S., 1950*
The Sign Of The Pagan   *U.S., 1954*
Taza, Son Of Cochise   *U.S., 1954*
A Time To Love And A Time To Die
  U.S., 1958

Schlesinger, John
Yanks   *GB, 1979*

Smight, Jack
Midway   *U.S., 1976*
The Secret War Of Harry Frigg
  U.S., 1967

Smith, Albert E.
see **J. Stuart Blackton**

Solntseva, Yulia
Battle For The Ukraine   *USSR, 1943*
The Flaming Years   *USSR, 1961*

Spielberg, Steven
Empire Of The Sun   *U.S., 1987*
Indiana Jones And The Last Crusade
  U.S., 1989
1941   *U.S., 1979*
Raiders Of The Lost Ark   *U.S., 1981*
Schindler's List   *U.S., 1993*
Saving Private Ryan   *U.S., 1998*
  (*see also* The Last Days)

Spigelgass, Leonard (prod)
Army-Navy Screen Magazine   *U.S., 1943 onwards*

Spottiswoode, Roger
Air America   *U.S., 1990*
Under Fire   *U.S., 1983*

Springsteen, R.G.
Battle Flame   *U.S., 1959*
Operation Eichmann   *U.S., 1961*
Red Tomahawk   *U.S., 1967*

Stahl, John M.
The Eve Of St Mark   *U.S., 1944*
The Immortal Sergeant   *U.S., 1943*

Steinhoff, Hans
Hitlerjunge Quex   *GER, 1933*
Ohm Kruger   *GER, 1941*

Stevens, George
The Diary Of Anne Frank   *U.S., 1959*
Gunga Din   *U.S., 1939*

Stevenson, Robert
The Battle   *U.S., 1934*
Forever And A Day (+ many others)
  U.S., 1942
Joan Of Paris   *U.S., 1942*
Johnny Tremain   *U.S., 1957*

Stone, Oliver
Born On The Fourth Of July   *U.S., 1989*
Heaven and Earth   *U.S., 1993*
Platoon   *U.S., 1986*
Salvador   *U.S., 1986*

Sturges, John
The Eagle Has Landed   *GB, 1976*
Escape From Fort Bravo   *U.S., 1953*
The Great Escape   *U.S., 1963*
Never So Few   *U.S., 1959*
The Scarlet Coat   *U.S., 1955*
Sergeants Three   *U.S., 1961*

Sturges, Preston
Hail The Conquering Hero   *U.S., 1944*

Summers, Walter see **H. Bruce Woolfe**

Syberberg, Hans-Jurgen
Hitler, A Film From Germany
  FRA/GB/FRG, 1977
Ludwig — Requiem For A Virgin King
  FRG, 1972

Szabo, Istvan
Colonel Redl   *FRG/HUN/AUS, 1984*
Confidence   *HUN, 1979*

Hanussen   *FRG/HUN, 1988*
Mephisto   *HUN, 1981*

Tarkovsky, Andrei
Ivan's Childhood   *USSR, 1962*

Tavernier, Bertrand
La Guerre Sans Nom   *FRA, 1992*
Life And Nothing But   *FRA, 1989*

Thomas, Ralph
Above Us The Waves   *GB, 1955*
Appointment With Venus   *GB, 1951*
Conspiracy Of Hearts   *GB, 1960*
The High Bright Sun   *GB, 1965*
A Tale Of Two Cities   *GB, 1958*
The Thirty-Nine Steps   *GB, 1958*
The Wind Cannot Read   *GB, 1958*

Thompson, J. Lee
Before Winter Comes   *GB, 1968*
The Guns Of Navarone   *GB, 1961*
I Aim At The Stars   *U.S., 1960*
Ice-Cold In Alex   *GB, 1958*
Kings Of The Sun   *U.S., 1963*
North-West Frontier   *GB, 1959*
The Passage   *GB, 1978*
Taras Bulba   *U.S., 1962*

Thorpe, Richard
Above Suspicion   *U.S., 1943*
Cry Havoc   *U.S., 1943*
Ivanhoe   *GB/U.S., 1952*
Knights Of The Round Table   *U.S., 1953*
Malaya   *U.S., 1949*
Quentin Durward   *GB, 1955*
The Tartars   *ITA, 1960*

Topper, Bert
Hell Squad   *U.S., 1958*
Tank Commandos   *U.S., 1959*
War Is Hell   *U.S., 1963*

Tourneur, Jacques
Days Of Glory   *U.S., 1944*
The Flame And The Arrow   *U.S., 1950*
The Giant Of Marathon   *FRA/ITA, 1959*
Great Day In The Morning   *U.S., 1956*

Trauberg, Leonid
  see **Grigori Kozintsev**

Truffaut, François
The Last Metro   *FRA, 1980*

Trumbo, Dalton
Johnny Got His Gun   *U.S., 1971*

Tuttle, Frank
Hostages   *U.S., 1943*
The Hour Before The Dawn   *U.S., 1944*
Lucky Jordan   *U.S., 1942*

Ucicky, Gustav
Heimkehr   *GER, 1941*
Morgenrot   *GER, 1933*
Tumult In Damascus   *GER, 1939*

Ustinov, Peter
Billy Budd   *GB, 1962*

Torpedo Squadrons Move Out
JAP, 1944
The War At Sea From Hawaii To Malaya
JAP, 1942

Yamamoto, Satsuo
General Yamashita   *JAP, 1952*

Yates, Peter
Eleni   *U.S., 1985*
Murphy's War   *GB, 1971*

Young, Harold
I Escaped From The Gestapo
U.S., 1943
The Scarlet Pimpernel   *GB, 1934*

Young, Terence
Inchon   *U.S., 1981*
No Time To Die   *GB, 1958*
The Red Beret   *GB, 1953*
Safari   *GB, 1956*
Storm Over The Nile   *GB, 1955*
They Were Not Divided   *GB, 1950*
Triple Cross   *GB, 1967*
Zarak   *GB, 1956*

Zampa, Luigi
The Difficult Years   *ITA, 1948*
The Honorable Angelina   *ITA, 1947*
Living In Peace   *ITA, 1946*

Zeffirelli, Franco
Tea With Mussolini   *GB/ITA, 1998*

Zinnemann, Fred
Behold A Pale Horse   *U.S., 1964*
From Here To Eternity   *U.S., 1953*
The Men   *U.S., 1950*
The Nun's Story   *U.S., 1959*
The Seventh Cross   *U.S., 1944*

Zwick, Edward
Courage Under Fire   *U.S., 1996*
Glory   *U.S., 1989*
Legends Of The Fall   *U.S., 1994*

Bibliography

A Biographical Dictionary of Film, David Thomson; André Deutsch, London, 1994
Brassey's Battles, John Laffin; Brassey's, London, 1995
Ciné Télé Guide, Eric Leguèbe; Solar, Paris, 1984
Empire, Denis Judd; HarperCollins, London, 1996
Encyclopedia of American War Films, Larry Lagman and Ed Borg; Garland Publishing, Inc, New York and London, 1989
The Film in History, Pierre Sorlin; Basil Blackwell, Oxford, 1980
Films and the Second World War, Roger Manvell; A.S. Barnes and Co, New York, 1974
The Guinness Television Encyclopedia, Jeff Evans; Guinness Publishing, London, 1995
Halliwell's Film and Video Guide 1999, John Walker, (Editor); HarperCollins, London, 1998
Halliwell's Who's Who in the Movies, John Walker, (Editor); HarperCollins, London, 1998
A History of Europe, J.M. Roberts; Helicon, Oxford, 1996
A History of the 20th Century, Vols I-3, Martin Gilbert; HarperCollins, London, 1997, 1998, 1999
History of the World, J.M. Roberts; Helicon, Oxford, 1993
Hollywood Goes to War, Colin Schindler; Routledge and Kegan Paul, London, 1979
The Hutchinson Encyclopedia, 1997. Helicon, Oxford, 1996
Leonard Maltin's Movie and Video Guide 1998, Leonard Maltin (Editor); Signet, New York, 1997
The Oxford History of England. Clarendon Press, Oxford. Various volumes, but especially: *The Fifteenth Century*, E.F. Jacob, 1961; and *English History, 1914-1945*, A.J.P. Taylor, 1965.
A Pictorial History of War Films, Clyde Jeavons; Hamlyn, London, 1974
Time Out Film Guide 1998, John Pym, (Editor); Time Out Magazine Ltd, Penguin Books, London, 1997
The Times Atlas of World History, 4th Edition, Geoffrey Parker (Editor); Times Books, London, 1993
Virgin Film Guide 1997, James Pallot (Editor); CineBooks, Virgin Books, London, 1997
War Movies, Jay Hyams; Gallery Books, New York, 1984
Warfare, Geoffrey Parker (Editor); Cambridge University Press, Cambridge, 1995
Wings on the Screen, Bertil Skogsberg; A.S. Barnes and Co, San Diego and New York, 1981
. . . and various articles from, among others, *Daily Cinema, Picturegoer, Empire, European Film Reviews, Kinematograph Weekly, Monthly Film Bulletin, Motion Picture Herald, Radio Times, Sight and Sound* and, of course, *Variety*.

Acknowledgements

I am deeply indebted to the staff and resources of the British Film Institute Library for helping an old duffer around the technological wonders of modern storage retrieval systems, and still having the courtesy and patience to orientate me again and again. The staff at my own local library, Central Milton Keynes, have suffered much too — with overdue reminders, exhorbitant requests, and for putting up with the locust who denuded their 'Cinema' shelves from time to time. Other libraries — particularly that of the Imperial War Museum, Essex County Central Library and Liverpool University (Lesley Butler was my chum there) — also weighed in when it mattered. My grateful thanks go to them all. My thanks also to Richard and Chris at Flashbacks, and Darren Thomas at Kobal, for their assistance in stills research.

Hellcats of the Navy
Reagan (left) in appropriately stiff pose.
Columbia

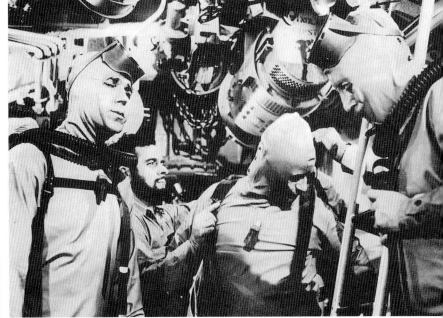